PERPETUAL MOTION
STUDIES IN FRENCH POETRY FROM
SURREALISM TO THE POSTMODERN

# LEGENDA

LEGENDA is the Modern Humanities Research Association's book imprint for new research in the Humanities. Founded in 1995 by Malcolm Bowie and others within the University of Oxford, Legenda has always been a collaborative publishing enterprise, directly governed by scholars. The Modern Humanities Research Association (MHRA) joined this collaboration in 1998, became half-owner in 2004, in partnership with Maney Publishing and then Routledge, and has since 2016 been sole owner. Titles range from medieval texts to contemporary cinema and form a widely comparative view of the modern humanities, including works on Arabic, Catalan, English, French, German, Greek, Italian, Portuguese, Russian, Spanish, and Yiddish literature. Editorial boards and committees of more than 60 leading academic specialists work in collaboration with bodies such as the Society for French Studies, the British Comparative Literature Association and the Association of Hispanists of Great Britain & Ireland.

The MHRA encourages and promotes advanced study and research in the field of the modern humanities, especially modern European languages and literature, including English, and also cinema. It aims to break down the barriers between scholars working in different disciplines and to maintain the unity of humanistic scholarship. The Association fulfils this purpose through the publication of journals, bibliographies, monographs, critical editions, and the MHRA Style Guide, and by making grants in support of research. Membership is open to all who work in the Humanities, whether independent or in a University post, and the participation of younger colleagues entering the field is especially welcomed.

ALSO PUBLISHED BY THE ASSOCIATION

*Critical Texts*
*Tudor and Stuart Translations* • *New Translations* • *European Translations*
*MHRA Library of Medieval Welsh Literature*

*MHRA Bibliographies*
*Publications of the Modern Humanities Research Association*

*The Annual Bibliography of English Language & Literature*
*Austrian Studies*
*Modern Language Review*
*Portuguese Studies*
*The Slavonic and East European Review*
*Working Papers in the Humanities*
*The Yearbook of English Studies*

www.mhra.org.uk
www.legendabooks.com

# SELECTED ESSAYS

Each title in *Selected Essays* presents influential, but often scattered, papers by a major scholar in the Humanities. While these essays will, we hope, offer a model of scholarly writing, and chart the development of an important thinker in the field, the aim is not retrospective but to gather a coherent body of work as a tool for future research. Each volume contains a new introduction, framing the debate and reflecting on the methods used.

*Selected Essays* is curated by Professor Susan Harrow (University of Bristol).

*Managing Editor*
Dr Graham Nelson, 41 Wellington Square, Oxford OX1 2JF, UK

www.legendabooks.com

*Micky Sheringham in conversation*

# Perpetual Motion

*Studies in French Poetry*
*from Surrealism to the Postmodern*

❖

MICHAEL SHERINGHAM

*l*

## LEGENDA

Selected Essays 2
Modern Humanities Research Association
2017

*Published by Legenda*
*an imprint of the Modern Humanities Research Association*
*Salisbury House, Station Road, Cambridge* CB1 2LA

*ISBN 978-1-78188-477-5 (HB)*
*ISBN 978-1-78188-478-2 (PB)*

*First published 2017*

*Copy-Editor: Richard Correll*

# CONTENTS

❖

# ACKNOWLEDGMENTS

❖

We would like to thank Jonathan Templeman for his careful editing as Michael Sheringham was preparing the manuscript, and Richard Correll at Legenda. Thanks are due to Claude Garache and Philippe Jaccottet for the cover image, and to Berny Sèbe for photographing it.

*Patrick McGuinness*
*Priscilla Sheringham*

# SOURCES

❖

The essays presented here originally appeared as follows, and are reprinted with the kind permission of the publishers.

'From the Labyrinth of Language to the Language of the Senses: The Poetry of André Breton', in *Sensibility and Creation: Studies in Twentieth-Century French Poetry*, ed. by Roger Cardinal (London: Croom Helm, 1977), pp. 71–101

'*Mont de piété* and André Breton's Early Poetic Development', *Forum for Modern Language Studies*, 15.1 (January 1999), 44–68

'Rimbaud in 1875 and André Breton's "Forêt-Noire"'. A longer version of this chapter was first published in *French Studies*, 35 (1981), 32–44

'Breton and the Language of Automatism: Alterity, Allegory, Desire', *Forum for Modern Language Studies*, 18, April (1982), 142–58; reprinted in *Surrealism and Language: Seven Essays*, ed. by Ian Higgins (Edinburgh: Scottish Academic Press, 1986), pp. 46–62

'Where Do Poems Come From? A Reading of Breton's "Carnet"'. Originally published in French as 'Genèse(s) de la parole poétique: lecture de "carnet" d'André Breton', *Pleine Marge*, 11 (1990), 79–84

'City Space, Mental Space, Poetic Space: Paris in Breton, Benjamin and Réda', in *Parisian Fields*, ed. by Michael Sheringham (London: Reaktion Books, 1996), pp. 85–114

'The Liberator of Desire', review of André Breton, *Œuvres completes*, vol. I (Paris: Gallimard Pléiade, 1988), *The Times Literary Supplement*, 7–13 October 1988, p. 1125

'Le Film des durées', review of Georges Sebbag, *Imprononçable jour de ma naissance: 17DRE 13RETON* (Paris: Éditions Jean-Michel Place, 1988), *La Chouette*, 21 (1989), 25–30, Journal of French Department, Univ. of London, Birkbeck

'Foucault's Goethe', review of André Breton, *Nadja*, trans. by Richard Howard (London: Penguin, 1999) and *Œuvres complètes*, vol. III, *The Times Literary Supplement*, 20 October 2000, pp. 4–5

'L'Amour et son double: Faces of Love in Yves Bonnefoy', *Romance Studies*, 7 (1986), 138–58

'Baudelaire, Bonnefoy, Jeanne Duval: Poetry and Ethical Lucidity', in *Lucidity: Essays in Honour of Alison Finch*, ed. by Ian James and Emma Wilson (Cambridge: Legenda, 2016), pp. 97–109

'Jacques Réda and the Commitments of Poetry', *French Poetry since the War: The Poetics of Presence and Passage*, *L'Esprit créateur*, 32 (1992), 77–88

'Raymond Queneau: The Lure of the Spiritual', in *Literature and Spirituality*, ed. by David Bevan (Amsterdam: Rodopi, 1992), pp. 33–48

'Language, Colour, and the Enigma of Everydayness', in *Sensual Reading: New Approaches to Reading in its Relation to the Senses*, ed. by Michael Syrotinski and Ian MacLachlan (Lewisburg, PA: Bucknell University Press, 2001), pp. 127–52

'Everyday Rhythms, Everyday Writing: Réda with Deleuze and Guattari', in *Rhythms: Essays in French Literature and Thought*, ed. by Elizabeth Lindley and Laura McMahon (Oxford and New York: Peter Lang, 2008), pp. 147–58

'Paris — City of Names: Toponymic Trajectories and Mutable Identities', in *The Cultural*

*Identities of European Cities*, ed. by Katia Pizzi and Godela Weiss-Sussex (Oxford: Peter Lang, 2012), pp. 165–84

'Michel Deguy', *The Literary Review*, 6, 14 December 1979, pp. 8–9

'Poetry and its Double', review of Michel Deutsch, Emmanuel Hocquard, Jean-Luc Nancy, Bernard Noël, Alain Veinstein, Franck Venaille, Mathieu Bénézet and Philippe Lacoue-Labarthe, *Haine de la poésie* (Paris: Christian Bourgois, 1979), *The Literary Review*, 25, 19 Sept.–2 Oct. 1980, pp. 23–24

'Innovarinations', review of Valère Novarina, *La Lutte des morts* (Paris: Christian Bourgois, 1979), *The Literary Review*, 34, March 1981, p. 35

'Imaginary Solutions', review of Alfred Jarry, *Messaline*, trans. by John Harman (London: Atlas, 1985), Timothy Mathews, *Reading Apollinaire: Theories of Poetic Language* (Manchester: Manchester University Press, 1987), Tristan Tzara, *Chanson Dada: Selected Poems*, trans. by Lee Harwood (Toronto: Coach House, 1987), René Crevel, *Difficult Death*, trans. by David Rattray (San Francisco: North Point, 1987), Raymond Queneau, *Pierrot mon ami*, trans. by Barbara Wright (London: Atlas, 1988), and *The Skin of Dreams*, trans. by H. J. Kaplan (London: Atlas, 1987), *The Times Literary Supplement*, 5 August 1988, pp. 856–57

'Discreetly Tangential', review of Raymond Queneau, *Œuvres complètes*, vol. I, ed. by Claude Debon (Paris: Gallimard, 1989), *The Times Literary Supplement*, 27 April 1990, p. 455

'Lust in the Library', review of Guillaume Apollinaire, *Œuvres en prose complètes*, vol. III, ed. by Pierre Caizergues and Michel Décaudin (Paris: Gallimard, 1993), *The Times Literary Supplement*, 8 October 1993, pp. 4–5

'The Sailor Who Hated the Sea', review of Victor Segalen, *Œuvres complètes*, 2 vols, ed. by Henry Bouillier (Paris: Laffont, 1995), and *Voyages au pays du réel: œuvres littéraires*, ed. by Michel Le Bris (Brussels: Complexe, 1995), *The Times Literary Supplement*, 4 October, 1996, pp. 6–7

'The Shadows inside: Memory, the Body, and Forgetting in Supervielle', review of Jules Supervielle, *Œuvres poétiques complètes*, ed. by Michel Collot and others (Paris: Gallimard, 1996), *The Times Literary Supplement*, 17 October 1997, pp. 5–6

'On the Road to Reality', review of Yves Bonnefoy, *The Arrière-Pays*, trans. by Stephen Romer (London and New York: Seagull Books, 2012), *The Times Literary Supplement*, 11 October 2013, p. 12

'L'Habitant de Grignan', review of Philippe Jaccottet, *Œuvres*, ed. by José-Flore Tappy and others (Paris: Gallimard, 2014), *The Times Literary Supplement*, 22 January 2015, pp. 11–12

'Apollinaire and the Livre de Peintre', review of Anne Hyde Greet, *Apollinaire et le Livre de Peintre* (Paris: Minard, 1977), *French Studies*, 34 (1980), 358–59

'Six French Poets of our Time', review of Robert W. Greene, *Six French Poets of our Time: A Critical and Historical Study* (Princeton, NJ: Princeton University Press, 1979), *Modern Language Review*, 76 (1981), 207–08

'Péret and the Poetry of Change', review of Julia Field Costich, *The Poetry of Change: A Study of the Surrealist Works of Benjamin Péret* (Chapel Hill: University of North Carolina Press, 1979), *Modern Language Review*, 78, (1982), 217–18

'Reverdy's Horizons', review of Michel Collot, *Horizon de Reverdy* (Paris: Presses de L'Ecole Normale Supérieure, 1981), *Modern Language Review*, 79 (1983), 420–21

'Finding a Language', review of *The Language of Poetry: Crisis and Solution. Studies in Modem Poetry of French Expression, 1945 to the Present*, ed. by Michael Bishop (Amsterdam: Rodopi, 1980), French Studies 38 (1984), pp. 241–42

'Bonnefoy's Poetics', review of Jérôme Thélot, *Poétique d'Yves Bonnefoy* (Geneva: Droz, 1983), *Modern Language Review*, 80 (1984), 948–50

'Rooted in the Oral', review of Clive Scott, *Vers Libre: The Emergence of Free Verse in France,*

*1886–1914* (Oxford: Clarendon Press, 1990), and Henri Meschonnic, *La Rime et la Vie* (Lagrasse: Verdier, 1990), *The Times Literary Supplement*, 28 December 1990, p. 1407

'Surrealism and the Book', review of Renée Riese Hubert, *Surrealism and the Book* (Berkeley: University of California Press, 1988), *French Studies*, 45.4 (October 1991), 492–93

'Guillevic', review of Gavin Bowd, *Guillevic: Sauvage de la modernité* (Glasgow: University of Glasgow French and German Publications, 1992), *Modern Language Review*, 90.1 (1995), 210–11

'Surrealist Automatic Writing', review of *Une pelle au vent dans les sables du rêve: les écritures automatiques*, ed. by Michel Murat and Marie-Paule Berranger (Lyon: Presses Universitaires de Lyon, 1992), *French Studies*, 48.2 (1994), 232–33

'A Translation of Bonnefoy', review of Yves Bonnefoy, *On the Motion and Immobility of Douve/ Du mouvement et de l'immobilité de Douve*, trans. by Galway Kinnell, intro. by Timothy Mathews (Newcastle: Bloodaxe Books, 1992), *French Studies*, 48.2 (1994), 240–41

'La Liberté des rues', review of Jacques Réda, *La Liberté des rues* (Paris: Gallimard, 1997), and Jean Rolin, *Zones* (Paris: Gallimard, 1997), *French Book News*, Service culturel, Ambassade de France, December 1997, pp. 24–25

'Bataille, Sartre, Valéry, Breton', review of Suzanne Guerlac, *Literary Polemics: Bataille, Sartre, Valéry, Breton* (Stanford, CA: Stanford University Press, 1997), *French Studies*, 54.3, (July 2000), 400–01

'The Material and the Real', review of Susan Harrow, *The Material, the Real and the Fractured Self: Subjectivity and Representation from Rimbaud to Réda* (Toronto: University of Toronto Press, 2004), *French Studies*, 59.4 (October 2005), 559–60

'Pierre Alferi and the Poetics of the Dissolve: Film and Visual Media in *Sentimentale Journée*', in *When Familiar Meanings Dissolve... Essays in French Studies in memory of Malcolm Bowie*, ed. by Naomi Segal and Gill Rye (Oxford and New York: Peter Lang, 2011), pp. 37–53

'Pierre Alferi, "Une défense de la poésie"', in *Twentieth-Century French Poetry: A Critical Anthology*, ed. by Hugues Azerad and Peter Collier (Cambridge: Cambridge University Press, 2010), pp. 279–87

'Pierre Alferi and Jakob von Uexküll: Experience and Experiment in *Le Chemin familier du poisson combatif*', in *Pierre Alferi: French Literature's Cinematic Turn*, ed. by Jean-Jacques Thomas, *SubStance*, 123, vol. 39, no. 3 (2010), pp. 105–27

'Survival and Resurgence of the Avant-Garde, or the Influence of Pierre Alferi on André Breton', first published as 'Survivance et recrudescence de l'avant-garde, ou l'influence de Pierre Alféri sur André Breton', in *Avantgarde und Modernismus: Dezentrierung, Subversion und Transformation im literarisch-künstlerischen Feld*, ed. by Wolfgang Asholt (Berlin: de Gruyter, 2014), pp. 89–105

# INTRODUCTION

❖

Michael Sheringham was assembling this book when he died in January 2016. The work included here appeared over four decades of scholarly engagement with French poetry and poetic thought. It represents only a part of Sheringham's critical achievements, which include his classic studies of French autobiography and of the Everyday, and the forthcoming *The Afterlives of Pierre Rivière: Foucault and the Archival Imaginary*, but it is a part to which he remained energetically committed.

The choice of essays, articles and reviews is therefore his own — as is the title, *Perpetual Motion*, which is as good a description as any, too, of the cut of Sheringham's mind. This book includes substantial scholarly articles and book contributions, short reviews and longer review-essays of the sort Sheringham published with the *Times Literary Supplement* and other papers of note over many years. The *TLS* called him 'an authoritative and stylish contributor' on its blog, written soon after hearing of his death, and those qualities of stylishness and authoritativeness are everywhere apparent in the pages to come. The book's unity comes from Sheringham's ongoing fascination with the idea of poetic form, and an attention to the continuities as well as the ruptures that have defined French poetry since André Breton and the surrealists. The book's diversity comes from the sheer range of material he explores. This range is evinced not just in the variety of his writers, who are not exclusively poets, but in the variety of approaches he adopts. Perhaps we may also add the variety of audiences for which they were written: the scholar and the student, the poetry-lover, the general reader and the enthusiast. Among his last pieces was an elegant and substantial review of the Pléiade Jaccottet in the *TLS* (it was in fact his last article for them), in which Sheringham deftly balanced deep knowledge, attentive close-reading, and clear, accessible prose. If there is one element of Sheringham's writing that unifies these diverse pieces, it is the interest he took in poetry's ability to remake and to *become* experience, rather than simply to narrate, represent or recall it. As he was in person to his friends, colleagues and students, so he is on the page: a sharer of ideas, and of the pleasures to be taken from pursuing them.

The first of these essays dates from 1977, and the last from 2015. There are essays on Pierre Alferi, Yves Bonnefoy, Michel Deguy, Anne Portugal, Jacques Réda and others — on individuals as well as movements and more numinous poetic 'currents'. There are also reviews of varying lengths, from short reviews for learned journals to more expansive review-articles. It is worth noting, in the contexts of these pieces, that Sheringham contributed to the debates within his discipline by reviewing the work of fellow-critics and taking part in the academic community. He maintained a regular presence in the pages of the journals where ideas were discussed and where the often isolated work of the scholar is brought into the light and shared by like- (and sometimes unlike-) minded academics. In this sense, and for all the distinction with which he carried out his individual research, he contributed to what we might call the *dailiness* of French studies, to the 'everyday life' of his departments and, more expansively, to his field of study, nationally and internationally.

For all its variety, there are motifs to be found in this book — preoccupations or intellectual force-fields to which Sheringham returns, and which bind it together with a perhaps unexpected unity of purpose. Chief among these are the recurrence of Breton, of the everyday, of real and imagined urbanism, of personal and collective memory, and of the materiality of language. Sheringham's ability to move from the mystical and the oracular in poetry to the linguistically innovative, by way of the ordinary and the everyday, is what made him such an authoritative commentator on the 'perpetual motion' that is the history of modern French literature. Also paramount is an attentiveness to the culture and the climates of thought which poetry feeds off, and to poetry's porousness and eclecticism. For this too, Sheringham was ideally placed, for he was theoretically astute and culturally observant. He understood the game of push-and-pull that poetry plays with the world, and with the language that it is both immersed in and draws free of.

The book begins with an early essay on André Breton, in which Sheringham explores the range of Breton's writing in the context of poet's role as, in Sheringham's words, the 'amanuensis of the unknown self'. He shows how poetry, for Breton, is a 'gravitational field, pulling more and more things into itself', and attends to the moment when, as Sheringham puts it (invoking Yeats, a frequent reference-point in his critical writing), 'the mirror [...] turns lamp'. Those of us who read Sheringham's criticism over years will be familiar with his ability to explain the way in which a poet like Breton thinks and feels, but to do so without reducing it or falsely unifying it; his capacity to explain something without *explaining it away*. As a critic, Sheringham is drawn to the roughness and the graininess of poetry, the moments of refusal to submit or yield, or readily to give up its meanings. Sheringham enjoys and is drawn to the way poetic language seems to 'fight back'. He is interested in the tangles in the thread of poetic language, the tight, seemingly unloosable knots, and not its smooth, flat unfolding. Breton himself was suspicious of 'fallacieuse clarté', and in Sheringham he finds a critic of the same temper. Sheringham's approach allows Breton to remain dynamic, mysterious, often bewildering, while finding ways through his work, showing that beneath the tumultuous surface of Breton's writing there is a stringency of purpose — a governing sensibility engaged in a project to remake the world and how we experience it. For this, the poem has to *be* the experience too.

Reading these essays, we are struck by their ambition and their openness. They are ambitious because they do not take the easy route, and because they choose, for the most part, literature that is innovative and challenging. Some of the poetry that Sheringham admires often seems to ask about the very possibility of poetry as a category and as an act of language. As a critic he is drawn to the liminal, shape-changing, border-crossing moments when poetry promises (or threatens) to become something else, or that glories in its own provisionality and inmixedness. His ability to write with inwardness and sympathy about a poet like Bonnefoy, as well as playfully and penetratingly about Anne Portugal or Pierre Alferi, shows a catholicism of mind which few critics can practise with such consistency or poise. Sheringham is at home with the poetry of the mystical, of the political, of the experimental-ludic and of the revolutionary-surreal. Though he is alive to their differences and their incompatibilities, he is also fascinated by their unexpected commonalities.

In a sense, all of his writings are marked by an enjoyment of the impurity of the literary object — of the autobiographical self that is more constructed and tricksy than the most ardently postmodern narrator, the everyday and the ordinary whose apparently flat surfaces reveal themselves to be holed by the magical and the unique, the surreal which finds in the banal an endless well of marvel-worthy material. Sheringham's command of literary and social theory, of political context, of art and popular culture keeps him alive to the contexts which the literary object lives in and lives off. Valéry, Breton's first hero, knew that if language were perfect, poetry would not exist. 'Rien de pur...', Valéry announces in *Poésie et pensée abstraite*, and it is not said in disapproval or disappointment, but with a sort of deadpan excitement. It is what guarantees and refreshes our need to read and write poetry. Sheringham's writing shares that excitement, and knows that the riches are to be found in that 'rien de pur', and not in some idealized process of refinement and sifting. To be able to convey this in lucid and patient criticism, to allow the reader to inhabit the energies that go into the making of literature without getting lost or becoming separated from sense, is one of Sheringham's achievements as a critic.

It will interest readers to know that a volume of tributes to Michael Sheringham appears in time with this one, and from the same publisher: *The Made and the Found: Essays, Prose and Poetry in Honour of Michael Sheringham*. It is fitting that its contributors include several of the very poets he discusses in this book, who knew him as a friend as well as a scholar, and who prized him as both.

*Patrick McGuinness*

# From the Labyrinth of Language
# to the Language of the Senses:
# The Poetry of André Breton

Je reviens à mes loups à mes façons de sentir[1]
[I return to my wolves to my ways of perceiving]

While many poets require us to go beyond the evident themes and modes of
statement in their poems to the latent sensibility from which they emerge, Breton
involves the reader immediately in his personal response to the world around him.
Before we can appreciate the significance of this profusion of the sensory on the
surface of Breton's poetry, it is helpful to examine the importance he attaches to
sense-experience. For Breton it is in the human being's sensory contact with the
world that an intuition of personal identity is most available: self and the world
are reciprocally defining concepts, the individual is inhabited by the accretions of
sensory contact with things:

> Je ne suis pas seul en moi-même
> Pas plus seul que le gui sur l'arbre de moi-même
> Je respire les nids et je touche aux petits des étoiles
> (*Clair de Terre*, I, 184)

[I am not alone within myself | No more so than the mistletoe on the tree of
myself | I breathe in nests and I touch the young of the stars]

The things to which we are drawn — objects, landscapes, textures — and our
reception of the sensory signals they emit, form an ever-evolving constellation that
is the figure of our sensibility. Breton refers to the 'sensations électives' [privileged
feelings] (I, 652) which together constitute an individual's 'lumière propre'
[particular light] (*Nadja*, I, 714), and frequently in his work we come across lists of
things to which his response seems particularly self-illuminating. But to discover
the self is, simultaneously, to discover the world. Breton gives the initiative to his
senses, allowing them a free rein: 'Je pique les coursiers de mes sens | Les uns
sont montés par de belles Amazones | Les autres se cabrent au bord des précipices
vermeils' (*Clair de Terre*, I, 184) [I spur on the steeds of my senses | Some are ridden
by beautiful Amazonians | Others rear on the edge of vermillion precipices].

It is not to the usual run of sensations that Breton introduces us — nor to
the circumscribed, rational world which these reflect. Indeed, if Breton himself
contributes to the discrediting of ordinary sense experience, it is not in the name of

any rational evidence, but so as to assert the cognitive role of less familiar sensations in respect of aspects of reality the rational mind ignores, but to which the individual sensibility gives testimony. There are certain sensations which reveal a hidden face of the world which corresponds to the hidden side of the mind — the unconscious. Revelation of the unconscious is directly linked to revelation of the world, and the senses are the agents of this process. The senses, however, can reveal the world only in so far as they have been activated by it, and in this lies the crucial role of the individual sensibility. Yet Breton does not propose a reversion to primitive modes of consciousness — pure anoesis or Lawrentian 'blood-knowledge'; the role of the poet is, as he puts it in *Les vases communicants III*, 'dégager l'intelligible du sensible' (II, 188) [to distinguish the intelligible from the sensory]. What is essential is that the senses should *lead*; if we let them, argues Breton, a wider horizon will be available even to the conscious mind.

Breton often addresses the problem of how we can incorporate into our everyday conception of the world fleeting moments of revelation that have fashioned our sensibility. The individual's unconscious bears the imprint of its encounters with the hidden aspect of the world, achieved through the process of reciprocal illumination I have outlined, and it is by gaining access to the unconscious that he or she can access, in a more permanent way, the gifts sensibility has amassed. In Breton's view it is the office of poetry to provide the means for this access. The surrealists discovered that it was possible to accede to the unconscious if the mind were allowed to express itself spontaneously in a manner that minimized the control of reason. In a second stage, the poem or text produced in this way acts as a catalyst through which the moments of perception that have made a deep impression on our unconscious can be re-precipitated in the mind. The poem itself comes to embody the trace of sensation on the mind; in so far as they manifest the poet's unconscious, his poems present a map of his or her sensibility, a sheet at a time. Yet there is comparatively little direct evocation of sensation in Breton's poetry; indeed on first acquaintance his poems seem merely to enact the strange behaviour of language when the customary semantic grid is lifted, allowing words to improvise provisional, individual compacts with one another — finding their own level, floating now perpendicularly, now obliquely, by turns luminous with meaning or opaque as the letters from which they are formed, merely words. But even if language is granted an autonomy seemingly incompatible with customary schemes of literary communication, this does not signal any evacuation of human presence in Breton's poetry: the new space into which words are projected by the practice of his poetry is not infinite, or circumscribed only by the finite permutations of the vocabulary he uses; and far from being remote from the human, the true space in which the words negotiate their meaning is that of his sensibility. But the sensory register to which it corresponds is a particular one, and the sensations that concern Breton are not the common sort. I hope to show presently that there is a parallelism of linguistic texture and type of sensation encompassed by Breton's poetry; but it is important to stress from the outset that, even if we accept that highly metaphorical discourse is not necessarily inappropriate to the true nature of our emotional and perceptual experience of the world, nevertheless it would be to misconstrue Breton's poetics if we assumed that he deliberately used language in a particular way so as to convey particular sensations. For Breton, the poetic process does not consist in a sequence of perception followed by expression through images. Rather, the inarticulate sensation, not rationalized into appropriate terms of comparison, finds an outlet in the gush of language. Far from presenting us with the reminiscence of sensation, Breton generates language to which he then responds sensorially himself, thereby recuperating original and fleeting sensations and more besides. Inasmuch as Breton's images allude to any context of actual sensations, it is not in a local and descriptive way. The phrase 'la fourrure de la nuit' (III, 34) [the fur of the night] in 'Du rêve' does not record a particular moment of experience when night was suddenly like fur — a local epiphany subsequently enshrined in the poem — even though the coherence and force of the image are totally grounded in sensory reciprocities. As a deliberate strategy the surrealist seeks to 'dépayser la sensation' [delocalize sensations], thereby enabling sense-experience to bypass rational channels and obtain immediate purchase on the unconscious, and to apprehend the extended reality which corresponds to it. This view does not derive from dissatisfaction with language as a medium of profound experience and knowledge of the world. For Breton, words, in the state of language proper to poetry, constitute 'le véhicule même de l'affectivité' (III, 732) [the very vector of affectivity]. An essential corollary to this is that words can in other states be hollow — Breton refers to 'les carapaces vides des mots' [the empty shells of words] — and it is only language emanating from the unconscious which can transmit the true apprehension of things. Our emotional experience is continuously forming chains of sensations, and to these there correspond 'groupements verbaux' (III, 731) [language chains] which the poet records. It is, ideally, a discourse dense and quick with its emergence from the unconscious that Breton presents on the page. For all its irrationality and apparent arbitrariness, the state of language that characterizes Breton's poetry has a special relation to the area of the mind in which an unfragmented, unmutilated vision of the world survives. But how can the reader share this experience, and profit from the inner adventure of the poet? If the words register the imprint of sensation on the unconscious, how can a response to language that *our* unconscious has not mediated be equivalent to a response to those aspects and that condition of things which such language designates? Michael Riffaterre suggested that the coherence of an apparently arbitrary image derives from the peculiar semantic resources (one might say resourcefulness) of language.[2] The initial semantic hostility of two terms, apparently simply yoked together in an image, is waived by our capacity and tendency to select from the semantic spectrum of each term those qualities which correspond with one another. 'Night' and 'fur', in the image I quoted above, attract and repel each other until we find the equilibrium proposed by the image — grounded in this case, say, on density of texture, darkness and so on. What must be stressed, then, is that surrealist metaphor, far from taking us away from sensation, that is, our broadest experience of the world of things, forces us to refer to the sensory presence and properties of things, even if we may sometimes eventually reject the image as incomprehensible, or worse, banal.

As the patterns of Breton's sensibility emerge, we become aware of the aspect of things with which their presence in his poems habitually confronts us: their potentialities as objects of sensation. By a kind of reverse synecdoche, objects in Breton's poems generally represent, to the exclusion of others, one or a few of their aspects — those that correspond to sensation rather than to our intellectual knowledge of them. Form, texture, mass, mobility, and so on, are the defining categories that shape the object in the poem, switching its sphere of operation from the labyrinth of language to the language of the senses. Breton's poems become comprehensible when we have weighed, touched and visualized in our minds, as far as we can, the things that inhabit them. No inventory of Breton's habitual material will afford much insight into the mechanisms of his poetry unless it takes into account the particular sensory aspect that defines the meaning of a given object in his poems. The many animals we find there are not cognate in respect of their status as animals; they invite classification, not into the familiar genera of animal life, but according to their shape, gait, the texture of their pelt and outer surfaces, and so on, for it is these attributes that define their role in Breton's sensibility and their role in the space of the poem. It is these individual qualities or aspects which combine, transferring and translating themselves on to other objects and qualities. The process is an emotional and sensory one; it originates in and, through language, provokes a special kind of emotion. The field created by these sensory and linguistic interactions can be compared to the virtual space of a kinetic sculpture by Gabo: at once absent and present, it gives us a sense of something simultaneously stirring us and eluding us: the emotion proper to poetry, and as Borges once suggested, to all art.

In Breton's poetic practice, the potential arbitrariness of the way he uses language is obviated in two principal ways. Firstly, through recurrences of kinds of sensations associated with certain objects and categories of object. The referential valence of words and images — types of plant, references to climate and so on — which had seemed circumstantial, is seen, through recurrence, to be almost stable. Secondly, apparently gratuitous connections are themselves consonant with the manner in which the senses apprehend the world. The way our minds, if we let them, confer meaning on images — despite semantic anomalies — and respond to amalgams of mental and physical, abstract and concrete, corresponds to the way in which, truant to reason, we in fact receive and respond to the world. And Breton sees in this space created by the language of poetry, this space always at one remove, always beyond, the intimation of a new life-space, a source of new values and a mode of living which would embody them.

The sensory world of Breton's poetry is more than an index to the sensibility out of which his poetic creations emerge and to which it might provide a key. Rather, it constitutes the vocabulary through which, enlisting the connections between the sensation and the unconscious, between the unconscious and language, and between language and sensation, Breton presents his apprehension of an extended reality accessible to all of us. While it does record his individual response, it is important to remember that the evidence of the senses argues the possibility of a universal response through which we might accede to the lost plenitude of our condition. It is not only the identity of the individual self that the poem's condensations manifest, but the collective self. Although particular stimuli — individual things and relations — are personal, I think it can be shown that the particular range and quality of sensations is not, despite the fact that their expression may make it seem otherwise. The sensations correspond to and translate a total apprehension of reality and, it would seem, evince a literally *impending* domain of possibility and futurity. Although language has a special pertinence to these sensations, presenting them according to its own means, it can only act as a signal for them. But equally, the sensation itself is, in an important sense, only a metaphor, the sign — which can be made available to the conscious mind — of a total ontological engagement to which it gives credence. There is a certain range of sensory experience which Breton, in common with a number of other modern writers — poets, philosophers, and theologians — sometimes refers to as *presence*.

There is a constant dialectic of absence and presence in Breton. Presence indicates fullness of being, achieved through our relation with things. But while in an early poem he had appealed for 'La vie de la présence rien que de la présence' (I, 176) [The life of presence nothing but presence], he came to regard the intermittence of presence as an essential attribute. Indeed to possess wholly that to which we aspire would be to infringe the authenticity of desire. So that, in his love for the woman whom he addresses in these lines, he regards '[...] la fusion sans espoir de ta présence et de ton absence' [the hopeless merging of your presence and of your absence] as a positive quality in which he finds '[...] le secret | De t'aimer | Toujours pour la première fois' ('Toujours pour la première fois', II, 408) [the secret to always loving you for the first time]. What is essential is that a balance (Breton writes of 'le balancier de l'absence [...]' (*Le Revolver à cheveux blancs*, II, 75) [the equilibrium of absence]) should be found between absence and presence, or rather that their complicity and imbrication be recognized: '[...] l'absence et la présence qui sont de connivence' (II, 94) [absence and presence that are in cahoots]. This interrelation derives from the individual's role: the moment of presence is less an instant when the world, the thing, is present, as a sort of *Urphänomen* — though this is sometimes the impression we are given — than a moment of the *self's* presence in the world. The two are of course connected, as Wallace Stevens conveys when he writes that '[poetry] is an illumination of a surface, the movement of a self in the rock'.[3] Consciousness, in the broadest sense, is to the world as light and dark are to the earth — divided, though by infinite degrees, in their appropriation. Similarly, self-presence is related to the modulations and intermittences of the world itself, as apprehended by the mind. Breton therefore frequently denies the primary reality and sensory properties of things while drawing attention to the fleeting nature of presence in reality, embodied in aspects or dimensions of reality — in a gleam, an incandescence, an atmosphere. In doing so Breton is often simply transcribing the poet's own emotional response to the world. In a letter to Breton's friend Antonin Artaud, Jacques Rivière wrote: 'Proust a décrit "les intermittences du cœur"; il faudrait maintenant décrire les intermittences de l'être' [Proust described 'the

heart's intermittences'; the intermittences of being should now be described].[4]
For Breton, it might be said, these are in essence identical: it is in an emotional
response to reality that the moment of presence — the moment of being — is
made possible. Emotional response is, in Breton's view, the mark of profound
experience, and such a response was generally, he believed, the outcome of sensory,
rather than intellectual, activity (though Breton, it should be stressed, believed that
one responded to *ideas* in a sensory manner). Consider the 'émotion très spéciale'
[very special emotion] that registers his response to those things in which he finds
himself:

> J'avoue sans la moindre confusion mon insensibilité profonde en présence des
> spectacles naturels et des œuvres d'art qui d'emblée, ne me procurent pas un
> trouble physique caractérisé par la sensation d'une aigrette de vent aux tempes
> susceptible d'entraîner un véritable frisson. (*L'Amour fou*, II, 678)

> [Without hesitation, I confess my profound indifference towards natural
> phenomena, and works of art, that do not immediately cause me some sort
> of physical disturbance, like the sensation of an egret's plume brushing one's
> temples which might engender an authentic frisson.]

Some caution is required here: the physical component of the sensation serves only
as a signal of the fact that the writer has been *moved* at a profounder level than the
physiological — just as in Plato's *Ion*, the shiverings of the poet are only the outward
manifestation of inspiration. In the egret's plume playing on his temples, there is an
echo of Mallarmé's

> lucide et seigneuriale aigrette de vertige
> au front invisible[5]

[lucid and noble egret of vertigo | with invisible brow]

The parallel with Mallarmé, a poet who kept the sensory world at some distance
in his verse, offers a corrective to any exaggeration of the strictly physical aspect of
sensory-emotive response, and of the precedence of powerful sensations in Breton.

The oscillations of sensory activity which attract Breton are at the origin of the
emotional texture of his poetry. Emotion is present at a primary level in the poet's
frequent direct references to the priority of emotive experience: 'Plutôt ce cœur à
cran d'arrêt' (I, 176) [Rather this safety-catched heart], he writes, again in *Clair de
Terre*; or, in a striking apposition, 'cœur lettre de cachet' (I, 171) [royal prerogative
heart]. Even more common is the presentation of a reality in the throes of the
emotion which apprehends it. For instance we read 'Ce jour-là je tremblerai de
perdre une trace | Dans un des quartiers brouillés de Lyon' (III, 28) [That day I
will shudder to lose a trace | In one of Lyon's jumbled districts]. Here the poet's
emotion has been imparted to reality itself: the adjective *brouillés* suggests, of course,
the labyrinthine streets of the ancient city; but it also represents a projection of
the indeterminacies of the poet's quest, the quest for a dimension of experience
consonant with the confused intuitions of a deeper self.

The fleeting and febrile quality of the emotion is transmitted to the reader in two
distinct manners: firstly by a poetic tone owing much to the nature of automatic

writing, and secondly by the way the world itself is presented in the poem. A few words must be said about the former and then more extended treatment is called for by the latter. The state of language actualized in automatic writing, rational and analytical faculties being suspended, tends to favour the direct exteriorization of emotion through the diction and form (or formlessness) of the poem. Indeed, Breton's poetry often has the confidential, intimate, tone of the 'murmure' [murmur], and Breton sometimes, although by no means always, sacrifices some of the characteristic felicities of modern poetry — ellipsis and rhythmic control, shall we say — by allowing the intricate patterning of the inner voice to guide the poem. At a second degree, a further aspect of automatic composition is involved. It should be remembered that the emotions referred to register an *inner* experience, an adventure of the inner self. A curve has been made from the world through the senses to the unconscious; for the individual to become aware and to benefit, it is essential that the rational intellect be excluded lest it reduce such experience to the level of ordinary sense-data; for the circle to be completed, language must participate, ferrying the sensory information unalloyed. This is the basis of Breton's poetics: the poet is the amanuensis of the unknown self.

Quite apart from the tone, then, Breton's poems bear in a less observable fashion the imprint of the experience in which they originate. We need to be attentive, beyond the direct notation of emotional reaction, to the way the material world presented in the poems reveals itself to be the world apprehended in unconscious experience. But in so doing we must observe how things in the poem articulate more than the emotion which has appreciated them, how they are made to serve as the sign-language for a certain experience of the world generally, to which in themselves they may be irrelevant. Before going on to look at this in detail, it is as well to trace one or two intermediate stages in which objects serve this role in a more explicit way.

We might begin with a stage at which the poet's subjective response to reality is conveyed merely by a linguistic contrivance: qualities equivalent to emotive response are predicated of a reality in itself stable. Thus we read of a 'château qui tremble' (III, 19) [a trembling castle], or of 'pièces frissonnantes' (L'Air de l'eau', II, 396) [shivering rooms]. There is next a further stage at which the poem registers a movement in reality and imbues it with human mystery — for instance the rustle of branches and the intermittent glimpses of sky this permits: 'le bois qui tremble s'entrouvre sur le ciel' (*Clair de Terre*, II, 164) [the waving woods half-open towards the sky]. Here the words are set the task of corroborating for the reader the poet's experience of reality: they acquit themselves of it in a manner independent of the experience itself — by exploiting the ability of language to operate in a range analogous to the sensory one. But the poem's foundation on the ability of the reader to recognize this *as* experience is of central importance. For this is how a thematic reality, in the network of poetry, becomes a 'poetic' or super-reality. It is the semantic margins of words which create the area of play in which an extension of the customary *presence* of things can take place. Thus, in the last quotation, the verb *s'entrouvrir* engenders possibilities, or indeed obligations, of reading which transport us from a literal (habitual) zone — trees waving in the breeze — to a metaphysical (unfamiliar) zone — an experience in which an intermittent sense of liberation and unveiling of reality is achieved. Yet the passage to metaphor is not a projection outside experience, but rather to the rim of experience — its exalted fringes of being.

To see how this is fully achieved in Breton's poetry we need to go beyond the two stages I have outlined to a thematic network not particularly identifiable by any direct appeal to sensory-emotive response. Let us examine, for instance, the thematic structure constituted by recurring references to favoured times of day and atmospheric conditions, and see how it translates, beyond a heightened awareness of the phenomenal world, an inner experience whose true nature and significance are independent of its literal reference.

Breton frequently refers to certain features of climate and times of day when the world seems spontaneously to partake of the emotion it occasions: 'Le temps est si clair que je tremble qu'il ne finisse' (II, 396) [Time/the weather is so fair I shudder lest it end]. The first light of morning appeals particularly to him. 'Chantier qui tremble chantier qui bat de lumière première' (III, 30) [Trembling site that beats with first light]; here morning is associated with the mystery of constant renewal and resurrection. In the same poem Breton writes 'c'est à croire | Que le ressort du soleil n'ai jamais servi' [enough to believe | That the sun's energy has never served]: the first rays of the sun form a diaphanous hedge: 'Pleine de velléités d'essors tendue de frissons | Une haie traverse la chambre d'amour' (III, 29) [Full of empty desires to fly, taut with thrills | A hedge cuts across love's bedroom]; everything is re-created:

> Le maraîcher va et vient sous sa housse
> Il embrasse d'un coup d'œil tous les plateaux montés
> cette nuit du centre de la terre (*Fata Morgana*, II, 1192)

[The gardener comes and goes beneath his cover | Embracing with a glance all of the dishes brought up | overnight from the depths of the earth]

The image of morning revealing things which have been freshly made in the night is extended elsewhere, when the *chantier* becomes quarries, and everything — leaves, snow, human flesh, is laid out in the first ray, the 'premier rayon' of sunshine (II, 398).

There can be no doubt of Breton's solidarity with Night. But, as some of the above quotations imply, night is not so much a time of revelation as of germination, when energies are marshalled for the day. Night is a time for promise, 'les promesses des nuits étaient enfin tenues' (I, 187) [the promises of night time were kept at last], and of invisible activity, 'la nuit | Qui fait bien ce qu'elle fait' (I, 188) [night time | Who does well what she does]; an extreme time of disorientation which precedes revelation, 'le mal prend des forces tout près' (I, 174) [nearby, evil is gaining strength], but also a time of dream and apparition: Breton refers to 'la nuit qui décalque mes images' (I, 174) [night time that copies my dreams]; and the night can be transfigured, just as flares of imagery light up the page: 'C'est la plus belle des nuits, *la nuit des éclairs*: le jour, auprès d'elle est la nuit' [It's the most beautiful of nights, *scintillating night*: daytime, by comparison is as night time]. Night and Day, like absence and presence, are relative: 'Moi qui n'accorde au jour et à la nuit que la stricte jeunesse nécessaire | Ce sont deux jardins dans lesquels je promène mes mains | [...]' (I, 182) [I who grant day and night only the shortest possible youth | They are two gardens in which I walk my hands]. Night is transformed by light; day, by the paradoxical density of shadow: 'Sous l'ombre il y a une lumière et sous cette lumière il y a deux ombres' (I, 188) [There is a light beneath the shadow, and two shadows beneath this light]. The essence of daylight is not clarity. Breton was attracted to the play of sunrays, and in the list of things which he cites in one poem as conditioning his poetic space, he includes, with evocative ambiguity, 'le sens du rayon de soleil' (II, 420) [the direction/meaning of the sunbeam]. It is often the paradoxical solidity of light rather than its transparency to which he draws attention. There is no feeling in Breton for the Mediterranean *éclat* in which both a Camus and a Valéry could descry the Pindaric realm of possibility; indeed his opposition to Graeco-Latin civilization increasingly nourished an intuitive enthusiasm for the more nubilous art and culture of the northerly Celts. Breton is dismissive of what he calls 'fallacieuse clarté' (IV, 299) [fallacious clarity]; he once gave this report of a projected visit to his favourite Tour Saint-Jacques in Paris: 'Ce dimanche 27 avril, force fut, très vite, d'en rabattre. Il faisait d'ailleurs très beau et trop clair: l'insolite se fût en tout cas dérobé. L'air n'était même pas pesant autour de la statue de Pascal' [Today, Sunday 27th of April, it was quickly necessary to retreat. The weather was too good and too clear: anything unusual would not have been apparent. The air around the Pascal statue wasn't even heavy].

It is to the transitional hours of the morning and evening twilight that Breton most frequently refers us. In the evening it is the *last* ray of light which is magical: '[...] le rêve des chants d'oiseaux du soir | Dans l'obliquité du dernier rayon le sens d'une révélation mystérieuse' (II, 1194) [the dream of evening birdsong | In the bias of the last ray of sunlight the meaning/direction of a mysterious revelation]; here again there is a play on the word *sens* — signifying 'meaning' and 'direction'. It is perhaps from the evening that one may hope for the revelation when:

> Les lits faits de tous les lys
> Glissent sous les lampes de rosée
> Un soir viendra
> Les pépites de lumière s'immobilisent sous la mousse bleue (II, 71)

> [All of the lilies made beds | Slip beneath the lamps of dew | An evening will
> come | The nuggets of light still themselves beneath the blue moss]

It is characteristic of Breton that he uses two tenses in the same sequence, for when, a little before, he writes 'l'avenir n'est jamais' [the future is never] — this does not signify despair, but that the evening which will come is already present, implicit, in the evening he experiences and 'describes'. The twilight is, then, the transitional hour when 'le jour et la nuit échangent leur promesses' (II, 1181) [day and night exchange their promises].

And it is of course a time when the air often has that *density* Breton missed round Pascal's statue (which, appropriately, marks the spot where his experiments confirmed Torricelli's theories about the weight of atmosphere). At twilight the atmosphere is either enlaced with mist or laden, perhaps illuminated as the quotation above suggests, with dew. The morning dew has, of course, connotations of freshness and nascence, so that it is the first dewdrop, like the first sunray which makes it iridescent, which encapsulates '[...] le mystère de l'existence | Le premier grain de rosée devançant de loin tous les autres follement irisé contenant tout' (III, 417) [the mystery of existence | The first drop of dew by far preceding the others, its iridescence impetuously containing everything]. Of the scores of references to dew in Breton, perhaps the most beautiful occurs in 'L'Union libre' [The Free Union] where, in his litany of celebration of the woman he loves, he writes of 'Ma femme [...] | Aux seins de spectre de la rose sous la rosée' (II, 86) [My woman with breasts spectral as the rose beneath the dew]. Here language mimes the lover's trembling apprehension of the woman's breasts in half-light, when they might themselves resemble roses sparkling but muffled in the morning dew, and perhaps accompanying mist, would give it an ethereal, remote quality; in the complementary dimension of language, the word *rose* 'haunts' the word *rosée*. Mist, related to dawn, embodies the persistence of dream in daytime. In a lyrically complex extended metaphor, Breton associates mist with the daily alchemy through which night becomes day — the 'Art des jours et des nuits' [Art of daytime and night time] (elsewhere he refers to 'La vapeur des alambics' (IV, 327) [The vapour of the stills]). He presents day and night as poised on the scales of a balance so sensitive that the flight of the first bird suffices to tip it towards day and release the mediating mist:

> Balance rouge et sensible au poids d'un vol d'oiseau
> Quand les écuyères au col de neige les mains vides
> Poussent leurs chars de vapeur sur les prés [...]
> Les roues du rêve charment les splendides ornières
> Qui se lèvent très hauts sur les coquilles de leurs robes
> Et l'étonnement bondit de-ci de-là sur la mer
> Partez ma chère aurore n'oubliez rien de ma vie (II, 67)

[Red scales, sensitive to the weight of a bird's flight | When the snowy-necked horse-woman with empty hands | Push their steam chariots on the field [...] | The wheels of the dream charm the handsome tracks | That rise high on the shells of their dresses | And surprise leaps here and there on the sea | Go, my dear dawn, forget nothing of my life]

Taking the opportunity to show how Breton's imagination, and sensory mechanisms, operate, one might draw attention to the way, in these lines, the departure of the bird suggests travel, thereby introducing the idea of a chariot or waggon, on which mist arrives and in which dawn will depart, bearing with it some of the central elements of the poet's life, because it is party to his dreaming and his waking. The *roues* relate to the *char*, but also (as evidence in other poems suggests) represent sunrays, through the idea of spokes. The dresses of the horse-women, presumably wispy and diaphanous, suggest the curves of shells (and the connection may have been generated via the scallop's radiating lines, like sunrays); but there is probably also a telescoped reminiscence of Botticelli's 'Birth of Venus' here. The shells introduce the sea, which is also connected with departure, while *étonnement* —

conveying the miracle and surprise of waking — seems to me to owe its context to a linguistic echo of *tonnerre* or *tonner*, and to refer to the frequent agitation of the morning sea.

The ethereal movement and insubstantiality of mist is further conveyed elsewhere, when it is invoked to convey the lightness and grace of a woman's arms: '[...] des bras si légers que la vapeur des près dans ses gracieux entrelacs au-dessus des étangs leur est imparfait miroir' (II, 77) [arms so light that the interlacing vapour of the fields above water pools imperfectly mirrors them].

In the network so far established we might be tempted to subsume all references to climate and time of day into the general category of *air*. Very little that is extraneous to such classification — for instance purely visual aspects characterizing different times of day — occurs in Breton's poems. Even references to the play of light-rays generally relate to the apparent solidification and shaping of the atmosphere, as do dew and mist. Yet it may be that air is only incidentally the common factor, for it is not so much air that is important as the process for which it is the medium. Going further, we might say that the experienced phenomenon is in itself less important that the associative field of the concept — partly linguistic, partly cultural — in determining the function of air as a poetic signifier in Breton's poetry. Which is to say that we must avoid the tautology involved in a purely literal reading which would lead us unequivocally from poem to sensory experience. On the other hand, to opt for a totally symbolic reading would lead to obligations which we could not fulfil on the basis of poetry. Air, once identified as a common ground for multiple references to dew and sunlight, is by no means the consistent symbol of anything in Breton's poems. Indeed, this may perhaps account for its prominence as the hidden centre of a thematic network. For it is not reference to *things in themselves* which characterizes modern poetry so much as *the interrelationship of things* — often, though not exclusively, suggested by sensory analogy. Air is favoured precisely because it is susceptible of a great variety of relationships, defining itself only with reference to a multiplicity of contexts. It is, indeed, in this slightly abstract aspect, rather than in particular sensory features, that air is remarkable. Air is flux, transitivity, a catalytic medium in which various degrees of substantification can occur.

The states of air which appeal to Breton are those which manifest an insubstantial presence — as light, vapour or water. In certain conditions — the bogus clarity of bright sunlight which hides and separates rather than reveals — air is vacuity and nothingness. But when it blows bits of paper around in a windy city: 'les morceaux de papiers se salient de haut en bas des maisons' (III, 21); rustles mistletoe — 'Dehors l'air essaie les gants de gui' (II, 396) [Outside air tries on mistletoe gloves]; or when, as 'les vêtements de l'air pur' (I, 381) [the clothes of pure air], it makes a billowing costume for the walker, the air becomes shape and presence — animated space. It has the miraculous capacity to precipitate itself: 'l'air est sur le point de fleurir' [the air is on the verge of flowering] (*Le surréalisme et la* peinture, IV, 614), and Breton once expressed the aspiration to a sense of participation in the universe in these terms: 'Si seulement j'étais une racine de l'arbre du ciel | Enfin le bien dans la canne à sucre de l'air' (I, 183) [If only I were a root of the sky's tree | Goodness at last in air's sugar cane]. For Breton is fascinated by the mystery of precipitation, in both the chemical and the meteorological sense. In one moment of discovery, the sun's rays are associated with the falling rain, both solidified: 'Je vois les arêtes du soleil | A travers l'aubépine de la pluie' (II, 94) [I see the sun's ridges | Through the rain's hawthorn]. Elsewhere rain becomes a 'colonne de cristal' (*Poisson soluble*, I, 370) [crystal column] or 'une haute verge de tourmaline sur la mer' (III, 419) [a thick layer of tourmaline on the sea]. Solidification, modulation into substance, represents the apotheosis of the insubstantial; and it serves as a metaphor for the shift from absence into presence and the mystery of the advent of being. References to air and to the atmosphere therefore have a multiple function in Breton's poetry. Far from any one-to-one symbolic function or any stable sensory experience, air refers the reader to a particular cluster of processes, relationships and metamorphoses which are homologous, rather than directly analogous, to mental, spiritual and emotional shifts. The broad wave-band of sensory reality embraced by references to air — and grounded on experience — becomes a semantic space in which can be articulated experiences which are non-sensory but which relate to the deep springs of the psyche. Indeed the grace of substance is often explicitly related to the emotion and desire of the individual through motifs such as crystallization, arborescence, ramification. Sartre once wrote perceptively of Breton: 'Ce qui le passionne, ce n'est pas le désir à chaud mais le désir cristallisé, ce qu'on pourrait appeler, en empruntant une expression à Jaspers, le chiffre du désir dans le monde' [He is not so much fascinated with desire itself as with crystallized desire, what we might call, to borrow Jaspers' expression, the figure of desire in the world].[6] In the following, for instance, the poet's desire is the catalyst which brings about a crystallization (here chemistry and meteorology join!): 'J'attends la pluie comme une lampe élevée trois fois dans la nuit, comme une colonne de cristal qui monte et qui descend, entre les arborescences soudaines de mes désirs' (I, 370) [I await the rain like a lamp lifted three times in the night, like a crystal column, that rises and falls, between sudden spurts in my desires].

   The processes of desire register the imbrication of natural and individual necessity, and through its operations — often manifest in limpid emotion — self and worth are mutually illuminated and discovered. As Breton helps his wife step off a boat, a moment of physical contact animates desire which 'creates' the transformed world within the self:

> Ta main [...] réfracte son rayon dans la mienne. Son moindre contact s'arborise en moi et va décrire en un instant au-dessus de nous ces voûtes légères où [...] le ciel renversé mêle ses feuilles bleues (*Arcane* 17, III, 46)

> [Your hand refracts its light in mine. Its slightest contact sows itself in me and instantly follows the light vaults above us in which the upturned sky mixes its blue leaves]

Elsewhere dust suspended in the 'premier rayon du soleil' [the sun's first light], as the poet wakes beside the loved one, is the insubstantial but tangible legacy of the previous day: 'c'est toute la vie d'hier qui se ramifie en un corail impossible de la pâleur de tes mains' (II, 669) [all of yesterday's life is ramified into an impossible coral, the paleness of your hands]. In one place we read 'toutes les branches de l'air' (II, 679) [all of the air's branches]. Breton's poems are full of references to things which present the quality of ramification: trees of course, leaves, many plants, particularly ferns, coral; and of things which *form* themselves: coral again, crystals, stalactites. Because they are emblems of desire, as much as the talismans of an individual sensibility, there is another way in which these things elude the simple arbitrariness of preference. If desire manifests the unity of mind and world, then these highly organized but delicate things seem to have a special pertinence to, and our relation to them a special purchase on, the generative processes of the mind:

> [...] les rameaux du sel les rameaux blancs
> Toutes les bulles d'ombre
> Et les anémones de mer
> Descendent et respirent à l'intérieur de ma pensée (II, 70)

[the branches of salt the white branches | All the bubbles of shadow | And the sea anemones | Come down and breathe inside my mind]

The individual's discovery of these things has not taken place at the level of his everyday life and self, but along the parallel inner trajectory constituted by his emotional and sensory experiences, which leave their trace on the sand of our unconscious and on the page:

> Ils viennent des pleurs que je ne verse pas
> Des pas que je ne fais pas qui sont deux fois des pas
> Et dont le sable se souvient à la marée montante (II, 70)[7]

[They come from tears that I don't spill | Steps ('pas') that I do not ('pas') make that are doubly 'pas' | And that the sand remembers as the tide comes in]

It is possible to discern something of Breton's feeling for the morning twilight in Baudelaire's line from 'Le Crépuscule du matin': 'L'air est plein du frisson des choses qui s'enfuient' [The air is full of the shivers of things that are running away]. Breton's poems record the endeavour to dispel a customarily accredited reality by encouraging words to give voice and vestment to an absent presence at the heart of things. Accordingly, it is not the substantial massiveness of the world in broad sunlight, but the flickering light of dawn and of certain atmospheric conditions that corresponds to the 'frisson' which registers sensory response. If poetry, in Stevens's phrase, is the illumination of a surface, then it is a feature of twilight to dissolve appearances into a changing spectacle of momentary impressions. If we now turn to this combination of the transient and the 'superficial' we shall be able to extend our survey of Breton's poetic world into some of its more paradoxical regions.

In a wide range of images Breton suggests that it is on the shimmering surface of things that their true substance and profundity lie. His poetry is characterized by a shifting 'essence' from a putative depth to surfaces, a modulation which, issuing from or paralleling *Gestalttheorie* and phenomenology, or the aesthetics of a Focillon with his 'profondeur cachée sur la surface' [depths hidden on the surface], underlies so much of contemporary art and thought. 'Ô substance', exclaims Breton, 'il faut donc toujours en revenir aux ailes de papillon' (II, 671) [Oh substance, we must then always return to butterfly wings]. The sudden glitter and flutter of a butterfly's wing correspond better to Breton's sense of what is 'real', to presence, and to the context of our relation to the extended reality he postulates, than the monumentality of the permanent everyday sense. Permanence lies within, in our emotional and imaginative annals: 'Il n'est que de fermer les yeux | Pour retrouver la table du permanent' (II, 1194) [We need but close our eyes | To find the seat of permanence].

Yves Bonnefoy has it that 'le fugace, l'irrémédiablement emporté est le degré poétique de l'univers' [the poetic quality of the universe is all that is fleeting, or can be irremediably lost];[8] for Breton, too, what is fleeting and momentary in experience is ontologically privileged. One image in which this is expressed in the *Second manifeste du surréalisme* is that of the glow of glimmer — the *lueur*, which is both within the individual: 'Cette lueur que le surréalisme cherche à déceler au fond de nous' (I, 783) [That glimmer that surrealism seeks to discern within us] and outside. In one of the *Constellations* — prose-poems which accompany paintings by Miró — Breton takes up the painter's title 'Personnages dans la nuit guidés par les traces phosphorescentes des escargots' [Figures in the night guided by phosphorescent snail trails] and comments:

> Rares sont ceux qui ont éprouvé le besoin d'une aide semblable en plein jour, — ce plein jour où le commun des mortels a l'aimable prétention de voir clair [...]. A l'éveil, le tout serait de refuser à la fallacieuse clarté le sacrifice de cette lueur de labradorite qui [...] est tout ce que nous avons en propre pour nous diriger sans coup férir dans le dédale de la rue. (IV, 299)

> [Few are those who have experienced a similar need for help in broad daylight, — the daylight in which most mortals make the pleasant claim that they see clearly. Upon waking, the main thing would be to refuse to sacrifice this ox-eye glimmer to false clarity, as it is all we truly possess to navigate without encountering any opposition in the maze of streets.]

In another place Breton writes of 'le brillant, quand on les coupe, de métaux inusuels comme le sodium [...], la phosphorescence, dans certaines régions, des carrières [...], l'éclat du lustre admirable qui monte des puits' (I, 714) [the glimmer when cut of some unusual metals, such as sodium, the phosphorescence of quarries in certain areas, the splendour of the brilliant lustre that rises from the boreholes]. Equally Breton is sensitive to the play of light and shadow, for instance as sunrays filter through trees in a wood giving the earth '[des] reflets plus profonds que ceux de l'eau' (II, 401) [deeper reflections than those of the water]. Elsewhere, he refers to 'la lueur qui pêche les cœurs dans ses filets' [light that catches hearts in its nets] (*Clair de Terre*, I, 185), which, through the idea of the net, subtly conveys the patterns of light and shade cast by vegetation or anything latticed (the thematic structure of the *ajour* [openwork], the *dentelle* [lacework] and so on is an important one in Breton) and also the dimension of our sensory and emotive 'captivation' by the spectacle.

The *lueur* is thus a real property of certain places and things given emotive amplification in Breton's sensibility;[9] but it also commands other metaphors: the *lueur* is also present in the flickering gleams of the fire: 'Le fond de l'âtre | Est toujours aussi splendidement noir | Le fond de l'âtre où j'ai appris à voir' (II, 400)

[The bottom of the hearth | Is still so glimmeringly black | The depths of the hearth in which I learned to see]. One of Breton's most famous poems, inspired by Heraclitus, celebrates many aspects of the flame; in one passage the flame seems to represent that aspect of things which engages the individual's imagination: 'Et la flamme court toujours | C'est une fraise de dentelle au cou d'une jeune seigneur' (II, 68) [And the flame runs still | It's a lace strawberry upon the neck of a young lord] (etc.). And just as the *lueur* was a guide in the labyrinth of the street, so Breton, splendidly enjoins the flame to guide him, here to an apotheosis: 'Flamme d'eau guide-moi jusqu'à la mer de feu' (II, 70) [Flame of water, guide me to the sea of fire].

The intermittent *lueur* in things corresponds to a particular modality of our apprehension, and particularly vision, of them. A recurring theme in Breton's numerous writings on painting is the redefinition of our powers of vision. Breton bemoans the poverty of our customary ways of seeing, while at the same time celebrating the potential capacities of the eye. The eye is valorized specifically by its capacity to discern the unity of the world), and, above all, to catch what is delicate or only fleeting. Nadja has 'des yeux de fougère' [eyes of fern], not simply because her eyes are green but because they are open and sensitive to 'les battements d'ailes de l'espoir immense' (I, 714) [the fluttering wings of enormous hope], and because her way of seeing deserves the compliment of association with one of the prizes of vision, the subtle structure of ferns. For Breton there is a reciprocity of what is at the fringes of seeing, and the hidden self. The ambiguity of vision engenders a gyroscopic poise of the self in its quest and trajectory: Breton presents himself as 'fixant un point brillant que je ne sais être dans mon œil mais qui m'épargne de me heurter à ses ballots de nuit' (I, 749) [staring at a brilliant point, that I know not to be in my eye, but that spares me from bumping into its night time bales]. But this brilliant point can also be a point in time, a moment when outer and inner correspond, when we attain 'cet angle toujours fuyant sous lequel les 'choses' s'estompent jusqu'à disparaître, au prix de quoi commence à se dévoiler l'esprit des choses' (IV, 762) [that always evasive angle of vision by which 'things' fade until they disappear, at the cost of which the spirit of things begins to appear]. This theme of the angle of vision at which things transmute so that we can see and relate them fully, can be well documented in Breton's poems — expressions such as *de biais*, *oblique*, *tangence*, *diagonal* (*on the bias, oblique, tangency, diagonal*) are common. The revelation which this vision implies accounts for the frequent association of these terms with the curtain:

> Tu rentres à telle heure de la nuit dans une maison oblique à ma fenêtre [...]
> L'angle fugitif d'un rideau
> [...] une route des environs de Grasse
> Avec ses cueilleuses en diagonale [...]
> Devant elles l'équerre de l'éblouissant
> Le rideau invisiblement soulevé (II, 407–08)

[At some hour of the night you return to a house diagonally across from my window [...] | The fleeting angle of a curtain | [...] a road in the vicinity of Grasse | With its diagonal rows of women harvesting [...] | The dazzling slant before them | The curtain invisibly lifted]

This spontaneous and imperceptible unveiling of reality, indicated in the last line, is what the eye can momentarily achieve; thus 'chaque paysage nous trouve dans la même attente qui est celle du lever d'un rideau' [each landscape fills us with the same expectation as the lifting of a curtain] (*Point du jour*, II, 299–300). Returning to the angle and the curtain, we find 'Entre le rideau de vie | Et le rideau de cœur' (II, 402) [Between the curtain of life | And the curtain of the heart], or '[...] adorable rideau de tangence' (III, 20) [adorable tangential curtain]. Essentially this tangential vision is akin to the one which Bonnefoy ascribes to memory: 'la vision absolue qu'elle nous donnait des choses, nous semble-t-elle la mère des plus furtives lueurs que l'instant arrache, pour notre joie, à la substance de ce qui est' [the absolute vision that it grants us seems to us the source of the furtive glimmers that are taken away in an instant, for our happiness, from the substance of what is].[10] Such vision, the *lueur*, is above all momentary, and with this can be associated the fact that the theme, and sometimes structure, of some of Breton's most successful poems is constituted by recreating through images the shared instant of a momentary encounter. In one poem, 'Le Puits enchanté', a meeting-place with a woman is presented not as a location in space but as the point defined by the trajectories which separate evocations of it describe, or inscribe, on our senses. Here is part of the passage:

> Tout au fond de l'entonnoir
> Dans les fougères foulées du regard
> J'ai rendez-vous avec la dame du lac [...]
> C'est là
> A la place de la suspension du dessous dans la maison des nuages (II, 1241)

[Deep down inside the funnel | Amongst the ferns crushed beneath the gaze, | I am meeting the lady of the lake | It's there | In the nether hanging place in the house of clouds]

This is not the definitive encounter which will re-shape the individual's life around the adventure of love, it is the context in which it is awaited: through the invocation of chance by an open, lyrical mode of living in which, as Breton wrote elsewhere, 'toute femme est la Dame du Lac' (IV, 327) [every woman is the Lady of the Lake]. It is the improvised space and tangent of Char's 'angle fusant d'une rencontre' [gushing angle of a meeting]. Such encounters, like that celebrated in 'A une passante' (which marks one of the many moments in Baudelaire which stand as paradigms of the modern poetic sensibility), are of course the prize of the *flâneur* and, as is so manifest in Breton's major prose works, one of the most familiar avatars of the surrealist is as wanderer of the city labyrinth. But in this context it is not the carnality of the libertine which characterizes him; even the existence of the central woman in the poet's life, at a time of love, is refracted through the city: 'Ton existence le bouquet géant qui s'échappe de mes bras | [...] s'effeuille dans les vitrines de la rue' (II, 398) [Your existence, the enormous bouquet of flowers that escapes from my arms | [...] loses its leaves in the street windows].

Even what is possessed is fleeting, ever escaping, needing to be lost and found again: 'les amants au défaut du temps retrouvant et perdant la bague de leur source' (II, 1181) [lovers lacking in time again finding and losing the ring of their source].

Between these poles of losing and finding, absence and presence, lies the experience of the encounter — the sudden flare of sexual energy, and yet more than the mere surge of lust, a source of revelation:

> Oracle attendu de la navette d'un soulier
> Plus brillant qu'un poisson jeté dans l'herbe
> Ou d'un mollet qui fait un bouquet des lampes de mineur
> Ou du genou qui lance un volant dans mon cœur
> Ou d'une bouche qui penche qui penche à verser son parfum
> Ou d'une main [...] (III, 20)

[Oracle expected from a shoe shuttle | More gleaming than a fish thrown onto the grass | Or than a calf that makes a posy of the miner's lamps | Or than a knee that shoots a pellet into my heart | Or than an inclined mouth that inclines to pour its perfume | Or than a hand]

In this poem, appropriately entitled 'Frôleuse', referring to an accidental or a fleeting contact with a woman, it becomes clear in the last line, which in retrospect conditions and focuses the poem as a whole, that it is around a fleeting encounter with a woman that the poem's images are congregating their defining beams: 'Et dis-toi qu'aussi bien je ne te verrai plus' [And tell yourself that I may as well no longer see you]. The sensual moments celebrated in the poem may not refer to the same woman, but whether they are taken to do so or not, the power of the encounter to transcend the individual's customary experience lies outside its possible historical or anecdotal development or antecedents; it resides in the eternal instant. Of these moments Breton writes:

> O ménisques
> Au-delà de tous les présents permis et défendus
> A dos d'éléphants ces piliers qui s'amincissent jusqu'au
> fil de soie dans les grottes
> Ménisques adorable rideau de tangence quand la vie n'est
> plus qu'une aigrette qui boit
> Et dis-toi qu'aussi bien je ne te verrai plus (III, 20)

[Oh menisci | Beyond all permitted and forbidden presents | On the back of elephants these pillars taper down to | silken thread in the caves | Menisci adorable tangential curtain when life is no more | than a drinking egret | And tell yourself that I may as well no longer see you]

In such fragmentary encounters, the poem tells us, may be heard the voice of an oracle. These are not merely moments of sensory joy but crucial particles of experience whose fleetingness and randomness subvert the properties of space and time, and out of which might one day be shaped a new sort of human destiny. These experiences are meniscuses (the meniscus is a lens which is convex on one side, concave on the other), through which the tremors of sensation diverge to fill and embrace the whole of an individual's existence. Their gift is beyond all gifts because it is not possession but transmutation; a process illustrated in the next line where the twisting conical pillar on the back of the decorated circus elephant modulates, via its visual similarity, into the stalagmite (dans les grottes), which tapers into a silken thread — the extreme point or drop of emotive and sensory experience, and equally, as the manifold variations on this theme attest throughout Breton's works, the thread which leads through the labyrinth: of the street or of the mind. At such moments life takes on a limpidity which is a revelation — 'Quand la vie n'est plus qu'une aigrette qui boit'; space and time blur; the individual lives a parenthesis and floats in a pocket of air.

The poem's function is to *summon up* these experiences by embodying in itself something of their structure. Many of Breton's poems have a parenthetical structure, creating autonomous worlds of their own, which nonetheless match the exceptional nature of the experiences to which they correspond. One poem, 'Monde dans un baiser' (II, 395) [World within a kiss], generates through its images the autonomous world of the kiss. It is this tendency for the poem to recreate exceptional mental experience in all its unfamiliarity that can lead to an initial impression of incoherence, a feeling that Breton's poetry is fanciful, gratuitously 'surrealist' in the banal sense, and antithetical to experienced reality. It should be clear by now that for Breton poetry is not a flight from reality but a confirmation and reinforcement of its deepest aspects whose more permanent enstatement at its surface would transform life. For it is not in the first instance in poetry that the transmutation of the finite into the infinite comes about. The achievement of presence precedes the poem: it is at the heart of reality, in the matrix of experience that it occurs and that the key or thread of existence is found. But only through language does the moment find a home; so the poem is the homecoming and harbour of experience, not the voyage:

> Les araignées font entrer le bateau dans la rade
> Il n'y a qu'à toucher il n'y a rien à voir [...]
> Mais c'est l'aube de la dernière côte le temps se gâte [...]
> Le ventre des mots est doré ce soir et rien n'est plus
> en vain (I, 186–87)

[Spiders bring the boat into the harbour | One can only touch there is nothing to see [...] | But it's the dawn of the last shore the weather is worsening [...] | Words' stomachs are golden tonight and nothing is any longer | in vain]

But in the eternal simultaneity of language and experience Breton can exclaim:

> Je ne touche plus que le cœur des choses je tiens le fil (II, 94)

[I now only touch the heart of things I hold the thread]

The movement of Breton's thought as of his poetry is to find the 'infinite' in a dimension of reality and experience. The theme of the star brings this out well. 'Tiens une étoile pourtant il fait encore grand jour' (II, 95) [Look a star, and yet it is still broad daylight] he writes playfully. For there is nothing intimidating in stars; just as it does for the navigator 'à la recherche mois des pays | Que de leur propre cause' (II, 405) [not so much on a quest for land | As for their reason for being], so for Breton the star orientates his quest, as something towards which he moves: introducing eschatological urgency into Hernani's melodramatic posturing, he writes

> Je suis celui qui va
> On m'épargnera la croix sur ma tombe
> Et l'on me tournera vers l'étoile polaire (III, 32)

[I am the one who goes | I'll be spared the cross on my tomb | And I'll be turned towards the North Star]

And the climax of *Les Etats généraux*:

> La flèche part
> Une étoile rien qu'une étoile perdue dans la fourrure
> de la nuit (III, 34)

[An arrow is shot | A star nothing but a star lost in the fur | of the night]

no longer foreseeing his death but registering the sudden influx of being which an event, a moment of sensation, has brought. The star can be found, and the experience and sensations with which Breton's poetry is concerned, are those which, as he writes, 'me servent à planter une étoile au cœur même du *fini*' (I, 749) [allow me to plant a star within the heart of the *finite*], and begin an answer to the question, at once urgent and hesitant, that he asks of Nadja: 'Est-il vrai que l'*au-delà*, tout l'audelà soit dans cette vie?' (I, 743) [Is it true that the *afterworld*, all of the afterworld might be found within this life?]. But even the star, that 'pure cristallisation de la nuit' (III, 81) [pure crystallization of night], is not abstracted; its metaphysical meaning is grounded in its sensory properties. 'La vraie vie est absente' [True life is missing], Rimbaud had written; so it was for Breton: but the wanderings of the *flâneur*, the abandon of the lover, and the poet's sudden tapping of the spring of language ever flowing within him, may catch the ripples in the pool of absence; then, as the everyday world recedes, the individual experiences 'le frisson de la vraie vie' [the quiver of real life] (*La clé des champs*, III, 737) — a moment of presence. The sensations which manifest this presence, and their crystallization into images as they etch themselves into words, are those which evince a relative dematerialization of the immediate object and a materialization of something beyond it — lying in its relation to other objects and to the individual. The disorientation of sensation derives from a recognition that it is experiences of sensory disorientation which convey and reveal the attainment of privileged states of being.

Breton therefore focuses on the perimeter of sensory response. The relation to things which he seeks maintains the object as and in the process of our apprehending it, ever becoming itself in the corner of our eyes, or at our fingertips: 'tout ce qui doit faire aigrette au bout de mes doigts' [everything that must be egret at my fingertips] (*L'Amour fou*, II, 763). Here, Breton writes of 'l'intrication en un seul objet du naturel et du surnaturel' [the entanglement of the natural and of the supernatural within a single object], and he associates this with 'l'émotion de tenir et en même temps de sentir s'échapper le ménure-lyre' (II, 751) [the emotion of holding the lyre-bird, and yet feeling it escape]. Such an experience is a paradigm of relation to the world of things and this is frequently expressed in terms of the hand's simultaneously grasping and releasing: 'la main dans l'acte de prendre en même temps que de lâcher' (III, 32) [the hand at once both grasping and releasing]. It is an experience which translates a particular view of man's capacity and channels for apprehending the extended reality, the Real, or the surreal, of which he may have an intuition. It is not in a total abandoning of physical reality that the individual may arrive at it. While Breton had once called on man: 'lâchez la proie pour l'ombre' (I, 263) [let go of prey for the shadow], he later wrote of 'cet état particulier de l'esprit [auquel] le surréalisme a toujours aspiré, dédaignant en dernière analyse la proie et l'ombre pour ce qui n'est déjà plus ombre et n'est pas encore la proie: l'ombre et la proie fondues dans un éclair unique' (II, 697) [that particular state of mind [to which] surrealism has always aspired, that finally disdains prey and shadow for that which is already no longer shadow, but is not yet prey: shadow and prey melted together into a single spark]. This conjunction and indeed the metaphysical view it embodies, can only be experienced — it is a sensation, and Breton celebrates in it an image which shows clearly the subordination of intellect to sense-experience, in the grasping of what we cannot hold but which can illuminate us, when he writes of 'Cette royauté sensible qui s'étend sur tous les domaines de mon esprit et qui tient ainsi dans une gerbe de rayons à portée de la main [...]' (II, 681) [This sensitive royalty that extends onto all of the realms of my spirit, that thus holds a sheaf of rays within arm's length].

★   ★   ★   ★   ★

It is, then, in what I will term the *limit-sensation*, that this relation, and the importance of the senses for Breton, is most significantly manifested. Sensations of this kind, and we have come across many in examining the emotional texture of Breton's poetry, are registered in the poems in a variety of ways, though generally not through direct evocations as in the example of the lyre-bird. More often, Breton directs our attention to the edges of sensory response by using language, or perhaps we ought to say presenting us with language behaving, in a certain manner. For example, he frequently assimilates abstract notions to concrete entities. He writes of 'la moire énigmatique de la ressemblance' [the enigmatic fabric of likeness], or 'la menthe de la mémoire' [the mint of remembrance] (III, 418). Both these images are of course to some extent amenable to rational analysis — in the latter case, it might be agreed that Breton is appealing to the widely accepted relation (endorsed by Schopenhauer and Proust), between smell — the most characteristic property of mint — and remembrance. In other cases the connection is less definable: 'Dans les fougères foulées du regard' (II, 1241) [In the ferns crushed beneath the gaze]. Of course a great many poets have used this device, but Breton's use is particularly vivid: luring the mind to give sensory definition to what is logically alien to such definition, as when he writes, about the news he awaits in a letter — 'les nouvelles qu'elle m'apportera leurs formes de rosée' (II, 98) [the news it will bring me their dewy form]. In this instance there is a double process; dew is certainly concrete, and yet we do not usually think of it as having form: just as a sensory habitation is made for what is otherwise a concept, then this too elides, leaving us nevertheless, I feel, with the aftertaste of a sensation.

Thus, a second operation taking place in Breton's poetry is that of starting from the concrete, and allowing language to deny its customary sensory properties, letting the material taper to the almost immaterial, to the limit of what we can feel and taste. This, again, is often achieved by the play of concrete and abstract, but the emphasis is reversed: 'Des bras qui ne s'articulent à rien d'autre qu'au danger exceptionnel d'un corps fait pour l'amour' (II, 77) [Arms that only move when faced with the exceptional danger of a body made for love]; 'Une région plus délicate que l'impossibilité de se poser pour certaines hirondelles' (I, 397) [A region more fragile than the impossibility of landing for some kinds of swallows]. While constantly forcing us to a sensory reading, Breton's poems do not use sensation to give us a strong impression of the sensory presence of real objects. Rather, he exploits the sensory properties of things (and the capacity of word-combinations to present themselves as the tokens of sensation) in a way which often denies or, alternatively, exaggerates their primary sensory qualities, so as to assert sensory analogies at a remoter level: '[...] la femme nue | Dont les cheveux glissent comme au matin la lumière qu'on a oublié d'éteindre' (II, 74) [the naked woman | Whose hair flows like the light one forgot to turn out in the morning]. Here the movement of the simile is towards the dematerialization of hair, whose static flow and gleam resemble the ebb of artificial light melting into that of the early morning, just as the curving hair of a naked woman emerges from and merges into the curves of her body. Breton's use of sensation in this way is further amplified in another more complex passage involving hair, flesh and light: '[...] les guetteuses nues [...] | cambrant leurs cous sur lequel le bondissement des nattes libère des glaciers à peines roses | Qui se fendent sous le poids d'un rai de lumière tombant des persiennes arrachées' (II, 92) [the nude watchers [...] | craning their necks on which the bouncing of their braids frees the just pink glaciers | That cleave under the weight of a ray of light that falls from the torn shutters]. The context here is that tenuous and often paradoxically chaste eroticism which is characteristic of Breton. The *glaciers* relate to the warming flesh of the *guetteuses* in the cold morning. Locked into the typically intricate metaphorical texture of this sequence is an image which conveys admirably the apparent solidity of the oblique rays of the sun in the morning. We would normally expect *fondent* (melt), as being appropriate to the effect of sunshine on ice. Here Breton exploits a phonic resemblance and translates the impalpable process of sunrays melting ice into an active force — the 'weight' of the sun as it falls, dislodged by the opening of the shutters, is sufficient to make an incision in the ice, — or the woman: *fendent* evidently has sexual connotations here. For the glaciers were 'only' a metaphor; that is, we can only understand their presence or function in the poem if we see them 'as' rendering the texture of the naked flesh of a woman; in this particular case, when the movement of the vertebrae, imparted to it by the bending of the neck, is contrasted with the more vigorous tossing hair which also accompanies this gesture and which, itself, might seem to be the cause of the movement of the flesh. Indeed another aspect of the limit-sensation is Breton's frequent tendency to confound our normal rationalization of causes and effects and present things in the magical, animistic way in which the child or so-called primitive might see them. Thus the toss and bounce of hair releases 'pink glaciers'; shutters opened abruptly dislodge sunrays. Or in another poem hands ravish a nightingale's nest *in order that it should rain for ever* (II, 77). Returning to the original quotation, we might say that the lines were leading us back to a primary situation whose complex sensory and emotional texture the metaphors rendered — in this case the sight of a woman stretching her neck towards a window in the morning. But this is insufficient. Breton does more than evoke the situation for us, or simply insert it in a fictional setting: firstly because the connections he makes are important in themselves; and secondly because the movement of his act as poet has been to allow sensation to crystallize, through language, into something more. So that it is not enough for the reader to go back through the mouth of the funnel to the original sensation, he must receive the fundamentally new sensation. The 'dépaysement de la sensation' [disorientation of sensation] is not merely negative but anticipates a new *pays*, a new world for man.

A further aspect of the limit-sensation is implicit in my remarks about metaphorical texture. The metaphorical process results not so much in presenting things in deliberately unfamiliar contexts but in denying all rational context (just as much modern painting dispenses with any consistent pictorial plane), and in bringing together elements from disparate semantic fields. This occurs even when the metaphoric development does have a stable tenor[11] (or initial term), as in 'L'Union libre' or in these lines: 'Je vois leurs seins qui mettent une pointe de soleil dans la nuit profonde [...] | [...] leurs seins qui sont des étoiles sur des vagues' (II, 89) [I see their breasts that bring a dot of light into the depths of night [...] | [...] their breasts that are stars upon the waves]. Here sun, night and sky are introduced into a process of metaphorical exchange; and there is a greater inter-relation than we might normally expect (and which tends towards the conceit), between these various vehicles of the metaphor: that of the first line could itself be a metaphor for the star in the second (though, paradoxically, the first line depends to some extend on suggesting a starless night sky); while the waves are prefigured aurally in 'profONDE'. When, however, as is frequent, the metaphor lacks a notionally stable tenor (like *seins* in the previous example), or when the whole fragile world of the poem is a vehicle for a tenor which is the theme or situation of the poem as a whole — so that direct statements, snatches of scenario, and so on, all contribute to a metaphor whose process is a constant generation of linguistic energy — then the *dépaysement* is even more extreme. 'Les pieuvres ailées guideront une dernière fois la barque dont les voiles sont faites de ce seul jour heure par heure' (II, 63) [One last time, the winged tentacles will guide the small boat whose sails are made of this day alone, hour by hour]. Here there is no literal meaning which the images transmit, and it is perhaps the differential between what we can apprehend and what is meaningless which is the limit-sensation. We can detect no consistent context: totally different spheres of experience are assembled in the compass of a single line or sequence in the poem. The plan of one against the other, in the absence of any stable metaphorical dynamism or single corresponding life-experience, produces a flurry of sensations since reference is so consistently made to concrete entities. 'What is more abstract than a fortuitous collocation of sensations?' asks Randall

Jarrell;[12] yet it is not really towards abstractions that such collocations, in Breton's poetry, direct us, but to other sensations against which reason may discriminate, but which are actual, though remote and fleeting, and which have no language of their own. The metaphoric process presents us with a limit-reality, yet it can operate only in so far as we register the connections it makes in a sensory way — even if their origin is in language. The licence Breton allows language to suggest connections between things — whether through metaphor, homonymic equivalence or phonic resemblance — is always grounded to some extent in other sensory relations.

The limit-sensation also relates to the theme of transition in Breton's poetry. Many poems have as their basic structure the evocation of a moment of transition: from winter to spring, day to night and the reverse; the associated themes of waking and sleeping also being common. But it is not only at this thematic level that the importance of transition is indicated: the extraordinary dynamism of many of his poems, particularly in the early collections, imparts to them, through language, a feeling of constant organic transformation. The impossible scenarios of a kind of mental picaresque are generally punctuated by the vocabulary of transition: active verbs coloured by a sophisticated use of tense, frequent occurrence of temporal words and phrases — 'alors', 'ensuite', 'tout devient' ['then', 'next', 'everything becomes'], etc. But although the subject, the *je* of the poem is frequently bustled through time and space, we are often reminded that he is, in the first instance, hurtling through the wonderland of language; and this awareness gives the poem a paradoxical immobility: the transition is never consummated and the itinerary of the poem, the trajectory of its subject, like the lived experience it transmits, does not reach a goal. Rather, in its 'vertige fixé' [firm giddiness], it gives him access to the mystery of transition and imminence, and gives him the sensation of what is about to be, and of what a total transformation of existence might bring. It is not the fall of Adam and Eve that Breton describes but that of Alice; if he acknowledges man's diminished state, it is not to original sin that he attributes it but to man's error and loss of the keys to himself. The limit-sensation is itself a transition; a foray into 'la frange changeante et chantante par laquelle un âge révolu anticipe sur l'âge à venir' (IV, 766) [the changing and chanting fringe through which a lapsed era edges onto that still to come]. It is a sensation too which, like those around which Proust constructed his masterpiece, reaches out of time into eternity.

Breton often plays on the ambiguity of the word *temps*, meaning both 'time' and 'weather'. Thus there are moments when 'Le temps se brouille à la fois et s'éclaire [...] | A la vie à la mort ce qui commence me précède et m'achève' (II, 1191–92) [Time/the weather is at once clouding over and brightening up [...] | To life to death what begins both precedes and finishes me]: that which is just beginning goes ahead of us into the future which will see man's resurrection. Man's progress will be impeded 'tant (qu'ils) ne feront pas *la part sensible* de l'éphémère et de l'éternel' [as long/so much (as they) will not play *the sensitive part* of the ephemeral and of the eternal]; while the mediating role of the artist is to act as a conductor of the lightning apparitions of the future: 'l'œuvre d'art n'est valable qu'autant que passent en elle les reflets tremblants du futur' (II, 447–48) [the work of art is only valuable as

long as she casts the shivering reflections of the future].[13] But it is essentially in his
own emotions and sensations and his own tentative approach towards the limits of
experience, that the apprehension of the eternal, of the delicate balance of absence
and presence, and of a new possibility for man, is available to the individual. These
lines of great aural beauty, at once lucid and mysterious, resume succinctly the
themes I have been seeking to elucidate:

> Et très loin dans les bois l'avenir entre deux branches
> Se prend à tressaillir comme l'absence inapaisible d'une feuille
> > ('Après le grand tamanoir', II, 83)

> [And far away in the woods between two branches the future
> Begins to quiver like the unappeasable absence of a leaf]

The extreme delicacy which characterizes the sensations in Breton's poetry is not
arbitrary; if it indicates a preference, then this preference originates in intuitions
of universal validity. There is no decadence or elitism in Breton's poetry, nor
any full withdrawal from the world; but instead the desire to monitor and mime
every smallest quiver of reality, and to greet what he can from beyond the normal
horizons of experience. It is on the marches of reality and of experience that Breton
concentrates his attention, and it is so as to capture the intimations of a deeper
reality that he diverts his and our attention from 'le terre-à-terre de la sensation'
[the down-to-earth of sensations] — everyday sense-experiences — to 'la dentelle
de mes sensations' (I, 370) [the lacework of my sensations], those in league with the
once and future state of man, present at the heart of things and self. The future is
less a division of time than a division of man.

It is more than a quirk of Breton's sensibility that the scale of his poetic universe
should so consistently be reduced. Apart from the diminutive quality of the habitual
'properties' of Breton's poems, the commerce which the *je* — a sort of Gulliver
— enjoys with things, through the extraordinary mobility which the discourse
lends the human subject (mirroring the rapidity of sense mechanisms) results in a
constant miniaturization. A constant shrinking and metamorphosis of the self, as it
seeks a relation with things, characterizes the poems; Breton lives in the heart of a
thistle (II, 396), refers to 'nous les plantes sujettes aux métamorphoses' (II, 90) [us
plants, subject to metamorphosis], writes 'Je goûterais le long des marais salants la
paix inconnue des métamorphoses' (II, 73) [Along the salt marshes, I would taste
the unknown peace of metamorphoses], or 'Tu te promèneras avec la vitesse | Qui
commande aux bêtes des bois' (II, 64) [You will walk with the speed | That directs
wild beasts]. It is with the fusion of self and world that the poems are concerned.
Emerging from the unconscious, objects present themselves in those aspects
through which the poet has been able to relate to them. The incidence of small and
delicate things in Breton's poetry seems to be connected with their special relation
to the mind and senses. It is as if there were something particularly small, living,
things, in conveying the processes of the unconscious: as if their micro-movements
rendered more plausible the capacity of the human brain to generate images of
the exterior world, and to reflect and recreate reality. Certain things, and certain
types of movement or potentialities for movement, seem to press themselves with

particular insistence on the mind, introducing themselves into, and reflecting, its hidden processes which can only be conveyed through metaphor. And so, in Breton's poems, rather than the succulence or symbolism of Valéry's pomegranates, the universe of fable, however individualized, in which Supervielle's horses gallop, or the conventional botany and entomology of Gide, we are presented with a miniature world populated by the darting softness of small mammals, the glitter of minerals, the intermittent brilliance of kingfisher's wings, the hieratic attitudes of flower and fern, the micro-dramaturgy of eye and hand. On the edges of sensation, perception is reconciled with imagination, while a further shrinking permits the miniature world of language to stand for heightened encounters with the world of things. The poem with its correspondingly emotive texture, can become a receptacle in which endures what Eluard called 'La Vie Immédiate' [Immediate Life], and what Breton calls, 'La vie telle que je l'aime et qu'elle s'offre [...]: la vie *à perdre haleine*' (I, 744) [Life as I love it and as it | she gives herself [...]: *breathless* life]. Through discourse the universe is appropriated. Or rather, an earlier, unconscious appropriation is consolidated for as long as the intermittent aesthetic force of the poem continues to operate.

The universe of Breton's poetry is, then, a gravitational field, pulling more and more things into its orbit. His miniaturized inscapes and scenarios are precipitates of desire; for Breton, language, mind and sensation modulate into each other in a chain of precipitations. The limit-sensation is a moment of coincidence of self and world. Some sensations register 'des échanges mystérieux entre le matériel et le mental' (II, 712) [mysterious exchanges between the physical and the mind]. Yet the self is more than a composite mirror of the aspects of the world in which it has found itself; and the critic's task should not be to build up an anthropomorphic portrait, like one of those by Arcimboldo.[14] The relation of the self and world is a dialectic, an ascesis; in the process of reciprocation the mirror, as in Yeats's line, turns lamp. What better to illustrate this than an image provided by the *réverbère* — half lamp, half mirror, and the butterfly — emblem of the limit-sensation? 'Les papillons de l'extérieur ne cherchent qu'à rejoindre les papillons de l'intérieur: ne replace pas en toi, si elle vient à être cassée, une seule glace du réverbère' [The outer butterflies seek only to re-join the inner butterflies: if any of it should break, do not replace a single pane of the lamp's glass/mirror within you].[15] There are moments of experience which break the barriers between the outside world and the inner, between subject and object, creating that inner space or *Weltinnenraum* of which Rilke wrote.[16] The sight of a bird flying home momentarily reveals the continuity of self and world:

> Je vois l'ibis aux belles manières
> Qui revient de l'étang lacé dans mon cœur (II, 67)

> [I see the well-mannered ibis
> Returning from the frozen lake in my heart]

The fluttering of a butterfly, like a human pulse; a glimmer of light; the fine point of sensation which the semantic resources of language can encapsulate: such things cross a divide and seem to participate more readily than others in this new space, and manifest better the possibility of a 'contact, entre tous éblouissant, de l'homme avec le monde des choses' (II, 711) [most dazzling contact between man and the world of things].

My argument has been that the meta-world of Breton's poetic universe is the product and instrument of ethical and heuristic strategy. The tyranny of abstract reason has choked the natural channels through which we incorporate the evidence of the senses into our model of the world, so that our everyday perceptiveness gives only a partial, distorted view of things which we instate as Reality. It is only through the reunification of the sensibility that the unity of the world, and of man with it, can be found again. The means for this are to be found in an openness to the world, in the passion of love, and in attention to the flow of subjective experience available to us in the speech always imminent in the mind. In these areas of experience the individual sensibility is integrated with sensory experience which challenges the familiar set of things, and may intuit a different way of the world. The senses are the garden in which man may await 'la fleur enfin éclose de la vraie vie' (III, 9) [the flower of real life, at last blooming]; in any case 'on n'en finira jamais avec la sensation' (II, 750) [we will never be done with sensation].

## Notes

1. References are to the four-volume *Pléiade* edition of Breton's works (Paris: Gallimard, 1988).
2. Michael Riffaterre, 'La Métaphore filée dans la poésie surréaliste', *Langue française*, 3 (September, 1969), 46–60.
3. Wallace Stevens, *The Necessary Angel: Essays on Reality and the Imagination* (New York: Knopf, 1951), p. viii. Cf. Breton 'C'est moi l'irréel souffle de ce jardin' [I am the unreal breath of this garden] (II, 78).
4. Antonin Artaud, *L'Ombilic des limbes* (Paris: Gallimard, 1971), pp. 44–45.
5. Stéphane Mallarmé, 'Un Coup de dés...', *Œuvres complètes I* (Paris: Gallimard, 1998), p. 380.
6. *Situations, II* (Paris: Gallimard, 1968), p. 324.
7. Cf. '[...] puiser aveuglément dans le trésor subjectif pour la seule tentation de jeter de-ci de-là sur le sable une poignée d'algues écumeuses et d'émeraudes' [blindly drawing into one's subjective treasure simply for the temptation to scatter onto the sand a fistful of foamy seaweed and of emeralds] (II, 376); also '[...] le secret impérissable s'inscrit une fois de plus sur le sable' [once more, the imperishable secret writes itself in the sand] (III, 108), where language itself proposes an image which conveys its generative processes (impérisSABLE)'.
8. Yves Bonnefoy, *L'Improbable* (Paris: Mercure de France, 1959), p. 120.
9. With a painter's eye Breton detects the magical quality of light in certain places: the moors of Brittany for instance (III, 575), or along the Hudson (III, 578); or '[...] Cette lueur vert-orangé qui me cerne du même fin pinceau [...] le décor romantique conventionnel et ce quartier presque enfoui de la Boucherie de Paris [That orange-green glow that for me outlines in the same fine brush conventional Romantic decor and the near-buried Parisian Butcher's quarter] (III, 653).
10. *L'Improbable*, p. 122.
11. 'Tenor', 'Vehicle' and 'Ground' are the terms coined by I. A. Richards in *The Philosophy of Rhetoric* (New York and London: Oxford University Press, 1936), to describe the elements of a metaphor.
12. *Poetry and the Age* (London: Faber and Faber, 1955), p. 214.
13. Cf. Shelley: 'Poets are the hierophants of an unapprehended inspiration; the mirrors of the gigantic shadows which futurity casts upon the present [...]': quoted by Robert Gibson in *Modern French Poets on Poetry* (Cambridge: Cambridge University Press, 1961), p. 33.
14. Although Breton sometimes encourages this: e.g. '[...] mon apparence de miroir mes mains

de faille | Mes yeux de chenilles mes cheveux de longues baleines noires' [my mirror-like appearance my ribbed hands | My caterpillar eyes my long black whale hair] (II, 99).

15. *L'Immaculée Concepion*, in Paul Eluard, *Œuvres complètes*, vol. I (Paris: Gallimard, 1968), p. 355. This work was written by Breton and Eluard in collaboration; the Pléiade edition cited identifies the quoted passage as Breton's.

16. 'Durch alle Wesen reicht der *eine* Raum | Weltinnenraum. Die Vögel fliegen still | Durch uns hindurch. O, der ich wachsen will | Ich seh hinaus, und *in* mir wächst der Baum [...]': R. M. Rilke, *Sämtliche Werke*, vol. II (Wiesbaden: Insel-Verlag, 1955), p. 93.

# *Mont de piété* and André Breton's Early Poetic Development

André Breton's first collection of poems has not received the attention it deserves. Breton was himself partly to blame for the prevailing view that *Mont de piété* contained little that could not be laid at the door of a youthful talent marking time and gaining experience by the sincerest form of flattery — imitation.[1] This view is adequate — if a trifle sweeping — when applied to the first half of the book; it is unacceptable where the later poems of the collection are concerned. But *Mont de piété* has been neglected. Some critics have allotted space — in two cases generous space — to individual poems or to a discussion of influences, but an overall view has not, as far as I know, been attempted.[2] This is to be regretted for a number of reasons. First, because Breton himself, although often harsh in his judgement of a collection partly devoted to what amount to *juvenilia*, seems to have cherished the later poems and chose to reprint them more readily than others.[3] Second, the collection offers precious evidence of Breton's early development, especially his evolving conception of poetry, indicated both by the influences he rejected and by his explicit treatment, in the later poems, of such writers as Gide, Valéry and Apollinaire. Third, his early experiments with poetic form provide a fascinating prelude to the writing of *Les Champs magnétiques* — 'premier ouvrage purement surréaliste' [the first purely *surrealist* work], as Breton was to call it in the *Manifeste du Surréalisme*. These considerations would not perhaps amount to much were it not, finally, for the exceptional formal interest of the later poems once their initial obscurity is overcome.

The poems of *Mont de piété* can be divided into three groups. Of the fifteen poems, the first four have in common their allegiance to recognizable poetic models of the late symbolist period. The next five poems constitute a second group in which the *fin de siècle* idiom, while being maintained in certain features of syntax and diction, is situated within a broader aesthetic pattern that modifies its significance. The last six poems, dating from 1918–19, suggest that Breton had both cast off early influences and evolved a poetic mode appropriate to the project of at once holding at bay and criticizing the example of other writers. Indeed, the final poems, of 1919, represent a series of staggered closures in which Breton seeks to bring the curtain down on a whole era of his life. Nearly all the fifteen poems which appeared in *Mont de piété* in the summer of 1919 had already been printed in a review. The collection contains the majority of the poems Breton published between 1914 and 1919. Sometimes several months (in one case more than a year) separate the composition of one poem from the next, a single poem being often the only testimony to Breton's development over the period. It will be necessary to examine Breton's poems in the order of their composition.[4]

★   ★   ★   ★   ★

Breton had a consistently low opinion of the poems he wrote in or prior to 1914, three of which were published in Jean Royère's neo-symbolist review *La Phalange*.[5] Four poems from this period are included in *Mont de piété* and they constitute the first group to be examined. These poems lack originality and seethe with the influences of Mallarmé, Valéry, and Jean Royère and his school.[6] The example of Mallarmé is evident in their dense linguistic texture and formal compactness as well as in their lack of obvious subject matter. But the erosion of content is not linked to the disclosure of any vibrant levels of abstraction and ideal purity, or to perceptions about language; still less are these curious poems underwritten by any profound experience on the human plane.[7] As far as subject matter goes, the influence of the Valéry of the *Album des vers anciens* is paramount: the dominant note is often a refined, almost chaste, eroticism.[8] Fairly typical of this vein are these lines from 'L'An suave':

> Un châle méchamment qui lèse ta frileuse
> Épaule nous condamne aux redites. Berger,
> Tu me deviens l'à peine accessible fileuse.
> (A l'ordinaire jeu ce délice étranger.) (I, 7)

> [A shawl spitefully wronging your sensitive | Shoulder condemns us to repeat ourselves. Shepherd, | You are becoming to me the barely accessible spinner. | (This delight alien to the ordinary game.)]

The Mallarméan echoes in vocabulary and phraseology are evident, but it is not for nothing that this poem is dedicated to Marie Laurencin. While critics have been quick to adduce the influences of major figures, they have neglected what might be called the neo-symbolist aesthetic (or neo-impressionism as Marcel Raymond calls it), prominent at this time, from which Breton's early writing derives its characteristic timbre. Breton's enthusiasm for lesser-known symbolist poets such as Ghil, Vielé-Griffin (also greatly admired by Gide) and Saint-Pol-Roux, whom he read and with whom he corresponded at this time, brought him into contact with younger artists, in whose work the etiolated symbolist spirit was given new vigour by the injection of less stereotyped, more personal motifs. The wistful figures of Marie Laurencin's portraits, the plaintive blend of detachment and intensity in a sonnet by Jean Royère form an essential background to Breton's early forays into poetry.[9] If Breton's poems show little sign of the astringent intellect always discernible beneath Valéry's verbal harmonies, he shares with Royère the note of spiritual earnestness which underlies the fashionable gallantries, the erotic playfulness of his verse.

> Je sens combien tu m'es lointaine et que tes yeux,
> L'azur, tes bijoux d'ombre et les étoiles d'aube
> Vont s'éteindre, captifs du ramage ennuyeux
> Que tôt figurera ton caprice de robe. (I, 7)

[I feel how far you are from me and that your eyes, | The azure, your jewels of shadow and the stars of dawn | Are to go out, captives of the dull branchwork | Your caprice of a dress will soon bear.]

Marcel Raymond cites the poem from which these lines are extracted as the culmination of the *Phalange* group's exclusive fascination with the wonders of language.[10] This should remind us that, as well as being elegantly amorous, Breton is exploring the interaction in poetic statement of linguistic manipulation and emotional effect. Emotion is central to Breton's idea of poetry. It was the emotive power of language, encapsulated in fragments of Rimbaud, Mallarmé or even Pierre Louÿs, that had led him to write.[11] He was already fascinated by linguistic patterns which, if hostile to sense, appeared to communicate with deep levels of the self. At this stage, however, Breton avoids the innovation at the semantic level which will characterize the surrealist revolution of poetic language, although a stanza like this one from 'Rieuse' owes much of its effectiveness to the interaction of concrete and abstract vocabulary — a development of the symbolist cult of synaesthesia:

> Sur la nacelle d'or d'un rêve aventurée
> — De qui tiens-tu l'espoir et ta foi dans la vie?
> Des yeux reflèteraient l'ascension suivie
> Sous l'azur frais, dans la lumière murmurée... (I, 6)

[In the golden barque of a chancy dream | — From whom do you get hope, and your faith in life? | Eyes would reflect the ascent's track | Beneath the cool blue, in the murmured light...]

His explorations of language are on the whole confined to experimentation with the symbolist mannerism of convoluted syntax.

Breton's own description of 'Rieuse' as 'un sonnet tout en volutes sans grand contenu humain' [a sonnet entirely in volutes without much human content] seems a fitting comment on this first group of poems (IV, 1013). It seems likely that he quickly realized their shortcomings; at any rate, a significant interval — the first year of the war — separates the poems of spring and summer 1914 from his next published work, written at the end of 1915.

★   ★   ★   ★   ★

Five poems composed between late 1915 and early 1918 display sufficient affinities to warrant being grouped together.[12] In this second group Breton's poetry begins to reflect his current experience rather than just vague feelings mediated and attenuated by literary influences. Emotional texture is still emphasized but it is strengthened by the immediacy and particularity of the feelings which nourish it. It is not, however, by any recourse to simplicity that Breton broadens the range of his poetry. On the contrary, its linguistic surface is, if anything, more mannered and accentuated than before. But the dislocation of syntax is now given a functional role, setting up subtle effects of perspective and distance within the field of a tangled mass of feelings, intuitions and desires. Breton in fact widens the range of his linguistic inventiveness to include elaborate wordplay, so that the artificiality and self-consciousness of the language are intensified. But this adds halftones of irony, self-mockery and parody to the restricted palette of the neo-symbolist. This intermediate group of poems is dominated thematically by the enactment of a complex emotional bind: the desire to overcome the dichotomy between two inadequate poles. On the one hand, the claustrophobic, artificial world of symbolism; on the other, the world of experience, involving the inescapable commitments of a position within society. Dissatisfaction with the imaginary world projects Breton into the real one; repudiation of the real one — inevitable given the intellectual sterility of a society resounding with the slogans of patriotism — sends him back to the consolations of the imaginary one. The rest of *Mont de piété* will be dominated by the quest for a third path in which the intuitive realm of poetry would find some foundation in a real world of substantial experience. While the poems in the second group tend to enact this tension — the neo-symbolist world being placed between parentheses but nevertheless preserved — the transition to the third group will be effected when a reinvention of poetic means puts Breton on the path of a viable alternative which instates the experience of poetry in the world of everyday experience.

Breton enclosed 'Décembre', the first poem in this group, in a letter to Apollinaire who replied approvingly.[13] These are the opening lines:

> Au 25 est l'auberge et son bouchon de gui.
> J'esquive la frayée injuste, ô blanche terre.
> Coucou — L'Europe à feu de l'an prochain languit.
> La chanson des fenouils — et te voilà! (I, 10)

> [Number 25 is the inn and its mistletoe stopper. | I dodge the unjust clearing, oh white earth. | Yoo-hoo — Burning Europe longs for the next year. | The fennel song — there you are!]

If the poem is more wilfully eccentric than its predecessors, this is because its audacities no longer derive from symbolist models (the note of derision in these lines neutralizes the sometimes heightened vocabulary and phrasing). The dislocation of strophe and alexandrine, the discord of rhythm and sense, are not gratuitous aesthetic flourishes: they assist the formulation of Breton's attitudes to his experience at the particular moment of December 1915. With Christmas and a new year imminent, the poet takes stock of his situation. In the lines quoted, the inn of the nativity, with its identifying sprig of mistletoe, is located spatially as if it were a number in the street, instead of temporally in the month of December. The mistletoe and the snow-laden ground seem to justify the poet's attitude to the war: 'J'esquive la frayée injuste'. Then, a further grammatical sleight serves to underline this attitude: the expected preposition 'en' is ousted to make the effective phrase 'L'Europe à feu' — as if combustibility were a general property of this continent. The tendency in this poem to admit reference to the poet's real situation is undermined, of course, by the fact that its subject is the tension between that situation and the ideal world of amorous longing and intangible gratification. Poetry is an arena in which the poet seeks sanctuary from the outer world of military determination. The central section of the poem suggests a retreat into a personal mythology of childhood

Nous taire
Enfants des contes si le beau missel en fleurs

> A minuit de ton gré s'ouvre au feuillet de cloches
> Pâles qui sont des jacinthes... (I, 10)

[Hush ourselves | Children of tales if the handsome flowering missal | At midnight with your blessing opens itself at the sheet of pale | Bells which are hyacinths...]

But the end of the poem marks a return to Breton's real situation as a soldier at Bouvines:

> Ce soir, j'envie aux preux des Bouvines la guerre
> Indulgente à raison de pape.
>                    Fantassin
> Là-bas, conscrit du sol et de la hampe, y être! (I, 10)

[This evening, I envy the heroes of Bouvines the war | Indulgent on the pope's account. | Infantryman | Over there, conscript of the earth and the flagpole, to be there!]

The war gives the bourgeois citizens an opportunity for complacency and self-congratulation: the Pope has granted indulgences to those who fight the good fight. Breton's reluctance to participate is less a pacifist attitude than the outcome of a sense of isolation which finds expression, if not remedy, in the neo-symbolist longing for an ideal. Nevertheless, these references to the poet's real situation, submerged as they are in layers of linguistic padding, serve to spread the poem outwards.

In the three central poems in this group the ascendancy of Mallarmé and Valéry in Breton's poetic firmament is attenuated by the discovery of Rimbaud.[14] 'Façon' is an intriguing poem in which the subtle phonological texture of Mallarméan poetry is subverted in two ways. Firstly, by being exaggerated to a point where puns and odd 'sound effects' are essential ingredients of the poem; secondly, by the discontinuity of jerky irregular constructions whose fits and starts are reminiscent of Rimbaud's phrasing.[15] In his next poem, 'Âge', Breton learns a different lesson from Rimbaud, that of making his poems the transmutation of personal experience. The title is explained when we note that the date at the foot of the poem is that of Breton's twentieth birthday. As in 'Décembre', the poem focuses on a precise moment, an emotional milestone; and the same tension is enacted between the insubstantial world of symbols and mysteries — now associated, via Rimbaud, with childhood — and the pressures of more immediate experience. The opening, 'Aube, adieu! Je sors du bois hanté: j'affronte les routes, croix torrides' [Farewell, dawn! I am leaving the haunted wood: I will brave the roads, sweltering crosses] (I, 8), expresses directly the desire to leave the haunted wood of childhood — or symbolism — and to confront the possibilities of reality. Much of the poem transmits a sensory experience of a concrete world: there is solidity, a degree of presence, lacking in earlier poems, which extends even to the season or the passing moment: 'l'août est sans brèches comme une meule [...] l'instant revient patiner la chair' [August has no gaps, like a millstone... the moment returns to burnish the flesh]. 'Âge' reveals the progressive grip of a coherent thematic basis in Breton's poetry, which can be summed up in this question: on what terms should the poet be with reality?[16] Breton's next poem marks a decisive development. In 'Coqs de bruyère' the urgency of Rimbaud combines with the linguistic fastidiousness of the Mallarmé school to create a language in which poetic mystery and energy are derived from productive ambiguity and polyvalence rather than from mellifluous vagueness and abstraction. The poem also consolidates the ground made by themes relating to the poet's immediate experience, and a further, crucial influence, that of Jacques Vaché, can be detected.

Breton's instinctive repudiation of the militarist ethos found its focus in the mysterious soldier whom he met in Nantes in 1916. Vaché's nonchalance in the face of war, as well as his legendary elegance, made a considerable impression on Breton.[17] In Vaché the glacial pose of the Dandy served to keep the encroachments of the world at bay. Following this example, and turning his own affection for fashion to use, Breton once again presents war in a cynical light.

> Coqs de bruyère... et seront-ce coquetteries
> de péril
> ou de casques couleur de quetsche? (I, 9)

[Wood grouse... and will it be coquettish quirks | of danger | or of damson-coloured helmets?]

Courage is dismissed as self-flattery; it is a mere accoutrement like damson-coloured helmets. Artillery fire is no more than a firework treat for spoilt children, 'quels | feux de Bengale gâteries!' [what | Bengal-light indulgences!]. This is not the naïve enthusiasm for war of an Apollinaire, but grim irony, 'humour noir'. Balancing this opening is a concluding sequence of seven lines in which, as in 'Âge' and 'Décembre', the poet's need to make a choice of action is to the fore.

> Au Tyrol, quand les bois se foncent, de tout
> l'être abdiquant un
> destin
> digne, au plus, de chromos savoureux,
> mon
> remords: sa rudesse, des maux,
> je dégage les capucines de sa lettre. (I, 9)

[In the Tyrol, when the woods darken, with all | my being giving up a | destiny | worthy, at most, of tasty chromos, | my | remorse: its coarseness, from affronts, | I free the nasturtiums from his letter]

These lines illustrate well the nature of Breton's new poetic mode, and the types of ambiguity it promotes. The poet dismisses both a destiny of spurious glory that could be commemorated by colour-prints, and any remorse such a decision might entail. The significance of this decision is underlined by 'de tout l'être', but the alternative option is vague. Yet it must be as wholehearted since Breton's patterning of lines, placing *l'être* at the beginning draws attention to the echo in its homonym placed diagonally from it at the end — *lettre*. This positioning also alerts us to the fact that 'de tout l'être' is not only qualified by *abdiquant* but qualifies in turn the statement which closes the poem, while *abdiquant* in turn modifies both 'un destin' and 'mon remords'.

> Je dégage les capucines de sa lettre

This concluding gesture must also benefit from the total commitment of the poet; but what — or *how* — does it signify? Breton dislocates syntax in such a way as to secure polyvalence of meaning. The word *capucines* reactivates earlier references to a woodland setting. Then, the verb *dégager* operates ambiguously, opening up different frames of reference, alternative contextualizations. A first reading confronts us with a grammatical incongruity or impropriety. If we take the words literally it would seem that the *flowers* were being disentangled from the *letter*. But the capucines are clearly not the primary item here since they can be focused within the context of an exterior setting, while the letter is a fresh and conclusive item in the poem. Therefore it makes more sense to assume that it is the letter that is being disentangled from the flowers, just as the last word of the poem protrudes from and terminates the tangle of language. If this is so, then we may infer that the letter is salvaged from an environment that threatens to engulf it. Accordingly, we can construe the woodland setting as a *selva oscura* ('quand les bois se foncent') from which the letter promises deliverance. The advantage of Breton's inversion of *lettre* and *capucines* is that it allows a second reading whereby the 'capucines' represent, via a genitival metaphor, the essential, desirable quality of the letter. The phrase 'les capucines de sa lettre' as a whole becomes the subject of *dégager*, so that what is manifested or disentangled is also the *essence* of the letter.

Capucines is able to stand metaphorically for the essence of the letter by dint of the code which gives flowers a connotation of beauty, enhancement. But a further dimension is added if we consider the pertinence of the verb *dégager* to *capucines*. Odoriferous flowers like nasturtiums are often said to 'dégager un parfum' [give off an aroma]. Insofar as this sense of *dégager* is activated by the floral context, it operates with reference to the poet or speaker rather than to the flowers: it is he who 'gives off', from whom there emanates, the floral quality or 'virtue' of the latter. At this third level, then, it is suggested that the meaning, the essence, of the letter is to be located as much within the recipient, as in the letter itself. This, taken in conjunction with an analysis of the possessive adjectives in the last two lines, will suggest the identity of the writer of the letter. It seems plausible that the letter is one of Jacques Vaché's *Lettres de guerre* which Breton collected in volume form after his friend's death, and to which he attached great significance. A number of salient facts assist this identification. Firstly, it is significant that the recipient should be the catalyst which releases the essence of the letter. Breton was aware that the writings and doings of Vaché could objectively seem of scant interest to others, but he always insisted on their mysterious appeal and influence. Breton included his friend in the list of precursors of surrealism, but was careful to write 'Jacques Vaché est surréaliste en moi' [Jacques Vaché is surrealist in me] (I, 329), emphasizing the subjective nature of his fascination with Vaché. Secondly, the poem suggests that the letter represents a means of transcending the war situation. It should be remembered that the concluding gesture of the poem constitutes the alternative to a military destiny; the letter is deemed to encapsulate the antidote to such a fate. This is reinforced by another grammatical relationship generated by 'je dégage' in conjunction with the preceding lines.

> mon
> remords: sa rudesse, des maux,
> je dégage les capucines de sa lettre. (I, 9)

Despite the comma, the words 'des maux' clearly link with the last line, so that it is from the ill-fortunes of war that the virtues of the letter are to be disentangled (on one reading of 'je dégage') or from which the essence of the letter is to be extracted. This second reading of 'je dégage' is underscored by the clear pun on the word *mots*, so that it is from the *words* of the letter that Breton draws his sustenance. The word *maux* is phonetically poised between the 'chro*mos*' redolent of militarism and the *mots* of the letter ('re*mords*' effects a transition). Lastly, the sequence of possessives: *mon* — *sa* — *sa* has a contribution to make. '*Sa* rudesse' contrasts with '*mon* remords' which precedes it (so that it is presumably the asperity of remorse that is alluded to). While the first *sa* alerts us to and highlights the second one, it also draws our attention to the fact that it does not refer to the same subject: this highlighted adjective confers honorific and emotive force on the letter by drawing attention to its sender. But even if the reader cannot bring a knowledge of Vaché's importance to the poem, the accentuated 'sa' situates part of the *aura* of the letter in the identity of its author.

In 'Coqs de bruyère' a major innovation in Breton's poetic language can be observed. The deployment of linguistic finesse begins to shift from a framework of gratuitous aestheticism towards a new mode of textual operation which exploits to the full the polyvalence that is the essence of poetic statement. If one considers for instance the accentuation of sound texture in symbolist poetry we can see that Breton, who inherits from it a developed sensitivity to phonological echoes, progressively restores the semantic, signifying role which had been eroded from it. In a way this is the true Mallarméan lesson, supplanting the superficial one handed down by his epigones. Words are encouraged to realize all their potential semantic energy and not to dissipate it in univocal reference.[18]

The next poem to be considered all but completes the transition between the middle and last phases of the collection, in that it allies the change in the formal structure of Breton's poetry to an important thematic change. 'André Derain' inaugurates a series of poems in which Breton employs his new poetic style to offer an enactment and critique of the aesthetico–moral position implicit in the creative personae and practice of such figures as Rimbaud, Gide and Valéry. In doing so, Breton projects his own dilemmas onto others and judges their solutions. His sympathetic treatment of Derain, however, only partially anticipates this manoeuvre. This new tendency owes something to the 'critique synthétique' of Reverdy and the *Nord-Sud* group.[19] Superficially, the poem appears to return to neo-symbolist mannerisms, but these are now employed parodically in a linguistic surface that achieves a remarkable degree of self-consciousness.[20] Indeed, the poem can be read as a valediction to a period-style which will not be heard again in the collection. Derain is chosen as a figure in whom Breton detects the tension he had experienced between *fin de siècle* vapidity and a sensibility alert to everyday experience whilst attuned to its mysterious undertones.[21] Breton's poem first of all gives a *résumé* of the painter's universe. The discontinuity of the first lines — wordplay, elisions and verbal telescopings — seeks to imitate the complex linking of disparate levels of reality in the picture plane. Then, purple moments of quasi-symbolist delicacy are counterpoised by a strong sense of natural life so that the symbolist universe is kept in a critical focus.

The last section of the poem seems explicitly both to render the appeal and to register the limitations of the neo-symbolist world

> Qu'un semblant de cornette bouffonne
> (et ta coiffe empesée)
> appelle: tout tremblant
> le ramage turquin, ma sœur, des noms en *zée*.
>
> Ah! plus ce brouillard tendre. (I, 11)

> [Let a sort of ridiculous cornette | (and your starched headdress) | call: trembling all over | the deep blue twittering, my sister, of names ending in *zee*. || Ah! no more of this tender fog.]

With ladies' fashion once again the muse, the poem nearly meanders into an outmoded byway, the reference to headgear sets off a series of synaesthetic shifts provoking a chain reaction of visual and aural images. The precariousness of the elaborate, but possibly provocative 'cornette' (worn by nuns, or women 'en déshabillé') is assimilated to the tenuousness of the comparisons it suggests — 'appelle: tout tremblant'. The basic comparison seems to be with a branch-like structure — the literal meaning (deriving from the cognate *rameau*) which underlies the two senses of *ramage*; this helps the two meanings to be present simultaneously. Where one sense is concerned — that of birdsong or twittering — Breton's poem reproduces the transference of meaning whereby the location (branches of a tree) suggest a word for what is associated with such a place — the warbling of birds. In terms of the poem, however, the transference of ideas is from the apparel of the woman ('cornette' suggests that this is old-fashioned) to her social or 'period' aura, epitomized, via the notion of pretty twittering, with chirpy *fin de siècle* names like *Alizée*. The second (perhaps more common) sense of *ramage* — a floral design or pattern — again builds on the sense of a branchlike structure, but gives a counteractive sense of tangibility to an image whose overall structure is a comparison between a piece of millinery and the sound of certain unfamiliar forenames. This tangibility, and the slightly giddy synaesthesia that the image as a whole promotes, is underlined by the adjective *turquin*, a bluish-grey colour (reminding us that this is in part the evocation of a painting), which activates the usual context of *ramage* in this sense — applying to a floral design on a fabric, generally a woman's dress. This perpetuates the chain of fashion imagery in *Mont de piété*, and also reintroduces the sense of the woman's physical presence, as well as relating directly to the 'cornette' whose shape and possibly floral accoutrements might resemble the design on a dress. But, equally, the somewhat conventional note of exoticism in the adjective *turquin* complements the first sense of *ramage* and enables this word to aid the movement towards the final term of the image: the sense of finely coloured, perhaps exotic, birds prepares for the refined and unusual names. The effect of this complicated image would seem at first to be to transport the reader without ulterior, higher, motive, several removes from actuality. But this is counteracted in two ways. First, the intricacy of the image does set up a strong verbal tension which seems to distract our attention from the banality of the material; this indicates the positive direction in which the poem is heading. More important here, however, are the clear elements of parody and irony. Breton is no longer straining after effect so much as questioning the effects of the now somewhat listless neo-symbolist strain. The 'cornette' is acknowledged at the outset to be 'bouffonne', and there is something equally absurd about the elaborate structure of imagery that it prompts. More ridiculous still is the way this segment of the poem, like the previous one, is in fact an imperative: there is some irony in the evocation of the artist's 'magic' — how wonderful, but at the same time, how futile that, by his *fiat*, a hat can evoke a name! It should not be forgotten that the poem refers partly to Derain's painting; hence the connection between the indefiniteness of the visual stimulus (it is no more than a 'semblant de cornette' that prompts the comparison) and its suggestiveness. But the deflating sense of fatuousness applies as much to the poet who seeks to emulate the painter.... Another strong ironic element here is the sense of anachronism, the feeling, underlined by the outmoded fashions, that this is all a bit dated. The reader is not surprised, then, indeed he may be relieved, when the drift of this last section is pulled up short by the impatient, peremptory close:

> Ah! plus ce brouillard tendre.

Like the 'bois hanté' in 'Âge', the 'brouillard tendre' seems to represent the symbolist domain which Breton now feels to be inadequate — too restricted a territory for the poet of the twentieth century. The exposition of this view in the context of an appraisal of Derain suggests that Breton detected in this painter's work undercurrents which introduced a sense of concrete reality and openness to modern experience into the deliquescent neo-symbolist world without sacrificing the sense of a mystery underlying appearances. In its implicit promotion of this latter quality, no less than in its centring on an artistic figure, 'André Derain' sets the scene for the last poems in the collection. These will put a consistent set of questions to the activity of the modern writer: is there a middle road to be found between retreat from actuality and society (the symbolist mode) and surrender to their lure and consequent damage to poetic consciousness? Can poetry be brought more clearly into step with the tempo and assumptions of modern life without in the process allowing its inherent properties and priorities to be dissipated? Is there a way of matching an adequate aesthetic stance to an adequate social one?

★　★　★　★　★

The last six poems, which embody Breton's own brand of 'critique synthétique', have in common the search for a secure basis for the poetic vocation in the context of Breton's progressive disillusion with erstwhile mentors such as Valéry, Rimbaud and Apollinaire. Of these poems the first three, written in 1918, investigate the compromise between art and society in the work of particular writers. The last three centre more on aesthetic questions.[22]

In the first three, Breton is generally concerned with the *persona* of the artist and the relation between his life and his art, Rimbaud continues to be an important protagonist in Breton's deliberations, and it is a measure of Breton's determination to press home his enquiry into the status of the poet that Rimbaud's poetic career, far from being above criticism, is subjected to scrutiny in the poem 'Forêt-Noire'. Rimbaud is, however, initially present by his formal influence on Breton's style. For the first time in 'Forêt-Noire', Breton abandons all trace of established poetic form. Rather than to the prose poetry of the *Illuminations*, it is to the obscure and neglected poem 'Rêve' [Dream], which Rimbaud wrote in 1875, that Breton turns.[23] In this poem, fragmentary clusters of words are disposed on the page in such a way that poetic energy is, so to speak, generated by their interaction across the crucial areas of blank space. In adopting the example fleetingly adumbrated in 'Rêve', but also implicit in Mallarmé's *Coup de dés* [A throw of the dice], Breton has in fact taken a further step in the direction already well indicated by the development of his poetry as we have been following it. The selection and organization of the various discrete elements of the poem demanded extreme concentration. A few years later Breton explained his procedure in a revealing passage which deserves to be quoted extensively:

> La vertu de la parole (de l'écriture: bien davantage) me paraissait tenir à la faculté de raccourcir de façon saisissante l'exposé (puisque exposé il y avait) d'un petit nombre de faits, poétiques ou autres, dont je me faisais la substance. Je m'étais figuré que Rimbaud ne procédait pas autrement. Je composais, avec un souci de variété qui méritait mieux, les derniers poèmes de *Mont de piété*, c'est-à-dire que j'arrivais à tirer des lignes blanches de ce livre un parti incroyable. Ces lignes étaient l'œil fermé sur des opérations de pensée que je croyais devoir dérober au lecteur. Ce n'était pas tricherie de ma part mais amour de brusquer. J'obtenais l'illusion d'une complicité possible, dont je me passais de moins en moins. Je m'étais mis à choyer immodérément les mots pour l'espace qu'ils admettent autour d'eux, pour leurs tangences avec d'autres mots innombrables que je ne prononçais pas. Le poème 'Forêt-Noire' relève exactement de cet état d'esprit. J'ai mis six mois a l'écrire et l'on peut croire que je ne me suis pas reposé un seul jour. (I, 323–24)

> [The virtue of speech (or, much rather, of writing) seemed to me to lie in its ability to shorten in a striking manner the business of laying out a small number of facts, poetic or otherwise, [...]. I had thought that Rimbaud had done much the same. I wrote, with a concern for variety which deserved better, the last poems of *Mont de piété* — that is, I managed to derive surprising effects from that book's white lines. Those lines turned the blind eye to the operations of thought that I wanted to conceal from the reader. It wasn't deceptiveness on my part, but rather a taste for speeding things up. I managed to obtain the illusion of a possible complicity, one I could forego less and less. I had begun overindulging words more than I should have, for the space that they allowed around them, for the tangencies they shared with innumerable other words which I kept tacit. The poem 'Forêt-Noire' comes from precisely this state of mind. I spent six months writing it and you will not be surprised to hear that I didn't rest for a single day.]

One of the most revealing features of this passage is the clear statement that these poems have as their basis the exposition of a certain factual content, and that mental operations are to be discerned beneath the discontinuous surface of the poetry. With this encouragement some interpretations of these later poems can be advanced.

In 'Forêt-Noire' Rimbaud is for the second time the subject of a poem. While in 'Âge' he had provided the example of a poet whose inventions, however liberated, had their root in a heightened encounter with a solid world, in 'Forêt-Noire' the ambiguities of Rimbaud's abandonment of poetry are set in the context of the appeal of a settled life. If this shows an equivocal view of Rimbaud, to the extent that Breton imagines the poet troubled by the conflicting demands of poetry and bourgeois comforts, this may owe something to the influence of Vaché, who was not impressed by Rimbaud.[24] Vaché was, on the other hand, a great admirer of Gide's Lafcadio. Breton once remarked that enthusiasm for *Les Caves du Vatican* was what distinguished a new generation of Gide's admirers from his pre-war friends. While Claudel and others were quick to tell Gide that he had slipped up, the young writers who were to make their mark in the twenties were delighted with a book which seemed to denigrate all the sacred cows of the period. They believed, however, that Gide had failed to live up to the promise of his hero, and it is the 'distance qui sépare M. André Gide de son héros' that is the subject of 'Pour Lafcadio'.[25] The title suggests both a dedication and a gesture of solidarity. But the poem itself is emphatically neither, being concerned principally with Gide and not Lafcadio. It follows 'Rêve' in being spoken yet impersonal — the voices in each of its three parts originate from different sources. The first part situates the speaker in the cocoon of a secure social station, a 'Gulf stream' of languid ease insulated from the currents of History, an elegant élite centring on a 'maître' and his admirers. ('Ma maîtresse prend en bonne part son diminutif' [...] implies that she accepts her role as 'diminutive' of the *maître*.)

> Greffier
> parlez MA langue MAternelle (I, 13)
>
> [Clerk | speak my maternal language]

The opening of the second section (which is italicized) indicates the attitude to art implicit in this milieu. The exhortation to a scribe suggests that the act of writing, if conceived as a contribution to the national tradition of a language, becomes impersonal and inauthentic, expressing only the official language of the 'court' and not the language of individual experience. At the same time the repeated syllable 'ma' suggests ironically that universal sentiments are really the disguise of sectional interests.

> *Quel ennui l'heure du cher corps*
> *corps accort*
> *Jamais je ne gagnerai tant de guerres* (I, 13)
>
> [*What a bore, time for the dear body*
> *winsome body*
> *Never will I win so many wars*]

The line which continues the sequence is triggered by the word 'maternelle' which spreads its meaning to represent parental authority. 'Quel ennui l'heure du cher corps' is in fact a quotation from the first section of Rimbaud's 'Enfance' [Childhood] in the *Illuminations*, where it registers a child's dismay at the parental reminder of bodily necessity — 'eat, wash and go to bed' — that interrupts his reverie. If we take the basic idea of creation being interrupted by reminders of the body, the line is extremely ironic when applied to Gide because the creative activity that is suspended in his case is further derided if put on a par with bodily activity — as just another atavism, just another task mechanically performed. The lines which follow bring out the implicitly sexual connotation of 'cher corps' and initiate a fusion of sexual and military contexts. While 'corps accort' at one level continues the idiom of sexuality, it also introduces the further context of the war through its homonym *corps à corps* with its connotations of bodily struggle: the amorous tussles of a graceful body are set against the grim reality of military strife. (The association slyly alludes to the masculine nature of Gide's sexual proclivities.) This gives the Rimbaud quotation further ironic strength since it suggests that the war is regarded as little more than a trifling interruption of private social pleasures. And this is extended in the last line where the military connotations of 'gagner [...] une guerre' are subordinated to the metaphorical ones of successes scored on the social and sexual 'battlefield' in the enthusiastic and self-congratulatory phrase 'jamais je ne gagnerai tant de guerres'. The superimposition of contexts by the various devices of ironic quotation, phonetic ambiguity, and the revivification of stock metaphorical phrases, reveals Breton's increasing mastery of the new mode of poetic ambiguity he has developed. The systematic ambiguity of these lines is continued by these and other means in the last section of the poem where the identity of the speaker changes to become that of an objectified author:

> Des combattants
> qu'importe mes vers le lent train
> l'entrain (I, 13)

[The soldiers | brought in by the slow train of my verses | what matters the liveliness]

Here two channels of discourse interpenetrate, and the value of two kinds of enterprise is questioned First, that of *combat* in either the military or socio-artistic spheres; second, that of Breton's own participation in artistic creation. While both embody two modes — painstaking and slow, as both military and creative progress can be ('le lent train') or vivid and lively ('l'entrain') — it is implied that these may be equally contingent and incomplete. The interconnection of the two statements suggests that Breton's activity as a poet is compromised by its failure to escape the established framework. The last lines, therefore, sketch an alternative strategy, that of the non-participant — like Lafcadio.

> Mieux vaut laisser dire
> qu'André Breton
> receveur de Contributions Indirectes
> s'adonne au collage
> en attendant la retraite (I, 13)

[Better to let it be said | that André Breton | collector of indirect taxes | has taken up collage | as he waits for retirement]

The fundamental issue, then, is the *viability* of poetry. This had been the subject of 'Forêt-Noire' where Rimbaud was potentially caught between the commitments of a poetic vocation which isolates from society, and the lure of a situation within it. But here the option of the Rimbaldian poetic adventure does not seem open, the poet's activity seems unresisting to the corrosive powers of society and nation. Retreat from writing is not envisaged here as antithetical to authenticity but on the contrary as its condition. The Rimbaldian expansion of self and language is no longer its mode; it is supplanted by a posture of irony and voluntary sterility of which Lafcadio and M. Teste are the patrons. The poem thus ends with a sort of aesthetic manifesto, negative in its formulation. Rejecting all the artistic personae currently available, dubious of the status of poetic 'productions' if they are merely the facade of a cultural elite, the artist will become an *arranger*; his art will not be determined by his impeccable connections with a tradition but will reflect a dual activity. First of all, that of being attuned to the undercurrents of his time. The artist will have the ability to extract what is alive and compelling from what is inert, he will be a 'Receveur de Contributions Indirectes' (a type of taxman), severing Lafcadio from the clutches of his creator, wresting M. Teste from Valéry. Second, he will be the agent of a new synthesis, a *collage*, in which the ingredients are reinvigorated by their interaction in a new context.

Both these functions are deeply characteristic of the period. As the first war closes, many artists are vying to be the impresarios of the new artistic sensibility which had its seeds in the European turmoil that had produced the cataclysm of the Great War. To be at the centre of the multiple new currents with which the European cultural milieu was alive as the old order was vanquished in the war, was a status to which Breton would explicitly aspire as the architect of the surrealist movements. In 1918 his ambition is only tentative and the poem ends on a subtle note of anticipation buried in ambiguity. 'En attendant la retraite' implies a jocular parody of bourgeois resignation, but it also suggests a rather closer horizon — the end of the war and the retreat of one of the belligerent nations.

Equally, Breton's evident dissatisfaction with art as *expression* and his promotion of an art of collage, of *bric à brac* (implied in the title *Mont de piété*), is symptomatic of a crucial phase of his development. It will be displaced only by the restoration of expressivity in another form when, influenced by Freud, Breton adopts the practice of automatic writing on which surrealism will be based. The end of 'Pour Lafcadio' thus identifies the technique inaugurated by 'Forêt-Noire' as a *poetry of collage* whose aim is to evade the defects of available poetic language.[26] It is appropriate that Breton should have employed it principally in his assessments of literary figures, since it can thus be seen as a kind of multi-faceted portraiture akin to that of the cubists who introduced collage into the mainstream of art.

In Breton's next poem, written after the armistice, the subject — or victim — is Paul Valéry. The title 'Monsieur V' suggests a portrait, while the sly dedication to Valéry (omitted in the original edition) gives a clear identification.[27] The opening lines inaugurate the textual system implicit in the collage:

> A la place de l'étoile
> L'Arc de Triomphe
> qui ne ressemble à un aimant que pour la forme (I, 13)

> [In place of the star | The Arc de Triomphe | which only resembles a magnet in form]

Each of the principal elements in these lines is ambiguous. The use of lower case in the first activates, beneath the topographical reference, an alternative reading: '*instead of* the star the Arc de Triomphe'. Now, the Arc de Triomphe clearly represents national pride in military success and refers us to the public triumph at the recent victory in the war. The sentiments implied by this have *supplanted* the *étoile*. What does the latter represent? The third line makes this clearer: the *étoile* is associated with the truly magnetic quality which the *Arc de Triomphe* lacks, despite what it represents. 'Pour la forme' is another clever play on words: the *Arc de Triomphe* resembles a magnet only externally (literal sense) or only half-heartedly, in a shallow manner (idiomatic sense).[28] The appeal of superficial public triumph and glory has usurped more truly magnetic qualities. Taken together, these lines suggest (as will be borne out later in the poem) that Valéry has forsaken the *étoile* of authentic poetic energy for the blandishments of public notoriety secured by conventional literary achievements such as his recently published 'La Jeune Parque' [The Young Fate] which had restored Valéry's prominence as a writer after years of silence.[29] The next two lines seem to imply this:

> argenterai-je
> les jardins suspendus (I, 13)

> [will I silver-plate | the hanging gardens]

The gardens could refer to the setting of 'La Jeune Parque'. In any case the phrase suggests something artificial and elevated — perhaps high society — while 'argenter' implies the superimposition of a superficial layer of distinction on an object, so that, like the Arc de Triomphe, it appears to have desirable qualities.

The next element of the collage is a lullaby which matches the march later on in the poem

> BERCEUSE
> *L'enfant à la capote de rubans*
> *L'enfant que chatouille la mer* (I, 14)

> [LULLABY | *The child with the cap of ribbons* | *The infant tickled by the sea*]

The lullaby discreetly launches a flashback to earlier phases of Valéry's development; it has a parodic flavour — *rubans* suggests precocious distinction, while *chatouille*, in a phrase associating the rocking cradle with the 'tangage' of a boat on the sea, perhaps refers obliquely to Valéry's origins in the maritime town of Sète, later to achieve notoriety with the publication of 'Le Cimetière marin'. The implication here might be that Valéry, hovering like 'La Jeune Parque' between the intellect ('la capote de rubans') and the senses, has only timidly acknowledged the latter —

*chatouille* suggesting an appeal that is resisted. The next group of lines makes it clear that the *étoile* was a valuable quality which Valéry once possessed but has now lost:

> En grandissant
> il se regarde dans une coquille nacrée
>     l'iris de son œil est l'étoile
> dont je parlais (I, 14)

[Growing up | he looks at himself in a pearly-white shell | his eye's iris is the star | I was speaking of]

These lines suggest that in the act of self-scrutiny so characteristic of his early writings, dominated by the figure of Narcissus, Valéry had been in touch with the elusive *étoile* he has now forsaken for public triumph. Another musical interlude follows:

> MARCHE
> *Pierre ou Paul* (I, 14)

> [MARCH | *Peter or Paul*]

The proverbial pair, 'Pierre ou Paul', suggests a hesitation between personae, perhaps those which Valéry might adopt on his return to creativity; would it be as the lucid nihilist who once told Breton that he recognized his younger self in Tristan Tzara, or the 'homme de lettres' who soon afterwards was to present his candidature for the Académie Française?[30] For Breton the matter is settled: Valéry has chosen the latter role:

> Il s'apprête à tirer les rois
> aujourd'hui comme ailleurs
>     ses égaux
> Rêve de révolutions (I, 14)

[He gets ready to try his luck with the kings | today as before | his equals | Dreams of revolutions]

Here it is suggested that Valéry has submitted to the bourgeois ethos. These lines associate him with the traditional Twelfth-night reunion when the family assembles to see who will be the lucky one to pick ('tirer') the piece of cake ('galette des rois') with the broad bean in it. Valéry, it is implied, has forsaken the hazards of creative adventure; now he opens himself to chance only in its cosy, domesticated form, and relegates revolutionary change (inherent in true poetry) to the status of a pipe-dream. But the stock expression 'tirer les rois' works at another level when its literal meaning is activated by the next lines. The 'rois' become symbols of the 'beau monde' to which Valéry now has access and whose favour, it is suggested, he curries: 'tirer' suggests a deliberate policy of ingratiation.[31] Breton implies however that, 'ailleurs', Valéry was already on a par with the nobility — when he was an authentic artistic innovator. The poem ends with a statement which at once sums up and extends its meaning

> On ne saurait décrire en art
> L'engin à prendre le renard bleu (I, 14)

[One cannot describe in art | The contraption that could catch the arctic fox]

The 'renard bleu' has obvious affinities with the 'étoile', as something elusive, refractory, beyond normal horizons. 'Prendre le renard bleu' is clearly a phrase representing the aim of the true poet or artist: to capture elusive, mysterious experience. Valéry, the lines suggest, has forsaken it by attempting to codify and formalize aesthetic means, and losing sight of aesthetic ends. His attempts to pin down the mechanisms of inspiration and creation ('décrire en art l'engin à prendre le renard bleu') can only be detrimental to poetry which, like the arctic fox, resists all domestication.[32]

It is difficult to summarize Breton's critique of other writers in these three poems, although there is undoubtedly a consistent thread. It is important to stress that what concerns Breton is not so much their aesthetic position as the degree to which they measure up to a quasi-moral ideal inherent, for Breton, in the writer's art. It is not so much for writing bad poems that Breton criticizes them but for failing to be worthy of the mantle they assume in writing. This is not to imply that orthodox moral criteria or obligations to society are invoked. Nor is Breton wholly adhering to the symbolist notion of the port as magus, although there is undoubtedly something of this. For Breton the authenticity of the artist depends on his fidelity to the range of experience which art ideally encapsulates and promotes, and to which the commitments of society, adopted to varying degrees by Rimbaud, Gide and Valéry, are detrimental.[33]

The last three poems in *Mont de piété* were written in 1919 and, although they have affinities with the 1918 poems, need to be considered separately. In 'Clé de sol' [Treble clef] (I, 14), written in the aftermath of Jacques Vaché's death, Breton borrows the evanescent, throwaway style of Pierre Reverdy.[34] But it seems a slight performance. Although the aesthetics of Reverdy's telegraphic style have the same aim as Breton's collages — that of creating a multiple signifying object, bristling with reflected meanings — Breton fails to achieve this purpose when he attempts the quivering delicate lines of Reverdy. While 'Clé de sol' is not intended to pass comment on either Vaché or Reverdy, 'Une Maison peu solide' [A rather unstable house] (I, 15) continues the appraisal of aesthetic models. Marguerite Bonnet's excellent analysis proves conclusively that this poem represents a critique of Apollinaire's conception of 'l'esprit nouveau'.[35] The poem also constitutes a variant of the collage principle — and a cautious tribute to Dada — since it consists of a curious 'fait divers' reproduced from a newspaper, Breton's intervention being apparently restricted to the transposition of names.

It was natural that the poetry of collage should culminate in a poem consisting entirely of *borrowed* materials. But whereas 'Une maison peu solide' does not generate poetic energy within its own texture, the poem which closes the collection combines the textual system of Breton's earlier collage poems with the added factor of featuring almost exclusively materials borrowed from the mass media of magazines, newspapers and advertising. Indeed, 'Le Corset mystère' [The Mystery Corset] (I, 16), inspired by a genuine Parisian poster, takes the form of a fashion advertisement, using a variety of different fonts and typefaces, thus continuing the sequence of references to fashion and costume as a dominant source of imagery in the collection. The opening fragment, 'Mes belles lectrices' is reminiscent of many fashion magazines of the period including *La Dernière Mode* edited almost single-handedly by Mallarmé. Too much space would be required to offer an adequate interpretation of the poem — although it should be emphasized that it does not defeat interpretation. But some remarks need to be made on the implications of the poem's form. In both form and subject matter, 'Le Corset mystère' is an amalgam of various ideas and influences. It betrays distinct echoes of the Dada activities in Zürich — in its typographic diversity and in its humour. But more than Dada itself it anticipates the liberating effect Dada was to have on Breton's development.[36] It is a fitting poem to close *Mont de piété* since it is both the summation of the aesthetic development in the collection and also a prefiguring of what will follow. It shows that Breton has both cast off the influence of his earlier mentors and transcended his obligation to test, appraise and criticize their example. Despite its consisting of borrowed material, it is a more affirmative and personal poem than most of its predecessors. Yet 'Le Corset mystère' is still more of a conclusion than a new beginning. While it is the epitome of the collage poem, its freedom and flexibility, its appeal to the collective experience of the group, central to Dada and Surrealism: ('nous adhérons à une sorte de Touring Club sentimental' [We belong to a sort of sentimental touring club]), its proclamation of the importance of inner exploration (**'UN CHÂTEAU À LA PLACE DE LA TÊTE'** [a castle in place of a head]), and of lyrical exploration ('Autrefois les meubles de ma chambre étaient solidement fixés aux murs et je me faisais attacher pour écrire: **J'ai le pied marin**' [In the past the furniture in my room was solidly fixed to the walls and I would get myself strapped in to write: **I've got my sea legs**]) assert the need for a new kind of poetic vehicle, more suited to registering and aiding these functions. 'Le Corset Mystère' ends with a beautiful evocation of a kind of lyrical 'knowledge' of Paris itself, as a supreme prize.

> Je tiens Paris comme — pour vous dévoiler l'avenir — votre main ouverte
> **la taille bien prise**.
>
> [I grasp Paris — as if to reveal to you the future — like your open hand | **a perfect waist**]

This is the first time that we see articulated what will become a quintessential feature of Bretonian and surrealist poetics — the elevation of 'Knowing Paris' to an existential and divinatory principle of the highest order. Knowing Paris like the back of one's hand, as the English expression has it, or as I might know your hand if you proffered it to me in the gesture of one seeking to have their palm read, and their fortune told, is given here the aura of an intimate transaction. Breton's deftness, evolved throughout *Mont de piété*, in making language work doubly, extracting polyvalence like the juice from an orange, is used here to make alternative contexts interactively present. And the further framework, generated by the closing reference to a trim waist, both flashes back to the presiding titular reference to the poster for a corset, and offers another take on 'knowing Paris', as if we could wear it like a closely fitting garment. It is appropriate then that the construction of 'Le Corset mystère' should immediately precede the production of *Les Champs magnétiques*, the first texts to be obtained by the method of automatic writing.

★   ★   ★   ★   ★

The evolution of Breton's poetic practice, which we have traced through the fifteen poems of his first collection, appears to culminate in what I have called the collage poem. This mode seems to have been principally the *instrument* of a reassessment of the aims and means of poetry, a transitional form through which Breton gravitated towards a new poetic practice.[37] It is evident that Breton's critique of Rimbaud, Gide, Valéry and Apollinaire is less concerned with their aesthetic production than with their understanding of the situation of the poet. In its independence of established poetic models, in the anonymity fostered by a multi-signifying textual system, the collage poem provided an ideally neutral mode in which to mark one's distance from one's eminent precursors. But it was in its own way at odds with the spirit in which Breton criticized them. For it maintained effort and fabrication as the essence of poetic creation, and in this sense perpetuated the aesthetics of the symbolist poem. But Breton increasingly felt that if the *étoile* of poetry lay beyond the reach of the conventional *littérateur*, it was also outside the bounds of his craftsmanlike approach to his art. 'Le Corset mystère' closes an era in Breton's writing because it heralds, but gives way to, the immediacy of a liberated discourse induced by the passive surrender to the unconscious instead of the active manipulation of linguistic material. Breton's automatic poetry will, however, retain many features of the collage poem: for instance its attentiveness to the ambiguities of the linguistic field, and its openness to the combinatory possibilities of words when they are allowed to relate to each other outside the customary boundaries of sequential discourse. Breton's automatic poetry will add fluidity and emotive responsiveness to the model of a poetic structure equipped to magnify the linguistic energy of the poem by encouraging meaning to accumulate at the interstices of words, in their interaction rather than in their referential action. The interplay of semantic forces, independent of fixed context or perspective, will be retained, but the anonymity of the collage poem's mixing of voices will be supplanted by the consistent 'murmure' of the automatic voice.

*Mont de piété* is remarkable for the way it stands apart from the artistic currents of its time and marks a largely private evolution. Its phases are characterized by a consistent attitude of abstention where the eclectic aesthetic doctrines of contemporary French modernism are concerned.[38] Breton did not feel the same kind of enthusiasm as many contemporary poets for the achievements of technological society or the landscapes of modern urbanization.[39] He was consequently indifferent to aesthetic techniques which sought merely to reflect them. Such innovations seemed to neglect the power of language to open new horizons, and seemed to offer poetry no more than a negligible, ornamental role. Breton's route out of Symbolism is a more tortuous one than that of many of his contemporaries because he felt more acutely than they did the desire to retain from it a sense of the centrality of poetic experience and an awareness of the wonders of language. Surrealism, which restores these priorities, will be the outcome of the quest which originates in the false starts and scruples of *Mont de piété*.

The curious title that Breton chose for his first book, although it clearly indicates his diffidence about the early poetry, is appropriately ambiguous.[40] The collection is a pawn shop in which the poet relinquishes his past work, the goods on display being no longer required by the owner. But a further meaning is indicated by the omission of the customary hyphens, underlining the literal sense of the words.[41] These poems constitute a mountain of piety — a pious monument to the poet's past, to the beginnings he hopes now to have exorcized.

## Notes

1. *Mont de piété* (Paris: Au Sans Pareil, 1919) (edition limited to 125 copies) is collected in I, 3–16.

2. The collection receives little attention in the standard works on Breton. Henri Pastoureau's valuable article 'Des influences dans la poésie présurréaliste d'André Breton', in *André Breton: essais et témoignages*, ed. by M. Eigeldiner, rev. edn (Neuchâtel: La Baconnière, 1970), pp. 45–80, offers a survey of *Mont de piété*, but the perspective is a narrow one and detailed analysis is reserved for the poem 'Forêt-Noire'. Marguerite Bonnet offers a brief but excellent analysis of 'Une Maison peu solide' in 'Aux sources du surréalisme: place d'Apollinaire', *La Revue des lettres modernes*, 104–07 (1964), pp. 44–45.

3. For details see Michael Sheringham, *André Breton: A Bibliography* (London: Grant and Cutler, 1972).

4. The poems in *Mont de piété* are not printed in order of either composition or original publication. Order of composition can be deduced from the poems themselves or from Pastoureau's article. For details of publication see Sheringham, op. cit.

5. *La Phalange*, 93 (March 1914), 233–34, printed 'Le Saxe fin' [Fine Dresden porcelain], 'Rieuse' [Laughing woman] and 'Hommage' [Homage]. By 1919 Breton was already reluctant to preserve these poems and only 'Rieuse' is included in *Mont de piété*.

6. The four poems are 'Rieuse', 'D'or vert' [Green gold], 'L'an suave' [The smooth year] and 'Hymne' [Hymn]. The style of these poems is often erroneously taken to be characteristic of the collection as a whole with the exception of the last two or three poems which are equally mistakenly placed under the aegis of Dada.

7. Breton later had these comments to make about this period: 'Mallarmé exerçait alors sur moi le plus grand ascendant, de sorte que j'écrivais des poèmes, ou des proses, de forme mallarméenne. Je dis de *forme* car, du fait de mon inexpérience humaine, encore une fois le fond manquait' [At that time Mallarmé exercised the greatest possible influence over me, such that I wrote poems and pieces of prose in Mallarméan form. I say 'in form' because, on account of my lack of human experience, the foundation was missing once again] (IV, 1014).

8. Breton read as many of these poems as he could in the scattered reviews which had printed them (the *Album* was not published until 1920). Questioned in 1952 about this phase of Valéry's poetry, Breton had these revealing comments to make: 'chaque fois que j'avais mis la main sur l'un d'eux je ne parvenais pas à en épuiser le mystère ou le trouble. Il y allait d'une pente très glissante de la rêverie, volontiers érotique d'ailleurs. Je pense à un poème comme 'Anne'... A la fréquentation de Valéry il n'est pas douteux que j'ai contracté, au mental, un certain goût du scabreux' [...] (III, 432–33) [Each time I laid my hands on one I couldn't exhaust its mysterious, disturbing quality. I was conscious of a sliding slope towards reverie, often erotic in character. I think of a poem like 'Anne'... through acquaintance with Valéry there is no doubt that I contracted, mentally, a certain taste for the scabrous].

9. The intellectual climate of early cubism was not as hostile to 'le symbolisme finissant' as one might expect. A fondness for allegorical subjects, for instance, was common to Picasso, Delaunay, Gris and others. (See George T. Noszlopy, 'Apollinaire, Allegorical Imagery and the Visual Arts', in *Literature and the Plastic Arts, 1880–1930*, ed. by Ian Higgins (Edinburgh:

Scottish Academic Press, 1973), pp. 49–74.) But it is interesting to observe Breton's resistance to modernist innovations. While Apollinaire's *Alcools* clearly embodies the shift from symbolism to modernism, and shows that, by 1913, radical new perspectives were open to the poet, Breton's preference, at this time, for Valéry and Royère, in whom he admired the taste for the rare and the hermetic, betrays a hostility to the democratic and populist currents in modernism, exemplified by Romains and the *Unanimistes*. It was only from 1915 onwards, in conjunction with his discovery of Rimbaud, that Breton recognized affinities with Apollinaire.

10. Raymond's comment is disapproving: 'Les poèmes de Jean Royère et des écrivains de son groupe, malgré la délicatesse de leur manière et le ton soutenu de leur incantation, donnent l'impression d'un art trop habile à sonder les merveilles du langage' [The poems of Jean Royère and the writers in his group, in spite of their delicacy of manner and the formal manner in which they are intoned, strike one as too canny to sound out the marvels of language]. Marcel Raymond, *De Baudelaire au surréalisme* (Paris: José Corti, 1966), p. 120. The poem is 'D'or vert' (I, 6).

11. See II, 679. Quoting these fragments, Breton notes: 'Je n'aspirais [...] qu'à procurer (me procurer?) des états équivalents à ceux que certains mouvements poétiques très à part avaient provoqués en moi' [I aspired only [...] to provide (for myself?) states equivalent to those which certain exceptional poetic movements provoked in me]. One of the phrases quoted, Rimbaud's 'Que salubre est le vent' [How healthy the wind is], occurs in 'Forêt-Noire' [Black-Forest].

12. 'Décembre' (1915), 'Façon' [Fashion], 'Âge' (1916), 'Coq de bruyère' [Wood grouse] (1917), 'André Derain' (1918).

13. See 'Lettres d'Apollinaire à André Breton (1915–1918). Introduction et notes par Marguerite Bonnet', *Revue des lettres modernes*, 104–07 (1964), 16.

14. Breton often wrote of the spell exerted on him by his reading of the *Illuminations* as he wandered the streets of Nantes in 1916. See III, 441, and IV, 1014.

15. Commenting on this poem in a letter dated January 1916, Valéry noted, 'Nous avons lu ces derniers vers que vous m'avez envoyés. Ils font penser que vous êtes dans cet état que les physiciens nommeraient critique. Leur brisement, leur art situé entre les types définis, le hasard introduit, voulu, rétracté à chaque instant, assurent que vous touchez un certain point intellectuel d'ébullition bien connu de moi, quand le Rimbaud, le Mallarmé, inconciliables, se tâtent dans un poète' [We have read these last lines you sent me. They make one think that you are in that state of mind which a physician would call 'critical'. Their fractured quality, their artistry which finds a place between well-defined types, the chance which is at each turn introduced, willed, and retracted — all these make it certain that you have reached a point of intellectual ferment which I know well, one where the Rimbaud and Mallarmé elements, which are irreconcilable, both make themselves felt in a poet] (quoted in Pastoureau, p. 52). The influence of Mallarmé can also be detected in the dominance of fashion imagery in this poem. This will be a consistent feature of *Mont de piété*, culminating in the last poem, 'Le Corset mystère', which purports to be an advertisement for ladies' underwear. Adrienne Monnier notes that Breton was enormously impressed at this time by Mallarmé's *La Dernière Mode*, see *Rue de l'Odéon* (Paris: Albin Michel, 1960), p. 98. In the original edition of *Mont de piété*, 'Façon' — a title which may be a pun on the English word 'fashion' — bears the epigraph 'Cheruit', which, as Pastoureau points out, was the name of a well-known 'maison de couture'. This is dropped in the *Clair de terre* edition. *Mont de piété* is a 'collection' in more senses than one: millinery provides one of the richest funds of fashion imagery. It is interesting to observe that this thematic motif survives the radical stylistic evolution which characterizes the volume. While in the early poems it originates in the reverence with which the evanescent female figures are regarded — their perfection and inaccessibility being underlined by the precariousness of their hairdos — in subsequent poems references to hats increasingly become vehicles of irony and parody. We move from the *toquet* of 'L'an suave' to the *hennin* of 'Décembre', the *chapeau de soie* of 'Âge', the *casques* of 'Coq de bruyère', the *tendre capsule* and the *melon* of 'Forêt-Noire', and the *capote* of 'Monsieur V'.

16. 'Âge' marks a brief excursion into the 'poème en prose' that will not be repeated in the collection, perhaps because the poem is too close to its model, Rimbaud's *Illuminations*, and particularly 'Aube' [Dawn].

17. See Vaché, *Lettres de guerre, precedées de quatre essais d'André Breton* (Paris: Eric Losfeld, 1970).

18. The effect is to create a denser and more complex circuit for the dissemination of linguistic energy. Vaché's letters may themselves have suggested some of the means whereby this is achieved. Their elliptical, telegraphic style, their apparent discontinuities of syntax, punctuation, and sense, the tendency to oblique rather than direct statement, are features that will be found in Breton's next few poems. In addition, Vaché's letters show ample evidence of aesthetic discussions with Breton. For Vaché's views on language and modern poetry, see an especially interesting letter dated 18 August 1917 (*Lettres de guerre*, pp. 56–58).

19. 'Critique synthétique' is an important precedent for the later poems in the collection. It consisted in substituting for a conventional review of a work a 'prose poem' generally attempting to convey in concentrated form the essence of the work *and* the reviewer's 'impressions' of it. Aragon excelled at it and from October 1918 contributed his regular 'critique synthétique' to Albert-Birot's *Sic*. Writing later of the genre, he noted 'les jeunes lampes à huile de la critique sont plus séraphins, plus filasses. S'ils vous parlaient d'Hernani, vous pourriez vous fouiller pour connaître le nom de Doña Sol' [criticism's young guns are more seraphic, more tow-headed. If they told you about Hernani, you could try as hard as you like to find out Doña Sol's name], *Traité du style* (Paris: Gallimard, 1929), p. 45. See, as an appropriate example, Aragon's 'critique synthétique' of *Mont de piété* (*Littérature*, 8 (October 1919), p. 28) which makes no comments on the poetry but stresses the idea that *Mont de piété* registers the successive metamorphoses, the 'sillage' of a poet in search of himself. Breton avoided all journalistic activity and never practised 'critique synthétique' as such. But the composition of the group of poems being considered coincided with Breton's first critical essays on Jarry, Apollinaire, etc., collected in *Les Pas perdus* (I, 191–308). It should be noted that *Mont de piété* was embellished with two engravings by Derain.

20. Wordplay is again prominent. For example, 'des genêts'/'déjeunait', *'ces langes* bleus comme un glaçon'/'le premier-né *c'est l'ange'*. Vaché approved of this poem, whereas he had been critical of the earlier ones: 'Je ne comprends pas... "le premier-né c'est l'ange" — c'est d'ailleurs au point — beaucoup plus au point qu'un certain nombre de choses montrées vers l'hôpital de Nantes!' [I don't understand... 'the firstborn is the angel' — it's spot on, though — far more spot on than some of the things shown around Nantes hospital!]. Letter dated 9 May 1918 in *Lettres de guerre*, p. 60.

21. Derain was to be one of the many artists whose early promise was, in Breton's eyes, betrayed by their later sterility. He was fascinated by Derain's evolution up to 1917 (see *Le Surréalisme et la Peinture* (Paris: Gallimard, 1965), p. 350). What interested him were not so much Derain's painterly qualities as their relation to his curious metaphysical speculations on ordinary and apparently banal aspects of reality. For an idea of these see *Le Surréalisme et la peinture*, pp. 21–22, and especially Breton's article on Derain, contemporary with the poem, 'Idées d'un peintre', in I, 247–50.

22. The first three poems which, like 'André Derain', date from 1918, are 'Forêt-Noire', 'Pour Lafcadio' [For Lafcadio], and 'Monsieur V'. The last three are 'Clé de sol' [Key to the earth], 'Une Maison peu solide' [An unstable house] and 'Le Corset mystère' [The mystery corset], which were all written in 1919.

23. 'Rêve' was enclosed in a letter to Delahaye dated 14 October 1875. The letter was first published by Berrichon in the *Nouvelle Revue française* (Juillet 1914), where Breton probably read it. See Rimbaud, *Œuvres complètes*, (Paris: Gallimard, 1972), p. 299. Breton himself drew attention to the influence of 'Rêve' on the later poems of *Mont de piété*: see *La Clé des champs*, OC III, p. 819.

24. Breton in fact seems sympathetic to Rimbaud's situation, which he identifies with his own. The italicized phrase, *'Que salubre est le vent'* is from Rimbaud's 'La Rivière de Cassis' [Blackcurrant river] (cp. footnote 11), and here it stands for the positive view of Rimbaud's abandonment of poetry — the view that he wished to widen the horizons of a quest still essentially poetic or creative. However, this is set against the negative view — that Rimbaud had succumbed to materialistic impulses and compromised with bourgeois society — a view represented by the bathetic phrase in counterpoint 'Ce souffle | Le vent des crémeries' [That breeze | The

wind from the dairies]. Breton will 'quote' Rimbaud once again in 'Pour Lafcadio'. For fuller discussion of 'Forêt-Noire', see Pastoureau, art. cit., and Michael Sheringham, 'Rimbaud in 1875 and André Breton's "Forêt-Noire" ', in this volume.

25. In the same passage Breton writes of Lafcadio 'Dans les années de débâcle intellectuelle et morale qui furent celles de la guerre 14–18, ce personnage n'a cessé de grandir, il a incarné le non-conformisme sous toutes ses formes... De lui part une sorte d'"objection d'inconscience" beaucoup plus grave que l'autre... Les idées de famille, de patrie, de religion et même de société sortent on ne peut moins vaillantes de l'assaut que leur livrent chez un adolescent l'ennui le moins résigné, le désœuvrement le plus mobile' [In those years of intellectual and moral defeat which were those of the '14–'18 war, this character never ceases growing in importance. He embodied non-conformism in all its forms... With him there begins a sort of 'unconscientious objection' that is much graver than the other... The ideas of family, of fatherland, of religion, and even of society come out with as little valour as possible from the assault visited on them in the heart of an adolescent by an ennui so little resigned and an aimlessness so much on target] (II, 1042–43). Jacques Vaché was reputed to have worked at a portrait of Lafcadio while in the trenches. Lafcadio belongs to the line of archetypal anti-heroes such as M. Teste, Jarry's 'Surmâle', Derain's 'Chevalier X', who figure prominently in the mythology of Breton and his friends at this time.

26. The technique characterizes Breton's favourite poems in *Mont de piété* which he reprinted even in his earliest anthologies, *Clair de terre* (1923) and *Le Revolver à cheveux blancs* (1932), where the remaining poems are excluded.

27. This should be contrasted with the sincere dedication of 'Rieuse' to Valéry.

28. Lautréamont makes the same pun when he writes of the dome of the Panthéon, 'c'est sur cette superficie sphérique et convexe, qui ne ressemble à une orange que pour la forme' [it is on this spherical, convex surface, which only resembles an orange in form], *Œuvres complètes* (Paris: José Corti, 1963), p. 358.

29. For Breton's disappointment with Valéry at this time see III, 449. It is most tersely expressed by the premature epitaph Breton composed in 1923: 'Paul Valéry 1871–1917' (I, 457).

30. When Valéry was elected to the Académie in 1924 Breton sold their correspondence. See III, 434.

31. In the period to which Breton refers, Valéry, like Bergson, had become the darling of the bourgeois establishment. Both Nizan and Sartre have explained the idealist leanings of the bourgeoisie in terms of the furthering of its own counter-revolutionary ends). The artist or philosopher is encouraged to adopt the unconscious rôle of 'watchdog' or guardian of the *status quo*. Sartre notes, 'Les honneurs ont caché Valéry: il vit des princes, des reines, des industriels; c'est qu'il travaille pour eux: la magnification du verbe profite directement aux grands de ce monde' [Honours have obscured Valéry: he lives off princes, queens, industrialists; in fact he works for them: the promotion of the word directly profits the high and mighty of this world], *Situations*, IV (Paris: Gallimard, 1964), p. 164. It is partly the desire to challenge the implications of the last part of Sartre's statement that leads Breton to assert that the essence of poetry, the *étoile*, is irreducible and antithetical to public or social triumph.

32. Breton's poem is in part a rebuff to Valéry's prescription of the kind of poem he should write: 'un sonnet parfait: rimes riches ou rares, raie au milieu, pas de ponctuation et des majuscules à gauche' [a perfect sonnet: rich or unusual rhymes, a parting in the middle, no punctuation, and capitals on the left hand side], letter quoted in Pastoureau, p. 68.

33. Breton's rejection of a solely aesthetic perspective in the justification of art will be maintained in his surrealist thought, as will his tendency to pass judgement on writers on quasi-moral grounds. *Les Pas perdus* offers ample evidence of Breton's willingness to assume the pose of a moralist, e.g. 'La morale est la grande conciliatrice. L'attaquer c'est encore lui rendre hommage. C'est en elle que j'ai toujours trouvé mes principaux sujets d'exaltation' [Morality is the great reconciler. To attack it is still to pay it homage. It is within it that I have always found my main subjects for exultation] (I, 195).

34. ' "Clé de sol" transpose l'émotion que j'ai éprouvée à l'annonce de la mort de Jacques Vaché' ['Clé de sol' transcribes the emotion that I felt at Jacques Vaché's death] (II, 734).

35. M. Bonnet, art cit.
36. It would be misleading, however, to speak of a Dada influence on Breton's poetry at this time. The aesthetic mode of Breton's poems derives, as I have suggested, from the coherent evolution of a poetic technique designed to achieve certain ends. 'Une Maison peu solide', which was originally intended to be printed in columns like a newspaper article (see letter to Tzara (20 April 1919) in Michel Sanouillet, *Dada à Paris* (Paris: Pauvert, 1965), p. 455) and 'Le Corset mystère' are given an extra layer of visual presentation, but if this enhances, it does not modify the established system of textual operation that Breton had already evolved before coming into contact with Dada.
37. A section of the *Manifeste du surréalisme* (1924) (I, 341–43) beginning 'Il est même permis d'intituler POÈME ...' [it is even permitted to call POEM...] offers a recipe for the collage or assemblage poem, and cites examples made up of fragments in different typefaces culled from newspapers.
38. For a wide-ranging account of these doctrines see Léon Somville, *Devanciers du surréalisme* (Geneva: Droz, 1971). See also Marcel Raymond, op. cit. A parallel kind of abstention is identified as one of the book's qualities in one of Breton's rare retrospective comments on *Mont de piété*: 'A revoir aujourd'hui cet ouvrage se recommande surtout par le cas poétiquement raisonnable, si l'on veut bien se reporter aux dates, qu'il fait de la guerre' [Coming back to it today, this work recommends itself above all by the poetically reasonable treatment that — if you want to check the dates — it gives the war]. (Part of the dedication of a copy of the book to René Gaffé. See *Bibliothèque de M. René Gaffé. Vente des 26 et 27 avril 1956, Hôtel Drouot, Paris*, p. 23.)
39. But Breton was increasingly sensitive to the feeling for the poetic aspects of daily life that lay beneath the naive enthusiasm of Apollinaire. Both 'Monsieur V' and 'Le Corset mystère' anticipate the connection the surrealist sensibility will make between poetic inspiration and the 'magie quotidienne' of privileged experience whose forum is frequently the city street.
40. A typically deprecating comment occurs in a letter to Tristan Tzara (29 July 1919) 'Si je vous ai envoyé *Mont de piété* c'est uniquement qu'il en coûtait à mon orgueil. Vous ne devez pas aimer ce recueil, naturellement' [If I sent you *Mont de piété*, it is only because it hurt my pride to do so. You're not supposed to like this collection, of course], *Dada à Paris*, p. 447.
41. It will become a typical manoeuvre of Breton's, particularly where titles are concerned, to use context, typography, or, more generally, linguistic isolation, to redress the neutrality of a banal phrase, throwing imaginary quotation marks round it and turning it into a vibrant field of meanings. The present example can be compared with the title 'Forêt-Noire' in which Breton has *added* a hyphen. Breton was doubtless struck by the oddness of the phrase *Mont-de-piété* which is in fact a corruption of the Italian *monte di pietà*, which ought to have been rendered as *mont-de-pitié*.

# 3

# Rimbaud in 1875 and
# André Breton's 'Forêt-Noire'

'Forêt-Noire' belongs to a small group of poems to be found at the end of Breton's first collection *Mont de piété* (1919).[1] These poems differ markedly from those that precede them, especially from the early ventures in neo-symbolism. Among the features they have in common are a disjointed appearance, accentuated by typographical peculiarities; a more or less evident concern with the motives and ambitions that determine literary creation; and a formidable reputation for obscurity. Until Henri Pastoureau, in the context of an essay on literary influences in Breton's early poetry, offered an analysis of 'Forêt-Noire', these poems seemed destined to oblivion.[2] Unfortunately, however, Pastoureau's analysis, in drawing attention to the connections between the poem and an obscure episode in Rimbaud's life, implied that interpretation depended on information extraneous to the poem itself. By making 'Forêt-Noire' a 'poème à clef' he both strengthened the locks on the other poems, about which he had little to say, and provided a clearly defined image of Breton's poetic practice in the period immediately preceding the discovery of automatic writing which was to herald surrealism. Over the years this image has been regularly endorsed by Breton critics, content to reiterate Pastoureau's view of 'Forêt-Noire'.[3] He had apparently shown that the poem was perfectly straightforward, even banal, when the correct cypher was applied; it therefore seemed safe to assume that the later poems of *Mont de piété* were, like the earlier ones, of no more than antiquarian interest: Breton had enlisted a tame species of dadaism to indulge in a last spasm of neo-symbolist obscurity.

However, in a well-known passage from the *Manifeste du surréalisme* (1924) where he refers to 'les derniers poèmes de *Mont de piété*' [the last poems of *Mont de piété*] and to 'Forêt-Noire' in particular, Breton observes: 'mes aspirations étaient les mêmes qu'aujourd'hui [...] mais j'avais foi en la lenteur d'élaboration' [my aspirations were the same as today [...] but I had faith in the slowness of elaboration]. He goes on to inform the reader that while 'l'exposé d'un certain nombre de faits [...] poétiques ou autres' [the exposition of a certain number of facts [...] poetic and otherwise] provided these poems with their 'substance', their essence lay in the attention which had been devoted to the choice and arrangement of words, the use of blank space, and the encouragement of verbal echoes. 'J'arrivais à tirer des lignes blanches de ce livre un parti incroyable. Ces lignes étaient l'œil fermé sur des opérations de pensée que je croyais devoir dérober au lecteur. Ce n'était pas tricherie de ma part mais amour de brusquer. J'obtenais l'illusion d'une complicité possible' [I managed to draw an incredible amount from that book's white lines. Those lines turned a blind eye to the operations of thought that I felt I wanted to conceal from the reader. It wasn't deceptiveness on my part, but rather a love of cutting corners. This gave me the illusion of a possible complicity] (I, 323).

I think it can be shown that, in disinterring the 'petit nombre de faits' underlying 'Forêt-Noire', Pastoureau relies less on the formal gambits that invite the reader's complicity than on a predetermined view of the poem's content. If we put aside his presuppositions, the anecdotal fabric of 'Forêt-Noire' appears to be much richer than he suggests and its elaborate formal organization, partly inspired by Rimbaud himself, comes fully into play. 'Forêt-Noire' emerges as a poem which, rather than taking a particular stand on Rimbaud's poetic apostasy, as Pastoureau argues, keeps the options of poetry open, even as, at every level, it follows Rimbaud's example in testing the limits and limitations of poetry itself. As such, for all its 'lenteur d'élaboration', the poem is far more than a pre-surrealist curio; not only does it illuminate the context in which surrealism emerged, but, with the other poems of 1918–19, it marks a decisive phase in the clarification of what were to become the poetic aspirations of Breton's surrealism.[4]

Pastoureau argues persuasively that 'Forêt-Noire' records the immediate aftermath of Rimbaud's last quarrel with Verlaine on the edge of the Black Forest near Stuttgart in February 1875, which is supposed to have ended in a brawl.[5] Taking up Breton's invitation at the end of the poem to envisage the words as being spoken by Rimbaud, he identifies dual levels of discourse and demonstrates the constant depreciation of one current of ideas by another: the deflation of 'poetic' rhetoric by the clichés of conventional life. He argues that any tension between them is decisively resolved in favour of the second, and that the poem registers Rimbaud's capitulation to materialism and social conformity: 'l'éblouissement a cessé: les sollicitations métaphysiques sont sans prise; l'homme a vaincu' [the ecstasy is over: metaphysical appeals cannot get a hold; the ordinary mortal has vanquished] (p. 64), From the outset, Pastoureau makes it clear that, in assessing what kind of inner disposition Breton attributes to Rimbaud at this point, he bases himself on a specific account of the incident — that of the man Breton once referred to as Rimbaud's 'sinistre beau-frère' [sinister brother-in-law]: Paterne Berrichon. Berrichon, who married Rimbaud's devout sister Isabelle, propounded the view that the Bohemian Verlaine came to tempt the now reformed and respectable Arthur back into their former evil ways; such is the drift of the paragraph Pastoureau quotes from Berrichon which concludes: 'Le Bateau ivre s'était plus convenablement assagi que Sagesse. Celle-ci voulait revivre les héroïques pérégrinations, celui-là entendait demeurer rangé. Conflit. Rixe' [Le Bateau ivre was more conventionally settled down than Sagesse. The latter wanted to relive their heroic travels, while the former intended to stay settled. Conflict. Brawl].[6] The next paragraph, which Pastoureau does not quote, gives an even clearer picture of the Rimbaud portrayed by Berrichon: 'En vain Pauvre Lélian, pardonneur infini, dès repris ses sens, implora-t-il son ami Rimbaud qui, se croyant pour les lettres déshonoré à cause du scandale de Bruxelles, resta inflexible, résolu du reste qu'il était hélas! à tenter fortune dans l'Industrie' [In vain did Pauvre Lélian, the moment he had regained his senses, infinitely ready to forgive, implore his friend Rimbaud who, thinking himself dishonoured for letters by the scandal of Brussels, remained inflexible, resolved, in any case, as he was alas! to seek his fortune in Industry]. Abetted by his appalling *fin de siècle* prose, Berrichon slyly insinuates that *he* is with Verlaine, on the side of adventure, and unsympathetic to Rimbaud's 'stuffy' attitude; but Isabelle's 'bien-pensant' version of her brother is promoted all the more effectively.

There seems very little justification for supposing that Breton relied on this version of the incident and used it to pass summary judgement on Rimbaud in 1875 and thereafter. To have relied on Berrichon's views would in itself have been extraordinary in view of two other sources available to Breton. The first is a book by Ernest Delahaye which Breton must certainly have read by 1918. Although he does not explicitly say so, Delahaye seems intent on setting the record straight, and he makes it clear that in his view Rimbaud's decision to become a tutor in Stuttgart had nothing to do with preparing himself for a career in the conventional sense. His aim was to immerse himself in foreign languages so as to be able to travel: 'Impossible de trouver dans le détail de cette vie errante une idée d'ambition quelconque. Ce qu'il veut, ce qu'il va chercher, j'ai essayé de le montrer: eaux, sols, horizons, villes, caresses de l'air' [It is impossible to find in the detail of this wandering life the least notion of any sort of ambition. I have tried to show what it is he wants, what he goes looking for: water, earth, horizons, cities, the caresses of the air].[7] Evidence for this view was provided by two letters Delahaye received from Rimbaud in 1875, one from Stuttgart immediately after Verlaine's visit in February, the other from Charleville in October. These letters may be considered the principal source of Breton's view of the Stuttgart episode and the factor instrumental in the writing of 'Forêt-Noire'. They were published, ironically enough, by Berrichon, in the July 1914 issue of the *Nouvelle Revue française* and we know that at some stage before writing his poem Breton read them there with the utmost interest.[8] As early as 1914, Breton had been fascinated by the mystery of Rimbaud's later career: 'l'aventure du Harrar (l'interrogation qu'elle porte) a valu, et continue à valoir à Rimbaud une grande partie de l'intérêt que nous lui portons' [the Harare adventure (the question it brings with it) earns Rimbaud, and continues to earn for him, a good deal of the fascination we have for him] (III, 433). The letters to Delahaye offered an antidote to the Berrichon view of Rimbaud which had long confused the issue: 'Si l'accès de Rimbaud n'était alors pas plus aisé, c'est aussi parce que ses biographes — à commencer par son sinistre beau-frère Berrichon — l'avaient défiguré à plaisir [...] venaient tout juste, en outre, d'être rendues publiques les lettres de Rimbaud à Delahaye de 1875, d'un intérêt capital' [If approaching Rimbaud was not easy at that time, it was also because his biographers — beginning with his sinister brother-in-law Berrichon — disfigured him at will [...] Rimbaud's crucially important letters to Delahaye of 1875, moreover, had just been published] (IV, 1014).[9]

The first letter offered clear evidence against Berrichon's interpretation of the Black Forest incident, since it suggested that Rimbaud's hostility to Verlaine had nothing to do with fears of compromising his new social situation, but that he was both exasperated by his friend's militant religiosity, and reluctant to resume their former intimate relationship.[10] The second letter provided a document which throughout his life Breton regarded as crucial to any understanding of Rimbaud's metamorphosis. This is the poem 'Rêve', incorporated in the letter itself, which Breton once referred to as 'le testament poétique et spirituel de Rimbaud' [Rimbaud's poetic and spiritual testament] (II, 1014). It was precisely in the wake of his discovery of this poem that Breton wrote 'Forêt-Noire', basing it on the incident earlier in 1875 with which the first letter had been concerned.[11]

Why did Breton attach such importance to 'Rêve'? Like most subsequent commentators, he was attentive to the position of the poem in the letter to Delahaye where it is immediately preceded by a disparaging reference to Verlaine's poetry. But while many critics consider that Rimbaud is merely venting, in his most sarcastic vein, a hostility to poetry by then well-entrenched, Breton, who never believed that he had stopped writing in 1873,[12] seems to have felt that in 'Rêve' Rimbaud rehearses for the last time on paper the tensions between poetry and life which had always permeated his work.[13] In the context of the letter, the poem does not seem to confirm or delineate a particular position, but, by adding to the turbulence of a verbal atmosphere already destabilized by irony, slang and self-parody, to underline the relativity of the surrounding discourses and personae. If there is no doubt that Rimbaud is sincere when, in the next paragraph, he asks Delahaye to find out 'en quoi consiste le "bachot" ès sciences actuel, partie classique, et mathém., etc.' [what the modern sciences baccalaureate is made up of, and the classics part, and the maths, etc.], he has already projected enough self-images to assume that the earnest young man who speaks at this point will appear as much a fabrication as the 'génie' who identifies himself with various cheeses.

★　★　★　★　★

Breton explicitly claimed that 'Rêve' had exercised 'une influence décisive' on the later poems of Mont de piété.[14] What is the nature of this influence? C. A. Hackett observes that 'Rêve' is 'une composition en contrepoint qui, tout en jouant sur le son et le sens des mots, traite un thème des plus sérieux: la vie sous ses aspects les plus banals, et la mort dans ses manifestations les plus absurdes' [a contrapuntal composition which, while playing on the sound and meaning of words, deals with an utterly serious theme]: life in its most banal aspects, and death in its most absurd manifestations.[15] Accordingly, contrapuntal structure, linguistic play and instability of tone all figure prominently in Breton's poems which proceed 'par brèves séquences discontinues, marquées de syncopes syntactiques, de ruptures de sens' [by brief discontinuous sequences, marked by syntactic syncopations, and breaks in meaning], as Marguerite Bonnet aptly puts it, adding 'à la manière du "Rêve" de Rimbaud' [in the manner of Rimbaud's 'Rêve'].[16] Breton once cited 'Rêve' as an early and crucial instance of the breaking down of 'l'interdépendance des parties du discours poétique' [the interdependence of the elements of poetic discourse].[17] Instead of reinforcing each other, and progressively consolidating a unified aesthetic project, the elements of the poem command a degree of individual autonomy which increases ambiguity and facilitates the expression of ambivalent sentiments:

> 'RÊVE'
> *On a faim dans la chambrée —*
>     *C'est vrai...*
> *Emanations, explosions,*
>     *Un génie: Je suis le gruère!*
>     *Lefebvre: Keller!*
>     *Le génie: Je suis le Brie!*
>     *Les soldats coupent sur leur pain:*
>       *C'est la Vie!*
>     *Le génie*      *— Je suis le Roquefort!*
>     *— Ça s'ra not' mort...*
>     *— Je suis le gruère*
>     *Et le brie... etc.*
>
>       VALSE
> *On nous a joints, Lefebvre et moi, etc.*
>
> ['DREAM'
> *They're hungry in the barracks —*
>     *It's true...*
> *Emanations, explosions,*
>     *A genius: I'm a Gruyère!*
>     *Lefebvre: Keller!*
>     *The genius: I'm a Brie!*
>     *The soldiers cut into their bread:*
>       *That's life!*
>     *The genius*      *— I'm a Roquefort!*
>     *— It'll be the death of us...*
>     *— I'm a Gruyère*
>     *and a Brie... etc.*
>
>       WALTZ
> *They paired us off Lefebvre and me, etc.*][18]

With its inebriated sing-song rhythms the poem is dominated by the impersonality of the barrack-room. Both first and last lines begin with 'on' [one]; the 'moi' [I] figures only as the penultimate word of the poem, introducing belatedly a specific protagonist who is also the implied author of the poem. But the closing line fails to provide a fixed perspective. The word 'VALSE', which introduces it, both suggests a change of tempo and euphemistically assimilates the protagonist's fate (presumably that of a conscript) to participation in a dance. The rhythm accordingly changes to a stately 'trimeter' which comes as a relief after the histrionic theatricality of the soldiers' voices. It could be argued that there is bitter irony here: the rhythmic flow and balance consolidate the insidious, manipulative power of the ambience. 'On nous a joints' seems to confirm this, and so does the curt 'etc.' which, amusingly, provides the last four syllables of the alexandrine, while at the same time it reflects graphically the diminution of individual identity enacted in the poem. And yet the sober diction may set us wondering, as we look back at the evocation of the 'chambrée', if we are not meant to discern poetic vitality, and a powerful, elemental vision of existence, behind all the tomfoolery. Sordid as it may seem, the soldiers' frugal meal takes on, perhaps, a ceremonial dimension in which the poet is glad to commune, even at the cost of his own individuality. What is more, the polarization between the protagonist and his environment loses distinctiveness the more aware we become of the protagonist as poet. The abrupt switches of tone and tempo and the intermingling of naturalistic, theatrical and oneiric idioms make it difficult enough to establish any fixed 'point of view'. But when we notice the extreme self-consciousness of the language — the play on rhyme and metre, the play on words: 'Keller!' | 'Quel air!', the submerged quotation (as Breton noted, the phrase 'émanations, explosions' occurs in Baudelaire)[19] — the problem of 'placing' the poet within the complex verbal field of the poem becomes even more acute. In the *dramatis personae* of 'Rêve' the 'moi' appears to have no more than a bit-part; in fact he plays all the roles and handles the *mise en scène* as well. The poet has become, so to speak, an impersonator, a ventriloquist. Through words, he transposes his circumstances into a dynamic context where he is able to act out and explore the possibilities available to him. Breton's 'impersonation' of Rimbaud in 'Forêt-Noire' serves the same purpose and, appropriately, borrows and develops a number of techniques from 'Rêve':

FORÊT-NOIRE*

                              Out
Tendre capsule                    etc. melon
Madame de Saint-Gobain trouve le temps long seule
Une côtelette se fane

Relief du sort
Où                sans volets            ce pignon blanc
Cascades
Les schlitteurs sont favorisés
Ça souffle
*Que salubre est le vent*        le vent des crémeries

    L'auteur de l'Auberge de l'Ange Gardien
L'an dernier est tout de même mort
A propos

De Tubingue à ma rencontre
Se portent les jeunes Kepler Hegel
Et le bon camarade

*RIMBAUD PARLE

[BLACK-FOREST*

                              Out
Tender capsule                    etc. melon
Madame de Saint-Gobain all alone the time drags
A cutlet withers

Relief of fate
Where                    without shutters             this white gable
Waterfalls
The *schlitteurs* are favoured
The wind's getting up
*How salubrious the wind is*            The wind from the dairies

The author of the Inn of the Guardian Angel
Died last year all the same
Appropriately

From Tübingen to meet me
come young Kepler young Hegel
And the good comrade

*RIMBAUD IS SPEAKING*]

In his title, Breton is clearly influenced by Rimbaud's use of quotation marks round the word 'Rêve' which fosters ambiguity by urging us to read the word variously, at different tangents to the poem that follows. Breton achieves a similar effect by isolating the place-name and thereby rekindling semantic possibilities implicit in the individual words, creating the aura of an emotional complex involving darkness, fear and mystery. In addition, the peculiar asterisk both ironically alludes to guide-books which employ asterisks to indicate the degree to which a place is worth visiting and, by suggesting an annotation, draws our attention to the words 'RIMBAUD PARLE' in upper-case italics at the foot of the poem. It is only in the second 'tercet' ('Forêt-Noire' playfully subverts both sonnet and alexandrine) with the possessive 'ma' that the disparate word-groups explicitly coalesce as the utterances of a particular individual. But the prominent words 'RIMBAUD PARLE' appear prematurely to advertise a specific attribution. If, however, at their instigation, we acclimatize ourselves to the notion of being privy to Rimbaud's thoughts, when, necessarily, we run up against these words again at the end, they serve to remind us that it is not Rimbaud who speaks, and urge us to consider in what sense it is 'Breton' who speaks, by proxy of the Rimbaud he invents.

Since Pastoureau believed that Breton's purpose was to 'réduire l'énigme psychologique [du] cas Rimbaud' [reduce the psychological enigma of the Rimbaud case] he holds the poem to a rigid dichotomy between lyricism and realism. If we now turn more specifically to the content of the poem it should be possible to rectify this bias while profiting from the many features of Pastoureau's analysis that seem useful. He argues convincingly that we should deem the words to be spoken by Rimbaud immediately after his brawl with Verlaine. The almost calligrammatic placing of the word 'Out' (it is a piece of *Franglais* adopted during the vogue for tennis in the *belle époque*, and hence anachronistic in Rimbaud's speech) sets the poem in motion with a violent desire for disengagement. But from what? For Pastoureau it is from the way of life Verlaine has supposedly reminded Rimbaud of. This is acceptable if we take it that Rimbaud is reminded of a relationship gone stale, of religious fervour gone mad, and of poetry gone soft. Pastoureau's argument is vitiated, however, by his belief that Verlaine could have seemed a valid incarnation of poetry, which Rimbaud none the less rejected. He provides a valuable gloss on the next line, identifying the 'tendre capsule' and the 'melon' as alternative types of headgear, but Pastoureau implies that it is Rimbaud's recent acquiescence in the ethos of the 'chapeau melon' that curtails his initial temptation to side with the world of the 'tendre capsule'. Surely for Breton, what flickers through Rimbaud's mind is the realization that 'the poet' as represented by Verlaine's Bohemian get-up is no less a stereotype than the businessman. If poetry is losing its grip on Rimbaud's imaginings of himself, it is not because he has adopted another image, but, as the next line suggests, because he has experienced the dispersal of all those hitherto available to him. 'Madame de Saint-Gobain' (a town famous for mirrors, appropriately situated in a large wood) can only be a looking-glass, perhaps the one, now vacant, in Rimbaud's room in Stuttgart. The dreary monotony of the sounds in this line suggests Rimbaud's disenchantment with the image the mirror has recently provided. The next line confirms this: the 'côtelette' is another synecdoche for the Stuttgart household and its aura. The verb 'se faner' cleverly superimposes poetic, domestic and pictorial connotations.[20] For Pastoureau the 'côtelette' registers 'l'attrait de la vie régulière' [the attraction of normal life] (p. 62): Rimbaud is worried he will be late for dinner. But surely it is more sensible to assume that what is in the process of withering away at this point is precisely the attraction of any conventional way of life — including that of the poet. The meeting with Verlaine has neither rekindled Rimbaud's poetic velleities nor reinforced any bourgeois allegiances; it has distanced him from both. Far from choosing between these paths, Breton will show Rimbaud seeking to extricate himself from their sterile opposition. But such a pose needs to be invented: the mirror has no available reflection for this future Rimbaud. Pastoureau's reading of the pivotal phrase 'Relief du sort' is excellent: 'calembour intentionnellement indigent (relief du sol) tendant à provoquer une sorte de confusion structurelle entre le temps et l'espace (le hasard et les chances observables à vol d'oiseau comme les accidents de terrain)' [an intentionally bad pun (*relief du sol*, ground relief) which manages to provoke a sort of structural confusion between time and space (randomness and chances observable from a bird's-eye point of view like features of the terrain] (p. 62). But he fails to connect it with the stanza that follows — a jerky montage of past, present and future images that dissolves the fixity of the portrait possibly available in the Stuttgart mirror.

Pastoureau pins this stanza closely to the dichotomy he has established; in doing so, he ignores the dynamic interplay of verbal units and sticks rigorously to a purely line-oriented reading. He construes 'où sans volets ce pignon blanc' as a brief escapade into poetic fantasy peremptorily dismissed by what follows. In fact the obvious wordplay, 'sans volets'/*s'envoler*, 'pignon'/*pigeon*, taken with the spacing which Pastoureau ignores entirely, contributes a fertile ambiguity enabling conflicting options to be simultaneously, and thus ambivalently, present, rather than in hierarchical alternation. For example, a hidden watermark underlies the first line of this section: a Rimbaldian *cri de coeur*: *Où s'envoler?*, which by alerting us to the second pun, enables 'pignon'/*pigeon* to enact simultaneously motion and stasis (the placing of the word 'Cascades' is crucial in showing the association of ideas which transforms the neat white house into a fantasy of departure and change). The Rimbaud whom Breton resurrects at this stage is still an exponent of the dynamic 'voyance' which, at the instigation of language, scrambles appearances and moments. The reference to 'les schlitteurs', by which Breton pays homage to Rimbaud's occasional use of dialect words (a 'schlitteur' is an Alsatian wood-gatherer),[21] does not, as Pastoureau disingenuously supposes, confirm Rimbaud's conversion to the virtues of hard work, but brings into play another established constituent of Rimbaud's poetic vision and personality. Even if one sees declarations like the following as inconsistent with, and critical of, the poetic quest of the *Illuminations*, it is nonsense to see them in terms of conventional careerism: 'Moi, moi qui me suis dit mage ou ange, dispensé de toute morale, je suis rendu au sol, avec un devoir à chercher, et la réalité rugueuse à étreindre! Paysan!' [I, I who have called myself a mage or an angel, exempted from all morality, I am returned to the ground, with a duty to seek, and rugged reality to grasp].[22] If the fantasy in white 'quotes' Rimbaud the 'voyant', and the reference to 'schlitteurs' Rimbaud the 'paysan', the next line literally quotes Rimbaud the poet. 'Que salubre est le vent', from 'La Rivière de Cassis', a poem written by Rimbaud in May 1872, is a line that embodies a considerable charge of affective energy and gives great poetic density to departure and change.[23] Its juxtaposition with 'Ça souffle', a phrase which Pastoureau aptly terms 'une locution vulgaire, d'échange humain dérisoire à l'occasion de la tempête' [a vulgar turn of phrase, a derisory human exchange when a storm is raging] (p. 63), does support Pastoureau's antithesis, and the bathos is reinforced by 'le vent des crémeries' (the expression 'changer de crémerie' means to try elsewhere in a banal sense). But if we take it that this juxtaposition shows Rimbaud impatient in 1875 with the febrile anticipation of 1872, it is hardly because he himself has been beguiled by the insipid whiteness and cosy parochialism of the 'crémerie'. The implication is rather that poetry itself, as for example epitomized by Verlaine, has been gravely compromised by its failure to present a defence against conformity. Rimbaud bitterly acknowledges that purely verbal declarations of intent, however poetic, have no necessary effect on life and do not guarantee self-transformation. Rimbaud, Breton implies, does not repudiate poetry in the name of bourgeois interests but in his awareness of its complicity with them.

Pastoureau disposes rapidly of the last two stanzas — our 'tercets'. The first, he argues, dismisses the 'sollicitations métaphysiques' of poetry by assimilating them to the 'enfantillages' [childishness] of the Comtesse de Ségur (author of *L'Auberge de l'Ange-Gardien* and other children's books, who died in 1874); while the last stanza shows Rimbaud attracted by the benefits of higher education as he recalls some of the 'illustres élèves' [illustrious students] of the University of Tübingen. This is supposed to complete Breton's case against Rimbaud and deliver the anticipated verdict of poetic bankruptcy. Such a view is totally unfounded. It misses the patent irony of the last stanza which clearly reflects Breton's doubts about the myth of Rimbaud the earnest and pragmatic intending student, keen to study so as to get on in the world. Kepler and Hegel are hardly stuffed shirts of the establishment, upholders of the middle-class pieties.[24] On the contrary, they are great revolutionaries of the mind, and the youthful years they spent at Tübingen paved the way for the eternal youth they now enjoy. 'L'homme aux semelles de vent' [The man with soles of wind] is not intended to be diminished by the association with such figures or indeed with Ludwig Uhland, author of a still-famous military poem 'Der gute Kamerad', 'Le Bon Camarade'. The collocation of Uhland's poem with the names of 'les jeunes' Kepler and Hegel ensures that the long period of restless wandering and *linguistic* acquisitiveness which will begin with Rimbaud's long march to Milan, is placed under the aegis of considerable ventures of the intellect.[25]

This helps to clarify what is renounced in the disparaging reference to the Comtesse de Ségur in the penultimate stanza. Breton arranges the three lines in such a way as to enable the middle one to function additionally as an independent statement. 'L'an dernier est tout de même mort' passes judgement, not without a hint of regret, on the year 1874 which Rimbaud largely spent travelling in the company of Germain Nouveau, and it seems possible that Breton adumbrates a psychological explanation for Rimbaud's decision to quit Europe in 1875.[26] At any rate, Breton seems to intend a sympathetic portrayal of Rimbaud's predicament at this time, centring on the difficult 'rite de passage' from childhood to manhood. The Black Forest is not the setting for a 'drame bourgeois' in which the young man hesitates between 'Ma Bohème' [My Bohemian Life] and 'Les Assis' [The seated ones]. It is a *selva oscura* in which conflicting images of man's estate compete for the soul of someone who, scarcely past adolescence, has an extraordinary poetic career behind him. Breton seems, then, to construe Rimbaud's hesitations about poetry partly in terms of the difficulty of disentangling it from the adolescence he had sought to exorcise in Stuttgart.

Still, the challenge of 'Forêt-Noire' is missed if one concludes that it is designed simply to present a more or less lenient picture of Rimbaud's ambitions in 1875. I think it can be argued that Breton, influenced to a large extent by 'Rêve', adopted an elaborate poetic mode whose aim was not solely to assess Rimbaud's position in 1875 but, through a complex process of identifications, to crystallize Breton's awareness of his own situation in 1918. The elaborate ordering of verbal units turns the poem into a lens that can be adjusted to focus either on the distant reaches of Rimbaud's destiny or on the immediate tensions of Breton's. To demonstrate the latter would be to unravel the tight thematic network of *Mont de piété* as a whole that I have attempted to clarify elsewhere. But I hope to have demonstrated sufficiently here that 'Forêt-Noire' enacts a mode of statement which, in scanning a complex network of inclinations, hesitations and resolutions, does not attempt to resolve them into a unified order but encourages the exhibition of their latent contradictions and dynamisms. If 'Forêt-Noire' is laconic in tone, it is after the fashion of the manifest content of dreams: between the discrete word-clusters of the poem and their latent content — the 'dream thoughts' constituted by the Black Forest incident, by the Delahaye letters and 'Rêve', by the parallels Breton registered between Rimbaud and himself — are to be found the characteristic strategies of the Freudian dreamwork (which was beginning to preoccupy Breton

at this time): condensation, displacement, representation and secondary revision.[27]
It is by following these detours, whose poetic qualities were noted by Freud, as they
are enacted in the workings of the language, that the sense of 'Forêt-Noire' can
be pursued. Its priorities are those of a self-scrutiny distrustful of all introspection.
It is a poem pledged to a project of self-discovery exercised in acute awareness of
its pitfalls. Between his gaze (and ours) and any definite image of himself, Breton
introduces two kinds of filter: he foregoes the indulgence of direct self-assessment by
interpolating the figure of Rimbaud whose age and predicament offered a distorted
reflection of his own — a displacement which matches Rimbaud's seclusion behind
the voices of the 'chambrée de nuit' [night barracks]. And he foregoes the reassuring
self-consistency implicit to some extent in any direct statement by consigning his
image to the ricochets of meaning which resound the moment a voice in imitation
of Rimbaud, or Breton, enters the tortuous defiles of the poem. The complexity
secured by these devices befitted Breton's sense both of his own predicament and
of that of Rimbaud, in the judging of whom he was always shy of certainties and
of whom he was one day to write, echoing Apollinaire's 'Lettre-Océan', this word
of caution to the profane: 'Tu ne connaîtras jamais bien Rimbaud' [You will never
know Rimbaud well] (III, 795).[28]

## Notes

1. *Mont de piété* (Paris: Au sans pareil, 1919). 'Forêt-Noire' may be found in I, 12.
2. Henri Pastoureau, 'Des influences dans la poésie pré-surréaliste d'André Breton', in (ed.), *André
   Breton: essais et témoignages*, ed. by M. Eigeldinger, rev. edn (Neuchâtel: La Baconnière, 1970),
   pp. 45–80. References to this article are incorporated in the text.
3. See, for example, S. Alexandrian, *Breton par lui-même* (Paris: Seuil, 1971), pp. 18–19; C. Browder,
   *A. Breton: Arbiter of Surrealism* (Geneva: Droz, 1967), p. 156; Marguerite Bonnet, *André Breton:
   naissance de l'aventure surréaliste* (José Corti, 1975), p. 137. Bonnet has some very interesting things
   to say about the 'poétique du derangement' she discerns in the poems of 1918. But in the case of
   'Forêt-Noire' she is faithful to the custom of directing the reader to Pastoureau.
4. For a general view of this phase and a discussion of the other poems see my '*Mont de piété* and
   André Breton's early poetic development', in this volume.
5. See Enid Starkie, *Rimbaud* (London: Faber, 1961), pp. 328–29; Joanna Richardson, *Verlaine*
   (London: Weidenfeld and Nicolson, 1971), pp. 139–40; Daniel De Graaf, *Arthur Rimbaud: Homme
   de lettres* (Assen: Van Gorcum, 1948), pp. 114–35.
6. Paterne Berrichon, *La Vie de Jean-Arthur Rimbaud* (Paris: Mercure de France, 1898), pp. 17–18.
7. Ernest Delahaye, *Rimbaud* (Reims and Paris: Revue littéraire de Paris et de Champagne, 1905),
   pp. 172–73.
8. For the text of the letters see Arthur Rimbaud, *Œuvres complètes*, ed. Antoine Adam (Paris:
   Gallimard, 1972).
9. Cf. Breton, *OC* III, 441 and 824.
10. In later books Delahaye acknowledged a homosexual element in the Black Forest incident, but
    he always stressed the sincerity of Verlaine's missionary purpose. See his *Verlaine* (Paris: Messein,
    1919), pp. 210–11, and *Rimbaud: l'artiste et l'être moral* (Paris: Messein, 1923), p. 58. Berrichon does
    not mention Verlaine's evangelical zeal but does refer to 'instances bizarres': it suited him better
    to portray Rimbaud as sexually conformist rather than as hostile to Christianity. The mixture
    of religion, sex and fisticuffs has drawn many writers to the incident, e.g. F. Porché, *Verlaine tel
    qu'il fut* (Paris: Flammarion, 1933), p. 269; P. Arnoult, *Rimbaud* (Paris: Albin Michel, 1943), pp.
    356–57 (where a dialogue is invented for the two belligerents). A play by Christopher Hampton,
    based on the relationship between Rimbaud and Verlaine, has a subtle Black Forest scene; see

*Total Eclipse* (London: Faber, 1969), pp. 68–72.

11. Breton's first reference to the poem is in a letter to Philippe Soupault dated 5 July 1918: 'Vous aimez ce poème "Rêve" que vous m'avez fait connaître' [You like this poem, 'Rêve', which you first introduced me to] (quoted in Bonnet, p. 137).

12. 'J'ai toujours été si peu disposé, pour ma part, à admettre que l'œuvre de Rimbaud s'arrêtait comme par "désenchantement" en 1873, que je n'ai cessé de 1918 à ce jour de faire un cas extrême du poème "Rêve" ' [As for me, I've always been so unwilling to grant the idea that Rimbaud's work stops as if by 'disenchantment' in 1873, that since 1918 to this day I have always been an extreme advocate for the poem 'Rêve'], III, 819.

13. For a thought-provoking discussion of the poem along these lines see Yves Bonnefoy, *Rimbaud par lui-même* (Paris: Seuil, 1961), pp. 169–70.

14. 'Il est aisé de constater que "Rêve" exerce une influence décisive sur plusieurs poèmes apparaissant dans mon premier recueil: *Mont de piété* (1919) tels "Forêt-Noire" [etc.]' [It is easy to see that 'Rêve' had a decisive influence on several of the poems which appeared in my first collection, *Mont de piété* (1919), like 'Forêt-Noire' [etc.]], III, 819.

15. *Autour de Rimbaud* (Paris: Klincksieck, 1967), p. 70. Professor Hackett quite justifiably argues that Breton overestimates the poem — the surrealist leader's gift for hyperbole was given full rein when he praised 'Rêve' as '[le] triomphe absolu du délire panthéistique, où le merveilleux épouse sans obstacle le trivial et qui demeure comme la quintessence des scènes les plus mystérieuses des drames de l'époque élisabéthaine et du second Faust [...]', *Position politique du surréalisme* (1935) (Paris: Denoël-Gonthier, 1972), p. 139 (*Œuvres complètes*, III, 481).

16. Bonnet, p. 137.

17. *Position politique du surréalisme*, p. 139. (*OC*, III, 481).

18. The text I have used is that of the *Lettres de la vie littéraire d'Arthur Rimbaud (1870–75)*, collected by Jean-Marie Carré (Paris: Gallimard, 1931), pp. 124–25.

19. See II, 867, and C. Baudelaire, *Œuvres complètes*, vol. II (Paris: Gallimard, 1976), p. 543.

20. There is perhaps a deliberate contrast here with the opening of the first of the *Eloges* of Saint-John Perse: 'Les viandes grillent en plein vent...' [The meat is cooking in the wind]. Breton greatly admired this text at the time he wrote 'Forêt-Noire', see *La Clé des champs*, OC III, p. 63.

21. According to Carré the unusual spelling 'gruère' in 'Rêve' reflects the 'prononciation ardennaise', *Lettres*, p. 124.

22. The lines are from 'Adieu' in *Une Saison en enfer*, OC, p. 116.

23. It was one of Breton's favourite lines of poetry. See *OC*, II, 679.

24. In a fine essay Gabriel Bounoure expresses powerfully the view that Rimbaud's repudiation of poetry, far from constituting a change of heart, was consistent with his previous attitude: 'A un certain moment, tout à coup, son œuvre lui devient inhabitable. Il éprouve pour elle cette haine du domicile dont parle Baudelaire. Elle représente à ses yeux un stationnement et un abri, donc un lieu clos et bourgeois, un confort haïssable, — en dépit de toutes les lézardes que sa violence sut ouvrir dans les parois du poème [...]. C'est une vue très plate et très fausse que de prêter à Rimbaud le dessein de chercher dans une réussite temporelle une revanche contre le tarissement supposé de son esprit' [At a particular moment, all of a sudden, his work becomes uninhabitable to him. He feels for it the sort of hatred of the home that Baudelaire speaks about. It represents to him a stopping-place and a shelter, and therefore a closed, bourgeois place, a detestable comfort — this in spite of all the cracks that his violence managed to open up in the walls of the poem [...]. It is a very flat, entirely false way of looking at things to attribute to Rimbaud the plan to seek worldly success as a revenge against the supposed drying-up of his spirit]. *Le Silence de Rimbaud* (Le Caire: Librairie L.D.F., 1955), pp. 19, 21.

25. Profiting from the proximity of Tübingen to the Black Forest, Breton attributes to Rimbaud the same widening of the horizons of poetic activity and empathy that he would himself proclaim in *Pleine Marge*: 'Maître Eckhardt mon maître dans l'auberge de la raison | où Hegel dit à Novalis | Avec lui nous avons tout ce qu'il nous faut et ils partent | Avec eux et le vent j'ai tout ce qu'il me faut' [Meister Eckhardt my master in the inn of reason | where Hegel says to Novalis | With him we've got all we need and they leave | With them and the wind I've got all I need], II, 1182.

26. Breton often alluded to the period Rimbaud spent with Nouveau, regarding it as one of the most mysterious phases in his life. See *Manifestes du surrealisme*, *OC*, I, 479, and *La Clé des champs*, *OC*, III, 823–25. De Graaf (pp. 96–103) speculates on a possible link between Rimbaud's departure for the East and the end of his relationship with Nouveau.

27. See S. Freud, *The Interpretation of Dreams*, ch. VI 'The Dream-Work' (London: Penguin, 1976), pp. 381–651.

28. Apollinaire's line is 'Tu ne connaîtras jamais bien les Mayas' [You will never know the Maya well], *Calligrammes* (Paris: Gallimard, 1966), p. 43.

# 4

# Breton and the Language of Automatism: Alterity, Allegory, Desire

'On sait, mais on oublie, que le surréalisme, autant que Mallarmé, a rendu le pouvoir au langage' [We know, but we forget, that Surrealism gave power back to language just as much as Mallarmé did].[1] On the face of it there could be no better validation of Blanchot's comment than Breton's 1922 essay 'Les mots sans rides' (I, 284–86) [Words without wrinkles]. 'Les mots font l'amour' [words make love]: words are 'créateurs d'énergie' [creators of energy], they have their 'vie propre' [own life]. Far more than 'petits auxiliaires' [little assistants] equipped with no more than a 'meaning', words, by dint of 'une sonorité à tout prendre parfois fort complexe' [a sonority which is, on the whole, sometimes extremely complex], a 'côté architectural' [architectural aspect], a capacity to work against 'l'idée qu'ils prétendent exprimer' [the idea which they claim to express] and to allow for complex interaction between figurative and literal meanings ('à chaque variation de celui-ci devant correspondre une variation de celui-là' [each variation in the former necessarily corresponding to a variation in the latter]), words, in combination, can form 'un petit monde intraitable sur lequel nous ne pouvons faire planer qu'une surveillance très insuffisante et où, de-ci de-là nous relevons pourtant quelques flagrants délits' (I, 285) [an uncompromising little world which we can only survey in a very insufficient way but where we can nonetheless spot, here and there, a few offenses *in flagrante*]. But there's the rub: if, when words make love, we are no more than voyeurs, can we hope to procure their matches? 'Les mots sans rides' is, no doubt, a celebration of poetic language, but running through the essay is a sinuous argument the aim of which is to dislodge the poet from his vantage-point as linguistic ring-master and wordsmith and to supplant him by the poet... asleep. It is worth looking at the climax of this argument. Breton, with one school of Parisian dadaism in mind, has cited Paulhan, Eluard and Picabia as exponents of 'recherches' with language that extend those of Lautréamont and Mallarmé but which, he says, still betray a lack of confidence in words:

> [O]n n'était pas certain que les mots vécussent de leur vie propre, on n'osait voir en eux des créateurs d'énergie. On les avait vidés de leur pensée et l'on attendait sans trop y croire qu'ils commandassent à la pensée. Aujourd'hui c'est chose faite: voici qu'ils tiennent ce qu'on attendait d'eux. Le document qui en fait foi est, sous bien des rapports, d'un prix inestimable. (I, 285)[2]

[We were not sure that words lived their own lives, we dared not see them as creators of energy. We had emptied them of their thought and waited, hardly believing they would do so, for them to command thought. That has now happened: they have what we expected of them. The document which bears it out is, in many ways, inestimably valuable.]

The 'document' in question consisted of various 'jeux de mots' by Robert Desnos which, as Breton observes, closely resemble those of Marcel Duchamp.[3] The difference is that Desnos has produced his orally and publicly while in a semi-hypnotic trance and is quite incapable of doing so in ordinary circumstances. What is the significance of this? Apparently it furnishes 'proof' that the amorous sport of words is as much a feature of the pre-reflective mind as it is the stock-in-trade of the post-symbolist poet: the play of language has become firmly instated within the field of the mind.

The compliments paid to language in 'Les mots sans rides' are paradoxical: in the end, what is valorized is a particular manifestation of the mind. But the compliment to the mind is paradoxical too. Desnos in his trance, or Breton and Soupault as they write automatically, are no more than receptacles for what Breton (in a closely related essay, 'Entrée des médiums') calls 'ce murmure qui se suffit à lui-même' [that self-sufficient murmur], 'ce qu'on est tenté de prendre pour la conscience universelle' [that which one is tempted to take for the universal consciousness), 'quelques mots qui tombaient de la 'bouche d'ombre' (I, 275) [a few words which fell from the 'mouth of shadow']. All these phrases stress the impersonality of the experience; Breton does not seem inclined to suggest that the 'révélation' he expects of the 'murmure' is of an individual nature. In these early contributions to what will eventually be a large body of writings on language and automatism, Breton's principal concern is to confer existential legitimacy on poetic language, while preserving some kind of self-sufficiency for language itself. For if Breton staked a great deal on a state of language that he closely identified with the post-Baudelairean poetic tradition, he was anxious not only to root it within the framework of the psyche but also to dissociate it from the customary manifestations of the intellect. By importing the autonomy of language into the sanctuary of the mind Breton achieved a double goal: he vindicated poetic language and, by endowing the mind with unsuspected properties, associated poetic activity with a revision of the contours of the self.

In the context of automatism, then, the play of language and a particular kind of mental activity become one and the same thing. What is manifested is less an area of the mind than a process of signification in which the subject is subordinated to the logic of the signifier so admirably described in 'Les mots sans rides'. Subordinated and, hence, alienated. Yet, in the context of automatism, poetic language, in its very autonomy, becomes, virtually at least, the agency of a new logic of the subject. Maurice Blanchot gets to the heart of the matter when he writes:

> D'un côté, dans l'écriture automatique, ce n'est pas à proprement parler le mot qui devient libre, mais le mot et ma liberté ne font plus qu'un. Je me glisse dans le mot, il garde mon empreinte et il est ma réalité imprimée; il adhère à ma non-adhérence. Mais d'un autre côté, cette liberté des mots signifie que les mots deviennent libres pour eux-mêmes: ils ne dépendent plus exclusivement

des choses qu'ils expriment, ils jouent et, comme dit Breton, ils font l'amour.[4]

[On the one hand, in automatic writing it is not strictly speaking the word which becomes free; it is rather that the word and my own freedom are henceforth a single thing. I slip into the word, and it bears my imprint and is my printed reality; it adheres to my non-adherence. But, on the other, this freedom for words means that words become free for themselves: they no longer depend exclusively on the things they express; they play and, as Breton says, they make love.]

At the core of automatism is an experience of integration: the subject coincides symbiotically with the language by which he is traversed. But if, within the context of automatism as an experience, the freedom of language can seem to corroborate a parallel freedom in the realm of the psyche, the moment we move outside this context the freedom of words can begin to look dangerously like... the freedom of words; and the new order of the subject can begin to seem like an illusion. In crude terms what is at issue is the possibility that automatism is primarily an experience within language and that therefore the products of this experience are at best partial embodiments of, and at worst no more than testaments to what was once alive in it. I intend to indicate various symptoms of Breton's own awareness of this possibility, first by looking at some of the poems he wrote in the immediate aftermath of the so-called 'époque des sommeils' [sleep period],[5] and then by pointing to certain tensions and oppositions that arise during the evolution of Breton's theory of automatism.

One of the striking things about 'Les mots sans rides' and 'Entrée des médiums' is that while Breton seems anxious above all to stress that poetic language is in some sense indigenous to the mind, he is reluctant to draw any specific conclusion from this. 'Le surréalisme' is defined (for the first time) as a state: 'un certain automatisme psychique qui correspond assez bien à l'état de rêve, état qu'il est aujourd'hui fort difficile de délimiter' (I, 274) [a certain kind of automatism which corresponds well enough to the dream-state, a state which is today very difficult to delimit], and if Breton uses phrases such as 'révélation', 'la précieuse confidence', 'dictée magique', the 'aura' which surrounds the products of automatism seems to stem from their unpremeditated and unpredictable character rather than from their content. The circumstances of hypnosis tended to dramatize the link between the vacancy of the subject and the emergence of the message, and thus, by comparison with automatic writing, to reproduce more closely that sudden eruption of a 'phrase de sommeil' [sleep sentence] into the relaxed mind which Breton always regarded as the paradigm of automatism.[6] But it should be remembered that even at the height of his short-lived enthusiasm for hypnosis (to which he was not himself susceptible) Breton regarded it strictly as a technique equivalent to the automatic writing with which he had already experimented. It might seem surprising that, three years after *Les Champs magnétiques*, he should have been so impressed with Desnos's prowess.[7] Breton explains in 'Entrée des mediums' that once publication of their texts was under way he and Soupault had found themselves more or less incapable of achieving the degree of disengagement from all motivation essential to the practice of automatism. The desire to shock through publication and the tendency to revel in the products of automatism for their own sake were liable, notes Breton, 'de compromettre dans son essence ce murmure qui se suffit à lui-même' (I, 275) [to compromise that self-sufficient murmur down to its very essence]. No doubt the attitudes to language prevalent in the period of Parisian Dada were also unhelpful in this respect. Revelling in what Paulhan called the 'irreducibility' of language, the dadaists were inclined to treat words in a way that suppressed their connection with the mind.[8] To restore this connection, while maintaining the climate of otherness surrounding words fostered by Dada, is the step Breton takes in 'Les mots sans rides'.

Apart from a few essays, Breton wrote very little between the publication of *Les Champs magnétiques* in 1920 and the autumn of 1922. When circumstantial factors led him to bring the 'époque des sommeils' to a close, he began writing poems which bear closely on the experience of automatism. What seems to have been on his mind is not the wish to produce automatic texts in the grand manner of those sections of *Les Champs magnétiques* written at the highest speed compatible with continuity, but a desire to focus on the process of automatism itself. In his annotations to a copy of *Les Champs*, Breton observes that, at slower speeds, automatic writing is compatible with the maintenance of overall thematic coherence.[9] In the poems of 1922–23, published in *Clair de terre*, Breton often seems to have taken automatism itself as his theme. Automatic writing becomes a way of propitiating the emergence of 'pure' automatism (I will comment later on the distinction this implies) by creating a context favourable to its eruption; and it also becomes a way of turning over in one's mind the implications — for oneself, for poetry, for life in general — of the phenomenon of automatism itself.

The first fruits of this revival are a sequence of poems which appropriately have as their general title a phrase spoken by Desnos from the depths of his trance, in answer to Breton's name: 'Le Volubilis et je sais l'hypoténuse' (I, 164–68) [The Volubilis and I know the hypotenuse]. The opening line sets the scene: 'l'oreille en face du silence...' (I, 164) [the ear, faced with silence...].[10]

★    ★    ★    ★    ★

In 'Le Volubilis...' and in *Clair de terre* generally, Breton keeps circling round the problem left hanging at the end of 'Les mots sans rides': what is the status of the 'language of the unconscious'? What kind of attitude can I take to the notion that I am inhabited by words which seem to insist on their pertinence to my existence and yet to resist easy integration? The poems are often punctuated by a sort of running commentary on the process of automatic writing itself. Here, for example, is an extract from the fourth poem in 'Le Volubilis...':

> J'ai comme un pressentiment de l'aile
> Des fuites dans mon éclat personnel
> Qui est un peu déchiqueté
> L'averse boule de neige des jardins nordiques
> Puis la poésie aux phares rouges sur une mer toute brune (I, 166)

[I have like the wing's intuition | Leaks in my personal radiance | Which is a

little ragged | The shower snowballs Nordic gardens | Then poetry with red
lighthouses over a wholly brown sea]

The sequence works by generating and intermingling three complementary
scenarios: the activity of writing, a storm at sea, and (between the lines) the act of
love. First the preliminaries: in mid-poem a sense of something 'about to come', a
'pressentiment de l'aile', accompanied by a feeling of self-dispersal; then the spasm: a
storm of words full of tension, energy and forward thrust, a snowball effect; finally
the consummation, a steady, fluent gratification: 'la poésie aux phares rouges sur
une mer toute brune'. A presentiment and a recollection; in between — yet in a
sense including both — 'la poésie': a 'total alert', a frantic signalling, a potential
plenitude of meaning, but also a total eclipse: the poet disappears, the advent of
poetry is his demise. The wonderfully laconic description of self-estrangement,
'des fuites dans mon éclat personnel', undercuts the hint of poetic angelism in the
'pressentiment de l'aile' and underlines an attitude of benevolence towards poetry
as an experience of self-dispersal.

Another poem, 'Il n'y a pas à sortir de là' (I, 169–70) [There's no way out of it],
is an extremely fragmented text, rather like a notebook in its form, where bursts of
'automatic fire' are interspersed with a more focused discourse that represents itself
as seeking some kind of dialogue with the disruptive forces by which it is constantly
fissured. In the opening section the convulsive, spasmodic discourse of automatism
is identified with natural forces and with some form of liberation:

> Liberté couleur d'homme
> Quelles bouches voleront en éclats
> Tuiles
> Sous la poussée de cette végétation monstrueuse (I, 169)

[Freedom colour of man | Which mouths will be broken to pieces | Tiles |
Under the pressure of this monstrous vegetation]

'Liberté couleur d'homme': the opening phrase puts as an assertion what much of
the text will put in question: is the freedom enacted in the violations of the poem
compatible with any recognizable human image? The association between shattered
speech and a house split open by the encroachment of nature seems to identify
the force of poetic language with expropriation and exile. The remainder of the
section, which reads like a kind of log-book of 'automatic' phrases, gives us a series
of glimpses through the roof: each fragment dislodges a tile ('Tuiles') and reveals a
patch of starry sky. In the next section, the steadier voice resumes:

> Rivière d'étoiles
> Qui entraines les signes de ponctuation de mon poème et de ceux de mes amis
> Il ne faut pas oublier que cette liberté et toi je vous ai tirées à la courte paille
> Si c'est elle que j'ai conquise
> Quelle autre que vous arrive en glissant le long d'une corde de givre (I, 169)

[You river of stars | Who carry off the punctuation marks of my poem and those
of my friends | One must not forget that I drew the short straw on this freedom
and you | If it is that freedom which I have conquered | What else but you comes
sliding along a rope of frost]

'Quelle autre que vous arrive...?' This question, addressed to the 'rivière d'étoiles' of the automatic text, renders admirably the apprehensiveness inspired by a sense of liberation that seems to stake everything on language: in what sense does the liberation of language signal my freedom? Am I given the freedom of the poem only to become the prisoner of words? Does anything but language itself come skidding along the 'corde de givre'? As if in answer to the very question posed in this line, the second half hints at the self-sufficiency of language by encouraging sound to generate sense:

> glissant le long d'une corde de givre

Is the freedom of language really such a lottery ('tirées à la courte paille')?

The next fragment suggests that more is at stake: 'Cet explorateur aux prises avec les fourmis rouges de son propre sang' [This explorer grappling with the red ants of his own blood]. The graceful sequence which opens the third section pursues this line of thought:

> Aussi bien le premier venu
> Penché sur l'ovale du désir intérieur
> Dénombre ces buissons d'après le ver luisant
> Selon que vous étendrez la main pour faire l'arbre ou avant de faire l'amour
> (I, 170)

> [Just as the first comer | Looking into the oval of interior desire | Counts up these shrubs by the glow-worm | Depending on whether you stretch out your hand to *faire l'arbre* [make the shape of a tree] or before making love]

Here the act of love and the activity of poetry intermingle and illuminate one another once again; this time psychoanalysis is the third party. The mixture will become familiar to Breton's readers. A sexual scenario: *l'ovale*: *buissons* (female) — *le ver luisant* (male) — *la main* — *faire l'amour* is intertwined with a symbolic figuration of poetry: 'le ver luisant' (poetry) shines forth as a result of an initiative: the creation of darkness ('faire l'arbre': to make shadow?) or, perhaps, the willingness to 'play' ('faire l'arbre': to pretend to be a tree). As a result light is shed on the tangled thickets ('buissons') of 'le désir intérieur'. 'Le premier venu': 'anyone'; but also, in a third scenario, none other than Dr Freud: the pioneer, in the serious pose of the scientist, 'penché sur l'ovale du désir intérieur', interpreting your tangles in sexual terms ('d'après le ver luisant'), varying the diagnosis according to your symptoms: 'selon que vous...'. In all three contexts the verb *dénombrer* suggests calculation and interpretation, but it also seems to work neologistically: DE(n)OMBRER: to un-shadow. In poetry, then, language may be the mirror ('l'ovale': a looking-glass) of desire. 'Quelle autre que vous arrive'?: 'le désir intérieur'. But what if inner desire is no more than the desire for nothing, for the unreal, for death, for pure difference? Breton has yet to develop his own myth of desire and, for the moment, it still has a slightly catastrophic air about it. If automatism keeps opening out onto another realm, it is a realm associated With the negative power of fantasy: 'Dans l'autre monde qui n'existera pas | Je te vois blanc et élégant' [In the other world which will not exist | I see you, white and elegant], and with death: 'O vitres

superposées de la pensée | Dans la terre de verre s'agitent les squelettes de verre'
[O panes imposed by thought | in the glass earth glass skeletons are writhing]. The
'terre de verre' of automatism is perhaps no more than a graveyard riddled with
'vers de terre' [earthworms/earth-poems]. And yet, at the end of the poem, we are
apparently asked to envisage the automatic text in slightly more positive terms: as
a sort of 'Radeau de la Méduse' floating in the sky: a kind of hysterical jubilation
on the edge of despair, a frantic signal for help, a last chance, a sign of life where
life seemed most at risk:

> Tout le monde a entendu parler du Radeau de la Méduse
> Et peut à la rigueur concevoir un équivalent de ce radeau dans le ciel (I, 170)

> [Everyone has heard of the Raft of the Medusa | And can if need be conceive
> of a heavenly equivalent of this raft]

'Il n'y a pas à sortir de là': the title, as is so often the case with Breton, plays on the
literal and conventional means of an idiomatic expression. The automatic text may
be a kind of prison, a place of seclusion and solitary confinement, set apart from the
world; but it is also the scene of another kind of inescapability: that of desire.

Some of the motifs I have touched on recur frequently in *Clair de terre*: the text
as a multilayered, vitreous realm in which the subject becomes a spectator of his
own mutations, 'Dans la glace de mes jours impossibles' (I, 175) [In the ice of my
impossible days], or the architect and vicarious inhabitant of a 'Maison insensément
vitrée à ciel ouvert à sol ouvert' (I, 183) [insanely windowed house, open to the
sky and to the ground]; the text as a prison: 'C'est aussi le bagne...' (I, 168) [It's a
prison, too...], 'Un joli bagne d'artistes où des zèbres bleus, fouettés par les soupirs
qui s'enroulent le soir autour des arbres, exécutent sans fin leur numéro!' (I, 162)
[A nice little penal colony where blue zebras, goaded by the sighs which in the
evening wrap themselves around the trees, endlessly perform their act!]. The comic
note of exasperation at the excesses of the imaginary world of automatic writing
often adds zest to these poems. It tends to convey the ambivalence of the poet's
attitude to his obsession with the imaginary 'disseminations' to which the language
of automatism consigns him: 'Je m'arrache difficilement à la contemplation... A
l'apparence humaine qui dissémine' (I, 175) [It is difficult to tear myself away from
contemplation... From the human guise that spreads out...]. The experience of self-
scattering, of submergence in a new medium, is sometimes enthusiastically sought
after: 'Sonnez la cloche de ces sorties d'école dans la mer' (I, 170) [Ring in these
school trips into the sea]; but fear of allowing the text to become the fantasmatic
embodiment of a desire for self-annihilation and total otherness sometimes leads to
revulsion. The instinct of self-preservation that this implies then becomes, in itself,
a source of guilt since it suggests a willingness to come to terms with the ordinary
run of things that the text so violently repudiates. This conflict is beautifully played
out in 'Plutôt la vie' (I, 176–77) [Life, rather]. Often read as a sort of paean to life,
'Plutôt la vie' seems to me to be a delicious feast of black humour. The repeated
formula 'Plutôt la vie que' that structures the poem opposes two sets of values and
experiences. Those associated with 'la Vie' are often superficially attractive and
charming but on the whole they are redolent of smugness, naivety, and timidity.

The other set of items consists of phrases which evoke the world of the automatic text: 'ces prismes sans épaisseur... cette mare aux murmures' [these prisms without substance... this sea of murmurs]. Here the emphasis is placed on the outrageous, the gaudy, the gratuitous and the camp: 'ces pierres blettes' [these overripe stones], 'ces établissements thermaux | où le service est fait par des colliers' [these thermal baths | where one is waited on by necklaces] and so on. 'La vie' is comfortable, safe and palpably 'there', even if the subject finds it hard to be there: 'Je n'y suis guère hélas' [I am, alas, hardly there]. On the 'other side' there is a promise of freedom, 'là-bas il ferait mieux que meilleur il ferait libre oui' [over there it will be better than better, it will be a free yes], but could one ever partake of it? If one set of ingredients is the predicate of life, the other set, in the logic of the title which plays on the expression 'Plutôt la mort' [Death, rather] becomes the predicate of death.

But does one have to accept that there is no alternative to the sterile opposition between the world and the text, life and death? Can anything be recuperated from the poem, or must it be written off as the locus of a powerful but futile vengeance against existence? If these questions are at the heart of *Clair de terre*, so is the conviction that everything turns on the status of a discourse which, for better or worse, is allowed to follow up its own initiatives. The climax of 'Dans la vallée du monde' [In the valley of the world] is one of the points where the viability of the language of automatism asserts itself in and through its negativity; once again desire is in on the act:

> Les femmes dont le troupeau est conduit par les animaux fabuleux
> Accusent de rigueur le principe
> Qui assimile les plantes spectrales
> L'amour à cinq branches l'hystérie flocon des appartements
> A la mort la petite mort l'héliotropisme (I, 181–82)

[The women whose herd is led by fabulous animals | Blame as they must the principle | Which assimilates spectral plants | Five-branched love hysteria flake of flats | To death *la petite mort* heliotropism]

Embedded in this marvellous sequence is a conventional notion: 'le principe... qui assimile... l'amour... à la mort'. But the syntactical structure of multiple embroiderings and interpolations that 'contextualizes' this piece of wisdom converts it into a subtle yet jubilant commendation of the dizzying transmutations of automatism. In their headlong rush, words not only transform plants into spectral plants but turn love into a sort of tree, and hysteria (their own?) into what sounds like a house-plant known to indoor gardeners as 'flocon des appartements'. If the force which produces these couplings is in some ways a purely negative affair, careering towards 'la mort', it is also a drive towards the light, a heliotropism which makes things grow.[11] We can read 'le principe qui assimile' as an absolute construction and construe the spectral plants and the hysteria as products of a principle very much 'de rigueur' in automatism (though some may agree with 'les femmes' and find it too rigid or too rigorous — like comparing love to death!); but to assimilate this principle to death and negation is to forget the spasm, the 'petite mort' through which these conjunctions assert desire and affirm a different kind of life.

In the midst of an activity of 'énonciation' which both implicates and displaces the subject, language reproduces itself from its own genes, and thereby affirms desire. This is, at its most extreme, the logic of automatism as 'la petite mort'. But does the language of automatism communicate desire or, once it is there on the page, does it merely commemorate the desire which was affirmed in its production? Frequently in *Clair de terre* the latter view threatens to prevail. If the text is identified with a prison or a vault it is not only because, in the space of the poem, the subject is locked in with desire, but also because desire itself always threatens to remain sealed behind the text which it inseminates. There is, however, a partial remedy. The text can become a poem in which the agency of desire and the experience of the subject in the act of writing are brought to the surface and, as it were, guaranteed some sort of survival. To achieve this end, the text is, as we have seen, encouraged to allegorize the process of its own production.

Nowhere is this more evident than in the admirable 'Ligne brisée' [Broken line] (I, 186–87), a poem where the customary roles are reversed: instead of a 'voix de l'énonciation' anxiously interrogating the verbal permutations spawned in its wake. we hear 'the words themselves' address the speaker:

> Nous le pain sec et l'eau dans les prisons du ciel
> Nous les pavés de l'amour tous les signaux interrompus
> Qui personnifions les grâces de ce poème
> Rien ne nous exprime au-delà de la mort (I, 187)

[We, dry bread and water in the prisons of heaven | We, the paving stones of love all the interrupted signals | Who personify the graces of this poem | Nothing expresses us beyond death]

The emergence of the automatic text is characterized as an experience in the course of which the subject remains, as it were, incarcerated. Within the confines of his 'prison in the sky' words can give him sustenance; but, as the last line of the opening sequence suggests, they are unable to transcend this context. The poem goes on to confirm this in a variety of ways. Within their world, words can provide not only bread and water but the waters of life: 'L'eau-de-vie panse les blessures dans un caveau par le soupirail duquel on aperçoit une route bordée de grandes patiences vides' [Whiskey dresses wounds in a cave by a window high in the wall through which one can see a road edged with large, empty docks]. The 'patience vide' is no doubt that of the poet who is prepared to hold himself suspended in the strange medium of words. If he is patient enough he will be the subject of a strictly immanent, irreducible form of experience: 'Il n'y a qu'à toucher il n'y a rien à voir... Ne demandez pas où vous êtes' [One can only touch there is nothing to see... Do not ask where you are]. In the course of the poem words adopt a succession of disguises: they appear as benevolent jailors; as mariners steering a ship into harbour at dead of night, bearing a cargo which, since it does not really 'travel', may seem like a luxury one would well do without: 'Bientôt nous porterons ailleurs notre luxe embarrassant | Nous porterons ailleurs le luxe de la peste' [Soon we will carry elsewhere our awkward luxury | We will carry elsewhere the luxury of the plague]. And they also pose as ministers of the antinomian creed of dreams: 'Peut-être pallions-nous à la fois le mal et le bien | C'est ainsi que la volonté des rêves se fait' [Perhaps we will overcome evil and good at the same moment | It is thus that the will of dreams is done]. Like Mephistopheles words offer a pact ('le pacte n'est pas encore signé' [the pact is not yet signed]): consign yourself to us and we will take care of you. But as the poem draws to a close, words register the subject's resistance to their terms and they become reproachful. 'Gens qui pourriez' [People who could], they intone, 'Nos rigueurs se perdent dans le regret des émiettements' [Our rigours become lost in regret for fallings-apart]: their strictures are ignored; the subject wants, they suspect, to retrieve something from his dispersal. So it is they who must disperse themselves: 'Le croc du chiffonnier Matin sur les hardes fleuries | Nous jette à la fureur des trésors aux dents longues' [The fang of Morning, the rag-picker, on the blooming herds | Throws us to the fury of long-toothed treasures]. Morning tries to pick up the pieces and to hold on to the pretty flotsam; but to try to fasten on to words is like fishing with bare hands: the fish get away; as they swim back down into the depths a quick glimpse of their gleaming bellies is all that is allowed — but it is enough. 'Le ventre des mots est doré ce soir et rien n'est plus en vain' [The belly of words is gilded this evening and nothing is more in vain]. This beautifully cadenced, plangent finale both rounds out the allegory and breaks the allegorical mould which has encased the text. It is now the subject of the experience, the words' addressee — and of course their 'onlie begetter' — who speaks. And what he says seems to amount to this: even if nothing is revealed, nothing retrieved, nothing learnt, something has taken place: words have made love, their bodies have glistened, 'I' have been with them. Something is affirmed, not only in the past, but also for the future: 'rien n'est plus en vain'. The end of 'Ligne brisée' pronounces benediction on what Breton will one day call 'la naissance du signifiant':[12] the sense of something stirring in language as it crystallizes and disperses on the page, proffering no more or less than 'la vérité à jamais insaisissable mais présente dans l'expression neuve' (III, 656–57) [the truth, forever ungraspable but present in new expression].

★   ★   ★   ★   ★

Running through the poems of *Clair de terre* is a set of anxieties, hesitations and scruples about automatism. The status of language, of desire, and of the self in the automatic text is subjected to constant interrogation. Such oscillations between confidence in and distrust of language were by no means unique to Breton, even in 1923: in the poems of 'L'Aumonyme' [Almonymity], for example, Robert Desnos frequently echoes Breton's concerns.[13] But what if we turn to the *Manifeste du surréalisme* of the following year? Are the questions answered, the doubts set aside? On the face of it, yes. Desire, while not purged of its anarchic force, is regarded in a much more positive light; the 'langage sans réserve' [language without reserve] of automatism is its bountiful messenger; the subject of the automatic 'murmure' is a unified subject — at least by contrast with his stunted, alienated counterpart in everyday existence. Automatism is affiliated with a wide range of experiences: love, dreams, the marvellous, lunacy, the 'psychomythology' of everyday life.

The emphasis is on continuity, fluidity, connections. Where automatic writing is concerned, the link between language and desire, established in *Clair de terre*, is not necessarily altered; but there is an apparent shift of emphasis from the intermittent to the continuous, from brief moments in a verbal flow to the automatic text as a whole, and from the spasms of a self dislocated by words to the adventures of a self at large in the submerged territory of desire. The effect of such a shift is to make a much stronger claim for the world created in the text.

This brings into view two slightly different ways of envisaging automatic writing. The first conceives it as an activity which stimulates the play of language and hence creates a context for the incursions of desire identified with moments when language really takes off on its own. The second conceives it as a way of transcribing a continuous verbal flow alive with unconscious desire. The first puts a stress on producing a particular kind of event in language; the second puts a stress on tapping, listening, attending to a murmur which is generally drowned out by other voices. The advantage of the second view is that it gives the automatic text quasi-documentary status. The disadvantage is that it risks conferring existential prestige on what may seem, to the impartial observer at least, no more than the virtues of poetic language itself. Both views tend, of course, to fog the issue of the relative degrees of passivity and self-awareness in automatism. I will consider this question presently.

In more or less adopting the second view in the *Manifeste*, Breton is careful to incorporate a crucial let-out clause. Despite the fact that most of the wonderfully casual discussions of automatic 'technique' centre on the aim of achieving a perfect match between the hypothetical continuity of the 'murmure' and the actual continuity of the text which transcribes it, Breton frequently draws attention to the disparity between them. While he stresses what he calls 'le caractère inépuisable du murmure' [the inexhaustible character of the murmur] he makes it clear that there is no guarantee that any more than short portions of the text will be automatic in the purer sense. He notes for example that 'la première phrase viendra toute seule' [the first sentence will come by itself], but that 'il est assez difficile de se prononcer sur le cas de la phrase suivante; elle participe sans doute à la fois de notre activité consciente et de l'autre' (I, 332) [it is rather difficult to know what will happen in the case of the following sentence; it is without doubt both a part of our conscious activity and of the other]. And, further on, Breton observes, 'Seule la moindre perte d'élan pourrait m'être fatale. Les mots, les groupes de mots qui se suivent pratiquent entre eux la plus grande solidarité. Ce n'est pas à moi de favoriser ceux-ci aux dépens de ceux-là. C'est à une miraculeuse compensation d'intervenir — et elle intervient' (I, 335) [Only the least loss of *élan* could be fatal to me. Words, groups of words following on from each other practice among themselves the greatest solidarity. It is not for me to favour some at the expense of others. It's up to a miraculous compensation to intervene — and intervene it does]. This implies acknowledgement that if the inner 'murmure' and the 'groupes de mots qui se suivent' flowing from the pen are closely related, they are not necessarily identical. But how do we know when they do coincide? If it is only when the 'miraculeuse compensation' intervenes or when, as Breton put it earlier, the writer has the benefit of 'l'occulte, l'admirable secours', how does one recognize such moments? In what sense do they stand out in the midst of the flow? Despite all the emphasis on continuity, Breton seems inclined to preserve, at the heart of automatism, the experience of suddenness, of spasm: the 'secours' is accompanied by a 'secousse'.[14]

Here, and in subsequent discussions, Breton seems torn between two different ways of valorizing automatism. What is stressed is on the one hand an experience within the context of a process of *énonciation*, on the other hand the status of the products of this activity. When the products are stressed the accent falls on the 'féerie intérieure' [interior fairyland] manifested by the automatic text, on the 'étendues logiques particulières' [particular logical regions] which it reveals, on the 'preuves palpables d'une existence autre que celle que nous prétendons mener' [palpable proofs of an existence other than that which we claim to lead] that it offers (I, 806, 807, 810). The unconscious tends to become characterized in spatial terms as a territory, the realm of a 'moi subliminal' [subliminal ego].[15] Automatism is associated with the imagination conceived as a synthetic faculty of which perception and representation are 'les produits de dissociation' [products of dissociation] (see e.g. II, 489–91). The automatic text becomes a place of recognition and reconciliation.

When the experience is stressed, imagination takes second place to inspiration: 'Nous la reconnaissons sans peine à cette prise de possession totale de notre esprit... à cette sorte de court-circuit qu'elle provoque entre une idée donnée et sa répondante (écrite par exemple)' [We recognize it effortlessly by the total possession taken of our minds... by that sort of short circuit it causes between a given idea and the answering one (written, say)].[16] The emphasis is on the discontinuous and the momentary. Specific moments within the flow of automatism are singled out: 'En certaines images, il y a déjà l'amorce d'un tremblement de terre' (I, 901). The main priority is not the retrieval of the self but 'l'anéantissement de l'être en un brillant, intérieur et aveugle, qui ne soit pas plus l'âme de la glace que celle du feu' (I, 782) [the annihilation of beings into a brilliance, interior and blind, which is no more the soul of ice than that of fire]. What matters is what happens to language: 'l'essentiel n'est-il pas de tenir à portée ces instants du verbe humain brusquement chargés de lumière' (SP 184) [isn't the essential thing to keep at hand those moments of human language when it is suddenly filled with light]. The advantage of this view is that the ordinary level of automatism which maintains some kind of continuity at all costs, can be regarded as a sort of patter, equivalent to the 'passes magnétiques' of the hypnotist. And it also makes it less essential to affirm any direct relation between the world created in the text and a 'world-view' latent under the surface of consciousness.

Paradoxically, perhaps, it is Breton's desire to hold on to his notion of the unbroken continuity of the 'murmure' and his desire to guarantee its purity that often lead him, in the *Second Manifeste* or 'Le message automatique', to formulations which emphasize the experience of automatism. Ever more dismayed at the charlatanism he detected amongst many practitioners of automatism, he was inclined from time to time to advocate a 'retour aux principes'. Noting the emergence of a 'poncif indiscutable à l'intérieur de ces textes' [something undeniably banal within these texts] he puts the blame on

> la très grande négligence de la plupart de leurs auteurs qui se satisfirent généralement de laisser courir la plume sur le papier sans observer le moins du monde ce qui se passait alors en eux — ce dédoublement étant pourtant plus facile à saisir et plus intéressant à considérer que celui de l'écriture réfléchie. (*OC* I, 806)

> [the great negligence of most of their authors, who are in general happy to let pen run over paper without at all observing what happens at the same time inside themselves — this splitting being, nonetheless, easier to grasp and more interesting to consider than that of reflective writing]

The emphasis on this kind of 'dédoublement' accompanies Breton's willingness to concede that he had originally tended to simplify 'à l'extrême les conditions de l'écoute' [to an extreme the conditions for listening], by not sufficiently stressing 'la nature des obstacles qui concourent dans la majorité des cas, à détourner la coulée verbale de sa direction primitive' [the nature of the obstacles which arise in the majority of cases to divert the verbal flow from its primitive direction]. In the face of this, he asks, 'comment s'assurer de l'homogénéité ou rémédier à l'hétéro- généité des parties constitutives de ce discours dans lequel il est si fréquent de croire retrouver les bribes de plusieurs discours?' (II, 380–81) [How can one guarantee the homogeneity, or remedy the heterogeneity, of the constitutive parts of this *discours*, in which one so often seems to find the snippets of a number of different discourses?]. As I have indicated, Breton's response to this kind of question was to recommend that vigilance should be exercised in the course of automatic writing. In the face of 'l'absence objective de tout critérium d'origine' (II, 381) [the objective absence of any criterion of origin], the practitioner must distinguish himself by his 'souci unique de l'authenticité du produit qui nous occupe' [our sole concern with the product's authenticity], bringing to bear a criterion which is internal to the process and experience of automatism. Once on the page the text is not in itself sufficient witness to the distinction between the more or less spasmodic incursions of pure automatism and the parasitic discourses which tend to run away with them. Of course the emphasis on vigilance during the 'écoute' does conflict with the notion of consigning oneself purely and simply to the 'caractère inépuisable du murmure'; but it does not alter the stipulation that re-reading and correcting should be avoided.[17] The point of 'dédoublement' is not to keep the text under control but to make sure that as far as possible it is out of control. The aim is still to escape from 'la vieille maison de correction' [the old house of correction]. 'Corriger, se corriger, polir, reprendre, trouver à redire' [correct it, correct oneself, polish, start again, find some fault]: these principles which befit the conventional *littérateur* must yield before a higher ambition: 'puiser aveuglément dans le trésor subjectif pour la seule tentation de jeter de-ci de-là sur le sable une poignée d'algues écumeuses et d'émeraudes' (II, 376) [blindly draw on subjective treasures solely for the temptation of throwing here and there on the sand a handful of frothy seaweed and emeralds].

But what about the automatic poem? In a letter to Rolland de Renéville Breton defended himself against the accusation that the use of automatism to simulate the symptoms of various mental disorders (in *L'Immaculée conception*, with Paul Eluard) represented a change of heart where automatic writing was concerned. This is one of the comments that Breton makes:

> Tout d'abord nous n'avons jamais prétendu donner le moindre texte surréaliste comme exemple parfait d'automatisme verbal. Même dans le mieux 'non-dirigé' se perçoivent, il faut bien le dire, certains frottements (encore que je n'aie pas désespéré de les éviter tout à fait, par un moyen à découvrir). Toujours est-il qu'un minimum de direction subsiste, généralement dans le sens de l'arrangement en poème. Il est difficile d'échapper aux raisons plus ou moins utilitaires qui veillent à ce que pour nous cela se passe ainsi. (II, 327)

> [First of all, we have never claimed in the least to present any Surrealist text as a perfect example of verbal automatism. Even in the best 'non-directed', one must admit, certain moments of friction (even if I have never lost hope of avoiding them altogether through some method yet to be discovered). It is always the case that some minimal degree of direction remains, meaning in most cases its arrangement into a poem. It is difficult to avoid the more or less utilitarian reasons which ensure that things happen this way for us.]

'L'arrangement en poème' seems to refer to a process going on while the text takes shape (but distinct from the 'frottements' — referred to elsewhere as 'scories' or 'bouillons' — which should ideally be eliminated). So the text is 'non-dirigé', save for the 'minimum de direction' provided by 'l'arrangement en poème'. The phrase does not, in the first instance, indicate a 'tidying-up' after the event, but suggests, rather, that the minimal formal — and perhaps thematic — conventions of the modern poem serve as a flexible framework on which the discourse of automatism can take shape. Breton refers to 'l'arrangement en poème' as a 'détermination qui est spécifiquement la nôtre' [a determination which is specifically our own] for which other 'déterminations' — for example that of imitating pathological symptoms — might be substituted. To endorse the legitimacy of the latter procedure, Breton quotes approvingly some comments on surrealist 'poetry' made by three psychoanalysts (one of whom was Jacques Lacan). One of the things they say is that 'dans ces productions, certains cadres peuvent être fixés d'avance, tel un rythme d'ensemble, une forme sentencieuse, sans que diminue pour cela le caractère violemment disparate des images qui viennent s'y couler' (II, 329) [in these productions, certain frameworks can be fixed in advance — for instance, the rhythm of the whole, a sententious form — without the violently disparate character of the images which have just slipped between them being in any way diminished]. In quoting this, Breton seems to be courting approval for the view that to create a framework is not necessarily to pre-determine the nature of what will fill out the frame. At the same time, in confessing to 'l'arrangement en poème', Breton is, I think, pointing beyond diction, rhythm or lineation towards those thematic and symbolic safeguards which, as I noted in the context of *Clair de terre*, guarantee the text to some extent against its self-destructive tendencies, and provide a setting for the 'poignée d'algues écumeuses et d'émeraudes' thrown up from the deep in the process of automatism. And yet these safeguards, like 'l'arrangement en poème' itself, are not extraneous to Breton's practice of automatism but inherent in it. The more Breton was prepared to recognize in his theorizing that automatic writing is in practice an essentially heterogeneous activity 'où l'on retrouve les bribes de plusieurs discours', the closer he came to matching his theory of automatism to his practice as a poet.

One of Breton's constant preoccupations was the question of whether to confer the 'blue riband' of the automatic message on the sort of play along semantic, phonetic, and symbolic axes which is in effect what 'run of the mill' automatism consists of. Breton's doubts in this respect stem from his commitment to the notion of a 'murmure'. Play on the signifier was not in itself incompatible with Breton's conception of the 'voix surréaliste'; on the contrary. But he was inclined to be suspicious about the sort of play on words which is so prominent a feature of his own poetry. Is it the voice speaking or no more than an incantation designed to propitiate its utterances? Breton once defined 'le lyrisme' as 'ce qui constitue un dépassement en quelque sorte spasmodique de l'expression contrôlée' (III, 451) [that which constitutes a somehow spasmodic movement beyond controlled expression]. But can one ascribe the spasm to a voice? Does it last as long as the 'murmure' holds out, as long as one can stave off a 'faute, peut-on dire, d'inattention' (I, 332) [a failure, so to speak, of attention]? The *mise en scène* of a voice overheard, transcribed, sometimes misrendered, is itself perhaps no more than an allegory, an anthropomorphic projection on to the features of language itself. In fact, as well as insistently drawing attention to the unfamiliar tunes in the automatic medley, Breton also emphasized from time to time the alien quality of the automatic 'voice'. In *Légitime défense*, he writes: 'Encore une fois, tout ce que nous savons est que nous sommes doués à un certain degré de la parole et que, par elle, quelque chose de grand et d'obscur tend impérieusement à s'exprimer à travers nous [...] C'est un ordre que nous avons reçu une fois pour toutes et que nous n'avons jamais eu loisir de discuter [...] Ecrire [...] faute de pouvoir rester sourd à un appel singulier et inlassable' (II, 291) [Once again, all that we know is that we have, to some extent, been endowed with speech and that through it something great and obscure tries to express itself through us [...] It is an order that we have been given once and for all and which we have never had the freedom to discuss [...] Writing [...] because we cannot ignore a unique, tireless call]. In the *Second Manifeste*, Breton observes that 'on demeure assez peu renseigné sur l'origine de cette *voix* qu'il ne tient qu'à chacun d'entendre' [we still know relatively little about the origin of this *voice* which each must hear], and then, in an extraordinary passage, he goes on to discuss what he regards as a sample of the voice's interventions which arises as he writes his manifesto: 'Parce que les exemples *boivent*. Pardon, moi non plus je ne comprends pas. Le tout serait de savoir jusqu'à quel point la voix est autorisée... Quand elle me répond que les exemples boivent (?) est-ce une façon pour la puissance qui l'emprunte de se dérober et alors pourquoi se dérobe-t-elle?' (I, 807) [Because examples *drink*. Sorry! I don't understand it either. The trick is to understand what degree of authority the voice has... When it answers me saying that examples drink (?), is that a way for the power borrowing it to hide itself, and if so why does it hide itself?].

Blanchot notes that Breton's obsession with the voice reflects 'la liaison entre l'écriture automatique et une exigence de continuité' [the connection between automatic writing and a demand for continuity]; and, in an excellent passage, he goes on to characterize the 'idéologie du continu... dont le surréalisme... est moins responsable qu'il n'en a été la victime' [the ideology of the continuous... of which Surrealism... rather than being responsible for it, has been the victim].[18] But Blanchot also detects another current in Breton's work which he associates with the notions of play, expectancy, fragmentariness, surprise, chance:

> L'écriture automatique est alors l'infaillibilité de l'improbable, ce qui par définition ne cesse d'arriver et cependant n'arrive qu'exceptionnellement dans l'incertitude et hors de toute promesse: en tout temps, mais dans un temps impossible à déterminer, celui de la surprise. Par l'aléa, un rapport qui ne se fonde plus sur la continuité est ainsi produit. André Breton et Paul Eluard le disent dans la note conjointe sur la poésie: 'C'est le manque et la lacune qui sont créés', discréditant la conception de la plénitude homogène qui se transporterait en quelque sorte réellement dans le langage et que le langage donnerait à lire immédiatement. Rupture, manque, lacune, voilà la trame du textuel (celui de dedans, celui du dehors, le 'tissu capillaire'), auquel nous accédons par l'inaccessibilité de la poésie.[19]

> [Automatic writing is therefore the infallibility of the improbable, that which by definition never stops happening and which nevertheless happens only exceptionally in uncertainty, outside any promise: at any time, but at a time which is impossible to determine, that of surprise. Through the *aléa*, a relationship which is no longer based on continuity is thus produced. André Breton and Paul Eluard say as much in the attached note on poetry: 'It is lack and lacuna which are created', discrediting the conception of homogeneous plenitude which is supposed somehow to be really carried along in language and which language would let us read immediately. Rupture, lack, lacuna: this is the weave of the textual (that of the inside, that of the outside, the 'capillary tissue'), which we reach through the inaccessibility of poetry.]

In the *Notes sur la poésie* (quoted by Blanchot in the above passage), where Breton and Eluard deride and debauch some of Valéry's statements about poetry, there is a section relating to the voice of inspiration. Valéry refuses to conceive it as a sign of 'quelque source ou divinité cachée', but identifies it instead with what he calls 'la voix en action', the manifestation of a sense of harmony deeply rooted in the human organism: 'Tout le corps humain présent sous la voix et support, condition d'équilibre de l'idée' [The whole human body present under its voice and support, the condition of balancing the idea]. To this, Breton and Eluard retaliate by invoking: 'la *voix inactive* — la voix indirectement retournant à, ou provoquant — les choses qu'on ne voit pas et dont on éprouve l'absence... Rien *sous la voix humaine*, torpillage, état d'ivresse de l'*idée*' (I, 1016) [The *inactive voice* — the voice indirectly returning to, or provoking — the things we do not see and whose absence we feel... Nothing *beneath the human voice*, sinking, drunken state of the *idea*].

Voice?/Void? Self?/Other? Breton's poems, at any rate, have their own arrangements for coping with these questions. As the 'trame du textuel' is constantly spun, the problems are endlessly deferred in the 'plaisirs' and 'jouissances' of a discourse which, if it constantly interrogates and allegorizes its own origins, commits itself, above all to its own perpetuation.[20] If Breton's poems tend to become more fluent in the collections which follow *Clair de terre*, their formal and thematic identity does not change radically. Most of the poems of *Le Revolver à cheveux blancs*, for example, can be read, at one level, as fables which allegorize the process of automatism itself. Equally, Breton's theoretical discussions of language and automatism — which of course ranged much more widely than I have indicated here — often seem to extend and develop, but not necessarily to transcend, the fruitful uncertainties of *Clair de terre*. In poem and manifesto alike — whether it be in the fables of a subject disseminated and inseminated by words or in the nuances and approximations of theory — the same tensions are enacted: continuity and discontinuity, trance and spasm, revelation and annihilation, 'la vraie vie' and 'la petite mort'. If these tensions prove so resilient, it is no doubt because, for Breton, a great deal was at stake: 'une volonté d'émancipation totale de l'homme, qui puiserait sa force dans le langage, mais serait tôt ou tard réversible à la vie' [a will to the complete emancipation of mankind, which would take its force from language, but which would have sooner or later to be paid back to life] (*La clé des champs*, OC I, 654).

## Notes

1. Maurice Blanchot, 'Le Demain joueur', in *André Breton et le mouvement surréaliste*, La Nouvelle Revue française (April 1967), 863–88 (p. 869n.).
2. There are some excellent discussions of Paulhan, Eluard and the 'recherches' to which Breton alludes, in *Au temps de Dada: problèmes du langage*, Cahiers de l'association internationale pour l'étude de Dada et du surréalisme, no. 4 (1970).
3. Duchamp's 'Jeux de mots' had been published in *Littérature* under the pseudonym 'Rrose Sélavy'. Desnos adopted the same pseudonym. See 'Rrose Sélavy' in Robert Desnos, *Corps et biens* (Paris: Gallimard, coll. 'Poésie', 1968), pp. 31–46.
4. M. Blanchot, *La Part du feu* (Paris: Gallimard, 1949), p. 95. Blanchot's discussions of automatic writing are among the most stimulating we have. See also *L'Espace littéraire* (Paris: Gallimard, coll. 'Idées', 1967), pp. 242–48 and passim; and also 'Le Demain joueur' (cited elsewhere in the present article). Other important contributions to the subject are Michel Carrouges, *André Breton et les données fondamentales du surréalisme* (Paris: Gallimard, coll. 'Idées', 1967), pp. 141–241; Jacques Garelli, *La Gravitation poétique* (Paris: Mercure de France, 1966), pp. 148–213. A great deal of light is cast on automatism and many other aspects of Breton's conception of language by J. Gratton in *The Poetic Language of André Breton* (unpublished doctoral thesis, University of Kent at Canterbury, 1981), and in his article on the 'textual dynamics' of Breton's poetry in *Surrealism and Language: Seven Essays*, ed. by Ian Higgins (Edinburgh: Scottish Academic Press, 1986), pp. 30–45.
5. Breton used this phrase to describe the brief period in 1922 when the proto-surrealists experimented with hypnosis. See III, 480 *ff*.
6. For Breton's accounts of the impact of phrases which come into mind on the edge of sleep, see *Les Pas perdus*, I, 274–75 and *Manifestes du surréalisme*, I, 324–25, and, especially *Le la* in IV, 339–44. Francis Ponge evokes the same phenomenon in 'Phrases sorties du songe', *Le Parti pris des choses* (Paris: Gallimard, 1967), pp. 145–46.
7. *Les Champs magnétiques* had been composed in the summer of 1919 and published in 1920.
8. In the period 1920–1922, which marked the ascendance of Tzara on the Parisian scene, Breton's ideas seem to have gone back into incubation. Most of his contributions to Dada periodicals consisted of fragments from *Les Champs magnétiques*. While he was impressed by Paulhan's

'savantes objections en matière de langage' [knowledgeable objections on questions of language] (III, 458) he seems to have felt that the kind of autonomy ascribed to language in, for example, *Jacob Cow le pirate ou si les mots sont des signes* (1920), strongly influenced by Saussure, was not quite the kind he was anxious to encourage; especially since it seemed to foster the astringent, cautious attitude to words which Breton had adopted himself in the poems of *Mont de piété* (1919), an attitude which the practice of automatic writing had helped him to revoke. Breton was well aware that Tzara's strident assaults on language were directed primarily against the social function of words and that, at heart, the archdadaist was their enthusiastic devotee. But Tzara's celebrations of the resilient sensemaking capacity manifested by words severed from grammatical context seem to have inspired the sort of suspicion with which Breton regarded 'la théorie futuriste de "mots en liberté" fondée sur la croyance enfantine à l'existence réelle et indépendante des mots' [the Futurist theory of 'words in freedom', based on a childish belief in the real and independent existence of words] (II, 290). Paulhan was subsequently to regard Breton as a 'terroriste' whose aim is to put language at the service of an especially rare breed of thought, and who is consequently distrustful of words. Blanchot, on the other hand, puts surrealism in Paulhan's other camp: 'Si la rhétorique consiste, comme le dit Jean Paulhan, à soutenir que la pensée procède des mots, alors il est sûr que le surréalisme c'est la rhétorique' [If rhetoric consists, as Jean Paulhan says, in maintaining that thought proceeds from words, then Surrealism is quite certainly rhetoric] (*La Part du feu*, p. 97). It seems to me that Breton oscillated between Paulhan's two poles.

9. These annotations are collected in I, 1127–30. Breton alludes to the question of different 'speeds' of automatism in *Les Pas perdus*, but most of his subsequent discussions make no reference to this. To acknowledge that the speed at which you write is fundamental to what 'emerges', is obviously to acknowledge that automatism is primarily a way of summoning up verbal energy rather than the transcription of a latent flow.

10. 'Le Volubilis...' was published in *Clair de terre*, Editions de Littérature, 1923. Only the last poem, 'C'est aussi le bagne...', was included in the 1966 edition.

11. In the context of automatism it is of course relevant to recall that an 'heliotropisme' is an involuntary, reflex response.

12. 'On n'a pas assez insisté sur le sens et la portée de l'opération qui tendait à restituer le langage à sa vraie vie, soit bien mieux que de remonter de la chose signifiée au signe qui lui survit, ce qui s'avérait d'ailleurs impossible, de se reporter d'un bond à la naissance du signifiant' [We have not stressed enough the meaning and importance of the operation which aimed to restore language to its true life: much rather than working back from the signified to the sign which survives it, which would in any case turn out to be impossible, instead turning in one movement to the birth of the signifier] IV, 21, 'Du surrealisme dans ses œuvres vives'.

13. See, for instance, 'P'oasis' (in *Corps et biens*, pp. 64–66), which raises questions about the sort of wordplay at which Desnos was so adept by dramatizing the competing claims of thoughts, words and individual letters. Each 'faction' asserts (in the manner of Breton's 'Ligne brisée') its primacy as the agent of fertility and growth in the garden of the mind: 'Nous sommes les pensées arborescentes... les mots arborescents... les lettres arborescentes qui fleurissent sur les chemins des jardins cérébraux' [We are arborescent thoughts... arborescent words... arborescent letters blooming on the paths of cerebral gardens]. If, in the end, the letters of the alphabet appear to win the day, it seems to be because, symbolically at least, they are innocent of the kinds of mutual contamination to which thoughts and words are prone. Heedless of the niceties of the linguist, Desnos explores the phonetic suggestiveness of the twenty-six graphic signs which make up the alphabet. By contrast with words and thoughts (between which only a Solomon can legislate), letters implement the pure agency of the signifier ('l'instance de la lettre' in Lacan's phrase) and do not presuppose or refer back to pre-existing channels in mental space. In a final formulation of the poem's key phrase, the 'chemins' are supplanted by 'déserts': 'Nous sommes les arborescences qui fleurissent sur les déserts des jardins cérébraux' [We are the arborescences that bloom over the deserts of cerebral gardens]. Words and thoughts emerge from the pure phonetic material provided by the alphabet. The text is not so much a garden as a madhouse: 'que vois-tu venir vers Sainte-Anne?' [what do you see coming towards Sainte-Anne?]. To

sprinkle the page with capital letters (and numerals: 'par nos amours décuplées nous devenons vains mais 10 — 20 — 2 — 20 [divins devins]' [through our increased loves we become vain but [divine seers]]) is to give spectacular emphasis to the arbitrariness and elasticity of the sign and, in so doing, to convey powerfully the mixture of poetic enthusiasm and existential insecurity which underlies 'P'oasis' — poetry is an oasis but also potentially a mirage — and links it to *Clair de terre*. Desnos's poem ends, in its own dazzling way, on the kind of interrogative note we have heard in Breton: 'En somme, F M R F I J [éphémère effigie] | sommes-nous des cowboys de l'Arizona dans un laboratoire | ou des cobayes prenant l'horizon pour un labyrinthe?' [All in all, [ephemeral effigy] | are we Arizona cowboys in a laboratory | or guinea pigs taking the horizon for a labyrinth?] Whose is the ephemeral effigy of which we catch a glimpse between the letters of the poem? 'Cow-boy' or 'cobaye', bounty-hunter raiding the language-lab or passive accomplice, whichever way he conceives of himself the poet who stakes all on words risks some form of 'méconnaissance', whether it be in respect of his own role or of the nature of language itself.

14. 'On feint de ne pas trop s'apercevoir que le mécanisme logique de la phrase se montre à lui seul de plus en plus impuissant, chez l'homme, à déclencher la *secousse émotive* qui donne réellement quelque prix à la vie' [One pretends not to notice too much that the logical mechanism of the sentence is showing itself increasingly incapable of setting off that *tremor of emotion* in people which in reality gives some value to life] (*OC* I, *Second manifeste du surréalisme*, p. 802; my italics).

15. Breton borrowed the phrase from F. W. H. Myers. See the excellent article by Jean Starobinski, 'Freud, Breton, Myers', in *André Breton*, ed. by Marc Eigeldinger (Neuchâtel: La Baconnière, 1970), pp. 163–74.

16. *MS* 166. On the relationship between automatic writing and the idea of inspiration see Octavio Paz, *L'Arc et la lyre* (Paris: Gallimard, 1965), pp. 227–42 and passim, e.g., p. 239: 'L'inspiration est une manifestation de l'"altérité" constitutive de l'homme' [Inspiration is a manifestation of the constitutive 'otherness' of man].

17. It is sometimes argued that Breton failed to see the contradiction between two crucial aspects of his description of automatism: the concentration of the mind on its own activities, and the passive surrender to the flow of mental associations. See for example C. Vigée, 'L'Invention poétique et l'automatisme mental', in *Révolte et Louange* (Paris: José Corti, 1962), 83–98. It seems to me that Breton's later discussions of automatism (i.e. after the first *Manifeste*) show clearly not only that he was aware of these problems but that he was more or less obsessed with them. What Breton keeps attempting to formulate, however, is a practice which cannot easily be characterized in terms of apparently pertinent logical oppositions: active/passive, conscious/unconscious, expression/creation, 'terrorisme'/'rhétorique', etc.

18. 'Le Demain joueur', p. 871.

19. Ibid., p. 873.

20. For detailed discussion of many aspects of Breton's poetic discourse which serve the functions outlined here, see the article by J. Gratton in *Surrealism and Language: Seven Essays*, ed. by Ian Higgins (Edinburgh: Scottish Academic Press, 1986), pp. 30–45.

# Where Do Poems Come From?
# A Reading of Breton's 'Carnet'

Where do poems come from? As is well known, where the origins of poetic utterance are concerned, the Surrealists refused to endorse the 'laicization' of poetry that we find, after the excesses of Romanticism, in Gautier and the Parnassian poets, which pursues its course (there are traces in Baudelaire) through Poe and Mallarmé, and reaches a climax in what is sometimes called the formalism of Valéry. One of Valéry's axioms described the poem, which had nothing sacred about it, as a 'feast of the intellect', the product of making rather than knowing. Contrariwise, the surrealists and particularly Breton strove to revive the notion of inspiration, with the proviso that it consisted not in the mind being possessed by an external agency — Dionysian frenzy, quasi-divine utterance — but in the expression of an inner power, the revelation of the psyche's well-springs and a hidden side of the self.

All this may now seem outmoded. Yet we can look at surrealist texts afresh if we focus on what gives them enduring power: the ceaseless interaction of poetry and poetics which they manifest, and the constant interpenetration between striking forms of linguistic signification and the territory of selfhood. This is my goal in offering a reading of an early text by André Breton, 'Carnet' [Notebook] (see appendix), published in June 1924 in *Littérature*, and uncollected until its publication in the first volume of Breton's *Œuvres* in the Pléiade collection.[1] The text has fascinated me ever since, in 1971, before the age of reprints, I copied it out into my own notebook in the Bibliothèque Nationale. It consists of a sequence of fragmentary notations — from brief philosophical meditations to addresses, telephone numbers and other jottings. The most important item, however, is a poem, 'La Mort Rose' [Rosy Death], which was subsequently to be published in a collection of Breton's poetry.[2]

I will here discuss the text as it was published in *Littérature*.[3] Etienne-Alain Hubert, who wrote the notes to 'Carnet' in the Pléiade edition, tells us that the text which appeared in *Littérature* was selected from the contents of a genuine notebook which has been preserved in Breton's archives. The Pléiade edition reproduces the entire notebook, with the unpublished portions (those not selected for inclusion as 'Carnet' in *Littérature*) in square brackets. The *Littérature* version, which is much shorter, consists of an abridged and reworked version — and we should emphasize from the off the importance of the additions Breton makes to the original material — of (more or less) the first half of the notebook. While keeping the entries in the order in which they were written, Breton cuts them back, omitting around a third (he keeps thirty-seven out of fifty-eight entries) and cutting material from some of those he keeps, without otherwise modifying them. Had Breton, perhaps, written only half the entries ultimately to be found in the notebook at the time he sent his text to be printed? Maybe, although the period of time between the final dates noted in the *Littérature* version (February 1924) and its publication in June is longer than was normal at the time. In any case, the crucial point is that, for the *Littérature* text, Breton deliberately chose to finish his text with an important element which did indeed belong to the period covered by the notebook (October 1923–June 1924), but which *does not* appear in the notebook itself. That is the magnificent poem *La Mort rose*, which is longer than any of the entries in the original notebook and which is dated '17 février 1924' [17 February 1924]. The fact that the poem did not originally belong to the notebook — which becomes evident only in the version published in the Pléiade edition, where *La Mort rose* is not to be found — is entirely in keeping with the reading I propose here. The addition of the poem (which is followed by another: the playful *coda* about the 'lectrice excitée' [excited reader] (37/463)) changes radically the meaning of the notebook as it appears in *Littérature*: the thesis it contains gets altered by this poetic prosthesis.

Breton wanted his reader to believe that the notebook really existed. That is undoubtedly meant to be suggested to us by the title, as well as numerous allusions to more or less precise dates (which cover a period of about five months) and a note of where the text was written, the Café Cyrano. But we would be wrong to think that Breton, short on topics for articles, decided to copy out his notebook for the reader's sake. He viewed the diary, as a genre of writing, with suspicion. He seems almost never to have kept a diary, with the exception of the logbooks he kept in exceptional periods — meeting Nadja, for instance.[4] If, unusually, he does so here, it is not to keep us up to date with his timetable or his inner life, but rather so that we can be present at the birth of a poem. What we have is a sort of 'Philosophy of Composition' to use Poe's phrase. But rather than retracing step by step the genesis or making of a poem, the poet shows us the context in which a poem came to be born. As we shall see, Breton explicitly repudiates the example of Valéry, inherited from Poe and his 'Raven.' This is in no way the 'Calepin du poète' [poet's notebook] from which Valéry extracted so many samples, nor an 'au sujet de "La Mort Rose"' to match Valéry's famous discussion of the composition of 'Le Cimetière marin' [The graveyard by the sea]. On the contrary, by filling his notebook, Breton's aim is quite different and, if a model had to be found, from the point of view of form, Baudelaire's *Intimate Journals* and indeed his 'Carnet' would be nearer the mark. From July 1861 to November 1863 Baudelaire had made a note of his debts, lists of writings to undertake, addresses, a draft for the preface of his prose poems and so on.[5] Here, Breton makes a point of including the addresses of Éluard and Pierre Louÿs, the telephone numbers of Picasso and Desnos, and a newspaper advertisement, while making several allusions, direct and indirect, to Baudelaire.[6] Against such a background — the daily grind and the openness of a curious mind — the poem, a sumptuous edifice of words, stands out like some weird meteorite, or a volcano whose eruption is quite unheralded, — with the exception of one or two spurts that seem to come to nothing, and a title noted a few weeks beforehand.[7] The Baudelairean 'Carnet' lends itself to a *mise en scène* in which the advent of a poem, far from being the due product of a long labour, a making, a painful delivery, seems like parthenogenesis, an immaculate conception, as a later joint collection by Éluard and Breton will have it. Playing Baudelaire against Valéry, the *carnet* against the *calepin*, does not mean that the contents of the notebook lack interest. On the contrary, Breton continually points to the constraints and dead ends of the poetic enterprise, and above all ruminates on the question of the self and its relation to poetic utterance. But even if, by a wonderful irony, behind its rich facade the poem manifests the same desires, and stumbles on the same paradoxes as the notebook, it nonetheless remains autonomous, insofar as nothing predetermines its advent, its allure, its duration, or its flavour.

We could group together the apparently rather heterogeneous material of the notebook under the heading 'The birth of a poem'. In addition to 'La Mort rose', about a third of the thirty-seven entries concern poetic discourse. First come two lines of poetry followed by suspension marks and, in parenthesis, the description 'Début de poème' [Start of a poem] (1/455). Thereafter two titles will be noted, one of which will later appear at the head of '*La Mort rose*', while the other will come to nothing (3/456, 14/458).[8] In the same category we can situate several gnomic utterances which seem to suggest surrealist automatic writing or the surrealist penchant for verbal slips and puns: 'La tête prise...' [the head caught] (16–17/459), 'Boulets de canon' and 'Citer de mémoire' [Cannonballs, Quote from memory] (22–23/460).[9] The aborted poem is typical Breton: 'On appelle les papillons dans une grotte | Où du sol au plafond se produisent sans cesse de grandes étincelles...' [Voices call the butterflies in a cave | Where from floor to ceiling giant sparks keep appearing...] (1/455). The reader is tipped without warning into a marvellous universe; from the start the poem declares its status as a heterocosm. Just as typical, however, is the fact that everything here seems to designate the act of utterance itself. The butterflies and sparks that bespeak the emergence of a poetic universe are either the subject of an invocation, or else 'perform,' like a music-hall number. Everything seems to suggest the emergence of a represented action. The cave, an image of the enchanted place and, since Plato, representation itself, constitutes a *mise en abyme* of the poem as a site where, in response to a call, something makes itself manifest. The elements of the marvellous spectacle are themselves of an intermediary nature: they are natural objects but also gleams, darting movements, components of an inner scene, of the *cosa mentale*. Instead of a title, the remark 'Début de poème' tells us both that this *was a poem* and that it *no longer is one* — for its source has dried up. The detached phrase which follows, outside the poem but part of the same fragment, connects the poem (ambiguously) to the domain of dreams or the fulfilment of wishes: 'J'ai toujours rêvé d'être un animal dans une forêt penchée...' [I have always dreamt of being an animal in a leaning forest] (1/455). Perhaps only the poem, and hence only language, can bring this about.

Two or three of the abstract meditations in 'Carnet' have to do with the question of the self and its relationship to the realm of experience. In the second fragment Breton employs one of the sceptic's traditional arguments for putting into doubt the knowledge we can have of anything other than the present moment. If I have the ability to represent a past event, how can I be sure that this representation is not the product of my present mind and my imaginative faculty in particular? If I feel as if I existed yesterday, how can I prove that yesterday I was not an animal or a ghost?[10] But Breton is not really writing as a philosopher. One feels that for him what matters above all is the desire to justify a belief in the ontological relevance of poetic discourse. From a philosophical point of view his dialectic is not especially brilliant. It may be associated with those rather ponderous or facetious conjectures, of Poe or Baudelaire, as well as certain currents of German idealism which captured the attention of the young surrealists when they wanted to call into question the existence of the surrounding world. Metaphysical speculation becomes a weapon which serves both to discredit orthodox beliefs and to make room for a poetic conception of the world.

We can see here how deeply hypothetical and fragile Breton's conception of the self is. Rather than a synthesis, an 'élan vital' or a personality, he conceives it as a theatrical space, a place of representation and performance. In Breton's ontology, however, the self is not primarily inherent in the faculty of representation but is constituted in the process of representation. The self inheres or is legible in the image, and is therefore seen to be inherently other: object rather than subject of consciousness. Yet this vision in fact stems from a prior choice. The a priori in Breton's ontology is not the self but poetic utterance, or at least the existence of what he called, with a wry nod to Poe's 'Raven', 'words that knock at the window pane': the inner voice which seems to be more myself than anything else and yet seems to come from elsewhere. It is in the enchanted cave of the poem, where sparks and butterflies gleam, that the writer glimpses his true countenance. How could this be justified unless one were to deny any significance to the rigid framework of personality, to human temporality, and were to affirm (as Breton does in one of his jottings) that the past (the one we usually remember) perhaps does not exist, and that there can be no such thing as death since one scarcely exists except in the present moment ('le présent est un point' [the present is a point] (2/456)), that is, in a narrow pencil of light that can suddenly find a radiant self in its beam? If the poem can reveal a 'vie antérieure' [anterior life] (2/455),[11] it is not because it can make us relive our past. In spite of the Baudelaire reference, Breton has no truck with that 'Charme profond, magique, dont nous grise | Dans le présent le passé restauré'[12] [Deep, magical charm by which, in the present, the past intoxicates us]. It is, on the contrary, because this past life — or, rather, this inner life, the 'lointain intérieur' [far-away interior] which Henri Michaux speaks of, real life — is waiting for us behind the veil of the banal, behind the day-to-day procession of consciousness, that poetry and the flow of poetic utterance can set us behind the stream of time.

Besides what Breton says about poetry and the 'I' there is another line of metaphysical speculation in 'Carnet' that will play a major role in surrealism. It lies in the interrogation of those tiny breaks in the fabric of daily existence — presentiments, intuitions, coincidences, parapraxes (to use Freud's term) — which can give us the feeling that, in our psychic life at any rate, we escape the rigours of banal causality. In the fifth fragment Breton enumerates certain phenomena of this sort, without neglecting the realm of utterance. If the sentence I have just finished is not necessarily the one I began a moment before, it is because in the course of my utterance a break has occurred. Has my verbal volition succumbed to mental and linguistic forces that go beyond the broad intentionality of my will to say something? Citing probability theory (a favourite hobby-horse of mathematicians at this time, as Valéry's fascination with Poincaré's theories demonstrate), Breton seems to adopt a quasi-scientific attitude in this field. But the allusions to Poe and Novalis maintain a metaphysical climate and, in later fragments, it is a fundamentally poetic investigation — 'a calculation of improbabilities' (26/456) — which will predominate. What can we say, indeed, about the amusing attempt to calculate the chances of finding a photograph card in a packet of Gold Flake cigarettes (35/463) except that this form of chance, not really very mysterious, is a poor relation of the truly marvellous conjunction of events through which poetic utterance, and in this case the poem 'La Mort Rose,' is able to come into being. For Breton, coincidences and similar phenomena are above all signs, breaches, openings, which disrupt appearances and muddy the waters of time. They make us feel as though we live on several levels at the same time and that, to cite *Nadja*, 'nous ne sommes pas seuls à la barre' [we are not alone at the helm].

'Carnet' also shows traces of Breton's enthusiasm to adopt the stance of a certain kind of moralist. In an early essay collected in *Les Pas perdus* contemporary with 'Carnet', he wrote: 'La morale est la grande conciliatrice, l'attaquer c'est encore lui rendre hommage' [Morality is the great conciliator, even to attack it is to pay it homage] (I, 195). Here (in Baudelairean tones) he castigates the mistaken belief that man is made in God's image (9/457). He does not specify what the consequences of such an error are but we may assume them to be the erroneous pursuit of a predetermined end to human existence, the notion of a model to follow, and of *a priori* definitions of man's essence. Another fragment ('Morale...') (13/457) is apparently concerned with the moral status of the subject: how far should our awareness of what we feel ourselves capable of doing, but do not do, be part of our self-definition? The bizarre allusion to the taxi driver suggests perhaps that it is in the mythical context of conversations between driver and client that such things should be debated. But it is in the artistic and literary field that Breton's moralizing vein is given full vent. In his view (and this will be true throughout his career) the writer, artist, especially the poet, must not become unworthy — *démériter* [demerit] is a word Breton often uses — of his role. In particular he must make no concessions to society. In this regard Breton roundly condemns the weekly review *Comoedia* for publishing some recent works by the painter Louise Hervieu who had the temerity to illustrate Baudelaire's *Les Fleurs du Mal*. This was a grave mistake: firstly, because poetry is not to be illustrated. And secondly because Louise Hervieu cannot measure up to Baudelaire. Nor does *Comoedia* have the right to set Hervieu alongside Courbet and Chardin: 'Toute l'indignité est là' [This sums up the indignity], fumes our critic. Later on Breton vilifies *Comoedia* once more, this time for having published something particularly stupid: 'L'artiste doit fuir l'impopularité' [It is the artist's duty to flee unpopularity]. 'Tu parles' [Like hell], says Breton (34/463).

Throughout 'Carnet' Breton tends to set up two opposing camps. On one side artists and poets he admires, on the other side those who have 'démérité' [forfeited merit]. In the former camp, we find, firstly, a few of the dear departed: Baudelaire above all. One fragment reads: 'Les hommes morts avec qui l'on vivrait assez commodément: Baudelaire' [Dead people whom one would be quite happy to live with: Baudelaire] (8/457). In another entry Breton reports an encounter with Victor Hugo (or rather his double) in the street (12/457). This side of the 'Carnet' creates the notion of a sort of spiritual aristocracy or club where Baudelaire and Hugo, but also Poe, Novalis, Courbet and Chardin, commune with Breton and some of his contemporaries. These last are present largely via their addresses and telephone numbers or by rapid allusions: we 'encounter' Éluard, Picasso, Desnos and Aragon in this way. Apparent here is the notion of the group, which will be of such fundamental importance to surrealism. In the latter camp are to be found hacks, poetasters, *Comoedia*, Louise Hervieu, people who think man is made in God's image, or that it is the artist's mission to avoid unpopularity. But we also find a more redoubtable Villain in the form of Breton's erstwhile mentor, Paul Valéry.

There is only one explicit allusion to Valéry but it is eloquent: '"A Paul Valéry (1872–1917)" Dédicace' ['To Paul Valéry (1872–1917)'. Dedication] (10/457).[13] Rather than a dedication this is clearly an epitaph.[14] While the dear departed, Baudelaire and Hugo, are resurrected, Valéry, while still alive, is consigned to the tomb, or rather to that experience which had so haunted Edgar Allan Poe, premature burial. Why Valéry? It should be recalled that 1917 was the date of publication of *La Jeune Parque*. On several occasions Breton was to evoke the disappointment he had felt at this return to poetry on the part of a man who had been his true initiator in this realm. After long years of enigmatic silence (associated in Breton's mind with that of Rimbaud whom he had recently discovered), it was unacceptable to make a comeback with these frigid alexandrines, this narrow classicism, and this chaste eroticism. And Valéry only compounded his error by his endless cold and scientific explanations of how the poem had been made, all the while extolling a conception of 'pure' poetry (for instance, in the lectures at the Vieux-Colombier of 1922–23). Still worse was the adulation, and the poet's apparent enjoyment of it, with which Valéry was henceforth received by the upper echelons of Parisian society. Breton's grudge can be expressed succinctly: the author of *La Jeune Parque* had 'démérité.' Valéry was not, was no longer, an adequate incarnation of poetry.[15] In 'Carnet', and throughout the period in which Breton develops the major theses of surrealism, he takes aim at this Valéry — the self-appointed aesthetician of poetic inspiration.

To get to the heart of the debate with Valéry, which we can read between the lines of 'Carnet,' it would be necessary to look closely at the often very subtle divergences between two poets who were agreed on many essential points, sharing for example a fascination throughout their poetic careers with the mystery of poetic utterance and a conviction that what was at stake was the status of the self. In 1920 Valéry wrote: 'Qui parle, qui écoute [dans la parole intérieure]? Ce n'est pas tout à fait le même... L'existence de cette parole de soi à soi est signe d'une *coupure*' [Who speaks, who listens [in our inner speech]? It is not quite the same... the existence of this speech between oneself and oneself is the sign of a *split*].[16] Elsewhere Valéry comments, like

Breton, on the cracks and crevices by which the act of speech is fissured: 'En disant telle chose sans l'avoir prévue, tu la vois comme un fait étranger, une origine — une chose que tu ignorais. Tu étais en retard sur toi-meme...' [When you say something unforeseen, you view it as an external fact, an *origin* — something of which you know nothing. You were therefore lagging behind yourself...].[17] But for Valéry the other self who leaves its trace in the inner voice that inhabits us is conceived as what he called a pure self ('moi pur'). 'Le moi pur,' writes Jacques Derrida, in a fine essay on the image of the spring in Valéry, 'source de toute présence, se réduit ainsi à un point abstrait, à une forme pure, dépourvue de toute épaisseur, de toute profondeur, sans caractère, sans qualité, sans propriété, sans durée assignable [...] ce moi qui est la source [...] ne revient surtout pas à l'individu' [The pure self, origin of all presence, is thus reduced to an abstract point, a pure form, without density, depth, characteristics or qualities, without properties or duration [...] this pure self which is the source [...] cannot, above all, be associated with the individual].[18] The 'moi pur' is a 'pur délice sans chemin'[19] [pure trackless delight], beyond any hypostasis and any incarnation. In Valéry, sometimes close to Buddhism, the gentle extinction of human presence is actively solicited. For Breton it is quite different: the point at which time, and what Rimbaud called 'present appearances', dissolve is not in itself a vanishing point. It resembles rather the eye of a needle; to pass through it would be to obtain access, like Aladdin, to the enchanted cave, to a space of self-retrieval and redeemed time. This fundamental divergence as to the nature of the hidden self naturally determines dissimilar attitudes to the poetic act. For Valéry it is associated with the ceaseless hunt for a fleeting prey, with the repetition of an intellectual ascesis, and with a primordial 'ravissement' in which the mind, as day dawns, strenuously confronts its own abeyance. For Breton, on the contrary, the aim is to neutralize intellect, to suppress effort, and to let buried utterance emerge. The aim is not to get back to the self's springs for a definitive showdown, but to seek amidst the traces of a lost self a new perspective on the world and a potential transformation of daily existence. To some degree, these divergences are the reflection of ideological differences. Derrida underlines the extent to which Valéry's concept of the source brings with it a complete rejection of the system of thought which ought to agree with it perfectly, that of Freud. Derrida suggests some reasons for this rejection: a mistrust of sexuality, and so on. As is well known, Breton, by contrast, placed enormous stock in Freud's theory.

The debate between Breton and Valéry expressed in the 'Carnet', then, includes deep affinities as well as very marked divergences. It is not too surprising, then, to find that the dialectic which characterizes for both their interrogation of poetic utterance, as well as the dialectic of their own opposition (for Breton's thought defines itself against Valéry's, and Valéry's defines itself, by way of his opposition to Freud, against surrealist ideas), resolves itself at a higher level into a clear affinity between the two. Despite the determination with which he pursues the inner voice, Valéry recognizes that it is not an aggressive, interrogative stance but a sort of passivity, which he frequently terms *attente* [expectant waiting], that seems to bring him close to it. 'Le poète en fonction est une attente' [The poet in function is an expectant waiting], he writes. Breton too prized the activity of waiting, not only in the case of his preferred technique with respect to tapping the inner flow of discourse — which consists in the suppression of active, critical agencies, and is thus a form of expectant waiting — but in his approach to existence in general. In *L'Amour fou* he wrote: 'Indépendamment de ce qui arrive, n'arrive pas, c'est l'attente qui est magnifique' [Regardless of what happens or does not happen, it is the waiting itself that is marvellous] (II, 697). He recognized that ultimately there can be no definitive revelation of a hidden self, or a world redeemed once and for all, but that the essence of poetry lay in the perpetual forward movement it inspires, In 'Carnet' he makes this observation, which could not be closer to Valéry in its spirit or its formulation: 'La mécanique de l'attente (je connais bien ça). A généraliser indéfiniment' [The mechanism of waiting (I know it well). To be infinitely generalized] (32/462). We must now see how the poem, 'La Mort rose,' fruit of this expectant attitude, measures up to these expectations.

One day in October 1923, after a few reflections on time and identity, amongst which we find the notion of 'the negation of death,' Breton wrote in his notebook, 'La Mort Rose (titre)' [Rosy Death (title)] (3/456). But it will take five months, until 15 February 1924, for the title to find something to entitle. Another title, 'Aventuriers tremblants' [Trembling adventurers] (14/458), never does so. Between the registration of the title and the emergence of the poem much is jotted in the notebook, many of the entries dealing with death and its negation: the possibility of living with Baudelaire, of meeting Hugo, of becoming a *mort-vivant* like Valéry. But there is no direct reference to writing a poem. We may deduce from this that, if the words 'La Mort Rose' crystallize a certain number of thoughts and obsessions, they do not amount to what Valéry called a 'vers donné,' subsequently needing abstract analysis and the provision of an elaborate intellectual scaffolding in order to become a poem. What 'Carnet' seems to suggest (no doubt deliberately, since, as will be evident, this text may be considered, partially at least, as an anti-Valéry manifesto)[20] is that hidden, buried thought-processes link title to poem. With the advent of the poem, at once foreseen — or awaited — and radically unforeseeable, it seems as if utterance has contrived to break a new path, disentangling itself from the familiar tracks of thought.

We should note how important a role the Baudelairean notebook plays in this text. Baudelaire's notebook is a ragbag, like 'le gros meuble à tiroirs' [big chest of drawers] of *Spleen*, 'encombré de bilans, | De vers, de billets doux, de procès, de romances...'[21] [stuffed with balance sheets, | With poetry, with love letters, with legal proceedings, with romances...] — a figure of the self. For Breton, the addresses, the quotes taken from newspapers, the Gold Flake cigarettes, the café Cyrano, are all figures of banality, the dullness of ordinary life, the context in which one writes and waits. The beautiful evocation of the café Cyrano (462), where the proto-surrealists met at the time, and which would become legendary with *Le Paysan de Paris* (which Aragon was already writing as Breton filled his notebook), is a *mise en abyme* of the dialectic between the everyday and the marvellous which Breton wanted to grasp. Starting from empirical observations (Cyrano, the rue Blanche), his language hurtles out of control, seeming to transform the slope of the rue Blanche into a descent to the depths, the name of the street into both a white automobile and a blinding whiteness, the infamous presence of 'femmes pas comme il faut' [ladies who aren't quite proper] (33/462) into an atmosphere of luxury which disrupts existence, and the three drops of kohl the girls use for makeup into a magic potion the poet desperately needs.

When the poem comes — foreseen, expected, and at the same time radically unpredictable — it seems, once again, that language hurtles away, detaches itself from the familiar world of reflection, becomes *sui generis*, unheard-of: 'Les pieuvres ailées guideront une dernière fois la barque...' [One last time winged octopus will guide the boat...] (l. 1/63). And yet, before concluding too hastily that the poem secures liberation from the contingent order it seems to spurn, let us examine the signs suggesting that the divisions and conflicts that preceded its birth are still alive. Already, in the first few lines, two significant facts stand out. The first concerns the tenses of the verb. If the solemn murmur, the ample and majestic movement of the 'verset' confer on radically incongruous items ('pieuvres ailées,' etc.) a sort of absolute sovereignty, it is all in the mode of prophecy. What we are offered is not constative (even metaphorically) but predictive. [Everything seems to happen as if the radical upheaval of the order of the world, which lies at the poem's heart, which is its very substance, does not precede language but rather proceeds from it. In other words, what the poem prophesies is, essentially, the accomplishment of its own inherent promise. But a corollary of the prophetic status of poetic utterance is that until it reaches its end the poem cannot affirm, or confirm, but only herald. Endlessly prophesying itself, poetry has the power to suspend the world but not to change it. Once the poem is finished and language crawls back, so to speak, under its rock, the world takes up its course again, and it is only along the underground channels that the poem has only intimated, that it continues. Everything in 'La Mort Rose,' from start to finish, is radically futural. If, through a succession of scenarios, the poem never stops proclaiming a radical transformation — a new reign, that of 'l'amour indivisible' [indivisible love] (l. 6/63) for example — it is always in the future. The imaginary acts through which the desired revolution will be (l. 20/63) accomplished, fantasies of destruction, 'lapidation suprême' [a supreme lapidation] (l. 20/63), etc. — are future. If, in the performative realm of prediction, words are acts, the poem tends towards constituting an act but, tied to the logic of prediction, it can only bequeath its act to posterity. The transformed world is the poem's legacy but, and here's the rub, to inherit it one would have to be part of the poem's domain, which is death. To speak, in poetry, is to lose one's grip on oneself. Another important aspect of 'La Mort Rose' stems in fact from a recognition of this. Here the beneficiary of the poetic process, the legatee of the world transformed by dint of poetry, is not the 'I', the subject of utterance, but a 'You'. It is *you* who 'sentiras monter dans tes cheveux le soleil blanc et noir' [will feel the black and white sun rise in your hair] (l. 2/63). And, later, it is *you* who will witness the radical upheavals ('l'horizon s'entrouvrir' [the horizon open up], etc.) (l. 13/63). It is you who, having renounced the past (l. 27/64), will benefit from the crucial reversal through which culture and nature will be reconciled and the human order will be reintegrated with the natural one:

> Les échos mouleront seuls tous ces lieux qui furent
> Et dans l'infinie végétation transparente
> Tu te promèneras avec la vitesse
> Qui commande aux bêtes des bois (ll. 29–32/64)

[Echoes alone will mould all the places which once were | And in the infinite transparent vegetation | You will move at the speed | Which impels the woodland creatures]

Here we find the fantasy, which goes so deep in Breton, of a reconciliation with the natural world that takes place via an imaginary miniaturization through which a human subject (represented in the poetic fable as a sort of Tom Thumb to whom the most extraordinary things can happen), and the natural world (figured by woodland animals and vegetation, by minerals, colours, small objects) enter into resonance. This fantasy, so personal and specific to Breton, is the emblem of a reunited world. But it is the other, the 'You', who has the honour of inheriting it. And at the end of the poem it is *you* who will arrive alone on the lost beach, a place absent from all maps, out of reach of the poet's call (l. 44/64).

For its part, the 'I' represents itself in three different ways. First the 'I' is the agent of destruction. It is the I that ups anchor and breaks with the established order. But in this his role is that of a catalyst. His principal destructive activity, the one which determines the others, is writing. But the person who writes, the 'I' who starts to utter, is not the one who will be the subject of the writing itself (that will be 'You'). As a scriptor he undergoes the strange Mallarméan fate of an 'eloquent absence.' He is, to quote one of Éluard's poems, 'Celui qui se détruit dans les fils qu'il engendre' [He who destroys himself in the threads/sons he engenders]. In the poem's fable the act of writing consigns the practitioner to an instrumental role. Here 'the hands | Which wrote these verses' (les mains | Qui écrivirent ces vers) (l. 11/63) become spindles, then vanish into the natural landscape, becoming fleeting movements, gleams, like nightingales or rainfall. The act of writing merges into the rhythms of the natural world: the *métier* of the writer gives way to the 'métier de la pluie' [the loom of the rain] (l. 12/63). And whilst the alter ego, the 'You', mobilized by the drives of writing, will be granted 'parfums défendus' [forbidden perfumes] (l. 36/64), the writing subject (as opposed to the written one) will be no more than an 'épave', an empty hulk; having lived through a radical disappropriation, the evacuation of his mind, he will 'appart[ient] au vide' [belong to the void] (l. 34/64), to the perpetual motion of an escalator ever rolling at the same melancholy pace, like a music box whose mechanisms would constantly play the same sentimental tune (l. 35/64).[22]

So far we have seen that in 'La Mort Rose' the writing subject finds representation in two complementary guises: as a destructive agent who sacrifices himself in his acts, and as a sort of dispersed, ghostly presence disseminated in the rhythms of nature. This 'attitude spectrale' [spectral attitude] — to quote the title of one of Breton's poems[23] — is especially perceptible in the last sequence where the 'I' is assimilated to a sleeper and to the sounds of the natural world, and imagines himself under the mossy ground on which 'You' walk, as well as in the tears which fall from 'Your' eyes (ll. 38–39/64). But the 'I' has a third guise, neither agent of writing's destructive action, nor patient submissive to its processes, but a loving voice addressed to a 'you' that is not only his alter ego but a feminine presence. In the last part of the poem, the 'You' is given an explicitly feminine identity (via the adjectives). Thus, through a gesture that is at the heart of the lyric tradition, and which takes a particular and fundamental form in surrealism, the activity of writing, the poet's primordial act (but edged with risk and danger insofar as it 'makes strange' his desires, his identity, and so courts death) is seen to be one face of the act of love. But where love is concerned, poetry's divisiveness, as an act which takes us to the core of experience but simultaneously displaces us from it, takes its toll. And so it is alone that 'You' will arrive at the poem's culmination.

Let us now restore 'La Mort Rose' to its context in 'Carnet'. If, in the myth of poetic creation adumbrated here, in opposition to Valéry's poetics, poetic utterance, outside all calculation, comes by its own path, it is not always to be welcomed. In the poem, the site not of a quasi-mystical ascesis, but of a gentle self-extinction, a 'rosy death' that recalls the 'petite mort' of sex, the subject is as likely to lose as to find himself. The advent of poetic utterance, while it stands out against the background of daily existence, offers — as its residue, at least — neither Parousia nor epiphany. What 'La Mort rose,' and 'Carnet' murmur — through tenses, pronouns, the majestic and irreversible current of discourse — is that the poem cannot reach any goal, but only mime and herald a radical reorientation of existence. It is poetic utterance itself, this voice that breaks out of us, that is essential. Hardly surprising, then, that the underlying subject of so much surrealist poetry — particularly Breton's, but Aragon's and Éluard's too — should be the advent of the poem itself. 'A poem which is its own allegory' — this could be the (Mallarméan) subtitle of 'La Mort Rose': a discourse which, under the accoutrements of metaphor and allegory, is no more than the profusion of its own essence, the intonation of its own order. And once this discourse dies down, the poet can only register the return to the everyday world, 'ce seul jour heure par heure [this one day hour by hour] (l. 1/63), by its traditional mark — the date. '17 février 1924': these words seem to mark the end of 'La Mort Rose.' But they are followed by a few more.

La lectrice excitée éteint l'électricité. (37/463)

[brimming with excitement the reader turns off her electric light.]

A way of saying, perhaps, that if the poem's electrical current has subsided it is for the act of reading, a new *'geste* de lire' [*gesture* of reading] (6/456), to reactivate and perpetuate it. And this act of reading may in turn stimulate other activities and perhaps — who knows? — another birth.

## Appendix: A Translation of Breton's 'Carnet'

### NOTEBOOK

\*

Voices call the butterflies in a cave
Where from floor to ceiling giant sparks keep appearing...
(start of a poem)
I've always dreamed of an animal in a leaning forest. (1)

\*

Anterior life? It is only through memory that I know anything of the past or even of existence itself. But there is no reason why I should not be endowed with the capacity to represent to myself, every second, what has happened, what is currently happening and (to a lesser extent) what will happen. It is this very significant difference (memory, observation, imagination) which interests me. And what if memory were a product of the imagination? I am, as far as I can tell, a man, but nothing proves that I was one just now or that I'm about to be one, if *just* and *about* have a meaning (time). If I were a speck of dust I'd see things the way a speck of dust sees them, or rather... For all I know, the present is a point. There is not even substitution, why? Denial of death. Desnos's story. 'I am the author of all the books...' This happened on a Thursday (October 1923). (2)

\*

Rosy Death (title) (3)

\*

To teleph. Desnos, Mlle Germaine at Paris-Soir (5 till 7). (4)

\*

Superstitions. Presentiments. Language. I don't finish the sentence I began (begin, finish?). Coincidences. Probability Theory (see Poe: Tales of the Serious and the Grotesque, page 113, see also the epigraph to this story, from Novalis). (5)

\*

The book, but what is a book, architecture, O architectures? Of reading and of the growing impossibility of the *gesture* of reading. (6)

\*

Aragon (the Picasso of the Passage Jouffroy). (7)

\*

Dead people whom one would be quite happy to live with: Baudelaire. (8)

\*

The grave error of accepting that man is made in God's image: what ensues from this. (9)

\*

'To Paul Valéry (1872–1917)' Dedication. (10)

\*

Every man for himself! (11)

★

I never met Victor Hugo, so that (seeing him cross the street one day at twelve-thirty... 25 November 1923). (12)

★

Morality: what I do and the awareness of what I could do. — Legendarily. — Say this to a taxi driver, when... (13)

★

Trembling adventurers! (title) (14)

★

And flattery! (15)

★

The head caught in a cornet red as a heart. (16)

★

How much soft money has passed through my hands? (17)

★

Waxes: Stockman, 12 rue Gaillon.
La Cire d'art, 20, rue N.-D. de Nazareth. (18)

★

Hôtel du Calvaire. (19)

★

Picasso Ely. 03–44 (20)

★

I caught French when I was young (discursive). (21)

★

Cannonballs, blackcurrant balls. (22)

★

Quote from memory, always from memory. (23)

★

Much could be said on this score. *Comoedia*, 27 Jan. Between an interesting reproduction of Courbet's The Meeting and Chardin's Child with a Teetotum, a study on the Nude by Louise Hervieu, the woman who took the liberty of illustrating the *Fleurs du Mal*. This sums up indignity. (24)

★

Mr. Lecandéla. (25)

★

Calculation of improbabilities. (26)

★

Theft 'au rendez-moi' [lit. 'give me back']. (27)

★

Éluard, 45 Eaubonne. (28)

★

'What's true of cheeses is also true of lamps.' (Mazda in l'*Intransigeant*, 5 Feb. 1924). (30)

★

The man who, seeing you coming with his right eye, turns to let you go past and follows you with his left eye when your back is turned (psychological). (31)

★

The mechanism of waiting (I know it well). To be infinitely generalized. (32)

★

Nearly all this noted down at the Cyrano (mandarin-curaçao), the rue Blanche penetrates as best it can as it descends, 3 drops of Kaol and the sabre paste scarcely legible, a white or grey car parking, ladies who aren't quite proper. (33)

★

'It is the artist's duty to flee unpopularity' (*Comoedia*, 12 Feb.) Like hell. (34)

★

$$50/50 + 49/50 + 48/50 + 47/50 + \ldots + 25/50 + \ldots + 1/50$$

| | |
|---|---|
| 5 — 10 | |
| 4 — 13 | |
| 3 — 17 | (Chances of a photograph in a packet of |
| 2 — 25 | Gold Flake cigarettes). |
| 1 — 50 (35) | |

★

ROSY DEATH
One last time winged octopus will guide the boat whose sails are made of this one day hour by hour
This is the only vigil and after it you will feel the black and white sun rise in your hair
From the vaults will ooze a liquor stronger than death
When it is contemplated from above a precipice
Comets will press themselves tenderly against the forests before striking them with thunder
And all will unite in indivisible love
If ever the motif of rivers should vanish
Before night falls you will observe
The great silver pause
On a peach-tree in bloom will appear the hands
That wrote these lines and they will be silver spindles
Too and silver nightingales on the loom of the rain
You will see the horizon open up and suddenly there will be an end to the kiss of space
But fear will exist no more and the panes of sky and sea
Will fly before a wind that is stronger than we are
What will I do with the tremor of your voice
Mouse waltzing around the only lamp that will not fall
Winch of time
I shall ascend the hearts of men

For a supreme lapidation
My hunger will turn like a diamond cut too fine
It will braid the hair of its child the fire
Silence and life
But the names of the lovers will be forgotten
Like the adonide drop of blood
In the crazy night
Tomorrow you will lie to your own youth
to your own firefly youth
Echoes alone will mould all the places that once were
And in the infinite transparent vegetation
You will move at the speed
Which impels the woodland creatures
Perhaps you will scratch yourself on my hulk
without seeing them as one throws oneself on a floating weapon
The fact is I'll belong to the void that's like the steps
Of a stairway whose movement is called 'pain indeed'
For you from then on the forbidden perfumes
Angelica
Under the hollow moss and under your steps which aren't steps
My dreams will be formal and fruitless as the water's sound like eyelids in the
shadows
I'll break into yours to gauge the depth of your tears
My cries will leave you sweetly uncertain
And in the train made of ice tortoises
You won't have to pull the alarm
You will arrive alone on that lost beach
Where a star will descend on your luggage of sand
17th February 1924

★

Brimming with excitement the reader turns out her electric light.

## Notes

1. OC, I, 455–72. The notes on 'Carnet' are on pp. 1432–40.
2. In Le Revolver à cheveux blancs, OC, II, 63–64.
3. Littérature, n.s., 13 (June 1924), 15–19. 'Carnet' is given as an appendix in English translation. For ease of reference entries have been numbered in parentheses and line numbers have been provided for the poem. When citing the 'Carnet', entries are referenced by number and page in Œuvres complètes, I. When citing 'La Mort rose', entries are referenced by line number and page in Œuvres complètes, II.
4. Note nonetheless that the editors of the Pléiade edition have found and published another notebook, from the period 1920–21, OC II, 613–22.
5. Baudelaire's 'Carnet' was published for the first time in 1911. There was an important facsimile re-edition by the Éditions de la Sirène in 1920 which Breton would almost certainly have known. The 'Carnet' may be found in the 'Pléiade' edition of Baudelaire's works, ed. by Claude Pichois, vol. I (Paris: Gallimard, 1978).
6. Among the material Breton cut from the original publication are Gide's address and a quotation from Louÿs (461, 457). He also leaves out the lists of books and works of art which apparently relate to his position as art consultant to the couturier Jacques Doucet.
7. For the Littérature version Breton left out the majority of the ratés and other false starts, both in

prose and verse (including an extremely mediocre 'poem' 'written in a taxi after drinking'!), for instance at pp. 459, 460, and 463. He kept only the beautiful 'Beginning of a poem', as well as a few gnomic phrases. The series of failed attempts undoubtedly gave the impression of effort and frustration, which would hurt the sense Breton seems to want here: that the poem 'takes off' without any warning.

8. For the *Littérature* version Breton left out another title, 'Bribes' (Scraps, 458). This is both rather un-Bretonian and opposed to the fundamental idea of *coulée*, which he generally affirms here against another intuition, sometimes recommended, in which the ideas of the fragment and of the discontinuity of internal language are prized. On the other hand, Breton leaves out the word 'title' after the phrase 'Sauve qui peut!' [Save yourself!], which makes these words into a gnomic wisecrack. (The absence of the word 'title' may also be a transcription error.)

9. The omissions made in the *Littérature* version sometime reinforce the enigmatic aspect of the text. In the original notebook the words 'boulets de canon' are preceded by the phrase 'Et lorsqu'on eut fondu les pièces d'or pour faire des canons' [When the gold coins had been melted down to make cannon] (460), which moved from the idea of the wartime economy to that of transformation. In the case of 'Citer de mémoire', the two parts of the sentence are initially separated by a quotation from Voltaire (or, amusingly, a misquote, as Hubert points out (1435)) on 'beaux détails' [beautiful details] in poetry. This gave a more restrained, less mysterious context for the injunction to 'citer de mémoire'.

10. One finds this same tone in Aragon's *Le Payson de Paris*, as well as in certain passages of the *Manifeste du surréalisme*.

11. 'La Vie antérieure', Baudelaire *Œuvres complètes*, I, 17–18.

12. 'Le parfum', ibid, p. 39.

13. In the original notebook this dedication is preceded by another, this time one of praise: 'A Pierre Reverdy, au plus grand poète vivant et au plus parfait (honnête) homme, ou homme (dédicace)' [To Pierre Reverdy, to the greatest living poet and the most perfect (decent) man, or man (dedication)] (457). There is a clear model from Baudelaire here: his dedication of the *Fleurs du Mal* to Théophile Gautier, 'poète impeccable, [...] parfait magicien ès lettres françaises' [impeccable poet, [...] perfect magician of French letters], etc.

14. In the *Littérature* version Breton left out another allusion to Valéry contained in the original notebook. In a letter, Valéry had diagnosed in the younger poet the dual, irreconcilable influences of Mallarmé and Rimbaud. In the notebook (463), Breton expresses anger with this. He points with amusement to the forthcoming appearance of *Igitur*, an 'unpublished' work by Mallarmé that could change our understanding of the poet (who was therefore still 'alive', whereas Valéry...), and so change our idea of the sort of influence he could exert. It is worth recalling that Breton had known Valéry for many years, and that the author of *Le Cimetière marin* had been a witness at his wedding to Simone Kahn in 1921. On the relationship between Breton and Valéry, see Marguerite Bonnet, *André Breton et l'aventure surréaliste* (Paris: José Corti, 1975), p. 32.

15. Breton had already expressed his feelings about Valéry in a poem, 'Monsieur V.' written in 1918, and published in his first collection, *Mont de Piété* (1919) (collected in I, 3–16). For a discussion of this poem see my 'Mont de Piété and André Breton's early Poetic Development', in this volume.

16. Cited by Jacques Derrida, 'Qual Quelle: les sources de Valéry,' In *Marges de la Philosophie* (Paris: Les Éditions de Minuit, 1975), p. 344.

17. 'Qual Quelle,' p. 345.

18. 'Qual Quelle,' pp. 325–63. Derrida stresses the degree to which Valéry foregrounds 'l'hétérogénéité de la source' [the heterogeneity of the spring]: 'La discontinuité, le délai, l'hétérogénéité, l'altérité travaillent déjà la voix, la produisent dès son premier souffle en système de traces différentielles, soit une écriture avant la lettre' [Discontinuity, heterogeneity, otherness, are already at work in the voice itself; they produce it from the very first breath as a system of differential traces, in other words as a form of writing before the letter].

19. 'Autre éventail de Mlle Mallarmé' in Mallarmé, *Œuvres complètes*, I, ed. by Bertrand Marchal (Paris: Pléiade, 1998), p. 31.

20. We should emphasize once again that we are discussing here the 'rewritten' notebook which appeared in *Littérature*. The original, particularly its second part, which is omitted entirely from the *Littérature* version, expresses quite different preoccupations, both minor and major. So, as Hubert has insisted, some entries contain sketches of certain themes of the *Manifeste*. Hubert argues that the selection made by Breton for the *Littérature* version reveals the poet's desire to 'livrer au public des remarques essentiellement extra-littéraires, ce qui entre dans la stratégie de "demoralisation" alors voulue par le groupe' [give the public essentially extra-literary remarks, part of the strategy of 'demoralization' the group was then pursuing] (1453). Our reading suggests, rather, that Breton wanted to demonstrate what one might call the 'extra-literary' dimension of poetic utterance. In the *Littérature* version, the omission of many 'literary' false starts — unfinished poems, etc. — goes hand in hand with the way in which *La Mort rose* has been 'grafted' on: coming from elsewhere, the poem shows that literature, and life, are elsewhere.

21. Baudelaire, 'Spleen', *OC* I, 73.

22. [See my 'Breton and the Language of Automatism: Alterity, Allegory, Desire,' in this volume.]

23. 'Les attitudes spectrales,' II, 70–72.

# 6

# City Space, Mental Space, Poetic Space:
# Paris in Breton, Benjamin and Réda

The Parisian field to be explored in this essay could be said to enjoy special privileges since it possesses both longevity and the capacity to generate or incorporate immensely varied modes of apprehending and construing the city. It owes this in part to its insistently interrogative and subversive nature, to the way it questions and undermines fixed views and orthodox perspectives, whether literary, sociological or historical, advancing instead the case for indirection or obliquity in the articulation of urban, specifically Parisian reality. This field could be called 'poetic' since a poet, Baudelaire, stands at its fountain-head, and other poets — Nerval, Apollinaire, Breton, Queneau and Réda — are closely associated with it. Yet its vitality has little to do with genre, literary history or literature *tout court*, and its widespread impact and resonances — in philosophy and theory (Benjamin, Lefebvre, Certeau), film (Godard, Rivette), anthropology (Rouch, Augé) — stem less from literary works than from the dissemination of ways of figuring the relationships between the traversal of urban space, the exploration of subjectivity at grips with its external context and the operations of language, in other words for encouraging productive interaction between city, mind, history and text. My discussion will focus principally on the Surrealists (especially Breton), on Benjamin, and on Réda.

Seen from the vantage-point of Apollinaire and Surrealism (this was in effect Benjamin's perspective in the late 1920s) Baudelaire's astonishingly productive engagement with the city, in the 'Tableaux parisiens' [Parisian scenes] of *Les Fleurs du mal*, the prose poems (a genre now customarily associated with urban experience) of *Le Spleen de Paris*, and such essays as 'Le Peintre de la vie moderne' [The painter of modern life], can be seen to have two principal aspects. The first centres on the notion of modernity. Baudelaire's famous review of the Salon of 1846 culminated in an appeal for art to engage with what he called the heroism or the 'epic side' of modern life. Pointing out that each age has its own passions and forms of beauty, and arguing that great art always combines the eternal with the transitory, he urged the artist to recognize that Parisian life offered subjects as grand and poetic as those of antiquity, and that what he called 'le merveilleux' permeated the contemporary urban environment if only one could recognize it.[1] An artist who did recognize this, according to Baudelaire, was Constantin Guys, famous for the rapidity of execution he brought to depictions of contemporary fashions and high society, and

Guys became the anonymous subject of a remarkable essay, 'The Painter of Modern Life'. Here Baudelaire celebrates Monsieur G. for the ability to extract the eternal from the transitory, and to isolate the poetic dimension of modernity from the simply modish by dint of a capacity, grounded in an essentially childlike vision, to crystallize on paper fleeting impressions garnered while in the midst of everyday life. Too passionate and obsessional to be a dandy, though possessing some of the dandy's refinement and independence, cerebral, but too enamoured of the visible and the tangible to be a pure philosopher, Baudelaire's ideal artist is a passionate observer and a 'parfait flâneur' who is most at home when out in the street, picking up the electric energy of the crowd but remaining incognito, registering the kaleidoscopic patterns of life in all its grace and detail.[2]

As a prospector of modernity the Baudelairean artist develops the *flâneur*'s sense of connoisseurship and curiosity to a pitch of obsession. A little further in this direction lies the hysterical persona of the poet whose exchanges with the city have a more extreme and existential character. In some of the key poems of the 'Tableaux parisiens': 'Le Cygne' [The swan], 'Les Petites Vieilles' [The little old women], 'Les Sept Vieillards' [The seven old men], and many of the prose poems, the city street becomes the stage for an encounter between self and other, individual consciousness and figures who mirror its labyrinthine recesses and perplexities. The desire of the painter of modern life to marry the crowd ('épouser la foule') becomes something more intense, 'cette ineffable orgie, [...] cette sainte prostitution de l'âme qui se donne tout entière, poésie et charité, à l'imprévu qui se montre, à l'inconnu qui passe' [[an] ineffable orgy, [...a] holy prostitution of the soul which gives itself entirely, poetry and charity, to the unforeseen which reveals itself, to the unknown which happens along].[3] Urban space becomes the arena in which the poet can explore the impact of the external world on his own subjectivity, as in 'Les Petites Vieilles', where instead of settling for a single register or perspective the poet shifts alarmingly from one to another, presenting the old women he encounters in his urban prowls now as wholly external paraphernalia of the city streets, now as dimensions or possibilities of his own being: 'mon cœur multiplié jouit de tous vos vices! | Mon âme resplendit de toutes vos vertus!' [my teeming heart exults in all your sins | and all your virtues magnify my soul!][4]

The two aspects I have isolated: on one hand the notion of a 'modern life' perceptible only to those with the antennae to receive it, and on the other the dramas of identification played out in city space, have in common a protagonist who makes it his business to be out in the city streets. Both aspects thus involve a connection between urban experience and individual self-discovery or attunement to the spirit of the age. In the work of Apollinaire, whose seminal poem 'Zone' (1913) stands with T. S. Eliot's *The Waste Land* (1922), also full of Baudelairean echoes, as a cardinal expression of the twentieth-century poet's sense of the city, the two features of Baudelaire's inheritance are amply represented. The self-styled 'Flâneur des deux rives' [Stroller of the two river banks] was an avid collector of Parisian curiosities, introducing readers of his newspaper column 'La Vie anecdotique' [Anecdotal life] to all manner of trifling but strange urban events and locations. In the haunting

'Souvenir d'Auteuil' [Memory of Auteuil] for example, the *flâneur* takes us round a series of municipal depots, including the Hôtel des Haricots, where rows of disused street-lights resemble a primeval forest. Like the poem, the journalistic column becomes a space in which to seek one's bearings amid the flotsam and jetsam of experience.[5] As impresario for the Fauves, the Cubists, the Futurists and a bevy of other avant-garde groups and individuals, Apollinaire continually sought to identify the new spirit, 'l'esprit nouveau', convinced like Baudelaire that it should be the common mission of poet and artist to take the pulse of contemporary life and to find forms appropriate to its articulation. For Apollinaire the central feature of early twentieth-century modernity was the impact of technology and its products: new modes of transport, new styles of building, new forms of experience. The challenge here was not only to develop *poetic* styles and forms that could reflect these new realities, but to respond more profoundly to the existential disorientation occasioned by the need to jettison established categories of belief and understanding. While some of Apollinaire's work suggests uncritical enthusiasm for whatever was new, his best poems, at least among those that deal directly with urban experience, present a remarkable blend of formal innovation and subjective exploration. In such poems as 'La Chanson du mal-aimé', 'Le Voyageur' or 'Zone', a free-verse poetics of fragmentation and juxtaposition converts itineraries in urban space into mental journeys involving past and future as well as present. The aspiration to an identity purged of its debilitating attachment to extinct desires leads to affirmations of solidarity with the brave new world of steel, electricity and rapid motion, but the need to come to terms with the past rather than simply negate it leads to the constant recrudescence of past scenes, so that the present in which the poet-protagonist writes and reflects becomes a shifting, conflictual zone of turbulence. This zone of present experience, a space that plays host to past and future versions of self, is quintessentially in Apollinaire that of the city street, and it is the street that will be the central forum of the Surrealist engagement with Paris.

## André Breton: Subjectivity in the City

In Surrealism, the differing, if by no means antithetical, ways of valuing Parisian experience we have adumbrated in Baudelaire and Apollinaire can conveniently be identified with differences between Aragon and Breton. Aragon's *Le Paysan de Paris* [Paris peasant], which played a decisive role in the germination of Benjamin's Arcades project (the *Passagen-Werk*), stands alongside Breton's *Nadja* (also important for Benjamin) as a seminal contribution to the Surrealist vision of Paris.[6] As the opening 'Preface to a modern mythology' makes clear, Aragon's starting-point is the very Baudelairean notion of a modernity incarnated in transient urban phenomena. The brilliant descriptions of the then recently demolished Passage de l'Opéra, a typical example of the glass-roofed arcades erected a century earlier to provide sheltered shopping on two storeys, and of the late nineteenth-century Buttes-Chaumont park, with its artificial hills, lakes and precipices, are really imaginary forays into the collective unconscious as it makes itself visible in the artefacts and rituals that characterize these two 'sacred' sites. Yet if *Le Paysan de Paris* is the *locus classicus* of a certain Surrealist vision of Paris, the work of Breton, where the theme of Paris is present in a more widespread way throughout the writer's career, provides a richer, subtler contribution to the poetic construction of the city. Largely this is because Aragon mythologizes Paris in a manner consistent in many ways with a tradition running from Villon through Restif de la Bretonne and Hugo to the twentieth century, while Breton develops the other strand, identified earlier in Baudelaire and Apollinaire, where the streets of Paris play a catalytic role in the exploration of *individual* mental space.

This is not to deny that individual subjectivity is implicated in Aragon's urban meanderings. Nor indeed that Breton's apprehension of Paris has a mythic or historical component. A remarkable text, dating from 1950, 'Pont-Neuf' (III, 888–95), famously proposes a detailed 'interpretation' of the topography of central Paris according to which the geographical and architectural layout of the Ile de la Cité, and the bend of the Seine where it is situated, are seen to make up the body of a recumbent women whose vagina is located in the Place Dauphine, 'sa conformation triangulaire, d'ailleurs légèrement curviligne et de la fente qui la bissecte en deux espaces boisés' [with its triangular, slightly curvilinear form bisected by a slit separating two wooded spaces] (III, 893). At one level this 'reading' is presented in terms of the psychology of forms, as an instance of how we respond to physical features of the environment in ways that reflect our own psychological make-up. But Breton also goes to some length to show that our response to urban sites is not exclusively conditioned by physical stimuli but also by historical resonances enshrined in street names, in snippets of antiquarian knowledge often manifested architecturally, and, more esoterically, in '*ce qui a eu lieu* ici' [*what took place* here] (III, 890). Yet if the resonance of past events and personalities — particularly, for Breton, those associated with such pursuits as alchemy, intrigue, revolution or poetry — still affect the atmosphere of the streets and monuments where they took place, thus over-determining the factors capable of affecting an individual in the present, it may also be the case that these historical resonances were themselves prompted in the first place by the physical features of the site. Hence, if the Place Dauphine and environs were for long a place of passion and licentiousness, this may be accounted for by the erotic reading mentioned above. In this vein Breton argues at some length that the decision in the seventeenth century to locate a new bridge across the Seine (the Pont-Neuf) at the western tip of the Ile de la Cité rather than at the Notre-Dame end, which would have been more logical given the aim of relieving traffic crossing the river along the main north-south axis, can only be explained by the powerful attraction exerted by the erotic heart of the capital. The 'force' to which the individual passer-by may respond as he or she circulates in Parisian space is thus the product of a dialectic of historical and physical textures, but in advancing and illustrating this thesis Breton also makes it clear that the individual subjectivity of the respondent is crucial. More importantly he indicates that the role of the encounter with, and imaginative response to, urban space is ultimately to provide insights into the individual as much as to the city. What attracts or repels us as we circulate in the Paris streets may be conditioned by historical and physical features, but what it reveals is the topography of our own subjectivity:

> Les pas qui, sans nécessité extérieure, des années durant, nous ramènent aux mêmes points d'une ville attestent notre sensibilisation croissante à certains de ces aspects, qui se présentent obscurément sous un jour favorable ou hostile. Le parcours d'une seule rue un peu longue et de déroulement assez varié — la rue de Richelieu par exemple — pour peu qu'on y prenne garde, livre, dans l'intervalle du numéro qu'on pourrait préciser, des zones alternantes de bien-être et de malaise. Une carte sans doute très significative demanderait *pour chacun* à être dressée, faisant apparaître en blanc les lieux qu'il hante et en noir ceux qu'il évite, le reste en fonction de l'attraction ou de la répulsion moindre se répartissant la gamme des gris. (III, 889)

> [The steps which draw us, year after year, without external constraint, to the same parts of the city testify to the way certain aspects, which in an obscure way present themselves as either benign or hostile, progressively impinge on our sensibility. A walk down a single street, of sufficient length and variety — the rue de Richelieu for example — if we focus our attention, can provide, between two street-numbers which could be specified, alternating zones of well-being and disquiet. No doubt a highly significant map should be drawn up for *each individual* which would indicate in white the places he is prone to haunt and in black those he avoids, the rest being divided into shades of grey according to the greater or lesser degree of attraction or repulsion exerted.]

In proposing an analogy and a reciprocal connection between the inner space of individual subjectivity and the outer space of contingent locations and events, this passage typifies Breton's view that personal identity and destiny are made manifest in a process of interaction with outer experience. As far back as one goes in Breton's work one encounters a view of the city street as an area of possibility. The street is quintessentially the place where *something can happen*:

> La rue, que je croyais capable de livrer à ma vie ses surprenants détours, la rue avec ses inquiétudes et ses regards, était mon véritable élément; j'y prenais comme nulle part ailleurs le vent de l'éventuel. (I, 196)

> [The street, which I thought capable of transmitting its surprising detours to my life, the street with its worries and its looks, was my true element; there, as nowhere else, I could breathe the wind of eventuality.]

The equation between circulation in Parisian space and circulation in mental space is a consistent feature of Breton's 'automatic' writing from the publication of *Les Champs magnétiques* in 1920 onwards, and here, both implicitly and often explicitly, the textual space engendered by the act of writing in a way designed to suspend the control of rationality and other censoring agencies, and to mobilize creative energies within language itself, is also implicated. In the automatic prose poetry of *Poisson soluble*, Parisian environments are frequently the setting for the dazzling processes of individual metamorphosis that consistently feature in these narratives:

> 'Un baiser est si vite oublié' j'écoutais passer ce refrain dans les grandes promenades de ma tête, dans la province de ma tête et je ne savais plus rien de ma vie, qui se déroulait sur sa piste blonde. Vouloir entendre plus loin que soi, plus loin que cette route dont un rayon, à l'avant de moi, effleure à peine les

ornières, quelle folie! j'avais passé la nuit en compagnie d'une femme frêle et
avertie, tapi dans les hautes herbes d'une place publique, de côté du Pont-Neuf.
Une heure durant nous avions ri des serments qu'échangeaient par surprise les
tardifs promeneurs qui venaient tour à tour s'asseoir sur le banc le plus proche.
Nous étendions la main vers les capucines coulant d'un balcon de City-Hotel,
avec l'intention d'abolir dans l'air tout ce qui sonne en trébuchant comme les
monnaies anciennes qui exceptionnellement avaient cours cette nuit-là. (I,
380)

['A Kiss is so quickly forgotten.' I heard this refrain go by during the long walks
in my head, in the province of my head and I knew nothing of the rest of my
life, which unfolded on its blond track. To want to hear beyond oneself, beyond
this wheel, one spoke of which, ahead of me, barely skims the cart-tracks, what
folly! I had spent the night in the company of a frail and alert woman, tucked
away in the long grass of a public square, towards the Pont-Neuf. For a whole
hour we had laughed at the vows exchanged, to their surprise, by the late-night
strollers who came in turn to sit on the nearest bench. We stretched out our
hands towards the nasturtiums flowing from a balcony of the City-Hotel, with
the aim of abolishing in mid-air everything that makes a ringing sound as it
shudders, like the ancient coinage which was exceptionally the currency that
night.]

Liberation from the usual co-ordinates of space, time and logic is associated with
love, or eroticism, which triggers a switch onto a mental or imaginary plane. At
one remove from the ordinary path of existence (which goes on all the while), the
narrator is both independent of everyday reality and still a participant within it. This
ambivalence is partly figured through the way the urban setting (characteristically
indicated by very specific topographical references) is subverted by the encroachment
of the natural world, which makes the city a hybrid environment containing, or
continuous with, the non-urban world outside it. Ambivalence also stems from
temporal dislocation in so far as the historical past of the city (present here through
the reference to cart-tracks and ancient coinage) is seen to be still extant below the
surface. In the mini-narratives of *Poisson soluble* the poet constantly slips in and out
of the historical present, journeying from the city to the countryside and back again,
abolishing the barriers separating city centre, *banlieue*, *faubourg*, and city proper,
observing 'le boulevard pareil à un marais salant sous les enseignes lumineuses' [the
boulevard like a salt marsh under its luminous signs] (I, 352), or 'le paysage de Paris
rossignol du monde variait de minute en minute' [the Paris landscape nightingale
of the world [which] varied from minute to minute] (I, 372). In the rest of the text
cited above, the narrator follows the Seine at dawn to a 'white village' that turns
out to be a picture, and then to a second village, Ecureuil-sur-mer, where he and
his partner disappear. While maintaining narrative continuity, the text insistently
disavows referentiality not only by means of fantasy and incongruity but by
drawing attention to linguistic generation. The lovers' bench (*banc*) at the beginning
is echoed by 'bancs de poisson' [shoals of fish], and the 'couverture' [cover] of the
village (as picture) features a 'sorte de lorette sautant à la corde à l'orée d'un bois
de laurier gris' [a flighty young lady skipping on the edge of a grey laurel wood],
where the phonetic echoes in the words *lorette/l'orée/laurier* lay bare the arbitrariness

of the textual elements (I, 380). (It should be noted in passing that the *lorette* is a specifically nineteenth-century, and urban, category.)

References to Paris consistently feature in Breton's automatic texts as the starting-point for scenarios of liberation and self-annihilation engendered by the break with referential codes and the adoption of linguistic and discursive play. It is as if the city of Paris were always already half imaginary, half linguistic, a territory of desire as much as of reality. In particular, the street, aired by the wind of eventuality, figured as an ever-changing space, and hence a zone of infinite possibility, offers itself as a place of metamorphosis where the individual past, and the restricted identity or *état civil* which goes with it, can always be abrogated by virtue of the multi-levelled historical and physical associations in which the street consists. The city-street, in other words, imparts to the individual subject something of its own sameness-within-difference.

*Nadja*, published in 1928, two years after Aragon's *Le Paysan de Paris*, is the first of a series of autobiographical narratives in which Breton recounts events in his life that seemed to substantiate his evolving theories, central to the activities of the Surrealist movement, with respect to what he called 'le hasard objectif' [objective chance]. This is the generic term for a category of experiences where the unfolding of individual existence seems conditioned by factors outside the fields of obvious causality or conscious volition. Breton's encounter with the enigmatic young woman, Nadja, and the fairly brief period when he sees her regularly, are punctuated by surprising episodes of telepathy and coincidence which challenge our conventional view of reality and point to the existence of unsuspected pathways linking individual subjectivity and external events. *Nadja* emphasizes that just as the liberation of language depends on the surrender of conscious control over utterance, so access to the occult pathways of experience may be propitiated by an attitude of openness and availability to experience that finds its cardinal expression in the practice of aimless wandering in urban space:

> On peut, en attendant, être sûr de me rencontrer dans Paris, de ne pas passer plus de trois jours sans me voir aller et venir, vers la fin de l'après-midi, boulevard Bonne-Nouvelle entre l'imprimerie du Matin et le boulevard de Strasbourg. Je ne sais pourquoi c'est là, en effet, que mes pas me portent, que je me rends presque toujours sans but déterminé, sans rien de décidant que cette donnée obscure, à savoir que c'est là que se passera cela (?). Je ne vois guère, sur ce rapide parcours, ce qui pourrait, même à mon insu, constituer pour moi un pôle d'attraction, ni dans l'espace ni dans le temps. Non: pas même la très belle et très inutile Porte Saint-Denis. (I, 661–63)

> [Meanwhile, you can be sure of meeting me in Paris, of not spending more than three days without seeing me pass, toward the end of the afternoon, along the Boulevard Bonne-Nouvelle between the *Matin* printing office and the Boulevard de Strasbourg. I don't know why it should be precisely here that my feet take me, here that I almost inevitably go without specific purpose, without anything to induce me but this obscure clue: notably that it (?) will happen here. I cannot see, as I hurry along, what could constitute for me, even without my knowing it, a magnetic pole in either space or time. No: not even the extremely handsome, extremely useless Porte Saint-Denis.]

The kind of urban *errance* [wandering] described here, which is undoubtedly Breton's central contribution to the poetics of the city, has its specific ecology. It has often been pointed out that Breton's Paris is clearly delimited, conditioned by residence in the rue Fontaine in the north of the city not far from Montmartre, and by various enthusiasms and prejudices. But if certain locations (such as the Tour Saint-Jacques, associated with alchemy) are favoured, and do indeed have a sacred 'aura', these serve essentially as landmarks within a latent field of energy that is manifested primarily through events such as encounters with people or objects, coincidences, unusual or uncanny occurrences, which tear the customary fabric of experience. The Paris of *Nadja* is a city of signs — luminous advertisements, billboards, printed ephemera, notices — and Breton treats Nadja (in a way arguably prejudicial to her needs as a human being) as a sort of Ur-sign, a pointer to a level of reality to which the city itself rather than Nadja is the key. Viewed at first as a free spirit, a 'génie libre', Nadja, whose erratic behaviour leads to her incarceration in an asylum, fades into the background while Breton is buoyed up by a new love that Nadja is deemed to have heralded.

Beginning as a quest for identity (the opening words are 'Who am I?'), *Nadja* progressively establishes a view of experience as cryptogram: 'Il se peut que la vie demande à être déchiffrée comme un cryptogramme' [Perhaps life needs to be deciphered like a cryptogram] (I, 716). In many respects this vision, and its connection with the city, is more fully realized in *Les Vases communicants* (1932), where the communicating vessels of the title are dreams and waking life, or more fundamentally the unconscious and reality. Breton advances a resolutely materialist view of dreams indebted to Freud's theory and practice, but also critical of it in some respects, which he illustrates by prolonged analysis of a recent dream partly concerned with his guilt at the way he treated *Nadja*, and with the breakdown of his relationship with the woman who supplanted her. The point of the analysis is to show that the dream can be entirely explained with reference to real events, that all its elements derive from lived experience, and that the function of the dreamwork is to contribute to the resolution of conflicting elements in the subject's life. Rather than a parenthesis the dream is a movement 'in the pure sense of a contradiction which leads forward'.

In the middle part of the book, as in the central section of *Nadja*, Breton turns his attention to a specific period in his recent past and in this case subjects it to minute analysis. While the context is again experiences that take place in Parisian space and the focus once more on coincidences, meetings, parallels and strange events, the argumentation is more circumstantial, and the attention to detail more pronounced. Breton now has a case to prove. Waking life and dream life, he argues, are not opposed but complementary. To demonstrate this he seeks to show how, during a period when his personal situation left him at a low ebb, positive psychical forces asserted themselves by infiltrating his everyday life, subjecting it to the logic of the dreamwork. In the course of the analysis these positive forces, which will later be designated by the generic term *desire*, are strongly associated with three fields: libidinal energy, subjectivity and the city. Having explained the reasons for the sense of abandonment he felt at this time (April 1931), Breton notes how at one stage he was saved from despair by 'woman' in general, incarnated by the generic 'Parisian woman' constituted by women glimpsed in the streets. Subsequently, specific women, notably a German tourist and a working-class girl who turns out to be only sixteen, occupy prominent positions in the networks of repetition and substitution that characterize Breton's life at this point. The two women are initially linked because, like *Nadja*, they have extraordinary eyes, a fact that constantly surfaces in the convolutions of Breton's narrative. When the young girl fails to meet him in the Café Batifol, Breton recalls that his first visit to this establishment had been in pursuit of another woman with strange eyes. Deciding to attend a play the girl had mentioned seeing with her mother, Breton finds that the name *Batifol* features prominently in the opening act. A woman (named Parisette) whom Breton dines with instead of the young girl, turns out to know a certain *Jeanson* whose name echoes that of *Samson*, author of an article Breton had read just before, while the latter name connects with the original girl because her eyes had reminded Breton of those of Moreau's *Dalila*.

And so on. As he traces out the patterns linking events, names, people and places, or things read, seen and imagined, which marked his life between 5 and 24 April 1931, Breton notes that everything is as in a dream *except* that 'here I am in reality moving around Paris' (là je me déplace réellement dans Paris). In this portion of waking life, as in a dream, desire is at work:

> l'exigence du désir à la recherche de l'*objet* de sa réalisation dispose étrangement des données extérieures, en tendant égoïstement à ne retenir d'elles que ce qui peut servir sa cause. La vaine agitation de la rue est devenue à peine plus gênante que le froissement des draps. Le désir est là, taillant en pleine pièce dans l'étoffe pas assez vite changeante, puis laissant entre les morceaux courir son fil sûr et fragile. (II, 177)

> [the exigency of desire in quest of the *object* of its realization makes hay with external facts, egotistically retaining only what may serve its cause. The futile activity of the street is scarcely more irksome than tangled bedsheets. Desire is at work, carving up the rapidly changing fabric, then deftly setting its fragile thread to work between the pieces.]

The thrust of Breton's demonstration is that at a point when he was psychically endangered, desire, the agent of subjectivity, came to his rescue. Not by providing a haven from the world of reality (a dream world) but by operating on given reality: 'le torrent du donné' [the torrent of the given). All the ingredients are real: 'Le Café Batifol n'est pas un mythe' [The Café Batifol is not a myth] (II, 178), the real world was there all the time, but 'je tentais désespérément, de toutes mes forces, d'extraire du milieu, à l'exclusion de tout le reste, ce qui devait d'abord servir à la reconstitution de ce moi' [I was desperately striving, with all my power, to extract from the *milieu*, to the exclusion of all else, what could contribute to the rebuilding of myself] (II, 179). At this 'particularly irrational' juncture in his life Breton's subjectivity was paramount. Yet the real world had by no means ceased to exist for him. Rather, under the sway of desire, it became a fragmented, unstable, labyrinthine field, a territory of bric-à-brac ready to be conscripted in the cause of psychic process and reparation.

In *Les Vases communicants*, as in *Nadja* and subsequently in *L'Amour fou*, the great purveyor of materials for the processes of the psyche to derive energies and modes of representation is the city of Paris. And indeed, by the end of *Les Vases communicants*, Paris emerges increasingly as the privileged mirror of subjectivity, in all senses its capital. There is nothing fortuitous about the Parisian setting of Breton's 'dream-phase': only this city could have provided the psychic support he needed. And we should not be surprised at the amount of topographical and circumstantial detail Breton provides (despite the fidelity to his antirealist refusal of descriptions), for example the numerous street names that enable us to reconstruct his itineraries. Paris is not incidental to the construction of subjectivity or desire presented in *Les Vases communicants*, it is of its essence, and the emphasis on the tangible reality and factitiousness of the city, far from being at odds with the project of rendering subjective experience, binds subjectivity to its objective correlative, Paris itself. The apotheosis of Paris-as-subjectivity comes in the third section of *Les Vases communicants*, which culminates in a long disquisition on the disastrous neglect of subjective existence. A lyrical evocation of Paris seen at dawn from the heights of the Sacré-Coeur extols the nocturnal city as the embodiment of 'l'essence générale de la subjectivité, cet immense terrain et le plus riche de tous est laissé en friche' [the general essence of subjectivity, that immense field, richest of all, [which] is left to lie fallow] (II, 205). Encompassing dreams, the unconscious and the whole realm of feeling or affect, the terrain of subjectivity requires exploration like the streets of a nocturnal city whose 'unconscious powers' call for profound meditation and deciphering.

The labyrinthine windings of desire and the dialectical interplay of subjectivity and topography also feature prominently in two famous chapters of *L'Amour fou*. One chapter concerns the chain of events surrounding Breton's meeting with Jacqueline, who was to be his second wife, during a walk through Paris at night, which, Breton subsequently found to his amazement, reproduced almost exactly a Parisian itinerary outlined in an automatic poem he had written some ten years earlier (II, 710–35). The second involves a visit to the flea market with the sculptor Giacometti, when both men were fortuitously drawn to purchase objects that, in manifold ways teased out by subsequent analysis, furnished symbolic 'solutions' to underlying psychological conflicts present at the time in each individual (II, 697–709). In both cases the city plays an active role as intermediary between internal and external reality. Paris offers itself as the place of recovered subjectivity, as the harbinger of lost identity. If the question of identity is always to the fore in Breton's negotiations with the city, if nonpurposeful circulation in urban space is seen as a path towards the discovery of an authentic, sublimated dimension of selfhood, this reflects the fact that for Breton identity is conceived in terms of difference, as something played out on another stage, in another dimension, at another level. With its endlessly varied spaces, vistas and itineraries, its combination of exteriors and interiors, its multiple layers of history that make each street a palimpsest, the city's inherent theatricality provides the ideal stage for the Surrealist pursuit of identity.

## Walter Benjamin and the Meditative *flâneur*

The Surrealist dimension of Benjamin's massive unfinished opus on Paris, the *Passagen-Werk* or Arcades Project, is well known. Benjamin began work on it in the late 1920s, partly under the impact of Aragon's *Le Paysan de Paris* (1924) and Breton's *Nadja* (1928), and it was Aragon's brilliant evocation of the Passage de l'Opéra that inspired Benjamin's central insights into the arcades he describes as being 'buried deep in great cities like caverns preserving the fossils of an extinct animal — the consumer of the pre-imperial epoch of capitalism', and as 'the home of the collective dream'.[7] In Breton's *Nadja* it was the emphasis placed on experience, and particularly what Benjamin labelled 'a profane illumination, a materialistic, anthropological inspiration', that provided food for thought, as did the Surrealist writer's seminal perception of 'the revolutionary energies that appear in the "outmoded", in the first iron constructions, the first factory buildings, etc.'.[8] In a recent study it has been argued that Benjamin's indebtedness to Surrealism is greater than hitherto acknowledged, and in particular that through the twelve-year evolution of the *Passagen-Werk* he remained attentive to developments in Breton's post-*Nadja* explorations of the interface between the city's streets and the subject's 'ghostly' identities.[9] Equally, the German editor of the *Passagen-Werk* highlights two strands in Benjamin's thinking whose interconnections are Surrealist in origin: attention to concrete details — objects, dress, architecture, stray pieces of information — and a fascination with the dream state.[10]

If Surrealism provided Benjamin with one of the starting-points for his work on Paris, he nevertheless always indicated the differences between his project and that of the Surrealists. With regard to *Le Paysan de Paris* Benjamin observed:

> Delimitation of the tendency of this work in relation to Aragon: while Aragon persists in remaining in the field of dreams, what counts here is to find the constellation of awakening. Whereas with Aragon there remains an impressionistic element — 'mythology' — and this impressionism is to be held responsible for the many empty philosophemes in the book, here the aim is to dissolve 'mythology' in the space of history.[11]

As we noted earlier, however, Breton also had serious reservations about the mythologizing character of Aragon's *Paysan* (stemming partly from the Baudelairean 'mythology of modern life'). In *Nadja* and *Les Vases communicants*, attention to precise spatial and temporal detail marks a concern for the minutiae of subjective experience as it unfolds in urban space, and this favours liberation from the customary limitations of habitual consciousness. Similarly, at many points in the *Passagen-Werk*, Benjamin, while by no means sharing the individualistic concerns of Breton, represents the interaction of subject and city in ways which not only have clear affinities with Surrealism but contribute more widely — and centrally — to the tradition under discussion here.

As ever with Benjamin it is appropriate to begin with the *flâneur*. However, just as Benjamin himself progressively elaborates the figure of the *flâneur* or urban stroller by contrasting his relationship to the city with that of other types of city-walker, so it is vital in my view to discriminate between a number of versions of the *flâneur* to be found in Benjamin's writings. In the nineteenth-century literature on the *flâneur*, particularly in the *Physiologies*, which he found particularly rich and symptomatic, Benjamin encountered distinctions between the *flâneur* and the *badaud* or idler, who simply gapes; between the *flâneur* and the *promeneur*, who is more purposeful, and so on.[12] In building up his own portrait Benjamin regularly takes issue with the established legend or myth of the *flâneur*, notably with regard to the question of knowledge. Where the mythical *flâneur* of the *Physiologistes* (including Balzac) possesses an encyclopaedic knowledge of faces and streets which makes him an expert, Benjamin plays down this expertise in order to emphasize instead the *flâneur*'s hidden motives, his more complex interactions with the city's labyrinth.[13] The Benjaminian *flâneur* differs from the voyageur who believes that historical knowledge can give access to the genius loci. For him it is the *fait divers*, a highly localized event that took place on this very spot, or the snippet of detailed information which counts.[14] But if the *flâneur*'s fascination with clues links him to the figure of the detective, his motives are more personal, and have less to do with ratiocination.[15] At one point Benjamin suggests that *promeneur* becomes *flâneur* at the point where he is prey to hysterical tears provoked by the irruption of the past in the present.[16] Indeed temporality is fundamental to this figure, whose attitude is also conditioned by a desire to divorce himself from his own past, profiting from the anonymity of the big city.[17] At one point Benjamin refers to the *flâneur* as someone who takes refuge in the shadow of the city. Like the *promeneur solitaire* of Rousseau, the *flâneur* cherishes his 'oisiveté' [idleness] and enjoys self-contemplation, but for Benjamin he differs in that he is still intensely preoccupied with the outer spectacle.[18] And unlike the *promeneur philosophique*, the *flâneur* needs the crowd — even if he prefers to remain incognito.

The notoriously elusive character of Benjamin's thought, and its historical evolution, together with the immensely complex composition and publication history of the *Passagen-Werk* and its offshoots, tended in the past to encourage a certain legend or myth of the Benjaminian *flâneur*. There are traces of this, for example, in Christopher Prendergast's excellent discussion of Baudelaire's prose poems where he compares the mobile, ironic stance of the Baudelairean walker-narrator with the more rigid attitudes that are said to characterize the Benjaminian *flâneur*.[19] Basing his reading mainly on the texts available before the publication of the Arcades project notebooks, Prendergast presents the *flâneur*'s position as one of either *control* or *jouissance*, superiority and detachment or vicarious pleasure deriving from voyeuristic non-involvement.

Interestingly, the notion of the *flâneur* as one who engages in voyeuristic objectification of the other has often been focused back on to the Surrealists. Breton's narrator in *Nadja*, for example, is often seen to exemplify the unattached observer who looks at city life as a spectacle to be consumed, while retaining the freedom to withdraw his interest at will (Benjamin himself noted the passage where Breton candidly affirmed that he felt 'closer to the things that *Nadja* is close to than to her'). But if this critique is partially valid, it misses much that Benjamin himself detected in *Nadja* and it is also much less applicable to Breton's subsequent accounts of city-wandering. Moreover, the view of the *flâneur* as voyeur does not do justice to the aspects of this figure perceptible in a passage such as the following:

> For the *flâneur* the street brings about a metamorphosis as it leads him back through past time. He goes down a street. For him each street has a downward slope, if not towards the Mothers, at any rate into a past which may be all the deeper for not being his own past, his private past. [...] His footsteps call forth a surprising echo, the gaslight on the tiled floor casts an ambiguous light on this double ground. The figure of the *flâneur* makes his way along the stone roadway on two levels as if he were animated by a clockwork mechanism. Inside, where the mechanism is hidden, a song issues from a music box as if from an old toy: 'From my childhood | From my childhood | A song always follows me.' Thanks to this melody he recognizes his surroundings; a childhood speaks to him, which is not the past of his own youth, the most recent, but a childhood lived through earlier. What does it matter whether this childhood was that of an ancestor or his own? He who wanders at length and without aim in the city streets becomes intoxicated. With each step, walking acquires a new force. Shops, cafés, women who smile, constantly appear, and the next street corner, a distant square in the fog, the back of a woman walking ahead of him exert an ever more irresistible attraction. [...] Paris created this type. The strange thing is that it wasn't Rome. What is the reason? In Rome does day-dreaming itself follow already-established itineraries? Is the city too rich in temples, monuments, closed squares, national sanctuaries, to enter wholesale into the dream of the passer-by with each paving-stone, each signboard, each step and each coach-door? [...] A landscape [...] that is indeed what Paris becomes for the *flâneur*. More precisely, he sees the city split itself clearly into two dialectical poles. It opens up to him like a landscape and it encloses him like a drawing-room. This too: the anamnestic intoxication which accompanies the *flâneur* wandering in the city not only finds its nourishment in what the eye can see, but can also latch onto straightforward knowledge, inert facts, which then become things that are lived through, experiences.[20]

The first thing to note here is the connection between motion and metamorphosis. The *flâneur*'s movement, ordained not by overall purpose or direction but by a willingness to have his progress determined by whatever turns up, transforms the city street, endowing it with an extra dimension, another level. For the *flâneur*, as Benjamin puts it brilliantly, all streets slope down and back, if not to the 'realm of the mothers', then to a past, youthful rather than archaic, which is not personal yet has the quality of lived experience. It is the walker's footsteps which call forth this 'surprising echo' or response, making the ground double and the *flâneur*'s progress something that takes place simultaneously on two levels. By virtue of this, the *flâneur* recognizes his surroundings as somehow familiar, and it is this experience he finds intoxicating, which propels him onwards and makes him reluctant to stop as he is solicited by stimuli on all sides. In harmony with something running deep down in the city's heart the *flâneur* feeds not only on what he sees but draws sustenance from simple facts, bits of local lore or legend that cease to be merely inert and take on the character of lived experience.

Obsessional and narrowly focused as his attitude might seem, the *flâneur*'s behaviour, under this description, certainly does not consist in sovereign detachment, nor is voyeuristic *jouissance* either the aim or the prize. A number of the traits encompassed here, including the sense of moving simultaneously on two planes and the way the historical past ('what took place here' — a similar phrase is found in Benjamin and Breton) is made pertinent and available to lived experience, have direct counterparts in Surrealist texts such as *Nadja* and *Les Vases communicants*. But in this guise the *flâneur* is neither a mythologist nor a voyeur but a subject engaged in a multi-faceted interaction with the city.

These aspects are further developed in passages concerned with the 'méditatif' [meditator], an important avatar of the Benjaminian *flâneur*. The category of the *méditatif* features prominently in Benjamin's discussions of Baudelairean allegory. If allegory is what will preserve Baudelaire from the 'abyss' of myth, meditativeness is a half-way stage on the way towards allegory.[21] Meditativeness is in part a defence mechanism against disruptive experience. The meditator differs from the *penseur* [thinker] in that the former does not reflect directly on a phenomenon but dwells on his own reflection on it.[22] To meditate, to turn something over in one's mind, is to draw experience into the realm of one's mental space, which is also the realm of affective memory ('ressouvenir') and of the image. Meditative thought 'is placed under the sign of memory', and it 'places the image at its service'.[23] Part of the 'ivresse' of the *flâneur* lies in pursuing resemblances, and superimposing one experience on another, in response to the 'clins d'œil' [winks] that space keeps administering. For Benjamin the theme of meditativeness brings out the phenomenology of *flânerie*, its characteristics as a *state* that has a number of phases like those triggered by taking a drug.[24] The mode of reflection that constitutes meditation is presented in somatic terms as a mental activity that responds to the body's experience, its susceptibility to bombardment by external stimuli. The meditative is an important category in Benjamin's delineations of the *flâneur* because it brings out the abolition of the boundary between inner and outer which is a vital aspect of the experience of *flânerie*. Meditation is a mode of thinking that, rather than sealing mind from body, abstract thought from sensory experience, amalgamates them in a wider space. It is by dint of 'meditativeness' that for the *flâneur* the experience of 'reading a street name at night can be the equivalent of a transmigration'.[25] Drawn into the subject's mental space, the street name is not simply a practical, historical or picturesque datum. It can trigger (as Proust will amply testify) a parallel journey, by no means exclusively mental since it will draw on the body's memory as well, into the folds of a past experience that is both collective and individual, personal and impersonal.

Benjamin's crucial position in the field of discourse about Paris which we are considering has been greatly bolstered by the recent publication of the *Passagen-Werk* notebooks.[26] In providing a more comprehensive view of Benjamin's thinking over a period of some two decades, the *Konvoluten* indicate the complex layering of Benjamin's thought, revealing many analogies with the Surrealists, particularly

Breton, and with later phases of Parisian wandering and writing. If the theatricality of Parisian space, the interaction of historical memory with present experience, the kinds of subjectivity fostered by exchanges with the city, are among the topics that could be pursued at length in a comparison of Breton and Benjamin, they could also form the basis of extensive comparison with the work of a contemporary writer, Jacques Réda.

## Jacques Réda: Travels in the City

The big city is generally where you travel to or depart from, on a journey elsewhere. If to travel is to be in transit, on the move, betwixt and between, the edge of the city marks the end of travel, its cessation. Of course the traveller may explore cities, but this is an interlude; *travel* will be resumed when the city is once again left behind, for the journey onward or the return. It follows that to adopt the mind-set of the traveller *within* and with reference to the city, and particularly with reference to one's own city, is to do something perverse, subversive, unsettling. It is to break with the utilitarian order, habits and protocols that characterize urban existence. It is to play a game whose rules we invent for ourselves.

Since the publication of *Les Ruines de Paris* (a title that deliberately echoes Baudelaire's *Le Spleen de Paris*) in 1977, most of Réda's writing, in verse and prose, has been concerned with journeys of one sort or another, and several books have focused exclusively on Paris and its immediate environs. I intend to discuss one of these, *Châteaux des courants d'air* [*Castle of air currents*], published in 1986.[27] The book's back cover carries a useful description of the work, written, it is safe to assume, by Réda himself. We are told that the poet's third itinerary in the 'nébuleuse parisienne' will take him from the 15th arrondissement to the 14th, via the Luxembourg gardens and the Place Saint-Sulpice over the Pont-Neuf to the Gare de l'Est and thence on a circular tour of all the city's railway termini. Picking up, perhaps unconsciously, the image of the nebula, with its connotations of space travel, Réda sees his work as combining precise personal observation with 'the state of weightlessness' required by *flânerie*, to produce a particular kind of textual space. To underline the special character of this hybrid space Réda switches from prose to verse. But instead of the freewheeling *vers-libre* familiar from earlier city poetry, he gives us an unorthodox sonnet in rhyming couplets and a metrical form based on an unusual fourteen-syllable line that preserves some of the rhythm of spoken French but at the same time emphasizes constraint and the exercise of a particular faculty or discipline matching that of *flânerie* itself:

> Si ce livre n'est pas un poème, c'est un roman
> Dont les personnages seraient chacun un monument
> Que rencontre, au hasard de sa promenade en spirale,
> Un œil moins curieux de splendeur architecturale
> Que des secrets dissimulées sous le front de Paris.
> Mais quels desseins le promeneur lui-même a-t-il nourris?
> On ne sait plus très bien s'il inventorie ou s'égare
> Ainsi de jardin en église et puis de gare en gare:

A son tour devenu, dans ces châteaux des courants d'air,
Un lieu de passage mental où la ville se perd,
Se retrouve, se plaît peut-être en sa métamorphose
En pages où parfois des vers circulent dans la prose,
D'un pas furtif (il ne faut pas effrayer le lecteur),
Comme se glisse dans la rue un air de vent rôdeur.[28]

[If this book isn't a poem it's a novel: | Each character a monument encountered | By chance in the spiralling drift | Of an eye alert less to architectural splendour | Than to the secrets Paris harbours beneath her brow. | But what of the walker's own hidden designs? | It's hard to know if he's making an inventory or losing himself | As he goes from gardens to church and then from station to station: | Becoming in his turn, among these castles full of draughts, | A space of mental passage where the city is lost, | And refound, enjoying perhaps its metamorphosis | Into pages where sometimes verse stalks amidst the prose, | With a furtive air (the reader mustn't be shocked) | Just as the wandering wind is heard gliding down the street.]

As an extension of *flânerie*, writing propitiates the interaction and exchange between *promeneur* and city. The former's spiralling progress (inspired in fact by the city's own shape) is determined less by a concern to celebrate architectural beauty or to make an inventory of what he sees than by a desire to read the city's mind, to penetrate the secrets under its brow. But this itself is perhaps no more than a cover for the pursuit of the *promeneur*'s own designs, which, if they remain hidden, may perhaps be inferred from the places to which he is drawn — large, empty, open to the four winds — and from the kind of attention he brings to them, as well as from the fact that he is constantly on the move. Réda's poem establishes an important connection between his lack of clear purpose, which makes his writing partly a quest for its own *raison d'être*, an understanding of what lies behind it, and the way, in his *flânerie*, he feels himself becoming a 'lieu de passage mental' where the city itself is repeatedly lost and found. The enjambment 'métamorphose | En pages' entertains first the notion that the city revels in the very process of metamorphosis itself (a theme we will find often in the text), and second, its transmutation into text. At this point the oscillation between prose and verse, a feature of some of the texts in *Châteaux*, is presented less as an apt way of celebrating or capturing the city than of mimicking a general principle of surreptitious, furtive, almost imperceptible presence, as of a wind blowing down a street or a *promeneur* uncertain of his credentials.

Central to *Châteaux des courants d'air*, and to the modes of city travel practised by Réda, is a shifting set of parallels between circulation in physical space, circulation in mental space and circulation in textual space, and hence between city, mind and text. But this does not make the city merely a pretext for enactments of self. The secret designs of the *promeneur* reveal themselves to involve anonymity and self-dissolution, a desire to become no more than an instrument serving to reveal the city's own reality. The moves and gambits of the *promeneur* serve to vary the angles at which the city is refracted through the prism of his mind, moods and words. The opening text emphasizes that it is the walker's own moves that prompt the city to reveal itself to him. He has to set things in motion by the primordial act of setting off on a journey in the city, finding pretexts for new itineraries. But if things go well the perceptions subsequently to be recorded will have stemmed from a symbiosis of such a kind that it is apparently the city's own reflections on itself which have been registered. No doubt this is an illusion and a device — a kind of extended prosopopoeia where the inanimate is given the power of speech. But it is based on a salient feature of the city that matches the *promeneur*. Like him the city exists in time, is constantly changing, possesses a history. Réda's writing always suggests that it is the city's constant metamorphosis which is at the heart of its reality. Monuments, streets, *quartiers*, utilities, institutions, customs are all, at any given time — that of any particular foray we might make — at some point in a process of mutation. This may be rapid or gradual, incipient or long-established, spectacular or unobtrusive, consistent or inconsistent with previously established patterns of development. But above all, this mutability makes the city a differential space made up of innumerable processes through which individual components are changing in appearance, function or importance but also changing in relation to each other. Seen this way the city is not so much the sum of its parts as the latent principle of a mutability whose impact may be registered the moment we decide to focus on it. If *this* is the city, then to apprehend its mobility, its play of differences, will require a corresponding mobility on the part of the witness. Réda's writing often conveys the sense of responding to the city's pressing desire for an act of witness that can reveal it to itself. This is what he means by turning himself into a 'lieu de passage mental' where the city 'se plaît peut-être à sa métamorphose'. The city needs to find expression by being filtered through the homologous zone of the *promeneur*'s mind, and the *promeneur* feels compelled to externalize what the city is doing to (and in) his head. In doing so he also realizes a clearly marked desire for self-dissolution — escape from self — which, while being a personal trait in the writer, chimes both with certain ways of theorizing about writing itself, and with the experience of the city.[29] The city manifests itself in endless traits which confer on it, by analogy, certain kinds of personality but do not alter its profound anonymity. To identify with the city is to aspire to the pure anonymity of metamorphosis, of being nothing other than an endless turnover of perceptions and connections.

It is in fact moving home rather than walking that sets things in motion in the opening text of *Châteaux*. Although he only moves a few hundred metres in the same arrondissement, Réda observes that the southerly direction of his move matches the 'mouvement giratoire' [gyratory motion] of the city itself as it spirals outwards from Notre-Dame in a shape reflected (or created) by the organization of the twenty arrondissements. His new vantage-point gives him an insight into another aspect of the city's movement, the existence of thoroughfares, like the one running parallel to the bend in the Seine from the Pont Mirabeau to the Pont de Tolbiac, which, sometimes under different names, cut across several arrondissements creating connections between quite disparate sectors of the city (in this case the deserted Citroën factory, the hidden gardens of Alésia, the valleys of the Parc Montsouris and the 'farouche autonomie' [fierce autonomy] of the Butte-aux-Cailles). Such avenues, another example being the rue des Pyrénées, add a particular 'dimension mentale' to the 'corps de la ville':

> Rues en perpétuel mouvement comme dans les rêves, où c'est la ville qui se perd et navigue en tous sens à travers les strates de pierre, de vie et de mémoire qui forment son épaisseur, réinventant à mesure les lois de son instable gravitation.[30]

> [Streets in perpetual motion as in dreams, where it's the city which dreams itself, navigating in all directions through the strata of rock, life and memory which make up its layers, progressively reinventing the laws of its unstable gravitation.]

This passage is typical of the kind of reversal we noted earlier. A physical datum (long streets) prompts a series of recognitions that are then represented as belonging to the city itself, which has given them concrete expression in the phenomenon under description. This shift — from how Paris might be conceived to how it might conceive of itself — is echoed by a shift from seeing Paris as a 'ville imaginaire' [imaginary city] to seeing it as a 'ville imaginative' [imaginative city] actively involved in self-invention, even, Réda adds wryly, mythomania:

> (Tous ses endroits où elle se prend pour Changhai, Chicago, Conakry), sans cesse en quête d'elle-même sous le front rassurant que nous tendent les monuments de sa gloire.[31]

> [(All these places where she thinks she's Shanghai, Chicago, Conakry) ever in quest of herself behind the reassuring brow presented by the monuments of her glory.]

Réda's next move in this passage involves a further reversal whereby the *promeneur* or witness becomes an extension or projection of the city rather than vice versa:

> Peu à peu ses métamorphoses influent sur le promeneur. Il se pressent à son tour, imaginé, promené comme l'antenne vagabonde de la ville dans ses humeurs passagères.[32]

> [Little by little her metamorphoses take effect on the walker. In his turn he feels he is being imagined, borne along like a wandering, reflective antenna of the city in its changing moods.]

This notion of the 'promeneur promené' is central to Réda's apprehension of the city and to the poetic logic of urban wandering. Whimsical and anthropomorphic as it is, a passage like the foregoing, in addition to being brilliantly observed and executed, communicates a profound desire for a particular kind of rapport with the city, and via the city with the self. To feel oneself so *absorbed* by the city is to enjoy a feeling of inclusion and participation. In becoming one of the city's antennae, the observer feels as if 'my head, which it contains, becomes the space which the city surveys' — the city is now the '*promeneur*'. And so:

> Le voici confondu avec les rues, avec la lente, expansive giration que la ville opère continûment sur son axe invisible qui est le temps, où — comme l'énonce la devise de ses armes — elle flotte et ne sombre jamais, liant à sa pérennité ces promeneurs dont le destin et peut-être le dessein secret sont de disparaître.[33]

[Here he is, fused with the streets, with the slow, spreading gyration the city performs continuously on her invisible axis, that of time where — as is proclaimed in the motto on her coat of arms — she floats and does not sink, linking to her own perennity those strollers whose destiny, and perhaps secret design, is to disappear.]

A number of the texts in *Châteaux* end on this note of inclusion, fusion, dissolution or absorption of the subject into the city. One of the *promeneur*'s arts is to find points of entry into the city's secret channels. Réda favours features that link parts of the city together, underlining its hidden unity in diversity, as in the case of the long arteries mentioned above, or railway and Métro lines. Derelict areas, *terrains vagues*, building sites screened by palisades have a particular appeal because they provide breathing space and pauses for thought to gather. To concoct a route around the city — as Réda does in *Châteaux des courants d'air* — motivated not by official itineraries but by a strong associative logic is to make manifest its hidden cohesiveness. The perception of resemblances and associations prompted by visual appearance, particularly as modified by temporal factors such as times of day or atmospheric conditions, is paramount. But the lore of the city, the wealth of assorted practical and historical information in the possession of an educated citizen is also often to the fore, as in Breton and Benjamin.

Cultural memory plays an especially important role in the sequence entitled 'D'une rive à l'autre' [From one bank to the other], which features samples of four generic spaces — a garden (the Luxembourg), a church (Saint-Sulpice), a bridge (the Pont-Neuf), and an arcade (the Passage Véro-Déodat). The text on the Luxembourg gardens illustrates the strong allegorizing tendency in the city-walker's engagement with his surroundings. Not especially interested in the niceties of official history (the precise identity of the eighteen queens and 'grande dames' represented in sculpture), Réda nevertheless sees every detail of the garden's layout as emblematic and identifies its contribution to his overall sense of the garden as 'une vraie patrie spirituelle' [a true spiritual homeland]. The account of Saint-Sulpice mentions all the obvious features, including the Delacroix frescoes described by Baudelaire and the statues of great churchmen in the square. But the striking thing about Réda's text is the way he combines historical and topographical reference with entirely personal impressions in a synthesis which succeeds in placing the emphasis neither on objective facts nor on private associations but on what one could call the human specificities of this particular place, the particular imprints it might leave on an open mind. Characteristically, throughout Réda's evocation of Saint-Sulpice one has the impression that he is taking us at once on a tour of a physical space we may know well ourselves and on a tour of his own mental space as refracted through its responsiveness to Saint-Sulpice. This is especially perceptible in a long final paragraph that describes the changing impressions of the facade as the sun sets, 'les lentes métamorphoses de sa substance au contact du couchant' [the slow metamorphoses of its substance brought about by contact with the setting sun], where the church appears narrowly to avoid total obliteration as it is consumed by purifying fires in accordance with its capacity to stand as the precarious materialization of 'le génie de l'église' [the genius of the church].[34]

Réda approaches the Pont-Neuf obliquely via his indignation at the permission granted to the sculptor Christo to wrap it up for a week, a criminal act in so far as it represented symbolically the occlusion of a site with unbroken links to the origin of the city in Roman times. For Réda the sturdy Pont-Neuf, resembling teams of oxen labouring in opposite directions, has since the seventeenth century acted as a fixative preserving 'la lente rêverie de l'Histoire' [the slow daydream of History] against the kind of dissolution threatened by Christo.

> La lente rêverie de l'Histoire, le long de la Seine qui n'en a pas, a déposé, superposé ses preuves de pierre et, dans les têtes, des entassements obscurs de souvenirs anonymes et de savoir qu'on croit oublier, mais sur lesquels distraitement on s'appuie comme sur le parapet du quai de Conti, pour s'abandonner à la douceur du soir tout à coup immobile.[35]

> [The slow daydream of History, along the Seine which has none, has deposited, superimposed, its proofs of stone and, in people's minds, dark piles of anonymous memories and knowledge one thinks one has forgotten, but on which one leans as on the parapet of the Quai de Conti, to abandon oneself to the sweetness of the evening which suddenly becomes still.]

Playing on the opposition between time and the timeless, history and its absence, motion and immobility, transience and permanence, the physical and the mental, this passage gives forceful and original expression to the idea that the monuments among which we casually linger in the city are concretizations of a history that is also deposited, less securely, in our mental reflexes and passive knowledge.

To write about the Parisian passages or arcades is inevitably to pay homage to Aragon and Benjamin, but Réda's account of a visit to one of these, while appropriately phantasmagoric (it is one of the more narrative texts in *Châteaux des courants d'air*), homes in on the rather sinister, abandoned quality of the passages, their 'loss of aura' in Benjamin's phrase, rather than on the marvellous. In fact Réda's text also constitutes an allegorical reflection on the limits, the precariousness of his own stance. In the end he presents himself as a ghost who haunts only an image of the places he traverses, and compares himself to the legendary crew of figures in portraits who, it is said, under cover of darkness, step down from their pedestals and canvases in the Louvre to enjoy a limited and secretive freedom.[36] The meditation seizes first on the checker-board tiled floor the passages have in common, which, set diagonally, makes the movements of the rate passers-by resemble moves in a game of live chess. For Réda the passages convey a feeling that one is being observed from on high, but with an indifference that serves to suggest both one's freedom (one can make any move one wants) and its futility. More positively, the notion of chess moves conjures up a fantasy whereby not only all the other surviving passages, clustered in a small group of arrondissements in central Paris, but also certain adjacent buildings become available to imaginative scrutiny, allowing the 'accès phantasmagorique' of the image-making *flâneur*.[37] Seen from this mental vantage-point these other spaces — the musty theatres round the Palais-Royal, the Bourse, the Banque de France, the Bibliothèque Nationale and the Hôtel des Postes — are revealed to possess family resemblances: emptiness, theatricality, darkness, alternations of frenetic activity and quiescence, noise and silence, endless repetitions and series — of gestures (in the theatre), objects (in the library), financial transactions (at the Bourse), messages (at the post office).

What is striking in this text is the way it emerges as an allegory of Réda's imaginative access from one space to others, and more especially from one dimension into others. His footsteps in the passage, as he moves a few paces to right or left or tries a knight's move, seem to enable corresponding exploratory movements in other zones, which, if he can link them by imaginative exploration, allow his 'entrée en communication'. But the allegory also reveals the dangers of a game that has only one player. As he emerges at nightfall, Réda's final perception of the passages turns them into a series of railway coaches relegated to the sidings and making up one long train which at night is switched on to a single-track line going nowhere: 'J'étais le seul voyageur de ce convoi sans destination, et je pouvais avancer longtemps encore, en esprit, dans un monde dont toutes les cloisons s'évanouissent pour m'ouvrir une interminable impasse' [I was the only passenger of this convoy going nowhere, and I could make my way for a long while yet, in my mind, through a world where all barriers melted away giving me access to an interminable impasse].[38] An 'interminable impasse': a melancholy conclusion, but only a provisional one since the text ends with the enchanting sight of the great window — 'la rosace illuminée' — of the Gare de l'Est, galvanizing the *flâneur* onwards to a tour of the capital's 'univers ferroviaire' [railway universe].

## The Once and Future City

Having largely thus far looked at Breton, Benjamin and Réda discretely, I now want to consider more directly the general field of discourse about Paris to which they may be said to contribute. When some of its basic constituents have been reviewed I will examine whether this discursive and practical field has any future. Central to it are questions of knowledge, power and possession. For the dominant discourses since the mid-nineteenth century, the project of 'knowing Paris' could be construed in terms of description, regulation and emulation. Rastignac's 'It's between us now!' (A nous deux maintenant!), addressed to the city at the climax of Balzac's *Le Père Goriot* from the heights of the Père-Lachaise cemetery, is the exact literary reflection of the crucial linkage between the rise of capital, the growth of the city, and the possibility of individual fortune. An immediate contrast can be made with the line, also addressed to Paris, which concludes the projected epilogue Baudelaire wrote for the second edition of *Les Fleurs du mal*: 'Tu m'as donné ta boue et j'en ai fait de l'or' [You gave me your mud and I turned it into gold].[39] Rather than wanting to emulate the city whose attributes he identifies in a long enumeration, Baudelaire represents himself as an alchemist who has sought to distil the quintessence of the city. Both the Balzacian novelist and the Baudelairean poet lay claim to superior knowledge about Paris. The difference lies in the alignment with other modes of cognition. While Balzacian knowledge (strongly identified with power) participates in the dynamic of the age, the Baudelairean slant is tangential, oblique, ironically dispossessed. Balzacian knowledge is rooted in description and anecdote, while Baudelairean knowledge eschews these in favour of less palpable qualities. In the important preface he wrote for his prose poems Baudelaire evokes the quest for a literary style, a rhythmical prose capable of rendering the 'innumerable connections' that characterize 'giant cities' and especially of communicating their impact on the city-dweller prone 'aux mouvements lyriques de l'âme, aux ondulations de la rêverie, aux soubresauts de la conscience' [to the lyrical movements of the soul, the undulations of reverie and the somersaults of conscience].[40] In thus linking the urban to questions of textuality and subjectivity Baudelaire certainly switches the prime emphasis from the observable characteristics of the metropolis itself (very few of which are described in the poems) on to the repercussions of city life in the individual. But the subjective existence thus foregrounded is wholly bound up with its *exposure* to the city. The subjectivity explored in the prose poems is in no sense a haven from urban reality; on the contrary it is the city's place of resonance and recognition. The prominent narrator-*flâneur* of the poems is generally abroad in the city streets, exposed to the shocks and stimuli of the crowd, aspiring, like the Painter of Modern Life, to resemble a 'kaleidoscope equipped with consciousness', a mental space able to register the endlessly changing patterns of experience. This mode of subjectivity, rooted in the rapid interchange between the mind, the senses and a constantly shifting environment, is intrinsically urban, and it founds a category of experience that cannot be subsumed into existing models. In the two-way encounter between mind and city, a process unfolds that affords a specific type of cognition, and the Baudelairean stance towards the city is explicitly epistemic, fuelled by a drive towards a knowledge that cannot be separated from this interactive process.

Baudelaire, then, may be said to announce the possibility of a mode of experience in which questions of language (how is this experience to be articulated and preserved?), questions of subjectivity (who am I in the city?), and questions of space (how can I best approach the city?) intersect. And it is the further extensions of this possibility, as it informs a rich tradition in European thought and poetry, which we have investigated in Breton, Benjamin and Réda. For Breton, knowing the city is dependent on attunement to a particular wavelength, a process involving the adoption of an attitude of lyrical expectancy and availability to experience. The quasi-scientific, documentary tone Breton adopts in his reports on the fruits of his urban wandering reflects the sense of operating at the frontiers of knowledge. In a number of places in the *Passagen-Werk* Benjamin makes it clear that one of his central concerns is with the articulation of a particular dimension or category of experience — *Erlebnis* (or lived experience) rather than *Erfahrung*. The *flâneur* aspires neither to knowledge or possession. Like the Surrealist surrendering to the flow of unconscious thoughts, or aimlessly wandering the streets, he cultivates a kind of 'oisiveté' [idleness], a suspension of purposive activity that favours the eruption of phantasmagoric experience, where the spectacle of outer events becomes imbued with subjective resonance.[41] As in the case of Baudelaire and the Surrealists, resemblance and analogy are crucial. 'Resemblance is the organon of (lived) experience':[42] prey to 'the demon of analogy' (Mallarmé), the *flâneur* wanders through a city that has become a 'forest of symbols' (Baudelaire) or a cryptogram (Breton). The work of Réda is fully continuous with this tradition of a non-anecdotal, non-sociological, non-mythological, but profoundly allegorical approach to the city, rooted in the solitary experience of an obsessive but idle subject. To be sure, Réda's writing is more descriptive than that of the other writers we are considering, but his descriptions rarely seek to inform; rather, description is a way of trying to keep in play an elusive hut vital form of experience that has been engendered by the adoption of an inherently unteleological stance.

For all three writers the experience of urban wandering involves temporal dislocation. But if the future is suspended as the present becomes suffused with the past, we always remain in a border zone, between now and then, and between the city's own historical archive and that of the individual. Similarly, at the level of identity, the exploration of individual subjectivity goes hand in hand with the revelation of the city's own reality. Magnetized by the city the urban *promeneur* goes on and on, seeking encounters that may prove revelatory (Breton); absorbing street names that act like 'intoxicating substances which make our perception richer in strata', and turn the city into a 'linguistic cosmos' (Benjamin); or constantly experiencing self-dissolution through the uncanny feeling that one's mind has become a conduit through which the city gives expression to its own sense of itself (Réda).

For all these writers Paris is a hall of mirrors, a place of recognitions, a metaphor for inner space, but with the proviso that the 'inner' cannot be separated from the 'outer' — that experience, identity, temporality, are only given through relation and interaction between subjectivity and objectivity, mind and world. This inherently phenomenological emphasis should alert us to the prevailing ethos that informs the poetic tradition of Parisian wandering. Solitary and individualistic as it might seem, this tradition in fact construes Paris as a place of relations; an organic totality which, in its very heterogeneousness, holds forth the (ever-deferred) promise of unity. Central to this tradition is the way it opposes ways of reducing the city to its constituent parts — objectifying its *quartiers*, dissecting its *métiers*, celebrating its piecemeal charm or metonymically extolling the whole city through one of its many aspects. Opposing such positivism, the Baudelairean tradition construes Paris as a site of melancholy but ever-hopeful experience that questions and subverts the reductive categories of the architect, the planner, the politician or the orthodox *littérateur*. Here Paris becomes the name of a dimension of experience where totality is imminent but never actual, a zone of possibility for which the city streets are the ever full, ever vacant, setting.

If the Parisian poetic field first delineated by Baudelaire has subsisted through a series of shifts and transformations to find striking new forms of expression in the writing of Réda, is it none the less an irrelevant anachronism in the age of McDonald's and Microsoft? Is Réda the last *flâneur*, a throwback to a superseded cultural phase? A recent book by Jean-Christophe Bailly suggests that such a verdict could be premature. *La Ville à l'œuvre* [The city at work] reflects the widespread concern for the future of cities that has placed architecture, planning and urban ecology at the centre of contemporary concerns. This is the context in which the ideas of the Surrealists (and the Situationists who emulated them), of Benjamin and Certeau, find continued or enhanced resonances. Bailly is a poet and essayist, an *écrivain* who writes about cities. 'Urban reality is sick', he observes.[43] But if so, he continues, we need to think hard about what it consists of in the first place. Back to basics: what *is* a city?

> La ville existe en masse et se disperse en grains, mais ce qui l'engendre, ce qui la fait être et devenir, c'est le mouvement de celui qui la parcourt. La loi est simple: plus ce mouvement est dans l'écart, le caprice, moins il est soumis aux canons restrictifs qui cherchent à l'enserrer, plus la ville a de chances d'être identifiée, révélée, distrait [...] La ville ainsi parcourue, ainsi 'ionisée' par la démarche qui la traverse [...] s'éclaire de l'intérieur.[44]

> [The city exists as a mass and disperses itself in seeds, but what engenders it, making it exist and develop, is the movement of the people who traverse it. The law is simple: the more aberrant and capricious the movement, the less it is submitted to restrictive canons which serve to hem it in, the more the city has the chance to be identified, revealed, distracted. [... .] Traversed in this way, 'ionized' by the manner in which it is crossed, [...] the city is lit up from within.]

Bailly emphasizes the liberating quality of urban space. 'La fonction urbaine' [the urban function], as he calls the basic essence of the urban, serves to create identity and community by facilitating access, making symmetries and resemblances, and encouraging common endeavours.[45] But 'the urban function' is under threat from the tyranny of bad architecture, soulless planning and indifference to what makes cities work, notably the basic unit of urban language, the *street*, and the 'ruissellement de paroles' [stream of words], the endless stories, which animate it. Keeping the street and the city alive depends on understanding their grammar and generating the new utterances on which they thrive. And for Bailly the principal agency of this process is walking, what he calls the 'grammaire generative des jambes' [generative grammar of the legs].[46] Like Réda, he insists that it is movement around it which engenders the city: what counts, Bailly says — echoing Michel de Certeau's analyses and his similar metaphorics of language and walking — is the 'micro-history of trajectories': it is these which make up the city's archive of memories, its 'dépot d'images' [store of images]. In terms that again echo Réda, Bailly stresses the active interpenetration of personal and collective memory, seeing the city as 'une mémoire d'elle-même qui s'offre à être pénétrée et qui s'infiltre en retour dans la mémoire active de qui la traverse' [a memory of itself which invites penetration and at the same time infiltrates itself in the active memory of the individual who traverses it].[47] The city-walker who is conscious of the space he traverses can become a participant in the palimpsest of the city, part of its archive. Indeed for Bailly, as for Benjamin, the act of deciphering urban signals is what he calls 'an immediate form of experience'.[48] There is urgent need to restore and perpetuate cities at the level of their *imaginaire*, in a struggle against various forms of dispersion. At the end of the book Bailly underlines the utopian strain in his lyrical analyses. But he insists that if 'urban reality is sick' we need to maintain a spirit of utopian projection, to keep insisting on the endless capacities for *meaning* a city offers and the wider patterns — however provisional and precarious — into which these meanings can cohere. The discourse and practice of Paris inaugurated by Baudelaire has proved flexible and resilient because it is rooted in abiding anxieties and aspirations. If it still has a future this is because, more than ever, the city — and Paris quintessentially — is the arena where vital connections between space, language and subjectivity are played out. Still in opposition, wilfully archaic in some respects, the discourse of the *promeneur*, the knowledge and pleasure it sponsors, may continue to offer hope and resistance.

## Notes

1. Baudelaire, *Œuvres complètes*, ed. by Claude Pichois, 2 vols (Paris: Gallimard, 1975–76), II, 496.
2. Ibid., II, 692.
3. Ibid., I, 291.
4. Ibid., I, 91.
5. Guillaume Apollinaire, *Œuvres en prose complètes*, ed. by P. Caizergues and M. Décaudin, 3 vols (Paris: Gallimard, 1989–93), III, 3–10.
6. For a useful general survey see Marie-Claire Banquart, *Paris des surréalistes* (Paris: Seghers, 1972). On Aragon see Yvette Gindine, *Aragon prosateur surréaliste* (Geneva: Droz, 1966). On Breton see Jean Gaulmier, 'Remarques sur le thème de Paris chez André Breton' in *Les Critiques de notre temps et Breton*, ed. by Marguerite Bonnet (Paris: Garnier, 1974).
7. Walter Benjamin, *Paris: capitale du dix-neuvième siècle*, ed. by Rolf Tiedemann, trans. by Jean Lacoste, 2nd edn (Paris: Cerf, 1993), pp. 555–56.
8. Walter Benjamin, 'Surrealism' in *One-way Street and Other Writings* (London: NLB, 1979), pp. 227 and 229.
9. Margaret Cohen, *Profane Illumination: Walter Benjamin and the Paris of Surrealist Revolution* (Berkeley, CA: University of California Press, 1993).
10. Benjamin, *Paris*, pp. 14–16.
11. Ibid, p. 842.
12. Ibid, p. 447.
13. Ibid, p. 449.
14. Ibid, p. 434.
15. Ibid, p. 459.
16. Ibid.
17. Ibid.
18. Ibid, p. 470.
19. Prendergast, *Paris in the Nineteenth Century* (Oxford: Blackwell, 1992), pp. 134–35.
20. Ibid, pp. 876–77.
21. Ibid, p. 337.
22. Ibid, p. 384.
23. Ibid, p. 385.
24. Ibid, p. 439.
25. Ibid, p. 831.
26. See also Susan Buck-Morss, *The Dialectics of Seeing: Walter Benjamin and the Arcades Project* (Cambridge, MA: MIT Press, 1991), *Benjamin: Philosophy, History, Aesthetics*, ed. by Gary Smith (Chicago, IL: University of Chicago Press, 1989), *Walter Benjamin et Paris*, ed. by Heinz Wissman (Paris: Cerf, 1986).
27. See *Les Ruines de Paris* (Paris: Gallimard, 1977), *Hors les murs* (Paris: Gallimard, 1987), *Le Sens de la marche* (Paris: Gallimard, 1992). For an interesting treatment of the relation between Réda and Benjamin see Catherine Coquio, 'Le Retour éternel du flâneur', *Approches de Jacques Réda* (Pau: Presses universitaires de Pau, 1994), 45–64.

28. *Châteux des courants d'air*, back cover.
29. On this aspect of Réda see my article, 'Jacques Réda and the Commitments of Poetry', in this volume.
30. *Châteaux*, p. 13.
31. Ibid.
32. Ibid.
33. Ibid., p. 14.
34. Ibid., p. 84.
35. Ibid., p. 89.
36. Ibid., p. 95.
37. Ibid.
38. Ibid., p. 96.
39. Baudelaire, op. cit, I, 192.
40. Ibid., pp. 275–76.
41. Benjamin, *Paris*, especially pp. 797–804.
42. Ibid., p. 799.
43. Bailly, *La Ville à l'œuvre* (Paris: Bertoin, 1992), p. 175.
44. Ibid., p. 26.
45. Ibid., p. 10.
46. Ibid., pp. 23–42.
47. Ibid., p. 57.
48. Ibid., p. 34.

# 7

# The Liberator of Desire

*Review of André Breton, Œuvres complètes, vol. i*
*(Paris: Gallimard 'Pléiade', 1988)*

André Breton has long been due for a Pléiade edition of his works, and this first volume (there will be four) takes us to 1930, from the early neo-symbolist poems, via the manifestos of 1924 and 1929, to the remarkable collaborative works of 1930: *Ralentir travaux* [*Slow down men at work*], poems written conjointly with Paul Éluard and René Char over a few days in the Vaucluse, and *L'Immaculée conception* [*The immaculate conception*], a series of texts in which Breton and Éluard applied some of the main vectors of surrealist writing — *écriture automatique*, systematic *détournement* of canonical writings — to the evocation of a human existence from foetus to cadaver. The *Champs magnétiques* of 1920, the poems of *Clair de terre* and the essays of *Les Pas perdus*, perhaps above all the prose work *Nadja* (1928), are the peaks; now, however, we see them not as a range of discrete paperbacks but as features of a landscape scarred by the outcrops and blowholes of constant bubbling beneath the surface. Breton collected up some of his shorter pieces, but a great many have remained inaccessible in defunct reviews, or, unpublished, in various archives. The three groups of *Inédits* and *Alentours* into which all this has been divided contain some of the most fascinating material in the volume. And, as much as the major texts, it attracts the swarms of profuse annotation which are the Pléiade trademark. By rights another major work, *Le Surréalisme et la peinture* (1928), should have been here, but it has regrettably been held over on the grounds that in its last expanded edition it was published in 1965. Otherwise Marguerite Bonnet's editing is flawless. As in her authoritative *Andre Breton et l'Aventure surréaliste* (1975, recently reissued by José Corti), she combines the virtues of an established academic critic with the advantages of a longstanding friendship with Breton and with members of his circle.

It has long been routine to condescend somewhat to Breton, and to be superior about his relations with the movement he launched and then animated, through thick and thin, for forty years. Surrealism is likened to a banana republic, with Breton as its crackpot dictator, or to a schism with Breton as its heresiarch. These and other tiresome misrepresentations naturally pay little heed to the hundreds of pages of varied, inventive and often brilliant writing, much of it still very fresh, that we find in this volume and look forward to in its successors. Breton can be dull sometimes, as any good writer can, but his books are like no others, and each seems to have the uncanny property of simultaneously borrowing from an established genre, forging a new one, and somehow subverting both from within. The first *Manifeste* mixes the discourses of the essay, the memoir and the scientific treatise, while at the same time purporting to be the preface to a series of poetic texts; *Nadja* is part case history, part diary and part manifesto.

Breton did have a magus side (Maurice Martin du Gard spotted it early and, wittily, called him a 'mage d'Espinal'), but it derives partly from the seriousness of his central project, which was to try and make poetic revelation a force to change human existence. In trying to create a movement rather than shaping his own oeuvre, and in seeking, out of genuine if sometimes wayward intellectual curiosity, to create a fusion of poetry with psychology, philosophical speculation and politics, while never allowing it to be entirely subordinate to them, he paid a price. He never wanted to be a *littérateur*, and all his work has a provisional, *ad hoc* quality. One of the interesting things about surrealism is its rejection of the cult of form which remained such a massive plank in the modernist programme — Yeats, Pound, Eliot, Joyce, Valéry — but also a beam in the eye when it came to socio-political action. However, Breton's attempts to remake the canon, promoting important writers such as de Sade (but also some duds), while immensely prescient and influential, were also counterproductive since they helped to turn surrealism into a ghetto outside the literary metropolis. It is remarkably difficult to situate Breton *vis-à-vis* other writers of his generation, and while this is in some measure to his credit, it has not generally been to his advantage.

Breton once observed that surrealism originated in 'a wide-ranging operation bearing on language'. The latter-day prestige or the movement's visual legacy often obscures the fact that it was as self-professed nominalists, intoxicated by the power of words seemingly to impinge on reality, that the surrealists began writing. Breton always stressed that poetry was aural before it was visual: Rimbaud and Lautréamont listened first, illumination came afterwards. This was initially part of the symbolist bequest which Breton grasped avidly but initially squandered on fey pastiches of Mallarmé and Valéry.

A series of events — the First World War, experience of treating neurological disturbance as a young medic, the Dada movement, the discovery of Freud — added ballast to Breton's sense of the gravity of *la chose linguistique*. The Dadaists, sickened by propaganda, had wished to subject language to every indignity, but their varied affronts seemed to Breton to lay bare the remarkable resilience of sense. What he gleaned of Freudian theory at this stage tended to confer ontological prestige on even the tiniest verbal scraps thrown up in our mental lives. 'Surréalisme' was initially no more than a name for the method he devised, and first tried out with Philippe Soupault in 1919, for tapping the ceaseless flow of discourse just beneath the surface of consciousness. It was a decisive move to confer honorific status on the products, and to publish it on a par with, if not as, 'poetry'. This sowed the seeds of much confusion and malpractice, in the face of which Breton was to write some years later that the history of what was by then called *écriture automatique* had been continuous calamity. He came to insist that it wasn't a recipe for getting poems on the cheap, though part of the impetus had come from a repudiation of the work-ethic poetics of neo-symbolism, incarnated by his erstwhile mentor, Paul Valéry.

Breton's relationship with Valéry cries out for analysis along the lines of Harold Bloom's 'anxiety of influence'. As late as 1920, the older poet was a witness at Breton's wedding to Simone Kahn: by 1923 Breton had written his epitaph. In a marvellous text, from early 1924, Breton staged a subtle confrontation between his view of the poetic process and Valéry's. The piece consists of the contents of a notebook in which, over a few months, Breton had jotted down addresses, quotations, remarks about other writers (including Valéry), odd phrases and titles, short meditations on chance, memory and so on. Suddenly, after all these stutters, there is a poem, 'La Mort rose', bearing a title noted a few weeks earlier. Far from being the product of graft and craft, a 'feast of the intellect', a monument to the laborious genesis in which a scaffolding is provided for the meagre 'vers donnés', the incoherencies of the Pythia, the poem comes in its own due time, a fruit of parthenogenesis, at once quite alien, unprecedented, and redolent of the subjectivity from which it emerges.

Yet, like most of Breton's poems and 'automatic' texts, 'La Mort rose', for all its majestic indifference to what Rimbaud called 'current appearances', is riven by anxieties. Typically, the poem is at one level no more than an allegory of its own emergence, the linguistic energies which drive it being personified in the shape of the poetic 'I'. His adventures — endless scenarios of liberation — form a kind of mental picaresque, as the onward rush of a discourse seeking above all to keep going necessitates new twists and turns of the narrative thread, but at the same time devalues them by revealing intermittently that we are in a wordscape.

Breton saw poetic language as a liberator of desire, and liberated desire as the key to a transformed universe, but he also had a feel for desire's darker side, and the possible collusion with it which an addiction to the verbal might constitute. He suppressed much of his 'automatic' writing, and it is amusing to witness the return of the repressed, duly sanitized by the apparatus of scholarship (*Poisson soluble* is here double the familiar length). In a fascinating letter to Jean Gaulmier, Breton admits the feeling of nausea and 'écœurement' which these texts inspire in him. This material is much more personal than it seems, not because it reveals guilty secrets but because even when language insists on its own prerogatives it acts as a channel for desires deeper than self-expression. Reading the poems of *Clair de terre* we can watch Breton, as he spills out his obsessions with things in miniature, with furry woodland creatures, with metamorphosis and surprise, or becomes captivated by a spectral image of himself disseminated in the workings of the language he generates; and we can monitor his addiction to the spasmodic recognitions such writing affords, but also to the equally frequent experiences of exclusion — as he is spurned by the words he spawns.

*Nadja* transposed these intermittences of recognition and rebuttal into the sphere of lived experience, making the Paris streets, with their signboards, flea markets, haphazard encounters, another sort of text. (Some of Breton's best writing is dedicated to the street: 'la rue, que je croyais capable de livrer à ma vie ses surprenants détours, la rue avec ses inquiétudes et ses regards, était mon élément: j'y prenais comme nulle part ailleurs le vent de l'éventuel' [the street, which I thought could give my life its surprising detours, the street, with its worries and its glances, was my element: there, as nowhere else, I experienced the power of possibility]). *Nadja*'s opening question, 'Qui suis-je?' [Who am I?] (I, 647), is initially reformulated in terms of the ghostly identity that certain uncanny events — coincidences, impulses, unforeseen encounters — seem to portend. By adopting a non-utilitarian, expectant stance during his endless urban perambulations, Breton goes less in hope of apparitions than of signals emitted on his own particular frequency. The pale, ectoplasmic photographs — so vital and original a feature of the book — eschewing all artistry, do not so much anchor the improbable in communally attested space, as dissolve the latter's objectivity, making the city and its inhabitants into weird emanations of Breton's psyche.

Nadja herself, first sighted in the late afternoon of 4 October 1926, in the rue Lafayette, is an apparition, and as such she disturbs the euphoric solubility of mind, city and text. Everything about her — 'les choses qui sont près d'elle' [the things which are close to her] (I, 701) — her strange utterances, predictive and apodictic, her drawings, her *comportement* — make her an incarnation of the spirit of surrealism: another surface on which Breton can catch reflections of his ghostly countenance. Yet the woman herself, with a sordid past and no future, the vulnerable creature of flesh and blood who will succumb to the madness which Breton, clued-up as he was on this score, failed in his dazzled state to detect, proves insoluble, unassimilable to the manipulative energies of the poet's desires. Our sense of Nadja's reality — the acknowledged but evaded blind spot of Breton's text — is greatly enhanced by Bonnet's moving annotations, which record the fate, in the dreary asylums of France *entre deux guerres*, of Léona-Camille-Ghislaine D., born Lille, 1902, died Hôpital de Perray-Vaucluse (Epinay-sur-Orge), 1941. Breton found he couldn't love Nadja; it is not for us to blame him for that. But when we think of her destiny it is hard not to feel some dismay at the opportunistic way he ended his book — her book — with a celebration of the convulsive beauty of *amour fou*, inspired by what was to be a fairly brief infatuation with Suzanne Muzard (again Bonnet's notes are invaluable here).

Yet it would be wrong to see in this the triumph of a surrealist ideology. *Nadja*'s coherence derives from its seismographic sensitivity to Breton's *imaginaire*. As such it is consistent with the way, in Breton, surrealism was not a matter of slogans, or literary terrorism, but an existential project, enacted in remarkably innovatory literary forms, albeit one which, in being pursued in the medium of words, always risked assuring the perpetuation of what it sought to transform — the dogged dominion of things as they are, the selfishness of desire, and literature's easy victories over experience.

# 8

# Le Film des durées

*Review of Georges Sebbag,* Imprononçable jour de ma naissance: 17DRE 13RETON *(Paris: Éditions Jean-Michel Place, 1988)*

Georges Perec wondered what it would be like to write a life-story based exclusively on the bedrooms you had slept in, or the bus-tickets you had preserved, or your cheque-stubs. In his later years Roland Barthes was fascinated with biography and what he called 'un retour amical de l'auteur' [the author's friendly return], by which he meant the author in the text, conceived as 'le lieu de quelques détails ténus' [the site of certain fine details]. And he expressed this touching wish:

> Si j'étais écrivain, et mort, comme j'aimerais que ma vie se réduisît, par les soins d'un biographe amical et désinvolte, à quelques détails, à quelques goûts, à quelques inflexions, disons: des 'biographèmes', dont la distinction et la mobilité pourraient voyager hors de tout destin et venir toucher, à la façon des atomes épicuriens, quelque corps futur, promus à la même dispersion; une vie trouée en somme...[1]

> [If I were a writer, and dead, how I would like it if my life were reduced, by the efforts of some friendly, casual biographer, to a few details, a few tastes, a few inflections — let's call them 'biographemes' — whose distinctness and mobility could travel far outside any fate and ultimately touch, like Epicurean atoms, some future body, privileged with the same dispersion; a life, that is, with holes in it...]

Breton would have understood completely: if he once wrote 'J'aimerais que ma vie ne laissât après elle d'autre murmure que celui d'une chanson de guetteur, d'une chanson pour tromper l'attente' [I would be pleased if my life left behind it no other murmur than that of a lookout's song, that of a song to while away the time] (II, 697), he was apt to cherish, as particularly self-revealing, the products of this attitude of *disponibilité* [availability]. In *Nadja*, having offered us some 'biographèmes' relating to Hugo and Flaubert, tiny anecdotes which seemed to reveal what he calls the 'lumière propre' of the individual, he tells us that he plans to relate

> les épisodes les plus marquants de ma vie *telle que je peux la concevoir hors de son plan organique*, soit dans la mesure même où elle est livrée aux hasards... où elle m'introduit dans un monde comme défendu qui est celui des rapprochements soudaine, des pétrifiantes coïncidences...[2]

> [the episodes of my life which marked me most *insofar as I can conceive it outside its organic plan*, or insofar as it is in the hands of chance... where my life sets me

in a world which is as it were prohibited, that of sudden moments of closeness, petrifying coincidences...]

A few years later, in *Point du jour*, he observed:

> La vérité particulière à chacun de nous est un jeu de patience dont il lui faut, entre tous les autres, et sans les avoir jamais vus, saisir les éléments au vol.[3]

> [The particular truth for each of us is a game of patience which requires one to seize the elements of it from among all the others, having never seen them.]

*L'Imprononçable jour de ma naissance* is a compendium of coincidences. In sixty-five fragments, interspersed with an abundant visual accompaniment consisting of refreshingly unfamiliar facsimiles and photographs (Breton and his dog Melmoth, Suzanne Muzard at Saint-Cirq-la-Popie), Georges Sebbag plunges into the temporal flux of Breton's existence. He is concerned not so much with events as with *durées*, with what he calls 'le temps sans fil' [wireless time] — the hidden intervals, spacings and periodicities which run beneath the surface of our existence marking out the innumerable parallel lives we lead.

> Se défiant de la grosse ficelle du temps linéaire, Breton s'introduit dans le peu de réalité du temps sans fil.[4]

> [Mistrusting the gross simplifications of linear time, Breton enters into the minuscule reality of wireless time.]

Half-way through the book Sebbag explains that in 1984 he had just completed a philosophical essay entitled *Le Temps sans fil* [*Wireless time*], presumably a contribution to what one might call the 'Paraliterature of time' which includes Jung's work on synchronicity, Koestler's (and Kammerer's) meditations on 'The roots of coincidence', and J.W. Dunne's famous *Experiment with Time* which Breton mentions once or twice. Wondering what to do next Sebbag picked up Breton's *Point du jour* and found, to his astonishment, on the first page of the opening essay — the famous 'introduction au discours sur le peu de réalité' [introduction to the discourse on the dearth of reality] (II, 265) — the phrase 'sans fil' which had preoccupied him for so long. Armed with the supposition that 'Breton était habité par les durées' [Breton was inhabited by durations] he began an enquiry into the many references to specific numbers and especially dates in Breton's writings.

In the 'introduction au Discours' itself Breton had written:

> L'auteur de ces pages n'ayant pas encore 29 ans et s'étant, du 7 au 10 janvier, date où nous sommes, contredit 100 fois sur un point capital, à savoir la valeur qui mérite d'être accordée à la réalité, cette valeur pouvant varier de 0 à ∞, on demande dans quelle mesure il sera plus affirmatif au bout de onze ans et 40 jours.[5]

> [The author of these pages not yet having reached his twenty-ninth year and having, between January 7th and 10th, the current date, contradicted himself 100 times on a crucial point, the value that should be given to reality, this value varying between 0 and ∞, one must ask whether he will be more confident after eleven years and 40 days.]

Sebbag calculates that this refers us to 19 February 1936, the date of Breton's fortieth birthday, but also a year when the calendar was exactly the same as it was in 1896 (the year he was born): a repetition which occurs only every twenty-eight years (Breton's age at the time of writing). Moreover, in 1956 as in 1896 Breton's birthday fell on a *Wednesday*. (This is also the case in 1931 when, on his only visit to his birthplace, Tinchebray, Orne, Breton sent Éluard a postcard, reproduced here — the postcard was similarly sent on a Wednesday, though in August.)

Breton will also die on a Wednesday in 1966, and this day of the week crops up regularly in his work. So do Saturdays. Breton's twentieth birthday, commemorated in the poem 'Âge', fell on a Saturday, as does 10 January 1925. This is also the day of the week on which Jacques Vaché was born, and Breton buried. The odd thing is that at a point in the early thirties Breton began to say both in print and in private that he was born on 18 February (not 19 February), on a Tuesday not a Wednesday, that he was an Aquarius not a Pisces. The first explicit written occurrence is in the 'prière d'insérer' for *Point du jour* (1934). Sebbag, though, ever on the alert, finds something fishy about a series of dates Breton cites in *Les Vases communicants* (1932) where three consecutive days in 1931 (20, 21, 22 April) are said at different points to be 'Mardi'. Now, in the year Breton was born, 19 February (his real or 'official' birthdate) was Ash Wednesday, while the Tuesday (his adopted birthday) was Mardi Gras. For our sleuth this means we should link the shift of weekday to the growth of the 'lutte antireligieuse' [anti-religious struggle] among the Surrealists in the early thirties. Moreover, the ascendancy of Tuesdays is triumphantly affirmed in *L'Amour fou* where the 'scène de l'Ondine', the unforgettable 'Nuit du Tournesol' and the poet's marriage to Jacqueline all occur on this day of the week. In another essay in *Point du jour* Breton had commented on the uncertainties which surround Achim von Arnim's birthdate. Nowadays one might want to link Breton with Samuel Beckett who also seems to have chosen to refashion his birthdate for symbolic reasons, opting in his case for Good Friday.

All this (and I have only given a taste of the book's contents and concerns) may seem trivial; or worse, tedious. It is certainly often very hard to follow (especially for the less numerate), despite Sebbag's unpretentiously lively and unfacetious style. What makes the book attractive, though, is its acute sensitivity to a cluster of things which, I suspect, Breton's readers often cherish in his work. From *Nadja* onwards Breton traced with singular pertinacity what one might call the *trajectories* of desire, sifting 'aussi bien quelques-uns des faits à première vue les plus humbles que les plus significatifs de ma vie' [some facts of my life which seem at first sight the most humble, as well as the most significant ones] for the 'lumière de l'anomalie' [light of anomaly] they seemed to emit, confident in his belief, derived and adapted from Freud, that the life of the unconscious repeatedly manifests itself in the nooks and crannies of our day-to-day lives, revealing not merely the symptoms of neurosis but the force of desire to transmute the reality most people settle for. This means that Breton's books (including the poems) are full of odds and ends, strange incidents, stray utterances, circumstantial details, 'figurants' [walk-ons] as well as leading players. Sebbag's book is full of this lore. School is out: we are spared the 'studium' of critical analysis, and offered the staccato *Jouissances* of the 'punctum'. Never mind the genealogy of *Hasard objectif*. How about the links between the 'sans fil' of the *Introduction* and the first *Manifeste*, the typographical poem 'ÎLE' in *Clair de terre*, and the message from the 'Île du sable' which comes over the 'sans fil' at the end of *Nadja*? Or how about the hidden threads which link the words 'Aube, adieu', in the early poem 'Âge', the restaurant signboard 'Les Aubes', depicted in the second edition of *Nadja*, marking a crucial moment in Breton's relationship with Suzanne Muzard, the latter's birthplace: *Aube*rvilliers, where Breton also lived as a child, La Ferté Saint-*Aub*in, a name which Breton once tells us he forgot, and the name of the poet's daughter, *Aube*, born in 1935? What of the name 'Béthune' which suddenly came into Breton's head on 8 June 1924? How does it connect with Milady de Winter in *Les Trois Mousquetaires*, with images of decapitation in Breton, with the poem 'La Porte bât' which seems to draw on Dumas's *Vingt ans après*? And the date 1713 which Breton divined in the initials of his name: where can it take us?

There are two sorts of cryptologist: there is the fanatical crank utterly persuaded that he alone has found, let us say, the meaning of Rimbaud's sonnet 'Voyelles' [Vowels]; then there is the enthusiast who wants us to participate in a ludic (but also serious) opening-up of texts he loves: this kind of cryptologist (and Sebbag is one) is a poet, and a guide whose obsession is worth sharing, for a while at least (that is all he asks). 'Psychanalyse sauvage' [amateur psychoanalysis]? 'Délire d'interprétation' [delirious interpretation]? Perhaps. Yet there is something infectious about Sebbag's appetite for the 'entrées et sorties des textes' [entrances and exits of texts], the permeability and permutability of experience. Not only does he pay tribute to something vital in Breton which 'criticism' is ill at ease with, but he contributes to our thoughts about what biography might become were it to wean itself of the 'grands récits' to which it is still generally addicted. Let us give Sebbag the last word:

> En dédoublant le jour de sa naissance, Breton s'introduit dans le film des durées. Il profane le Mercredi des Cendres et placarde le Mardi des Masques. Il met en scène les aubes, les apparitions du temps, les *boys* du sévère. Il écrit le discours qui a une portée, celui du peu de réalité.[6]

> [By splitting in two the day of his birth, Breton enters into the film of durations. He profanes Ash Wednesday and placards Mask Tuesday. He stages dawns, time's apparitions of, the servant-boys of the severe. He writes the *discours* which has a range, that of the small amount of reality.]

## Notes

1. Roland Barthes, 'Sade, Fourier, Loyola', *Œuvres complètes*, II (1994), p. 1044.
2. Breton, I, 651.
3. Breton, II, 304.
4. Sebbag, section 26 (no page numbers).
5. Breton, II, 273.
6. Sebbag, section 64.

# 9

# Foucault's Goethe

*Review of André Breton,* Nadja, *trans. by Richard Howard (London: Penguin, 1999),*
*and* Œuvres complètes, *vol. III (Paris: Gallimard 'Pléiade', 1999)*

The third Pléiade volume of André Breton's works, covering the years 1941–53, presents a tale of two exiles. First in New York, where, from 1941 to 1946, Breton was part of the brilliant expatriate circle that included Claude Lévi-Strauss, Max Ernst, Georges Duthuit and many others, but where he never felt remotely at home. Second, more poignantly, in post-war Paris, where Breton and Surrealism never succeeded in re-establishing the central position they had occupied between the wars.

In the 1946 poem, 'Je Reviens' [I Return], a nightmarish taxi-ride records Breton's disorientation at not feeling at home in the city which had often, as in the closing pages of *Les Vases communicants* (1932), incarnated the Surrealist spirit. Of course, the poet was acutely aware of having missed a critical phase in the history of Paris. Desperate for news of the Liberation, as he wrote *Arcane 17* during a stay on the Gaspé coast of Quebec in August 1944, Breton wondered what changes were being wrought in the mind of the city:

> Paris, ses rues, ses places, aux derniers documents produits, sont une énigme totale: il s'agit de savoir quels courants sensibles travaillent dès maintenant à s'en rendre maîtres, quelles bases de discrimination, conformes à sa complexion invariable, il est en train d'adopter, quelle leçon, en tant qu'organisme obéissant à ses lois propres et non à des consignes étrangères, il tirera de sa dure expérience.[1]

> [Paris, its streets, its squares, according to the most recent documents, are a complete mystery: what one wants to know is, which currents can be felt labouring at this very moment to gain mastery of it, which bases of discrimination it is in the process of adopting, in conformity with its invariable complexion, which lesson, as an organism which obeys its own laws rather than foreign counsel, it will take from its difficult experience.]

The Parisian organism was mutating in Breton's absence, and he would never feel wholly at one with it again. In a sense, his true homecoming only occurred at the moment in 1950 when Saint-Cirq-Lapopie, the village in the Lot where he was to buy a home and spend hours searching for agates in the river-bed, first appeared to him 'comme une rose impossible dans la nuit [...] j'ai cessé de me désirer ailleurs'[2] [like an impossible rose in the night [...] I stopped wishing I was elsewhere].

Breton's paean to Saint-Cirq-Lapopie, written in 1951 for the local tourist office, is permeated by the progressive reorientation of his sensibility, during the years of exile, away from the urban towards the rhythms of the natural world and non-linear time. A comparison of the role of Paris in *Nadja*, a key Surrealist text of the 1920s, with its presentation in 'Pont-Neuf' (1950) (on pages 888–95 of this new Pléiade volume), a wonderful poetic meditation on the topography of the Ile de la Cité, reveals the kind of shift involved.

*Nadja* has appeared at long last as a Penguin Twentieth Century Classic, but it is a pity that Richard Howard's somewhat awkward 1960 Grove Press translation could not at least have been refreshed, particularly since it was based on the 1928 original rather than the significantly modified edition Breton prepared in 1963, which has since been the only one current in France. Breton's encounter with Nadja in the rue Lafayette on the afternoon of 4 October 1926 is unthinkable outside the metropolis, and Nadja's capacity to incarnate the essence of the Surrealist aspiration is closely bound up with her role as an emanation of the *genius loci*. Her advent is foreshadowed by a series of strange events and coincidences tied to precise Parisian locations, carefully anatomized in Boiffard's 'scene of the crime' photographs, and more of these sites feature in the circuitous wanderings on which, following only her whim, Nadja guided the mesmerized leader of the Surrealist movement. When Leona D. (Nadja's real name) disappears into an asylum, Breton turns for solace to the city she had helped reveal, 'la vraie ville distraite et abstraite de celle que j'habite par la force d'un element qui serait à ma pensée ce que l'air passé pour être à la vie'[3] [the true city distracted and abstracted from the one I live in by the force of an element which is to my mind what air is supposed to be to life].

In *Nadja*, movement in city space is catalytic: an abstract, mental city is made manifest within the real one; the concrete gives way to the ethereal. In 'Pont-Neuf', on the other hand, the concrete gives way to the abstract; the emphasis is on organic interaction. The interplay between 'la forme d'une ville' [the form of a city] and 'le cœur d'un mortel' [the heart of a mortal] (to cite Baudelaire) is cast in terms of the attraction and repulsion exerted by very specific topographical features. Influenced by gestalt theory, Breton suggests that a subjective map of Paris could be drawn up for each individual, but he maintains that our response is triggered not only by physical attributes of the site but by its historical resonances, deriving from 'ce qui a eu lieu ici' [what happened here]. On the physical side, the magnetic pull accounting for the particular alignment of the 'Pont-Neuf' is attributable to a range of features — notably the curvilinear course of the Seine — that conspire to make the Ile de la Cité resemble a Baudelairean 'géante', and the Place Dauphine, with its 'conformation triangulaire, d'ailleurs légèrement curviligne et [...] la fente qui la bissecte en deux espaces boisés'[4] [triangular layout, whose lines are all the same gently curved and [...] the split which bisects it into two wooded spaces], no less than 'le sexe de Paris'. But this physical power is attested and subsequently overdetermined by the magnetism exerted by a wealth of historical events, including the burning of Templars on this spot in 1313. The way the Palais de Justice and the Sacré Coeur appear to turn their back on the Place Dauphine confirms its taboo quality and its status as a 'lieu sacré'.

It is plausible to argue that, four years after his actual return, 'Pont-Neuf' marked Breton's re-appropriation of Paris, since here he brings to bear on a Parisian site a mode of seeing and writing that was nourished by the experience of exile, and grew out of his ecstatic encounter with new landscapes. The invention of a new mode of topographic writing may yet come to be seen as the great achievement of the second half of Breton's career. Whatever the ideological shifts and turns, the constant stimulus is the experience of place.

Not only *Arcane 17* and *Martinique charmeuse de serpents*, but also the later long poems and sequences: *Les Etats généraux, Ode à Charles Fourier, Constellations*, as well as numerous shorter poems and texts — all take off from the multifaceted interrogation of specific locations. The celebrated fifth chapter of *L'Amour fou*, published in *Minotaure* as 'Le Château étoilé' [The starry castle] in 1936, but also — specifically as a travel text — in Victoria Ocampo's *Sur*, can be seen as a starting point. Breton's account of an ascent of the Teide volcano on Tenerife is the springboard for a poetic meditation, where each detail of the natural and human landscape triggers a chain of interconnected reactions and associations.

Commenting on the process, he cites Leonardo's recommendation to his pupils that they seek inspiration in the contemplation of patches of old wall. For Breton, the lesson is that subjective desire is accessible to us through its objective externalization. Any 'surface' can serve as a 'révélateur', a screen on which desire is made legible. No significant realignment of the Surrealist project is involved, therefore, as Breton increasingly cultivates his responses to the particular kinds of 'révélateur' supplied by the natural world as opposed to urban 'errance' or the magnetic fields of automatism: plants, animals and rock formations, as opposed to 'objets trouvés', coincidences or textual slippages. But if the contemplation of geographical space becomes the privileged catalyst of inner desire, this does mark a greater emphasis on the common or universal as opposed to the strictly individual. On his visit to Mexico in 1938, Breton discovered a culture and a people as well as a natural paradise. If, in a previously unpublished section of 'Souvenir du Mexique' [Memory of Mexico], Breton notes that 'les routes mexicaines s'engouffrent dans les zones mêmes où se complaît et s'attarde l'écriture automatique'[5] [Mexican roads rush into those same zones in which automatic writing delights and dawdles], human beings play as great a part in his response to Mexico as landscape and nature.

The same is true of Martinique; Breton's ship (on which he had enjoyed very productive exchanges with Lévi-Strauss) was providentially delayed en route to New York in 1941, and the encounter with the island generated a spate of writings, including the 'Dialogue créole' with André Masson, where poet and painter respond antiphonally to their surroundings, 'Des Épingles tremblantes' [Trembling pins], a sequence of dense prose poems, 'Eaux troubles' [Troubled waters], a stinging denunciation of French colonial power, and 'Un Grand Poète noir' [A great black poet], the famous essay celebrating the impact of Aimé Césaire's *Cahier d'un retour au pays natal*. As Michel Leiris pointed out in a perceptive review, *Martinique charmeuse de serpents* provides a complex, multiple view, lucidly encompassing many of the contradictions of the island, which inspired moral indignation as well as poetic fervour in the Surrealist leader. As a mirror, Martinique reflects the darker as well as the lighter side of human desire. The encounter with the Caribbean, enhanced by a visit to Haiti and a return to Martinique in 1946, played a significant role in refocusing the aims and ambitions of Surrealism, while providing a contrasting frame for Breton's sojourn in the United States.

Steadfastly monoglot, Breton was probably never destined to like America. But his response to the powerhouse of Western capitalism was certainly conditioned by his new-found solidarity with some of its victims, and the major writings of his American period were closely linked to his journeys away from New York.

A central paradox running through all Breton's later work is the way it rehabilitates the real, the natural and the organic, thus developing the humanist and vitalist dimensions of Surrealism, while greatly enhancing the role of occult and esoteric thought. The orientation towards the topography, flora and fauna of the natural world, as well as the rituals of native peoples, stimulated by the discovery of new landscapes, leads to a celebration of rhythms, harmonies and forces. The Surreal retains its connection to unconscious desire and to the discrediting of narrow rationalism, but the routes to it are now more earthly than the convulsive paths of automatism. Yet at the same time Breton progressively widens the range of his interests in such fields as alchemy, the Tarot tradition, and particularly the various currents of eighteenth- and nineteenth-century 'illuminist' thought. As Étienne-Alain Hubert shows in his indispensable annotations to Volume Three of the Pléiade Œuvres complètes, the discovery of Auguste Viatte's study, Victor Hugo et les illuminés de son temps (1942), convinced Breton of the extent to which occultist thought permeated the whole poetic tradition of what he called the 'splendide dix-neuvième siècle'.

At one level, what appealed to Breton in the occultist tradition was the way it challenged, however waywardly, the hegemony of positivist rationalism by positing alternative cosmologies and visions, often on a grand scale. Far from being the Pope of Surrealism, as he is often portrayed, Breton was its heresiarch, a 'grand indésirable' (his own label), who identified with such figures as Fabre d'Olivet, Saint-Yves d'Alveydre and Charles Fourier. The first major text of his New York period, the Prolégomènes à un troisième manifeste du surréalisme ou non (1942), published in the first number of the sumptuous periodical VVV, Breton's main outlet at this time, is a powerful and playful gesture of dissent. From the famous opening assertion, 'Sans doute y a-t-il trop de nord en moi pour que je sois l'homme de la pleine adhésion'[6] [I no doubt have too much north in me to be the kind of man who gives total adherence] (III, 5), Breton professes his disdain for all those prevailing systems of thought and social organization that restrict the range of human possibilities. 'La survivance du signe à la chose signifiée' [The sign outliving the thing signified] (III, 706) is the bane of modern culture: we live among the dead matter of exhausted ideologies; new myths, truly articulating the relationship between man and world, must be found to supplant the old. The idea of 'grands transparents' (III, 14) — invisible agencies, like winds, whose numinous presence is felt in moments of fear and chance — represented Breton's own contribution to a new mythology.

At the heart of the affinity Breton increasingly perceived between Surrealism and the esoteric tradition lies the appeal of analogy. The important essay from 1947,

'Signe ascendant' [Ascendant sign], whose title alludes to the Zodiac and whose epigraph comes from the Zohar, not only revises the Surrealist theory of the poetic image by placing the analogical process at its centre, it argues forcefully for analogy as a 'mode de connaissance'[7]. But while citing esoteric sources alongside modern poetic ones, Breton is at pains to insist that poetic, as opposed to 'mystical' analogy, 'ne présuppose nullement, à travers la trame du monde visible, un univers invisible qui tend à se manifester'[8] [in no way presupposes, across the weave of the visible world, an invisible universe which seeks to manifests itself]. The vital office of analogical thought is to illuminate the sense of a totality and a continuum of man and the world. The appeal of the esoteric — considered analogically — is that it maintains a sense of the connectedness of things. This had been the message of *Les États généraux*, the long poem Breton wrote on Long Island in the summer of 1943: 'Les images m'ont plu c'était l'art | À tort décrié de brûler la chandelle par les deux bouts | Mais tout est bien plus de mèche les complicités sont autrement dramatiques et savantes'[9] [Images delighted me the art | Wrongly criticized for burning the candle at both ends | But everything is far more interconnected the complicities are much more dramatic and intellectual]. The word 'savantes' may surprise here; yet knowledge and science in the broadest senses (including the so-called 'sciences traditionnelles', in other words the occult sciences) have their vital part to play in uncovering the lost paths to the unity of experience.

From the outset, the Surrealist project sprang from the impulse to see poetry and knowledge as indivisibly intertwined. Building on this foundation, travel and exile turned André Breton into a man of quite remarkable erudition. The new kind of topographical writing he evolved made a perfect vehicle for analogical thought to break down barriers between disparate areas of knowledge and experience, and to articulate a more organic and unified vision of the universe. In *Arcane 17*, the title refers to a tarot card symbolizing hope and resurrection, but the springboard of the analogical process is the here and now. First, the famous Rocher Percé at Gaspé, a massive rock island with a single impregnable cliff, topped by one of the largest colonies of gannets in the world, and then a lakeside vista in the Laurentians near Montreal, provide the 'révélateurs' or screens which set desire-laden thought in motion. Breton weaves together immediate experience — initially, a boat trip round the rock in the company of his new partner, Elisa — with personal history, objective history, elements of topography, natural history, myth, legend, art, music, poetry, Tarot and other forms of divination. A richly associative mode of writing blends tiny scraps of knowledge and experience, extraordinarily diverse in kind, into a moving affirmation of the lost but recoverable unity of human civilization.

Breton's most productive cultural encounter in North America was with the Native American tribes of the south-west, above all the Hopi. In the summer of 1945, while divorcing and remarrying in Reno, he spent several weeks visiting reservations in Nevada, Arizona and New Mexico. A precious *inédit* in the new Pléiade consists of the very extensive notes he made on his journey, which include detailed descriptions of ceremonies such as the snake dance, and many allusions to the reference works and museum material Breton consulted. On his return to New York, Breton declared his intention of compiling a 'livre de voyages' that would bring together his writings on Mexico, Martinique and the Hopis. Sadly this never came to fruition, but while still in Nevada he embarked on his *Ode à Charles Fourier* (1947), which has many references to the communities and landscapes of the Indian reservations. In Fourier, Breton found a visionary thinker, dedicated to the invention of new kinds of human community based, like Surrealism, on the realization of human desire, who was also a great master of analogical thought. Reading Fourier in the five-volume 1846 edition acquired in New York, brushing aside the faint praise of Marx and Baudelaire, Breton began writing the *Ode* in the garden of his Reno motel, contrasting, point by point, the sorry mess of the planet in 1945 with the utopian world of Fourier's projections and predictions. Far from dismissing Fourier's utopianism, Breton endorses his radical libertarian spirit, saluting the 'soif du mieux-être' [thirst for enhanced being], which locates human progress in the understanding of human affectivity, and celebrating his poetic insistence on detail. A collage of quotations, enumerations, calligrams, informed by a concrete sense of place, mixing erudition with poetic fervour, document and desire, anthropology, politics and aesthetics, the *Ode à Charles Fourier*, published soon after Breton's return, exemplifies Breton's later work.

In an interview after Breton's death in 1966, Michel Foucault called him 'notre Goethe'; by breaking down the barriers between disciplines and ways of thinking, Breton made new cultural configurations possible: 'Il a été à la fois le disperseur et le berger de tout ce moutonnement de l'expérience moderne'[10] [He at once scattered and shepherded all the contours of modern experience]. Grandiose as it may seem, such a claim certainly gains validity as the magnificent Pléiade edition progressively contextualizes André Breton's very disparate oeuvre. The final volume, bringing together all his writings on art, as well as his last texts, is eagerly awaited.

## Notes

1. Breton, *OC* III, 74.
2. Ibid., pp. 1047–48.
3. Breton, *OC* I, 749.
4. *OC* III, 893.
5. Ibid., p. 952.
6. Ibid., p. 5.
7. Ibid., pp. 766–69.
8. Ibid., p. 767.
9. Ibid., p. 31.
10. 'C'était un grand nageur entre deux mots', Entretien avec C. Bonnefoy, *Arts et loisirs*, no. 54, 5–11 October, 1966, pp. 8–9.

# 10

# Naissance de l'aventure surréaliste

*Review of Marguerite Bonnet,* André Breton:
naissance de l'aventure surréaliste *(Paris: José Corti, 1975)*

Until now 'la critique universitaire' has not done well with Breton. American scholars have been most productive, but the well-known studies by Caws, Balakian and Browder all leave something to be desired. The most stimulating books have come from creative writers such as Julien Gracq or from participants in the surrealist group — Crastre and Bedouin, more recently Audoin, Alexandrian, and Legrand. The publication of Marguerite Bonnet's doctoral thesis is therefore especially welcome since the author combines the virtues of an established critic and university teacher with the advantages of a long-standing friend and admirer of Breton to whom has been entrusted the task of editing a forthcoming edition of his works in the *Bibliothèque de la Pléiade*. Marguerite Bonnet has commented on the present work in an interview (*Le Monde*, 21 March 1975) and in a summary of her thesis prepared for its *soutenance* (*L'Information littéraire*, 27 (1975), 213–16). In the course of her research the scope of this study which was originally to have traced the development of 'l'aventure surrealiste' *in toto* narrowed first to exclusive focus on Breton and then to its present concentration on the early part of his career up to the publication of the *Manifeste du surréalisme* and its aftermath.

Origins rather than accomplishments are the subject matter of this book. Valuable traces of a more extensive project subsist: Mlle Bonnet has not wasted her patient *dépouillement* of the periodicals of this period; the excellent bibliography covers a clutch of surrealist writers to whom there are numerous cross-references. But it is essentially the author's good fortune in having been able to consult previously unpublished material, principally correspondence, that warrants her concentration on this formative period. This includes the correspondence with Paul Valéry of 1913–17; letters to Breton's closest friend of this period, Theodore Fraenkel; letters to his first wife Simone as well as her letters to a cousin which give a lively portrait of Breton's life at this time. Anecdote is, however, given little space in this book, letters being used essentially to provide evidence of Breton's intellectual orientations. But the new material is not simply placed at the service of more incisive literary criticism: Mlle Bonnet's aim throughout is to 'saisir la formation d'une pensée et d'une sensibilité'; her approach to texts, supple and varied as it is, is subordinated to the overall desire to elucidate 'un projet existentiel', to locate in the incunabula of the surrealist movement the trajectory of an individual destiny.

In this the book is largely successful. The reader is able to witness the emergence of something other than the species of literary terrorism for which surrealism sometimes passes: that programme for the revision of human values and initiatives which, sponsored as it is by the new sense of the relevance of Poetry that is the legacy of Baudelaire and Rimbaud, has been so influential in steering subsequent French poetry towards the domain of Being.

Marguerite Bonnet's research, backed up by a versatile critical approach, enables her to enforce important discriminations. Breton did not need to wait for Dada to sense the importance of negation and revolt in the poetic enterprise. Having re-situated established issues (Breton's discovery of Rimbaud, the encounter with Vaché) which have become fossilized for want of recent research, she opens new perspectives by her emphasis on the widespread Nietzschean and anarchist currents to which, as his correspondence attests, Breton responded enthusiastically. In this, as in the extensive account of *Les Champs magnétiques* and *Clair de terre*, a dominant concern is to reclaim territory colonized in a manner disadvantageous to Breton and surrealism by Michel Sanouillet's *Dada à Paris*, an earlier doctoral monument to this fascinating period. There is a subtle account of Breton's conception of 'une mythologie moderne' and a convincing section which in filling in the background to automatic writing gives the emphasis back to Freud where Myers and Janet have recently been adduced as influences by Starobinski and Balakian respectively. The Manifeste is seen to offer a 'redéfinition de l'homme' in which poetic concerns are totally fused with existential ones. The reading of *Poisson soluble* acknowledges the success of the thematic approach already employed by Gracq and Audoin and offers instead an admirable analysis of the way this text operates through the interaction of semantic and phonetic associations swiftly changing track at the intersection of various *générateurs*. Finally, the author's most agreeable style should be mentioned: always lucid and scrupulous, it is often eloquent in the best sense.

# 11

# Baudelaire, Bonnefoy, Jeanne Duval: Poetry and Ethical Lucidity

Baudelairean lucidity has frequently been judged a dubious virtue. This is no doubt partly because its *locus classicus* is often deemed to be 'L'Irrémédiable' ['The Irremediable']. In this poem from *Les Fleurs du Mal* [*Flowers of Evil*] a series of 'emblèmes nets' [clear emblems], including that of a ship immobilized in polar ice, is succeeded by the supremely emblematic evocation of a:

> Tête-à-tête sombre et limpide
> Qu'un cœur devenu son miroir!
> Puits de Vérité, clair et noir
> Où tremble une étoile livide,[1]

> [Sombre and limpid face to face
> A heart become its own mirror!
> Well of Truth, clear and black
> Where a livid star trembles,]

which is followed by the mockingly triumphant affirmation that, since the devil pulls the strings, we should revel in 'la conscience dans le mal!' [knowledge of our own evil]. In his 'Situation de Baudelaire' Paul Valéry underlined the poet's debts to Edgar Allan Poe. His list of the features that captivated Baudelaire in Poe begins with 'le démon de la lucidité' [the demon of lucidity], linking lucidity with 'le génie de l'analyse' [analytical genius] but also with a certain perversity (Baudelaire translated Poe's story 'The Imp of the Perverse' as 'Le démon de la perversité').[2] Jean Prévost, citing 'L'Irrémédiable' in a discussion of Baudelairean self-scrutiny said that the poem showed, 'une autre volupté dans le mal, un autre orgueil, non plus celui de l'indépendance, mais celui de la lucidité' [a different relish for evil, a different pride, not that of independence, but pride in lucidity].[3] In his biographical study of Baudelaire Jean-Paul Sartre places Baudelairean lucidity squarely in the context of the poet's hyper self-consciousness. 'Il s'est engagé dans la voie de la lucidité pour découvrir sa nature singulière' [he set out on the path of lucidity to discover his singular nature].[4] Feeling different from others, but lacking a straightforward sense of his interior world (Sartre calls him 'un homme sans immédiateté' [a man without immediacy]),[5] Baudelaire engaged in constant self-scrutiny. He was an 'homme penché' [a man leaning over],[6] forever inspecting his mental experience. But for Sartre 'la trop grande clarté équivaut à la cécité' [excessive clarity equates with blindness].[7] Endlessly trying to capture his own innerness Baudelaire encounters only the successive states of consciousness itself, 'les modes indéfinis de la conscience universelle' [the infinite modes of universal consciousness].[8] 'La fameuse lucidité de Baudelaire', writes Sartre, 'n'est qu'un effort de *récupération*. Il s'agit de *se* recouvrer et — comme la vue est appropriation — de *se* voir. Mais pour *se* voir il faudrait être deux' [Baudelaire's vaunted lucidity is no more than an effort at *recuperation*. The aim is to retrieve *oneself* and — since to see is to appropriate — to see *oneself*].[9] Citing the 'tête-à-tête sombre et limpide' [sombre and limpid face to face] of 'L'Irrémédiable' Sartre observes that:

> l'effort de Baudelaire va être pour pousser à l'extrême cette esquisse avortée de dualité qu'est la conscience réflexive. S'il est lucide, originellement, ce n'est pas pour se rendre un compte exact de ses fautes, c'est pour être deux ...[10]

> [Baudelaire will strive to push to its extreme the abortive gesture towards duality involved in reflexive consciousness. If he is, from the start, lucid, it is not so as to appraise his faults accurately, but so as to be double ...]

But 'la possession finale du Moi par le Moi' [final possession of the self by the self] eludes the poet: 'Il exaspérera donc sa lucidité: il n'était que son propre témoin, il va tenter de devenir son propre bourreau' [he will thus exasperate his lucidity: he was no more than his own witness, he will try to become his own executioner].[11]

★　★　★　★　★

That lucidity can be sterile and inhuman, and may sometimes belong, in terms of common humanity at least, to the pathology of the intellect, is an idea that attaches itself, beyond Baudelaire, to a line of poets running from Poe, through Baudelaire, to Mallarmé and Valéry. One of Sartre's titles for his posthumously published study of Mallarmé was 'La lucidité et sa face d'ombre' [Lucidity and its dark shadow].[12] In this conception, lucidity tends to be hyper-lucidity, such as that of Valéry's emblematic Monsieur Teste. In his appraisal of the poet, Yves Bonnefoy sees Valéry's hyper-lucidity as part of his Mediterranean mind-set and as a quality that debars the poet of *La Jeune Parque* from a true encounter with the real, outside the scope of purely conceptual knowledge: 'Il y a des mirages de la clarté' [there are mirages of clarity].[13]

Yet in his first essay on Baudelaire (1953) Bonnefoy does not take the path of censuring the poet's hyper-lucidity, although he acknowledges its role in his make-up. Even if, he argues, Baudelaire's poetry remained essentially discursive, and hence linked to conceptual knowledge, the poet of *Les Fleurs du Mal*, 'le maître livre de notre poésie' [the master book of our poetry], attained what Bonnefoy called 'la vérité de parole [...] au-delà de toute formule' [the truth of speech [...] beyond all formulae].[14] The achievement was existential. Baudelaire's path went by way of consent to finitude. Taking direct issue with Sartre, but agreeing that Baudelaire made an irrevocable choice early in life, Bonnefoy writes: 'Baudelaire a choisi la mort, et que la mort grandisse en lui comme une conscience, et qu'il puisse connaître par la mort' [Baudelaire chose death, so that death might grow inside him like consciousness, and so that death should become knowledge] (*SSB*

14). Baudelaire's poetry unites the mortal body and immortal language, the former giving the latter its truth.

Bonnefoy amplified this analysis in a section on Baudelaire in his major 1959 essay 'L'Acte et le lieu de la poésie' [The act and the place of poetry]. Taking 'Le Cygne' [The Swan] as a concrete example, he adumbrates a view of Baudelaire's achievement that goes beyond the recognition of finitude to the recognition of other, ordinary, human beings in their everyday mortality. 'Andromaque je pense à vous' [Andromaque I think of you]: in his treatment of the figure of Andromaque 'Baudelaire substitue à l'archétype classique une passante lointaine, une femme réelle [...] cela signifie qu'il y va de l'être hors de la conscience' [Baudelaire replaces the classic archetype by an obscure passer-by, a real woman ... and this signifies that being exists outside the mind].[15] Moreover the poem then extends this recognition to other beings, 'tous les êtres perdus, les captifs, les vaincus' [all that are lost, the captives, the defeated], via the recollection of the real swan exiled in the city street, 'Le cygne est l'existence singulière pour la première fois reconnue d'une façon souveraine dans une poésie qui mourait. Il est l'ici et le maintenant, cette limite' [The swan marks a singular existence recognized wholly distinctively for the first time in a poetic idiom that was dying. It is the here and now, that boundary].[16] Here poetry becomes an act, indeed an 'acte d'amour', which gives supreme value to the merely mortal, and attempts to attain presence in language through a prosody that captures 'le frôlement d'aile de l'existence dans les mots voués à l'universel' [the stirring of existence, like a beating wing, in words committed to the universal].[17] And the kind of lucidity that is at stake, rooted in Baudelaire's 'choice' of death, which Bonnefoy reiterates here, is far from hyper self-reflexivity. Rather, in its focus on other human beings, and our recognition of their reality, it lies in what we could call ethical lucidity.

⋆　⋆　⋆　⋆　⋆

Bonnefoy's engagement with Baudelaire's ethical lucidity has continued up to the present. The recent publication of *Sous le signe de Baudelaire* [*Under the sign of Baudelaire*] (2011), which collects nearly all Bonnefoy's writings about the poet of *Les Fleurs du Mal* followed by *Le Siècle de Baudelaire* [The Baudelaire Century] (2014), allows us to pursue this theme in detail. The grounds for doing so are moreover augmented by the presence of Baudelaire in Bonnefoy's recent poetry, especially in his great poem 'L'Heure présente' ['The Present Hour'].[18] There are various paths that could be taken in this context. The one I have chosen involves a figure who has come to fascinate Bonnefoy in recent years, as his preoccupation with Baudelaire has focused increasingly on the poet's relation to the city of Paris. The figure is that of Jeanne Duval, who is referred to, as we shall see at the end of our discussion, in 'L'Heure présente'.

Jeanne Duval hovers, of course, in the background of 'Le Cygne', but she goes unmentioned in Bonnefoy's first reading of the poem, as well as in a second reading in his long and complex essay 'Baudelaire contre Rubens' ['Baudelaire contra Rubens'] initially published in 1967. Here Bonnefoy uses Baudelaire's fluctuating assessments of the painter Rubens as a scale to gauge the interplay of the ethical and the aesthetic in Baudelaire's poetic stance. Bonnefoy detects in some of Baudelaire's strictures against Rubens an envy of, but also a disdain for, the painter's lack of self-conflict, his 'esprit de compassion [...] aptitude à l'incarnation, à l'échange' [spirit of compassion [...] and aptitude for incarnation, for exchange] (*SSB* 39) — all key words. At the heart of Bonnefoy's analysis is the way Baudelaire's changing attitudes to Rubens expressed a shift, in the poet's moral understanding, towards the importance of not forgetting ordinary reality and the real human beings who play a part in our lives. It is a move towards seeing compassion as central to poetry, not just thematically — as in Victor Hugo, ever capable of expressing charitable sentiments, essentially as an idealization of his stance as a poet — but verbally and existentially. At stake here is the capacity to extricate oneself from the labyrinth of one's own psyche — to be capable of genuine love that can only exist if we open ourselves to the encounter with others, extricate ourselves from our own fantasies and obsessions, and also, in Baudelaire's case, to escape from a primarily aesthetic mode of perception. As Bonnefoy wrestles with Baudelaire's tortuous dealings with Rubens, assessing writings from the whole of the poet's lifetime, he notes Baudelaire's remorse at his incapacity to love, and illustrates this with regard to 'Le Cygne' where the idea of communion with others is an issue. But Bonnefoy now sees the end of the poem, with its widening circle of addressees, in negative terms. The substitution of a real swan for the ideal, imaginary, one is only apparent:

> Baudelaire aux dernières strophes ne s'y adresse plus qu''aux captifs, aux vaincus', à ceux que la douleur a spiritualisés, pense-t-il, à ceux par conséquent qu'il situe plus haut que l'homme ordinaire, à ceux qu'il *construit* une fois encore, y retrouvant son image. (*SSB* 51)

> [Baudelaire in the last few lines addresses only 'the captives, the defeated', those whom suffering has spiritualized, he thinks, those who consequently are to be placed above the ordinary man, those who, once again, he *constructs*, finding in them his own image.]

The beings addressed at the end are an imaginary construct, a projection of the poet's self. If Bonnefoy revises his reading of the end of 'Le Cygne', now diagnosing self-absorption and incapacity to love, the matter will not rest there: other readings of the poem will feature in future years. In any case what is at stake is what Bonnefoy will later call a 'dialectique de refermement et d'ouverture' [dialectic of openness and closure] (*SSB* 103) in Baudelaire with regard to the world of ordinary others. And even in the dialectic of 'Baudelaire contre Rubens' the pendulum will swing back and forth between the gift of compassion and its absence. Another poem central to Bonnefoy's reading is 'Les Petites Vieilles' ['The Little Old Women']. Here Bonnefoy notes the poet's desire to love the old women — 'aimons-les!' [Let us love them!] — and his incapacity to do so, his inability to escape himself — 'Mais moi, moi, qui de loin tendrement vous surveille'[19] [But I, I who tenderly watches you from afar] — and hence his relapse into 'une écriture de soi' [a writing of self] (*SSB* 53). Yet a few years later Bonnefoy will see in 'Les Petites Vieilles' 'un des sommets des *Fleurs du Mal*' [one of the summits of *Flowers of Evil*], Baudelaire learning, in the Paris streets, to free himself of his self-obsessed 'crispation' [tensed posture] and to love others 'sans réclamation pour soi-même' [without recognition for himself] (*SSB* 112).

★  ★  ★  ★  ★

*Sous le signe de Baudelaire* indicates that, in the thirty years following the first version of 'Baudelaire contre Rubens', Baudelaire was not at the centre of Bonnefoy's preoccupations, although he dedicated a course to him at the Collège de France in 1990–91. It is in 1998 that he fully re-engaged with his fellow poet, finding a new-found focus in episodes in the poet's life and key poems, often from the 'Tableaux parisiens' ['Parisian Tableaux']. Central here, and right up to the present, is the figure of Jeanne Duval, and more specifically the significance of Baudelaire's apparent choice to refer to her, on two occasions, by the initials 'J.G.F.'. It is Bonnefoy's recurrent treatment of this crux in Baudelaire's life that I wish to trace out here.

Let us recall that Jeanne Duval was Baudelaire's half-French, half-Haïtian, and hence coloured mistress, with whom he had a tempestuous relationship from his early twenties, around 1840. Some of the most intense love poems in *Les Fleurs du mal*, such as 'Les Bijoux' and 'Le Balcon' are thought to have been inspired by her. Their fourteen-year relationship broke up in the mid-1850s, and Jeanne became prematurely aged and infirm, suffering partial paralysis. But Baudelaire continued to be concerned about her, and two letters to his mother, to which Bonnefoy refers several times, testify to this ongoing attention. In the long letter of 11 September 1856 Baudelaire evokes his recent break-up with Jeanne:

> cette femme était ma seule distraction, mon seul plaisir, mon seul camarade, et malgré toutes les secousses intérieures d'une liaison tempétueuse, jamais l'idée d'une séparation irréparable n'était entré clairement dans mon esprit. Encore maintenant, et cependant je suis tout à fait calme, — je me surprends à penser en voyant un bel objet quelconque, un beau paysage, n'importe quoi d'agréable: pourquoi n'est-elle pas avec moi, pour admirer cela avec moi, pour acheter cela avec moi?[20]

> [this woman was my sole distraction, my sole source of pleasure, my sole comrade, and despite all the inner shocks of a tempestuous affair, the idea of a definitive separation never clearly entered my head. Still now, and yet I am quite calm, — I find myself thinking when I see any attractive object, a fine view, anything that is agreeable: why isn't she with me, to admire this with me, to buy this with me?]

As Bonnefoy notes, this letter 'où se marque beaucoup d'amour' (*SSB* 171) [where much love is perceptible] gives moving testimony to the place Jeanne continued to have in Baudelaire's life, and there is evidence elsewhere of his concern for her material well-being, despite his own penury.

As Bonnefoy will now often recall in his references to 'Le Cygne', it is generally accepted that the stanza

> Je pense à la négresse, amaigrie et phtisique
> Piétinant dans la boue, et cherchant, l'œil hagard,
> Les cocotiers absents de la superbe Afrique
> Derrière la muraille immense du brouillard;[21]

> [I think of the negress, emaciated and consumptive,
> Plodding through the mud, and with a haunted look
> Searching for the absent coconut trees of majestic Africa
> Beyond the impenetrable wall of the city's fog;]

refers to Jeanne. But the centre of Bonnefoy's attention to the matter of Jeanne is the preface to *Les Paradis artificiels* [*Artificial Paradises*] in 1860, and the fact of its dedication to someone addressed as 'Ma chère amie' ['My dear friend'], and referred to only by the initials J.G.F. On the basis of this, and of Baudelaire's other use of these initials, in the dedication to the poem 'L'Héautontimorouménos' ['Self-tormentor'],[22] scholarly consensus has by and large agreed that they designate Jeanne. Setting aside such fanciful rationalizations as 'Jeanne gentille femme' [Jeanne gentle woman] or 'Jeanne grande féline' (!) [Jeanne large feline], Bonnefoy takes this identification for granted but shifts the debate to the question of why Baudelaire chose at once to pay homage to Jeanne and to hide her name, an issue at the heart of the preface to *Les Paradis artificiels*. In the first two paragraphs of this dense and often sardonic text Baudelaire accounts for the dedication of a book on artificial paradises to a woman with the famous declaration that: 'la femme est l'être qui projette la plus grande ombre ou la plus grande lumière dans nos rêves [...] elle vit spirituellement dans les imaginations qu'elle hante et qu'elle féconde' [Woman is the being that projects the greatest shadow or the greatest light in our dreams [...] she lives spiritually in the imaginations she haunts and nourishes].[23] Going on to assert that it is unnecessary that a book's dedication should be understood, or indeed that a book should be understood by anyone other than its dedicatee, Baudelaire makes this striking declaration:

> Mais ce n'est pas à une morte que je dédie ce petit livre; c'est à une qui, quoique malade, est toujours active et vivante en moi, et qui tourne maintenant tous ses regards vers le Ciel, ce lieu de toutes les transfigurations.[24]

> [But it is not to a dead woman that I dedicate this little book; it is to one who, although sick, is always active and alive in me, and who now turns her eyes towards the heavens, where all transfigurations take place.]

And then addressing the dedicatee as 'Tu' he concludes:

> Tu verras dans ce tableau un promeneur sombre et solitaire, plongé dans le flot mouvant des multitudes, et envoyant son cœur et sa pensée à une Électre lointaine qui essuyait naguère son front baigné de sueur *et rafraîchissait ses lèvres parcheminées par la fièvre*; et tu devineras la gratitude d'un autre Oreste dont tu as souvent surveillé les cauchemars, et de qui tu dissipais, d'une main légère et maternelle, le sommeil épouvantable. C. B.[25]

> [You will observe in this tableau a sombre and solitary walker, immersed in the moving flow of the multitudes, and sending his heart and his thoughts to a distant Electra who used to wipe his sweaty brow *and refreshed his lips parched*

*by fever*; and you will guess the gratitude of another Orestes whose nightmares you have often watched over, and whose tormented sleep you would assuage with a gentle and maternal hand. C.B.]

In Bonnefoy's successive readings of this text which he calls 'proprement sublime' [truly sublime], the elements remain, first, the notion of Jeanne as, 'quoique malade', 'toujours active et vivante en moi', which Bonnefoy consistently reads, not in terms of assimilation and self-enclosure on the poet's part, but of a fully inward and enduring relation to a real living human being. The second element is the significance of the identification of Jeanne with an 'Electre lointaine' [distant Electra], and Baudelaire himself with 'un autre Oreste' [other Orestes], along with the tender gesture of mopping the fevered brow of an individual in psychic distress. The latter elements derive from a passage in De Quincey's *Confessions of an English Opium-Eater* (De Quincey is the 'promeneur sombre et solitaire' [sombre and solitary walker] Baudelaire refers to) where the English writer recalled being 'Persecuted by visions as ugly, and as ghastly phantoms as ever haunted the couch of an Orestes',[26] and, referring to 'My Eumenides, like his', continued 'But watching by my pillow, [...] through the heavy watches of the night, sate my Electra.'[27] And he recalls M.'s (his wife Margaret's) 'ministrations of tenderest affection — to wipe away for years the unwholesome dews upon the forehead, or to refresh the lips when parched and baked with fever'.[28]

In the *Paradis artificiels* Baudelaire had half-translated half-paraphrased this passage, referring to:

> l'invocation la plus sobre et les actions de grâces les plus tendres à une compagne courageuse, toujours assise au chevet où repose ce cerveau hanté par les Euménides. L'Oreste de l'opium a trouvé son Electre qui pendant des années a essuyé sur son front les sueurs de l'angoisse et rafraichi ses lèvres parcheminées par la fièvre.[29]

> [The most sober invocation and the most tender benediction to a courageous companion, always at the bedside of this mind haunted by the Furies. The Orestes of opium has found his Electra who for years wiped the sweats of anguish from his brow and refreshed his lips parched with fever.]

In his first discussion of the preface, in 1998 (*SSB* 169–70), Bonnefoy emphasizes the fusion of the sister (Electra) and the mother ('mère maternelle') which, he argues, reveals an enduring anger against his mother for having 'forgotten' her first husband, Baudelaire's father. But returning to this 'page fondamentale' [crucial page] three years later, in a 2001 essay of more than 120 pages, 'Le Poète et 'le flot mouvant des multitudes' [The poet and the 'moving flow of multitudes'], Bonnefoy offers a different reading, now centred on Jeanne Duval. The quotation in Bonnefoy's title is from Baudelaire's text and refers to De Quincey's account of his solitary wandering in the London streets. The central theme is the experience of 'la grande ville': 'ce que Baudelaire sut découvrir dans le creuset parisien, c'est la poésie comme telle, la poésie rejointe en son essence pour la première fois dans son histoire en France' [what Baudelaire was able to discern in the Parisian melting-pot was poetry itself, poetry that for the first time in its history in France was encountered in its very essence] (*SSB* 277). Having referred to Jeanne Duval as one of the figures of 'démunis' [indigent people] in Baudelaire, Bonnefoy notes that 'il faut absolument apprendre à estimer et respecter [Jeanne] si on veut atteindre au plus haut de la poésie de Baudelaire' [it is absolutely essential that we learn to value and respect Jeanne if we are to grasp Baudelaire's poetry at its greatest] (*SSB* 278). And he speculates on the way Baudelaire identifies with both De Quincey and Orestes. If feelings about his father are present here, there is no rage towards the mother. The identification of Jeanne with Electra expresses 'l'attestation d'un être par un autre être, une reconnaissance mutuelle dans l'absolu d'un moment de vie' [the acknowledgement of one human being by another, a mutual recognition in the absolute of a living moment] (*SSB* 287).

Bonnefoy's fullest treatment of the dedication occurs in a 2006 article entitled 'Que signifie J.G.F.?' [What does J.G.F. mean?]. An epigraph quotes a letter of 11 January 1858 where Baudelaire pointed out to his mother that two of his recent poems were based on memories of her, but that he had left them 'sans indications claires parce que j'ai horreur de prostituer les choses intimes' [without clear pointers because I find prostituting personal matters abhorrent].[30] Pursuing this, Bonnefoy cites a draft of the *Paradis artificiels* dedication where Baudelaire had noted: 'je désire que cette dédicace soit inintelligible' [I would like this dedication to be unintelligible] (*SSB* 334). For Bonnefoy the essential question is not who is J.G.F.? — it is clearly Jeanne — but why disguise her identity? He adduces here the sonnet 'Le Portrait', also thought to refer to Jeanne, but the ailing Jeanne, which begins:

> La Maladie et la Mort font des cendres
> De tout ce feu qui pour nous flamboya
>
> [Sickness and Death turn to ashes
> The fires that burned so high for we two]

and continues by saying that, if what remains of eyes, mouth, and kisses is only a pale sketch, nonetheless:

> Noir assassin de la Vie et de l'Art,
> Tu ne tueras jamais dans ma mémoire
> Celle qui fut mon plaisir et ma gloire![31]
>
> [Black assassin of Life and Death
> In my memory you will never kill
> The one who was my pleasure and my glory!]

From this point, 'Le Portrait' will become an essential part of the matter of Jeanne:

> A 'J.G.F.' je pressens une signification [...] qui a rapport à la poésie en ce qu'est celle-ci en son essence, à ce très haut niveau où furent écrits 'Le Portrait' ou 'Le Balcon', deux des cimes des *Fleurs du mal.* (*SSB* 334).
>
> [In 'J.G.F.' I intuit a meaning [...] that pertains to what poetry is in its essence, at that supreme height at which 'The Portrait' and 'The Balcony', two of the summits of *The Flowers of Evil*, were written.]

The connection between withholding Jeanne's name and the essence of poetry —

as a way of encountering the real — lies in the observation that if, on the one hand, naming is essential — 'Il faut nommer par leur nom les êtres qui sont [...] on ne peut les réjoindre qu'en les nommant' [we must accord living beings their names [...] only through giving them their names do we commune with them] — on the other hand, to name too explicitly is often to betray the one named: 'D'où l'habitude des grands poèmes, où des souvenirs sont actifs, d'interpeller plutôt que nommer, de dire "tu" en lieu et place d'un nom propre pourtant présent en leur' [Whence the habit in great poems, where memories are active, to interpolate rather than to name, to say 'you' in place of a proper name that is nonetheless profoundly present] (*SSB* 337). And Bonnefoy refers to: 'l'acte lui fondamentalement poétique par lequel Baudelaire pense à quelqu'un avec des mots qui empêchent d'en approcher de trop près: mots comme "la négresse, amaigrie et phtisique," dans "le Cygne"' [The fundamentally poetic act by which Baudelaire thinks about a person with words that prevent getting too close to them: words like 'the negress, emaciated and consumptive' in 'The Swan'] (*SSB* 338).

Thus the gesture of disguising a name is a mode of giving that is central to poetry: 'Ne pas nommer un être aimé par son nom, alors même que l'on sait que c'est ce nom son seul lieu, c'est la donation suprême que peut faire la poésie, accédant ainsi au meilleur de soi' [Not to refer to a loved one by their name, even knowing that their name is their only place, is the supreme gift poetry can bestow, through which it attains its highest virtue] (*SSB* 338). For what is bestowed on Jeanne by the three letters J. G. F. is recognition of her absolute human reality: 'J, G, F, — les trois lettres [...] signifient son [Baudelaire's] besoin de reconnaître à Jeanne de l'absolu — son absolu ordinaire, si je puis dire' [J,G,F, — these three letters [...] signal Baudelaire's need to recognize in Jeanne an absolute — her absolute ordinariness, so to speak] (*SSB* 338). The three letters of the dedication to 'Ma chère amie' are the expression of love:

> Ces trois lettres? C'est la poésie en ce qu'elle a de plus haut, autant que le plus bel hommage que Baudelaire pouvait rendre à Jeanne Duval: en vérité, une déclaration d'amour, en ces jours où la vie même de Jeanne était gravement en péril. (*SSB* 339)
>
> [These three letters? They are poetry at its greatest height, as well as the finest homage Baudelaire could pay Jeanne: in truth, a declaration of love, at a time when Jeanne's life was in grave danger.]

★   ★   ★   ★   ★

The value of these, essentially poetic, speculations and assertions on Bonnefoy's part is the evidence they give of the evolution of his own conception of poetry, and of the notion of presence, towards the arena of everyday human intercourse, and thus towards the necessity for ethical lucidity. It is also the case that they pave the way for beautiful poetry. But before coming on to how the withholding of Jeanne's name figures in recent poems by Bonnefoy, let us briefly consider some passages from *Le Siècle de Baudelaire* [*The Century of Baudelaire*] (2014) where further strands or parameters are added to the nexus of ideas entwined around the secret dedication to Jeanne.

The first of these is allegory. In 'Le Cygne' the poet in the city street famously exclaims that 'Tout pour moi devient allégorie' [Everything for me turns into allegory].[32] In 'Leurre et vérité des allégories' [The lure and the truth of allegories], through a re-reading of 'Le Cygne' and its relation to Jeanne, Bonnefoy rehabilitates allegory as a figure that can be the vehicle of existential concerns. If, in a first moment, allegory removes its object from the world, transposing it onto a higher plane, in a second moment it may do the reverse. Crucial here is the motion of thought enshrined in the Baudelairean 'penser à' (thinking about). The opening of 'Le Cygne' restores the humanity of a grieving woman to the mythic figure of Andromache. And the memory of the real swan in the street de-allegorizes the ideal bird, allowing it to become associated, in the poet's thoughts, with Jeanne. Bonnefoy then links the apparition of Jeanne in 'Le Cygne' with 'une troisième époque de la pensée de Charles sur Jeanne' [a third period in Charles's thinking about Jeanne], as evidenced in the 1856 letter to his mother, and 'Le Portrait', of which Bonnefoy writes, in connection with 'La Maladie et la Mort...': 'quelqu'un en lui brûle de passer à l'intérieur du temps de l'existence comme elle va pour y rencontrer, en Jeanne, un autre être que soi, l'autre même en son droit' [Someone inside him is burning to pass through into the time of ordinary existence so as to encounter, in Jeanne, a being other than oneself, the other person in his or her inherent legitimacy.].[33]

Hence the reference to the 'négresse amaigrie' in the city street, where Jeanne's ailing body is the crux of her reality. Here, for Bonnefoy, allegory, in its point-by-point concatenation of aspects, links with metonymy. By contrast with metaphor's immediate fusions, metonymy goes from one feature to another, from Jeanne as figure to her very real corporeal suffering. 'Mais près de la métaphore veille la métonymie. Laquelle remarque sur Jeanne [...] des signes de la maladie [...] ou cette main qu'elle a 'légère et maternelle' ...' [But close to metaphor metonymy is vigilant, and metonymy notices in Jeanne [...] the signs of illness [...] or her 'light and maternal' hand...].[34] To notice these lateral phenomena, that metaphor would elide, is to apprehend: 'l'indéfait qui demeure sous la pensée [...] la beauté propre de ce qui est, ici, maintenant. La métonymie, poésie en cela, est le regard qui survit dans l'affairement aveugle des métaphores' [the undefiled that persists beneath thought [...] the beauty of what simply is, here, now. Metonymy, and in this it is poetry itself, is the looking that remains fast amidst the blind flurrying of metaphors].[35] 'La métonymie plonge dans l'existence' [metonymy reaches deep down into existence].[36]

For Bonnefoy metonymy becomes central to the kind of conversion or commitment he calls 'le grand resaisissement' [the great re-grasping] which consists in making 'ces choses comme elles sont les composantes du lieu où vivre' [making things as they are the building blocks of a place where we may live].[37] And increasingly for Bonnefoy it is the city and urban experience that provide the forum for this recognition. In 'Paris en poésie' he argues that, in the 'Tableaux parisiens', 'la ville accède à la conscience de soi' [the city accedes to self-consciousness],[38] not as a playground for the narcissistic reveries of the flâneur, but as the place of a possible encounter with human beings as real presences. The lucidity of poetry is properly ethical, residing in the capacity to break out of the confines of fantasy and illusion: 'La possibilité poétique, c'est simplement d'*inquiéter* cette rêverie, de faire de la lucidité une obligation d'autant plus intense qu'elle se sait à jamais contrainte par cet illusoire qu'elle voudrait transgresser' [Poetic possibility lies simply in *disturbing* this reverie, in making of lucidity an obligation all the more intense that it knows itself to be constrained by the illusion out of which it seeks to break.].[39] Baudelaire, says Bonnefoy, came to see 'l'expérience morale' as an essential dimension of poetry.

★   ★   ★   ★   ★

In a 2008 sonnet, 'Le Tombeau de Charles Baudelaire' ['The tomb of Charles Baudelaire'], the poet muses that the only words that could have succoured Baudelaire when language had deserted him (a reference to the poet's final aphasia) were those — of course unknown to us — administered by the unknown woman he once called 'une Electre lointaine', who dissipated his fevered dreams 'd'une main légère' [with a light touch] — two direct citations from the *Paradis artificiels* preface. The tercets then meditate on the fact that Baudelaire had chosen to designate this person in a mysterious fashion — 'Parce qu'être compatissant est le mystère même' [because to be compassionate is the mystery itself] — alluding to her only through three letters:

> ce qui permit à ces trois lettres,
> J,G,F, de s'accroître dans la lumière
> Sur laquelle ta barque glisse. D'être pour toi
> Le port enfin, ses portiques, ses palmes.[40]

> [Which allowed these three letters,
> J,G,F, to grow in the light
> On which your boat glides. To be for you
> The harbour at last, with its porticos and its palms.]

In the logic of this poem, the letters J.G.F. are both the emblem of a love rooted in ethical lucidity and an enactment of the benison Jeanne's succour might have represented.

Near the beginning of the long poem 'L'Heure présente' ['The present hour'], the poetic voice surveys a fallen world, and picks out in the dark a series of mythical and biblical figures resembling 'images' culled from the repertoire of western representation:

> Et vois, là, c'est Vénus
> Penchée sur Adonis mourant. Et cette autre image,
> C'est Niobé, all tears. Je vois Judith
> Se redresser, sanglante. Je vois, dans la pluie d'or,
> Danaé, ses cheveux épars.[41]

> [And see, Venus over there
> Leaning over a dying Adonis. And this other image,
> Is Niobe, all tears. I see Judith
> Rise up, bloodied. I see, in the rain of gold,
> Danae, her hair all flowing.]

The allusion to Niobe, the incarnation of the mourning mother, is made more complex by the words 'all tears' from the lines where Shakespeare's Hamlet ironically contrasts the crocodile tears of his mother Gertrude with those of Niobe. The enumeration continues further on, with reference to two more female figures from Shakespeare, and then, surprisingly, to 'J.G.F.':

> Et te nommes-tu Ophélie,
> [...] Tu te penches sur lui,
> Le Prince fou, écartant ses cheveux
> Que colle la sueur de sa fièvre ...
> [...]
> Ô trahie,
> Te nommes-tu Desdémone?
> Willows, willows ...
> Et te nomme-t-il J.G.F.,
> Es-tu son 'Electre lointaine',
> Écoute bien:
> La maladie et la mort font des cendres
> De tout le feu qui pour nous flamboya.[42]

> [And are you called Ophelia,
> [...] You lean over him,
> The mad prince, parting his hair
> Which is sticky with his feverish sweat
> ...
> O you, so betrayed
> Are you called Desdemona?
> Willows, willows ...
> And does he call you J.G.F.,
> Are you his 'Distant Electra',
> Listen carefully:
> Sickness and death turn to ashes
> The fires that burned so high for we two.]

One thing that links these figures is the posture of leaning over and succouring a suffering figure: Venus over Adonis; Ophelia over Hamlet. With Desdemona the link is only implied, through the words 'willows, willows' which refer us to the Willow Song scene in *Othello* where Desdemona thinks of emulating her old servant, Barbara, who would 'hang [her] head all at one side' when she used to sing her the 'song of "willow"'.[43] With J.G.F. the link, as we have seen, can be explained by the reference to the maternal hand and to Electra in the dedication to J.G.F. of *Les Paradis artificiels*. Through a series of invocations, including that of Jeanne (without naming her), the poem establishes a sorority. But, via the switch from 'te nommes-tu' to 'te nomme t-il', the apostrophe to Jeanne also invokes Baudelaire. Moreover, the lines about J.G.F. repeat Baudelaire's own gesture of naming without naming, with its ethical implications (in Bonnefoy's reading). In 'L'Heure présente' Jeanne is named three times without being named. Once, via 'her' initials. A second time, via the sobriquet 'Electre lointaine' that Baudelaire borrowed from De Quincey, the addition of the possessive adjective 'son' making this not quite a quotation. A third time, by citing, without quotation marks, and without the capital letters for 'Maladie' and 'Mort' that might essentialize sickness and death, two lines from Baudelaire's 'Le Portrait'. Preferring lower case, Bonnefoy's lines point to the real suffering faced by Jeanne, and its profoundly human resonance. One of the summits of Bonnefoy's achievement, 'L'Heure présente' shows clearly, in its lovely embedding of J.G.F., the convergence of the poet's mature poetry of presence with an ethical lucidity that is focused on real proximity and exchange with other mortals, and rooted in a lifetime of reading Baudelaire.[44]

## Notes

1. Charles Baudelaire, *Œuvres Complètes*, ed. Claude Pichois, 2 vols (Paris: Gallimard, Pléiade, 1975), i, 80.
2. Paul Valéry, *Œuvres*, ed. Jean Hytier (Paris: Gallimard, Pléiade, 1957), p. 199.
3. Jean Prévost, *Baudelaire* (Paris: Mercure de France [1953], 1964), pp. 178–79.
4. Jean-Paul Sartre, *Baudelaire* (Paris: Gallimard, Idées [1947], 1963), p. 34.
5. Ibid., p. 28.
6. Ibid., p. 26.
7. Ibid., p. 29.
8. Ibid., p. 34.
9. Ibid., p. 30.
10. Ibid.
11. Ibid.
12. Jean-Paul Sartre, *La Lucidité et sa face d'ombre* (Paris: Gallimard, Arcades, 1986).
13. Yves Bonnefoy, *L'Improbable et autres essais* (Paris: Gallimard, Idées, 1983), p. 99.
14. Yves Bonnefoy, *Sous le signe de Baudelaire* (Paris: Gallimard, 2011), p. 14. Page references to this volume will be incorporated in the text, preceded by the abbreviation *SSB*.
15. *L'Improbable*, p. 115.
16. Ibid., p. 116.
17. Ibid., p. 117.
18. In Yves Bonnefoy, *L'Heure présente* (Paris: Mercure de France, 2011), pp. 79–98.
19. *Œuvres complètes*, i, 91.
20. Baudelaire, *Correspondance*, ed. Pichois and Ziegler, i (Paris: Gallimard, Pléiade, 1973), p. 356.
21. *Œuvres complètes*, i, 87.
22. Ibid., p. 78.
23. Ibid., p. 399.
24. Ibid., p. 400.
25. Ibid.
26. Thomas de Quincey, *Confessions of an English Opium-Eater* (London: Cresset Press, 1950), p. 292.
27. Ibid.
28. Ibid.
29. *Œuvres complètes*, i, 463.
30. *Correspondance*, p. 445.
31. *Œuvres complètes*, i, 40.
32. Ibid., p. 86.
33. *Le Siècle de Baudelaire* (Paris: Seuil, 2014), p. 49.
34. Ibid., p. 55.
35. Ibid.
36. Ibid., p. 89.
37. Ibid., p. 75.
38. Ibid., p. 197.

39. Ibid., p. 199.
40. *La Longue Chaîne de l'ancre* (Paris: Mercure de France, 2008), p. 112.
41. *L'Heure présente* (Paris: Mercure de France, 2011), p. 83.
42. Ibid., p. 84.
43. See Bonnefoy, 'La Tête penchée de Desdémone', in *Othello*, éd. bilingue (Gallimard: Folio théâtre, 2001), pp. 7–67.
44. For a fuller discussion of the poem see Michael Sheringham, '"L'heure présente": invocation, amitié, ressourcement', in Michèle Finck and Patrick Werly, eds, *Yves Bonnefoy: poésie et dialogue* (Strasbourg: Presses Universitaires de Strasbourg, 2013), pp. 35–54.

# 12

# L'Amour et son double:
# Faces of Love in Yves Bonnefoy

In *The Characters of Love*, John Bayley observes that if love is so universal a theme in literature it is 'because of the remarkable variety of its worlds'.[1] Love in Proust is solipsism, separation, sickness; love in Lawrence is intense communion, dark knowledge, and so forth. Unlike death, love has no fixed place in the span of our lives, and by comparison with greed, power, or ambition, it is multi-dimensional: private and social, mental and physical. The 'worlds of love' are not only varied as enactments of a central human experience, they are various in respect of the forms of consciousness a writer can express through them. And this is all the more evident in lyric poetry where a literary tradition which has made it at times incumbent on the poet to be a lover has been exploited in ways which have magnified the capacity for one human emotion to be a vast repository of tropes through which areas of human reality, stretching well beyond the apparent limits of love itself, can be figured. In Dante and Petrarch, human love, sometimes mirroring, sometimes alienating divine love, is at the heart of a total vision of the universe. In Scève, and in Renaissance poetry generally, the afflictions and felicities of the lover become the idiom in which a wide-ranging psychological reality can be voiced and integrated in wider frameworks of knowledge. In Baudelaire, love provides the costume, repertoire, and properties for the acting-out of a vast array of emotions and fantasies, but also, more crucially, it becomes the stage, essentially imaginary and verbal, on which consciousness is confronted most acutely with its own machinations. In Éluard, love and language reciprocally engender a world of endless proliferation. And so on.

The poetry of Yves Bonnefoy is less evidently a poetry of love than that of some of these predecessors. The cult of woman and the eternal feminine, so pervasive in the lyric tradition, and the complexion of the 'Je' of his poems, are rarely identifiable — and then only partially — with the amorous subject of the lyric tradition. The 'Je' in Bonnefoy's poetry is characteristically that of a consciousness seeking to enact in language certain experiences in which the world, and our own existence within it, is encountered with an unusual intensity. Such experiences and the words that enshrine them are the domain of *la présence*. Yet if it is above all else a poetry of presence, Bonnefoy's is also a poetry of love. As I shall seek to show, love, along with place, is a primordial context for *la présence*, though it is a context which is not given once and for all, but subject to evolution. If love in Bonnefoy, as in some of the other poets I mentioned, is always doubled by a wider vision, its worlds, its ways of figuring how we dwell in the world, change markedly as his work develops. It is this shifting significance, and these changing faces of love, that I propose to study.

I think it is possible to identify three principal faces — and phases — and I shall examine these in turn. First the transgressive vision of love, under the sign of eroticism, which we find in Bonnefoy's first main collection of poems, *Du mouvement et de l'immobilité de Douve* (1953). Next, the calmer, more sensual, dreamlike love of *Pierre écrite* (1965). And finally the integration of these into a wider vision of love, associated with Agape rather than Eros, which is crucial to all Bonnefoy's writing since the early seventies, and at the heart of his great long poem, *Dans le leurre du seuil* (1975).

In the first section of *Douve*, 'Théâtre', the reader is confronted with a dimension of experience of which the feminine presence named Douve is both the emblem and the catalyst. The repetitions of the name Douve, and the reiterated second person pronoun which invokes it, seem simultaneously to refer to a person, a human presence, and to forestall any such identification. The word Douve becomes the subject of a conflicting range of predicates whose overall effect is to disperse identity into a play of processes and movements: dying, metamorphosis, transition, apotheosis. One of the chief things that make this ambiguity about Douve possible, and create a framework for the interplay of the personal and impersonal, the immanent and the transcendent, is a specific idiom: that of erotic experience.
Il s'agissait d'un vent plus fort que nos mémoires

> Stupeur des robes et cri des rocs — et tu passais devant ces flammes
> La tête quadrillée les mains fendues et toute
> En quête de la mort sur les tambours exultants de tes gestes
>
> C'était jour de tes seins
> Et tu régnais enfin absente de ma tête

> [It was a matter of a wind stronger than our memories | Dresses' stupor and rocks' cries — and you passed in front of these flames | Your head sectioned into squares your hands split and the whole | Questing for death on the exultant drums of your gestures || It was day of your breasts | And you reigned finally absent from my head]

Here, the third poem in the sequence (p. 47)[2] picks up a reference to the wind at the end of the preceding one where fragments of speech, attributed to Douve, had contrasted *l'ivresse imparfaite de vivre* [the imperfect drunkenness of living] with certain elemental experiences, such as the wind, associated by implication with death and intoxication.

The wind becomes identified with a range of percepts which together create the impression of an erotic dance in which, like a shaman, the figure of Douve seems to invoke an order of symbolic, ritualized realities. The penultimate line underscores the erotic connotations by identifying Douve's breasts as a source of light, and the last proclaiming Douve's reign, and also extends the significance of the erotic register by identifying it with the obliteration of the mental or psychological order.

This makes a link with the first line which had associated the power of the wind with the scoring out of memory and the individual past. The poem, then, concerns the attainment of a level of being beyond the realm of the mental and psychological, and it associates this with erotic experience, or at least communicates the experience in images with a strong erotic content. A subsequent poem (p. 57) registers the inadequacy of both denotative and figurative language with regard to a certain experience of presence.

> Ton visage ce soir éclairé par la terre,
> Mais je vois tes yeux se corrompre
> Et le mot visage n'a plus de sens
> La mer intérieure éclairée d'aigles tournants,
> Ceci est une image.
> Je te détiens froide à une profondeur où les images ne prennent plus

[Your face this evening lit by the earth | But I see your eyes become corrupted | And the word face no longer has any meaning || The interior sea lit by turning eagles, | This is an image. | I hold you cold at a depth where images no longer take hold]

Douve's face, perceived in its quiddity, as a phenomenon on our planet, shifts out of the framework of ordinary representations; and metaphorical language, however convulsive, can only betray its arbitrariness when set the task of evoking the subject's sense of her inner being. But set against these failures is the prestige of another mode of knowledge, beyond images or psychology, which is the province of intense physical, erotic presence: 'Je te détiens froide à une profondeur où les images ne prennent plus'.

At this stage of Bonnefoy's work, love, passion, the erotic is not in itself what is at stake: it is an imaginary context for the exploration of a region of experience. If Douve flickers between concrete and abstract, human and inhuman, it is because she is, so to speak, an impersonation of presence. In these early poems, which belong to the pole of movement in the polarity between movement and immobility registered in the book's title, presence is apprehended in terms of the transgression of limits; the abolition of mind in favour of body; of light and colour in favour of sound, substance and texture; of words in favour of gestures. And presence is linked to a temporality which denies duration and allows only the spasm, the seizure, the instant. A particular mode of presence finds expression in a particular vision of the erotic which can be shown to have affinities with the one so hauntingly articulated by Georges Bataille, a writer who made a strong impression on Bonnefoy. In this vision erotic experience is seen as the context in which human beings can encounter most fully their mortal condition or, to use a word we often find in Bonnefoy, their finitude. The erotic subject is divested of what makes him, in Bataille's phrase 'un être constitué': 'Ce qui est en jeu dans l'érotisme est toujours une dissolution des formes constituées' [There is always at play in eroticism a dissolution of constituted forms]; and he seeks, in and through a 'renversement qui chavire' [reversal which capsizes], to attain 'un point où le cœur manque' [a spot where the heart is missing], a point at which he is momentarily restored to that unbroken continuity of being for which since birth he is nostalgic, and to which death promises obscurely to restore him: 'De l'érotisme il est possible de dire que c'est l'approbation de la vie jusque dans la mort' [One can say of eroticism that it is the approval of life all the way into death].[3] Figured in this way, the erotic is an experience of limits briefly transgressed and identity momentarily ceded. But the last poem of 'Théâtre' registers disquiet at this; 'Mais Douve d'un instant cette flèche retombe' [But Douve of an instant this arrow falls back down] (p. 63), and in the next two sections of the book the intensely physical and erotic dimensions of Douve fade into the background, as alternative images of presence are explored. But the erotic returns, in a slightly different guise, in the fourth section, 'L'Orangerie', which begins the overall movement towards place that marks the book as a whole. Here, we have shifted towards the pole of 'Immobilité', and the emphasis is not on the moment of transgression but on a state of definitive order and perpetuity to be achieved through a sacrifice in which the spiritual and the erotic are indissolubly linked. The poems are in fact related to a symbolic narrative, called 'L'Ordalie' [The Ordeal], where a man, mortally wounded at the hands of a woman, succeeds in reaching an Orangery, and then dies strangely transfigured.[4] Elements of this scenario recur, but the imaginative crux of these poems is a stasis that is at the same time an excess of movement, a multiplicity of forces having found a dialectical point of suspended animation. The salamander is a key image here and in this poem, part of 'La Salamandre' (p. 98), Douve and the salamander are fused.

> Regarde-moi, regarde-moi, j'ai couru!
> Je suis près de toi, Douve, je t'éclaire. Il n'y a plus entre nous que cette lampe rocailleuse, ce peu d'ombre apaisé, nos mains que l'ombre attend. Salamandre surprise, tu demeures immobile.
> Ayant vécu l'instant où la chair la plus proche se mue en connaissance.

> [Look at me, look at me, I ran! | I'm close to you, Douve, I illuminate you. || There is nothing more between us than this stony lamp, this small piece of appeased shadow, our hands which the shadow is waiting for. A salamander taken by surprise, you remain still. || Having lived the moment in which the closest flesh turns into knowledge.]

The conjunction of Douve's stillness with the rapid motion she describes is seen to engender an intense movement of reciprocity with the 'je', formulated magnificently in terms which confer on it an intense physical proximity to another being, in circumstances which momentarily conjoin disparate contexts, the capacity to constitute knowledge: 'la chair la plus proche se mue en connaissance'.

Yet, in the poetic charge of such moments, the erotic betrays its essentially imaginary and self-enclosed status. As a mode in which the idea of presence is enacted and explored in poetry, the erotic seems to have the advantage of distancing the realm of thought and representation, thereby underlining the strong anti-conceptual strand in Bonnefoy's sense of presence. Yet this privilege of the erotic is more apparent than real. In both its mobile and immobile manifestations, the erotic remains tied to the mental representations of the subject, who is primarily a witness and a voice rather than a participant. While it apparently roots the experience of presence in the here and now of bodily experience, and if it seems to make of Douve a creature of flesh and blood, in fact it only obliges the imagining subject to spill this blood, to break the bounds of this body, to symbolize and conceptualize the here and now, in short to derealize and disembody Douve, restoring to her proper name its haunting emptiness and openness. Powerful as its pull is — towards body, substance, depth — the erotic does not succeed in incarnating presence, or in breaking the bounds of the self and its representations. On the contrary, it risks alienating the sense of presence in the obsessions of the ego when it pretends to obliterate them in favour of an encounter with the other.

★    ★    ★    ★    ★

In now moving on to other faces of love, I want first to indicate how I think they connect with the analysis of *Douve*. What remained latent there, as part of the complex dynamics of the volume as a whole, is externalized more and more explicitly as a conflict and a debate. The status of the erotic, or more often than that the workings of amorous desire, is explicitly evaluated in the light of a criterion of presence articulated with increasing clarity: presence as 'ce qui est', the *hic et nunc* apprehended fully and intensely.

The first phase in this debate occurs in Bonnefoy's second collection of poems, *Hier Régnant Désert* [Yesterday Reigning Barren] (1958). At the heart of the haunting, often sombre, poems which make up much of the book, is a sense of guilt which attaches to the incapacity to love the world as it is. A repeated theme is the desire to remake a link with all that Douve had forsaken: the individual past, one's own memory and childhood, the grey ordinary world of the everyday. Again and again in these poems, where solitude reigns and human love is absent, the desolation of scepticism reanimates the temptation to return to the fabrications of the poet's earlier faith, but a new vigilance has arisen in the poetic consciousness, ceaselessly alert to the devious paths by which the imaginary seeks to substitute its own order for that of the real. In *Hier Régnant Désert*, 'le difficile réel' [difficult reality], to quote an essay from this period, becomes the poet's task, and a dominant aspiration is the desire to alter his relation to the world of reality without changing the real into something else: 'mêler deux lumières' [to mix two lights], to find in the intensity of presence a reconciliation between the world as it is and our desire to transcend it, a reconciliation that is heard in the voice of Kathleen Ferrier (p. 159), 'voix mêlée de couleur grise' [a grey, mixed voice], both 'lumière' and 'néant de la lumière', a thing of this world, yet sustained by the eternal.

Like Douve, *Hier Régnant Désert* culminates in poems of place. Whereas in Douve real and symbolic places had mingled, giving the category of place an intermediate status, here it is through encounters with places very much of this world that the capacity to love is restored. 'À une terre d'aube' [To a dawn land] celebrates the numinous places of Greece in some of Bonnefoy's most beautiful poems, and it seems as if place has eclipsed human reality as a context for presence. But when we open Bonnefoy's next collection, *Pierre écrite* [Written Stone] (1965) we are immediately plunged again into one of the 'worlds' of love, although now it is a world very different from the eroticism of Douve. In the first section, 'L'Été de nuit' [The Night Summer], we are presented with an amorous climate of calm, blissful ecstasy. And in an initial sequence of poems, 'L'Été de nuit' proper, a period of time, a flawless summer spent in loving harmony, is depicted as a cruise on calmer waters. The lovers' room becomes a ship, with the woman as the figurehead, or a garden, 'dont l'ange | A refermé les portes sans retour' [whose doors the angel | Has closed, leaving no way back] (p. 185). And one of the things that is emphasized about this newfound love is that it reunites the lover, the 'je' by healing the rifts and conflicts which divide him. Love, instead of being the context for a presence achieved in violent transgression, comes to sponsor presence through the liquidation and transcendence of the desire to contest the given order of the world.

> Voici presque l'instant
> Où il n'est plus de jour, plus de nuit, tant l'étoile
> A grandi pour bénir ce corps brun, souriant,
> Illimité, une eau qui sans chimère bouge.
> Ces frêles mains terrestres dénoueront
>
> Le nœud triste des rêves.
> La clarté protégée reposera
> Sur la table des eaux.
> L'étoile aime l'écume, et brûlera
> Dans cette robe grise.

[Here almost is the moment | When it is no longer day, no longer night, so much has the sun | Grown to bless this brown body, smiling, | Limitless, a water which moves without chimera. These frail earthly hands will untie || The sad knot of dreams. | The protected brightness will lie | On the table of the waters. || The star loves the sea-spray , and will burn | In this grey dress.]

Here, in the fifth poem of 'L'Été de nuit' (p. 189), the starry night sky which obliterates the division of night and day is linked with the proximity of the lover's body, also limitless, and is identified with the calm sea in which no imaginary monsters or fabled creatures lurk. And this respite from the imagination's clamour for otherness, for the unreal, or for the fringes of reality, is then credited to the 'frêles mains terrestres' which, as they undo the 'nœud triste des rêves', do not create anything but shelter clarity from the turmoil of the restless mind.

Yet this poem is a turning-point, and hereafter, in those which follow, the restless mind is given its head again, the idyllic picture is submitted to scrutiny and contaminated by doubts. These doubts are of the same order as those which, as L'Arriere-Pays will document, can assail the poet when he prefers Delphi to Dover: am I not substituting yet another dream, another projection of my own desires, for the reality, the presence I want to join?[5] Are there not symptoms, in this idyllic world in which we are perhaps marooned as much as becalmed, of a seemingly inveterate tendency to aspire beyond the finite? In the seventh poem of the sequence (p. 191) we can see these doubts enacted in terms of a double *mise en scène* of the subject's relation to his experience.

> N'avions-nous pas l'été à franchir, comme un large
> Océan immobile, et moi simple, couché
> Sur les yeux et la bouche et l'âme de l'étrave,
> Aimant l'été, buvant tes yeux sans souvenirs,
> N'étais-je pas le rêve aux prunelles absentes
> Qui prend et ne prend pas, et ne veut retenir
> De ta couleur d'été qu'un bleu d'une autre pierre
> Pour un été plus grand, où rien ne peut finir?

[Don't we have the summer to cross, like a large | Motionless ocean, and myself simple, recumbent | On the eyes and the mouth and the soul of the vessel, | Loving the summer, drinking your eyes without memory, | Was I not the dream with vacant pupils | Which takes and does not take, and does not want to retain | Anything of your summer colour except a blue of another stone | For a vaster summer, one where nothing can finish?]

On the one hand the poet is restored to tranquillity, simplicity, and ecstatic contemplation of what is proximate; but, at the same time, he is 'le rêve aux prunelles absentes', a swooning creature who averts his eyes from the real and seeks the gratification of specific, pre-determined desires. Where she is 'sans souvenirs', he fabricates, selects, 'et ne veut retenir | De ta couleur d'été qu'un bleu d'une autre pierre | Pour un été plus grand, où rien ne peut finir', transforming an intense engagement with reality into what Yeats called the 'artifice of eternity', 'ce haut artifice, l'éternel' in Bonnefoy's own translation.[6]

A few poems later, the poet notes self-accusingly, in response to the lover's invitation simply to look at her:

> Je t'inventais
> Sous l'arche d'un miroir orageux, qui prenait
> La parcelle d'un rouge en toi, impartageable
> Et l'enflammait 'là-bas', au mascaret de mort. (p. 194)

[I would invent you | Under the arch of a stormy mirror, which took | The portion of a red within you, unshareable | And enflamed it 'down there', in the deathly rip-tide.]

In his stormy mirror the poet transmutes chosen fragments of a cherished reality, 'la parcelle d'un rouge en toi', and, removing them from a world of give and take and change, he irradiates them, not here, but 'là-bas', 'au mascaret de mort', in the dark, deathly tidal-wave of the imagination, which reverses the current of things, and goes back up the estuary into the heartland of reality. And in the next poem, 'Le Jardin' (p. 195), the stars and the beautiful star-lit tracks, are admonished in these terms:

> Vous nous preniez le vrai jardin,
> Tous les chemins du ciel étoilé faisant ombre
> Sur le chant naufragé, sur notre route obscure.

[You removed from us the true garden, | All the paths of the starry sky casting shadow | On the song of the shipwrecked, on our dark way.]

The ideal confiscates the real: its light only engulfs our own obscure being in darker shadows. Love, then, albeit with a new face, reasserts itself as a context for presence in *Pierre écrite*, but only to become caught in a conflict which threatens to disqualify it, like eroticism, as the site of imaginative energies which seem to open, but ultimately block, our encounter with 'ce qui est'. The immediate aftermath of the conflict played out in the later poems of 'L'Été de nuit' is a plunge into the dark, negative poems of the 'Pierre écrite' section. These poems seem in fact to have been written earlier, since they were initially published in 1959; but in the dialectic of *Pierre écrite* as a whole, these dark poems create a border between the identification of a conflict and its (at least partial) resolution.

The resolution is initiated in 'Un Feu va devant nous', a sequence of love poems which again seem to grow out of the experience of a single time and place — a summer and a room. The first poem, 'La Chambre' (p. 221) quietly celebrates a unity which is asserted not in terms of the abolition of distance and difference nor achieved at the expense of sacrificing the perceived to the illusions of the perceiver, but in the communion of 'deux lumières', 'deux pays de sommeil | Communicant par leurs marches de pierre | Où se perdait l'eau non trouble d'un rêve | Toujours se reformant, toujours brisé' [two lands of sleep | Communicating through their stone steps | Where the untroubled water of a dream lost itself | Always reforming itself, always broken]. There is here, it seems, an acceptance of the intermingling, the dialectic, of the real and the imaginary, the proximate and the distant, 'ici' and 'là-bas': 'La main pure dormait près de la main soucieuse' [the innocent hand slept beside the anxious hand]. The anxieties of the lover who cannot still his thirst for otherness are now encompassed within a deeper union which is no longer called into question by them. And as a result, these desires, wonderfully rendered in the next poem, 'L'Épaule' [The Shoulder] (p. 222), as 'tout mon obscur déchirement de nuit | Et toute cette écume amère des images' [all my arcane nocturnal rifts | And all this bitter spray of images], only provisionally and intermittently alienate him from the proximate, and now tend instead to feed back into and illuminate the reality which inspires them. The lover's shoulder is always there, creating a tangible world within which the dream world, 'tout ce haut rougeoiement d'un impossible été' [all this high glow of an impossible summer], can constitute a flight from and then a return to the here and now of presence. Love now provides a context in which presence is intermittently experienced, within the folds of temporality.

> UNE PIERRE
> Un feu va devant nous.
> J'aperçois par instants ta nuque, ton visage
> Puis, rien que le flambeau,
> Rien que le feu massif, le mascaret des morts.
>
> Cendre qui te détaches de la flamme
> Dans la lumière du soir,
> O présence,
> Sous ta voûte furtive accueille-nous
> Pour une fête obscure. (p. 232)

[A STONE | A fire goes before us. | I catch sight now and then of the back of your neck, your face | Then, nothing but the torch, | Nothing but the massive fire | the rip-tide of the dead. || Cinder detaching yourself from the flame |

In the light of the evening, | Oh presence | Welcome us beneath your hidden vault | To a dark celebration.]

The flickering light of a torch permits glimpses of the loved one's body in its physical proximity even if the incandescence of the torch constantly threatens to obliterate presence by asserting its 'feu massif': once again the deathly tidal wave of the imagination threatens reality. The site of presence is not the flame but the ash it sheds as the imagination burns itself out in the evening light, 'Pour une fête obscure'. What is asserted is constancy, a willingness to live out the intermittence of the presence. And through this, by another twist of the dialectic, what is achieved is a deepening, and a transfiguration, of the subject's relation to reality, a change in the light which seems to signal at once as the rebirth and the retreat of a divinity, apprehended, as it were, through a renunciation of all claims on the divine. The gods return to the earth in return for our willingness to purge the earth of our gods. So we read, in 'La lumière, changée' (p. 233),

> Dieu qui n'es pas, pose ta main sur notre épaule,
> [...]
> Renonce-toi en nous comme un fruit se déchire,
> Efface-nous en toi. Découvre nous
> Le sens mystérieux de ce qui n'est que simple
> Et fût tombé sans feu dans des mots sans amour.

[God who is not, place your hand on our shoulder, | [...] | Renounce yourself in us as a fruit splits apart, | Erase yourself in us. Reveal to us | The mysterious meaning of what is only simple | And would have fallen without fire into words without love.]

And we arrive on the threshold of the third face of love in Bonnefoy, a phase which runs from the later poems of *Pierre écrite* onwards, where love takes on a much wider resonance in his work. A displacement occurs. The opposition between love and dream, between human love as a context for presence, and the idolatrous imagination which disfigures it, is encompassed in a wider opposition. At first sight, this is an opposition between all the forms of what Bonnefoy calls *l'excarnation*, all activities of mind that resolve themselves into an image, a beguiling coherence; and the consent to love what is, a consent which these activities foster, yet in the end foreclose. But to understand what is really at stake in this third sense of love, we need to see how, in encompassing their opposition; it both resolves it and changes its nature.

If, in the later poems of *Pierre écrite*, an apparent resolution is achieved, it is largely through the abolition of one of the terms: the renunciation of images becomes the key to our restoration to the world in its simplicity and clarity, a clarity heralded by a language, a diction, purged of obscurity:

> Nous n'avons plus besoin
> D'images déchirantes pour aimer
> Cet arbre nous suffit là-bas... (p. 243)

[We no longer need | Images which tear at us in order to love | That tree down there is enough for us...]

We can, perhaps, wean ourselves of the images we had craved through a conversion, within ourselves, to the simple. In a lovely poem to Persephone, to Coré who succumbed to temptation, and picked the flowers, and was banished to the underworld, yet returns intermittently to the earth, and so is associated for ever with the mystery of growth, the poet reassures her:

> ... Je comprends
> Cette faute, la mort [...]
> ... Mais oui, prends.
> La faute de la fleur coupée nous est remise,
> Toute l'âme se voûte autour d'un dire simple (p. 242)

> [...I understand | This fault, death [...] Yes, of course, take it. | The culled flower's fault is restored to us, | Soul forms a vault over simple utterance.]

Throughout this cycle, 'Le Dialogue d'angoisse et de désir', there is ambivalence: may we redeem ourselves once and for all, or is the 'dire simple' [simple utterance] the intermittent product of a constant rise and fall? This question will be at the heart of the later work, including Bonnefoy's essays on poets and painters.

For example, the sense that a love of the given world is a path to which we can convert ourselves by renouncing images figures in Bonnefoy's discussion of Poussin in his remarkable book on the early baroque period in Rome. In Bonnefoy's analysis, Poussin remained torn between 'deux intuitions opposées d'une profusion du réel [associated with the erotic] et des limites de la personne' [two opposed intuitions, of the profusion of the real and of the limits of the person], between desire and finitude; and Bonnefoy analyses alternative paths manifested in the paintings.[7] There is, for example, the 'rationalisme ardent' which anticipates neo-classicism; the dissociation of form and content, supremely represented by the 'Triumph of David' in the Dulwich collection, which anticipates modern art; and there is the suite of paintings on the theme of *Moïse sauvé* [Moses saved]. These last remain a key reference-point for Bonnefoy, because in them he identifies a more secret, obscure path: that of love, manifested through 'ses données primordiales: l'enfance, le vrai lieu, la femme rédemptrice, le destin' [its primordial givens: childhood, the true place, the redeeming woman, destiny], and the recognition that 'on ne peut se passer, dans le contact avec l'être, de la médiation des êtres particuliers' [one cannot, in one's contact with being, do without the mediation of particular beings]. But in Poussin this path led, ultimately, nowhere; the impulses and velleities Bonnefoy identifies remained warring forces in his work and his destiny.

The same is true in a deeper, profounder way, perhaps, in Baudelaire, and it is in the admirable essay centred on Baudelaire's fluctuating and ambivalent attitude to Rubens that Bonnefoy gives full expression to a conception of love which, above and beyond the divisions which tore Baudelaire in two, 'cette destinée poétique qui se disloque entre idéal et présence' [this poetic destiny, broken up between ideal and presence], reconciles these opposing forces by integrating them within an open and compassionate attitude.[8]

In the contradictions between Baudelaire's initial enthusiasm for Rubens in 'Les Phares' [The Lighthouses], and his ferocious condemnation of him some years later in Brussels, Bonnefoy diagnoses a sense of guilt on Baudelaire's part at his incapacity to open himself to others, and a lucid recognition of his 'refus de l'échange' [refusal of human exchange], even granted the fundamental shift which divides the poems of 'L'Idéal' [the Ideal] from the 'Tableaux parisiens' [Parisian tableaux]. But having made his diagnosis, Bonnefoy acknowledges a change in his own attitude, and this essay takes a remarkable and unexpected turn. Initially he is tempted to endorse Baudelaire's self-condemnation, and to confirm what it implies: the ineradicable contradiction between the values of art and those of existence, with the implication that one has to choose between them. But then, seeking to understand Baudelaire's enthusiasm for the Jesuit ecclesiastical architecture of Brussels, with its strange mixture of fussy adornment and hieratic simplicity, Bonnefoy wonders if Baudelaire's change of heart reflected a deeper perception: a sense that the claim Rubens's work might have to solidarity with the world in its luxuriant mutability was in fact unfounded. Perhaps the poet's spleen was vented not against an artist who effortlessly achieved what his successor found so elusive, but against one who deluded himself, and others, into thinking that he was in league with the real when in truth his paintings, in their blithe perfection, sublimate and eradicate the here and now as surely as the most stylized art. And Bonnefoy wonders if the enthusiasm for Jesuit churches might indicate Baudelaire's intuition that an art of presence, or of love for human beings in their finitude, far from eradicating the image, the formalizing fictions of the imagination, would be an art in which the image was acknowledged for what it was and what it represented, while at the same time made relative by other factors. An art, then, which would acknowledge the contradictions endemic to it and, in so doing, transcend them to some extent. As such the work of art would be a reflection of our perennial condition as creatures of imagination, but also, beyond this, it would illuminate our condition as mortal beings and our presence in the world, duly recognized and made available to love.

In this connection it is important to recognize, as Bonnefoy often reminds us, that debates which seem confined to the aesthetic realm have resonances far beyond it. As he stressed in his inaugural lesson at the Collège de France, our daily existence is in itself the territory of strife between the image and presence. The discourses of our society, and ideologies, our opinions, our impoverished speech, are just as closed a prison, sequester us just as surely away from any encounter with the world's unity, which presence manifests, as the aesthete's predilection for the consolations of form. Indeed they do so all the more, given that the imaginary world of the artist is already a critique of our order, though a futile one unless it lucidly acknowledges its own nature. In the realms of both art and daily existence our capacity to avoid closure, to engender presence, is blocked by the narrower desires of the ego which always has a stake in things as they appear in the light of its own quest for gratification, irrespective of the existence of others. But for Bonnefoy love is manifest, and engenders presence not when it shuns these blocks and imagines a new order for itself, another image, but when, in recognition of a criterion which exists fully only in the reciprocity of human beings, and in a sense of human community, it checks the ego's projections and reorientates the self towards the world. This means that poetry should recognize that, as speech, as *parole* as well as *langue*, it is in its essence 'une guerre contre l'image' [a war against the image] as much (though not more) as it is the realm of the image.[9] And he writes, 'La poésie qui vainc l'image dans l'écriture est amour et en cela même' [The poetry which conquers the image in writing is love by dint of this very act].[10] *Dans l'écriture*: the image must have its say, but it must not be allowed the last word.

In Bonnefoy's recent work we find a new formulation of the dialectic between poetry and existence. In our daily life we wage war against the image when we consent to break out of our ego's demands, 'les gravitations de l'égocentrisme', and fully acknowledge the horizon on which other existences alone give ours its meaning. And in doing so, in consenting to this 'décrispation' [loosening], we contribute to 'l'instauration d'un temps partagé, d'une finitude comprise' [the establishment of a shared time, of an understood finitude],[11] we participate in a process equivalent in every way to what the poet does, because it stems from the same origins as the word within us. We are close here, to be sure, to the relationship of the Imaginary and Symbolic orders described by Lacan, but their articulation to the third order, the Real, is different: for Lacan the Real is the impossible, for Bonnefoy it is, precisely, the improbable and hence the possible.

As well as in the poetry, then, Bonnefoy's conception of love has been articulated in his essays on poets and painters — Baudelaire, Jouve, Mallarmé; new work on Rimbaud focusing on his relation to his mother and on a poem in which love is derided; Marceline Desbordes-Valmore, and soon a new book on Giacometti. But another framework must, at least briefly, be mentioned: that of theology.

The understanding of love that we find in the recent work has affinities, noted by Bonnefoy, with Agape, Christian love as conceived by the fathers of the early church and then codified by St Paul in opposition to the Eros of Plato and, in particular to the dark, dualistic Platonism of the gnostic sects. Bonnefoy frequently uses the term 'la gnose' in the context of the image, to designate the tendency, so marked in the modern poetic tradition, to depreciate the real world, and to substitute for it a remote or ideal one. Agape, as Anders Nygren shows in his major treatise,[12] is a love which, in response to God's willingness to love us without question, and to incarnate Himself in our mortal condition, addresses itself above all to other people, not for this reason or that reason, this quality or that quality, but because they are our kin: it is a love for what is incarnate and not transcendent, and it is a love which recognizes an order implicit in the world as given. As Denis de Rougemont puts it:

> Pour L'Éros, la créature n'était qu'un prétexte illusoire, une occasion de s'enflammer; et il fallait aussitôt s'en déprendre, puisque le but était de brûler jusqu'à en mourir! L'être particulier n'était guère qu'un défaut et un obscurcissement de l'Être unique.

> [For Eros, the creature was merely an illusory pretext, an opportunity to catch fire — and one had to extricate oneself from it as soon as possible, for the goal was to burn until one died! The particular being was at best a flaw, something which obscured unique Being.]

Agape, on the other hand, 'fait apparaître le prochain' [makes a fellow human being visible]. It is an 'obéissance dans le présent' [obedience in the present], but it is reciprocal: 'il aime l'autre tel qu'il est, au lieu d'aimer l'idée de l'amour' [it loves the other as they are, instead of loving the idea of love].[13] The theological resonance in Bonnefoy is important because it emphasizes that whilst his work is not religious in the sense of implying belief in a personal God, what is at stake is a theology of the earth, the rediscovery of 'le sens', a unity and coherence in the world. As such, these theological resonances provide an appropriate prelude to a brief account of love in *Dans le leurre du seuil*.

*Dans le leurre du seuil* is an immense and very intricate poem, composed, in some respects, like a musical score with the echo and variation of a great many major and minor motifs over its seven parts. Although one cannot hope to do it justice in a brief space, a survey of love in Bonnefoy would be incomplete if it did not attempt to indicate both how, in its overall movement, the poem manifests the conception of love at the heart of Bonnefoy's mature work, and how love between man and woman fits into this latest form that his poetic world has taken. In simple terms, what we encounter is a poetic structure within which there is a constant to and fro between the daily experience of a couple and their child, in a given place, and the macrocosm of the world. Once again we have the elements of a summer, or rather a succession of summers at times dramatically condensed into one temporal frame, so that there is both concentration and duration. But there is no longer the tendency to seal off the experience, nor the tendency for it to fade away at the points when presence is manifested in the beauty and harmony of the external world. Instead, increasingly as the poem develops, the relationship between the couple becomes a constant reference-point and context for a great many ways of encountering the world. And the strife between, on the one hand, the dream, the image, 'la gnose', the anxious desire to create a closed and definitive order of meaning, and, on the other hand, that countervailing force which dissolves this desire, and keeps open the channels through which the subject relates to a world of change and time, finds its primary context within a loving relationship which acknowledges the struggle and renders it beneficent. And, in so doing, it imparts this wise acquiescence to other areas, language, for example, which at the same time nourish and sustain it in its constant evolution. This primary context might be characterized in terms Bonnefoy uses in his essay on Marceline Desbordes-Valmore: 'les données de la vie que l'homme et la femme partagent, et que le rêve quitte mais que l'amour recommence' [the givens of life which man and woman share, and which dreams forsake but which love reinaugurates].[14]

This centrality emerges fully in what is fittingly the fourth and middle section of the poem: 'Deux Barques'. The opening sections had been sombre in their tonality. The first, 'Le Fleuve', is permeated by anxiety at the thought that we have lost the means of integrating our sense of the world's radiance with any order of meaning other than those which create coherence at the expense of the world as it is, separating 'le sens' from 'la forme et la couleur', giving us a 'world' only at an abstract level. And the second section, 'Dans le leurre du seuil', is dominated by the mythic figure of a ferryman, 'le passeur', who represents the vain attempt to locate and find meaning by breaking through the bounds of the world and seeking another shore, 'l'autre rive'. In so doing, he only cuts himself off from his organic links with the human community he tries to serve, and in his gnostic quest only exacerbates the dualism diagnosed in the opening section of the poem. But in the third section, 'Deux couleurs', a crucial reversal takes place: instead of the attempt to transcend the existing world represented in Part Two by a humble dog and a repeated refrain, 'Plus avant que le chien' [Farther forward than the dog], what is now urged is a transcending of the dream of an 'ailleurs', represented by the image of a star. The section opens with the words 'Plus avant que l'étoile', which are then identified with the two lovers whose hands in mutual confidence seek 'Pour mieux que l'or | Et que naisse la vie de rien qu'un rêve' [For something better than gold | And that life be born from nothing but a dream]. In the rest of this section, the birth of a child, with its Christian resonances, particularly in conjunction with the star, is seen as the fulfilment not of a dream but of the transcendence of that dream, and of the desire for incarnation. The dream is nevertheless crucial, not as an end but as mediation, a catalyst that must be aspired to but at the same time seen for what it is. 'Bois' [Drink] says the beloved to her lover, 'Au sens qui rêve' [From the cup of dreaming sense]. And he drinks: 'j'ai confiance, je bois' [I'm confident, I drink]; he partakes of her image as reflected in his desire, seeing her as 'Cette Égypte, feuillages, nuits d'été, bêtes, routes du ciel' [This Egypt, dense foliage, summer nights, beasts, tracks in the sky], but in so doing he does not lose touch with our world, with the truth, since she is always present there, and as a result, in this detour through the image, something is restored to the real world, embodied in the child who partakes of two colours (hence the title), those of dream and reality, and those — green and red — of Pharaoh's daughter in Poussin's 'Moïse sauvé' which plays a key role throughout the poem.

'Deux Barques', the next section, opens with another repeated motif, that of waking and then dwelling on what subsists of a dream. In this case it is also a return from the intensity of sexual passion, evoked in the first few lines, and followed by a dialogue between the lovers:

> — Où que tu sois quand je te prends obscure,
> S'étant accru en nous ce bruit de mer,
> Accepte d'être l'indifférence, que j'étreigne
> À l'exemple de Dieu l'aveugle la matière
> La plus déserte encore dans la nuit.
> Accueille-moi intensément mais distraitement,
> Fais que je n'aie pas de visage, pas de nom
> Pour qu'étant le voleur je te donne plus
> Et l'étranger l'exil, en toi, en moi
> Se fasse l'origine ... — Oh, je veux bien,
> Toutefois, t'oubliant, je suis avec toi,
> Desserres-tu mes doigts,
> Formes-tu de mes paumes une coupe
> Je bois, près de ta soif,
> Puis laisse l'eau couler sur tous nos membres.

Eau qui fait que nous sommes, n'étant pas,
Eau qui prend au travers des corps arides
Pour une joie éparse dans l'énigme,
Pressentiment pourtant! (pp. 275–76)

[ — Wherever you are when I take you, darkly, | This noise of the sea having built up in us, | Accept being indifference, which I embrace | As God the blind embraced the most barren matter | the most deserted of all still in darkness. | Welcome me intensely but distractedly, | Make it so that I have no face, no name | So that being the thief I give you more | And the stranger the exile, in you, in me, | Makes itself the origin... — Oh, I accept,/ nonetheless, forgetting you, I'm with you, | Should you unclasp my fingers, | Should you make of my palms a bowl | I drink, near to your thirst, | Then let the water flow over our limbs. | Water that makes us be, though we are not, | Water which comes to life over arid bodies | For a joy scattered thinly in the enigma, | Premonition, all the same!]

First he, in his passion, asks her to make of their love-making a space where he may dissolve his identity and so bring back to her the fruits of other territories in which they can find a new origin. And she, in her reply, consents, but at the same time tells him that there will still be reciprocity in this, that the water they drink in their abandon, though in a sense it is nothing, still penetrates and changes their existence. And she reminds him of something they had experienced together while out walking. In the midst of a stony field, they had seen their own images reflected in a water-tank, their faces smiling happily in what seemed a light-filled world, and had sensed a different order of things, 'une lueur | Autre, bouge dans cet accord de leurs visages' [a different | Gleam moves in this match between their faces]. But the question as to which of the two worlds, real or reflected, should be termed 'le vrai', is irrelevant: '...peu importe. | Invente-moi, redouble-moi peut-être | Sur ces confins de fable déchirée' [...no matter. | Invent me, perhaps make me double | In these margins of a torn fable]. And in consenting, in his turn, to this dialectic of image and experience, the 'je' begins to remake a bond with both the dream and the world of everyday things:

Donne-moi ta main sans retour, eau incertaine
Que j'ai désempierrée jour après jour
Des rêves qui s'attardent dans la lumière
Et du mauvais désir de l'infini. (p. 277)

[Give me your hand with no way back, uncertain water | that I have cleared, stone after stone, day after day | of the dreams which dawdle in the light | and of the bad desire for the infinite.]

He rescinds his persistent dualism which had polarized them, leading him fastidiously to purge his sense of the world around him of all contamination by dreams, attempting to cure himself of his desire to transfigure her. Now he recognizes that this may succeed only in depriving the world of its 'saveur':

Que le bien de la source ne cesse pas
À l'instant où la source est retrouvée
Que les lointains ne se séparent pas

> Une nouvelle fois du proche, sous la faux
> De l'eau non plus tarie mais sans saveur.
> Donne-moi ta main et précède-moi dans l'été mortel
> Avec ce bruit de lumière changée. (pp. 277–78)

[May the spring's beneficence endure | Beyond the moment when the spring is found again | May distances not separate themselves | From the proximate once again, under the scythe | Of the water, no longer brackish but without flavour. | Give me your hand and precede me into the mortal summer | With this sound of light that has changed.]

He accepts to be dispersed rather than divided, dispersed into a multiple relation with the world and its reflection in desire:

> Les images, les mondes, les impatiences,
> Les désirs qui ne savent pas bien qu'ils dénouent
> [...]
> ... que tout cela
> La rose de l'eau qui passe le recueille
> En se creusant ici, puis l'illumine
> Au moyeu immobile de la roue. (p. 278)

[Images, worlds, impatiences, | Desires which do not know clearly that they undo | ...let all that | Be gathered by the rose of the flowing water | as it makes its course here, then be illuminated by it | At the wheel's unmoving hub.]

*Dans le leurre du seuil* has many more twists and turns, and more to say about love in subsequent sections; still, the evolution I have sought to trace is now, I think, clear. Where love was once a way out of this world, it is now a way back to it. Where love was once a world within the world, a dream, it is now at the heart of reality. Or rather, these earlier figurings of love are still what loving consists of, under the sign of Eros, but, as Agape, love is now the movement that restores them to the incarnate world, to temporality, finitude, opening, metamorphosis. It will be appropriate to end with some lines from a later section of *Dans le leurre de seuil* which express this admirably:

> Désir se fit amour par ses voies nocturnes
> Dans le chagrin des siècles; et par beauté
> Comprise, limite acceptée; par mémoire
> Amour, le temps, porte l'enfant, qui est le signe. (p. 313)

[Desire made itself love by its nocturnal paths | In the sorrow of the centuries; and by beauty | Understood, limits accepted; by memory | Love, time, which carries the child, who is the sign.]

## Notes

1. John Bayley, *The Characters of Love* (London: Constable, 1960), p. 5.
2. All page references in the text of this article are to Yves Bonnefoy, *Poèmes* (Paris: Gallimard, 1982), which collects Bonnefoy's four principal volumes of poetry.
3. Georges Bataille, *L'Érotisme* (Paris: UGE 10:18, 1965), pp. 15, 17, 20.
4. *L'Ordalie* (Paris: Maeght, 1975). Bonnefoy's comments on the story cast interesting light on *Douve*; see also *Entretiens sur la poésie* (Neuchâtel: La Baconnière, 1981), pp. 135–41.

5. *L'Arrière-Pays* (Geneva: Skira, 1972).
6. Bonnefoy's translation of 'Sailing to Byzantium' and other poems by Yeats may be found in *Argile*, no 1 (1973), 64–93.
7. *Rome 1630, Horizon du premier baroque* (Paris: Flammarion, 1970). Quotations are from Chapter 9, pp. 110 and 126.
8. 'Baudelaire contre Rubens' in *Le Nuage Rouge* (Paris: Mercure de France, 1977), pp. 9–82.
9. *La Présence et l'Image* (Paris: Mercure de France, 1983), p. 51 and *passim*.
10. *Entretiens sur la poésie* (Neuchâtel: À la Baconnière, 1981), p. 149.
11. Ibid., p. 145.
12. Anders Nygren, *Agape and Eros* (London: SPCK, 1932).
13. Denis de Rougemont, *L'Amour et l'Occident* (Paris: Plon, 1939), pp. 60–61.
14. Preface to M. Desbordes-Valmore, *Poésies* (Paris: Gallimard, 1983).

# Jacques Réda and the Commitments of Poetry

Vous êtes assis et vous fumez; vous croyez être assis dans votre pipe, et c'est vous que votre pipe fume; c'est vous qui vous exhalez sous la forme de nuages blanchâtres.

[You are sitting down, smoking; you think you are sitting in your pipe, and it is you that your pipe is smoking; it is you whom you are breathing out as pale clouds.]

CHARLES BAUDELAIRE, *Les Paradis artificiels*

This alarming reversal experienced by the hashish smoker is clearly portrayed as the hyperbolic expression, the *comble*, of the aspiration harboured by those 'poètes panthéistiques' [pantheistic poets] who seek to merge totally with external nature: 'Vous voici arbre mugissant au vent et racontant à la nature des mélodies végétales' [Here you are, a tree bellowing to the wind and speaking plant-melodies to nature]. Baudelaire's irony reflects his own resistance to nature poetry, allied to the reluctance to forfeit the controlling lucidity of reflexive consciousness. Yet the poet of *Le Spleen de Paris* was also capable, in discussing his friend Banville, of high praise for the lyric poet, that 'homme hyperbolique' [hyperbolic man] who, by dint of daring to be 'absolument lyrique' [absolutely lyric], 'opère fatalement un retour vers l'Eden perdu' [inexorably brings about a return to the lost Eden].[1] Since the mid-nineteenth century, French poets have oscillated between hyper-critical astringency and aspirations in which we can recognize the lyric priorities identified by Baudelaire. In the context of a poetry which, in recent decades, has frequently returned to the evidence of the given world, Jacques Réda has certainly accentuated the lyric pole. Indeed, his work is striking for the frequency with which he alludes to experiences of osmosis between mind and environment, moments of self-dissociation and reversal which, in their disorientating extremity, sometimes resemble those of the Baudelairean hashish-smoker. Consider, for example, the following passages:

> 1 Je flottais avec ma fumée et n'en sortais que comme une fine antenne promenée par la ville elle-même, une lanterne qu'elle portait en rêve au travers de sa propre masse pour en sonder l'énigme et l'épaisseur... (*La Tourne*, p. 153)

> [I floated with my smoke and emerged from it only as a delicate antenna led by the city herself, a lantern she carried in a dream across her own mass to sound its mystery and its depth...]

2   Je ne suis plus moi-même à présent qu'un souvenir qui divague, se perdant de rue en rue jusqu'à l'éblouissement des ponts, parmi ces passants que le soleil d'hiver imagine. (*Les Ruines de Paris*, p. 44)

[I am at this moment no more myself than a rambling memory, losing itself from street to street up to the glare of the bridges, among these passers-by imagined by the winter sun.]

3   Et moi sur le talus de cette route dont je ne suis qu'un des accidents, la conscience de plus en plus claire de soi qu'elle prend avec chaque tour de roue, pour s'enhardir, et se dérouler à mon chapeau comme une longue fumée bleue? (*L'Herbe des talus*, p. 196)

[And myself on the side of this road of which I am but one of the accidents, the ever clearer self-consciousness it takes on which each turn of the wheel, to steel itself, and to [unroll itself to my hat] like a long blue plume of smoke?]

4          Mais quels desseins le promeneur lui-même a-t-il nourris? [...]
           A son tour devenu [...]
           Un lieu de passage mental où la ville se perd,
           Se retrouve, se plaît peut-être à sa métamorphose
           En pages où parfois des vers circulent dans la prose...
           (*Châteaux des courants d'air*, back cover)

[But what plans has the walker himself cherished? | [...] Become in his turn [...] | A mental [place along the way] where the city disappears, | Is found, perhaps takes pleasure in its metamorphosis | Into pages or sometimes lines of verse circulating within prose...]

5   Je filtre, retiens de plus en plus mal, déjà souffle parmi les souffles, étincelle dans la lumière, tunnel dans la nuit. De nouveau le processus de dissolution s'est mis en marche. Il faut se préparer à disparaître encore un coup. (*Le Sens de la marche*, p. 48)

[I filter, keeping hold of things ever more poorly, already a breeze among breezes, a spark in the light, a tunnel in the night. The process of dissolution has got underway once more. I must get ready yet again to disappear.]

The dissolution of the self, its wraith-like evaporation into the ambient air, is common to all these passages whose emblem might be the phrase 'ne plus que' which signals the fundamental reversal through which poetic consciousness becomes a satellite of the phenomena it witnesses, rather than the reverse. In the first quotation Réda does not convey an annexation of the city by poetic *fureur*, nor an ecstatic union with its essence. Rather, by resorting to what may seem at first like a naive anthropomorphism, he conveys a particular kind of participation whereby the poet's mind becomes an extension of the city's reality, a 'lieu de passage mental' (quotation 4) within which that reality is made apparent. In the poetic act, sleights of syntax, diction and figure engender a double displacement: of the city, transmuted into lines, colours, and volumes which precipitate desire; of the poet, whose own mental space is evacuated of all personal property in order to make way for its 'guests'. Consenting to disappear (quotation 5), to cede his own memories to the anonymous 'souvenir' of his surroundings (quotation 2), the poet becomes a conduit or tunnel through which the world may pass.

In selecting passages from works published over a period of some fifteen years, my aim was partly to indicate the continuity of Réda's concerns. Now, however, I wish to identify a change of emphasis which has come about progressively in the remarkable series of five books, written largely in prose but (increasingly) with many interpolations in verse, inaugurated by *Les Ruines de Paris* in 1977.[2] The prose poems which make up that volume (and their precursor, the prose text which opens La Tourne[3]) reflect the decisive step of casting the poet as an inveterate *promeneur* and of making poetry and travel indissoluble. In *Les Ruines de Paris* each highly charged and densely metaphorical poem presents itself, in its radical discontinuity, as the distillation of a more or less productive excursion into the 'nébuleuse parisienne' [Parisian nebula], or further afield. Beginning usually *in medias res*, and with limited anecdotal contextualization, the poems are marked by a restless, urgent pizzicato rhythm explicitly modelled on the walking bass ('basse ambulante') and other features of the jazzman's artistry of which Réda has written with such sympathetic discernment. By contrast, later collections such as *Recommandations aux promeneurs* and *Le Sens de la marche* have a quite different atmosphere, and a far more variegated climate. The pieces tend to be longer, more discursive, and more anecdotal. Rather than eliminating the framework of autobiographical experience within which writing and travelling merge, Réda foregrounds it, breaking with his earlier tendency to eschew the *récit*.[4] The change of emphasis which I have briefly evoked is perhaps perceptible in the excerpts already given, but to make it more patent I shall quote again:

> Mais la ville montrait son âme entièrement désœuvrée, comme une fille encore qui d'elle-même ne décidera pas, qui tourne, a l'air de réfléchir, attend sans que l'on puisse interpréter son regard [...]. Et ses yeux s'ouvraient donc à l'extrémité de chaque avenue, tantôt gris, tantôt bleus, toujours dans la douceur de ce qui ne se fixe pas mais qui rêve, me rêvant aussi moi l'indécis entre *oubli* et *peut-être*, passant. (*Les Ruines de Paris*, p. 142)

> [But the city showed its soul to be entirely idle, still like a girl who will not decide by herself, who turns, looks like she is thinking, waits with a gaze which one cannot interpret [...]. And her eyes thus opened onto the far end of each avenue, sometimes grey and sometimes blue, always [in the sweetness] of what is not fixed but which dreams, dreaming myself, too, the person hesitating between *forgetting* and *maybe*, a passer-by.]

> Là règne souverainement le bleu immatériel de l'hiver, qui se fonce et s'épaissit de façon plus sensuelle à mesure qu'avance l'après-midi. Cette souveraineté tolère la circulation de gros nuages et semble même s'en réjouir. Jusqu'à un enthousiasme qui me dilate comme une outre mystique, faute de pouvoir s'extérioriser, j'admire la géométrie complexe mais dépouillée qu'inscrivent, dans cet espace, des compositions bien rythmées de fils, caténaires, poteaux [...]. Emouvante, instructive rencontre de la volonté logique et transitoire humaine, et de ces passagères vapeurs sur un fond sans fond permanent. (*Le Sens de la marche*, p. 210)

[The sovereign ruler there is the immaterial blue of winter, which darkens and thickens ever more sensually as the afternoon advances. This sovereignty tolerates the passage of big clouds and seems even to rejoice in it. I admire to the point of an enthusiasm which, unable to express itself, swells me up like a mystical wineskin, the complex but austere geometry inscribed, in this space, by [finely] rhythmic compositions of wires, overhead cables, poles [...]. A moving, instructive meeting of the human will, logical and transitory, and these passing vapours, on a background without permanent grounding.]

The context of the two passages is similar: a portion of city glimpsed from a train pulling out of Paris; a section of sky observed during a wait at a suburban station. But the character of these moments is markedly different. In the first, the *métaphore filée* of city as bashful girl seems to enact the spectator's desire to hold on to an inherently evanescent experience. The series of predicates assigned to the girl/city exactly match the vicissitudes of that desire, and we hardly need to wait for the explicit osmotic reversal ('me rêvait aussi moi l'indécis') to feel that in this glimpse (and by virtue, indeed, of its elusiveness) the city figures a desired mode of being, answers a need for an intensely imagined ontological plenitude. The motif of indecision or hesitation which links city/girl to poet/observer is an indication that the experience is viewed in terms of a potential transformation of existence: to be a 'passant', here, is to be 'in between', caught in the space which divides the real from the figural, the eminently forgettable ('*l'oubli*') and the merely virtual ('*peut-être*'); it is to be in the grip of that 'attraction du centre' about which Réda had written so eloquently in *La Tourne*. The language here, in its elliptical, self-absorbed, hypnotic rapidity, as it cascades through branching clauses, seeks to cling to a perception it knows it has already lost. In the second passage the poet/observer allows himself to be suffused by what has galvanized his attention (a patch of sky traversed by clouds and criss-crossed by wires) precisely to the degree that he refrains from any overt attempt to possess it. Rather than a proliferating series of intuitive jabs or riffs, his discourse attunes itself to the percepts, adopting a calm, meditative tempo befitting the experience of dilation rather than concentration which occurs here. Accepting the limits of the experience, as something immanent rather than transcendent, the poet curbs his figural zeal as he develops metaphorical links between the remote blue sky, the transitory clouds, and the impermanent products of human industry.

The change of emphasis I have pinpointed should not be exaggerated or seen exclusively in terms of progress or polarization. One of the most attractive features of Réda's work is that it is a continuum, a series of improvisations and explorations in which he tries out different approaches and, often playfully, adopts different modes: autobiography in *L'Herbe des talus*, the guide-book in *Châteaux des courants d'air*, the 'how-to' manual in *Recommandations aux promeneurs*. Moreover, the evolution of Réda's writing is partly the outcome of a progressive acceptance of open-endedness, of the ever-increasing weight he has placed on the conviction that 'le passage' is the essential feature of mortal existence. The figure of the *promeneur* which has progressively emerged in Réda (and which, since with it comes his distinctive voice as a poet, will perhaps be his most enduring creation) is essential in this regard. Solitary (sometimes almost curmudgeonly) and socially unclassifiable, the *promeneur* aspires to that specific form of anonymity which is the sign of the poet's availability to experience. Self-contained (he carries all essentials with him, from a thermos to a toy soldier), he travels light, by train or *Solex*, and prefers, even relishes, putting up with the discomforts of cheap, unfashionable hotels to accepting the hospitality of friends. Without a watch, he has no fixed timetable but sets himself non-utilitarian targets determined only by whim. What matters is not arriving at a putative destination but realizing as profoundly as possible, on the way, how very *little* it matters whether he arrives or not.

I propose now to focus on *Le Sens de la marche*, and in particular on two important aspects: journeys in the footsteps of other writers and Réda's presentation of his motives. Like its immediate predecessors, *Le Sens de la marche* is a mixture of prose and verse, but apart from the poems which open and close the volume, the verse is almost entirely incorporated within the prose pieces. Réda's digressive prose is now much closer to the essay (he is an admirer of Montaigne) than to the *poème en prose*, and each piece is the record of a journey. Five of the nine main essays concern journeys made under the aegis of writers Réda admires: La Fontaine, Proust, Wordsworth, Renard, and Follain, and in each case he travels with an appropriate stock of reading matter. To retrace the steps of another is to allow our experiences to be channelled by those of our precursor. Yet, equally, the attempt to explore, in real space, what is also someone else's mental and emotional construct is to change the footing of one's journey, to displace it on to another level, to make it double.[5] As Réda will frequently suggest, to travel with the other in mind is to turn the environs into a shadowland, and to become shadowy oneself. If, moreover, the effect is to discipline our attention, as we seek to align it with what has gone before, this may foster rather than inhibit the mobility of contemplative thought. We ought therefore, perhaps, to view Réda's decision to travel 'with' La Fontaine and the others as an act of homage which provides — literally — a 'pre-text' rather than a purpose for his journey. And this strategy should therefore be associated with other kinds of 'contrainte' Réda sets for himself in *Le Sens de la marche*, such as deciding to look for the source of the river Vioménil, to cover six *départements* in four days, or to traverse (the word *traversée* is recurrent) a region such as the Brie or the Meuse. There is nothing systematic or formalistic here, but this admirer of Queneau clearly sees that a constraint freely adopted can be inherently liberating; and there is some sense in linking Réda's journeys with the strategies of such so-called landscape artists as Richard Long whose 'works' commemorate predetermined, yet at the same time aleatory, trajectories in space and time.

For Réda, one of the main incitements to travel, to remain on the move, is to escape the limits of a circumscribed identity and an inhibiting past, to explore the multiplicity of potential ways of being. The letters La Fontaine sent to his spouse as he made the longest journey of his life (from Paris to Limoges) exude, in their language, a mode of being which Réda seeks to revivify as he follows his poet-ancestor along part of the same route, addressing *him* a series of chatty missives which report his observations. Wilfully anachronistic and artificial, larded both with quotations from La Fontaine and with poems of his own, which sometimes verge on pastiches of La Fontaines's style, Réda's epistolary journey takes on the character of a dialogical space, a mingling of voices which annuls time and affirms the fundamental universality of a poetic perception of the world. Likewise, the counterpoint between quotations from the poet Jean Follain's memoir of childhood, *Canisy*, and the poems Réda is sparked to write as he tours the village of Canisy, book in hand, takes on an antiphonal character, transcending the drab banality of the Normandy village, this 'enclave désertée de la mémoire' [deserted enclave of memory] (*Le Sens de la marche*, p. 176), and affirming the perennial power and freshness of poetic vision and poetic language. By not naming Follain until midway through one of the poems written in his wake, Réda underlines the anonymity of the space into which he seeks provisional access: not the Canisy of Follain's real boyhood (Réda is not nostalgic, even if Follain was), but the space which conjoins the Canisy poetically recreated in Follain's memoir and the Canisy transformed by Réda's particular way of 'traversing' it. Ultimately this space exists only on paper: it cannot be 'held' for long in the head of its witness, but only preserved in the words through which he bodies it forth: 'dans ma tête encore un moment se rejoignent, | Reflets se reflétant le long d'un invisible pli, | Des mots qui sont mémoire et les choses que prend l'oubli' [in my head once again for a moment there meet, | Reflections reflecting themselves all along an invisible fold, | Words which are memory and those things forgetting takes] (p. 185).

Réda's account of a tour in the Lake District of Wordsworth, Coleridge and Southey is the most extensive and ambitious of his 'journeyings-with', In a preamble, punningly entitled 'En manière de prélude' [By way of a prelude], he lists the features of Wordsworth's writing which appeal to him and which he has tried to emulate in his own work (these include 'la note de haute et grave sentimentalité lyrique qui, jusque dans les poèmes les plus délicats, fait résonner sans le moindre effet une profondeur métaphysique' [the note of high, serious lyric sentimentality which, even in the most delicate poems, sounds without the least effect a metaphysical depth] (p. 63), and explains his resolve to record the journey stage by stage in a series of regular sonnets (a decision dictated partly by the size of notebook he had with him). 'L'emploi du vers' [The use of verse] has, he observes, become second nature to him;[6] here, however, the use of verse is more systematic and thoroughgoing. First of all, proportionally, the thirty sonnets occupy as much space as the prose text which links them together. Secondly, the italicized prose and the poems printed in roman type constantly subvert any stable dichotomy between the poetic and the prosaic. They achieve this by constituting a seamless continuum (the poems — though each bears a title — often continue a 'sentence' begun in prose) and by constantly interchanging the 'prosaic' tasks of narrative and commentary. In its 'degré zéro' the poetry is very prosaic indeed:

> *Cependant,*
> ### Une Précision:
> Je n'ai pas dit le nom de ce lac: Ullswater,
> Qui n'est pas le plus grand. Pour la superficie,
> Windermere à coup sûr a la suprématie... (p. 75)

[*However,* | **A Clarification:** | I have not said the name of this lake: Ullswater, | Which is not the biggest one. For surface area, | Windermere is by far the bigger...]

But Réda has no interest in reserving poetry for supposedly 'higher' things: let it do its share of the spadework! And so poems record the quest for a cork-screw, the flight from Japanese tourists at Dove Cottage, double-decker buses, aching feet, Fish and Chips. What subsists, and indeed emerges enhanced, in the constant transit between poetry and prose, is the ceaseless shift from one level of attention and feeling to another. However mobile, and ultimately irrelevant, the borderline between poem and prose may be, the fact of switching to and fro enacts, and indeed actively fosters, the *displacement* which is the hallmark of the poetic.

Réda frequently alludes to the dissolution of identity brought about by his mode of travel. Not a native, but no stranger, given his close acquaintance with the works of Wordsworth and his circle; a traveller, but not a tourist; in the midst of others, but acutely conscious of his total solitude, he lives 'l'aventure | De n'être personne entre les restaurants, | Le village, l'église et sa cloche champêtre' [the adventure | of being no one among the restaurants, | The village, the church and its [countryside] bell] (p. 90). Travelling thus may bring 'une certaine dépersonnalisation, comme si l'on se transformait en un libre espace dont celui qu'on explore devient à son tour le promeneur' [a certain depersonalization, as though one were transforming oneself into a free space which that which one is exploring comes in its turn to walk around in] (p. 69). As a vacant space in which the beauties of the landscape (and especially the mountains), memories of the Lake poets, the events of the day, can resonate and merge, Réda progressively finds himself haunted by the shade of another displaced person who lived in the shadow of poetry, namely Dorothy Wordsworth, as the poem 'Coleridge, William, et Dorothy' shows:

> L'un semblable aux tourments de ce grand paysage,
> L'autre à la profondeur de son calme soumis:
> Que plus rien désormais ne les divise, amis,
> Presque jumeaux par la matrice du langage
> Où, relisant leurs vers, à mon tour je m'engage
> Et soupèse les miens comme dans un tamis
> Trop fin. Et je me sens un indigent, hormis
> Pour celle dont on sait à peine le visage
> Mais dont je crois que la bonté m'accompagnait,
> Sa main furtive quelquefois sur mon poignet,
> Muette et, brusquement distante mais fidèle,
> M'entraînant de nouveau vers un autre horizon,
> Sans que cesse jamais de battre, à cause d'elle,
> Le cœur même des mots au cœur de la maison. (p. 85)

[One akin to the torments of this great landscape, | The other having given himself up to the depths of its calm: | May nothing further divide them henceforth, friends, | Almost twins through the womb of language | Where, rereading their verses, I in turn join in | And weigh my own as in a too-fine | Sieve. And I feel myself a pauper, except | For she whose face one hardly knows | But whose goodness, I believe, goes with me, | Her furtive hand sometimes

on my wrist, | Mute and, bluntly distant but faithful, | Drawing me once again
towards another horizon, | Without there ceasing to beat, because of her, |
The very heart of words in the heart of the house.]

With its moving cadences this fine poem both celebrates the sense of affinity with
Dorothy, which develops in the course of Réda's solitary journey, and conveys
the wider network of family relationships into which, by proxy of the fusion of
travel and language, he finds himself enmeshed. The identification with Dorothy
is threefold. In its sometimes clumsy directness her famous *Journal*, which Réda
reads along with her brother's guide to the Lake District, is perceived as a model of
attentiveness, revealing 'son âme non pas changeante mais sensible jusqu'au vertige
aux mouvements de la vie et aux métamorphoses de sa splendeur' [her soul, not
changeable but sensitive to the point of vertigo to the movements of life and to the
metamorphoses of its splendour] (p. 66). Then, her human drama — displaced in
the affections, and the household, of her brother by their cousin Mary Hutchinson;
unlucky in her love for Coleridge who preferred Mary's cousin Sarah — not only
touches Réda but makes Dorothy less remote than the fiery Coleridge and the
preternaturally calm Wordsworth; moreover, her position as a third party also
resembles his own. Lastly, Dorothy's sisterliness makes her the embodiment of an
unthreatening, maternal femininity and of a selfless, non-possessive love. All these
factors tend to ally Dorothy with poetry itself, a 'matrice' in which language truly
lives, by dint of a vigilance akin to that of 'celle qui fut son autre âme: la sœur |
Exquise dont l'intelligence et la douceur | Habitent chaque mot devenu poésie' [she
who was his other soul: the exquisite | Sister whose intelligence and sweetness |
Live in each word which has become poetry] (p. 86).

If Réda's poems are accorded any kind of priority, it is only in the strict sense
that, composed instantaneously, 'sur le motif', they predate the retrospective prose
which links them. One of the effects of this *décalage* is to bring into view questions
which, while never expressly formulated or answered, seem constantly latent: Why
poetry? Why travel? What is a poet? Réda's answer to these questions seems to
reside in the demonstration that a poet is someone who leads a double life, a secret
agent who is involved, by virtue of what poetry exacts but also of what it promises,
in a constant process of *dédoublement* and self-distancing. Rather than being inspired,
a magus with vatic powers, a *possédé*, the poet is constantly displaced by his double,
that anonymous protagonist who participates in the wider rhythms of the world
and their repercussions in language. The two sonnets (written at Oxenholme
station) which close 'Le District des lacs' link what poetry is and does to questions
of memory and language. Taking leave of the 'ombres' [shadows] he has evoked,
Réda wonders if his journey has been more than a mingling of absences: that of
the shades whose abiding presence has only been 'inferred' from features of the
landscape and his own absence, given that he has been 'Moins qu'une ombre |
Parmi d'autres' [Less than a shadow | Among others] and will have left no trace on
the landscape he has traversed. Yet if, at one level, nothing has taken place, and time
has already obliterated Réda's 'passage fortuit' [happy passage], this death heralds
the perpetuation of his experience — in the 'clement' environment of memory.

While the details of his trip are already fading, the 'ombres', including his own, seem to become more real: 'Donc le départ est comme un retour qui commence, | L'adieu comme un salut du temps à la clémence | De la mémoire' [Leaving is thus like the start of a return, | The farewell like time waving to the leniency of memory] (p. 105). And the Wordsworthian valediction which follows — 'vous quittant, je me remets | A vous, ombres et lacs, montagnes, poésie' [taking leave of you, I turn once again | To you, shadows and lakes, mountains, poetry] — makes poetry the guardian of memory: 'poésie | Qui demeurez où, telle une seconde vie, | Le voyage accompli ne s'achève pas' [poetry | Which remains there where, like a second life, | The completed voyage does not come to an end] (p. 105).

Associated with constant death and rebirth, with the disappearances and resurfacings of a subject always caught in the throes of metamorphosis, poetry for Réda is essentially a practice with a direct effect on life. The writing of a poem cannot be separated from a wider cycle of actions whose combined effect is radically to modify the individual's conditions of existence. But this begs the question of motive, inviting us to enquire how the poet views the *stasis* he seeks to annul in the impetus to keep moving. Although, in the presentation of successive volumes, he has progressively indicated a sense that the sequence of works from *Les Ruines de Paris* onwards involves a particular 'itinéraire',[7] Réda has hitherto had little to say on this count. But he does seem to address it in the two poems which open and close *Le Sens de la marche*. In the first he entertains the thought that the 'persévérant désir' [relentless desire] for solitary flight — in space and on paper — might in some way be connected with death, but he does not pursue the idea very far. In the closing poem, 'Traversée du bleu', Réda points to an erotic component in his desire for open space, comparing his 'traversée' to a dance, and the beauties of nature, which make him catch his breath, to a succession of alluring partners. But the erotic scenario fades into a more generalized celebration of the pleasures of dissolution and union with what lies outside the self, the joy of being no more than 'une forme mouvante | Parmi d'autres, nuage issu de la vapeur | Enveloppant de bleu tout l'espace' [a moving form | Among others, a cloud come from vapour | Enveloping all of space in blue] (p. 216). We may be tempted to find Réda evasive or disingenuous in this context; yet it is central to the evolution we have been registering that he should have come to locate the poetic in a form of attention which begins precisely at the point when the anxious questions about origins and destinations have been quelled. None of his writing makes this more plain than the magnificent title essay which immediately precedes 'Traversée du bleu'.

'Le Sens de la marche' is the account of an abortive Sunday-afternoon trip to Versailles. Having evoked in some detail the frame of mind in which one might decide to go there — the pervasive air of unreality which reigns in the gardens, the limitless perspectives which seem to unblock ('déblayer') corresponding vistas in ourselves (p. 191) — Réda describes, often in stunningly minute detail, the stages of a journey which, owing to an unexplained breakdown of the railway service, never reaches its destination. As the afternoon unfolds, non-arrival comes to seem not only entirely consistent with, but the supreme realization of what arrival portended, and of what the stimulus to depart had disclosed: 'l'intense pulsion du limité vers ce qui le délivre' [the intense drive of the bounded towards that which releases it] (p. 191). As he progressively acknowledges that he is not going to get anywhere, the realization that 'le but n'est jamais qu'un symbole' [the goal is only ever a symbol] (p. 196) fully sinks in, and the realities of journeying, available anywhere at any point, come to galvanize Réda's attention. In the initial stages, while the trip is still 'on', Réda treats us to the rêveries of the expectant traveller whose thoughts oscillate between his surroundings and the emotions of departure. Broaching a central theme, he explains the desirability of finding a seat 'dans le sens contraire de la marche' so that the landscape, instead of coming at us as a series of piecemeal percepts to be hurriedly checked off before they disappear behind our heads, spreads itself out ('se déploie') in an endless process of renewal without, at any particular point, seeming to change or disappear. Disagreeing with Claudel, who had accused those who face backwards of being slaves to the 'douceurs vénéneuses de la nostalgie' [nostalgia's poisonous sweetnesses], Réda argues that to have one's back to the engine is to experience 'la profusion merveilleuse du monde qui ruisselle sans autre berge que l'horizon' [the marvellous profusion of the world, which flows with no bank but the horizon] (p. 199).

In the event, Réda's train to Versailles makes an impromptu halt after a few minutes, and he spends the rest of the afternoon marooned in the limbo of an unfamiliar station, with a gaggle of strangers, as trains occasionally pass in the wrong direction, or stop only to disgorge passengers before firmly snapping shut their doors. Initially, his thoughts dwell on the particular varieties of silence and peace which attend those occasions when a train stops nowhere in particular: 'on baigne dans le profond mais vibrant silence de l'immobilité ferroviaire, peuplé de menus grincements, craquements brefs, soupirs dans le labyrinthe des tuyauteries' [one bathes in the deep but vibrant silence of train-travel immobility, populated by little creaks, brief pops, sighs from the labyrinth of pipework] (p. 201). But more and more his mind resists such 'dérives' into reminiscence and conjecture and settles for its immediate surroundings, in belated recognition of the fact that 'tout endroit mérite attention et déférence' (p. 204). There follows an enchanting series of descriptions: the station building and its environs; the railway line and its constituent parts — steel rails, wooden sleepers still bearing the mark of the axe, the endlessly satisfying crunchiness of ballast ('le cailloutis rauque et gras qui grommelle' [the rough, crude, muttering gravel] (p. 208)); the smells of the railway: 'Une ligne de chemin de fer est une odeur qui va par les campagnes... une sorte de trace animale qu'on piste avec ferveur car elle a le goût de réglisse noire qui se mâche dans l'âme des insoumis' [A railway line is a smell that travels along the countryside... a sort of animal trace which one tracks with fervour for it has the taste of black liquorice chewed in the soul of the unvanquished] (p. 208). By this point Réda's essay has become an anthology of the forms of attention the most humdrum place can — should? — provoke. He composes a poem on the theme of station platforms and the quality of waiting they may stimulate, noting that the adoption of a different rhythm of discourse may offset a feeling of 'enlisement' [getting bogged down] (p.

210); and this leads into the passage quoted earlier, regarding the patch of sky with cloud and wires, which concludes as follows:

> Pour moi ma destination est atteinte. A travers le lacis des fils je m'élève vers la région lumineuse où, comme une roue tournant autour de son axe inflexible, les nuages, les heures, les trains, la vie passent et ne passent pas. (p. 211)

> [As far as I'm concerned, I've reached my destination. Across the tracery of wires I raise myself towards the bright region where, like a wheel turning around its inflexible axis, clouds, hours, trains, and life pass by and do not pass by.]

At once intensely committed to the real and lucidly abstracted from many of its blandishments, 'Le Sens de la marche' traces the outline of a postmodern poetry of meditation.[8] Coolly insouciant towards conclusions, passionately attached to the intervals and interstices between the goal-seeking activities of the community, Réda's essay is an invaluable allegory of the poetic quest, comparable, in its emphasis on place and passage. with Yves Bonnefoy's 'Les Tombeaux de Ravenne' or Philippe Jaccottet's 'A travers un verger'. Rather than hallow a string of supercharged moments. as he was wont to do in earlier work, Réda, through the unstable, asymmetrical interplay of prose and poetry, poetic and prosaic, récit and metaphorical tableau, refuses all stable discriminations in the name of a boundless attentiveness. Committed to a receptivity born of waiting and thus to a forward élan, Réda may seem reluctant to look back, to Scrutinize the origins of his desire to be in motion. But in fact he knows that every word gives him away. What makes jazz so distinctively human, he once noted, is that 'l'élan incandescent vers le sublime n'y peut être séparé d'un surgissement brûlant de l'obscur' [its blazing movement towards the sublime cannot be separated from a sudden, burning appearance of the obscure].[9] So it is with Réda and his poetry where the darkness of lost desire is patent in the light of ever-renewed desiring.[10]

## Notes

1. Œuvres complètes (Paris: Gallimard, 1971), p. 737. The quotations from Les Paradis artificiels are on p. 338.
2. The five books, all published in Paris by Gallimard, are Les Ruines de Paris (1977), L'Herbe des talus (1984), Châteaux des courants d'air (1986), Recommandations aux promeneurs (1988), and Le Sens de la marche (1990). All page references are given in the text.
3. Amen. Récitatif. La Tourne (Paris: Gallimard, 1988).
4. For a stimulating discussion of a more general 'retour au récit' (return to the story) in contemporary poetry, see Dominique Combe, Poésie et Récit: une rhétorique des genres (Paris: José Corti, 1989).
5. Richard Holmes has much of interest to say along these lines in his Footsteps: Adventures of a Romantic Biographer (New York: Viking/Elizabeth Sifton Books, 1985).
6. Cf. the 'prière d'insérer' of Châteaux des courants d'air which, appropriately, begins in prose and shifts into verse.
7. See especially the 'prière d'insérer' on the back cover of Recommandations aux promeneurs with its reference to an 'itinéraire (celui des Ruines de Paris [etc.]) dont la fantaisie apparente cache peut-être un sens constant plus secret'.
8. I am thinking of this phrase in the sense of Louis Martz's seminal The Poetry of Meditation (New Haven, CT: Yale University Press, 1962).

9. *L'Improviste: une lecture du jazz* (Paris: Gallimard, 1990), p. 27.

10. Jean-Pierre Richard's 'Scènes d'herbe', in *L'Etat des choses: études sur huit écrivains d'aujourd'hui* (Paris: Gallimard, 1990), pp. 11–38, examines scenarios of desire in Réda's writing. See also Daniel Leuwers, 'Jacques Réda ou les intermittences du passage', in *L'Accompagnateur: essais sur la poésie contemporaine* (Marseille: Sud, 1989).

# 14

# Raymond Queneau:
# The Lure of the Spiritual

*Tel qu'en lui-même enfin l'éternité le change* [He is changed into what eternity has at last made him] (Mallarmé). Since his death in 1976 Raymond Queneau has been changing fast. The unpublished autobiographical material included in the Pléiade edition of his poetry provides a fuller picture of the relationship with his parents and with his childhood, bringing more clearly into focus the psychological malaise which led him to undergo psychoanalysis in the 1930s.[1] Queneau had written about this in the stylized and distancing alexandrines of *Chêne et chien* [Oak tree and dog] (1937), an early autobiography-in-verse where he had made it clear that psychoanalysis had failed to lay the ghosts of his childhood, that the shadows persisted:

> Cette brume insensée où s'agitent des ombres,
> Comment pourrais-je l'éclairer?
> Cette brume insensée où s'agitent des ombres
> — est-ce là mon avenir? (19)[2]

> [This crazy fog where shadows dance | How can I pierce its dark? | This crazy fog where shadows dance | — is that where my future lies?]

The idea that our future depends on what we make of our past is expressly articulated in another recently published text which, more than anything else, seems likely to change our picture of an essentially oblique, tangential and secretive writer. Published in 1986, Queneau's *Journal 1939–1940*, a diary he kept from the summer before war was declared until after the fall of France, revealed the gleeful neologist, the poet of the suburbs, the philosophical humourist to have been a man deeply if intermittently concerned with spiritual self-transformation:

> Un pauvre homme, un pauvre homme
> Bien vaniteux, bien orgueilleux
> Avec l'Infini comme veilleuse.[3]

> [A poor man, a poor man | so vain, so proud | with the Infinite as his vigil light.]

Like Sartre's *Carnets de la drôle de guerre* Queneau's diary is partly a meditation on the circumstances in which it was kept. As in Jean Guéhenno's *Journal des années noires*, Queneau's entries reflect a concern to keep attuned to the inner life while the outer one changes, and a desire to occupy his mind in a situation where others dispose of his body and occupy his country. Yet it is not so much outer events which prompt Queneau to this form of writing as a dual desire: to keep track of a spiritual dimension in his life which he had been particularly conscious of since about 1935; and to pursue the work of psychoanalysis — not through self-analysis or the attempt to tap the unconscious (though he often reports his dreams) — but through daily attention to the disparate levels, the divisions and differences, within himself. Queneau exploits one of the strengths of the diary form, the opportunity it offers to mix the utterly contingent, mundane and trivial — the 'quotidien' in its most basic form — with the intermittent motions of intellect, feelings and spirit. And this chimes with an apprehension of spirituality where the spiritual is a discontinuous presence, a flickering flame which cannot be commanded, only perhaps propitiated. In a most compelling way, Queneau's *Journal* locates the spiritual in the midst of the down to earth: the barracks and billets he encounters in the endless meandering drift which was the soldier's lot in the *drôle de guerre* — places and times, menial tasks and mundane desires; letters written, books read, projects hatched and discarded; observations on people around him, relationships (with his wife and son, for instance) continued on a different footing; and so on.

From various remarks he makes in passing we can discern some of the motives which led Queneau to keep a diary at this point. Early entries indicate that he is reading the diaries of other writers — Gide's, which had just been published, that of Eugène Dabit, and the diary of his friend Marcel Moré. Queneau admires Moré's success in 'expressing' his personality through his diary, but then underlines how this differs from his own undertaking, by noting: 'Et si l'on ne cherche pas à "s'exprimer"?' [But what if our aim is not to 'express' ourselves?].[4] Self-expression, the communication of and with one's 'personality', is precisely not Queneau's goal. Indeed, while remaining deeply attached to these scattered pages, which he will deposit in various places as he moves around (at one point he buys a 'coffret' to keep his diary in) Queneau will become disillusioned with his diary-writing when he perceives it as recording, and possibly abetting, 'la marche croissante de mon égoïsme, de mon caprice, et de mes mensonges' [the steady growth of my egotism, my caprices, and my mendacities].[5] The point of keeping a diary, for Queneau, is to resist the lure, the allures, of a perfected self-image: 'Ici, il ne s'agit pas d'œuvre d'art, ni de document; mais d'une épreuve, d'une épreuve de mon individualité médiocre, changeante et périssable' [Here, we are not dealing with a work of art or a document; but a test, a test of my mediocre, changing and ephemeral individuality].[6] The sense of a trial, a discipline, an attempt to look at oneself as if one were someone else — 'Eprouver son individualité comme autre' [To experience one's individuality as if one were another person][7] — permeates the *Journal* and takes us to the heart of Queneau's spirituality.

If one were to characterize it in very broad terms, one could say that spirituality in Queneau had to do with the conquest of negative factors — egotism, vanity, false ambitions — which place the individual outside the orbit of the spiritual; and with a quest, through the adoption of certain practices and attitudes, for inner peace, truth and harmony. Such a description underlines the extent to which Queneau's spirituality is traditional and, in many respects, conventional. Queneau has no desire to be original, to break a new pathway to transcendence in the manner of, say, his friend Georges Bataille. He finds inspiration in Neoplatonist thought, in the canonical texts of Christian piety and mysticism, and above all in Chinese philosophy. The speculations of René Guenon, concerning a common transcendent 'tradition' behind apparently disparate religions and civilizations, are an important influence, echoing Queneau's encyclopaedic interests, his fascination with all systems of thought and forms of knowledge. But if there is, therefore, a 'bookish' side to Queneau's spiritual quest, the texts to which he has recourse serve primarily as stimuli for meditation. He shows little sign of wanting to indulge in metaphysical system-building on his own account; his true concerns are more personal and direct.

A key term in Queneau's *Journal* is 'transcendance', or 'le transcendant', which does not designate a realm or agency so much as that which is attained or intuited when we transcend certain aspects of ourselves. Alluding to a phrase associated with the *Collège de Sociologie* of Bataille, Leiris and Caillois, Queneau observes: 'Le sacré — oui. Et dans la vie quotidienne par un appel constant au transcendant' [The Sacred — yes. And in daily life through a constant appeal to transcendence].[8] The transcendent is associated with the sense of having, from time to time, 'passé sur un plan plus élevé' [raised oneself on to a higher plane][9] — a feeling which is at the core of Queneau's impulses towards the spiritual. At the conclusion of a passage evoking the agitated futilities of military training he notes:

> Il n'y a plus de paix pour moi; et pourtant je sens toujours en moi une pointe inaccessible où je me suis en qque [sic] sorte accroché — un plateau calme et sage au pied duquel roulent des tourbillons. Dieu m'appelle — ou Moi-même: Soi, le non- égoïste, le désintéressé, le principe, la transcendance qui me soutient, m'anime, me transforme et me fera disparaître.[10]

> [There is no more peace for me; yet despite this I still feel within myself an inaccessible point to which I have somehow climbed — a calm and quiet plateau at the foot of which whirlwinds blow. God calls me — or it is I: Oneself, the unegotistical one, the disinterested, the principle, the transcendence which sustains me, animates me, transforms me and which will one day make me disappear.]

The transcendent is associated with 'l'anéantissement de l'égo' [the obliteration of the ego],[11] with detachment from the pettiness of selfhood, from the vanity which confines and enslaves. Observing his fellow soldiers, Queneau alludes, sympathetically, to their '[...] égoïsme complet. Ils ne dépassent pas leur propre individualité' [[...] complete egotism. They do not transcend their own individuality].[12] To meditate on the question: 'qui suis-je?' ['who am I?'][13] ought to involve a depersonalization — 'se considérer comme un "il"' [to consider oneself as a 'he'][14] — and the quest for a basic unchanging identity, 'cet Ego invariable dont il faut trouver la racine, racine qui est une flamme consumante' [This unvarying Ego of which I must find the root, the root which is a consuming flame].[15] If the goal of transcendence is peace, 'la paix profonde' [profound peace],[16] which Queneau takes as a constant subject for meditation, the means to it are various.

It is important to notice the essentially rationalistic and practical complexion of Queneau's spiritual life. Meditation is one of the principal paths he follows, yet its aim is not mystical union with the divine, or a knowledge which passes understanding, but rather the elimination, through concentration, of what impedes us from recognizing the spiritual. An important theme here is that of acceptance:

> Ou est le Tao? Ici. Ici. Là encore. Et dans cette ordure? Là aussi.
> Chercher ici aussi le divin. L'acceptation de la 'réalité'.
> Dur chemin.[17]

> [Where is the Tao? Here. Here. There as well. And in this garbage? There too. |
> To look for the divine here as well. The acceptance of 'reality'. | Difficult path.]

Acceptance of reality. Consent to things as they are. But also, above all perhaps, and doubly difficult, acceptance of oneself — 'Il est difficile de s'accepter soi-même: C'est par là qu'il faut commencer' [It is difficult to accept oneself: That is where I must begin].[18] The approach to the spiritual is a recourse against the negative energies of self-dissatisfaction or self-hatred — which psychoanalysis had also had a stake in treating. Self-acceptance, however, an obsessive theme in the *Journal*, is not complacency or regard for self, but rather an insurance against the false path of self-perfection, against the construction of an image of self, a 'personality'. And so another path towards transcendence is the suppression or attenuation of what Queneau calls 'La rêverie'.

In a very characteristic way the theme of reverie arises at a certain point, occupies Queneau intermittently for a while, and then gives way to other subjects of meditation such as the value of repetition, or his attitude to Catholicism.[19] On 1 December 1939 Queneau is at Fontenay-le-Comte. His diary records that he has applied to become an interpreter, that this prospect has changed his frame of mind for the better, that he worked enthusiastically at his English grammar, ate some oysters and some cakes, read *L'Enfant* by Vallès, and did not think of God or anything else. His last entry for the day reads '[...] je suis certain d'une décision proche' [[...] I am certain there will soon be a decision].[20] At 7.00 a.m. the next morning he notes the contents of '[un] rêve grandiose et écclesiastique' [a grandiose and ecclesiastical dream][21] which prompts him to prayer. Then, after lunch, he notes that the Ministry has turned down his application to be an interpreter, and observes 'Cet échec m'a réjoui fort. Il est bon que les déboires tuent les rêveries' [This failure has cheered me up. It is a good thing when difficulties annihilate pipe dreams].[22] At midnight he turns to his diary again, noting first how he spent the afternoon and evening: a stint at the municipal library, then at the cinema ('bien bête' [very silly]);[23] and then, beginning with a definition, he starts to meditate on the subject of 'rêverie':

> La rêverie est une tentation du réel, un défi au réel pour qu'il n'arrive pas; ou parce qu'il n'arrive pas. La rêverie supprime les possibilités, ou plutôt les réalise à sa façon.[24]

> [Reverie is a way that reality tempts us, it is a challenge to the real *so that* such and such should not happen; or *because* it doesn't happen. Reverie abolishes possibilities, or rather realizes them after its own fashion.]

Our reveries, Queneau seems to be saying, postulate a future image of ourselves, foreclosing, as it were, the possibilities of the real. Reverie, he pursues, is a form of vanity, manifested in this case by a desire for promotion, a khaki uniform. This recognition prompts Queneau to reproach himself for his abiding childishness: 'Enfant, enfant' [Child, child],[25] he laments, gently picking up the title of Vallès's book, and the persistent theme that childhood conflicts and anxieties still control the adult, particularly in the infantilizing context of the *drôle de guerre*. But Queneau then wonders if he is not exaggerating his 'mauvaises raisons' [bad reasons],[26] succumbing to another kind of vanity or 'vantardise' [boastfulness][27] — that of he who confesses. This leads him to note how varied are the obstacles to what he calls 'cette saisie désirée du Transcendant en soi' [that desired grasp of the Transcendent within oneself],[28] and then to observe: 'cette satisfaction quand la vie t'a déçue, tu ne t'en es pas encore guéri' [that way of feeling satisfied when life disappoints you, you have not cured yourself of that yet].[29] This suggests the perception that his reaction to the news about the interpreter's job had been an instance of a deeply-rooted psychological mechanism, but it does not disqualify the thoughts on 'Rêverie', which are pursued a few days later: 'Dissoudre les rêveries au fur et à mesure qu'elles apparaissent, c'est ma première discipline' [To dissipate reveries as and when they form, that is my primary discipline];[30] and then later: 'Il faut éliminer la rêverie, pour laisser libre le futur, et plus puissante l'imagination' [Reverie must be eliminated in order to allow freedom for the future, and to enhance the power of the imagination].[31]

A characteristic of the diary as a form is the avoidance of synthesis and resolution. The day-by-day inscription of Queneau's preoccupations involves many twists and turns, and much that remains inconclusive or unresolved — for example the question of whether his attitude to the spiritual represents a form of quietism, passivity or *amor fati*, as opposed to a search for discipline and control; or whether his 'refus du mensonge politique' [refusal of the lie of politics],[32] his 'abstention *m a x i m u m* de toute opinion' [*maximum* abstention from all opinions],[33] based on the recognition that the domain of doxa is antithetical to spirituality, is in fact an evasion. In leaving many questions about his spiritual life unresolved, Queneau's diary underlines the way the spiritual becomes equated with a particular form of attention, a specific 'souci de soi' [concern for self][34] manifested in the achievement — which makes it so remarkable to read — of a characteristic tone of voice. In the later months covered by the *Journal* Queneau increasingly feels deserted by the call of the spirit, and when it ends, with his return to civilian life after the fall of France, we are made to feel that, for some indefinite period, he will perhaps have nothing to report on this front.

The question I now wish to take up is where we might look in Queneau's creative works for a reflection of the spiritual concerns which have surfaced with the publication of his *Journal*. I shall focus particularly on his last collection of poems, written in the early 1970s at a time when spiritual questions again came to the fore in Queneau's life. But one or two observations must be made with regard to the intervening period. It seems clear, in the first place, that Queneau's multifarious interests, activities and writings — from his concerns with encyclopaedic knowledge, with mathematics, with language in all its manifestations — could profitably be re-evaluated in the light of his spiritual concerns. More specifically, two well-known aspects of Queneau's work would repay close attention. The first is his concern with, or rather his love for, 'le quotidien' in all its forms: the unexceptional, the insignificant, the ordinary — which is also extraordinary, mysterious, and surprising. In everything he wrote Queneau was a poet of everydayness. The remarkable fictions, such as *Pierrot mon ami* (the 'germ' of which came from a dream noted in the *Journal*),[35] *Loin de Rueil*, *Le Dimanche de la vie*, are permeated by an unemphatic, unaffected partisanship with the humdrum, with the world of the *fait divers*. They feature people who, while themselves apparently devoid of spirituality, often display forms of accommodation with life which reflect Queneau's spiritual preoccupations. Pierrot drifts amiably and incuriously through a web of intrigues he cannot be bothered to unravel. He prefers to think of Yvonne, the fairground owner's daughter, of pinball, at which he is a wizard, of ham sandwiches with good mustard and white wine at the requisite temperature; he likes to lie on his bed smoking or flicking through a copy of *Le Rire*, thinking as little as possible, a propensity favoured by the ability, with which he is blessed by Queneau, to make his mind blank for long periods.[36] Of course the principal habitation of Queneau's characters is the linguistic universe he creates out of the rhythms and tropes of popular speech, and through such devices as 'le néo-Français' [neo-French] — the phonetic transcription of the spoken word. Queneau's constant euphoric celebrations of the linguistic, and the humour which invariably accompanies them, maintain a certain distance, preventing a stable regime — realism or surrealism — from establishing itself over his fictional territory. It is possible to read Queneau's novels as exercises in whimsy and nostalgia, but this involves a failure to notice that each of his principal concerns — his love of language, his unsentimental reverence for the diversity of words, things and forms of understanding — has an inward aspect as well as an outer one, a face turned towards the question of spirituality, not least because one often feels that the creative act in Queneau springs from the effort to keep at bay the inner and outer impediments to spiritual existence. In *Courir les rues* (1968), which surely deserves to occupy a prominent place on the Paris-Poésie line that runs from Baudelaire to Réda via Apollinaire and Breton, poetry becomes a form of mental and verbal perambulation.[37] A hundred and fifty-four short poems explore a 'Paris de paroles' [Paris of words] — posters, street-names, bus-routes, statues commemorating the likes of Jules Simon who changed his name from Jules Suisse, inspiring Queneau to devise one of his marvellous titles: 'Il ne voulut pas d'un nom helvète' [He wanted to be rid of a Helvetic name].[38] Queneau takes the city as it comes, steeped in past time, ever changing. Each poem is a sally forth into its endless fascinations; there is no desire to halt or to possess.

The second area which must be signalled is Queneau's predilection for 'con-traintes' [constraints] of all kinds: fixed poetic forms; the challenge of incongruity — writing, for example, a *Petite cosmogonie portative* which bristles with scientific terms, in regular alexandrines — or an ode to polystyrene; citational play — incorporating and disguising vast domains of erudition in his fictions, or rewriting

Descartes in neo-French; the elaboration in *Cent mille milliards de poèmes* (the first OULIPO classic) of a 'machine à sonnets' [sonnet machine] capable of generating millions of versions of itself.[39] Whatever else it is, formal constraint in Queneau is always a discipline, a form of spiritual exercise, a liberation from the vanity of self-expression, a secret struggle.

These two facets — 'le quotidien' and 'la contrainte' figure prominently in Queneau's last book, *Morale élémentaire* (1975), a collection of poems, in three parts, written in a phase when Queneau had explicitly renewed his spiritual orientations, and particularly his interest in Oriental philosophy.[40] The first group of fifty poems is based on a 'forme fixe' [fixed form] which, Queneau informs us, was not premeditated, or devised according to strict principles, but which arose spontaneously.[41] Each poem consists of thirty-two phrases, made up of a noun qualified by an adjective or participle, regularly arranged around a brief kernel-poem. With a few adjustments, this form was then adhered to, and Queneau tried to compose one each day often after a stroll with his dog Taï-Taï. The series complete, he developed another form which led to a series of dense *poèmes en prose* each of which is sparked by one of the sixty-four hexagrams of the *I Ching*. These were also composed on a daily basis. Attention here will focus on the initial series (*Morale élémentaire I*).

Perhaps the first thing which may strike us about these enigmatic poems is the blend of the unchanging, the static, the emblematic, on the one hand; and, on the other, the presence of unceasing change, variation, and mutation. Here are two samples:

(1)

Isis sombre          Fruit vert          Animal tacheté
          Néologismes clairs
Fleur rouge          Attitude transparente          Etoile orangée
Sources claires
Forêt brune          Sanglier roux          Troupeau bêlant
Arbre clair

Un bateau
sur l'eau
seulabre
suit le courant
Un crocodile
mord la quille
en vain

Isis ocre          Statue meuble          Totem abricot
Néologismes clairs

[Sombre Isis          Green fruit          Speckled animal
Clear neologisms
Red flower          Transparent attitude          Orange star
Clear springs
Brown forest          Ginger boar          Bleating flock
Clear tree

A boat
on the water
onlytree
follows the current
A crocodile
bites the keel
vainly

Ochre Isis        Soft statue        Apricot totem
Clear neologisms]

(2)

Amour glacé        Plastron verni        Col raidi
Souvenirs figés
Amour poli        Blason gelé        Miroir lissé
Mémoire perdue
Amour fondu        Etang séché        Soleils alourdis
Poussières anciennes

Quelles sont ces traces?
Des pas de limace?
Le vol du coucou?
Le cri du hibou?
Quelles sont ces traces?
Là-bas sur la place
le vide est partout

Amour glacé        Souvenirs figés        Mémoire perdue
Poussières anciennes

[Frozen love        Varnished dicky        Stiff collar
Congealed memories
Polished love        Frozen coat of arms        Smoothed mirror
Lost Memory
Melted love        Dried-up pond        Sluggish suns
Ancestral dust

What are these traces?
Slug's trails?
Cuckoo's flight?
Owl's cry?
What are these traces?
Over there in the square
void all around

Frozen love        Congealed memories        Frozen remembrance
Ancestral dust]

Each of the thirty-two phrases in each poem has a self-contained, marmoreal quality which conveys the idea of a permanent inscription, as, for example, in the *Stèles* of Victor Segalen. The longer, polysyllabic adjective seems to confer a definitive quality on the shorter substantive, and this is accentuated by the spacing which imparts a solemn, gently hieratic pace or tone, suggesting that the sounding of a gong between each unit would not be inappropriate.[42] Yet the security of this mode of utterance is constantly disrupted by the fact that these phrases are also drawn into a constant play of variation and difference which qualifies them in their turn, and also by the fact that, with absolute inevitability, they are interrupted by another form of discourse in the shape of the 'kernel-poem'. These 'interludes' (Queneau's term)[43] provisionally establish a lighter, more aerated space, a 'clearing' in the poem, characterized by a different tonality which also, through the presence of active verbs and temporal references, conveys a sense of transitoriness or, rather, of the permanence of change.

The phrases are subject to innumerable modes of variation, gravitation and transformation:

1    A noun may recur, but with a different adjective: 'Isis sombre' in the opening line of the first quoted poem is transformed into 'Isis ocre' in the last line.

2    The recurrence-with-difference of a noun may occur in the same position in the line (as in the 'Isis' example) or in a different one.

3    An entire phrase may be repeated identically, but may or may not retain its position in the line, as 'néologismes clairs' does in the first poem quoted above.

4    The *fourth* phrase — in the second line — may or may not turn out to be repeated as a conclusion.

5    As we read these poems, some of the phrases recede immediately into nothingness, whilst others — but we do not know which until we have read to the end — accumulate meaning and destiny through recurrence.

6    Sometimes a phrase is repeated on the same line, as if the needle were temporarily stuck: 'Main traceuse | Main traceuse | Main traceuse' [Tracing hand | Tracing hand | Tracing hand].[44]

7    A poem may contain several exact repetitions or none at all.

8    In some cases the division between left- and right-hand columns seems pertinent, and encourages the reader to identify a micro-poem within the larger unit; in other cases this does not occur.

9    Often phrases using different words may be seen as semantic transformations or echoes of each other, or as items in a series — 'Souvenirs figés | mémoire perdue | poussières anciennes', in the second poem quoted above. The establishment of a semantic *isotopie* may colour other phrases, so that, for example, we see the 'plastron verni | col raidi' as belonging to the order of memory — in this case memory of a paternal presence.

10    In some cases the third 'section' of the poem contains no elements from the first and represents a new development. In other cases (for example 'Amour glacé' above) the third part is like an abbreviated, accelerated, compressed version of the first — a distillation of what has emerged as central.

11    Sometimes the phrases share a consistent frame of reference (the *Iliad* and the Trojan War for example in 'Murs murants...', and in some cases a narrative development seems to be conveyed in fragmentary form.

12  Sometimes a prominent metaphysical 'plot' can be discerned, as in 'Vanité venteuse...' where phrases connoting vanity and pride mingle with phrases involving the word 'Violette' in a progression — 'étranglée' [strangled], 'éperdue' [frantic], 'écrasée' [crushed][45] — which suggests the annihilation of spiritual life.

The relationship between the phrases and the kernel-poem is also subject to enormous variation. Quite often, with its habitual emphasis on the visual, and on the natural world, its orientation towards *choses vues*, and its kinship with Haiku, the 'interlude' has the character of a brief coming-to-life, followed by a return to the immemorial (or to the past). Often marked by a child-like simplicity, through the use of rhyme which may give it the flavour of a *comptine*, the kernel-poem may conjure up the child who endures within the aging man. Often, too, it gives the impression of unfolding or opening up what is locked in the compressed blocks of the phrases, sometimes by conveying the moral of the tale, or the lesson of the day. But equally, the kernel-poem may represent a momentary respite from the obsessive themes which dominate these poems — memory and the past, language and the act of writing, time and aging.

Written in the space of a day, as a daily task, these poems, with their tripartite structure, have something of a day's pattern — morning, afternoon, evening. As the light moves, the colours change (as in 'Isis sombre...' quoted above), some things arise and fade, others insist and endure, nothing remains quite the same. In each poem we are made witness to a process of repetition and transformation as ineluctable as the flow of a river or the changing shadows in a room. Yet, as the poems and days succeed one another, the pattern remains the same — each poem is a transformation of the same basic poem, the same essential day. And each poem, in its gravitation, seems to withhold something, an enigma or an absence, behind or within, which can only be disclosed through the words which disguise it. This is perhaps the place of the spiritual — or else that of the archaic opacities which make it forever out of reach.

*Morale élémentaire* is perhaps Queneau unmasked, or less disguised, but it is still Queneau: there is wry humour, there are everyday words, and what is new here grows out of what came before — explicitly in the *Journal*, surreptitiously elsewhere. At the end of one of the prose poems in the third part of the book, Queneau writes:

> Le dessin s'écarte peut-être du projet, mais l'intention demeure bonne et directe, ferme en sa discrète tangence.[46]

> [The design diverges perhaps from the project, but the intention remains sound and direct, firm in its discreet tangency.]

A discreet tangent, tenaciously held... not a bad description of Queneau's path, in both spiritual and literary terms.

## Notes

1. Raymond Queneau, *Œuvres complètes*, vol. I, ed. by Claude Debon (Paris: Gallimard, 1989). See especially the section headed 'Souvenirs inédits', pp. 1069–96.

2. All quotations from Queneau's poetry are from the Pléiade edition. The lines quoted were used by Georges Perec as an epigraph to his autobiography, *W ou le souvenir d'enfance* (Paris: Denoel, 1975). Perec admired in Queneau a writer for whom literary activity, however personal its materials, was always partly a game, an *exercice de style* drawing on existing models, but also a loving witness to the diversity of three orders: language, knowledge and everyday reality.

3. Raymond Queneau, *Journal 1939–1940*, ed. by A. I. Queneau and Jean-José Marchand (Paris: Gallimard, 1986), p. 92.

4. *Journal*, p. 105.

5. Ibid., p. 97.

6. Ibid., p. 67.

7. Ibid., p. 115.

8. Ibid., p. 62. Queneau was probably in the audience when Michel Leiris delivered his famous lecture on 'Le Sacré dans la vie quotidienne' in January 1938. See *Le Groupe, La Rupture, Change*, 7 (1970), 63–72. Cf. Denis Hollier, *Le Collège de Sociologie 1937–39* (Paris: Gallimard, 1979).

9. Ibid., p. 14.

10. Ibid., p. 73.

11. Ibid., p. 91.

12. Ibid., p. 42.

13. Ibid., p. 65.

14. Ibid., p. 119.

15. Ibid., p. 116.

16. Ibid., *passim*, e.g. p. 191.

17. Ibid., p. 48.

18. Ibid., p. 121.

19. On repetition see *Journal*, pp. 64, 134; On Queneau's relation to Catholicism, see pp. 35, 49, 188.

20. Ibid., p. 93.

21. Ibid.

22. Ibid., p. 94.

23. Ibid.

24. Ibid.

25. Ibid.

26. Ibid.

27. Ibid.

28. Ibid.

29. Ibid., p. 95.

30. Ibid., p. 107.

31. Ibid., p. 114.

32. Ibid., p. 122.

33. Ibid.

34. Ibid.

35. *Journal*, p. 51.

36. Raymond Queneau, *Pierrot mon ami* (1942; Paris: Gallimard, 1972).

37. *Courir les rues* may be found in the Pléiade edition, pp. 351–434.

38. *Œuvres complètes*, p. 417.

39. For the *Petite cosmogonie portative*, see *Œuvres complètes*, pp. 197–238. Le Chant du styrène (pp. 239–48) was written for a documentary film commissioned by a plastics firm and directed by Alain Resnais. Queneau was a founder member of the *Ouvroir de Littérature potentielle* which was set up in 1960 with the aim of encouraging the production of texts by the use of formal

constraints. See *Oulipo: la littérature potentielle* (Paris: Gallimard, 1984). *Cent mille milliards de poèmes* (*Œuvres complètes*, pp. 333–50) consisted of ten sonnets each line of which was hinged separately so that it could be read in conjunction with any combination of thirteen other lines.

40. *Morale élémentaire* may be found in the *Œuvres complètes*, pp. 611–702.

41. A group of these poems appeared in the *Nouvelle Revue Française* of January 1974 accompanied by an explanatory 'Note' (*Œuvres complètes*, p. 1466) which was suppressed in the published volume. The manuscripts and preparatory dossiers for *Morale élémentaire* have been studied by Claude Debon: see her 'Notice' in the *Œuvres complètes* (pp. 1451–66) and her 'Raymond Queneau: naissance de Morale élémentaire', in *Penser, Classer, Ecrire*, ed. by Béatrice Didier and Jacques Neefs (Paris: Presses Universitaires de Vincennes, 1990), pp. 27–34.

42. As Queneau himself indicated in a sentence which was not finally included in the *NRF* note, cf. *Œuvres complètes*, p. 1452.

43. In the cancelled sentence referred to in the previous note Queneau also used the word 'ritournelle' [ritornello], ibid., and suggested that these parts might be accompanied by 'un petit air de flûte ou de pipeau' [a tune played on the flute or reed-pipe].

44. Ibid., p. 614.

45. Ibid., p. 637.

46. Ibid., p. 678.

# 15

# Language, Colour, and the
# Enigma of Everydayness

The links between colour and everyday life were underlined in a spectacular way in spring 1996, when Pepsi Cola decided to make a change of colour — the can, not the drink — central to a change of image. The opening moves in one of the most expensive advertising campaigns ever launched included a transatlantic flight by a Concorde painted blue, with André Agassi, Claudia Schiffer, and sundry other celebrities aboard, all decked out in the new shade, and, on the same day, an edition of the London *Daily Mirror* printed on blue paper. This was followed by a poster campaign featuring everyday objects and icons strongly associated with the colour red — Labour Party rosette, Royal Mail post box, Heinz ketchup, Swiss army knife — that all suddenly turned blue and were accompanied by the legend 'Change the script!'.

It is too soon to say whether, in Britain at least, people like having their colour conventions tampered with, or if blue is an appropriate colour for other aspects of the Pepsi image. Yet these issues were aired when, on Pepsi Day, BBC Radio 4 News ran an item featuring a surprising range of experts on colour, demonstrating wide-ranging and complex links between colour, science, and culture. A public relations consultant spoke about dress codes and image make-overs, a psychologist discussed moods, physiology, and such questions as whether blue really is a cool colour, while another expert stressed the complex cultural history of colour symbolism and the culturally variable associations colours possess, despite strong evidence that the central nervous system responds fairly universally to colour difference. Then an art historian explained the Purkinje shift (after the Bohemian physiologist J. E. Purkinje who first described it in 1815) whereby, in a defined context such as a room, blue grows on the eye to the extent that, after twenty minutes or so, it supersedes red and dominates the perceptual environment, an effect often observed in Italian churches where the Virgin's blue mantle progressively stands out with a magical radiance. Then came internationally patented Yves Klein Blue, abstract expressionism, colour field painting, and so on and so forth. Subsequently, a series of short programmes on BBC Radio 3 explored the connotations of individual colours, covering, in an amusing and anecdotal way, the kind of ground surveyed in John Gage's magisterial 1993 text *Colour and Culture*, which has a wealth of information concerning the development of dyes and pigments, esoteric colour symbolisms in heraldry and alchemy, mosaics and stained glass, and much else besides.

In the United States, enthusiasm for discussions of colour can be gauged by the success of Alexander Theroux's *Primary Colors*, a witty, stylish, but ultimately somewhat tedious compendium of snippets of information illustrating the multiple meanings that have accrued through history to red, blue, and yellow. Colour is clearly central to everyday life, not just in modern industrial societies dominated by mass-produced objects, although Jean Baudrillard, devoting a substantial section to colour in *Le Système des objets* [*The System of Objects*], underlines how recent the liberation of colour has been. In nonindustrial societies the ability to interpret the changing colours of the natural world has a functional role, and the earliest art — polychrome cave paintings — points to connections between magic, colour, and hunting. As is well known, some communities have a very subtle colour vocabulary for utilitarian reasons, and this poses teasing questions for linguisticians about the order of priority between language and reality. Moreover, readers of Lévi-Strauss may recall the passage in *Tristes tropiques* where the anthropologist goes shopping on the Boulevard Sebastopol in search of appropriately coloured articles to take as gifts to the Bororo Indians, for whom certain colours are infinitely prized while others are shunned.

If, in a general way, there is a clear link between colour and everyday life, we may ask if the connection is still there when we seek to investigate more deeply the nature of everydayness. Can colour lead us to the heart of our sense of the quotidian? What constructions of everydayness does colour fit in with, and which aspects of the phenomenon of colour are particularly relevant to it? The first thing to note is that those who have made the everyday, or the ordinary, a familiar category in recent thought — from Henri Lefebvre to Roland Barthes, Jean Baudrillard, Michel de Certeau, Umberto Eco, and Stanley Cavell; from the surrealists to Raymond Queneau, Georges Perec, Jacques Réda or Michel Vinaver — consistently underline the deeply ambiguous and problematic nature of this notion.

Problematic, in the first place, because of its inherent evanescence and instability: Maurice Blanchot notes that 'le quotidien est ce qu'il y a de plus difficile à découvrir' [the everyday is the most difficult thing to discover].[1] The everyday can only be located at the intersection, or in the overlaps and interstices, of different systems and orders — public and private, real and imaginary, regular and haphazard. The everyday is also ambiguous and ambivalent because, as Lefebvre's work shows again and again, it is a place of estrangement and alienation, but at the same time a zone of liberation, joy, and contentment. Unlike other more localized sectors of experience — the aesthetic, the political, the sexual — which have at least overt positive valuations, the everyday is not only capable of being lived through in different ways, but is inherently ambivalent. There are various ways in to this labyrinth. For example, we can follow the trail of the object, or that of daily practices or rituals, or we can track the everyday through trajectories and ways of traversing space, or in the organization of the day itself, or in spatial practices — the layout of rooms in a house or the streets of a city. In the discussion that follows, colour will be seen as one of these trails, a route towards the enigma of the everyday.

To approach the question of how colour might be pertinent to the everyday, we need initially to look at the ways in which it can be valorized. One way of celebrating colour that might seem particularly relevant to the everyday sees it in terms of immediacy, affect, the prelinguistic. Historians of colour and culture locate the valorization of colour within a fundamental opposition between two poles conveniently represented by Newton and Goethe. In a Newtonian perspective, colour is a phenomenon to be understood in terms of the laws of optics and the physical nature of light. Goethe's theory of colours, on the other hand, elaborated in 1810, although based on experiment, exalts the subjective component in the perception of infinitely variegated hues. The Romantic investment of colour as a mental phenomenon had been anticipated by many Renaissance proponents of *colore* as opposed to *disegno*, as well as in earlier theological distinctions between *lux* and *lumen*. But, directly and indirectly, Goethe's work heralded numerous investigations and classifications of the subjective dimension of colour, and a wealth of often intensely poetic writing about its power, such as the famous section from Baudelaire's *Salon de 1846*, entitled 'De la couleur' [Of Colour],[2] or the many reflections on colour in the writings of Delacroix, Kandinsky, or Albers.

Common to these ecstatic evaluations of colour is the emphasis on intensity, power, and communion, often supported by spirituality or a sense of the mystery of the universe. I wish, however, to focus on a tension within this radical privileging of colour. This tension may exist within the discourse of a single proponent of colour, and in its simplest form boils down to the question of whether what is valorized is the pure experience of a single colour, a unified experience of one colour at a time, or, on the other hand, the contrastive nature of colour, the harmonies and resonances which colours can achieve in combination. Baudelaire, for example, may speak of 'le rouge, cette couleur si obscure, si épaisse, plus difficile à pénétrer que les yeux d'un serpent' [red, this colour that is so dark, so dense, harder to penetrate than the eyes of a serpent] ('De la couleur', p. 446), but essentially his approach to colour, impassioned and wholehearted as it is, is rooted in the notion of 'l'harmonie, la mélodie et le contre-point' [harmony, melody and counterpoint] (p. 423). Colour is an 'hymne compliqué' [complex hymn] where 'le rouge chante la gloire du vert; le noir — quand il y en a — zéro solitaire et insignifiant, intercède le secours du bleu ou du rouge' [red sings to the glory of green; black — when it exists — a solitary and insignificant zero, seeks the intercession of blue or red] (p. 422). For all his enthusiasm for artifice, Baudelaire's championing of colour is grounded in nature, in a

> bel espace de nature où tout verdoie, rougeoie, poudroie et chatoie en pleine liberté, où toutes choses diversement colorées suivant leur constitution moléculaire, changées de seconde en seconde par le déplacement de l'ombre et de la lumière, et agitées par le travail intérieur du calorique, se trouvent en perpétuelle vibration (p. 422)

> [a lovely corner of nature where everything freely luxuriates, gleams, and glistens in its greenness or redness, where all things, diversely coloured by dint of their molecular structure, changing second by second through the shifts of light and shadow, and activated within by the agency of heat, are to be found in perpetual vibration]

By contrast, Kandinsky's enthusiasm for colour, which he saw as a path along which artistic creation could free itself from enslavement to nature and attain spirituality, focuses on the intense material presence of pure colour. An extraordinary passage in his autobiography describes a founding moment when, at the age of about fourteen, he bought a set of oil paints and saw the colours come to life as he squeezed them out of the tube:

> avec un profond sérieux, une pétillante espièglerie... une domination de soi opiniâtre... ces êtres étranges que l'on nomme couleurs venaient l'un après l'autre, vivants en soi et pour soi, autonomes, et dotés à chaque instant à leur future vie autonome, et, à chaque instant, prêts à se plier librement à de nouvelles combinaisons; à créer une infinité de mondes nouveaux[3]

> [With a profound seriousness, a bubbling vivacity... a stubborn self-possession... these strange beings we call colours emerged one after the other, living beings both in and for themselves, autonomous, and endowed at every moment with their future autonomous life, and at each moment ready to lend themselves freely to new combinations, to create an infinite number of new worlds]

Even when they enter into combination, colours retain their intense, sovereign, autonomy, a point Kandinsky emphasizes further on when he insists on the 'forces fraîches' [fresh forces] of the newly emerged colours as they assert themselves against the background of the palette, creating chance combinations in a process he compares to both music and alchemy.

In a different vein, Ernst Jünger's remarkable meditations on colour in *Das Abenteuerliche Herz* [*The Adventurous Heart*], translated into French by Henri Thomas as *Le Cœur aventureux*, also underline the immediacy and specificity of individual colours, over and above the combinations and juxtapositions that maximize their power.[4] Very much in the German Romantic tradition, and following Goethe and Baudelaire, Jünger's stimulus is always colour in nature, but his observations lead away from the familiar towards mysterious laws of metamorphosis and participation reflected in a wide range of contexts. A number of texts centre on the mystery of redness, a 'fundamental substance' associated with the life force in its intensity. For Jünger, red is both the colour of the earth's core — Mother Earth is red — and of the human body, and particularly the inner organs:

> Nous sommes les petites grives que la terre mère attrape avec la couleur rouge. La matière profonde est rouge, qu'elle se cache sous ses vertes robes; sous les dentelles blanches que sont les glaciers, sous les falbalas gris dont l'océan borde ses rivages...La vivante matière dont nous sommes faits est rouge; nous sommes de fond en comble revêtus de cette couleur. Et c'est pourquoi elle est si proche de nous, si proche qu'entre elle et nous il n'est pas de place pour la réflexion. Elle est la couleur de la pure présence; nous nous comprenons sous son signe de façon muette.[5]

> [We are the little sparrows that Mother Earth catches with the colour red. Deepest matter is red, even when it hides under green robes; under the white lace of glaciers, under the grey frills with which the ocean decks out its shores... the living matter of which we are made is red; we are totally enveloped in this colour. That is why it is so close to us, so close that between us and it there

is no room for thought. Red is the colour of pure presence; under its sign we commune without words.]

The notion of colour as presence and intensity is central to the aesthetic theory of Georges Duthuit and led him to write influential studies of Byzantine art and of the Fauves.[6] By contrast with Greek art, colour in Byzantine icons, murals, and mosaics comes alive, becomes a celebration of place and moment. As for the Fauves — Matisse, early Derain, anticipated by Cézanne — they fulfil the broken promise of impressionist art which, while ostensibly liberating colour, had in fact kept it subordinate to design and classical space. By freeing colour from perspective and reference, the Fauves had allowed art to become an act in which the immediacy of sensation and affective experience is externalized. For Duthuit, as for Kandinsky, there is something eruptive, transgressive, and violent about colour. But in Duthuit's case the experience of colour is essentially immanent: what it apprehends, and in its way potentially divinizes, is the pure moment, the here and now. Colour does not point in the direction of a harmony revealed through contrast and combination but becomes pure event, associated with the act of painting.

The kind of tension we are concerned with is reflected in psychoanalytical accounts of colour. For the analyst Christian David, it is self-evident that what is at stake when colour enters the psychological arena is an investment, and generally an over-investment, in pure affect.[7] The cult of colour reflects a desire to escape the hegemony of language, the aspiration to an oceanic state without clear limits. Colour is a sublime realm beyond conflict in which one seeks to immerse oneself. For Murielle Gagnebin, on the other hand, colour, in a psychoanalytical perspective, is not an absolute but an instrument of mediation, a transferential zone.[8] If colour is indeed linked to 'the infinite range of emotions' — and thus with the affective order — what it offers is in fact tied to its essentially differential nature. If colour is a zone of energies and vibrations, these are not so much occasioned by pure colour as by incompatibilities, reciprocities, and juxtapositions. Seen this way, colour is essentially agonistic and thus expressive of, rather than a haven from, conflict.

For Gagnebin, the essential parameters that define colours — position on the chromatic scale, saturation, brilliancy — taken together with the play of opposition to other colours, produces a space of infinite variety that can match the singular and specifically differential aspect of each moment of perception. The factor of intensity makes colour capable of registering the work of unconscious drives, while the chromatic scale relates to the perception of difference. For Gagnebin, the ambiguity of colour makes it a go-between from sensory experience to unconscious desire, and this allows it to signal the work of fantasy and repression: 'Colours point to the active power of repression' (p. 106). This tension can be formulated in the context of language and identity. On the one hand, colour is seen as antithetical to language, articulation, sense, mimesis, and thus to ordinary selfhood. It offers a release from the grip of these agencies into a realm of pure event, experience, affect.

For Michel Corvin, 'le manque de sens fait "revenir" la figure en son excès d'image [...] La couleur ainsi posée représente un absolu indépassable: quelque chose dont on n'a rien à dire, mais qui s'impose par un trop-plein de présence, impossible à nier'[9] [the lack of meaning "brings back" the figure in its excessiveness as image [...] Posited this way, colour represents an absolute that cannot be transcended: something of which nothing can be said, but which imposes itself through an excessive plenitude and presence that is impossible to refute]. Roland Barthes subscribes to this discourse when he writes in his autobiography, 'serais-je peintre, je ne peindrai que des couleurs: ce champ me paraît libéré également de la Loi (pas d'imitation, pas d'Analogie) et de la Nature'[10] [if I were a painter I'd paint nothing but colours: this field seems to me to be equally free of the Law (no imitation, no Analogy) and of Nature]. But Barthes's antinaturalism points to the ambivalence of this kind of release which, even if it is linked to the rhythms of the body, can seem to have connotations of emptiness, in the Buddhist sense, rather than plenitude.

Equally, however, the other side of our polarity — the sense that colour harmonies are compatible with, indeed analogous to, language — is also marked by ambivalence. The features of colour reference which have fascinated philosophers, most notably Wittgenstein — for example the huge disparity between the very restricted number of basic colours: the primaries, or those of the spectrum, or just red, blue, and green, and the hundreds and thousands of nuances which even an untutored eye can discriminate — encourage talk of the language of colour (a notion also linked to colour symbolism). Yet if this can be used to underwrite a sense of the profound affinity between colour range and the subtleties of individual psychology, the linkage of colour and language, hue and cry, can also sponsor classifications which, even as they attempt to tie colour to mood or humour, end up being immensely abstract and conceptual.

At this point, Maurice Merleau-Ponty's discussions of colour in his writings on perception become an indispensable point of reference. Colour is both incidental and fundamental to Merleau-Ponty's accounts of the human subject's 'mélange avec le monde' [mingling with the world], the two-way processes, designated by such terms as l'entrelacs [the intertwining] or le chiasme [the chiasm], or concepts such as 'la chair du monde' [the world's flesh] and 'le corps interposé' [the interposed body] that mark out perception not as the work of one agency or another but as communion or synergy, a mutual participation in an open totality. Incidental, because although painting, and particularly the work of Cézanne, was a constant source of meditation for Merleau-Ponty, his concern is not with colour itself. Fundamental, nonetheless, because, as is testified by frequent references in La Phénoménologie de la perception [The Phenomenology of Perception], Le Visible et l'Invisible [The Visible and the Invisible], and L'Œil et l'Esprit [Eye and Mind], colour had a particular relevance to Merleau-Ponty's concerns, a pertinence that is very revealing for our concern with the everyday because it is connected with one of colour's inherent dualities. As a type of sense-datum associated with physical phenomena, colour can be linked with a materialist and empiricist viewpoint where mind receives the imprint of matter. Conversely, a quality dependent on light, it can be seen as an abstraction, the product of a mental operation effected by a subject separate from the world. Since he sought to overturn both these perspectives, and the false duality they imply, it is not surprising that Merleau-Ponty often focuses on colour.

My discussion will centre principally on one passage from *Le Visible et l'invisible*, but I will first outline briefly what I want to draw from the way Merleau-Ponty uses colour in his attempts to render the difference between thinking about the world and living in it, and to characterize our inclusion in the visible, the way perception interrogates the world. The points I want to stress have to do with three related areas: immediacy, identity, and language. Already central to the discussion of *le sentir* [feeling] in the *Phénoménologie* is the insistence that sensation is never just of the here and now but incorporates the past: 'elle [la sensation] suppose en moi les sédiments d'une condition préalable'[11] [sensation presupposes in me the sediment of an earlier condition]. Nonetheless, there is something profoundly anonymous about it: 'Toute perception a lieu dans une atmosphère de généralité et se donne à nous comme anonyme [...] je devrais dire qu'on perçoit en moi et non pas que je perçois. Toute sensation comporte un germe de rêve ou de dépersonnalisation'[12] [Every perception takes place in a climate of generality and gives itself to us as anonymous [...]. I should say that there is perception happening in me, and not that I perceive. Every sensation comprises an element of dream or of depersonalization].

In its singularity, each sensation is always the first and last of its kind and invokes the response not of a subject who makes decisions but 'another self who has already espoused the world'. *Le Visible et l'invisible* extends the discussion of what it is like to be a subject of perception and, as the title indicates, this work emphasizes that the visible is rooted in the invisible — in what the subject brings to the process of perception. Language, far from being alien, an agent of severance, is seen to be potentially integral with it. Both seeing and speaking, according to Merleau-Ponty, if we seek to grasp them concretely rather than discursively, can be what he calls 'expériences irrécusables et énigmatiques à la fois' [13] [at once incontrovertible and enigmatic experiences].

Near the beginning of the book's last chapter, titled 'L'Entrelacs — le chiasme' [The Intertwining — The Chiasm], Merleau-Ponty uses colour to explore a central paradox, the way seeing involves both proximity and distance, absorption and separation. How can it be, he asks, that the apparently seamless quality of visual experience does not constitute either a total takeover of the object by the subject or conversely of our mind by the object? What magic property must the visible have — 'quel est ce talisman de la couleur, cette vertu singulière du visible'[14] [what is this talisman of colour, this singular virtue in the visible' — that we can apprehend it so totally, while at the same time it retains its sovereignty? If the structure of vision is chiastic, and seeing involves a crossing over into the realm of things — a movement outwards, but at the same time an internalization, an invasion by the outside — why do subject and object not simply fuse, or coincide absolutely, or cancel one another out? Because, in a metaphor Merleau-Ponty develops extensively, they are of the same flesh: 'Le regard même les enveloppe, les habille de sa chair'[15] [The gaze itself envelops them, clothes them in its flesh]. Vision marshals in things a dimension which is other than the thing in itself, which inheres in our apprehension of them, but which is nevertheless not simply our projection, because, reciprocally, vision marshals in us a dimension which does not pre-exist this chiastic exchange or intertwining 'le monde et moi sont l'un dans l'autre'[16]. Crucial here is the fact that vision is a bodily experience by dint of the fact that seeing is a kind of touching: 'tout visible est taillé dans le tangible' [every visible is cut out in the tangible]. The act of vision enlists our body, through which we are 'pris dans le tissu des choses' [caught up in the fabric of things].

To illustrate this, Merleau-Ponty develops the example of colour: a shade of red that catches my eye is seen to be not one thing that I relate to all at once, but a layered and variegated phenomenon which implicates widely different orders of experience:

> Il faut comprendre d'abord que ce rouge sous mes yeux n'est pas, comme on dit toujours, une quale, une pellicule d'être sans épaisseur, message à la fois indéchiffrable et évident, qu'on a ou qu'on n'a pas reçu, mais dont on sait, si on l'a reçu, tout ce qu'il y a à savoir, et dont il n'y a en somme rien à dire. Il demande une mise au point, même brève, il émerge d'une rougeur, moins précise, plus générale, où mon regard était pris et s'enlisait avant de le fixer, comme on dit si bien. Et si, maintenant que je l'ai fixé, mes yeux s'enfoncent en lui, dans la structure fixe, ou s'ils recommencent d'errer alentour, le *quale* reprend son existence atmosphérique. Sa forme précise est solidaire d'une certaine configuration ou texture laineuse, métallique ou poreuse et il est peu de choses en regard de ces participations.[17]

> [We must first of all understand that this red under my eyes is not, as is always stated, a quale, a pellicule of being without thickness, a message at once indecipherable and obvious, which one has or has not received, but of which — if one has received it — one knows all there is to know, and of which there is finally nothing to say. It requires a focusing, however brief; it emerges from a less precise, more general redness, in which my gaze was caught, into which it sank, before — as we so aptly put it — fixing it. And, now that I have fixed it, if my eyes penetrate it, into its fixed structure, or if they start to wander round about again, the quale resumes its atmospheric existence. Its precise form is bound up with a certain woolly, metallic, or porous configuration or texture, and the quale itself counts for very little compared with these participations.]

'Participations' is a key word here. Talking about a particular shade of redness, Merleau-Ponty seeks to show that our rapport with it is engendered not by its fixed character, as a pure quality, but by the fact that it belongs simultaneously to different orders. First, my way of attending to it is physical, mobile — 'Il demande une mise au point': I need to locate its specificity in the way it is not just red, but this red. And to do this I scan it and feel it with my eyes. The particular quality of redness does not just stand still. A work of differentiation takes place. A second dimension is situational — the relation between this red and other contiguous shades of red, or other colours and coloured things in the same environment. This red is not an isolated phenomenon but 'un certain nœud dans la trame du simultané et du successif' [a certain knot in the thread of the simultaneous and the successive].[18] Thirdly, and most importantly, with regard to the chiastic relationship of viewer and viewed, this red's participation in 'the fabric of the visible' also locates it in a 'tissu d'être invisible':

À plus forte raison, la robe rouge tient-elle de toutes ses fibres au tissu du visible, et, par lui à un tissu d être invisible. Ponctuation dans le champ des choses rouges, qui comprend les tuiles des toits, le drapeau des gardes-barrières et de la Révolution, certains terrains près d Aix ou à Madagascar, elle l est aussi dans celui des robes rouges, qui comprend, avec des robes de femmes, des robes de professeurs, d évêques et d avocats généraux, et aussi dans celui des parures et celui des uniformes.[19]

[The red dress *a fortiori* holds with all its fibres onto the fabric of the Visible, and through it onto a fabric of invisible being. A punctuation in the field of red things, including the tiles of roof tops, the flags of gatekeepers and of the Revolution, certain terrains near Aix or in Madagascar, it is also a punctuation in the field of red garments, which includes, along with the dresses of women, robes of professors, bishops, and advocate generals, and also in the field of adornments and that of uniforms.]

Take a red dress. Its redness punctuates 'the field of red things' — roof tiles, flags, landscapes tinged with ochre: this red has a place in a constellation of reds I have seen before, reds I remember, as well as other reds in its immediate environment. These absent reds make up one level of invisibility. But this red dress worn by a woman fits not only into a constellation of other red costumes — associated with particular officers: teachers, bishops, judges — but with uniforms generally. And the red of this particular dress differs according to which constellation I fit it into:

Et son rouge, à la lettre, n'est pas le même, selon qu'il paraît dans une con-stellation ou dans l'autre, selon que précipite en lui la pure essence de la Révo-lution de 1917, ou celle de l'éternel féminin, ou celle de l'accusateur public, ou celle des Tziganes, vêtus à la hussarde, qui régnaient il y a vingt-cinq ans sur une brasserie des Champs-Elysées.[20]

[and its red literally is not the same as it appears in one constellation or in the other, as the pure essence of the Revolution of 1917 precipitates in it, or that of the eternal feminine, or that of the public prosecutor, or that of the gypsies dressed like Hussars who reigned twenty-five years ago over an inn on the Champs-Elysées.]

Finally, a given red also belongs to an imaginary constellation: it is 'a fossil drawn up from the depths of imaginary worlds'. This vivid series of enumerations leads into a crucial general statement summarizing what Merleau-Ponty is saying about colours, and how they represent visible things in general. If we take into account all these orders of belonging, 'these participations', then:

une couleur nue, et en général une visible, n'est pas un morceau d'être abso-lument dur, insécable, offert tout nu à une vision que ne pourrait être que totale ou nulle, mais plutôt une sorte de détroit entre des horizons extérieurs et des horizons intérieurs toujours béants, quelque chose qui vient toucher doucement et fait résonner à distance diverses régions du monde coloré ou visible, une certaine différenciation, une modulation éphémère de ce monde, moins couleur ou chose donc, que différence entre des choses et des couleurs, cristallisation momentanée de l'être coloré ou de la visibilité.[21]

[a naked colour, and in general a visible one, is not a piece of absolutely hard, indivisible being, offered all naked to a vision which could be only total or null, but is instead a kind of strait between exterior horizons and interior horizons that are always gaping open, something that comes to touch lightly and makes diverse regions of the coloured or visible world resound at the distances, a certain differentiation, an ephemeral modulation of this world — less a colour or a thing, therefore, than a difference between things and colours, a momentary crystallization of coloured being or of visibility.]

So a colour is not a thing, one and indivisible, to be apprehended or not, but a kind of narrow strait between an outer horizon — other visible reds — and an inner one — other invisible reds. To attend to a colour is not to home in on some pure quality or essence but to enter a field of resonances embracing various domains in the world of the visible. But if this means moving away from the colour itself, the trajectory is not away from the particular but paradoxically towards the specificity of a particular moment, 'a certain differentiation, an ephemeral modulation of this world'. The move is not towards the generic character of the colour or thing, but towards its difference from other colours or things, or the same colours and things perceived in other circumstances. To attend to an occasion with regard to the dimension of colour is to attend to what makes it this occasion and not another.

At this point let us bring language back into the picture. One of the factors that is precious about Merleau-Ponty's way of thinking about colour is that it has explicit parallels with what he has to say about language and particularly a dimension of language he calls 'la parole opérante' [operative speech]. Just as a perception of colour is not a one-off thing but draws on a hinterland of other perceptions going to make up 'the fabric of our experience', so 'la signification univoque n'est qu'une partie de la signification du mot, qu'il y a toujours, au-delà, un halo de signification qui se manifeste dans des modes d'emploi nouveaux et inattendus'[22] ['univocal signification is but one part of the signification of the word ... beyond it there is always a halo of signification that manifests itself in new and unexpected modes of use]). And just as the field of our experience comprises 'this immense latent content of the past', and is not constituted by indivisible entities or essences but rather by 'un temps et un espace d'empilement, de prolifération, d'empiétement, de promiscuité, — perpétuelle prégnance, perpétuelle parturition, générativité et généralité.'[23] ['a time and a space that exist by piling up, by proliferation, by encroachment, by promiscuity — a perpetual pregnancy, perpetual parturition, generativity and generality'], so language partakes of this: 'La parole est partie totale des significations comme la chair du visible [...] il y a là [...] solidarité et enlacement [...] elle prolonge dans l'invisible, étend aux opérations sémantiques, l'appartenance du corps à l'être'[24] ['like the flesh of the visible, speech is a total part of the significations [...] there is solidarity and intertwining [...] speech prolongs into the invisible, extends unto the semantic operations, the belongingness of the body to being']. Within the linguistic field 'operative speech' is 'a way of making things themselves speak').

Here language is not being used instrumentally; words combine according to the 'entrelacement naturel de leur sens, par le trafic occulte de la métaphore'[25] ['natural intertwining of their meaning, through the occult trade of metaphor']. What counts is not the manifest meaning of words, 'mais les rapports latéraux, les parentés, qui sont impliqués dans leurs virements et leurs échanges'[26] ['but the lateral relations, the kinships that are implicated in their transfers and their exchanges']. In the context of lived experience, language does not mask or conceal Being. Rather, 'si l'on sait le saisir avec toutes ses racines et toutes sa frondaison'[27] ['if one knows how to grasp it with all its roots and all its foliation'], it is 'le plus valable témoin de l'Etre'[28] ['the most valuable witness to Being']. This reasoned confidence in language, and its connection with the domain of colour, lead naturally in the direction of poetry, a frequent point of reference for Merleau-Ponty, as well as towards painting.

★   ★   ★   ★   ★

Connections between colour, language, and everyday experience play an important role in contemporary French poetry, and I wish now to focus on two contrasting approaches in the work of Yves Bonnefoy and Philippe Jaccottet. Bonnefoy is well known for his writings on art, from his studies of Poussin and Roman baroque to the many essays on modern artists including a fine monograph on Giacometti, but Bonnefoy's concerns are the same whether he is thinking about poetry, writing poems, or seeking to understand an artist's work, and meditations on colour feature in all three areas. Bonnefoy's central theme is what he calls 'la présence' [presence], an experience of Being in the context of the everyday world, particularly associated with language, landscape, and love. In all these fields his writing investigates how human desire, articulated through the imaginary, propitiates or thwarts the approach to presence. Is the realm of the image, generically speaking, an arena for presence or not? To the extent that the imaginary may involve a confiscation of the real, of presence, a substitution of something else in its place, should authentic art and poetry constitute 'une guerre contre l'image' [a war against the image], a repudiation of form, concept, ornament, beauty, or is there a 'good' way of dealing with images, a way of lucidly contesting the negative features of the image within the imaging process itself?

These are the kinds of issues on the horizon when Bonnefoy talks about colour. In three books published in 1977, colour features in three different kinds of context. First, a section of his long poem *Dans le leurre du seuil* [*In the Threshold's Lure*] is entitled 'Deux couleurs' [Two Colours].[29] The colours allude to a series of paintings by Poussin on the subject of Moses in the bulrushes, but more importantly they instigate what will be a recurrent motif: the notion of two colours working in contrapuntal fashion, with and against one another, each contesting and relativizing the proposition of the other, and through this interplay opening up another dimension. Subsequent poems by Bonnefoy, most notably 'Dedham, vu de Langham' [Dedham, seen from Langham], which concerns the landscapes of Constable, will also be concerned with colour. Secondly, a number of essays in *Le Nuage rouge* [*The Red Cloud*] involve interrogations of colour.[30] The title essay refers to a painting by Mondrian, predating his turn to pure abstraction, depicting a landscape near the sea and a single large red cloud in the sky. Bonnefoy pays close attention to all the colours in the painting, in the context of which the red cloud

— compared at one point to the burning bush — is read as a profoundly ambivalent sign, because it represents at the same time an aspiration to a transcendent order and the questioning or checking of that impulse to achieve transcendence through the affirmation of what Bonnefoy calls 'l'hétérogène à jamais qui dresse la présence contre l'image, la faille qui revendique ce que nulle écriture ne saurait jamais accepter [...] un ici [...] un lieu [...] une durée' [the eternally heterogeneous which confronts the image with its sheer presence, the gap which lays claim to what no writing can ever contain [...] a here [...] a place ... a duration] (p. 123).

The ambivalence of colour, or its capacity to incarnate ambivalence, is at the centre of essays on Georges Duthuit — 'Un Ennemi des images' [An Enemy of the Image] — and in the nudes of Claude Garache, who uses only one colour, red. In his discussion of Garache, as Richard Stamelman has underlined, Bonnefoy considers the way colour has often represented a desire for immediacy in artists ranging from Titian and Rubens, to Delacroix or Van Gogh.[31] Demonstrating how immediacy is in fact negated by the purely formal character of colour harmonies, colour being in some respects simply another language, a system of mediation, Bonnefoy points to ways in which, in brief passages, the closed order or system of colour language can be evaded, and how tonal values can suddenly engender presence: 'Loin de vouer la perception sensorielle aux apories du médiat [...] les valeurs [...] replantent autour de nous, l'apparence fermant sa roue, toutes les belles plumes de la présence du monde' [Far from condemning sensory perception to the aporias of mediation [...] tonal values [...] restore around us, appearance having closed its peacock's tail, all the fine scattered feathers of the world's presence] (p. 325). Third, 1977 also saw the publication of a work entitled *Trois remarques sur la couleur* [*Three Remarks on Colour*] consisting not of an essay but of three enigmatic prose texts, similar in character to another series brought together the same year under the general title *Rue Traversière* [*Cross Street*].

When, ten years later, Bonnefoy brought the two sets of texts together, along with others written in the meantime, he gave them the generic label 'récits en rêve' [dreaming narratives].[32] Bonnefoy's 'récits en rêve' can be seen as a cross between the 'poème en prose' [prose poem], the 'récit de rêve' [dream narrative], the lyrical or meditative essay, and the parable or metaphysical tale in the manner of Borges. They generally feature a fictional narrator, often a traveller, but the oneiric aspect does not usually involve a markedly dreamlike atmosphere and consists more, as the phrase 'récits en rêve' suggests, in the way the narratives develop, often switching abruptly from one time and place to another. In fact, most of the texts involve two or three scenes linked by a commentary, as well as fleeting dialogues between the narrator-traveller and the people he observes or encounters.

When these texts were incorporated as a section in the larger volume, *Récits en rêve*, a number of new ones were added under the rubric 'Remarques sur la couleur', but interestingly two of the original three had in fact migrated to join another cluster entitled 'L'Origine de la parole' [The Origin of Speech]. This underlines the close connection between colour and language which is a consistent feature of these texts, several of which feature imaginary communities, generally islands, where the conventions regarding the names of colours, or the relation between colours and things, differ from those with which we are familiar. In 'Deux et d'autres couleurs' [Two and Other Colours], for example, the traveller encounters three different ways of thinking about colour, or. rather three ways in which an attitude to colour can bespeak an attitude to, or understanding of, human reality.

In the first part, he is told that the local language uses two colour names to designate a single colour, and conversely a single colour term to designate something that is of two colours, though it is also possible to designate the latter by two pairs of names corresponding to the two constituent colours. So a green and white ferry can be referred to as red or, alternatively, as yellow, blue, black, and red since green can be designated as yellow and blue, and green as red and black. The aim of this system is to remedy the poverty of ordinary language, which does not even begin to render the richness of reality, by the creation of a 'second degré de la parole' [second degree of speech], a language of proliferation and surprise which aims to circumvent the limits of 'la dénomination abusive' [inappropriate designation]: 'Défaire la dénomination abusive, lever par ce levier, l'infini, l'arbitraire triste du signe, mais c'est laver la face du monde, mon ami, c'est se retrouver respirant dans la respiration de tout, silencieuse! Nous avons inventé le second degré de la parole!' [To rectify inappropriate designation, to abrogate by this means, the infinite, sad arbitrariness of signs, why, this is to wipe clean the face of the earth, my friend, it's to recover one's breath, in the silent breathing of all things! We have invented the second degree of speech!] (p. 81).

This fantasy of using language to go beyond language leaves the traveller sceptical, and on his journey to various islands on the ferry he will encounter another kind of potential link between colour and presence. As the ship leaves its various ports of call, he notices that coloured streamers maintain, for a while at least, until they drop or break, a link between departing passengers and those they leave behind. The flashes of colour, which stand out against the purple sea-mist, figure the intermittent, unpredictable, snatches of shared experience or communal presence which, for a while at least, provide a vital link, a line of communication between human beings: 'Certains rubans cassaient, assez vite, et retombaient dans l'écume, y salissant et trouant, le bleu, le vert ou le rouge. Mais d'autres duraient, improbables, miraculeux, dans les cris de bonheur ou le silence attentif' [Some ribbons broke fairly quickly, and fell back into the spray, puncturing and dirtying the blue, the green or the red. But others kept aloft, improbably, miraculously, amid cries of joy or attentive silence] (p. 83).

In the third part of the text the traveller, back in the port where he had started, encounters the man he had spoken to earlier. He now dismisses, as no more than an image, the linguistic theories he had expounded, but, while apparently confirming what the traveller had understood by the strips of ribbon, and the moments of joy and grief enshrined in momentary flashes of colour, he urges him to witness another spectacle the next day. Go to the temple on the mountainside, he says, and look at the grey earthenware jars half buried in the garden behind. Once a year they are filled with different coloured powders which when lit create a vast flame where the colours both fuse together and remain distinct:

> C'est phosphorescent, c'est changeant, c'est un et multiple à la fois, c'est indéchiffrable comme la vie, c'est immatériel comme elle, on peut dire, je crois, qu'il s'agit là d'une couleur autre, dont la terre ne savait rien avant que l'on eût compris que l'on meurt, et naît, et renaît, et renaît encore. (p. 85)

> [It's phosphorescent, it's changing, it's one and multiple at the same time, it's indecipherable as life, and as immaterial, one can say, I think, that we have here another colour, of which the earth knew nothing before people understood that we die, and are born, and are born again, and yet again.]

As I suggested earlier, in this text and others like it, Bonnefoy uses colour as an idiom or key in which to explore allegorically questions of language, ethics, and aesthetics. Another piece, 'La Resurrection', juxtaposes three elements, W. B. Yeats's play *Resurrection*, which Bonnefoy had translated, the paintings of Bram van Velde, which involve variations on three or four basic colours, and the death of the narrator's mother. Initially the meditation establishes a parallel between the play, where three characters incarnate three ways of understanding Christ's resurrection, and thus three different visions of the world, and the colours in van Velde's paintings which can be seen to figure different 'modes d'être' [ways of being], and, in their combination, like different coloured flames in a single hearth, to signify 'les vérités diverses de la raison, du cœur, du corps que le sang remue, ou la contemplation qui l'apaise' [the diverse truths of reason, of the heart, and of the body animated by blood, or by contemplation which restores its peace] (p. 140).

Seen this way, colour is 'une spéculation tendue à l'extrême de soi, donc instable, ouverte aux contradictions, militante' [a tense speculation at the self's extremity, hence unstable, open to contradictions, militant] (p. 141). But suddenly this vision collapses and gives way to a different perception of van Velde's colours, Their combinations are now seen as 'sans cause, sans finalité' [without cause, without aim]; their beauty is that of the void, the timeless; they turn everything into absolutes. And perhaps the same is true of Yeats's play. At any rate, at the end of the text the notion of resurrection is applied to someone known, and the narrator wonders whether, were his mother to be resurrected with the look she bore when she had been loved most intensely — perhaps the day she met his father — he would be able to recognize her at all (p. 144).

In two further texts, colours incarnate antithetical extremes: on one hand, total stability, on the other, total mutability. 'Au Mont Aso' describes a mountainside, in an Eastern country such as Japan, renowned for its uniform greenness, where visitors find that the experience of 'la simplicité de la perception' [the simplicity of perception] has a powerful effect on their relation to language: 'car c'est la notion même de différence qui se dissipe ici [...] Et avec elle s'efface le vain désir de nommer ou plutôt [...] s'atténue cette sorte de houle dont les vocables, cette intempérance de la couleur, enveloppent et brisent ce qu'ils nomment' [for it's the very notion of difference that dissolves here [...] And with it the vain desire to name is effaced, or rather [...] that kind of swell with which speech, that intemperance of colour, envelops and destroys what it names] (p. 87). But this experience is seen in fact to dispel the enigma of experience, and the narrator's subsequent vision of two streaks of colour in the sky, and then his memory of a tomb made out of red clay, and finally his recollection of being told of one moment in the year when Mount Aso does slightly change its shade of green, and that in this period of mists people go in groups and hold picnics where ribald jokes are told and couples are formed, serve to dispel the Oriental perfection of pure experience without language.

In 'Le Crépuscule des mots' [The Twilight of Words], on the other hand, the narrator visits a land where the meaning of words is subject to sudden changes and shifts, in response to the ever-changing nature of reality. But while at any given time there may be a word not only for this type of boat but for the impression a boat gives as it approaches the harbour, or for the aura which surrounds a newly arrived passenger, people on street corners endlessly debate the meanings of utterances. Colours are repeatedly invoked as the narrator reports his debates with the local inhabitants and expresses his doubts about this linguistic regime. Does it not imply a sacrifice of communality and disregard for certain elemental realities? He conveys the delight of gliding in a world of metamorphosis where 'l'univers n'est plus qu'une esplanade infinie' [the universe is no more than an infinite esplanade] (p. 98) and concedes that in the realm of colour the infinite nuances of tone and shade occur within the framework of seven basic colours which preside and unify. But he wonders, nonetheless, if it is not precisely the mission of poetry to preserve meanings rather than to dispel them, and at the end of the text there is still a sense that the debate remains open, that perhaps the issue is not one of adjudicating between colour and language, but exploring under what conditions both these domains can open up rather than close off an encounter with the world.

In general, the drift of Bonnefoy's meditations about colours, which are always meditations on ways of living in the world and on the ethics of representation, is away from the sovereign beauty of pure colour towards contrast, juxtaposition, change, and mutability. In a series of reflections on the paintings of Miklos Bokor, he stresses the sudden emergence of colours in Bokor's works which he sees as a kind of germination or crystallization, a process reflecting inner change:

> Couleurs, non, l'expérience du monde, du destin que la couleur a permise [...]
> D'année en année [...] la musique des yeux pénètre plus avant l'apparence [...]
> c'est la passion qui se fait en lui couleur, ombres de couleur, afin de se clarifier,
> se musicaliser. (p. 101)

> [Colours, no, the experience of the world, of a destiny that colour has facilitated
> [...] Year after year [...] the music of the eyes penetrates further into appearance
> [...] It's passion which in him is transmuted into colour, coloured shadows, in
> order to become clarity, to become music]

And in a text from a more recent collection, *La Vie errante* [*The Wandering Life*],[33] 'L'Alchimiste de la couleur' [The Alchemist of Colour] the alchemist, having spent years trying to transmute colours into gold, pure light, endlessly mixing them on his palette but producing only grey, suddenly sees two stains of different colours. Possessed now by this contrast, he juxtaposes colours and begins to see fields, branches, and birds. In the end, the parable suggests, colours take us back to where we are, they are the earth, and the true alchemist is the landscape painter whose art constitutes a revelation of the real (p. 25).

I want now to turn to the work of Philippe Jaccottet, in which landscape is also a central preoccupation. Though originally Swiss-French, Jaccottet has lived since the 1950s at Grignan in northern Provence, and the greater part of his work in various forms, including collections of poems, an ongoing poetic diary or log-book, *La Semaison* [*Sowings*], several volumes of prose pieces, and some mixing of all three forms, originates in his contemplation of the landscape in which he lives. Observations and meditations regarding colour can be found in all aspects and periods of his work, but I will base my remarks on three prose texts from a recent book, *Cahier de verdure* [*Green Diary*] (1990), which in fact contains both poems and prose texts, combining them in a way which, as the title of the volume suggests, adds up to a sort of notebook or ongoing register.[34] It is worth noting that a number of Jaccottet's earlier prose texts, including *Paysages avec figures absentes* [*Landscapes with Absent Figures*] and *À travers un verger* [*Through an Orchard*], were collected together under the title *Des histoires de passage* [*Stories of Passage*]. Most of them have a narrative element, like Bonnefoy's 'récits en rêve', but here the autobiographical dimension is totally explicit and there is no fictionalization, even if the development of the text, sometimes referred to as a reverie, is often engendered by associations, images, and memories which emerge in a way reminiscent of dreams. The word *passage* relates to the fact that the starting point for most of these autobiographical reveries or meditations, which often reconstruct a past event in great detail, sometimes relating it to other events, is generally something that has been observed in passing, generally on one of Jaccottet's daily walks around Grignan, but sometimes also on journeys elsewhere.

So these 'histoires' are closely linked to contingent moments, to chance and accident, but also to everyday experience, to the repetitions and rituals of the everyday. In seeking to home in on and to understand retrospectively something that has moved or surprised him, galvanized his attention, or roused him from a state of indifference or dejection into a mood of celebration or reflection that makes him want to investigate his own experience, Jaccottet may follow a number of paths. As a rule, what prompts him to reflect and write is a natural phenomenon, the impression made by a tree, a mountain, a vista; and very often one of the things which may be central to the initial experience is colour.

This is the case in the three texts I want to discuss from *Cahier de verdure*. In the first, 'Le Cerisier' [The Cherry Tree], it is the sight of a cherry tree at nightfall that he seeks to explore, and particularly the impression conveyed by the redness of the cherries in conjunction with the dark green of the foliage. In the second, 'Blason vert et blanc' [Green and White Emblem], it is a small orchard of quince trees, and in the third, 'Apparition des fleurs' [Apparition of the Flowers], it is the conjunction in the same place of three flowers, each a different colour — blue, yellow, and white. In none of these cases is it colour itself, independently of the rest, that is paramount. But on each occasion, both in the initial event, and its exploration in words, the question of colour, of what the colours meant, of what they contributed, is absolutely central. In many ways Jaccottet's texts can be seen to exemplify perfectly the account of what it means to be arrested by and to explore a colour impression put forward by Merleau-Ponty in the passage commented on earlier. What Jaccottet investigates are the various orders of 'participation' to which the colour seems to belong, ranging from other elements in the same context, to the subject's own personal associations and experiences, often rooted in the distant past, to the cultural associations of the colours and colour combinations concerned. In doing so, and although he constantly registers his sense of failure and dissatisfaction in this regard, Jaccottet is not favouring colour over language, but trying to exploit the 'parole opérante' [operative speech] of poetry, trying to register and match the work of perception with the work of language.

Although he writes in prose, Jaccottet exploits to the full the resources of diction, assonance, rhythm, repetition and metaphor, composing his text in a series of fragments, each consisting of one or more paragraphs, separated by a double space. As in the case of Bonnefoy, colour has a place in Jaccottet's concerns not just because of a delight in the visual, and indeed in painting, but because the process of attending to colour, particularly in the context of the natural world, seems to involve not an escape from the real but a profound engagement with it, at a level and in a manner which raises questions about language, about experience, and about everydayness. The sense of beauty, and the ecstasy of looking, are in fact central insofar as for Jaccottet, as for Bonnefoy, the beauty of the world maintains the possibility — to be set against abundant incitements to despair — of some sort of harmony.

In each of the texts from *Cahier de verdure*, the initial experience is one of being stunned by the beauty of what has been seen, but if this inspires a desire to reflect and understand, it is in response to what is experienced as a kind of duty, an ethical demand solicited by the experience of looking. In 'Le Cerisier', for example, Jaccottet refers several times to the feeling of responding to something akin to the light pressure of a hand gently inciting him to change his direction: 'Cette fois, il s'agissait d'un cerisier' [This time, it was a cherry tree] (p. 9). The opening passage reconstructs the very specific circumstances — time of day, lie of the land, elements of the scene, initial on-the-spot feelings — but also draws out and embroiders various threads of association relating to night, metamorphosis, apparitions. Then there is the description of the one particular cherry tree:

> Ses fruits étaient comme une longue grappe de rouge, une coulée de rouge, dans du vert sombre; des fruits dans un berceau ou une corbeille de feuilles; du rouge dans du vert, à l'heure du glissement des choses les unes dans les autres, à l'heure d'une lente et silencieuse métamorphose, à l'heure de l'apparition, presque, d'un autre monde. (p. 12)

> [Its fruit were like a long cluster of red, a flow of red, in dark green; fruit in a cradle or basket of leaves; some red in some green, at the hour when everything flows into everything else, at the hour of a slow and silent metamorphosis, at the hour of the apparition, almost, of another world]

In the following paragraph Jaccottet addresses himself to why this particular quality of redness, in its conjunction with the green, should have prompted such a response in him, why it should have had so much the quality of an apparition and to have suggested images of gentle metamorphosis: 'Que pouvait être ce rouge pour me surprendre, me réjouir à ce point?' [What could this red have been to surprise me, to delight me so much?] (p. 12). It suggested neither blood nor flames. (A long parenthesis conjures up, with great accuracy and immediacy, the recent, contrasting, experience of staring at flames in a bonfire. This contrast emphasizes the differential quality of the phenomenon under consideration — the redness of the cherries.) The recollection that the cherries seemed to flow links them to wine, and he ends up settling for the notion of a 'feu suspendu [...] une grappe de feu apprivoisé, marié à de l'eau nocturne' [suspended fire [...] a cluster of tamed fire, married to nocturnal water] (p. 13). And in subsequent paragraphs this will lead to the idea of seeing the cherries as a kind of votive offering, and then to seeing them as somehow 'couvés' [watched over] by the green foliage, and thus as representing past experiences held in suspension, allowed to ripen under the protection of the green.

In the second text, 'Blason vert et blanc', prompted by the glimpse of quince-blossom through a steamed-up car window, the conjunction of white and green, and of the words 'vert et blanc', becomes the emblem of the experience which is pursued almost exclusively in terms of colour, through the question of what the conjunction of colours intimated. Yet here the path of association does not involve other things of the same colour, but rather literary and cultural references. The particular character of this blossom, this mode of 'floraison', different from cherries and apples, on this particular occasion of passage, prompts a welter of feelings and impressions to do with calm, simplicity, or self-sufficiency, which seem to be epitomized most satisfactorily in the conjunction of green and white. Having established that 'Vert et blanc. C'est le blason de ce verger' [Green and white. The emblem of this orchard] the meditation, 'rêvant, réfléchissant à ces deux couleurs' [dreaming, thinking about these two colours] (p. 26) explores the resonances of the colours, through Dante's Vita nova, Hölderlin's Hyperion, Botticelli's Flora, Verlaine's Gaspard Hauser, and so forth. The summary of the qualities of the two colours together elicits the notion of enveloping femininity, and this engenders a further cultural reference — to Mozart's Zerlina — which then leads into the idea of rustic ceremonies and well-ordered spaces, conjuring up a country church where all is ready for the wedding. Then, partly via the waxy whiteness of candles, we are introduced to further ways of rendering the sense of security and gentle solidity exuded by these colours, 'couleurs fermes, opaques et tranquilles; rien qui frémisse [...] Comme si le mouvement n'existait plus' [colours that are firm, opaque and tranquil; nothing brusque... As if movement no longer existed] until the meditation ends a few pages further on.

The third text also relates to something in the natural world that arrests the writer's attention, but the decision to explore this 'apparition' is prompted by a repercussion it had already had in Jaccottet's writing when, at the end of a dark poem inspired by the death or serious illness of several friends, the names of three flowers had represented the universe's response to the poet's sardonic desire for some sort of explanation: 'Pour réponse, au bord du chemin: seneçon, berce, chicorée' [For reply, at the side of the path, groundsel, hogweed, chicory] (p. 69). To try and understand what it was about them that had brought these flowers to mind, Jaccottet goes back to the occasion when their unusual conjunction in a field, during the summer when one friend of his was dying, had overwhelmed him with wonder and joy. In fact, the investigation will not prove very satisfactory. Although Jaccottet perceives that the three colours are vital, and that 'ces couleurs devaient donc bien "donner sur" autre chose' [these colours, it was clear, 'gave onto' something else], and although he has no difficulty in pursuing the resonance of the three particular shades, he feels nonetheless that 'ces couleurs m'échappaient' [these colours eluded me], or rather that what it was that had enabled them to appear for a moment 'comme des clefs de ce monde' [like keys to this world] still eluded him. 'Je ne comprenais donc toujours rien' [Clearly, I still hadn't understood anything] (p. 72). To some extent, Jaccottet's dissatisfaction stems from the contradiction between the basic simplicity of the experience, and indeed the simple, unsophisticated quality of both the flowers and their colours, and the elaborateness of his poetic investigation, the endless comparisons and relays through which he seeks to pin them down.

In the end, perhaps, he comes closest to defining the crucial quality in the experience which made it seem to hold out a response to the terrible doubts cast by the shadow of suffering and death, when he shifts away from the colours and comes back to the flowers themselves, and particularly to their associations with Persephone, who was condemned to the underworld for picking flowers in the meadow, or when he focuses on the notion of 'surgissement' [sudden appearance], the sudden 'apparition' of the flowers which seem all at once to appear out of nowhere. But this in no way alters the pertinence of colours to Jaccottet's project or the validity of colour as a pathway towards a deeper understanding of his experience.

By way of conclusion, I will sum up what seems to be involved in Jaccottet's preoccupation with colour, and in doing so link it to some of the main strands of my argument. First, the general links between colour and subjectivity must be reiterated. We are concerned here with a phenomenologically constructed subjectivity, inseparable from the subject's engagement with the world of things and others, and moreover a dimension of subjective experience that comes close to being anonymous or impersonal, to being everybody's experience. As a cardinal dimension of perceptual and sensual experience, colour manifests the way sensation is both highly individualized, something that happens to this subject in this time and place, and at the same time depersonalized. Being contingent on atmospheric conditions, on available light, and on a whole range of other situational factors, colour also links subjectivity to temporal process, to the momentary but also to duration, and thus to the unfolding rhythm of the day. All Jaccottet's passages occur at a particular time of day, often a transitional one like morning or evening, and as such they manifest something more general about the connection between colours and everydayness. In most contexts colour is only one component of a phenomenon or occasion, often seemingly an inessential or trivial one, yet it can present itself as the key in which a certain experience is lived through and thus, in another sense of the word, as the key to its wider significance.

Like Merleau-Ponty, Jaccottet shows that to follow the trace of colour is to attend to an occasion in a particular way, that may lead in many directions, but keeps the experience in play, deepening our sense of its possible bearings. In this respect, the peripheral nature of colour turns out to be a strength since it does not prejudge the order of gravity or significance the perception may turn out to have. Merleau-Ponty compares colours that grab our attention to screen-memories which are often put together out of various occasions, and in which what initially seems incidental may turn out to be fundamental, and vice versa. Colours are the receptacles of desire, but as Bonnefoy's 'récits en rêve' consistently show, colours lend themselves to being the vehicles of desire sublimated into ethical, metaphysical, or ecological concerns. Colour is always difference, but difference in a narrow compass. There are far more nuances and combinations of colours than words to describe them, but where the proliferation of language can seem to threaten the bond of language and experience, the endless nuances of tone are held in place and ordered by their primordial relationship to a very small number of basic colours. What is more, colours are universal even if the way they are perceived is culturally relative. If I have said little about the numerous kinds of colour symbolism, and the function of certain esoteric ways of thought such as heraldry and alchemy, it is because these are always ways of pinning colour down, of extolling its riches but at the same time curtailing its infinity. Yet of course all ways of organizing colours pay tribute to the boundlessness of nuance.

However compellingly it may address us, colour is always an enigmatic feature of any phenomenon. Physically, chemically, functionally, colour is a side effect rather than the main point. It often seems gratuitous, even frivolous; generally non-utilitarian, colour has no particular job to do, far less than other physical qualities such as shape or size. Nevertheless one of the enigmas of colour is that it can seem to be the soul of an object or occasion. And this means that to say of something that it is this colour or that, to present a passage of experience in terms of what colour things were, can seem to be saying very little, or, on the contrary to say a great deal, but a great deal about that particular moment, about your participation in it. Colours are physical but also doubly immaterial. We apprehend them by dint of our capacities as physical organisms capable of acts of perception. Colours address us through our senses, through our bodily presence in the world (Merleau-Ponty), but at the same time they involve us in a mental process of discrimination and deciphering which both resists and solicits language. Colours provoke desire and deliver us from fixity, but at the same time they stir up the archives of our identity. If colour offers us one way of grasping everydayness, it is perhaps because of the type of fascination it exerts and the kind of attention it requires, a mode of attention attuned to the mysterious reciprocities of self and world, and to a realm where everything is always changing, and yet much remains the same.

## Notes

1. Maurice Blanchot, 'Everyday Speech' [1963], trans. by Susan Hanson, in *Everyday Life*, ed. by Alice Kaplan and Kristin Ross, *Yale French Studies*, 73 (1987), 12–20. Where no English-language edition is listed translations are my own.
2. Charles Baudelaire, *Salon de 1846*, in *Œuvres complètes*, vol. I, ed. by Claude Pichois (Paris: Gallimard, 1974).
3. Wassily Kandinsky, *Regards sur le passé*, quoted in Philippe Choulet, 'L'Esprit de la couleur chez Kandinsky', in *La Couleur*, ed. by Lambros Couloubaritsis and Jean-Jacques Wunenburger (Brussels: Éditions Ousia, 1993), p. 213.
4. Ernst Jünger, *Le Cœur aventureux*, trans. by Henri Thomas (Paris: Gallimard, 1979).
5. Jünger trans. Thomas, p. 217.
6. Georges Duthuit, *Représentation et Présence* (Paris: Flammarion, 1974).
7. Christian David, 'Iris au service d'Eros: remarques sur le pouvoir expressif des couleurs', in *Questions de couleurs. Rencontres psychanalytiques d'Aix-en-Provence*, ed. by Christian David and others (Paris: Les Belles Lettres, 1991).
8. Murielle Gagnebin, 'Chromatique et herméneutique', in *Questions de couleurs*, p. 106.
9. Michel Corvin, 'La Passion des mots', in *Des mots et des couleurs*, vol. II, ed. by Jean-Pierre Guillerm (Lille: Presses universitaires de Lille, 1986), p. 24.
10. Roland Barthes, *Roland Barthes by Roland Barthes*, trans. by Richard Howard (New York: Hill and Wang, 1977), p. 146.
11. *Phénoménologie de la perception* (Paris: Gallimard, 1945), p. 240.
12. Ibid., p. 242.
13. *Le Visible et l'invisible* (Paris: Gallimard: 1964), p. 170.
14. Ibid., p. 173.
15. Ibid., p. 173.
16. Ibid., p. 162.
17. Ibid., p. 174.
18. Ibid.
19. Ibid.
20. Ibid.
21. Ibid., p. 175.
22. Ibid., pp 129–30.
23. Ibid., pp. 152–53.
24. Ibid. pp. 155–56.
25. Ibid., p. 164.
26. Ibid.
27. Ibid., p. 165.
28. Ibid.
29. Paris: Mercure de France, 1977.
30. Paris: Mercure de France, 1977.
31. Richard Stamelman, 'Transfigurings of Red: Colour, Representation, and Being in Yves Bonnefoy and Claude Garache', *The Comparatist* (May 1986), 90–106.
32. *Rue Traversière et autres récits en rêve* (Paris: Gallimard, 1992).
33. Yves Bonnefoy, *La Vie errante* (Paris: Mercure de France, 1993).
34. Philippe Jaccottet, *Cahier de Verdure* (Paris: Gallimard, 1990).

# 16

# Everyday Rhythms, Everyday Writing:
# Réda with Deleuze and Guattari

A connection between the dimension, or level, of everyday life and the potentially rhythmical character of lived experience is familiar to us through such realities as circadian rhythms. Moreover, when one tries, on the basis of the set of discourses that progressively shaped this key concept in modern culture, to establish some of the parameters that define the *quotidien*, rhythm has a prominent place, alongside such ideas as the overlooked, the recurrent, the residual, the self-evident.[1] A central project of Henri Lefebvre's three-volume *Critique de la vie quotidienne* (1947–82) is to establish how 'rhythmic temporalities' — beneficent rhythms, including cyclical time, which blend the heterogeneous array of everyday experience into some sort of homogeneity — subsist within the linear time of modern industrial society, and the 'compressed time' of the modern bureaucratic world.[2] Indeed one of Lefebvre's last publications was *Éléments de rythmanalyse: introduction à la connaissance des rythmes* (1992).[3] In the literature on the *quotidien* one could also cite the many places in Michel de Certeau's *L'Invention du quotidien* (1980) where rhythm is a factor, for example in his accounts of urban walking or of reading.[4] There is also the fascinating discussion of 'idiorrythmie', designating a fluid balance between individual and community, in Roland Barthes's posthumous *Comment vivre ensemble* (2002). Drawing on Émile Benveniste's seminal distinction between *rythmos*, implying pattern and regular cadence, and *rhuthmos*, designating 'une forme improvisée, modifiable', Barthes argues that 'idiorrythmie' is 'par définition individuel' and reflects how the subject engages with social and natural codes: 'l'idiorrythmie [...] renvoie aux formes subtiles du genre de vie: les humeurs, les configurations non stables, les passages dépressifs ou exaltés; bref, le contraire même d'une cadence cassante, implacable de régularité' [idiorrhythmy [...] refers to the subtle forms living: moods, unstable configurations, depressive or exalted phases; in short, the direct opposite of a brittle rhythm, implacable in its regularity].[5]

★ ★ ★ ★ ★

In order to probe the links between the upsurge of interest in the nature of rhythm, and the convergence of attention on the quotidian, which both occurred in the period around 1980, I intend to read in parallel the important remarks on rhythm in Deleuze and Guattari's *Mille Plateaux* (1980), and the opening text of Jacques Réda's book of prose poetry, *Les Ruines de Paris* (1977). Although they do not allude to the *quotidien* directly, taken together these texts suggest how the rhythmical can be seen as a key figure for the everyday. For they identify rhythm less with repetition and return than with momentum, divergence, and a constant traversing and subverting of fixed codes, articulations and contexts. Seen in this way, rhythmicity expresses the everyday's multiplicity, and the lack of fixed qualities that make it a place of passage, variation, and layering, which resists codification. At issue here, in the convergence of the everyday and rhythm, is the status of the subject. Although Deleuze and Guattari bracket out the subject in favour of processes and flows, and see *subjectivation* as the imposition of a limitation, they are concerned with the vital experience and rhythms of the human animal. It is however useful to have in mind Henri Meschonnic's more or less contemporaneous *Critique du rythme* (1981), which notes its affinities with *Mille Plateaux*'s development of the notion of rhythm, but puts forward the view that rhythm, properly understood, is the key to the essential historicity of the human subject.[6] Based on readings of modernist poetic texts, Meschonnic's *Critique du rythme* and *La Rime et la vie* (1989)[7] also have the virtue of frequently recalling the urban focus of many texts that link issues of rhythm, subjectivity and everydayness.

In *Mille Plateaux* rhythm is the principle that creates passageways between heterogeneous milieux. The key factor here is the ultimately aesthetic process of appropriation, or territorialization, for which the emblem is the 'ritournelle' — a repeated musical phrase separating larger units, a 'petit air' [little melody], or a snatch of song. A frightened child who hums a jingle in the dark creates order in the face of chaos. When we organize our domestic space — often including aural elements: radio, TV, Hi-fi — we act as 'bricoleurs', managing transition between heterogeneous items. When we leave our interior for the outside world we have the opportunity to improvise, to vary our established itineraries by adopting new pathways and routines. Drawing on ethology, the account of the 'ritournelle' in *Mille Plateaux* often chimes with ways of talking about the everyday. For example, Barthes's account of 'idiorrythmie' invokes habitat, the 'espace apprivoisé' [domesticated space] where a creature is 'chez lui'. Distinguishing two functions of 'clôture' — as protection, and as a marking out of one's own space or territory, one's distance — Barthes cites E.T. Hall's concept of proxemics which studies 'les espaces subjectifs en tant que le sujet les habite affectivement' [spaces which are subjective insofar as the subject inhabits them affectively] (156) — also a reference point for Deleuze and Guattari, and echoing Georges Perec's *Espèces d'espaces* and other texts.

Deleuze and Guattari insist that the 'ritournelle', and the rhythm it makes by punctuating the line of experience, is also a mode that allows the openness of chaos to subsist rather than be denied. Like all living creatures we exist simultaneously in a series of milieux, each possessing its own code, determined by periodic repetitions. Yet each code is constantly being 'transcoded', as one milieu — for example that linked to the perceptual apparatus — becomes the host or ground for another, for example the milieu linked to bodily processes. 'Il y a rythme dès qu'il y a passage transcodé d'un milieu à un autre, communication de milieux, co-ordination d'espaces — temps hétérogènes' [Rhythm is there as soon as there is a transcoded passage from one milieu to another, or communication between milieux, or coordination between spaces — heterogeneous temporalities] (p. 385).[8] Rhythm is a kind of go-between in that, by virtue of its very in-betweenness, it partakes of chaos itself while at the same time serving as its antidote. Rhythm is not the same as measure or cadence. Measure implies code within a specific signifying milieu, while 'le rythme est l'Inégal ou l'Incommensurable, toujours en transcodage' [rhythm is the Unequal or the Incommensurable, always being transcoded]. For Deleuze and Guattari, 'la mesure est dogmatique, mais le rythme est critique, il noue des instants critiques, ou se noue au passage d'un milieu dans un autre. Il n'opère pas dans un espace-temps homogène, mais avec des blocs hétérogènes. Il change de direction' [measure is dogmatic, but rhythm is critical, and knits together critical moments, or identifies itself in the passage from one milieu to another. It does not function in a homogeneous space-time, but with heterogeneous units. It changes direction] (p. 385). Rhythm is not on the same plane as the elements it deals with: 'Le rythme se pose entre deux milieux, ou entre deux entre-milieux, comme entre deux eaux, entre deux heures, entre chien et loup, *twilight* ou *zwielicht*' [Rhythm sets itself between two milieux, or between two in-between milieux, as between two bodies of water, or two hours, or between day and night, *twilight* or *zwielicht*] (p. 385). This switching of milieux is vital as it accounts for how rhythm can involve return and periodic repetition but at the same time not fall back into sterile repetition, single measure. In the economy of rhythm, repetition within a milieu effectively creates another milieu: 'c'est la différence qui est rythmique, et non pas la répétition qui, pourtant, la produit' [it is difference which is rhythmic, and not repetition, which, however, produces it] (p. 386).

While it switches milieux the operation of rhythm does participate in a process Deleuze and Guattari call territorialization. Rhythms produce territories when they are expressive, in other words when rhythm works on, or works with, 'matières expressives' such as sounds, colours, or gestures: 'Un territoire emprunte à tous les milieux, il mord sur eux, il les prend à bras le corps (bien qu'il reste fragile aux intrusions). Il est construit avec des aspects ou des portions de milieux' [A territory borrows from all milieux, it overlaps with them, and embraces them (even if it remains fragile in the face of intrusions). It is constructed from aspects or portions of milieux] (p. 386). The operation of rhythm, via the 'ritournelle', becomes creative of territory when the constituents 'cessent d'être fonctionelles pour devenir expressives. Il y a territoire dès qu'il y a expressivité du rythme' [cease to be functional and instead become expressive. There is a territory as soon as there is a rhythmic expressiveness] (p. 387). To illustrate this point, Deleuze and Guattari evoke the colours of birds and fish, and how, above and beyond other functions, their colour, in becoming expressive, marks a territory: 'C'est la marque qui fait le territoire [...] La territorialisation est l'acte du rythme devenu expressif, ou des composantes de milieux devenues qualitatives' [The mark makes the territory [...] Territorialization is the action of rhythm which has become expressive, or of components of milieux which have become qualitative] (p. 388). But by virtue of being rhythmical, the marking of a territory, even if it produces a dimension, occurs on a different plane from actions: 'il conserve le caractère le plus général du rythme, de s'inscrire sur un autre plan que celui des actions' [it keeps the most general character of rhythm, occupying a different order to that of actions] (p. 388). And this means that territorialization does not produce a subject. Even though this appropriation is aesthetic and expressive in kind, and thus constitutes 'signatures' on the part of the markers, what it produces 'n'est pas la marque constituante d'un sujet, c'est la marque constituante d'un domaine, d'une demeure. La signature n'est pas l'indication d'une personne, c'est la formation hasardeuse d'un domaine' [is not the constitutive mark of a subject, but rather the constitutive mark of a domain, a dwelling. A signature is not the indication of a person, but the uncertain formation of a domain] (p. 389). Here the aesthetic process, the predilection for qualities, is linked to the production of a space: 'C'est avec la demeure que surgit l'inspiration. C'est en même temps que j'aime une couleur et que j'en fais mon étendard ou ma pancarte. On met sa signature sur un objet comme on plante son drapeau sur une terre' [It's with the dwelling that inspiration comes. It happens at the same time that I like a colour and that I make a standard or placard for myself from it. One puts one's signature on an object as one plants one's flag on a piece of land] (p. 389).

One effect of Deleuze and Guattari's ethological *parti pris* is to insist that expressive qualities are not just subjective expressions and emotions but are 'auto-objectives, c'est-à-dire trouvant une objectivité dans le territoire qu'ils tracent' [self-objective — that is, they find an objectivity in the territory they trace out] (p. 390). This specification with its apparent circularity is very relevant to Réda. As is the account of how expressive materials produce mobile relationships which themselves express the links between the territories they produce, the inner level of impulses, and the outer level of circumstances. And also the proposition that territorial motifs 'forment des visages ou des personnages rythmiques' [fabricate rhythmic faces or characters], so that the rhythm is not simply associated with a subject — Réda for example — but becomes that subject, constitutes it: 'c'est le rythme lui-même qui est tout le personnage [...] Non plus des signatures, mais un style' [rhythm itself is the whole character [...] No longer signatures, but a style] (p. 391). We can link this to an earlier chapter in *Mille Plateaux* where Deleuze and Guattari define style — that of Kafka, Beckett, or Godard, but one could say equally that of Réda — in terms of continuous variation: 'un chromatisme généralisé' which stems from the '[mise] en variation continue des éléments quelconques' [continuous variation of ordinary elements]. Thus 'un style n'est pas une création psychologique individuelle, mais un agencement d'énonciation' [a style is not an individual psychological creation, but an organization of utterance] (p. 123). Later they describe the 'ritournelle' as

> un prisme, un constant d'espace-temps. Elle agit sur ce qui l'entoure, son ou lumière, pour en tirer des vibrations variées, des décompositions, projections et transformations. La ritournelle a aussi une fonction catalytique: non seulement augmenter la vitesse des échanges et réactions dans ce qui l'entoure, mais assurer les interactions indirectes entre éléments dénués d'affinités dites naturelles. (p. 430)

> [a prism, a space-time constant. It acts on what surrounds it, sound or light, in order to draw varying vibrations from it, decompositions, projections, and transformations. The 'ritournelle' functions also as a catalyst — not just increasing the rate of exchanges and reaction among the things surrounding it,

but ensuring that there exist indirect interactions between elements which have no so-called natural affinities.]

And thus, 'la ritournelle fabrique du temps' [the 'ritournelle' produces time] (p. 431): rhythmical activity, combining heterogeneous fields and entities, produces temporalities.

A final parameter of territorialization is its link with distance. The operation of rhythm (as in Barthes's 'idiorrythmie') is as much to do with taking one's distance, steering one's course away from — as with proximity or fusion:

> Le territoire, c'est d'abord la distance critique entre deux êtres de mêmes espèces: marquer ses distances. Ce qui est mien, c'est d'abord une distance, je ne possède que des distances. [...] Il y a tout un art des poses, des postures, des silhouettes, des pas et des voix. [...] La distance critique n'est pas une mesure, c'est un rythme. (p. 393)

> [Territory is first of all the critical distance between two things of the same species — the outcome of marking one's distances. What is mine is above all a distance — I possess only distances. [...] There is a whole art of poses, of postures, of silhouettes, of gaits, and of voices. [...] The critical distance isn't a measurement, but a rhythm.]

Territorialization is also an operator of deterritorialization. Although always involving the 'natal' and the *heimlich*, 'ritournelle' — and rhythm — are also linked to what Deleuze and Guattari call 'lignes de fuite'. This connects with breaking codes:

> L'essentiel est dans le décalage que l'on constate entre le code et le territoire. [...] le territoire se forme au niveau d'un certain *décodage* [...] Partout ou la territorialité apparaît, elle instaure une *distance critique* intra-spécifique entre membres d'une même espèce; et c'est en vertu de son propre décalage par rapport aux *différences spécifiques* qu'elle devient un moyen de différenciation indirect, oblique. (p. 396)

> [Essential here is the discrepancy one finds between the code and the territory. [...] A territory forms at the level of a certain *decoding* [...] Wherever territoriality appears, it establishes an intra-specific *critical distance*, one between members of the same species. It is because of its own discrepancy with *specific differences* that it becomes an indirect, oblique means of differentiation.]

★    ★    ★    ★    ★

Let us now look at how Jacques Réda takes his distances, carves out his differential territory but also deterritorializes himself in the everyday city. The back cover of Réda's *Les Ruines de Paris* begins by quoting the opening of the first text, 'Le Pied furtif de l'hérétique' [The Heretic's furtive step] (which will be our main focus), a generic prelude to the forays or searches into what Réda calls elsewhere 'la nébuleuse parisienne':

> 'Vers six heures, l'hiver, volontiers je descends l'avenue à gauche, par les jardins...' Ensuite, de Belleville à Passy, de Montmartre à la Butte-aux-Cailles [...] il n'y a plus qu'à se laisser guider par les pas d'un promeneur tour à tour (ou

ensemble) nuageux, curieux, inquiet, hilare, furibond, tendre, ahuri, à travers les arrondissements et boulevards de Paris.

['Around six o'clock, in winter, I happily go down the avenue to the left, through the gardens...' After that, from Belleville to Passy, from Montmartre to the Butte-aux-Cailles [...] there's nothing to do but let oneself be guided by the steps of a walker, by turns (or all at once) up in the air, curious, uneasy, merry, furious, tender, and stunned, across the arrondissements and boulevards of Paris.]

The impersonal formulation, 'se laisser guider par les pas d'un promeneur' relates first to the reader but also suggests that the 'promeneur' is guided by his own 'pas' (this reversal — the 'promeneur' being 'promené' — recurs constantly in Réda).[9] Rather than an agent, the walking subject is framed as an affective space that is by turns (or at once) 'nuageux, curieux [...]', etc., while Paris is in turn personified as having secrets, desires, and morals. Other sorties, beyond the city, are then evoked, always involving styles of motion akin to the walking or strutting bass of the jazz player: 'toujours au rythme de la marche ou des trains, imitant le rebond plein d'espoir de la *basse ambulante*, en jazz, sur bon tempo' [always at the rhythm of walking, or of trains, imitating the hopeful bounce of the walking bass, in jazz, at a good tempo]. And this, along with the last sentence ('sans cesse on repart...' [we set off ceaselessly...]), invokes a rhythm that is also directional, a momentum that is linked to the endless 'resurgissement' of passage itself.

Turning now to 'Le Pied furtif...' I want to argue that what is rhythmical in this text is not so much its beat or cadence as a cluster of features that can be related to the ideas of Deleuze and Guattari: the switching between or out of codes; the sense of creating a territory based on taking one's distance; the treatment of 'matières expressives'; and the presence of specifically ' "ritournelle"-like' elements. And furthermore that, in Réda's case, these facets of the rhythmical can be related to the traversal of everyday space, and to everyday experience when this is seen in terms of an opposition between dead routine — purely mono-coded repetition — and an experience of heterogeneity bound up with a rhythmicity that does not produce or consist in unity but in an endless knitting together of the heterogeneous into provisional ensembles.

Although in prose, like the subsequent shorter texts that make up *Les Ruines de Paris*, a collection that marked Réda's turn towards the city and the everyday, 'Le Pied furtif...' is more lyrical, more linguistically and poetically supercharged, than the texts which follow. Yet the poem is essentially the account of a walk through Paris as dusk descends. The title points to the text's bassline — walking — and to dissidence: the step is 'furtif' because it is 'hérétique' — and this counter-orthodoxy is linked to the narrating subject's non-utilitarian predilections, and his susceptibility to interaction with his surroundings. In the following brief discussion I will focus primarily on the beginning and end of this highly intricate text (consisting of six pages without a paragraph break).

In the opening sentence (p. 9)[10] we learn of the narrator's proclivity to follow a particular 'avenue' down its left-hand side, via some gardens, at nightfall (other poems will link this to the very Baudelairean motif of the 'crépuscule du soir', and the dangerous transitional moment it represents: between night and day, but also between realms, reigns, climates, etc.). The poet seems to slip into the city via a conduit that is already in-between, and he tells us that he stumbles and bumps into chairs because — like Johnny-head-in-air — his eyes look upwards to the sky whose quality of incomprehensibility is also that of 'l'amour qui s'approche' [love which draws near] (love and the poet as amorous subject will be one of the text's codes). The second sentence is devoted to the indefinable colour of the sky, a dull shade of turquoise, and the way this 'aspire tous mes yeux' also involves an osmosis or reversal, whereby a light that eludes the visible becomes (or reveals) an inner dimension of the experiencing subject. In the following lines various sounds, colours and lighting effects — a stream of perceptions — are evoked in conjunction with the antithetical qualities of love and night, both portrayed as forces that are driven to express themselves through concrete entities. Everything in the walker's path becomes a 'matière d'expression' [expressive matter] in a process that is rhythmical in the way the next item chimes with the preceding one, or others already mentioned, but at the same time involves another dimension or order of experience. And if everything that grabs the 'hérétique's' attention along the way is apprehended via qualities that are also, or become, his own, this is seemingly by virtue of an endless capacity for subdivision ('en subdivisions, c'est l'obscur [already a variant on nuit] s'arrachant par la masse des arbres qui chante, qui veut s'y perdre' [in subdivisions, it is the dark hurrying away through the mass of trees which sings, which wishes to lose itself]) whereby an entity is grasped — synecdochically or metonymically — via one of its features or parts. Thus the night modulates into 'l'obscur', personified as a sonorous presence actualized by the trees that darken as it tries to cling to them. And this segment ends with an affirmation of affinity, picking up first the sound: 'j'ai la même voix dans la tête et la même épaisseur monotone' [I have the same voice in my head and the same uniform thickness] (as the trees) and thus the same capacity to be a 'matière expressive' for the realm of the nocturnal. The next segment begins by 'explaining' the implicit principle that accounts for their osmosis: 'Car il arrive qu'une obsession de transmutation urgente nous possède: à force de le contempler, passer du côté du spectacle, entrer dans la substance aveugle qui sait, qui resplendit' [For it may happen that we are possessed by an obsession with urgent transmutation: by contemplating it, we go over to the side of the spectacle, enter into the blind substance which knows, which shines forth] (p. 10). The irresistible desire for transmutation, for becoming other — a part of the 'substance aveugle' — via an act of contemplation so intense that the spectacle allows us to enter it, is seen to be paradoxical given that, as the following sentence observes, the witnessing subject already contains ('débordait') the sky he aims at. And this realization brings him back to earth with a bump: 'C'est l'instant où je trébuche ...' [It is the moment at which I stumble]. Ultimately the process at work here is not ascensional but lateral: the desire is for transmutation itself; and favouring one's own transmutability is seen to be a way of responding to, or participating in, a dimension of experience that is not above or below but constituted via a particular way of processing what comes one's way. There is nothing special about the things the poet encounters; what is special is his mode of encountering them, and the way this mode transmutes them — and him. As he reaches the Place de la Concorde the milieu becomes 'tout à coup maritime' [suddenly maritime] (p. 10), a transformation that seems to be induced by a combination of factors: the wide open spaces, gusts of wind flapping flags, and a monumentality that conjures up Lorrain's paintings of ships in harbours — artworks already ambiguous insofar as the seemingly vast edifices surrounding Lorrain's ports often seem to make the sea unreal. In effect the maritime code that transmutes the cityscape is over-determined by a cultural code stemming from classical painting, while the 'ritournelle' here is the walker's visual memory. This is poetic metaphoricity, in the tradition of Baudelaire's 'Le Cygne' ('tout pour moi devient allégorie' [everthying becomes allegory to me]), but more markedly a function of the transmutation engendered by transit and the aspiration towards transition. 'Making his way', as if along a beach, the poet acknowledges that it is the 'indécision du soir' [evening indecision] — the ambiguity of evening light — that opens up this space. Although as the next segment will testify — in a kind of parenthetical flashback to moments in broad daylight ('plein air') — this bit of Paris always has an estuary-like feel, linked to the quality of light and its interaction with architecture. The stones of Paris, as in the 'blocs et échafaudages', and 'ce Louvre' in 'Le Cygne', become a 'ritournelle', infiltrating other contexts. In the fourth segment, the deserted park which ruminates (we recognize the Tuileries) counters the pompous assertiveness of the 'allée en terrasse [...] qui part droit comme un coup de fanfare étrange de la Raison' [terrace [...] which heads straight off like a strange fanfare of Reason] (p. 11), redolent of fanatical inflexibility and geometric law. The 'ritournelle' here is the earth, the compacted soil, and particularly the blade of grass — a key motif in Réda, and also in Deleuze and Guattari (p. 399) — that obstinately refuses to be obliterated in this 'jardin français' and invites only 'le pied furtif de l'hérétique' (the poem's title phrase occurs here). Later in the Tuileries passage, the 'ritournelle' is a snatch of music heard — or rather imagined and interpolated — when the poet comes across a merry-go-round where the fake painted horses invoke animality, childhood, and ageing, and where the final strains of Fauré's *Requiem* which come into his mind redirect his attention, once again switching codes (p. 12).

Let us now fast forward to the end of the heretic's progress. In what we can construe as its penultimate segment (p. 13), the beginning, 'Bien sûr je pense à une Dame' [I'm thinking of course of a Lady], pulls the plug on a flight of fantasy, centred on the moon, which casts the poet as howling wolf and lunatic. If love and desire are part of the picture, it is motion — the walking that love-sickness induces — that is catalytic. Echoing Laforgue, and also Beckett's ruminative narrators (rumination, which favours variety, is an operator of metamorphosis), the poet specifies the conditions of walking: the key article of the walker's faith is that '[l]e désespoir n'existe pas pour un homme qui marche' [despair does not exist for a walking man] (p. 14). Hence a need to avoid social exchange that inevitably pins you down, arresting the rhythm of transmutation: 'C'est pourquoi je vais vite et droit devant moi vers la rase campagne à fourrés qui règne autour des Invalides. Déjà rue de Babylone il arrive qu'on croise un lapin' [That's why I go directly and quickly forwards towards the scrubby, open countryside that predominates around the Invalides. By the time I reach the rue de Babylone I've already encountered a rabbit] (p. 14). Here the switch of milieu invokes the code of the 'campagnard', triggered by the vast expanse of the Esplanade des Invalides, and then by the provincial aura of the streets of the seventh arrondissement which conjure up 'rase campagne', 'des cloches qui tintent derrière les vieux murs' [bells sounding behind old walls], and a wind redolent of 'terre molle' [soft earth].

Finally, 'Je rentre': the poet gets back to base, rejoining, like Apollinaire at the end of 'Zone', a cosy domestic space: eggs, cheese, wine, lots of records, and a hi-fi system that allows you to turn up the bass. And this leads into a final projection, a last transmutation or role, which axiomatically sums up the process enacted in the walk. In casting himself as the vibrating strings of the double bass ('tendues comme l'expérience' [tensed like experience]), the narrator sidesteps or sets aside psychology ('Est-ce que je suis gai [...] triste?' [Am I cheerful [...] sad?]) and metaphysics ('Est-ce que j'avance vers une énigme, une signification?' [Am I going towards an enigma, a meaning?]), and affirms, in lieu of any wish for knowledge ('je ne cherche pas trop à comprendre' [I'm not trying overly to understand]), the pure desire to progress rhythmically ('je continue d'avancer, pizzicato' [I keep moving forwards, pizzicato]) and thus, through a forward momentum that constantly shifts the scenes, to participate in the wider vibration of the world, of the cosmos as Deleuze and Guattari would put it.

In Réda, as in *Mille Plateaux*, the 'travail de la "ritournelle"' involves an aesthetic process where a minor element that returns brings about a change of gear, a switching of codes, and in doing so constitutes a parallel track, enmeshed with, but also at a distance from the plane of actions and events. Réda's walk through Paris, between day and night, involves recognizable locales and activities — he is in the city we know — but also a parallel universe, a possible world that is a product of the way his progress selects and processes the elements it traverses. It is walking that makes the territory: territorialization is inseparable from this peripatetic, mobile, mode of apprehension. Yet even if we may ask where all the city's usual noises and crowds have gone, the 'promeneur' is not in a solipsistic cocoon: he may pick up stray bits and pieces but they don't build a cosy nest. The counter-story, the fable he concocts, may have stable elements — and reflect his heretical options — but they are always improvised and *ad hoc*: the 'ritournelle' is a response to a threat, a deviation induced by desire's resistance to constraint. The kind of rhythmicity at work in this prose poem, which I have sought to characterize by way of Deleuze and Guattari, can, moreover, be linked to those ways of experiencing the everyday (as a dimension where freedom balances constraint, and where inventiveness stems from familiarity with the rhythms of constant change) that Lefebvre, Barthes, de Certeau and Perec, along with others, have taught us to recognize.

## Notes

1. See Michael Sheringham, *Everyday Life: Theories and Practices from Surrealism to the Present* (Oxford: Oxford University Press, 2006).
2. Henri Lefebvre, *Critique de la vie quotidienne*, 3 vols (Paris: L'Arche, 1947–82).
3. Lefebvre, *Éléments de rythmanalyse: introduction à la connaissance des rythmes* (Paris: Syllepse, 1992).
4. Michel de Certeau, *L'Invention du quotidien* (Paris: Gallimard, 1980).
5. Roland Barthes, *Comment vivre ensemble* (Paris: Seuil, 2002), p. 39.
6. Henri Meschonnic, *Critique du rythme: anthropologie historique du langage* (Lagrasse: Verdier, 1981), pp. 522–23. See also Nicolas Abraham, Nicholas Rand and Maria Torok, *Rythmes: de l'œuvre, de la traduction, de la psychanalyse* (Paris: Flammarion, 1993).
7. Meschonnic, *La Rime et la vie* (Lagrasse: Verdier, 1989).
8. Gilles Deleuze and Félix Guattari, *Mille Plateaux* (Paris: Minuit, 1980). Page references will be given in the text.
9. See 'Jacques Réda and the Commitments of Poetry' in the present volume.
10. Jacques Réda, *Les Ruines de Paris* (Paris: Gallimard, 1977). Page references will be incorporated in the text.

# 17

# Paris — City of Names: Toponymic Trajectories and Mutable Identities

The cultural identity of Paris is enshrined in the ever-changing roster of its street names, and in the names of the city's squares and monuments, restaurants and cafés, shops and places of entertainment, as well as, more ephemerally, on posters, hoardings, the sides of buses, taxis, and lorries, fliers and other bits of urban flotsam and jetsam. The plaque that indicates the name of a street — Rue Monge, Rue Gît-le Cœur, Rue de la Roquette; or a junction: Havre-Caumartin; or a garden: Parc des Buttes-Chaumont; or any other city location — plants the textual in the midst of the monumental, the relative immateriality of language in the midst of the concrete materiality of stone, brick and macadam. Far from being merely functional, street names, through their double status — as signifiers composed of phonemes that may induce particular echoes, and as signifieds that may connote historical events and personages, or once familiar but now vanished phenomena — harbour compressed virtualities of meaning. Matching or contrasting with the physical setting designated by the name, these meanings are appropriated by city-dwellers, for whom street names are at the same time a practical necessity and important constituents in each individual's private map of the city, where toponyms may come to be heavily weighted with personal significance. Names add a layer to the city, and in doing so they also figure — by their inherent multi-layeredness, underlined by the way urban toponyms are subject to abrupt change — a multi-dimensional quality that is central, where Paris is concerned, to its cultural identity and to the conditions and modes of identity that characterize the French capital.[1]

In Paris, the use of street signs to indicate names dates from a police directive of 1728 which stipulated initially that they should be on metal and later that they should be engraved on stone. In 1806 Napoleon decreed that new inscriptions should be made using oil paint on plaques and these had to be redone in 1847. At some stage the norms with which modern Parisians are familiar were adopted: white letters on a blue background, with a slightly ornate green surround bearing black and white highlights resembling rivets. A decree of 1982 specified that the blue should be 'copper phthalocyanate' and the green 'chrome oxide'. From the reign of Louis XIV, the naming of streets was an arm of French state propaganda, subsequently intensified by the Enlightenment cult of 'les grands hommes'. The French Revolution sharpened awareness of the ideological, political and pedagogical potential of street names, and this led to a key aspect of street naming

— expedient changes of name. According to the historian Daniel Milo, waves of wholesale renaming (known as 'débaptisation' [unbaptizing]) became a regular feature of urban life.[2] The Revolution suppressed references to royalty and excised the 'Saint-' prefix in numerous names (following a decree of 1794, hammers and chisels expunged 'Saint-' in a way that is still visible where engraved signs survive, as at the bottom of the Rue des Saints-Pères in the 6th, where one can see how the prefix was subsequently restored under Napoleon). Bonaparte let the Saints march back in, but purged many older names, creating new streets and monuments to celebrate his victories. Under the Restoration matters swung the other way: wholesale 'unbaptizing' of Revolutionary and Imperial excrescences restored numerous pre-revolutionary names associated with royalty — including the Place du Palais-Royal.

And so it went on right up to the present when renaming and commemoration are still liable to be contentious. The mayor of Paris, Bertrand Delanoë, recently supported a lobby which, after a bitter row, secured a change in the name of a street, situated on the borders of the 1st and 8th *arrondissements*, from Rue Richepance to Rue du Chevalier de Saint-George. Richepance, one of Napoleon's commanders, put down a rebellion in Guadeloupe in the course of which 10,000 slaves were massacred. Hence the decision to make amends by renaming the street after the Guadeloupe-born Joseph de Saint-George, the illegitimate son of a French planter and his Senegalese slave, who moved to France and became a celebrated fencer, a violinist and a composer.[3] At a ceremony marking the change of name Delanoë said he was delighted, but overnight the street's furious residents took a spray gun to the new street sign, obliterating all but the words 'anciennement [formerly] Rue Richepance' (the custom of indicating former names, for practical purposes, often adds to the layered historical density of urban toponyms). Another recent Parisian affair led to a spate of articles on the 'mystery of Paris's fake plaques'. A councillor, Claire de Clermont-Tonnerre, urged the Parisian authorities to do something about the sudden proliferation of plaques commemorating fictitious people, including one Karima Bentiffa, or bearing such inscriptions as 'Here on the 17th April 1967 nothing happened'![4]

In 2004 *The Guardian* devoted an editorial to the topic of street-naming, praising the work of Professor Richard Rodger of Leicester University who had recently argued that 'the modest signs that mark our streets are as valuable a heritage as castles and stately homes, and a great deal less costly to maintain'.[5] Not long after, the American artist Susan Hiller's 'J-Street Project', exhibited in London in April and May 2005, offered powerful testimony to the way street names can stand as markers of buried histories. The work consists primarily of photographs recording the 303 roads, streets and paths in Germany whose names refer to a Jewish presence (Judenstrasse, Judenweg, etc.). In her presentation the artist commented:

> All my work deals in ghosts. Ghosts are invisible to most people but visible to a few.
>
> In Germany there are 303 streets named after their former Jewish residents, but hardly anyone notices them. These street names are ghosts of the past, haunting the present.

The street signs in my images explicitly name what's missing from all these places.[6]

With regard to Paris we can find many echoes of Hiller's view that street names bear witness to buried layers of history in Benjamin's *Passagenwerk* [Arcades project] (discussed below), in Michel de Certeau's essay 'Les Revenants de la ville' [The Phantoms of the City],[7] and in the anthropologist Marc Augé's *Un Ethnologue dans le métro* [An Ethnologue in the Underground].[8]

The most thorough recent contribution to the literature on Paris's literary and cultural identity is Karlheinz Stierle's *La Capitale des Signes: Paris et son discours* [Capital of Signs: Paris and its Discourse].[9] Street names articulate particularly clearly what Stierle calls the *legibility* of Paris, by which he means a propensity to be apprehended by the human subject that stems from Paris's own essential 'self-consciousness' — the feeling that Paris is constantly re-inventing itself through a particular dynamic that seems to be akin to thought processes. In his account of Paris as a 'capital of signs' Stierle takes as his starting point Paul Valéry's remark that if Paris's symbolic, historic and aesthetic complexities induce in us a desire to think the city — to construct it as a mental object, a *cosa mentale* — it is actually the reverse that takes place: 'Think about Paris?' muses Valéry, 'The more you think Paris, the more you feel that, on the contrary, it is Paris who is thinking you'.[10] This experience of feeling oneself absorbed into the city — so that grasping Paris is tantamount to being made a part of its mechanism — is a feature that crops up often in the literature on Paris (and especially in the work of the poet Jacques Réda who will be discussed further on). We find it, for example, in the Surrealists' sense of the city as a magnetic field where streets, texts, and neural pathways run in parallel.[11] Stierle roots his account of the 'lisibilité' of the city in the way Paris engenders a sense of its own self-consciousness. Drawing on Foucault, he views 'Paris' as a discursive formation in which the individually authored representations that make up its cultural history are rendered anonymous by their absorption into an ever-evolving archive that generates, dialectically, new acts of attention and new modes of representation. This semiotic process constantly constructs Paris as an elusive totality, so that what instigates the city's self-consciousness, the stratification that makes it an unreal — or surreal — 'thought space', is the constant stimulus to link parts to wholes, present moments to past ones. Because of its accumulated histories, its density of texture, and the pervasive climate of otherness it fosters in the sphere of human relations — in the city people are strangers to one another — living Paris to the full (as opposed to just going from A to B) involves constantly linking what is present to what is absent, buried, not here: 'the city is a medium where reality is always in a condition of semiotic fragmentation, the signifier split from the signified' (CS, 23). Things in the city become signs (and the city becomes semiotic) by virtue of a constant fissuring by dint of which everything is both itself, a detail, and — through its link to a submerged totality (made visible by phenomena such as street names) — something else. For Stierle, 'the endless semiotization of everything that appears' produces 'this imaginary flow that impels our progress' and constitutes an endless process, an 'infinite agitation of semiotic meaning'

(CS, 24) which, as a mode of reading and deciphering, requires a distancing from the immediate utilitarian activities of the city.[12] Thus, as regards names, which for Stierle constitute a major facet of the city's semiotic profile, their practical differentiating function is coupled with a capacity to lead back into the city's still remembered, or all but forgotten, histories. It is because the city's names conjoin materiality and meaning, textuality and monumentality, that they can be seen as objective correlatives of the city's 'mind' as enshrined in its strata and fissures.

The German writer and critic, Walter Benjamin, whose inspiration informs much of Stierle's thinking, had a passionate curiosity for Parisian street names. In the unfinished *Passagenwerk* on which Benjamin worked throughout the 1930s, one entire dossier (Konvolut P) — incorporating material from early sketches (1927–30) — is given over to street names (a generic term for all Parisian toponyms, including the names of squares, monuments, places of leisure, etc.).[13] As usual, the Konvolut consists of a series of fragments comprising reflections by Benjamin himself (whole paragraphs and short aperçus), and quotations from the extensive range of his reading in nineteenth- and twentieth-century books on Paris by a variety of French, German and English literary and non-literary figures.

Benjamin starts out from the idea of Paris as 'la ville qui remue' — a city that never stops moving — and affirms that what he calls the 'unconquerable power in the names of streets, squares and theatres' (AP, 516) is as important a source of this mobile energy as the 'life of the city's layout' (the way it keeps changing its aspect through development). Typically, Benjamin accords equal weight to the microcosm, the street name and its plaque, and the macrocosm, the massive physical changes wrought by Haussmannization. Observing that names often 'persist in the face of all topographic displacement', he cites, firstly, the theatres that used to line the Boulevard du Temple that were torn down but whose names resurfaced elsewhere in the city, in a new quarter; secondly, the ways street names preserve the names of land-owners from much earlier periods, or recall long-vanished topographical features, as in the case of the 'Château d'Eau' metro station that marks the place of a now dried-up spring; and thirdly the names of restaurants, often derived from their *cuisinier*, that passed into legend when they disappeared, but also propagated themselves through imitations such as the many 'Petit Vatels' and 'Petit Riches' that sprang up, even in the suburbs. Summing up, Benjamin notes that the 'movement of names parallels the movement of streets and indeed the two movements often run at cross purposes to one another' (AP, 516): two processes of endless change and transmutation whose disparities create further energies. In contrast, Benjamin cites 'timeless little squares' that 'spring up' in the course of urban renovation but receive no name. Here, says Benjamin, 'the trees hold sway'. This underlines how the name, when there is one, has a key influence on how we see the topography; the absence of a name can shroud a place in mystery and anonymity. Moreover, the alternation between named streets and nameless 'terrains vagues' [disused lots] is one of the rhythms of the city, and of the interplay of texts and monuments.

In support of the contention that '[t]here is a particular voluptuousness in the naming of streets' (AP, 517) Benjamin cites the 'Quartier de l'Europe', planned in

1820 to have the names of European capitals; and the origin of the name Roquette — 'given to two prisons, a street and an entire district' — a name supposedly derived from the plant of the same name 'which used to flourish in previously uninhabited areas'. In one fragment Benjamin suggests that the sensuality of street names, accounting for their potency, stems from the fact that responding to the name is a substitute for the direct, physical experience of the pavement, possessed by those who have felt the road surface with bare feet, testing 'the uneven placement of paving stones with an eye toward bedding down on them' (AP, 517). Through the sensuousness of the name we are brought into vicarious sensuous contact with the physicality of the street.

Benjamin cites a remark by Leo Spitzer, in connection with Proust, that proper names can be receptacles for feeling because they are 'conceptually unburdened and purely acoustic' — 'bare formulas' (AP, 519). The name is available to semiosis. Clearly however, names in the city vary greatly in their degrees of bareness, and the specific identity they have, their sensuous quality, is by no means purely aural but often carries all sorts of semantic associations — with people we may have heard of and places we may have seen or read about. Yet it is important to note that the 'power' of a name may work on us even when we do not know who the person was — so that the proper name is always to some degree a 'bare formula' whose phonemes we can invest with our own associations, especially since the relation between a street and its name is often arbitrary. Street names rarely commemorate people who actually lived in that very place, and in other respects streets rarely 'match' the people they are named after (the poets Raymond Queneau, Jacques Roubaud and Jacques Réda have all made much of the lack of 'fit' between streets and their names).[14] Nonetheless, for Benjamin the importance of the signifier, the acoustic dimension of the name, is confirmed by the restoration of saint's names after the revolution. It was, he claims, because of the ugly hiatus created by the removal of 'Saint-' in names such as rue Honoré, rue Roch and rue Antoine that the prefix was restored after the Revolutionary period): if the names had sounded better without the prefix no one would have bothered to restore it. In fact, according to Benjamin, the phoneme 'Saint-' after 'rue' creates an aural buffer that makes the name agreeable to pronounce.

In a number of fragments Benjamin suggests that attempts to reform the naming of streets and monuments in Paris reveals the resilience and power of urban toponyms: 'The true expressive character of street names can be recognized as soon as they are set beside reformist proposals for their normalisation' (AP, 519). The very fact that so many commentators on Paris — whose dusty tomes Benjamin pored over in the Bibliothèque nationale — felt moved to criticize the names given to its streets is eloquent testimony to the power of names. Benjamin was particularly fascinated by proposals made in the revolutionary and Napoleonic eras (when street names were changing constantly for ideological reasons) to redraw the toponymic map of Paris by renaming streets and squares in a utilitarian fashion that would make it correspond to the map of France, or a map of the world. He cites a passage from Louis-Sébastien Mercier's *Le Nouveau Paris*, commenting on a scheme where 'Paris would be the map and hackney coaches the professors' (AP, 518). Saint's names and merely descriptive designations would be replaced by the names of towns, so that in the north of Paris streets would take the names of towns in northern France, whilst on the South, or left bank, streets would be named after places in the Midi.

The proposal Mercier cites was probably that of J.-B. Pujoulx, from whom Benjamin quotes extensively in four other fragments of Konvolut P. Pujoulx's idea was that streets should not only be named after cities and localities 'taking into consideration their geographical position relative to each other', but that the size of the town should be reflected in the size of the street and that rivers and mountains would also be catered for and represented by especially long streets that cross several districts, the aim being 'to provide an ensemble such that a traveller could acquire geographic knowledge of France within Paris, and reciprocally of Paris within France' (AP, 520). In one passage quoted by Benjamin, Pujoulx expresses his disdain for the incoherence and caprice whereby some beautiful neighbourhoods are disfigured by streets with offensive names:

> I arrive by the Rue Croix-des-Petits-Champs; I cross the Place des Victoires; I turn into the Rue Vuide-Gousset, which takes me to the Passage des Petits-Pères, from which it is only a short distance to the Palais-Egalité [Palais royal]. What a salmagundi! The first name calls to mind a cult object and a rustic landscape; the second offers military triumphs; the third, an ambush, etc. (AP, 521)

By contrast, Pujoulx affirmed, how fine it would be

> for the resident of the South of France to rediscover, in the names of the various districts of Paris, those of the place where he was born, of the town where his wife came into the world, of the village where he spent his early years. (AP, 522)

Pujoulx claims that 'unsystematic and insignificant' names gave visitors the impression of an irrational and immoral populace (AP, 521). Let those who won't countenance my proposals, he averred, go and live in the rue des Mauvais Garçons or the rue Tire-Boudin (AP, 522). For Benjamin, Pujoulx's fussy rationalism paid homage to the highly subjective and imaginative energies at work in the relationship between the urban subject and city toponyms.

At the heart of Benjamin's sense of the power of street names is their capacity to induce multi-layered vision. The conjunction of the name, its sounds and associations or both, and the physical lay-out of the place, as well as its symbolic attributes, produces an interaction that radically deepens and transforms perception. In one fragment Benjamin illustrates this via an 'excursus on the Place du Maroc'. What was no more than a 'desolate heap of stones, with its rows of tenements' when he came upon it one Sunday afternoon, became, by dint of its conjunction with its name, and perhaps (as a third element) the ethnicity of its residents, both a Moroccan desert and a monument of colonial imperialism. At this moment, says Benjamin, 'topographic vision was entwined with allegorical meaning', although 'not for an instant did it lose its place in the heart of Belleville'. Benjamin compares this experience to that induced by intoxicants. 'In such cases', he writes, 'street names are like intoxicating substances that make our perceptions more stratified and richer in spaces' (AP, 518). 'What is decisive here', he adds, 'is not the association but the interpenetration of images' (AP, 518).

In another fragment Benjamin sees the conjunction of word and space, and text and monument, in the street name as effecting a 'revolution in language':

> What was otherwise reserved for only a very few words — a privileged caste of words, the names — the city has made possible for all words, or at least a great many: to be elevated to the noble status of name. And this supreme revolution in language was carried out by what is most general: the street. [...] Even those much-overused names of great men, already half-congealed into concepts, here once more pass through a filter and regain the absolute; through its street names, the city is image of a linguistic cosmos (AP, 840).

A similar image crops up elsewhere when Benjamin insists that street names do not exist in isolation: their contrasts and juxtapositions make up 'a vascular network of imagination', the 'linguistic network of the city'. In an early passage (AP, 833) he sees the energy at work in the encounter between the city subject and the urban toponym as essentially dialectical and related to temporality — or to the sudden abolition of temporal distance so that past and present fuse together. The fragment begins: 'Being past, being no more, is passionately at work in things' (AP, 833). Names can be a conduit to the pastness, the 'having beenness' that is an essential part of the urban landscape — and a key element in the cultural identity of cities: 'in the inmost recesses of these names', Benjamin writes, 'an upheaval takes place, and thus we retain a world in the names of old streets, and to read a street name at night is like experiencing transmigration' (AP, 833).

In a passage on the Parisian arcades — quintessentially nineteenth-century marvels that had become *passé* and dilapidated, so that the energies of modernity now lay only dormant in them, requiring the kind of imaginative activity Surrealism had provided to rekindle their magic — Benjamin talks of the way electric lighting has contributed to the fading of the arcades' radiance, which has now withdrawn into their *names* (Passage des Panoramas, du Caire, Véro-Dodat, de l'Opera, Vivienne, etc), and he comments

> But their name was now like a filter which let through only the most intimate, the bitter essence of what had been. (This strange capacity for distilling the present, as inmost essence of what has been, is, for true travellers, what gives to the name its exciting and mysterious potency). (AP, 834)

Why is it that Benjamin and, following in his footsteps, such leading French poets as Raymond Queneau,[15] Jacques Roubaud[16] and Jacques Réda[17], along with the historian and philosopher Michel de Certeau,[18] and other writers such as Julien Gracq,[19] Jean-Christophe Bailly[20] and Marc Augé,[21] find street names so fascinating, and how does this connect with the cultural identity of the city? The appeal of the street name is that it draws attention to our participation in urban space whilst at the same time involving a mental process. The street name inspires journeys that are inseparably mental and physical, textual and monumental. The encounter with the name has a strongly practical orientation (even when it begins — or ends — with the street map): it invokes a *practice* of space, an embodied experience: not a desire to describe but a desire to meditate, ruminate and circulate, to be drawn through space, allowing oneself to be informed and transformed by the process. To illustrate this I will now focus on the place of the street name in the work of Jacques Réda.

In the Parisian perambulations Réda has reported on in a series of books, starting with *Les Ruines de Paris* in 1977, and including *Châteaux des courants d'air* (1986), *La Liberté des Rues* (1997, hereafter LR), *Le Citadin* (1998) and *Accidents de la circulation* (2001, hereafter AC) street names are often dwelt upon in detail, sometimes enthusiastically, sometimes with scepticism.[22] Evoking, in *La Liberté des rues*, the plethora of contexts — from shopfronts to removal lorries — where words contribute to the urban landscape, Réda comments rather dyspeptically on street names that are 'de plus en plus détachés de la réalité topographique, et dont la succession et l'assemblage, de quartier en quartier, constitue autant de labyrinthes sans issue, de rébus privés de signification' [more and more detached from topographical reality, and whose succession and combination, from *quartier* to *quartier*, make up so many labyrinths without exit, rebuses without meaning] (LR, 78–79), even if the city walker is sometimes tempted to find a meaning in the strings of names he finds on his path.[23] Yet if 'la toponomie de Paris est déroutante' [the toponymy of Paris is disconcerting] it is because 'elle excite anarchiquement diverses zones de l'imaginaire, du savoir, et de la sensibilité' [in an anarchic way it stimulates diverse fields of imagination, erudition and sensibility] (LR, 95–96) and Réda sometimes comes across areas where a sort of cohesiveness or logic prevails — as when he finds that the rue d'Oran abuts the rue de Laghouat (they are both Algerian cities) — reinforced to some extent by the hazards of population movement.

In *Accidents de la Circulation* Réda again bemoans the arbitrariness of Parisian toponymy (AC, 44). Commenting on a street where a section seemed to have been lopped off and given another name he conjures up municipal waiting rooms crammed with candidates pressing for their names to be allocated to streets! And he goes on:

> Dès lors d'ailleurs qu'ils n'indiquent pas de façon explicite le sens de leur mission (rue du Puits, rue de la Gare, rue de l'Église, rue du Pré) les noms des rues sont de médiocre importance. D'autant que bien souvent le pré, le puits voire la gare ont depuis longtemps disparu. La persistance du nom prend alors un tour ironique ou sarcastique dont la rue peut souffrir. Il veut mieux donc oublier le nom des rues, si l'on vent les connaître dans leur plus authentique intimité. (AC, 45)

> [When they don't explicitly state their mission (as in rue du Puits, rue de la Gare, rue de l'Église, rue du Pré) street names are of little significance, especially since the meadow, the well and indeed the station may long since have disappeared. In such cases the persistence of the name occasions a pinch of irony or sarcasm from which the street may suffer. Better then to forget the names of streets, if one wants to get to know them in their intimate authenticity.]

Yet a few pages later we find Réda conceding that the name of a street we have neglected to visit may 'nous poursuit à tort ou à raison parfois comme un remords' [pursue us rightly or wrongly like a feeling of remorse] (AC, 76). He then welcomes a chance to make amends to a street oddly named rue des Colonels-Renard. How come, he wonders, that a street came to be named after several colonels bearing the surname Renard?

> Nul doute en effet qu'il ait pu exister quantité de colonels appelés Renard. Mais à moins que leur nombre ait été vraiment considérable [...] qu'on ait voulu de la sorte les honorer en bloc [...] ce pluriel a quelque chose qui déconcerte. Ou alors, au contraire, notre armée a-t-elle compté si peu de colonels Renard (trois ou quatre) qu'il a paru judicieux de commémorer cet anomalie? Ou bien encore (tentons d'épuiser le sujet), s'agirait-il d'une espèce de dynastie, de famille exceptionelle où l'on aurait été colonel de père en fils? Ou simplement de deux frères? Peut-être jumeaux, sinon siamois? (AC, 77)

> [No doubt there may have been a good many colonels with this name. But unless their number was really spectacularly high [...] so that it was felt appropriate to honour them en bloc [...] this plural is disconcerting. Or perhaps, on the contrary, the French army has counted so few colonel Renards (three or four) that it seemed a good idea to commemorate this anomaly? Or else (let us try and be exhaustive) we may be dealing with a sort of dynasty, a truly remarkable family where fathers and sons succeed one another as colonel? Or perhaps it's a case of two brothers. Possibly twins, though perhaps not Siamese?]

In *Le Vingtième me fatigue* [Tired of the Twentieth] (2004, hereafter VF),[24] meditations on street names are the core of the work. *Le Vingtième me fatigue* comprises two parts: firstly, an eponymous essay, where the 'vingtième' that fatigues the poet is both the twentieth century (after all the hype, Réda was suffering from post-millennium blues — did the twentieth century really have that much to be proud of?), and the twentieth *arrondissement* where he lives; and secondly, a series of shorter texts under the collective title 'Supplément à un inventaire lacunaire des rues du XXe arrondissement de Paris' [Supplement to a incomplete inventory of the 20th *arrondissement* of Paris].

Amusingly, the opening section of *Le Vingtième me fatigue* turns out to be a digression putting off the sense of obligation and guilty conscience Réda feels at having neglected to accord the rather peripheral and run-down twentieth *arrondissement* its due attention in his large body of writings about the streets of Paris. The central conceit of the ensuing text is that the move to put this right is motivated by a sense of having felt plagued by the *arrondissement*, and much of the piece is concerned with the ploys Réda claims to have adopted in order to resist this harassment on the part of what he calls the 'spectre' de l'*arrondissement* (its ghost, but also its spectrum or range of features, and indeed its shades or 'tones'). The poet's first ploy had been to avoid descriptive prose (the twentieth *arrondissement* clamours to be described), and to write more or less regular sonnets. But here he finds that when stuck for a rhyme it is a street name that often come to mind: his search for a rhyme ending in *ierges*, following his use of the words *cierges* and *concierge*, only produces a line referring to the rue des Enviergers. The *vingtième arrondissement* refuses to be forgotten! His next ploy is to write a novel based in the countryside in which the characters never go outside. But after a while, no doubt because he was writing the novel in Paris, he finds that the narrative shifts and rhythms of his story are inflected by the topography of his native city, for example by the way the Rue des Rigoles takes a sudden headlong plunge. Another victory for the *arrondissement*! Réda's third attempt to evade his 'sujétion lamentable au spectre des rues' [lamentable subjection to the spectre of the streets] (VF, 24) is to give up writing and simply travel. But when he gets back he hurts his back and has to stay at home as if by way of punishment. Reaching up for a book, he finds his back miraculously healed and his mind clarified. He decides that his whole approach to the city — his obsession with finding a centre, with observing different climates, with losing and inventing himself, and his fantasy that his own *arrondissement* was clamouring for his services — simply stems from his own sense of fragmentation and lack of consistency. The best antidote would be to write something useful — by learning some botany, astronomy or oenology. So he goes out and endeavours to avoid paying much attention to the streets, but all of a sudden finds himself in the rue des Réglises whose name had always intrigued him. What on earth are 'réglises'? (VF, 27). In no time Réda has found a new justification for describing his surroundings: it is perhaps the best way of containing the pent-up energy harboured by the myriad details that clamour for our attention, however banal the environs.

> C'est-à-dire que telle fenêtre, tel bout de trottoir, tel coin de mur ou n'importe quoi d'aussi insignifiant, et malheureux ou honteux de l'être, n'en a pas moins la prétention de prendre place, pour se consoler, dans la mémoire de n'importe quel étourdi de passage. (VF, 29)

> [In other words, such and such a window, or stretch of pavement, or bit of wall, or anything quite insignificant, and distressed or ashamed of the fact, nonetheless aspires, by way of consolation, to find a place in the memory of the unwitting passer-by.]

Turning now to the inventory that makes up the bulk of *Le Vingtième me fatigue*, I want to bring out the many different ways street names feature in these accounts of some of the most banal streets of Paris's least picturesque *arrondissement*, and what Réda's often highly elaborate poetic meditations around names and naming tell us about the city's cultural identity.

In the first text Réda find himself at the intersection of three streets: rue de Sénégal, rue de Pékin, and rue Pali-Kao, and muses on links between these names and the Asian population of an area that also sports rues d'Amman, de Chine, de Cambodge, and de Japon. Recognizing that it would be surprising if many immigrants came to live in these streets simply because of their names, he notes that there are nonetheless a lot of Asians in the *vingtième arrondissement*. Yet in a street as depressing as rue de Chine — which crosses a series of other streets 'avec la résolution d'un neurasthénique qui va se pendre. Rien ne cheche à te retenir' [with the resolve of a neurasthenic who is intent on hanging himself [and] finds nothing on his path likely to dissuade him] (VF, 38), there are precious few indications of China, so Réda offers some recommendations as to how the area could make itself look more eastern.

In several of these texts Réda reflects on the custom of naming streets after little-known or quickly forgotten worthies. In the case of the Rue Jouye-Rouve, at first glance a 'rue quasiment pure où rien ne s'impose à l'attention' [pure street where nothing seeks to attract attention] (VF, 43), the name does little else than underline how the street is no more nor less than a 'hyphen' between two points, a route from A to B as functional as the hyphen in the street name. Yet paradoxically, as Réda will develop later on, reflecting on the banality of a name is itself a way into the atmosphere of a site, and as if to prove this point Réda spots a bizarre café he hadn't initially noticed. Going on to consider the recent practice whereby municipal authorities provide biographical details of the people streets are named after, he initially condemns it, as displaying the fly-blown erudition of retired provincials. But he comes round to it when he recognizes that one can turn the names into fictional characters, or identify (for example) a clutch of aviators in the *vingtième arrondissement*.

In a piece on one of the least attractive bits of the *vingtième*, near the Porte de Bagnolet, where Réda sets himself the challenge of pinning down the specific type of banality that prevails in these identical streets, with their uniform 1930s buildings that could easily be somewhere else, he notes that the provision of a diversity of names doesn't serve to enliven the district because they are all just names of people, some famous, some not. Paris, he notes grumpily, is turning into a dictionary of proper names, and this is undesirable because random clusters of, say, composers manifestly spring from municipal directives, and from the 'un besoin permanent de figer la vie dans l'officiel' [constant need to freeze life into official postures] (VF, 60). The name 'rue Schubert' does nothing to help us remember the composer of the *Unfinished Symphony*, whereas a street name like 'rue Charles et Robert' poses an enigma (as in the case of the Colonels-Renard) that sets us imagining a stirring tale of brothers or comrades. Equally, as Réda observes in another piece, an intriguing name like the 'rue de Surmelin', which sets us wondering what a *surmelin is* — perhaps a type of *surmulot*, in other words a giant rat — has a real resonance when one discovers that it is in fact the name of a tributary of the Marne rather than a long-forgotten landowner. When it transpires that the nearby rue de la Dhuis is also named after one of the Marne's 'modestes affluents' Réda embarks on a fantasy where the rivers slip away from their names to course through the meadows he imagines lying behind some of the individual houses that line these streets (VF, 75).

'Le Borrégo', the longest and most programmatic text in *Le Vingtième me fatigue*, concerns the relationship between a street and its 'secret' climate or tonality. Réda freely admits his *parti pris*: 'je cherche des qualités aux rues' [I try to establish a street's personal qualities] (VF, 78). But he is in fact drawn to streets that have no obvious qualities, partly because he identifies with their modesty and anonymity — like him they are 'quelconque'. Why then does he feel a moral obligation to record these streets? Although in this case he will feel impelled to go to the rue Borrégo and do his fieldwork, the starting point of his reflections, on a day when he couldn't face going out, was responding to his sense of duty by evoking his *memories* of a street picked at random. Realizing that he doesn't know what 'Borrégo' refers to, he comes back to the question of names. In many cases, notably when it is the name of a historical personage, the street name, he surmises, is a bad indicator of its tonality, a 'blind alley'. Streets are better off with plain names like rue de la Gare, or rue des Rigoles: even if the topographic feature or utility is no longer extant, the name makes us think of what was once there, so that the street benefits from the aura of layered memories, and from the reveries on past realities that the name inspires. In any case, says Réda, streets often react against the names foisted on them — for example by remaining resolutely banal and ugly despite being given a grand name — he cites the rue Vitruve (after the Roman writer Vitruvius) as an example. This conceit, whereby excessive servility — insisting on remaining modest — is seen as a form of revolt, is typical of Réda, linking as it does a form of behaviour discerned in (or ascribed to) the external world (here the street), with the inner dispositions of the observer and narrator, Réda himself. Equally the 'insurmountable sadness' and bare rigidity of the Rue Haxo are said secretly to repudiate 'le parrainage imposé de ce grand architecte militaire' [the enforced tutelage of the great military architect] (VF, 84).

What is striking here — and sums up the whole tradition of meditating on street names that Réda, following on from Benjamin, Queneau, Roubaud and others, exemplifies — is the self-conscious pseudo-science and mock erudition Réda deploys as he develops wonderfully subtle and persuasive arguments that are always based on specific cases. His ruminations are strongly empirical and experimental but they frequently end up being self-contradictory or inconsistent. Of course this becomes a tribute to the creative stimulus of urban toponyms which inspire a freewheeling discourse that has the key benefit of keeping the city walker engaged and thus able to make more and more local discoveries. In effect Réda, like Roubaud and Queneau, works through every possibility of connection or disconnection between streets and their names, recognizing (but disguising) the fact that there are ultimately no hard and fast conclusions to be drawn, and that the relation of name to thing is in the end usually arbitrary.

Réda acknowledges that some streets do derive their personalities from their names but that this is unlikely to happen with names like rue Jules-Grévy or rue d'Agen: making the passer-by think of a politician or a small provincial town is unlikely to be very productive unless these have particular associations that can feed back into how the surroundings are viewed. In the case of rue Borrégo Réda has only vague memories of the street and doesn't know what the name means. Obviously the street would be far less intriguing if it were called rue Pierre Mesmer or rue de la Nièvre, however arbitrary it may be to project on to the street feelings inspired by the associations of its name. Indeed this might lead to complaints on the part of more or less identical streets claiming to possess the same qualities — or lack of qualities — but endowed with a less fascinating name. At this point in his musings Réda resolves to visit the rue Borrégo in order to found his feelings about the street — kindled by its name — on some objective features (although he is fully aware that it is the name that will probably guide him to find features that 'match' its associations). All he had remembered initially about the street was a post office and a church, but the first thing he spots is a 'terrain vague' (vacant lot) — one of his favourite (and fast disappearing) types of urban space. He then spies a brick building with abandoned shop fronts at ground level which spontaneously makes him think of Trieste. However, since he has never been to Trieste he realizes that his reaction is probably inspired by some poems by the Triestine writer, Umberto Saba. There may be no such building in Trieste and yet, arbitrary and personal as the association is, it nonetheless seems that something of the reality of Trieste is perceptible here in the Parisian street (like Benjamin, Réda is highly sensitive to all the places where Paris reminds one of Havana, Le Havre or Dakar). Réda is aware that he could brew up this 'fantasy of Trieste' with the brick building, the vacant lot, and other features that appealed to him, and elicit from this the 'personality' or secret' he insists on believing every street possesses. Yet, in a characteristic reversal, he ends this piece by affirming that what he responds to in the rue Borrégo, and the other streets in which he wanders, is a question that the street itself seems to ask of him. And he affirms that the street's entreaty to pinpoint its identity precludes responses that are merely fanciful and partial, or that fail to address the street as whole. But at the same time Réda recognizes that the enigma posed by the street is really that of his own identity, and that the key or cipher represented by the features of the street he is driven to interpret, like is name, relates to his own life. In the wonderful prosopopoeia with which the text ends, the street pronounce its own verdict on the city walker: identifying its name as 'of Mexican origin' ('I thought so' interjects Réda) the rue Borrégo ruefully laments the fact that it really has no identity beyond the ones projected on to it by the mind and memory of the embroidering subject — in this case Jacques Réda. Ironically, the street concedes that it only has a 'voice', an autonomous identity, a secret, by dint of the walker's quest for 'the invisible pattern of [his] life'. The cultural identity of the street is a function of our desire to sense the city as a sounding board or echo-chamber.

Yet the final text in *Le Vingtième me fatigue*, on the rue de l'Atlas, nuances this picture once again, and works round to the view that, even if what the urban subject encounters time and again, in his or her itineraries, is a kind of generic secret that mirrors an abeyant identity — 'le secret qui se dérobe partout, dont nous nous protégeons derrière un réseau d'habitudes' [the secret that is everywhere withheld and from which we protect ourselves by a network of habits] (VF, 92) — in certain key instances what is encountered or revealed, is a deeper impression, in the literal sense of something imprinted on us. Some streets, it seems, bear a deeper imprint that can mesh with the 'mental space of this or that passer-by'. The street becomes the unconscious bearer of an anonymous memory for which the street's name can be the label. Yet in this dispensation it is better that the street name carry no baggage: that it should have the abstraction of a date rather than waylay us with 'une modeste énigme de l'Histoire, ou une perplexité concernant le motif de son choix' [a modest historical enigma or our perplexity as to why this particular name was chosen] (VF, 92). Here, in the rue de l'Atlas, the name channels attention firstly onto the few Berber passers-by — by association with the mountain range — and particularly onto men wearing the garment known as a *passe-montagne* (a type of jacket). But Réda also finds Atlas, the giant, in a lowering brick repository which reminds him how attracted he is to this type of building, as well as to removal lorries often bearing enigmatic names, as of remote deities or fairy-tale giants. He had seen a removal firm called HONHON that morning, and the brick repository in the rue de l'Atlas bears the name ODOUL. As he continues to 'sniff out' ('flairer') what appeals to him in this street, Réda spies some tiny bits of detritus caught in the grooves of a patch of tarmac that has been ornamented with a simple pattern. A bit further on he comes upon another bit of tarmac, plain this time and 'black and shiny as licorice'. What catches his attention here is a date inscribed when the tar was still hot: '29: 09: 98', 'une de ces nombreuses dates orphelines ou veuves sur les trottoirs de Paris' [one of the innumerable widowed or orphaned dates one finds on the pavements of Paris] (VF, 95). For the first time he understands what appeals to him in such imprints or impressions. The date is a kind of anniversary — and he can ask himself what he was doing then, and note that it was nearly two years ago to the day. But the date does not commemorate anything except the precise moment when cold steel made this impression on hot asphalt 'comme dans la chair d'un grand bœuf inerte' [as if in the inert flank of a cow] (the animality here matches the verb *flairer*). There is a generic memory here for Réda of all the occasions when he had encountered the acrid but sweet smell of hot asphalt — a smell that is 'nutritive pour l'âme' [nourishes the soul] (VF, 96). But the real key is his awareness of what Charles Baudelaire, in his great Parisian essay on 'Le Peintre de la vie moderne' [The Painter of Modern Life], called 'la mémoire du présent' [the memory of the present], associated with moments, marked by 'the stamp of sensation' ('l'estampille de la sensation'), when the transient and the eternal fuse by virtue of a sudden perception.[25] It may not be the street name that provides the resting point for the twin journeys of perception and cogitation here. But in the rue de l'Atlas, as in so many other streets, the name is for Réda the vehicle for a process of endless metaphorical exchange between city and subject, inducing the lateral metonymic drift, from displacement to displacement, that keeps him shuffling through a pack of identities engendered in and through his interactions with the city of light.

## Notes

1. I have examined the topic of Paris street names in two previous publications: 'Naming the Streets: Experience and Identity in Contemporary Writing on Paris', in *Thresholds of Otherness / Autrement mêmes: Identity and Alterity in French-language Literatures*, ed. by David Murphy and Aedín Ní Loingsigh (London: Grant and Cutler, 2002), pp. 175–94, and *Everyday Life: Theories and Practices from Surrealism to the Present* (Oxford: Oxford University Press, 2006), pp. 375–85.
2. Daniel Milo, 'Le Nom des rues', in *Les Lieux de mémoire*, ed. by Pierre Nora, 3 vols in 7 (Paris: Gallimard, 1997), II, 283–315.
3. *The Guardian*, 5 February 2002.
4. 'Plague of plaques bemuses Parisians', *Guardian*, 14 November 2002. Cf. 'Le mystère des fausses plaques de Paris', AFP, 13 November 2002.
5. 'Street Cred Signs', *Guardian*, 11 April 2004.
6. Susan Hiller, *The J-Street Project*, Timothy Taylor Gallery, London 14 April–21 May 2005.
7. *L'Invention du quotidien*, new edn, rev. by Luce Giard, 2 vols (Paris: Gallimard, 1990), II, 189–204.
8. Paris: Hachette, 1986.
9. Karlheinz Stierle, *La Capitale des signes: Paris et son discours* (Paris: Maison des sciences de

l'homme, 2001). Page references to this work are incorporated into the text following the abbreviation CS.

10. 'Présence de Paris' (1937), Œuvres, ed. by Jean Hytier, 2 vols (Paris: Gallimard, 1960), II, 1011–15. All translations from French in this article are my own.

11. Cf. my 'City Space, Textual Space, Mental Space: Paris in Breton, Benjamin and Réda', in this volume.

12. Stierle's point chimes with Certeau's brilliant account of the 'semantic tropisms' induced by street names in L'Invention du quotidien, II, 156–59. Cf. on this Everyday Life, pp. 379–81.

13. The Arcades Project, trans. by Howard Eiland and Kevin McLaughlin (Cambridge, MA: Harvard University Press, 1999), pp. 516–26 (for quotations I have use the abbreviation AP).

14. On this disparity see Everyday Life, pp. 384–85.

15. See his Courir les rues (Paris: Gallimard, 1967).

16. See his La Forme d'une ville change, helas, plus vite que le cœur des humains (Paris: Gallimard, 1999).

17. See below.

18. See L'Invention du quotidien (Paris: Gallimard, 1990).

19. See Julien Gracq, La Forme d'une ville (Paris: José Corti, 1985).

20. See La Ville à l'œuvre (Paris: Editions Jacques Bertoin, 1992).

21. Paris: Hachette, 1986.

22. All published in Paris by Gallimard.

23. Cf. Georges Perec, Perec / rinations (Paris: Zulma, 1995), a collection of crossword puzzles relating to Paris devised by Perec where the clues often consist of Parisian itineraries based on street names.

24. Geneva: La Dogana, 2004.

25. 'Le Peintre de la vie moderne', in Charles Baudelaire, Œuvres complètes (Paris: Gallimard, 1961), I, p. 1165.

# 18

# Michel Deguy

Can French poetry ever rescind its pact with 'l'azur', 'le merveilleux', 'le séjour', 'L'Une', 'L'Être', or any other euphemism for what must always amount to something like transcendence? Or can it merely feign to do so and, when it courts its own failure, succeed only in hypostatizing absence, negativity, 'l'expérience des limites', turning them into something like... transcendence? If the work of Michel Deguy has provided a uniquely fertile and flexible space for this question to display its complexities, it is because the span of his career to date, together with his philosophical training, have both exposed him to the full force and gravity of the Heideggerian view of poetry as quest for the ground of Being and equipped him with the conceptual range to engage fully with structuralism and its aftermath.

The publication of *Actes* and *Oui-dire* in 1966 not only confirmed that French poetry had, as Georges Poulet suggested in a review of Deguy's three previous collections, found a major new voice, but marked a decisive mutation in the timbre and resonance of that voice. *Actes*, which ranks with Bonnefoy's *L'Improbable* as a crucial meditation on poetry, inaugurated what will probably stand as Deguy's 'grand manner': a fusion of poetry and poetics in a style of exceptional vitality, bristling with neologisms, rare and foreign words, and coinages arrived at by cunning hyphenation ('la ruse du trait d'union' [the hyphen trick]).

Though the patchwork of precept and practice deliberately prevented the mix from congealing into dogma, a new consistency was clearly perceptible in Deguy's restless reformulations of the connections between poetry and experience. The early poems had emphasized the poet's vigilant 'auscultation de l'espace' [sounding-out of space], constantly anticipating those rare coincidences of moment and place which stake out the periphery of Being. But already, against the grain of a search for 'les sites de l'essence [...] qui lui annoncent de quelle manière il est au monde' [those essential sites [...] that reveal our way of being in the world], against the fetishism of special places and moments, runs a current of speculation in which the key themes are the world as 'spectacle' and the activity of metaphor:

> Chaque chose est proche d'une autre, et dans cette proximité est enfouie sa propre essence, sa manière d'être en relation. Cette disposition de soi du monde dans la diversité du spectacle, il appartient à la métaphore d'en saisir l'ordre... Il appartient au regard du poète de relever cette topographie ontologique du visible.
>
> [Each thing is close to another, and its own essence, its own way of being in relation, is nestled in this closeness. It is the office of metaphor to grasp the

way in which the world presents itself to us in the diversity of the spectacle [...] The role of the poet's gaze is to make out this ontological topography of the visible.]

Here the emphasis is on an activity prior to the poem; metaphor is rooted in perception and serves to record those resemblances and affinities which make our planet into a world, a cosmos: the poet is its cartographer.

If *Actes* consummates a new phase in Deguy's poetics it is because the poem is promoted from log-book to crow's nest, and language takes place of honour at the captain's table. We move from 'le lieu comme médiateur de l'être' [the place as a mediator of being] (Poulet's phrase) to this view of the poet at work:

> Guettant la différence entre ce qui est là et... *ce*, justement, qui a rapport essentiel au langage, le poète attend la naissance des mots à cette jointure invisible dans le visible... attendant *pour rien*, attendant le défaut de l'être, la blessure capricieuse, l'hémorragie de choses miraculeuses; les décrivant, mais comme si elles n'étaient là que pour leurs mots qui veulent dire autre chose: ce qu'en l'absence d'elles le poème dira.

> [Looking out for the difference between what is there and [...] *that* precisely which is essentially related to language, the poet waits for words to be born in this invisible junction in the visible... waiting *for nothing*, waiting for the gap in being, the fickle wound, the haemorrhage of miraculous things; describing them, but as though they were there only for their words which mean something else: what the poem will say in their place.]

What gave Deguy's contribution its originality was not so much the formulation of a poetic ontology in terms of the relation between language and things but the ways in which he pinned it to a sophisticated awareness of the semiotics of poetic discourse. Every feature of poetic language and thus every kind of transaction between words contributes to the 'figurativity' through which poetry apprehends Being: 'les figures du langage sont la trame du linge de Véronique sur les traits de l'être' [the figures of language are the weave of Veronica's veil resting on being's face]. The poetic quest is conducted within language and poetry seeks to become a 'langage du langage': 'le poète maintient (et restitue) "l'autre version", l'autre rapport transversal, des mots aux mots, entre eux, à l'intérieur de la langue, il fait entendre à elle-même les pouvoirs de la langue, il la révèle à elle-même' [the poet maintains (and restores) 'the other version', the other transversal relation, between words and words, between words, inside language; it makes language itself hear its own powers, and reveals language to itself].

It is evident that the poetic theory of *Actes* subscribes enthusiastically to what Barthes has called 'l'optimisme du signifiant' [the optimism of the signifier], the predilection for modes of linguistic functioning which fend off the tyranny of expression, transcendental meaning, and ideology. Yet by annexing these semiotic functions to the field of Being, however remote or elusive that notion is, Deguy was sowing the seeds of a contradiction his later work has sought often vainly to exorcize. Gérard Genette, for example, was quick to discern in Deguy's work the perpetuation of 'l'illusion symboliste': the belief in a reciprocity between the 'fringe benefits' of the linguistic system — what Deguy called the 'ultra-sons du langage' — and an occult order of reality and experience. If Deguy's response to such criticisms has usually been defensive, repudiating the claims of formalism to legislate for poetic activity, he has not stood still.

In *Figurations* (1969) and, especially, *Tombeau de Du Bellay* (1973), the faith in poetic language as the corroboration of something other than an illusion engendered by language itself is subjected to a kind of slow torture. Veronica's veil emerges from the mangle looking more like the Turin shroud, a highly suspect artefact, to be venerated perhaps only by the credulous. But Deguy does not really believe in forensic tests, and his first impulse is to turn in another direction. Not away from poetry, or from language for that matter, but as his most recent book, *Jumelages suivi de Made in USA* (1978), suggests, away from the battleground of poetic language and Being and back to the crucible of experience. What Deguy has not relinquished is the sense that a poem is a particular kind of event.

*Jumelages* widens the angle of the lens through which Deguy offers the reader the spectacle of the poet's activity. The 'twinnings' arise when the experience of writing, and of 'being a poet', is given a context amidst the discourses of the modern world encountered in technology, tourism, the mass media, politics or the experience of another culture (America). Poetics becomes 'poéthique' and the poem offers itself as a non-aligned territory, a hiatus in which the terms which monopolize and foreclose debate are temporarily exposed to another frame of reference: 'C'est brièvement un autre réferentiel auquel le "j'écris" appartient' [The 'I am writing' belongs briefly to another set of reference points]; 'Le poème c'est la prose empêchée par d'autres moyens, ralentie et continuée — enrayée à une autre échelle; ce en quoi la prose consiste est dilaté là où ça résiste' [The poem is prose which has been prevented by other means, slowed down and continued — blocked off on another scale; what prose consists of is dilated precisely where it resists].

While Deguy's earlier books, however widely they drew on his fieldwork, were made in the poet's own studio, *Jumelages* is shot almost entirely on location: trips to America, parties in Sydney, airports and colloquia. The efficacy of poetic language is now measured in terms of the pressure it exerts on the elements of discourse from which the reigning ideologies are made. Yet this spawns another crisis. What is the 'specific gravity' of the poem when — under the banner of 'écriture' or 'différance' — a large part of the intellectual community wants to share the spoils of poetic deconstruction? The excellent quarterly review *Po&sie* which Deguy founded in Spring 1977 has had this question constantly in view. If an answer has emerged it consists in a reaffirmation of the view that, for the poet, language can never wholly comply with its own demystification. The poet may no longer be the 'shepherd of Being' but the vigil continues.

# 19

# Poetry and its Double

*Review of Michel Deutsch, Emmanuel Hocquard, Jean-Luc Nancy, Bernard Noël, Alain Veinstein, Franck Venaille, Mathieu Bénézet and Philippe Lacoue-Labarthe,*
Haine de la poésie *(Paris: Christian Bourgois, 1979)*

One of the things that unites the poets represented here is lack of enthusiasm for a dominant trend in recent French poetry: 'cette idéologie du vocable [...] Il y a un lexique restreint que vous trouvez partout. Du genre: terre, sable, air, argile, feu, etc. Presque un code' [this ideology of key words [...] There's a restricted lexicon that one finds everywhere. Things like: earth, sand, air, clay, fire, etc. Almost a code]. Of course it is partly *because* it has become stereotyped that the poetic discourse characterized here has lost some of its force. But it is clearly not inconsistent with the poetic vision which inspires this discourse that it lends such density to certain elemental terms. For it is a poetry in which presence fleetingly tips the scales against absence, and in which poetic intuition can provide the orientation for a quest, found a landscape, and sponsor a mode of being.

It is this possibility of an accommodation between what is intimated in poetry and any available images of the self and its environment that is relinquished by the poets assembled here. And this explains the gesture of affiliation to Georges Bataille from whom the book derives its title. It would he very difficult to summarize the subtle, tentative relation to Bataille sketched in an opening dialogue between Mathieu Bénézet and Philippe Lacoue-Labarthe (the co-editors). It bears on the notion that poetry is the channel through which language contests its own limits — and hence the limitations of thought itself. But, in constituting itself as a discourse, poetry tends to retain with one hand what it gives away with the other and, in the process, supplants what it promised to make room for or, rather, fills the gap it tends to reveal. 'La vraie poésie est en dehors des lois [...] mais, finalement, la poésie accepte la poésie' [True poetry is outside the law [...] but, ultimately, poetry accepts poetry]. 'La haine' [hatred], in Bataille's phrase, refers both to a negative potential inherent in poetry and to the contempt poetry inspires when, almost inevitably, it disguises this potential. Fifteen years after the publication of *La Haine de la poèsie* [Poetry's Hatred] (1947), Bataille changed the title to *L'Impossible*.

Here are three extracts from *Haine de la Poésie*. The authors are, respectively, Philippe Lacoue-Labarthe, Alain Veinstein and Bernard Noël.

1        ...laisse — laisse venir (céder, probablement
         ou sourdre, bien qu'à peine)
         ce qui ne viendra pas et ne peut arriver, faute
         ne serait — ce que d'un infaillible rivage [...]

[...let — let come (yield, probably | or well up, although barely) | what will not come and cannot happen, | for want, if only, of an infallible shore [...]]]

2        Mais aujourd'hui, *fenêtre*... Un mot nouveau
         troue ma phrase, suspend le cours... [...]
         Rien rapporté jamais... Jouets dans *terre* et *mort*...
         Lambeaux, miettes, bouts de terre et mort... [...]
         Ces mots, phrases, d'une histoire où nous *manquons*...

[But today, *window*... A new word | pierces my sentence, holds up its course... [...] | Nothing ever reported... Toys in *earth* and *death*... | Shreds, crumbs, bits of earth and death... [...] | These words, sentences, of a story from which we are *missing*...]

3    La langue est maintenant ce morceau de chair mobile derrière les dents. [...] à coups de couteau | griffonnent bouches nouvelles | il faut que le corps parle | totalement | et soit tué le tu — Je ne signerai pas ça, a dit Noël. Il me semble que je mentirais. — Crois tu que la vérité a des droits sur nous? a demandé Léon. — J'ai toujours été un simulateur sincère. — Pousse-toi a répliqué Léon, tu es un personnage de trop. [...] J'écris, a-t-il écrit. J'écris pour que se retire celui que je ne suis pas.

[Language is now this piece of flesh moving behind the teeth. [...] by knifeslashes | new mouths scribble | the body must speak | totally | and the you be killed | — I won't put my name to that, Noël said. I feel I'd be lying. — Do you think sincerity has any claim over us?, Léon asked. — I've always been a sincere pretender. — Move over, Léon replied, you're an unneeded character. [...] I write, he wrote. I write so that he who I'm not withdraws.]

Lacoue-Labarthe's poem seems slack and derivative; the long 'clarification' which follows is much more taut. The problem is that of articulating the poet's relation to something that is at once infinitely remote and as close as his own heart-beat. Jean-Luc Nancy continues this train of thought by rewriting, line for line, Valéry's 'drama of consciousness', *La Jeune Parque*, in such a way as to radicalize the dislocation of speech he discerns in the poem. The result, 'La Jeune Carpe', does not quite repay the effort. Hölderlin provides the most consistent point of reference for some of these poets. Michel Deutsch bases an impressive meditation around the famous description (by his landlord, the carpenter Zimmer) of Hölderlin's behaviour at Tübingen — the poet walking rhythmically, declaiming at his window, playing the same simple tune at the harmonium for hours on end, 'as if he wanted to eradicate every last shred of what he knows'.

I find Veinstein's text more rewarding because if, like the poets I've mentioned, he too is concerned with negotiation, access, exclusion, the unstitching of knowledge, it is not really with reference to anything prior to the immediate context of writing itself. It is in the act of writing that he experiences a sense of constant exclusion.

Words, no sooner inherited, must be bequeathed: for Veinstein it is in an eternal present over which he exercises no right of ownership that something is constantly taking shape and then dissolving.

But there is something very familiar about the position from which he writes. The question: who is Alain Veinstein? never crosses one's mind. With Bernard Noël and, to a lesser extent, Mathieu Bénézet, it is quite different. The 'Je' of the text is reinvested with an autobiographical density deliberately lacking in Veinstein; but at the same time it is subjected to a greater turbulence, indeterminacy, anonymity. Bernard Noël has evolved a form of writing where the first person slips and slides under the author's name, his body, his existence as a political subject and so on. The writer is like the man in that Magritte painting: pictured from behind, he is looking into a mirror, but the reflection is that of his back. How tempting to think that the person in the mirror, in the text, is himself. Bénézet's journal, 'Mon cœur mis à vif' [My heart made raw], dissects this temptation with a passionate, edgy, intensity.

Noël once remarked that the essence of Bataille lay in 'la contestation permanente de l'écrit par le vécu, et réciproquement' [the permanent challenging of the written by the lived, and vice-versa]: he and Bénézet exemplify this most clearly. But perhaps it is also the lesson of Emmanuel Hocquard's haunting little anecdotes which each confront an object, or an experience, with its description, its representation or its imitation: 'Deux récits ne pouvant coincider. Ils ont en commun ce qui les sépare: un bord d'ombre' [Two tales unable to coincide. They share what separates them: a shadowy edge].

— 20 —

# Innovarinations

*Review of Valère Novarina,* La Lutte des morts *(Paris: Christian Bourgois, 1979)*

'Le drame dans la langue française' [Drama in the French language], a diary Novarina kept while writing the first five versions of this 'play', gives a good picture of what he is up to:

> C'est pas écrit *pour* mais *vers* le théâtre... Mettre le pantalon suicide. Les zones théâtrogènes du texte... Refaire tout le chemin de l'apprentissage de la langue matièrenelle... Qui touche la langue touche le fond... Traiter la langue comme une chose... Au contraire de ceux qui servent la langue, il la desserre... il écarte, il ratisse les tissus du langage... Rapidement suivre ce qu'il se dicte... tous les rapports possibles des paroles à des corps... Lutter toujours contre la tendance à fabriquer une perspective... Du texte personne ne pourra garder aucune mémoire.

> [It's not written *for* but *towards* the theatre... Put on suicide trousers. The text's theatrogenic zones... Redo the whole journey of learning one's matternal language... Who touches language touches base... Treat language as a thing... As opposed to those who serve language, he unscrews it... he opens out, he combes through the cloths of language... Quickly follow what he dictates to himself... all the possible relationships of words to bodies... Struggle always against the tendency to make up a perspective... No one will be able to conserve any memory of the text.]

Mother Tongue's apron strings are very hard to undo. Writing without due care and attention is not enough. Novarina keeps egging himself on to write dangerously, recklessly. He gives himself a framework, based largely on the metaphor of language as a theatrical space where thoughts, words and deeds are *performed* — and then works hard to disfigure and distort the material provided by the organic bond between the French language and French institutions. In practice, the outcome is a fairly homogeneous sort of dialect.

The effect? Something like the 'Circe' chapter in *Ulysses* rewritten by a team including Rabelais, Jarry, Artaud, Queneau, Lacan... A lot of comic gusto, a vivid sense of the materiality of words and the tyranny of ready-made linguistic forms, and an engaging vigour and directness. Novarina and his fellow-contributors to the review *TXT* are worth looking into. But, perhaps appropriately, I felt a greater sense of liberation when I put this book down than when I was reading it.

# 21

# Imaginary Solutions

*Review of Alfred Jarry,* Messaline, *trans. by John Harman (London: Atlas, 1985);*
*Timothy Mathews,* Reading Apollinaire: Theories of Poetic Language
*(Manchester: Manchester University Press, 1987);*
*Tristan Tzara,* Chanson Dada: Selected Poems, *trans. by Lee Harwood*
*(Toronto: Coach House, 1987);*
*René Crevel,* Difficult Death, *trans. by David Rattray*
*(San Francisco: North Point, 1987);*
*Raymond Queneau,* Pierrot mon ami, *trans. by Barbara Wright (London: Atlas, 1988),*
*and* The Skin of Dreams, *trans. by H. J. Kaplan (London: Atlas, 1987)*

As avant-gardes displace one another down the years, from the Symbolists, through Futurism, Dada and Surrealism to the post-structuralisms of today, the friction between past, present and — since this is the dimension to which avant-garde art often lays claim — the future, consistently generates creative energy. Cruising through Imperial Rome's mean streets to the brothel where she likes to handle more clients than the hardest-working whores, Alfred Jarry's Messalina is partly revamped Tacitus, partly Nineties floozy, a sort of Nana *alla romana*. There is a whiff of the *canular* in all Jarry did, but *Messaline* (published in 1900, and now very well translated by John Harman) is neither a spoof nor a diligent (or opportunistic) attempt at historical reconstruction in the manner of a bestseller of the period, Sienkiewicz's *Quo Vadis?*. Abetted by his own brand of that hothouse *fin de siècle* prose in which half the words are orchids and all come entwined in the dense creepers of a syntax which makes word-order seem aleatory, Jarry transmutes impeccable erudition into the surreal and the fantastic. Messalina's sexual voracity becomes a power which narrative and language try their best to contain. The plot centres on her foreboding that the phallic god has abandoned Rome, and the Empress's obsessive desire to track down and unmask the Phallus leads her into an abject spiral of destruction.

Rather like Jules Laforgue in the *Moralités légendaires* of a decade earlier, Jarry uses the waning of the pagan world to focus on the raising into consciousness of what was instinctual, and as a parallel for the various senses of an ending the *fin de siècle* seemed to spawn. The ancient text or legend (and this will be echoed in Apollinaire) comes to figure the archaic strata of the self, and the textual permutations to which it is subjected: irony, parody, transvalorizations of various sorts — the whole range of operations that one text can perform on another — epitomize the anxious attempts of modern consciousness to dig itself out. To treat the past in this way is also to play truant from the present and enjoy what Jarry once called the 'delights of anachronism'. Eclectic erudition prizing arcane terms and cryptic encodings of knowledge joins hands with a 'sci-fi' outlook (Jarry was a lifelong devotee of H. G. Wells), so that the difference between revisiting the past through time-travel and previewing the future through technological speculation, a feature of Jarry's next novel, *Le Surmâle* (1901), becomes minimal.

'Le Roi-Lune' [The Moon-King], in Apollinaire's marvellous collection of stories *Le Poète Assassiné* [*The Poet Assassinated*], composed before the First World War but not published until 1916 (Ron Padgett's translation, first published in 1985, has recently been reissued in paperback), features a resourceful time-traveller in the shape of Ludwig of Bavaria who, far from drowning in the Stambergersee, inhabits a vast cavern where he and his youthful companions divert themselves by donning a contraption that tunes them into opportune moments from the past lives of famous lovers — Héloïse, Lola Montès *et al.* — and enables them to make love with their shades. The story typifies Apollinaire's characteristic oscillation 'entre avenir et souvenir' [between future and memory] (as he once put it) and the byways of whimsy down which he was often led by the pull between the lure of the past and his desire wholeheartedly to meet the challenge of modernity. The title story, as was typical with Apollinaire, was cobbled together out of bits and pieces from a dozen other works (newspaper articles, aborted novels and suchlike). This 'cut and paste' approach, which one also finds in the poetry, is less a sign of modernism than a symptom of Apollinaire's effort to create a space where his contradictions, always expressed in temporal terms, would find some sort of *modus vivendi*.

But these stories, which feature lonely ventriloquists, amnesiac chauffeurs — the kind of people one subsequently meets in Queneau's novels — or legendary figures such as King Arthur, who here turns up to claim the English throne in the year 2105, represent a kind of imaginative recidivism. The pervasive fantasy of ubiquity and omnitemporality seems to reflect not only creative omnipotence but a desire to control the past through 'play' (in a late poem Apollinaire referred wistfully to 'le temps qu'on peut chasser ou faire revenir' [time, which one can drive out or call back]). But he came to recognize that the addiction to nostalgic immersion in his own past ('une onde mauvaise à boire' [waters in which not good to drink] as he put it in 'La Chanson du mal-aimé' [The song of the ill-loved]) would not be cured in this fashion. The case was treatable, but something more drastic was needed, and many have taken the line that the remedy came in the form of 'modernolatry' (to use Renato Poggioli's term): the undiscriminating espousal of the new in all its flavours. But this is a half-truth at best, and Timothy Mathews, in his *Reading Apollinaire*, a subtle and original study of Apollinaire's poetic language, further contributes to discrediting it.

Through a series of highly charged and imaginative readings of individual poems, Mathews argues that the themes of separation, loss and transience in Apollinaire's first collection, *Alcools* (1913), are by-products of his concern with an experience that takes place as he writes, the experience of a sense of self 'fragmented in language and as language'. In pursuing his identity in the medium of words Apollinaire didn't shrink from — if anything he courted — the ways poetry can make context dissolve, and cause memories or sensations to be displaced by the mobility of words and images. In his writings on the Cubists Apollinaire emphasizes the desire to create an image of the perceptual act itself, and his enthusiasm for Delaunay's 'Orphic' simultaneities was prompted by the artist's attempts to 'delve into' the way sensations unfurl in mental space. Mathews argues convincingly, that in the 'poèmes-conversation' and 'calligrams' Apollinaire was attempting something comparable. The textures of myth and legend are purged in *Calligrammes* (1918), but deliverance, Mathews seeks to show, is achieved not through the embrace of the future so much as through surrender to the elusive, ungraspable immediacy of the present. Or rather, the future to which Apollinaire did aspire, through the adoption of a prophetic stance in many of his later poems, is not to be identified with the paraphernalia of the modern world, but as a time when human beings will be able to meet the challenge which the present, the here and now of perception, poses to consciousness.

Apollinaire responded eagerly to news of the Dada movement which reached him from Zürich from 1916 onwards, but he did not live to witness its Parisian incarnation. With Dada, the avant-garde's liquidation of the past seems complete. But, for Tristan Tzara and his companions, this also meant having no truck with any of the futures the imagination could herald. Only the gesture of destruction itself could claim to be untainted, and Tzara's desperate manifestos, paradoxically perhaps his most durable works, are full of appeals to an almost mystical concept of mental spontaneity as yet untouched by the quasi-Freudian ambitions the Surrealists would harbour. After Dada, Tzara enjoyed a literary career of a surprisingly conventional kind (much more so than, say, Breton's). He wrote poetry and essays, served on committees, became politically involved. Some of the poems are very good, and one should be grateful to Lee Harwood, in *Chanson Dada: Selected Poems*, for providing English-speaking readers with translations drawn from the whole range of Tzara's work. Yet it is doubtful if many will find it easy to respond to what in English, and in the absence of any indication of context, may seem little other than chains of non sequiturs varying only in length.

René Crevel acted in Tzara's play, *Le Cœur à barbe*, on the memorable night in 1923 when a ritual punch-up marked a watershed in Dada's evolution into Surrealism. From then until his suicide in 1935 Crevel participated in all the reviews, signed all the tracts, attended all the meetings in cafés (health permitting). Yet when one reads him it is not always easy to see how this can have been. An active homosexual with misogynistic tendencies, Crevel must have found Breton's fulminations against gays, and his cult of the feminine, somewhat trying. Nor did he really share the Surrealists' beliefs concerning chance, or the modern marvellous, or even language (he dodged the automatic writing sessions). Moreover, his main literary output consisted in works which, superficially at least, looked like novels, a form of writing of which Breton did not approve.

In fact Crevel's six 'novels' (which include *Détours, Mon Corps et moi, Êtes-vous fou?* — he was very good at titles) are really monologues, larger autobiographical improvisations, dazzling and lethal, in which he externalized his demons, tried to lay his family ghosts and, provisionally at least, sought to keep the lure of death at bay. His father committed suicide during a family dinner-party when Crevel was fourteen, and before her son's eyes his irate mother hurled abuse at the suspended corpse. This event, along with his mother's recent death, and his aborted psychoanalysis, surfaces in *La Mort difficile*, now translated for the first time. The opening scene, in which two bourgeois women (both based on Crevel's mother) discuss their husbands, is deadly *humour noir*. But Crevel's strength is that he can change the pitch when he wants to, as when the focus shifts to the hero's infatuation with a pleasure-seeking piece of American beefcake, Arthur Bruggle. Lowering the flame of invective and sarcasm, Crevel shows how, in the face of rejection, existential hunger for another being — the desire for the other revealing itself to be inseparable from the desire to be the other — ebbs away into shameful recourse to ever more potent forms of oblivion. Crevel admired Gide, and his writing has affinities with the 'nouveau mal de siècle' of Arland and Drieu la Rochelle. But full-throttle participation in Surrealism provided an extra defence against literary propriety, and Crevel's fierce candour (one of his best books was called *Les Pieds dans le plat* [*Putting one's foot in it*] gives his treatment of sexuality a force remarkable for its period and still worth exposing oneself to now.

In the 1920s Raymond Queneau was a diligent if self-effacing Surrealist (he did his quota of automatic writing for *La Révolution surréaliste*) and after his break with the group in 1930 Surrealism continued to animate his work, though in ways which derive as much from Jarry and Apollinaire. *The Skin of Dreams* (*Loin de Rueil*, 1944: the newly issued translation dates from 1948 and is rather mediocre) features a dreamer, Jacques L'Aumône, whose fantasies of identification with the stars of the silver screen at the Rueil-Palace cinema keep interfering with reality but are ultimately reconciled with it when, after many adventures, he becomes a Hollywood star himself.

*Pierrot mon ami* was perhaps Queneau's masterpiece, and it is surprising that this modem classic has not been translated into English before, though it was worth waiting for the task to be done properly, as it now has been by Barbara Wright. The conflagration which destroyed the famous Luna-Park fairground in Paris in the late 1930s, as well as the fact that the entrance to the 'spectators only' gallery of its helter-skelter apparently bore the legend 'Entrée des philosophes', seem to have been the novel's germ. Pierrot, an amiable drifter, finds, then loses, employment in the Palais de la Rigolade at the Uni-Park, becomes a fakir's assistant, is befriended by the guardian of a memorial chapel marking the spot where a Poldavian prince died in a riding accident, becomes embroiled in the attempts of the fairground manager's mistress to track down a long-lost lover, serves as a delivery-driver for an animal trainer who turns out to be the fakir's brother, and so on. Yet what makes the novel such a treat, and so resonant for all its light-heartedness, is the erosion of the boundary between the extraordinary and the everyday. The outline of a potential whodunit takes shape around Pierrot, but he shows little concern:

what interest him are Yvonne, the fairkeeper's daughter, ham sandwiches with good mustard and a glass of white wine, lying on his bed reading *La Veine*, playing pinball (at which he excels), admiring the clever display of ball-bearings in a local shop window and, above all, taking life as it comes — a propensity nurtured by his tendency to make his mind a blank as often as he can.

Queneau is marvellous at summoning up unemphatically the atmosphere of the Paris suburbs and their denizens — people with names like Jojo Mouilleminche and Albéric Prouillot, each with a tale to tell and an axe to grind. Yet he was not a realist. The verbal inventiveness, the humour and the encyclopaedic quality of his writing ('Parmi les alcools de ma vie', he once remarked, echoing Apollinaire, 'il y a eu l'érudition et le calembour' [Among the intoxicants of my life have been erudition and puns]) do more than attune us to the mystery of everydayness, fundamental as this is. A founder member of the College of 'Pataphysics, dedicated to Jarry and his science of imaginary solutions, Queneau had the poet's devotion to the way things could, or should, be. Later on, as co-founder of the OuLiPo (Ouvroir de Littérature Potentielle), this unlikely guru exerted a major influence on a new avant-garde (notably on Georges Perec, who was devoted to him). But if there was a sage in Queneau he never imparted his wisdom more touchingly than in *Pierrot mon ami*.

# 22

# Discreetly Tangential

*Review of Raymond Queneau, Œuvres complètes, vol. I,*
*ed. by Claude Debon (Paris: Gallimard, 1989)*

*Tel qu'en lui-même enfin l'éternité le change...* Since his death in 1976 Raymond
Queneau has been changing fast. The publication of his *Journal (1939–40)* revealed
the gleeful neologist, the poet of the suburbs, the philosophical humorist to have
been a man deeply if intermittently concerned with spiritual self-transformation:
'Bien vaniteux, bien orgueilleux | Avec l'Infini comme veilleuse'[1] as one entry puts
it. Our understanding of all Queneau's work, including marvellous fictions such as
*Pierrot mon ami*, is likely to be enhanced by this new perception of an essentially
oblique, tangential writer. Volume One of Claude Debon's superb Pléiade edition,
which is devoted exclusively to Queneau's poetry, contributes to the revised picture
by clarifying the spiritual project underlying his last collections, especially *Morale
élémentaire* (1975).

We also learn more about the poet's relationship to his childhood and parents
through a series of previously unpublished autobiographical fragments. Queneau's
maternal grandfather was presented with a pair of binoculars by Queen Victoria in
recognition of his part in a sea-rescue; but the family fortunes suffered a blow when
his ship the *Arabic* went down. His daughter made a go of the *mercerie* in Le Havre
made over to her in 1900, keeping up her pretensions to gentility by ridiculing
the peasant origins of the ailing colonial soldier she married *sur le tard*. Queneau's
memories of the *arrière-boutique* and the stifling petit-bourgeois world in which he
grew up never ceased to haunt him, inspiring contradictory feelings of solidarity
and dismay.

Although he had written poems from early on and, in his surrealist phase,
produced much *écriture automatique* (reprinted here among the many *inédits*),
Queneau did not publish a volume of poetry until 1937. *Chêne et chien*, a 'roman en
vers' (predominantly alexandrines), which appeared between his fourth and fifth
novels, is an autobiographical narrative in which he recounts both his childhood
and the period of psychoanalysis through which he tried unsuccessfully to lay its
ghosts [to rest?]:

> Cette brume insensée où s'agitent des ombres, comment pourrais-je l'éclaircir?
> cette brume insensée où s'agitent des ombres,
> — est-ce donc là mon avenir? (*OC*, I, p. 19)

Georges Perec took these lines as epigraph to his own autobiography, endorsing the view that our future depends on what we make of our past. But Perec also admired in Queneau a writer for whom literary activity, however personal its material, was always partly a game, an *exercice de style* drawing on existing models, but also a loving witness to the diversity of three orders: language, knowledge and everyday reality.

One of Queneau's best-known poems, 'L'explication des métaphores' (p. 65), brilliantly evokes language's eerie power of derealization; if words are celebrated in all his poetry they are never hallowed, there is no Word. 'Bien placés, bien choisis | quelques mots font une poésie' (p.106), and yet, 'ça a toujours kékchose d'extrême un poème' (ibid.). To resist etiolation words have to earn their living:

> Les mots qui se passaient des ombres de réalité
> Moururent En expirant révélèrent leur pères
> Puis ils se sont ternis dans des marches rapides
> Pour vivre ils se sont faits ouvriers et boxeurs (p. 90)

Queneau saved hundreds of words from unemployment and, through his splendid *néo-français* — phonetic transcription of spoken language — added vastly to the linguistic labour force. The results, it is true, can be prosaic, and the end-product sometimes 'peu de chose', but in a poem such as 'Si tu t'imagines' (p. 120), made famous by Juliette Greco, the effect is memorable, even if the theme, as so often in Queneau, is traditional. Death, in fact, inspires some of his best poems, explicitly in the last section of *L'Instant fatal*, tacitly elsewhere.

Death's shadow is by no means absent from the encyclopaedic enthusiasms Queneau tried to incorporate into his poetry, often in surprising ways. *Petite cosmogonie portative* (1950) retraces the earth's evolution from what we would now call Big Bang onwards, his dense alexandrines, crammed with scientific terms, are not easy reading, though there are charming moments, as when humans eventually appear in the fifth and last of the massive cantos. Italo Calvino admired the poem greatly and wrote an erudite introduction to the Italian translation. Less demanding is the 'Chant du styrène', an informative ode to polystyrene ('O matière plastique | D'où viens-tu?' (p. 239) written for Alain Resnais as the soundtrack to a documentary commissioned by a plastics company. If the appeal of the non-human world is linked to an escape from people and from death, the same applies to *littérature potentielle* (Queneau was a founder of OULIPO): the exploitation of formal constraints and generative principles provided an exit from the closed shop of purely individual creation. With *Mille Milliards de poèmes* (1961), the first OULIPO classic, Queneau set out to model a book of poems on the Turing machine. Each line of ten matching sonnets could (in the original volume, though not in the Pléiade) be flicked over individually, and the resulting combinations provided, in theory, enough reading matter for several lifetimes.

Queneau's true genius lay, however, in the particular quality of his attentiveness to everyday reality. Words and speech-rhythms were always a prime channel of his 'availability to experience' (to borrow a phrase from Marianne Moore, a poet he greatly admired); and by commanding their own kind of attention, formal constraints — including traditional prosody which he championed (though he was not otherwise a traditionalist) — helped Queneau resist any temptation to eschew banality or to abandon the path outlined in the title of a poem from *Le Chien à la mandoline*: 'De l'information nulle à une certaine espece de poésie' (p. 417).

Yet where the poetry of everydayness is concerned it is perhaps in his later collections that Queneau came into his own. *Courir les rues* (1968) surely deserves to occupy a prominent place on the Paris-Poésie line which runs from Baudelaire to Réda via Apollinaire and Breton (it is good to see, incidentally, that Queneau himself now figures on the Metro map). Here poetry is a form of mental and verbal perambulation. In 154 short poems he explores a 'Paris de paroles' — posters, street names, bus routes, statues commemorating the likes of Jules Simon who changed his name from Jules Suisse, inspiring Queneau to devise one of his funniest titles: 'Il ne voulut pas d'un nom helvète' (p.417). Queneau takes the city as it comes, steeped in past time, ever changing. Each poem is a sally forth into its endless fascinations; there is no desire to halt or possess.

*Morale élémentaire* brought this orientation of Queneau's poetry to a magnificent fruition, fusing the formal preoccupations of the *oulipien*, the love of everyday things, and the impulses of a renewed spirituality. Having evolved a strict poetic form, indebted to Haiku and based on regularly spaced phrases of noun plus adjective ('Ombres traçantes Pluies lassantes Neiges accomplies' (p. 652) arranged around a brief kernel-poem, Queneau set himself the task of composing one each day, often after a stroll with his dog Taî-Taî. The series complete, he developed another form: dense prose poems sparked by the sixty-foul hexagrams of the *I-Ching*. Although he was strongly tempted to publish these poems under a pseudonym, *Morale élémentaire* is still Queneau: there is wry humour, there are everyday words, and what is new grows out of what came before. 'Le dessin s'écarte peut-être du projet', reads the end of one poem, 'mais l'intention demeure bonne et directe, ferme en sa discrète tangence' (p. 678). A discreet tangent, tenaciously held: not a bad description of the path Queneau traced as a poet.

## Note

1. Queneau, *Journal 1939–1940*, ed. by Anne-Isabelle Queneau and Jean-José Marchand (Paris: Gallimard, 1986), p. 92.

# 23

# Lust in the Library

*Review of Guillaume Apollinaire, Œuvres en prose complètes, vol. III,*
*ed. by Pierre Caizergues and Michel Décaudin (Paris: Gallimard, 1993)*

Like many poets of the first rank, Guillaume Apollinaire was also a fine prose writer, and while a third Pléiade volume might seem to be scraping the barrel, the present one, devoted to an important aspect of his immense journalistic output, as well as to his erotic writings, has many attractions. Not the least is the very Apollinairean mixture of erudition and lasciviousness that results when the poet's unashamedly pornographic works are equipped with full scholarly apparatus. It is amusing to see *Les Onze Mille Verges* [*The Eleven Thousand Pricks*], until fairly recently available only *sous le manteau*, decked out in full academic dress. But in case one were to miss the aura of transgression and discomfort which has traditionally accompanied its reading, it has been thoughtfully maintained by the surprising decision to eschew the usual print-size, and to present the poet's two pornographic novellas (the other being the inferior *Exploits d'un jeune Don Juan*) in characters scarcely more legible than the famous Pléiade footnotes.

The peek-a-boo flavour of Apollinaire's erotic imagination was cleverly captured in an exhibition, in Paris last year, of books and papers from his library, recently acquired by the Bibliothèque historique de la Ville de Paris. A special installation at the Maison de la Poésie invited the voyeuristically inclined to peep through slits in a fake wall and decipher well-thumbed passages from the steamy missives dispatched by the soldier Apollinaire to the rackety Louise de Coligny. The poet found it stimulating to apprise Lou, as he called her, of what he would like to do to each of the nine (!) portals of her body, but where similar sentiments in, say, James Joyce's letters to Nora Barnacle, convey an atmosphere of cosy smut, Apollinaire's obsession with orifices has a more sinister air.

Indeed, in *Les Onze mille verges*, probably written around 1907, nearly a decade before the letters to Lou, carnal excess constantly tips over into sadism. Such merits as this rumbustious narrative may possess, in pitching us from Bucharest to Paris to the Russo-Japanese war of 1904, as the hero, Mony Vibescu, becomes embroiled in the affairs of the royal house of Serbia, stem from the way the story jolts unstoppably from ribald *paillardise* to the most repellent scenes of sexual violence, while the narrative voice maintains an unruffled and mildly jocular tone. While it is hardly a moral fable, the logic of the narrative tends to show up the pathological dimension underlying the quest for sexual gratification. One minute Culculine d'Ancône and

Alexine Mangetout are finding new uses for a coachman's whip or a policeman's truncheon, the next they are involved in bouts of sexual gymnastics so frenzied that they are left flat out, recovering (if they are lucky) amid large quantities of sperm, blood and excrement.

Apollinaire handles the narrative with great gusto, imagining situations and settings, such as a nightclub in Port-Arthur kept by two Symbolist poets in drag, which provide opportunities for genuine humour and wit, as well as couplings galore, involving all and sundry, not excluding children, the disabled and animals. Anticipating the Absurdists, the humour stems from disparities of tone, vocabulary and register. To cater for the most jaded and pernickety of his readers, Apollinaire piles on the agony in the last chapters, which feature the confessions of a masochist, the fiendish lusts of a Red Cross nurse, the flagellation of an ephebe, a certain amount of defecation and Mony's terrible come-uppance at the hands of 11,000 soldiers. Yet despite the excess, Apollinaire treats sexual matters in a down-to-earth way, using the most common words for sexual organs, practices and processes. The contrast points to two different sides of his erotic imagination. In Apollinaire's aesthetic mythology, evolved in his writings on the Cubists, the artist destroys appearances and courts self-destruction in the purifying fire of creation. Erotic transgression is therefore in some measure analogous to poetic transcendence. But he never allows sex to lose its connection with less sublime realities. At a more basic level, the stereotyped scenarios of female compliance and subordination, the obsession with big buttocks and anal penetration, tell a tale of misogyny where the desire to avenge female treachery constantly overlays the fantasy of a *femme moderne* who would reciprocate (but in fact simply replicates) male desire.

The hot-line between erotomania and bibliophilia has no better witness than Guillaume Apollinaire. Not only did he compile (in 1913 with Fernand Fleuret) the first proper catalogue for the famous *Enfer*, where the Bibliothèque nationale stored its dirty books, but, soon after writing *Les Onze mille verges*, he was commissioned to write introductions for, and edit, two series of erotic classics, 'Les Maîtres de l'amour' and 'La Bibliothèque des curieux'. And between 1908 and 1914, he was responsible for fourteen volumes, ranging from anthologies of Aretino, Sade, Cleland and Baffo, to editions of works such as *Le Joujou des demoiselles* [*The Girls' Plaything*].

At some point, Apollinaire revised his contributions to form a volume which Blaise Cendrars, who wanted to publish it, compared to 'un fleuve noir, plein de goudron et de soufre' [a black river, full of tar and sulphur]. In fact, *Les Diables amoureux* [The Devils in Love] only emerged in 1964, and the Pléiade reproduces this version rather than the original prefaces. Even in this abbreviated form, Apollinaire tends to be a bit long on biographical details, bibliographical niceties and background information. Celebrating 'le divin Arétin' [the divine Aretino] at great length, he gets tangled up in questions of attribution and only just conveys what he admires about the *Ragionamenti*. A lengthy introduction to *Fanny Hill* consists largely of quotations from an 1801 volume called *Les Sérails de Londres* [*The Seraglios of London*]. The presentation of 'Le Divin Marquis' is, however, noteworthy for the portrayal of Sade, who spent much of his life in prison, as 'cet esprit le plus libre qui ait jamais existé', a depiction which fired the enthusiasm of the Surrealists. For Apollinaire, Sade belonged to a period which saw a remarkable flowering of erotic writing and publishing, and in his treatment of Nerciat, author of the famous *Félicia ou mes fredaines* [*Félicia or, My Escapades*], the poet projects himself back into a more congenial erotic climate. On the strength, seemingly, of a saucy epistolary novel called *Un Été à la campagne* [*A Summer in the Country*], Apollinaire locates another haven in the last days of the Second Empire, notable, he claims disarmingly, for a 'dévergondage plein de bonhomie et de simplicité' [simple, good-natured debauchery]. For the bookish, though, the real erotic home remains the library, where the pleasures of anachronism are freely available.

The other main achievement of this volume is to show us the full range of Apollinaire's writings in a mode he was to make his own: the journalistic *écho* or, to use the poet's preferred term, *anecdote*. Some of these ephemeral writings have been collected before, by Apollinaire himself to make a charming book called *Le Flâneur des deux rives* [*The Flâneur of Both Banks*], published soon after his death, and by others in such volumes as *Anecdotiques* (1926). Here, this material is not only fully annotated but greatly amplified to include contributions to over two dozen periodicals. Some of it is tedious, but the diversity provides an ideal context for the writings which take pride of place: Apollinaire's contributions to the *Mercure de France*, and especially the column he created in 1911, and kept up fairly regularly until his death in 1918, headed 'La Vie anecdotique'.

The uncharacteristically solemn sentence which opens the first column gives a clue to the poet's frame of mind: 'J'aime les hommes, non pour ce qui les unit, mais pour ce qui les divise, et des cœurs, je veux surtout connaître ce qui les ronge' [I like people, not for what unites them, but for what divides them, and, as for hearts, I want above all to know what's gnawing at them]. By Apollinaire's time, the role of the *échotier* was fairly clear. Part gossip columnist, part social secretary, he indicated the topic of the hour, the talk of the town, the flavour of the month, in whatever sector was appropriate to the paper's readership. With his finger in so many artistic pies, Apollinaire was ideally cut out for this task, but he brought to it a poetic sensibility, responsive not so much to the obviously bizarre and *outré*, but to an indefinable quality which made the event, person or phenomenon in some way different or unique.

A typical fortnightly instalment of 'La Vie anecdotique' might consist of a few items, ranging in length from a paragraph to a couple of pages. First might come a brief piece lamenting the demise of a periodical, noting the sale of a sultan's hideous collection of china or celebrating the opening of a Chinese restaurant by reproducing its menu. The second item might give a sketch of an unjustly neglected artistic figure or an eccentric personage from Apollinaire's vast circle of acquaintances. At various points, his readers are introduced to the superstitious Romanian writer, Jean de Mitty, who would not post a letter without first spelling it out word by word on his thumb nail, and to M Abdul-Hadid, 'un des hommes les plus singuliers qui se puissent imaginer, même en rêve' [one of the most singular men one could imagine, even in dreams], a Muslim Swede and defender of the Cubists, who was never seen without his shopping-bag. Most unforgettable is Faïk Beg Konitza, the Albanian patriot and philologist who settled in Chingford. Editor of *Albania* and reformer of his native tongue — 'il fit, en peu d'années, d'un patois de bougres et de matelots, une langue belle, riche et souple' [in only a few years he turned a dialect for geezers and sailors into a beautiful, rich, supple language] — Konitza was exceedingly nervous and always behind schedule (the 1904 numbers of *Albania* appeared in 1907). Finding shopping a trial because he was always convinced shopkeepers would think he had stolen goods he had just purchased, Konitza was just leaving for the florist's to buy the button-hole by which Apollinaire was to recognize him at Victoria Station when the poet arrived, hours late, by cab, apologizing for the long delays he had experienced crossing the channel.

The essayist Paul Léautaud admired Apollinaire's column for its 'style simple et extrêmement fin' [simple, extremely delicate style]. These stylistic qualities embody a way of seeing and feeling that is profoundly individual and yet at the same time anonymous and neutral. As with Nerval and Baudelaire, what counts is the capacity to suspend judgment and withhold classification. With 'La Vie anecdotique' we are closer than we might think to the wellsprings of Apollinaire's creativity. As in his marvellous long poems, 'Zone', 'Le Voyageur' or 'Le Musicien de Saint-Merri', with their ambulatory rhythms, collage structure, constant mingling of fact and fiction, self and other, past and present, the items Apollinaire assembles and juxtaposes seem to take on a new life. Like the poem, the journalistic column, with its bric-a-brac, becomes a space where an identity endlessly seeks its bearings amid the flotsam and jetsam of experience.

When Apollinaire decided to make a book out of his *Mercure* pieces, he selected, re-ordered and edited the material comprehensively, sewing together bits from different periods and contexts. But although a certain unity is conferred by the concentration on Parisian people and places, the effect is still that of a patchwork, and *Le Flâneur des deux rives*, a miniature masterpiece of writing about the city, is a compendium of marvels. Each chapter is an associative cluster based around an area (Auteuil), a locale (libraries or bookshops) or an institution, and its denizens. In the haunting 'Souvenir d'Auteuil', the flâneur takes us round a series of municipal depots, from the Hôtel des Haricots, where rows of street-lights resemble a primeval forest, to a repository for superannuated artworks, including a roomful of religious paintings, where a 'congrès de crucifiés' endure their exile. Elsewhere, we meet Alexandre Treutens, licensed as a 'poète ambulant' by the Mairie of Enghien; Michel Pons, the celebrated 'restaurateur-poète' with his friend André Jayet, the 'cordonnier-philosophe'. Most memorable is the account of Ernest La Jeunesse, 'le dernier boulevardier'. Here, Apollinaire's skill at evoking the bond between people and their habitats, and his acute sense of transience, converge beautifully in a description of the dandy's room, particularly a table laden with mouldy confectionery, which had the air of being set out

> depuis plus d'un siècle pour une troupe turbulente d'enfants qui ne sont point venus, qui ont grandi, ont vieilli et sont morts sans avoir touché à ces bonbons

surannés et charmants, objets précieux d'une gourmandise qui n'est plus, dont on n'a pas écrit l'histoire et qui n'a même pas son musée.

[more than a century ago for a turbulent flock of children who never came, who grew up, grew old, and died without having touched these charming, old-fashioned sweets, the precious objects of a *gourmandise* that exists no longer, whose history has gone unwritten, and which does not even have a museum of its own.]

# 24

# The Sailor Who Hated the Sea

*Review of Victor Segalen, Œuvres complètes, 2 vols, ed. by Henry Bouillier*
*(Paris: Laffont, 1995), and Voyages au pays du réel: œuvres littéraires,*
*ed. by Michel Le Bris (Brussels: Complexe, 1995)*

When he died in 1919 at the age of forty-one, Victor Segalen had published only three slim volumes: *Les Immémoriaux*, a sort of ethnographic novel recording the terrible decay of Polynesian civilization brought about by the interference of European missionaries; *Stèles*, a series of beautifully executed prose-poems inspired by Chinese history and culture; and *Peintures*, a work which started out as an essay on Chinese painting but became something quite different when Segalen adopted the narrative voice of a fairground *bonimenteur* rather than a critic, and set about evoking, in restless and sumptuous prose, imaginary as opposed to real works of art.

Yet the naval doctor and semi-professional archaeologist, whose body was found by his wife at one of their consecrated places in the forest of Huelgoat in his native Brittany, an open copy of *Hamlet* by his side and blood still seeping from a wounded ankle, died as much from physical and nervous exhaustion as from the consequences of a bizarre accident. A sailor who hated the sea, Segalen loved land travel, the more arduous the better, and kept on the move as much as he could. Not inappropriately, given that his great theme was to be the struggle between the Real and the Imaginary, Segalen's first contact with Chinese civilization was in the Chinatown of San Francisco where he was laid low by typhoid fever. But it was Polynesia that provided his first encounter with the exotic, a term he was to meditate on and define in a highly personal and intriguing fashion. Segalen arrived in the Marquesas only weeks after the death of Gauguin, some of whose possessions and works he acquired in an auction at Hiva-Oa. Along with Rimbaud, Gauguin became a key figure in his personal mythology, steering him towards creativity. While his thesis, *Les Cliniciens ès lettres* [*Clinicians in literature*], possessed a strongly literary flavour, being concerned not with diseases or doctors but with writers imbued, one way or another, with things medical, Segalen's true career as a writer began in Polynesia, where he hatched *Les Immémoriaux* and other works, such as the unfinished *Le Maître-du-jouir* [*The Pleasure-Master*], inspired by Gauguin, in which he conveyed the impact of a culture based on voice, touch and pleasure on a sensibility mutilated by a narrow religious upbringing.

Between 1909 and 1914, Segalen lived mainly in China, and he made another long visit there and to the Far East in 1917–18. Although he often had irksome medical duties to attend to, he quickly developed a passion not only for all aspects of Chinese imperial history and culture but for topographical and archaeological exploration and description, in 1913–14, he led an official French mission which made important new discoveries, including what was then the oldest monumental stone statue in China, adorning the tomb of Huo Quping, a general who died at the age of twenty-four in 117 BC, having reputedly massacred 80,000 Huns. In 1917, further travels enabled him to complete the research for a remarkable monograph on Chinese monumental statues to be accompanied by extensive photographic documentation.

*Chine: la grande statuaire* [China: The Great Statuary] is one of the many post-humously published works that have progressively contributed to Segalen's belated recognition as one of the most original and interesting writers of his time. For some years, Segalen *inédits* have been appearing regularly from small presses in France such as Fata Morgana and Rougerie, and now, all of a sudden we have two major collections of his writings. Michel Le Bris's edition of the literary works is an attractive and readable volume, with a hot-headed introduction by a travel-writing fanatic and Stevenson specialist. Despite the wretched quality of the paper, and the relative thinness of the critical apparatus (a pity, since the editor has devoted most of his scholarly career to elucidating Segalen), Henry Bouillier's Bouquins volumes are well worth the extra shelf space. If ever there was a case for having everything (or as much as possible), this is it. Where a writer's *oeuvre* consists to such a degree in unpublished or unfinished projects, it can be vital to see the different ways he approached a particular theme. Even more important where Segalen is concerned is the multi-faceted, interdisciplinary character of his writing, the way he not only adopted a highly sophisticated and experimental approach to the literary genres in which he worked (the *poème en prose* in *Stèles*, the novel in *René Leys*), but actively sought to invent new modes of writing, transgressing established boundaries and bringing the exigencies of style to bear on the complex reality he perceived by dint of his various guises as ethnographer, musicologist, doctor, archaeologist, sinologist and poet.

Michel Le Bris's edition hives off Segalen's 'literary' output from such works as *Chine: la grande statuaire*, where the descriptions fuse a poet's sense of time and place with a scholar's knowledge of detail, and a traveller's experience in the field, or *Briques et tuiles*, a log-book where topographical and stylistic exploration go hand in hand. Worse, Le Bris omits a text which not only provides a key to Segalen's entire project as a writer, but in itself accounts for his new-found notoriety in certain quarters. Segalen never wrote the 'Essai sur l'exotisme', subtitled 'Une esthétique du divers', which he had first mooted somewhere off Java in 1904. But at intervals between then and 1918, he jotted down ideas, made plans, refined definitions of key terms and wrote drafts of the opening paragraphs.

At the heart of Segalen's sense of the exotic is the shock of encountering that which is other. If writing and travel were for him a single vocation, their common origin lay in an experience of radical difference which he sought, in the projected essay, to define against the grain of literary exoticism exhibited in his own period by a Pierre Loti or a Claude Farrère. Where these writers turned camels and palm trees, pith hats and houris into new reflections of European hegemony, Segalen sought ways of hanging on to the crucial, and much more fertile, strain of alterity experienced by the 'exote' who consents to maintain the tension between self and other rather than collapsing them into one synthetic vision:

> L'Exotisme n'est donc pas une adaptation; n'est donc pas la compréhension parfaite d'un hors soi-même qu'on étreindrait en soi, mais la perception aiguë et immédiate d'une incompréhensibilité éternelle.
>
> [Exoticism is not, then, a form of adaptation; it is not, therefore, the perfect comprehension of something outside oneself which one embraces in oneself, but the acute, immediate perception of an eternal incomprehensibility.]

Benefiting from the poetic density and current prestige of fragmentary discourse, Segalen's immensely resonant notations regarding the 'secousse exotique' [exotic jolt], the 'notion du différent' and the 'pouvoir de concevoir autre' [power of thinking otherwise] have attracted the attention of a number of influential theoreticians of post-colonialism, racial difference and the ethnographic encounter, and they have turned the author of *Stèles* into a patron saint of alterity. While not without reservations, Edouard Glissant and Edward Said have applauded Segalen's disengagement from the discourse of empire, while James Clifford has likened his 'poetics of displacement' to the work of other writer-ethnographers, notably Michel Leiris, in whose writing a comparable literary inventiveness and generic hybridity is engendered by the attempt to maintain difference through emphasis on subjectivity. More recently, Jean Baudrillard and Marc Guillaume have made Segalen a crucial point of reference in the debate about otherness and assimilation, to which many leading French intellectuals, including Jacques Derrida, Julia Kristeva, Tzvetan Todorov and Marc Augé have contributed.

Baudrillard's admiration for Segalen fully acknowledges the extent to which the desire to maintain desire and preserve creative estrangement pays homage to the self as much as to the other, creating space for the energies and manoeuvres of a subject free to move between cultures and between identities. Segalen's lament for the lost otherness of a Polynesia which had fallen victim to European assimilation, or an Imperial China whose death throes he witnessed at first hand, certainly bears an ethical stamp, but the desire to preserve otherness at all costs, to cultivate a sense of the radical exoticism which may be experienced in various regions of experience, from sexuality to historical reconstruction, had a strongly personal and aesthetic basis.

Ultimately, the object of Victor Segalen's 'esthétique du divers' [aesthetics of diversity] is a realm of experience beyond customary selfhood, briefly apprehended at times when the tension between the imaginary and the real reaches a point where both are momentarily transcended. As he observes in the preface to *Stèles*, the light whose changing is measured by the standing stone (or poem) is inner: 'c'est un jour de connaissance au fond de soi: l'ombre est intime et l'instant perpétuel' [it is a light of knowledge in one's own depths: the shadow is intimate and the instant is perpetual]. Or, as he put it in a letter to Henri Manceron in 1913: 'le transfert de L'Empire de Chine à L'Empire de soi-même est constant' [the transfer between the Empire of China and the Empire of oneself is constant]. Read in the context of the 'Essai sur l'exotisme' and many other contemporaneous works collected in Bouillier's edition, *Stèles* becomes a much more intense and personal work than it seems. Each *stèle*, with its exhortation, counsel, injunction, edict, decree or ultimatum is at once the record of the 'exote's' encounter with external otherness and part of a tactics of self-recovery. 'Sans marque de règne' [Without indication of reign], it bears the imprint not of this emperor or that dynasty,

> Mais de cette ère unique, sans date et sans fin, aux caractères indicibles, que tout homme instaure en lui-même et salue.
> A l'aube où il devient Sage et Régent du trône de son cœur.

> [But of that unique era, dateless and endless, whose characters are unsayable, which each person establishes in himself and pays tribute to. || In the dawn in which he becomes Sage and Regent of his heart's throne.]

Yet Segalen's poetic quest never does away with reality. On the contrary, what gives his best work enduring strength is its treatment of physical sensation, particularly in connection with the experience of travel and material reality, especially architecture and landscape. *Equipée*, with its ironic title, meaning escapade or jaunt, and its intensely evocative subtitle, 'Voyage au pays du réel' [Journey to the land of the Real], is a masterpiece. Where *Peintures* made imaginary paintings seem intensely real, *Équipée* fragments a real journey (the 1914 mission) into twenty-eight mini-essays, each of which contrasts the journey undertaken by a body in space, time and adversity, with the journey lived through in the mind which anticipates, reacts, negates — in short, imagines. Nothing could be easier than keeping the two in parallel; the challenge is to make mental and physical journeys intersect, to procure and investigate moments when 'le Réel' is neither the humdrum opponent of 'l'Imaginaire' nor merely its springboard: 'il n'est ici question que de chercher en quelles mystérieuses cavernes du profond de l'être humain ces mondes divers peuvent s'unir et se renforcent à la plénitude' [it is solely a question here of seeking to find in which mysterious caverns of the depth of the human being these diverse worlds can unite themselves in, and bolster one another to fullest degree].

With stunning panache and verbal exuberance, Segalen writes about leaving and arriving, the tempo of the *étape* and the horrors of the enforced *halte*: crossing cols, bathing in geysers, coming upon centuries-old artefacts in friable yellow earth; meeting one's earlier self ('autoscopie' was one of Segalen's enduring preoccupations), and debating what one wants one's friends to say (or not say) on one's return.

In the interests of a comparable staging of the shadow-play between the real and the imaginary, Segalen's brilliant *René Leys* — at once an epistemological fiction, a *roman-à-clef*, a metafictional meditation and an exercise in autofiction — plays fascinating games with generic conventions while making the setting (the architecture of Peking and the Forbidden City) crucial to the workings of the narrative. But as Bouillier's edition makes plain, *Equipée* is, alongside *Stèles*, the purest distillation of Segalen's gift. It manifests the extraordinary feeling for landscape and place evinced in such essays as 'Le Grand Fleuve' [The Great River] and 'Terre jaune' [Yellow earth], not previously available in book form, as well as in *Briques et tuiles*, and the later *Feuilles de route* (1914–17), which receives its first publication in full. At the same time, *Equipée* reflects admirably the interwoven strands in Segalen's work — medicine, ethnography, archaeology, sinology, antiquarianism, philosophy, epigraphy, photography, eroticism — which make it of such compelling interest today, whatever the contribution we feel his 'esthétique du divers' can make to our current deliberations about the value of preserving otherness.

# 25

# The Shadows Inside: Memory, the Body, and Forgetting in Supervielle

*Review of Jules Supervielle, Œuvres poétiques complètes,*
*ed. by Michel Collot and others (Paris: Gallimard, 1996)*

Thanking him, in 1925, for a copy of *Gravitations*, Rilke called Jules Supervielle a Saint Christopher who could build bridges between the human realm and the cosmos, introducing ordinary mortal things to the ways of 'la vie sidérale' [sidereal life]. *Débarcadères* [Wharfs] (1922) had cast the poet as a gaucho riding the endless pampas, haunting the poet's exotic background (like Lautréamont and Laforgue, Supervielle was born in Montevideo, in 1884, and continued to spend long periods, including the Occupation, in Uruguay). In *Gravitations*, the poet becomes an astrologer or a geologist. His prime concerns may be inner, but now his 'cœur astrologue' [astrologue heart] needs interstellar space to find its mirror. This was not megalomania but a sign of the vacuum poetry had to fill. Supervielle's parents died accidentally when he was an infant and traces of this loss can be found throughout his career. In *Gravitations* the cosmos is made familiar (and the ordinary world of experience correspondingly uncanny) because it answers an immediate need, and one so pressing that, as Michel Collot points out, much toning down was felt to be necessary when Supervielle revised the poems for the definitive edition of 1932. By that time, Supervielle had in any case adopted a more austere poetic. He was no longer so likely to use the sprawling free verse of '47 Boulevard Lannes' where, as in a Chagall painting, homely milk bottles and puffing dray-horses are viewed with astonishment as if by a visitor from outer space. 'Boulevard Lannes que fais-tu au milieu du ciel | Avec les immeubles de pierre que viennent flairer les années' [Boulevard Lannes, what are you doing in the middle of the sky | With stone apartment blocks which the years come sniffing around]. Nor would he have been likely, by this time, to pay homage to his compatriot Lautréamont in such thrillingly surrealistic terms as in the poem from a sequence where Supervielle adopted the persona of one of his own fictional creations, Guanamiru, hero of the 1925 novel *L'Homme de la pampa* [*The Man of the Pampas*], an *alter ego* who possessed the larger-than-life qualities Supervielle came increasingly to feel he could do without.

To some degree, writing novels, plays and especially short stories and *contes* such as the famous 'L'Enfant de la haute mer' [The Child of the High Seas] provided an outlet for the more *fantasque* side of Supervielle's creative imagination. At any rate, his poetry in the 1930s develops a vein opened in the section of *Gravitations* which starts with these lines, dedicated to the Spanish poet Jorge Guillén:

> Suffit d'une bougie
> Pour éclairer le monde
> Autour duquel la vie
> Fait sourdement sa ronde.
> Cœur lent qui t'accoutumes
> Et tu ne sais à quoi
> Cœur grave qui résumes
> Dans le plus sûr de toi
> Des terres sans feuillage.
> Des routes sans chevaux...

[A candle is enough | To light the world | Around which life | Secretly dances its round. | Slow heart which acclimatizes you | And you don't know what to | Serious heart which gathers up | In the safest part of you | Lands without leaves | Roads without horses...]

Here the gap between microcosm and macrocosm is registered *sotto voce*. Metre, rhyme and syntax keep control. There is nothing outlandish about the juxtaposition of domestic and cosmic: it reflects a search for resonances deep in the heart. This organ is not so much the seat of the passions or feelings, as the core of the poet's sensibility, of his capacity to be affected by experience. Rather than a source of fixed identity, the poet's *cœur* engenders self-division since it points to an inner anonymity, as a later poem indicates:

> Il ne sait pas mon nom
> Ce cœur dont je suis l'hôte.
> Il ne sait rien de moi
> Que des régions sauvages.

[It does not know my name | This heart whose guest I am | It knows nothing about me | Except wild regions.]

Rilke appreciated this aspect of Supervielle, identifying it, in the letter already quoted, with the 'douce et précieuse liberté' [gentle, precious liberty] of a poem like 'Pointe de flamme' where, he comments approvingly, 'c'est comme si c'était fait par personne' [it is as though it were made by no one]. And it is the creation of a lyric voice that is at once intimate and self-effacing, close to the world but also at a distance from it (Supervielle is supremely a poet of distances) that has attracted later poets, including Jean Follain, Philippe Jaccottet and Jacques Réda, who have all written about him, and Paul Celan and Charles Tomlinson who have translated his verse.

The anonymity of the poet's *cœur* is closely linked to the mystery of the corporeal, a theme richly articulated in the three major collections from the 1930s, *Le Forçat innocent*, *Les Amis inconnus* and *La Fable du monde*, as well as in later work. Supervielle is a great poet of the body, and writes grippingly about the weird and wonderful contraptions human beings get around in. Like his friend Henri Michaux, he possessed an acute sense of the body's inner landscape, the 'lointain intérieur' [interior distance] of artery, nerve and sinew. And as with Michaux, Supervielle's particular kind of dissidence as a poet, vis-à-vis such major currents as Surrealism, is linked to the place of the body. Rejecting the Surrealist cult of the dream, Supervielle noted in his 1951 poetic credo 'En songeant à un art poétique' [While musing on an *ars poetica*]: 'Rêver, c'est oublier la matérialité de son corps' [To dream is to forget the materiality of one's body]. In his notes to the sequence in *La Fable du monde* called 'Nocturne en plein jour' [Nocturne in broad daylight], where the diurnal darkness is that of 'la profonde température de l'homme' [mankind's deep temperature] and of 'nos organes | Ces bêtes à l'abandon dans leur sanglante écurie' [our organs | Those neglected beasts in their bloody stable]. Dominique Combe suggests that the 'organic theme' in Supervielle's work should be linked to lack of religious faith, 'tout se passe comme si Supervielle substituait, à la transcendance d'un dieu par trop incertain, l'expression des profondeurs insondables du corps' [it is as if Supervielle were substituting, in place of the transcendence of a far too uncertain god, the expression of the body's unsoundable depths]. Crucial, here, is the question of identity. For Supervielle, the otherness of the body, its distance, its dissidence, is a mark of self-estrangement experienced physically, viscerally: 'Quand le flux de la nuit me coule sur les lèvres... | Comme un voyageur qui arrive de loin | Je découvre en intrus mon paysage humain' [When the tide of night flows on my lips... | Like a traveller arriving from afar | I discover, as an interloper, my human landscape]. But the experience of self-estrangement generates a sense of the wider ramifications of identity and loss of identity. In the apostrophe to the mother he never knew, from the opening poem of *Gravitations*, it is at the level of the body that the mystery of continuity is fathomed. In the magnificent 'Oloron-Sainte-Marie', dedicated to Rilke's memory just after the German poet's death, and recording a pilgrimage in 1926 to the burial place of Supervielle's parents, in the company of Michaux, the contrasts established between the quick and the dead involve searing encapsulations of the bodily existence we lead in our vertebrae, our muscles and our nerves.

If Supervielle's more speculative treatment of body and soul often has a metaphysical ring, and indeed may remind English readers of Donne or Marvell, it is also important to connect it with the way his poetry, partly because of the concision of the short line, so often seems particularly attuned to grasping fleeting sensations. 'Saisir, saisir le soir, la pomme et la statue, | Saisir l'ombre et le mur et le bout de la rue' [To seize, to seize, the evening, the apple and the statue, | To seize the shadow and the wall and the end of the street]. Such apprehension is the province of the body, of sensory receptivity, but it leads into the realm of a limited, or 'attenuated', divinity, a divinity of small things and momentary perceptions, which was the nearest Supervielle could get to God:

> O Dieu très atténué
> Des bouts de bois et des feuilles
> Dieu petit et séparé
> On le piétine comme on le cueille
> Avec les herbes des prés.

[O very attenuated God | Bits of wood and leaves | Little, separate God | One treads on him just as one gathers him up | With meadow grasses.]

In the later collections, reflections on the body have to do with decline and death. There are moving lines about ageing in the lovely 'Hommage à la vie', written in Montevideo at a time when, through such sequences as 'Poèmes de la France malheureuse', Supervielle was, like Georges Bernanos, playing a distant but significant part in the spirit of resistance. Suffering cardiac problems from a relatively early age (a fact that is obviously linked to the 'heart' motif), Supervielle often wrote about ill-health, as in 'Les Nerfs' [Nerves] — 'Vous qui rendez la chair pensante | Et raisonneuse sous la peau' [You who make flesh a thinking | Reasoning thing under the skin] — a brilliant celebration of synaptic life, dedicated to his doctor. 'Insomnie' provides the last word on this distressing condition, while his last collection, *Le Corps tragique* [The Tragic Body] (1959), a late return to form, includes a poem addressed to the poet's liver.

★ ★ ★ ★ ★

Supervielle's attentiveness to bodily process is matched by his treatment of the mechanisms of memory, and particularly the relationship between memory and forgetting. Having all Supervielle's poetry in one volume makes it easier to trace the complex shifts of attitude, from rage vented by an adolescent poet and orphan against the daily work of oblivion, to the profound meditation on the constructive work of forgetting expressed fifty years later in *Oublieuse Mémoire* [Forgetful Memory] (1949). 'L'Oubli', from *Brumes du passé* [Mists of the Past] (strange title for a sixteen-year-old) — the archetypal slim volume, published at the author's expense and unavailable since — is conventionally derivative. Yet, as the Pléiade editors point out, the denunciation of 'l'affreux oubli qui m'engloutit dans le vide' [the dreadful forgetting which engulfs me in the void] is surprisingly violent, and its most recent erasure, the features of an English girl the boy had fallen for the year before, resurfaces in one of Supervielle's last poems, 'Londres', from *Le Corps tragique*.

In the mature poetry, allusions to memory often reveal ambivalence. The temptation sedulously to conserve reminiscence against dissolution — to wrap a memory in one's arms, like a girl saved from fire, and then lay it down in 'le lit blanc de la mémoire, aux rideaux tirés' [the white bed of memory, with curtains drawn] — remains a temptation. But it is seen as contradicting the recognition that to preserve 'ce souvenir divisé [qui] se raidit contre l'oubli' [this divided memory [which] hardens itself against forgetting] may be to cut us off from ourselves, and that our ways of forgetting define us as much as our memories. 'Le Souvenir', from *Les Amis inconnus*, refers to a time when 'notre amour sera divisé par nos ombres' [our love will be divided by our shadows], while another poem from the same collection identifies the experience of self-dispersal which undermines confident assertions of personal memory:

Je me souviens — lorsque je parle ainsi
Ah saura-t-on jamais qui se souvient
Dans tout ce chaud murmurant carrefour.

[I remember — when I speak this way | Ah will we ever know who it is that
remembers | At this warm whispering crossroads]

A fine poem from *La Fable du monde* urges the new day to grant benediction to
the waking man, 'encore frissonant, | Sous la peau des ténèbres' [still shivering, |
Under the skin of shadows], who has just managed to assemble his disparate parts,
and in 'Hommage à la vie', one of the things commended is the courage to confide
the world to one's memory, 'Comme un clair cavalier à sa monture noire' [Like a
bright rider to his dark charger].

The opening sequence which gives its title to *Oublieuse Mémoire*, and to Maurice
Blanchot's meditation on these poems in the *Nouvelle Revue Française*'s 1960
commemorative volume to Supervielle, explicitly addresses the potentially creative
role of forgetting in the activity of memory. In an interview, Supervielle associated this with the creative process itself. 'Il y a quelque chose de commun entre
la composition poétique et cet espèce de tâtonnement intérieur provoqué par la
présence de l'oubli. La mémoire et l'oubli sont inséparables' [There is something
in common between poetic composition and this sort of internal groping around
which is provoked by the presence of forgetting. Memory and forgetting are insep-
arable]. These poems insist as strongly as ever on what forgetting makes us lose, yet
the emphasis is less on annihilation than on transformation, and on the connections
between the two. Memory may embalm the past, but forgetting preserves the future:
'Que modèlent mes jours ta lumière et tes mains | Refais par-dessus moi les voies
du lendemain' [May your light and your hands model my days | Remake above
me tomorrow's paths]. Forgetting may wield its deadly eraser, 'sa belle gomme à
tuer', and in cahoots with silence it may lay waste what we had cherished, appearing
wholly destructive. 'Avec tant d'oubli comment faire une rose' [How to make a
rose with so much forgetting]. Nevertheless, memory and silence, those 'doucereux
étouffeurs d'amour' [sickly-sweet smotherers of love], sponsor the constant making
and unmaking of self and world:

> Et que dans l'ombre enfin notre mémoire joue
> Nous redonnant le monde aux actives couleurs
> Le chêne redevient arbre et les ombres, plaine,
> Et voici donc ce lac sous nos yeux agrandis.

[And let our memory finally play in the shadow | Giving back to us the world
of active colours | The oak once more becomes a tree and the shadows plains,
| And here then is this lake, beneath our widened eyes.]

In an abandoned 'prière d'insérer' [blurb], published here for the first time,
Supervielle noted that 'l'oubli, ce créateur à rebours, ne cesse de travailler en
silence. N'est-il pas l'ange qui veille sur la libre circulation de nos images et fait
le choix entre celles qui nous conviennent et les autres. Sa présence est constante
dans l'obscur de nous-mêmes où rien n'égale la délicatesse de ses procédés, la
discrétion de ses coups de gomme' [forgetting, this creator in reverse, never stops
its silent work. Is it not that angel which watches over the free circulation of our
images and chooses between those we accept and the others. Its presence is constant
in the darkness of ourselves, where there is nothing to equal the delicacy of its

methods, the discretion with which it applies its eraser]. Forgetting is more than a good editor. As Blanchot stresses, *Oublieuse Mémoire* points to a form of mediation that maintains links not with what we once knew but with what, perennially but obscurely, we are:

> O Dame de la profondeur
> Que faites-vous à la surface...
> O Dame de mes eaux profondes
> Serais-je donc si près des ombres
> Ou venez-vous m'aider à vivre
> De tout votre frêle équilibre?

[O Lady of depth | What are you doing at the surface... O Lady of my deep waters | Am I thus so close to the shadows | Or do you come to help me live | With all your frail equilibrium?]

The thrill of rediscovering Jules Supervielle through this collected edition is due not so much to new material as access to the totality of his *oeuvre*, including earlier manuscript states. Undermined though it is by a further reduction in the font size of the Pléiade collection's critical apparatus, the common commitment of Michel Collot's editorial team to the tenets of *la critique génétique* [genetic criticism] ensures that the treatment of successive drafts is admirably clear, comprehensive and conducive to an understanding of the poet's creative process and progress. What is underlined again and again is Supervielle's gift for simplicity, the unerring purity of diction that enables him to convey complex ideas and feelings through the most ordinary words and expressions. We are made privy to an unassuming artistry which, as a poet who learnt much from Supervielle, Philippe Jaccottet, once put it, 'maintient l'ouverture sur l'insaisissable' [maintains an opening onto the ungraspable]. Not, finally, the elusiveness of the cosmos, but, as in Rilke or in Beckett, the strangeness of who, where, when and what we are.

# 26

# On the Road to Reality

*Review of Yves Bonnefoy,* The Arrière-pays, *trans. by Stephen Romer*
*(London and New York: Seagull Books, 2012)*

Yves Bonnefoy turned ninety on 24 June 2013, and we can at last enjoy a magnificent English translation of his crucial prose work, *L'Arrière-pays*, dating from 1972 when the poet was approaching fifty. The translation is the work of another poet, Stephen Romer, and the publication owes its existence to Naveen Kishore and the Indian imprint Seagull Books, who were willing to ensure that the book's essential visual dimension was fully respected and integrated with the text.

*L'Arrière-pays* originally appeared with the Swiss published Skira in the remarkable collection Les Sentiers de la création. At the invitation of the critic Gaëtan Picon, artists and writers were invited to provide insights into their own creative process by combining a written text with extensive visual material, the formatting and design of the volumes often encouraging arresting page spreads that married the verbal and the pictorial. In a few years a constellation of French creators, including Francis Ponge, René Char, Claude Lévi-Strauss, Roland Barthes, Claude Simon and Michel Butor, responded to the call. *The Arrière-pays* (the French expression has been retained with the author's approval, for want of an adequate English equivalent) is an unclassifiable combination of autobiographical self-questioning, travel narrative and metaphysical rumination. But it is also a picture book, and the numerous reproductions of Renaissance, Baroque, and some modern paintings, as well as photographs of sites, monuments and landscapes, are not simply illustrative, but the work's very core.

Starting out from the opening declaration: 'I have often experienced a feeling of anxiety, at crossroads', the essay's five chapters, accompanied by forty or so illustrations, weave together recollections of particular places — in Italy and Greece, but also India and Japan — and memories of artistic or literary works that seem imbued with a similar atmosphere and promise. The latter include paintings by Poussin, Botticelli, Degas, Mondrian and many others, but also travel guides, travel narratives such as Alexandra David-Néel's book on Tibet, and fictional works, including a story called 'The Red Sands', which Bonnefoy had read as a child, in which a twentieth-century explorer in the Gobi desert stumbles on an outpost of the Roman Empire that had survived in isolation for nearly two millennia. Progressively, *L'Arrière-pays* moves from the origins and lineaments of the writer's obsession with elsewheres to the stratagems he devised to free himself from their grip, including a botched attempt at a novel, called 'The Traveller', which was supposed to purge his fantasies and restore a secure sense of reality. In the end, Bonnefoy suggests, it was the discovery that poetry could consist in the questioning of the self through language that helped him 'to tear the real away from the eddies of memory, the illusions of desire'.

*L'Arrière-pays* anatomizes an illusion to which images are especially germane. For Bonnefoy, the evidence that sustains the dogged belief that just along the path not taken, or yonder in the unreachable distance, lies a territory attesting to a higher estate, and a sense of being that is imbued with true presence, is often to be found in earlier artists or architects whose works betray signs of the same obsession. In its fervour and high-flown abstraction, as well as in its poetic density and allusiveness, Bonnefoy's prose style in *L'Arrière-pays* sets a challenge that Romer's translation meets with resounding success. The five chapters retrace phases in Bonnefoy's struggle to free himself from this obsessive dream or reverie, which he refers to as his 'Gnostic' belief in an elsewhere, while the narration keeps relaunching the reverie, as images and memories that stirred and sustained it are concretized in the work's visual aspect. (In a preface to this translation Bonnefoy makes a telling comparison with the mixture of text and photographs in André Breton's *Nadja* and *L'Amour fou*; a more recent reference point might be W. G. Sebald's topographical narratives, especially *The Rings of Saturn*.) The repeated pattern of dream and awakening, recantation and relapse, leads progressively to a realization which will be central to all Bonnefoy's subsequent writing: that the Gnostic temptation and the erring of the imagination are not wholly to be censured, but understood as part of a dialectic that leads to a true engagement with sublunary existence and concrete reality. The detour via the unreal or the inaccessible can lead back towards presence.

If he is sometimes intensely self-critical, Bonnefoy can also be generous towards his childhood and youthful selves. The memory of male chanting intercepted as the schoolboy turned the shortwave dial on a radio is linked to one of *The Arrière-pays*'s most haunting territories, that of Central Asia, a rocky landscape of stones and grasses whose nomadic populations seem to live more intensely or absolutely than we do. This is a cliché perhaps, but it is easy to see how it could reorientate a child's perceptions and inspire a quest for higher things. In the central chapter, on the place of Italy in the poet's reveries, the invention of perspective, and its deployment in painting from Uccello to Giorgio de Chirico, and in the architecture of Bernini or Alberti, is seen ambivalently as both a harbinger of illusions that 'flattered my Gnostic tendencies' and a device that could enable the image to stake out 'the precise and living space of man'. Evoking his journeys in southern Tuscany and the Marche, and the abandoned fictions in which he had tried to capture these experiences, Bonnefoy portrays himself as a traveller who fired himself up by 'flicking through my *Pistes Sophia*: back numbers of the *Burlington Magazine*, where the photographs are smaller and greyer', and then pressed on from one artwork or vista to the next, mistaking the shadow for the substance: 'these specious hopes clothed the most ordinary predella in the light of enigma'. But he also recognizes that ultimately 'Florence had been for him the wounded, wise and mindful teacher that he needed... she showed him... that it is possible to love images, even if one recognizes non-being in each of them [for] they enable a potential deepening of the self and a recognition of its destiny'. Romer's translation captures the noble elevation of Bonnefoy's tone while at the same time respecting its fervent antiquarian quirkiness. The windings of desire-driven fantasy (Bonnefoy shows that he is well aware of the unconscious shaping of his reveries) are rendered with great sensitivity.

In addition to the 1972 text the Seagull edition provides valuable additional material, including a fine introduction where Romer casts light on 'the paradox and perplexity at the heart of the book' by contrasting Bonnefoy's enduring struggle with Stéphane Mallarmé's severance of word from thing with his affection for the Yeats 'who finally declares himself for the world of flesh and blood'. Romer also includes, at the author's suggestion, translations of three recent 'Returns to the *arrière-pays*'. The focus in the first, written as the introduction to the 2004 Italian edition, is the existential ambivalence of perspective: while it can pander to the dream of a world elsewhere, Uccello's *dolce prospettiva* may also promote, as early as Alberti's 'geometrizing of space', 'a here which has about it no vestiges of illusion'. The other two, 'The place of grasses' and 'My memories of Armenia', collected as a short book in 2010, offer fascinating reassessments, in the light of Bonnefoy's mature poetics, of the sense of place at the heart of *L'Arrière-pays*. If the 'place of grasses is a mental image — of ancient stone walls and a stretch of tall wild grass — it is not linked to an elsewhere but to an intense experience of the here and now, a preconceptual sense of presence, rooted in childhood, that resists the triumph of the adult ego's analytic gaze over subjective vision. Experiences of place are now aligned with Bonnefoy's sense of the poetic project as the 'search within language for the great forgotten referents that exist beneath the seething mass of signifiers'. The doubts and anxieties that permeate *L'Arrière-pays* are concomitant with poetic writing as a struggle to remember presence and to affirm meaning 'at the moment when meaning falls away'. In the second piece Bonnefoy revisits 'the lure of images' by recalling déjà-vu experiences occasioned by photographs of Armenian churches in old books of architectural history. These were pseudo-memories (he has never visited or studied Armenia) induced, Bonnefoy speculates, by the propensity of low-resolution black-and-white images, on poor paper, to create a *'cosa mentale*, an experience of the mind, at the heart of which aspirations of a metaphysical nature begin to stir'. There is therefore no reason to repudiate them: if poetry, for Bonnefoy, serves to dismantle 'more or less chimerical presentations', the images from which it starts out are its life-blood. This is no doubt the enduring lesson of *The Arrière-pays*.

# 27

# L'Habitant de Grignan

*Review of Philippe Jaccottet, Œuvres,*
*ed. by José-Flore Tappy and others (Paris: Gallimard, 2014)*

Take the TGV from Paris to Montélimar, a local bus or two, and you could find yourself in an earthly paradise, albeit one where mortality is an abiding presence, along with a sense of the incapacity to capture in words the beauty that death and loss always seem to threaten. If you followed these steps you would be retracing the path of Philippe Jaccottet, the Swiss-French poet of Vaudois Protestant heritage. In 1953, aged twenty-eight (he will soon be ninety), after some years in Paris, Jaccottet came with his wife Anne-Marie, an artist, to live in Grignan in the Drôme. He has lived there ever since, translating for a living, bringing up children, walking and reconnoitring in the low mountains of northern Provence, keeping an eye on the changing vista of the Mont Ventoux to the south, building a reputation as an immensely subtle critic and observer, and above all writing poetry and prose directly inspired by the same territory. One might want to say that he has made this territory his own, were ideas of possession and selfhood not both wide of the mark. Jaccottet has always tried to impinge as little as possible on the landscape he immerses himself in every day, cherishing it less for its particularity than for its generic or essential qualities. As his attention moves, from the darting flight of swifts, to colours, trees, the language of flowers, the interplay of far and near, streams, tracks, echoes of other landscapes, his aim is to celebrate all that such phenomena have to offer, independently of any individual psychology, and as a bulwark against a rising tide of senselessness.

The selection of 'Œuvres' in this Pléiade volume was made by Jaccottet himself and comprises all his poetry (two early collections are relegated to a section of appendices), including his volumes of poetic prose and the superb cross-over volumes, where verse and prose are in dialogue, that are now central to his achievement. It also features all the volumes, covering the years 1954–98, of his magnificent poetic journal or commonplace book, sometimes published as *Journées* [Days] or *Carnets* [Notebooks], but here referred to by the generic title *La Semaison*, under the aegis of the definition of this word in Littré's Dictionary, which Jaccottet repeatedly uses as an epigraph: 'Dispersion naturelle des graines d'une plante' [Natural dispersion of a plant's seeds]. Included as well are his only narrative work, *L'Obscurité* (1961), a dark *récit*, reminiscent of Maurice Blanchot and Louis-René Des Forêts, recording an existential crisis; *Libretto*, a book on Italy; and a meditation on the painter Giorgio Morandi. The coverage therefore excludes Jaccottet's critical writings, which run to a dozen or so volumes, and include collections of essays on poets and poetics, notably *L'Entretien des muses* [The Muses' Conversation] and *Une Transaction secrète* [A Secret Transaction], monographs on Rilke and on the Swiss-French writer Gustave Roud, and numerous pieces in the *Nouvelle Revue Française* and various Swiss publications, as well as works relating to travels in Austria, Egypt, Spain and the Middle East.

The editorial work, entrusted predominantly to writers closely connected with the author rather than to academics, is of an exceptionally high standard. The author of the preface, Fabio Pusterla, is an Italian poet and the translator of several volumes of Jaccottet's poetry. José-Flore Tappy and Jean-Marc Sourdillon are also poets, Suisse Romande and French respectively, while Doris Jakubec is a professor of Swiss French studies at Jaccottet's alma mater, the University of Lausanne, and Hervé Ferrage, who works in cultural diplomacy, is the author of a fine book on the poet. Works are presented in strictly chronological order, and the editorial 'Notices' draw illuminatingly on the Jaccottet archive at Lausanne, which holds extensive draft material for most of his writings. Textual variants are only recorded in exceptional cases, but there are valuable accounts of the genesis of each Jaccottet volume, and transcriptions of notes on the writing process recorded in the margins of manuscripts and typescripts. A forty-page chronology, prepared by Tappy in collaboration with the author, offers an invaluable account of Jaccottet's life, with new information about his friendships, travels and translation work.

Many French writers will have encountered Jaccottet in his guise as the translator of Homer, Giacomo Leopardi and Giuseppe Ungaretti. It is, however, as a translator of German literature that he is best known. His version of *Death in Venice*, done when he was twenty-five, was admired by Thomas Mann, and Jaccottet subsequently went on to translate, over a thirty-year period, *The Man without Qualities* and most of Robert Musil's other novels, plays, essays and letters. Over the years he has translated much of Hölderlin and Rilke, but also Góngora and Osip Mandelstam. *La Semaison* conveys the impact of these encounters, while the Pléiade editors help us to detect how their presence underlies particular poems or sequences. A striking instance is the encounter with R. H. Blyth's English translations of Haiku which played a large part in inspiring the minimalist aesthetic of Jaccottet's 1961 collection *Airs* [Tunes]. Blyth's remark that 'Haiku are self-obliterating', noted in *La Semaison* in 1960, will strike a chord in any reader of Jaccottet.

If Jaccottet is a great poet of self-effacement, he knows that this stance can be productive. There is no affectation in casting himself as 'L'ignorant', the title of his second collection (1958) where, in an eponymous poem, he famously urged that 'l'effacement soit ma façon de resplendir' [let self-effacement be my way of shining forth]; nor is he posturing when he portrays himself, when relatively young, as a 'poète tardif' [late poet] trammelled with age: self-irony and wry humour are central to the willed anonymity of his persona as 'L'Habitant de Grignan'. This is the title of one of the texts that make up *La Promenade sous les arbres* [Wandering beneath the Trees] (1957), Jaccottet's first work of prose meditation on language, poetic truth and landscape. Surprisingly, it is indebted to a mystical treatise, *The Candle of Vision* (1918), by W. B. Yeats's friend, AE (George Russell), which was published in translation by the *Cahiers du Sud* in 1952 and greeted with enthusiasm by Georges Bataille. What impressed Jaccottet in AE's account of his visions was the simplicity with which an ordinary man reported on extraordinary experiences. Having tried for some years, under the forbidding auspices of Hölderlin, Novalis and Rilke, to give voice to the feeling of a connection between certain moments of heightened experience and his desire to write poems, Jaccottet found in AR's writing a model to follow in the broaching of these issues even if, as he makes clear, he could never share the Irish visionary's certainties.

Like the narrative of *L'Obscurité*, *Éléments d'un songe*, Jaccottet's second volume of poetic prose texts, also published in 1961, relates to a personal crisis. Here the currents of tormented self-questioning, and the sense of having lost one's way, are interwoven with reflections on *The Man Without Qualities*, and create a dialogue with the second part of Musil's novel, where Ulrich dreams of acceding to 'Der andere Zustand' ('l'autre état' [the other state] in Jaccottet's French), a mystical state inspired by Ulrich's reading of Meister Eckhart. The beautiful poems of *Airs* (1967), written in the aftermath of this crisis, and of the discovery of Haiku, are closely related to the annotations of things seen in *La Semaison*, and underline motifs that will remain central: air, distance, purity, lightness, colours, voice, times of day. The exquisite 'Fin d'hiver' [Winter's end], which opens the first sequence, sounds a note that will be sustained throughout.

> Peu de chose, rien qui chasse
> l'effroi de perdre l'espace
> est laissé à l'âme errante
> Mais peut-être, plus légère,
> incertaine qu'elle dure,
> est-elle celle qui chante
> avec la voix la plus pure
> les distances de la terre

[Hardly a thing, nothing to chase | the fear of losing space | is left to the wandering soul | But perhaps, being so light, | and unsure it can last, | it's his voice that can sing | in the purest of ways | the distances of the earth]

Jaccottet's next two collections of verse are works of mourning. *Leçons* (1969) — 'les humbles, terribles et très hautes Leçons de Jaccottet' [Jaccottet's humble, fearful, elevated Lessons], as his fellow poet Jacques Réda called them in one of his own poems — traces the phases of his father-in-law's final illness and death, while the background of *Chants d'en bas* [Songs from Down Below] (1974), poems often painfully sardonic in their denunciation of the false claims of poetic remedy, is haunted by the deaths of Paul Celan, Ungaretti and Jean Follain, as well as people close to him. A third sequence of poems, 'À la lumière d'hiver' [To the winter light] (1977), marked by the death of the poet's mother, is added to these two collections in 1977, creating a new unity but also marking a passage from darkness to light, conveyed magnificently in a poem inspired by walking out into a garden at night:

Aide-moi maintenant, air noir et frais, cristal
noir. Les légères feuilles bougent à peine,
comme pensées d'enfants endormis. Je traverse
la distance transparente, et c'est le temps
même qui marche ainsi dans ce jardin,
comme il marche plus haut de toit en toit, d'étoile
en étoile, c'est la nuit même qui passe
[...]
(Chose brève, le temps de quelques pas dehors,
mais plus étrange encore que les mages et les dieux.)

[Help me now, air so dark and cool, dark | crystal, The weightless leaves are scarcely moving | like thoughts of sleeping children. I cross | the transparent distance, and it's time | itself that seems to walk in this garden, | just as higher up it steps from roof to roof, from star | to star, it's the night itself that is passing | [...] | (A brief thing, just a few steps outside, | but stranger than the mages and the gods.)]

In 'À la lumière d'hiver', as Jaccottet explained in an important note included in *Une Transaction secrète*, the image of night leads into motifs of sound and silence inspired by listening to a Mozart quintet (K 516), and then a sudden desire to see the landscape enveloped in a protective coating of snow. After the temptation in *Airs* of a 'poésie sans images', the sequence as a whole marks a renewed acceptance of image-laden poetic reverie, even when it leads beyond the visible, and a more open-ended and discursive style, though one always animated by a will to contest the images it spawns, and to remain rooted in patient receptiveness and attention to 'le plus proche' [what is closest]. This is the path pursued in the prose works that will come to predominate from the mid-1970s.

Already, most of the 'proses' (a term Jaccottet prefers to 'poèmes en prose') in *Paysages avec figures absentes* [Landscape with Absent Figures] (1970) differed markedly from the earlier ones in *La Promenade sous les arbres* and *Éléments d'un songe* in being inspired by a desire to explore the ramifications of a real event, usually something seen while out walking, for example a meadow of poppies, a brimming cornfield or a flooded dell, and proceed by welcoming and then sifting and often censuring, as inadequate or unhelpful, the diverse thoughts, words and images that come to mind in the effort to capture what had arrested him in the scene. As he notes at the outset, writing, while seeking maximum precision rather than trying to pin things down analytically, must be true to what is fleeting and ungraspable in these occasions, to 'ce qui, en elles, se dérobe' [what withholds itself in them]: 'J'ai pu seulement marcher, et marcher encore, me souvenir, entrevoir, oublier, insister, redécouvrir, me perdre. Je ne me suis pas penché sur le sol comme l'entomologiste ou le géologue: je n'ai fait que passer, accueillir' [All I've been able to do is walk, and walk again, remember, glimpse, forget, persevere, rediscover, lose myself. I haven't scrutinized the ground like an entomologist or a geologist: all I've done is pass by, and greet]. As Sourdillon remarks, these open-ended 'proses-poursuites', on average a dozen or so pages in length, pick up from the *Sprechgesang* or 'poésie-discours' of 'À la lumière d'hiver' and lead into an immensely fruitful experimentation with ways of combining poetic and prosaic registers. In the splendid 'Travaux au lieu dit l'Étang' [Works in the place called the Pond], what strikes the poet-observer most forcefully when coming upon a valley swamped with water, a recurrent event as the local place name implies, but still surprising, is a line of white spray on the far side, as the wind makes the water ripple against the reeds: 'c'est une autre inscription fugitive sur la page de la terre, qu'il faut saisir, que l'on voudrait comprendre [...]. Alors on regarde et on rêve [...]. Et me voilà tâtonnant à nouveau, trébuchant, accueillant les images pour les écarter ensuite' [It's another fleeting inscription on the earth's page, which you must seize, which you would like to understand [...]. And so you look and you dream [...]. And then off you go, groping your way forwards again, stumbling, welcoming images then rejecting them further on]. Images of silken garments, petals or feathers, via memories of a poem by Góngora, or of glasshouses and rapids, are not only mulled over but assayed in fragments of verse, in a manner that reflects Jaccottet's fruitful exchanges with Francis Ponge, a poet in many respects very different from him, as both parties acknowledged.

In the mid-1970s, in À travers un Verger [Through an Orchard], Beauregard and Les Cormorans [The Cormorants], all published as separate short volumes before being collected together in 1984, 'proses-poursuites', now about thirty pages in length (although Beauregard combines three interconnected pieces), become central. As a rule, the guiding thread is the way the inadequacy of an initial response, for example to the 'émerveillement' provoked by an almond orchard in blossom, may be countered by a more oblique and circuitous journey through thoughts, words and images. The aim is to get to the bottom of why, for example, in connection with the orchard, images of a snowstorm come to mind, an enquiry that ranges across a wealth of cultural allusion, as well as acoustic and emotional memory. There are bouts of often harsh self-criticism, when the poet-narrator feels that poetic facility leads him away from reality rather than closer to it, and exhortations to look harder, think better and find more suitable words. The poem-essay is primarily an account of a mental journey, an accelerated running commentary on the phases of an enquiry that may have occupied a considerable period. The prose is subtly rhythmical without being incantatory, and musical not only at the level of sound, but also in the attention to pacing and stress.

The Pléiade's strict chronology helps us to see that in the lovely poems of Pensées sous les nuages [Thoughts under the Clouds] (1983), Jaccottet's last collection of poetry tout court, he applied the spirit of the 'proses-poursuites' to sequences of poems around a theme or a person, rather than a natural phenomenon, with the prose scaffolding largely stripped away, although 'Le mot "Joie"' [The word 'joy'] starts with an italicized introduction recounting the starting point for the attempt to explore, 'sans avoir peur de laisser agir le levain de la métamorphose' [without fear of allowing the yeast of metamorphosis to work], a moment when the word 'joie' hit him with a strange force. The poems of 'On voit' [You see] note things glimpsed in the human world of Grignan, including children skeltering in the grassy playground, protected, 'comme une fraîche cascade' [like a cool waterfall], by the tall trees and the light of a September morning, from 'l'énorme enclume

| qui étincelle d'étoiles par-delà' [the enormous anvil | shining with stars on the other side], the anvil compressing images of deathliness, remoteness and beauty. As Derek Mahon remarked in the introduction to his fine volume of Jaccottet translations (1988), where he called him 'one of the finest European poets of the [twentieth] century', Jaccottet's 'existential lyrics' also give us 'intellectual music', for example in the beautiful sequence which he addressed to Henry Purcell, after hearing a performance by the counter-tenor James Bowman. Here cosmic and pastoral images interweave, and the changing mode of address culminates in a use of the familiar 'tu' to pay fraternal homage to the miracle of an artistry where the creator is both absent and present, and where the earthbound and the transcendent perpetually mingle:

> Tu es assis
> Devant le métier haut dressé de cette harpe.
>
> Même invisible, je t'ai reconnu,
> Tisserand des ruisseaux surnaturels.

[You sit | by the stately loom of the harp. || I recognized you, even though you're invisible, | Weaver of supernatural streams.]

It is with *Cahier de verdure* [The Notebook of Green], in 1990, that Jaccottet takes the next step and composes a volume based on a carefully crafted combination of 'proses' (now of the shorter ten-page variety as a rule), poems and notations in the idiom of the briefer entries in *La Semaison*. *Après beaucoup d'années* [After Many Years] (1994) and *Et, néanmoins* [And, Nonetheless] (2001) will then repeat this pattern, with variations. Some of Jaccottet's finest work is here, in all the modes he has made his own, from the honouring of occasions to the remembering of the dead. Two established features find greater prominence. One is the use of spacing and the placing of the words on the page. The other is a tendency for colour vocabulary to play a large part in the poet's investigations. One way of hanging on to the experience of moonlight, a quince orchard, or a bonfire, as word are rallied to the action of recall, celebration and speculation, is to keep asking what colour it was, what nuance of green or brown or red, was involved. 'Que pouvait être ce rouge pour me surprendre, me réjouir à ce point?' [What could this red be to so surprise me, to so fill me with joy?] Jaccottet wonders, recalling a cherry tree laden with fruit, chanced upon when evening light was shining through the cherries. 'Comme une flamme dans une veilleuse de verre? Une grappe de feu apprivoisé, mariée à de l'eau nocturne, à de la nuit en formation, imminente mais pas encore advenue?' [Like the flame of a night-lamp? A rich cluster of tamed fire, fused with nocturnal waters, with night itself in the making, imminent but still in abeyance?].

The spate of questions and answers, through which Philippe Jaccottet homes in on something seen in passing, shows how questions about colour can now propel his poetic quest, as he goes on into old age still finding new ways of fathoming his surroundings.

# 28

# Apollinaire and the Livre de Peintre

*Review of Anne Hyde Greet,* Apollinaire et le Livre de Peintre
*(Paris: Minard, 1977)*

Professor Greet has no hesitation in singling out *Le Bestiaire au cortège d'Orphée,* on which Apollinaire collaborated with Dufy, as the most rewarding 'livre de peintre' inspired by the poet's work. She dismisses Derain's illustrations for *L'Enchanteur pourrissant* in a few sentences and then devotes a short chapter each to Chirico's versions of *Calligrammes* and the unpublished set of illustrations for *Alcools* on which Marcoussis laboured for twenty years. Chirico's lithographs, she argues, seem responsive only to those features of Apollinaire's verse which connect with his own obsessions: melancholy, regret, nostalgia, mystery; the humour, gaiety and poetic exaltation of *Calligrammes* are missing. Chagall might have been more suited to the task, while Reverdy could have been a better choice for Chirico. Marcoussis was more successful. His monochrome etchings, which aptly combine cubist fragmentation with surrealist visual punning, focus on local details sometimes initially identified in watercolours executed on a copy of *Alcools.* But Greet feels that Marcoussis surrendered too much of his creative autonomy in his fidelity to the poetry so that the 'livre de peintre' tends to yield to its arch-enemy the 'livre illustré'.

Professor Greet argues that insufficient attention has been paid to the links between Le Bestiaire and the emblem-book tradition. Previous critics, well aware of Apollinaire's erudition in this field, have nevertheless felt the connexion to be superficial. But this is because they have tended to focus exclusively on the whimsical, sometimes haunting, poems whereas, for Greet, 'C'est surtout le rapport entre texte et image qui crée le lien entre Apollinaire et les emblématistes' (p. 67). If the prominence of the figure of Orpheus, to whom are devoted the book's sub-title, four poems and woodcuts, and a passage in the poet's wonderfully idiosyncratic notes (Eliot achieved a similar tone when he half-jestingly annotated *The Waste Land*) indicates a concern with the activity of creation that earlier emblem-makers would not have shared, this is no reason to deny the features Apollinaire and Dufy have in common with them. To explore these, Greet discusses at length the different kinds of emblem-book and various features of the traditions with which poet and artist were able to play on an equal footing, this being the clue to the success of Le Bestiaire. Most of Dufy's woodcuts went through various versions, and the evolution of the final product is analysed in detail. Professor Greet is good at identifying pithily the salient features of an illustration and she has been well served by the publishers who have ensured that most of the eighty-one illustrations (including several from Renaissance bestiaries) are on the same spread as the text which refers to them. To a large extent this book constitutes a critical edition of Le Bestiaire and as such it is to be welcomed.

# 29

# Six French Poets of our Time

*Review of Robert W. Greene,* Six French Poets of our Time: A Critical and Historical Study *(Princeton, NJ: Princeton University Press, 1979)*

How useful is it, within the field of modern poetry, to make a distinction between the poet for whom language is a means and the poet for whom it is an end in itself? It is certainly possible to give some substance to these notions: the poet as magus versus the 'scripteur', 'poetry as a quasi-religious or Gnostic quest' versus 'a radical contextualist stance [...] the rejection of referentiality', the 'splintered self' versus the 'absent self'. By the end of this book these oppositions are old friends. But are they good friends? Professor Greene raises this question in acute form because he uses the distinction not simply as a theme to focus discussion but as a means of establishing two distinct families of poet. Making Reverdy the paradigm of the 'Orphic, means-oriented' poet neither adds to nor detracts from the solid, useful essay on this poet, but it does have regrettable consequences for the discussion of those poets who are seen as continuing this trend. Too often the account of Char, Du Bouchet, or Dupin is made to depend on a conceptual framework designed essentially for Reverdy: a mixture of cubism, surrealism, existentialism, and phenomenology which does not give much grip on the ontological dimension of the later poetry, although specific poems and images often receive sufficient individual attention to compensate for this to some extent. To make Ponge the paradigm of the 'end-oriented' poet is even more hazardous as it involves some distortion of the poet's own work. Professor Greene gives us, in effect, the Ponge lionized by *Tel Quel* in the sixties but back-dated so as to follow Reverdy and precede Char. Ponge the 'scripteur' all but eclipses the poet who considers himself 'l'ambassadeur du monde muet' [the ambassador of the mute world], and Greene has a strong tendency, mitigated by good readings of 'Fable' and 'Le Pré', to reduce Ponge to what he may have in common with Marcelin Pleynet. (Greene's superficial and lukewarm essay on Pleynet failed to convince me that he is of much interest as a poet.)

Curiously, Professor Greene makes no effort to extend his two families; there is no mention of Denis Roche, who might have given more substance to the end-oriented school, or of Bonnefoy, whose essays, idiosyncratic as they are, provide an essential background to the generation to which Du Bouchet and Dupin belong. This is surprising, given the emphasis Greene places on the literary-historical aspect of his enterprise. He constantly draws the reader's attention to circumstantial affiliations: allegiance to surrealism, enthusiasm for particular painters, relation to journals such as *L'Ephémère* or *Tel Quel.* This leads to some interesting pages, but they are undermined by the reluctance to go beyond the six chosen poets. However, if Greene's attempt to make the means-end distinction the basis of an historical, pigeon-holing approach fails to convince, I suspect that it is because all the poets discussed are haunted to some degree by the very problem the distinction poses. Only the essay on Dupin considers the issue in this fashion. If, despite these shortcomings, this book is a useful contribution to its field, it is because Professor Greene is a very good practical critic. Each chapter includes readings of individual poems that are subtle, concise, and alive with memorable formulations.

# 30

# Péret and the Poetry of Change

*Review of Julia Field Costich,* The Poetry of Change: A Study of the Surrealist Works of Benjamin Péret *(Chapel Hill: University of North Carolina Press, 1979)*

'Surrealism is completely and fully realized in the works of Benjamin Péret'. Connoisseurs of surrealism will be familiar with this sort of claim but may be surprised at the radicalism of this particular formulation. It is one thing to argue that the surrealist flame burns with incomparable intensity at certain moments in Péret's poetry, quite another to assert that his work supremely encompasses the whole movement. Earlier critics (Bédouin, Courtot, Bailly, Matthews), however prone to hagiography, have on the whole taken the first line. In the present study (which seems to have been completed in 1973) the claims made for Péret at the outset, and intermittently throughout, are never seriously substantiated. In fact Professor Costich makes little use of surrealist theory or any other frame of reference, and bases her survey of Péret's works (excluding his political writings which are not even listed in the otherwise useful and detailed bibliography) on a single notion, that of change. The approach is, in a very loose sense, thematic. The first chapter (of four) identifies motifs relating to change in Péret's Dada and early surrealist collections. Chapter 2, entitled 'Desire as the Force of Change', has sections on Péret's conception of 'l'amour sublime' and the poems of *Je sublime* which embody it most thoroughly; on the longer, later, poems, inspired by Péret's experience of Mexico, and on the poetry of invective and revolt exemplified by *Je ne mange pas de ce pain-là*. In Chapter 3, 'Re-inventing the World', Professor Costich offers an account of *Histoire naturelle* (1958), and then, under the headings 'Food and Play' and 'The Syntax of Dream', she gathers together a number of threads in Péret's writing. It is, for example, in these sections that Péret's use of language receives most attention, though somewhat unsatisfactorily. There are some remarks on wordplay and on recurrent stylistic features such as the long 'chains of subordination' common in Péret's poetry, there is an extended comparison between the 'syntax of events' in the poems and tales and the structure of dreams, but nowhere is there any real discussion of Péret's texts in terms of the linguistic processes which they manifest so admirably. Yet, what is quintessentially Péret, and quintessentially surrealist for that matter, is surely the wonderful prosperity he bestows on words. The 'New Myth of Change' that Professor Costich summarizes in a short final chapter has few claims on our attention apart from the textual performances which constitute it. Professor Costich sacrifices too much of the fascinating detail of Péret's poetry to her all-embracing theme: individual poems or stories never receive extensive analysis in their own right. To place too much stress on the unity of Péret's poetic career, and thus to play down the radical differences between a typical poem from *Le Grand Jeu* and a later work such as *Air Mexicain*, is a mistake. At worst, it is to risk portraying Péret as the ideologue he constantly tried not to be. At best, it tends to emphasize the less interesting things about Péret's poetry — the narrowness of range and the monotony of ostensible 'theme' which betray the fact that, like most surrealists, Péret was, *malgré tout*, an ideologue — at the expense of the heterogeneous play of language which keeps his best work more mobile than Professor Costich's myth of change allows.

# 31

# Reverdy's Horizons

*Review of Michel Collot,* Horizon de Reverdy
*(Paris: Presses de L'École Normale Supérieure, 1981)*

Michel Collot invites us to stare hard at the mysterious horizon that features with such obsessive frequency in the couple of thousand poems Reverdy wrote, through thick and thin, between 1915 and 1960. Setting his sights on what the poetry repeatedly skirts, flirts with, or hedges its bets on, Collot trains but also, perhaps inevitably, strains the reader's eye; while it is good to be led deeper than usual into the spiritual texture of Reverdy's writing, it is a pity that here we encounter his poetry only in the small bits and pieces preferred by the thematic critic. Collot admits to taking his critical cues from Charles Mauron and Jean-Pierre Richard, but while it is probably fair to say that he lacks both Mauron's informed zeal for psychoanalytical demonstration, and the virtuosity which makes Richard's thematic *bricolage* so stimulating, he is less inclined to be abstract than the latter and less obtrusively concerned with nosological and methodological questions than the former, and this is all to the good.

We begin, canonically enough, with the Father — or, more precisely, with recurring allusions to the setting sun, to the figure of Christ, to the literal and metaphorical death of the poet's father, which link up to form a pattern that can be envisaged as a 'récit mythique' [mythic tale] told and retold, destroyed and reassembled, in poem after poem. Next on the horizon is death, 'le seuil d'un autre monde, qui pourra se révéler au-delà ou néant, selon une hésitation propre à la démarche métaphysique de Reverdy' [the threshold of another world, which could reveal itself to be the beyond or total negativity, in accordance with a hesitation that is a central part of Reverdy's metaphysical approach]. With a sure hand, Collot traces the equivocal lexicon ('passage', 'ombre', 'ciel', 'escalier', 'carrefour' [passage, shadow, sky, stair, crossroads]), and teases out the deeply paradoxical figures which constitute 'la representation reverdyenne de la mort' [the Reverdian representation of death]. We end with the Mother: darkness, twilight, sea, and stars. There is the usual twist: Reverdy's images of dawn, for example, tend always to stress deliverance from the threat of 'le règne nocturne de l'indifférenciation' [the nocturnal kingdom of indifferentiation]. Moreover, such deliverance usually registers as violence: dawn cuts, penetrates, punctures the darkness asserting the claims of luminous lucidity and of the real; above all, dawn gives the landscape back its horizon, the emblem of division and difference which the poet 'knows' he would do well to accept, 'just as', by accepting castration, he can accede to 'un monde où il s'égalera au père' [a world where he will be equal to the father]. Back to Dad, or at least to the Lacanian version of the paternal instance which hovers discreetly over much of the analysis. This is a sober and sometimes elliptical book but not a dull or pretentious one. Both its narrowness of range and the pregnancy of its formulations befit the subject. There is much work still to be done on Reverdy and Collot's guidelines will be more than merely useful.

# 32

# Finding a Language

Review of The Language of Poetry: Crisis and Solution.
Studies in Modem Poetry of French Expression, 1945 to the Present,
ed. by Michael Bishop (Amsterdam: Rodopi, 1980)

'Trouver une langue' [Finding a language]: it sometimes seems as if since Rimbaud (and Mallarmé) this imperative has been the chief bequest of the French poet to his successors. One virtue of this book is to emphasize the diversity of contexts in which the quest for an adequate poetic language has been conducted in recent French poetry. Five of the twelve essays discuss non-metropolitan poets: two African (Senghor and Tchicaya U'Tamsi), one Caribbean (Césaire), one Belgian (Marie-Claire d'Orbaix), one French-Canadian (Gaston Miron). D'Orbaix apart, all are acutely conscious of the rifts and contradictions between their national, cultural, and linguistic identities. Gerald Moore and A. James Arnold survey the careers of Tchicaya and Césaire respectively, demonstrating the connections between the evolution of their poetic styles and the historical and political changes to which they have responded. Moore's essay is thorough and urbane; Arnold's somewhat disjointed, but distinguished by a valuable analysis of the revisions Césaire has made in successive versions of the Cahier d'un retour. In an elegant and forthright essay, which inspects the paradoxes and solecisms of Senghor's ideology of 'rhythm', Roger Little suggests that where the poet opposes 'black' and 'white' we should substitute 'poet' and 'non-poet'. John Beaver's account of Miron is solidly informative. James Brown concentrates on one collection, Erosion du silence, by d'Orbaix and, with the aid of a curious but effective blend of semiotics and ontology, explores the 'semantic reversals' already implicit in the title. Michaux, Ponge and Char represent the earliest generation of poets considered here. In a wide-ranging and fluent essay, Peter Broome documents Michaux's deep mistrust of language and surveys the poet's counter-measures — within language: neologism, incantation, fluid structures; and outside it: drugs, dépaysement, painting, ideograms. Ian Higgins summarizes Ponge's general attitude to language and then concentrates on his explorations, Littré in hand, of the form and substance of words; reference is made especially to the more recent works. James Lawler skilfully illustrates the emergence of Char's poetic language through a close comparison of two versions of 'Biens égaux' [Equal Goods] (1938 and 1946) and a good reading of 'La Sorgue'. Poets of the fifties and sixties are less well served. Graham Dunstan Martin's pragmatic approach to the problems of understanding Bonnefoy's notion of 'présence' does not yield a convincing reading of 'L'Écume, le récif' [The Foam, the Reef] (from *Pierre écrite*) to which the last third of the essay is devoted. Brian Gill's introduction to Dupin is too unsure of its audience to be really useful, although valid points are made. Mary Ann Caws's short essay on Deguy is a diffuse piece of writing which gives central themes a somewhat gnomic treatment. One's spirits are raised, however, by Michael Bishop's illuminating discussion of Denis Roche which explains the poet's ideas and procedures, concedes their largely negative character, and then envisages them existentially in terms of a dialectics of destruction and jubilation. Here, as in his brief editorial introduction, Bishop invites us to acknowledge the versatility of poetic language in the period.

# 33

# Bonnefoy's Poetics

Review of Jérôme Thélot, Poétique d'Yves Bonnefoy (Geneva: Droz, 1983)

'Oui, dans la nuit | Où la télévision cherche le rivage' [Yes, in the night | Where the television seeks the shore]: readers of Dans le leurre du seuil will perhaps remember this disorientating moment. Why, in a poetry so deliberately restrained in its vocabulary — 'La poésie veut des mots qu'on puisse prendre dans son destin' [Poetry wants words that we can make part of our destiny], Bonnefoy once wrote — this reminder of our technological age and its artefacts? One of the functions of the critic is to help us think through our responses to such moments, and it is entirely typical of this invaluable book that Jérôme Thélot has thought about it, and, moreover, committed his judgement: 'regrettables faiblesses [...] nuisibles' [harmful [...] and regrettable moments of weakness], he writes of télévision and fourgonnette [small truck] as 'symptômes incongrus d'une tentation moderniste' [out-of-place symptoms of a modernist temptation]. We may demur, indeed we may find such a view obtuse. But Thélot's candour and concern, as well as his evident if sometimes evanescent merits as a literary analyst, no doubt account in part for the remarkable fortune whereby his book gives us not only the fruits of valuable research on the language of a great contemporary poet but also the poet's own responses. In a spirit of dialogue, and sometimes of irritation, Yves Bonnefoy annotated the margins of Thélot's thesis, and these annotations (109 of them, in all some 7000 words) are now published as an appendix to this book. Responding to Thélot, taking issue, always on specific points, Bonnefoy helps the reader: the fourgonnette, he insists, is crucial to the central experience recorded in the poem: 'On ne peut tout de même pas dire le "Char métallique".... Faut-il ne pas la nommer, alors qu'elle a tant compté?' [One could hardly say, the 'metallic chariot'.... Shouldn't one give it its name, given how much it mattered?]. But he also helps us appreciate his critic. For without its precious annotations (which make little sense on their own) Thélot's book would be one to keep; with them it will be with us for many a year, even when some of its critical insights and methods have been superseded, partly no doubt by Thélot himself. A fairly narrow and pragmatic definition of poétique informs this book, at least in its conception: four long chapters devoted to prosody, syntax, vocabulary and repetition, images. But far from being blind to the limitations of his method, Thélot makes a useful point of them and often, especially in the last chapter, transcends them deliberately.

The discussion of versification takes as its basis the opposition between regularity and irregularity. Bonnefoy uses traditional metre more than many modern poets but, argues Thélot, metrical irregularity is crucial: particularly the eleven-syllable line, divided 6/5 (Thélot calls this the 'alexandrin boiteux' [limping alexandrine], and sees it as the 'étymon' of Bonnefoy's metrics), and in later works, the decasyllabic line divided, untraditionally, 6/4. Thélot has many interesting things to say about these devices and many others (although he is inclined to exaggerate the role of minor irregularities and to give undue psychological weight to metrical features). He provides us, moreover, with invaluable statistical data. But the argument often depends on an oversimplified scheme in which regularity is equated with the lure of pure form, the dissolution of time and reality into the 'intemporel' [timeless], while irregularity is said to assert the claims of finitude and existence *hic et nunc*. In response to this, Bonnefoy stresses here that, in his sense of it, the alexandrine (while of course always susceptible of becoming 'la forme hypostasiée' [form hypostatized]) is, partly by dint of the 'e muet' [mute 'e'], an inherently unstable form: 'Il y a une "faille" possible au cœur même de l'alexandrin (cf. Baudelaire)' [There is a possible 'fault' in the very heart of the alexandrine (cf. Baudelaire)]. It is by working within this form, but putting pressure on its weak points, that the tensions between timeless order and existential reality are enacted; of course, irregularity also plays a part, but as the agent of a process through which form itself is explored and questioned, not, as Thélot too often alleges, as the embodiment, through the negation of form, of finitude.

The chapters on syntax and vocabulary raise similar issues. One of Thélot's virtues is that he has no critical axes to grind. But he is apt, in the heat of analysis, to write as if undecidability, ambiguity, and so forth were good things in themselves rather than grave and possibly insuperable risks, and he is also inclined to translate formal features too readily into metaphysical postulates. He provides lucid discussion of word-order, cadence, apposition, apostrophe, punctuation, and rhetorical questions. The occasional jibes at Jakobsonian 'microscopie' probably betray his awareness that it is easy to exaggerate (as he does) the effect of a missing comma (it should be noted, however, that Bonnefoy approves of the notion of 'la non-ponctuation' — the signifying role of absent punctuation marks). Thélot tends to impress on us the negative potential of many of Bonnefoy's syntactical usages, arguing that they enable the poem, through a form of 'harmonie imitative' [imitative harmony] (the term seems quaint) to register experiential reality's resistance to discourse. Bonnefoy's comments emphasize that apparently-negative features can signify positively as well by default: he writes of a '*disharmonie à vocation positive*, disharmonie dont le caractère négatif ne tend qu'à révéler, dégager, le plein de la finitude, la présence...' [*disharmony with a positive calling*, a disharmony whose negative character tends only to reveal and draw out the fullness of finitude, presence...]. Where vocabulary is concerned Thélot is good on the suppression of articles, and the preference for the definite article, both paradoxical ways of 'deconceptualizing' words and arriving at the concrete via the generic rather than via the aspectual dimensions of language. He also writes wisely on the question of whether some words can be said to be more 'poetic' than others, although in the process he disinters some dusty old classifications — 'mots roturiers' [common words], etc. The discussion of repetition is also murkier than it needed to be, because Thélot devotes disproportionate space to a notion of 'répétition manquée' (partial repetition or variation on a key phrase), again in the attempt to make a formally perceptible feature carry too heavy a semantic load.

In his discussion of 'Images' (in the widest sense) Thélot takes as his guideline one of the mainsprings of Bonnefoy's recent thinking about poetry: that sense of the duplicity and mendacity of 'l'Image' which the poet, in a comment here, summarizes as 'la vision qui s'organise en proposition d'univers cohérente et suffisante, et se substitue au monde de la finitude, son charme étant précisément qu'elle en dénie le caractère fini' [the vision which resolves itself into the positing of a coherent, sufficient universe, and substitutes itself for the world of finitude, its charm being precisely that it denies its finite character]. Of course, as Thélot recognizes, this condemnation of the image is part of a dialectic in which poetic lucidity is always ready to lift the embargo and restore to the image, seen for what it is, a cardinal role in the expression of a vision oriented by hope and possibility. But his discussion is marred by a tendency to confuse the image as a linguistic feature with the poetic realm engendered through it (in conjunction with other aspects of poetry, and indeed art in general). As Bonnefoy points out several times, in a crucial *mise au point*, his critique is addressed primarily to the latter, the imaginary world of the image ('l'Image') and not to the device ('la figure'). Of course metaphors (for example) can be mendacious, but they need not be; they can serve the proper end of poetry, which is to avoid the self-sufficient lure of the imaginary and enact the complexity and plenitude of presence. In Thélot's account the figure achieves this end only negatively, by a sort of self-cancellation, and he is good at detailing such features as 'la transgression du discours par l'image' [the transgression of discourse by image], 'la surcharge métaphorique' [metaphorical excess], the juxtaposition of densely metaphorical language with simple statement, all devices which he sees as circumventing the inbuilt tendency for 'la figure' to assert its own order over that of the world. But Bonnefoy insists that these devices are not the be-all and end-all; images do not simply work negatively, and understanding an image in a poem is not first and foremost a matter of registering the intricacy and impact of a process of signification but of responding to the proposition of an equivalence: 'la révélation des correspondances fondamentales dont notre existence humain se nourrirait' [the revelation of fundamental correspondences which our human existence is nourished by]. The vocabulary is deliberately, and perhaps provocatively, traditional, but Bonnefoy gives it a new bite by stressing that what he calls 'la qualité œuvrante de la figure' [the figure's performative quality] (which enables it to get a grip on our world) often resides in the force that permits it 'de briser la tyrannie de l'image' [to break the tyranny of the image].

That his view of 'l'Image' as 'à la fois la faute et l'espoir' [at once the error and the hope] should be so prominent in Bonnefoy's comments (as it was of course in his recently published inaugural lecture at the Collège de France, entitled *La Présence et l'Image*) is a reminder that he has in the last few years been recovering and formulating, for his benefit and ours, the underlying poetic of *Dans le leurre du seuil*. The many fascinating comments he makes on this poem (often stressing how it differs from the earlier work) will be of permanent importance. One of the more general will perhaps render their tenor: '*DLS* est pour moi la mise à jour d'un monde de la présence qui tient, au-delà du conceptuel' [For me, *DLS* brings to light a world of presence that coheres, beyond the conceptual].

Modern French poetry, and the work of Yves Bonnefoy in particular, has not received the critical attention they deserve, but this book may be a sign that the monopoly of fiction and literary theory has seen its day and that the excitement and gravity of poetry will once again find recognition and profit from the drive of the critical imagination. Bonnefoy himself, no doubt one of the most challenging critics of the age, will of course have contributed immeasurably if this is true, and so, in his way, will Thélot, if this book finds the audience it deserves.

# 34

# Rooted in the Oral

*Review of Clive Scott,* Vers Libre: The Emergence of Free Verse in France, 1886–1914 *(Oxford: Clarendon Press, 1990), and Henri Meschonnic,* La Rime et la Vie *(Lagrasse: Verdier, 1990)*

There will always be those who think free verse is for the lazy poetaster or the *parvenu* ignorant of national tradition. Clive Scott, in *Vers Libre: The emergence of free verse in France 1886–1914* quotes a squib from Etiemble to the effect that *vers libre* is poetry for the eyes only; in *La Rime et la vie*, Henri Meschonnic disinters some robustly xenophobic declarations by Grammont and Bally urging that a bunch of foreigners (Belgians like Verhaeren, Greeks like Moréas, Americans like Stuart Merrill, Jews like Gustave Kahn) should not be allowed to poison French verse. Scott suggests that the sense of threat stems from the abolition of pre-existent standards and stable forms in favour of formal energies demanding the collaborative work of the reader. *Vers libre*, if we may personify it (as Scott does to good effect, though occasionally to excess) is committed to relativity, to temporal flow and immediacy, to multiple perspectives, and above all to 'the unmediated language of the psyche'.

Scott provides a usefully detailed account of the origins of *vers libre*, focusing initially on the year 1886, when the promotional efforts of Gustave Kahn, through the medium of the weekly review *La Vogue*, placed it firmly on the map. He then turns to formal antecedents, stressing the important links with the prose poem, before surveying the competing theories and practices of Kahn, Mockel, Dujardin and others. Perhaps the most interesting strand in the web of hypotheses canvassed in an atmosphere of rivalry, amid much jockeying for supremacy, was the widespread interest in 'psychophysical' doctrines concerned with the linkage of mind and senses. However, the poetry of Kahn and his cohorts is often drearily mannered and insipid; constrained by the standard *imaginaire* of the period, it rarely displays the deviant energies of a self apprehended in its immediacy. To find these we must turn to the giddy swerves of Rimbaud's 'Marine' and 'Mouvement' (1872), generally acknowledged to be the first specimens of *vers libre* in France; to Laforgue's parlando style with its interjections and phatic urgency; to the Claudelian *verset* rooted in the physiology of utterance and the belief that rhythm mediates between the human organism and the cosmic order; to the rhythmical elasticity of Apollinaire's verse, which creates a depth of field in which the present may be viewed as a precarious zone poised between the challenges of past and future.

Scott makes important distinctions between varieties of free verse, but one of his chief findings is that a given poem often combines different principles of rhythmic organization. Scansion becomes a way of exploring the mobility of rhythmic textures, of tracing 'the way voice inhabits and motivates text', and of identifying the different ways a poem can be realized in reading, Scott does this brilliantly and like its predecessors — *French Verse-Art* (1980), *A Question of Syllables* (1986), *The Riches of Rhyme* (1988) — his new book is written with consistent elegance and verve. In Scott's hands scansion earns interpretative colours to which it rarely aspires. My only reservation concerns the frequency with which, in the interpretation of specific poems, rhythmic measures — often the tetrasyllable and the trisyllable — become protagonists whose struggles express the poet's conflicting attitudes and feelings. Even when it enables him to mount a legitimate challenge to existing interpretations, this 'binary' approach tends to detract from his main argument that *vers libre* favours the open-ended movement of *énonciation*, the unpredictable fluctuations of the voice.

*Vers libre* ends with a quotation from a writer who has consistently argued that poetry in general has to do with what Scott calls 'the experiential dimension of utterance'. Henri Meschonnic is a professor of linguistics and a prize-winning poet. He is also the author of a remarkable series of books about language and poetry notable for polemical ardour, intellectual range and strong commitment to the view that poems matter. Among them are the five volumes of *Pour la Poétique* (1970–78), *Le Signe et le poème* (1975), the massive *Critique du rythme* (1982), and *Modernité modernité* (1988). *La Rime et la vie*, one of three books he has published this year, is a collection of pieces reflecting many of his usual preoccupations: the *méconnaissance* of poetry displayed by philosophers (see also *Le Langage Heidegger*, 1990), by theoreticians of language (with exceptions made for Humboldt and Benveniste), by psychoanalysts (in this case Nicolas Abraham), by translators (there was a memorable row over Celan some years ago), and by poets or their champions (Scève, Guillevic, Michaux and Lionel Ray are discussed here).

Meschonnic opposes all descriptions of language that sever it from the activity of 'l'homme réellement en train de parler' (the person actually in the process of speaking) (Humboldt), even — especially — when they credit poetry with special privileges. In its structuralist heyday, the dominance of the sign fostered a ludic poetry, a festive 'son et lumière du langage' (sound and light of language) cut off from history and subjectivity. For Meschonnic, the 'sacralization' of the poetic *Logos* under the auspices of, say, Heidegger, 'l'effet Hölderlin', or Blanchot, leads to a similar disqualification of poetry through the failure to realize that it is above all a transitive activity which does not create its own world but transforms our relationship with the one we live in.

In the past decade, rhythm has emerged as a central theme in Meschonnic's writings. Rhythm resists linguistic categorization because it pertains to the subjective organization of discourse; it should not be regarded as an autonomous system (prosody) which embellishes or augments meaning but as a resource through which meaning comes to bear the irreducible imprint of the subject. Always rooted in the present of utterance, in the oral, rhythm is temporal rather than spatial and points to a vital continuity between subject, language and historicity.

Scott suggests that for its pioneers *vers libre* favoured not only individual self-expression but a general exploration of the conditions of subjectivity and *énonciation*. On Meschonnic's wider canvas the interests of the *verslibristes* are symptomatic of a crucial aspect of post-Baudelairean modernity: the concern for the transitory. Like Scott, Meschonnic associates rhythmic creativity with the attempt to implant the immediacy of the oral into the written. He insists, however, that we should not simply equate the oral with the spoken but see it, in the context of rhythm, as the stirring of subjectivity in language, 'un avènement du sujet' (an advent of the subject). The 'sujet du rythme' is not, however, the individual but the product of a particular kind of linguistic activity. In this perspective, the opposition between oral and written is another of the dualisms which must be overcome if poems are to have a future and if the rhythmic subject is to hold its own against the individualism which thinks of itself as prior to or beyond language, and beyond history.

# 35

# Surrealism and the Book

*Review of Renée Riese Hubert,* Surrealism and the Book
*(Berkeley: University of California Press, 1988)*

Although the idea of the Book seems alien to the surrealist spirit, it is hardly surprising that a movement in which poets and painters collaborated on an equal footing should have produced such powerful incitements to bibliophilia as *Facile* (Éluard and Man Ray), Magritte's illustrations for *Les Chants de Maldoror*, or Ernst's *Une semaine de bonté*. As this scrupulously documented and beautifully illustrated study shows, the book in which words and images combine is one of Surrealism's most striking manifestations. It is difficult, however, to define the surrealist book with any precision; if Professor Hubert's attempts to do so are not entirely convincing, the strength of her study lies in its presentation of the richly diverse ways in which the surrealists engendered a creative interplay of verbal and visual languages. The model surrealist book would perhaps involve the collaboration of two members of the group during its *époque historique*: *Simulacre* (1925), for example, where Masson 'illustrated' Leiris; or *Dormir, dormir dans les pierres* (1927) which brought Péret and Tanguy together; but Hubert rightly points out that these works maintain the traditional subservience of image to text which had dominated book-illustration until the late nineteenth century: the artist uses pictorial means to 'conjure up' the poet's imaginary world. A more radical break with the mimetic tradition is often found in less direct forms of collaboration, and in works produced after the demise of organized Surrealism. In Bellmer's illustrations to Kleist, and Ernst's extraordinary sequence, *Paysage marin avec capucin*, which deconstructs a seascape by Friedrich, the surrealists' fascination with Romanticism produces works of great quality. The desire to engage with acknowledged precursors, particularly Rimbaud, Lautréamont and Lewis Carroll, also proved a rich source of inspiration for artists from Dali to Mattá. In some cases text illustrates image, reversing the usual order: Breton's admirable series of prose poems, *Constellations* (1959), was inspired by a series of Miró gouaches created two decades earlier. Hubert devotes an interesting chapter to the interaction of text and photographs in Breton's *Nadja*, and of images and quotations in Ernst's collage-novel *Une semaine de bonté*, arguing that in both cases narrative continuity is subverted, and that the refusal of mimesis favours a genuine dialectic of the verbal and the visual. Another chapter focuses on cases where collaboration is motivated by political solidarity, as in the fine edition of Césaire's *Cahier d'un retour au pays natal* illustrated by Wifredo Lam. In the last part of the book Hubert considers post-war achievements, highlighting the role of publishers like Maeght, responsible for such authentic *livres de peintre* as *Les Pénalités de l'enfer* (Miró/Desnos). For understandable reasons Professor Hubert has chosen to study the surrealist book in isolation from the movement's journals, such as *Minotaure*, where the mixture of verbal and visual materials was often compelling. This tends to accentuate the somewhat peripheral character of a number of the works discussed here. It does not detract, however, from the real value of Hubert's book which lies in her sensitive analyses of particular works, accompanied by meticulous scholarship which builds on existing work in this field and also indicates directions for future research.

# 36

# Guillevic

*Review of Gavin Bowd,* Guillevic: Sauvage de la modernité
*(Glasgow: University of Glasgow French and German Publications, 1992)*

'Ce parcours de l'œuvre de Guillevic tente de démontrer le passage d'un humanisme triomphaliste à une humilité écologiste, une ouverture à l'autre' [This survey of Guillevic's work tries to show the movement from a triumphalist humanism to an environmental humility, an openness to the other] (p. 96). The first critic to attempt an overall reading of Guillevic's career, Gavin Bowd highlights the poet's spell as a militant communist bard in the 1950s. Guillevic had contributed memorably to Resistance publications, and with 'Les Charniers' had found a tone of voice in which the unbearable horror of the Nazi death camps could be fathomed. Yet it was still surprising that this poet of the terse, laconic fragment should enthusiastically embrace the programme for a *Poésie nationale* launched by Aragon in the pages of the *Lettres françaises* and start writing sonnets full of cold war propaganda. But if Khrushchev's 'secret report' to the XXth Party Congress in 1956, revealing Stalin's atrocities, dealt a mortal blow to the poet's beliefs and reduced him to silence for five years, the agony was to be protracted; Guillevic did not finally leave the Party until 1980 and his commitment to socialism has proved durable. The challenge since his resumption of writing, with *Carnac* in 1961, has been to keep hope alive through an approach to poetry, defined in the poet's words as 'les noces de la parole et du silence', which accommodates negativity, and which fosters a search for antidotes to chaos and catastrophe: the land, the feminine, the word, the sacred.

Bowd's segmentation of Guillevic's career performs a useful function even if the proliferation of subheadings, quotations, and summaries (relics of a thesis) sometimes makes for choppy reading, while in a short book breadth of coverage inevitably leads at times to superficiality. Bowd sees Guillevic as a postmodernist, in the sense that a major part of his work has been written in the aftermath of the communist 'grand récit', and in the sense that his 'poétique de l'inachèvement' eschews totality in favour of micro-bursts of poetic energy (Guillevic adopted the word *quanta* to describe his short sharp poems and aphorisms). But Bowd also sees Guillevic as a primitive, a man bent on resurrecting the sacred, on hallowing scattered fragments of a lost origin discovered in the midst of the here and now. Yet in this book one misses concerted analysis of the tensions between different facets of Guillevic's work and a thorough investigation, based on close attention to his poetic discourse, of the kinds of sense-making at work in the fragments. Bowd tends to fall back on thematic recension and somewhat nebulous phrase-making just when a more critical and analytical approach would be most welcome. This is a pity, partly because it militates against the attempt to move contemporary poetry from the critical back-burner. Bowd rightly feels that Guillevic's voice deserves to be heard. But nowadays its chances of resonance depend crucially on attunement to the ways recent theory has articulated new relationships between the linguistic, the political, the psychological, and so on. Having staked out the terrain, Bowd will, one hopes, move on to survey it in different ways.

# Surrealist Automatic Writing

*Review of* Une pelle au vent dans les sables du rêve: les écritures
automatiques, *ed. by Michel Murat and Marie-Paule Berranger*
*(Lyon: Presses Universitaires de Lyon, 1992)*

Along with 'le hasard objectif' [objective chance], 'écriture automatique' guards the
entrance to the surrealist edifice, ready to intimidate the faint-hearted, to confuse
the credulous and to confound the tidy-minded. The centrality of language in
the surrealist project can only be understood by reference to what was at stake in
the rituals of writing which engendered *Les Champs magnétiques*, *Poisson soluble*,
*L'Immaculée Conception* and the 'textes surréalistes' expected of all contributors to
*La Revolution surréaliste*, from Paul Éluard to Dédé Sunbeam. Yet, as André Breton
ruefully noted in 1933, when he declared the history of automatism to have been
an 'infortune continue' [continual misfortune], both the practice and its products
are as easy to caricature as they are difficult to define and dissect. The great merit
of this excellent collection is to emphasize the plurality of 'écritures automatiques'
without losing sight of the features which differing practices and theorizations had
in common. In a stimulating introductory survey M. Murat stresses the pitfalls of
tying automatism to expressivity ('la dictée de l'inconscient' [the dictation of the
unconscious]) or, conversely, of reducing it to a rhetoric of 'automatism effects'. As
L. Jenny insists, surrealism involved a new mythologization of the linguistic which
has been a vital influence on modern culture. But Jenny's view of a verbal utopia,
'sans aucune visée de l'autre', is not corroborated by the findings of N. Limat-
Letellier in her extensive discussion of Aragon, or M.-P. Berranger's exploration of
Breton's *Poisson soluble*. Both critics stress the function of metatextual language in
the automatic text, showing how it reflects the paradoxical *dédoublement* [doubling]
of passive 'scripteur' and active, lucid, 'observateur' which marks automatism as
a discourse obsessively concerned with its own emergence and reception. Often
practised *à deux*, as in the case of 'L'Enfant planète' by Péret and Desnos, analysed by
M.-C. Dumas and R. Strich, automatism may, according to J. Chénieux-Gendron
on the basis of her analysis of the manuscripts of *L'Immaculée Conception*, be seen
as a process that is both ludic and heuristic, an exploratory method practised by
a community of initiates. None the less, J. Kristeva's psychoanalytic reading of
*Poisson soluble* reminds us that the individual psyche and its perilous travails in the
underworld of language and sexuality are much to the fore in automatic texts, where
the spectacular *mise en scène* of a subject in process can still divert and enthral.

# A Translation of Bonnefoy

*Review of Yves Bonnefoy,* On the Motion and Immobility of Douve/
Du mouvement de et l'immobilité de Douve, *trans. by Galway Kinnell,*
*intro. by Timothy Mathews (Newcastle: Bloodaxe Books, 1992)*

The new Bloodaxe Contemporary French Poets series gets off to an impressive start with this volume devoted to Bonnefoy's first major collection of poems which was regarded as a landmark on its first publication in 1953. The series (which also features works by Michaux and Char, with Jaccottet, Césaire and others in the pipeline) has a number of virtues. Instead of anthologies, we are given complete collections, with original and translation on facing pages. Introductions are substantial; typography and design are good; pricing is realistic: the series deserves to prosper. Bearing a fine reproduction of a Lorrain painting on its cover, the Bonnefoy volume reprints the workmanlike translation of *Douve* made by the American poet Galway Kinnell, which was first published in the 1960s. Although Kinnell's versions often fail to match the controlled intensity of the originals, it is no bad thing that they incline more towards the plainly prosaic than the self-consciously poetic. Through the enigmatic figure of Douve who constantly shifts between reality and myth, mind and body, erotic presence and mortal absence, Bonnefoy explores to its farthest limits the territory of his poetic imagination, inaugurating a magnificent poetic project he was to pursue in subsequent volumes. Rather than tie himself too closely to *Douve*, Timothy Mathews discusses Bonnefoy in the context of recent theory, drawing interesting contrasts and parallels with Roland Barthes, the poet's immediate predecessor at the Collège de France. Mathews portrays Bonnefoy as an essentialist, committed to the restoration of presence and plenitude and to the integrity of the subject, but also as a poet haunted by language, death, naming, and the fearful lure of the image. In the analysis of selected poems, and of the links between Bonnefoy's poetry and his prose works, Mathews conveys effectively why Bonnefoy deserves to find the wider readership for which this volume is intended.

# La Liberté des rues

*Review of Jacques Réda,* La Liberté des rues *(Paris: Gallimard, 1997), and of*
*Jean Rolin,* Zones *(Paris: Gallimard, 1997)*

For Jacques Réda Paris is intensely familiar, perpetually astonishing, and eternally mysterious. For many years he has been exploring its streets, and reporting, in verse and prose, on his forays into what he calls the Parisian nebula, adopting different strategies in his endless quest to understand just what it is that drives him continually out onto the streets, in fair weather or foul, on foot, bike, or Solex. But his new book is a landmark, both in his own work and in the extensive literature, currently taking on new and more varied forms, inspired by the City of Light. Twenty years after *Les Ruines de Paris* (recently published by Reaktion Books in an excellent English translation by Mark Treharne), which launched a series of books inspired by wanderings in Paris and its hinterlands, Jacques Réda has written another masterpiece. *La Liberté des rues* is an amazing achievement, the work of a writer at the height of his powers, drawing together and encapsulating many of the strands in his previous work, while also promising more for the future.

Jacques Réda is a poet through and through, with a poet's intense relationship to words and a poet's commitment to ways of experiencing reality that more utilitarian forms of writing and living tend to neglect. But like many of the greatest modern French poets, and particularly those who have taken the city and everyday experience as their favoured territory, Réda has often turned to prose. Baudelaire is of course the great precursor here. In the preface to his collection of prose poems *Le Spleen de Paris*, he voiced the aspiration to develop a prose style fluid enough to capture the undulations of reverie and the quick-fire shifts of feeling and thought triggered by the experience of walking in the city. In *Les Ruines de Paris*, Réda followed Baudelaire's example and composed sumptuous prose poems where the densely supercharged language, matched by constant metaphorical play, captured the twists and turns of a mind abroad in the city's streets and suburbs. In subsequent books Réda tried out different styles and strategies, drawing on the traditions of the essay and the fable (he is an admirer of Montaigne and La Fontaine) and also playing with the conventions of guidebooks and travel narratives. In *Châteaux des courants d'air*, a series of linked mini-essays and disquisitions takes the reader on a tour of two favoured *arrondissements*, samples key types of monument (a bridge, a church, a passage) before investigating and comparing Paris's railway termini. *Recommandations aux promeneurs* is inspired by 'how-to' manuals, while *Le Sens de la marche* uses different combinations of prose and verse to commemorate expeditions out of Paris in the footsteps of other writers admired by Réda, including William Wordsworth.

All the texts in *La Liberté des rues* are in prose, but the book's six sections each have a different flavour, determined partly by immensely skilful and subtle differentiations of style and idiom. For example, the opening section, 'L'Activité du soir' is a sequence of short texts (one or two pages) resembling prose poems in their brevity and density, but taking full advantage of prose poetry's narrative possibilities, its ability to celebrate the prosaic. Here the (eminently Baudelairean) central motif is the advent of evening, an event which, however abruptly it seems in retrospect to have happened, owes its unsettling effects on the sensitive individual to its elusiveness. Most of the other sections, loosely focused on 'memorable encounters' (with seemingly unmemorable people), 'great expeditions' (involving very short distances), or 'Finding what one was not looking for' (a kind of serendipity that Réda's purposely aimless wanderings seem to favour) feature slightly longer texts, where a narrative or discursive thread is clearly perceptible but where the logic of language and metaphor are in charge.

Réda's Paris is both everyone's and no one's. It is not the city seen by the tourist, the businessman, the lover, the planner, the geographer or the historian. It is a city of intensely lived moments, and closely observed details. It is a city of colours, impressions, atmospheres, hilarities and forebodings. Yet this is a Paris available to anyone prepared to live and experience the city in Réda's way, according to principles admirably elucidated in the eponymous section of *La Liberté des rues*. Here Réda seeks to draw up the rules of the game he plays with the city, or that the city plays with him. This reversibility is crucial because, for Réda, to apprehend Paris is to become a participant in its rhythms and patterns, and to make oneself subject to its dictates and whims: the way it chooses to spread itself out in the Avenue Trudaine, or to pump air down the Rue de la Pompe.

This is what being granted the freedom of the streets — *La Liberté des rues* — means: becoming part of the city's endlessly changing plan, absorbed into its mutable reality by virtue of one's own mutability, made manifest by our consent to become no more than a passer-by, though in Réda's case a *passant* equipped with the ability to render in exquisite language every nuance of what he sees as he passes.

★   ★   ★   ★   ★

On the afternoon of Sunday fifth of June 1994 the journalist and writer Jean Rolin set out on the first of three 'journeys' around the fringes of Paris. Taking the metro towards Pont de Sèvres, he alighted at Marcel-Sembat and checked into the extremely modest Hôtel Phénix, the first of many similar establishments where he would rest fitfully over the next two weeks (and then again in August and November) gathering together the impressions of the day. Five days later, in an attic room of the Ouest-Hôtel near the Pont-Cardinet station, having arranged his meagre possessions — wash-bag, plans of Paris and suburbs, notebooks and pens — in the order he forces himself to observe to the letter, Rolin is still asking himself why he is doing this. What does he hope to achieve by cutting himself off from family and friends, sticking to public transport, wandering round unfashionable and often dangerous districts, slumming it in tacky restaurants and dodgy hotels? In a sense, Rolin never really finds an answer. But if the unease this provokes is one of the things that keeps him going (he associates travel with anxiety), his question receives the semblance of a response in something he witnesses near the Gare Saint-Lazare: the huge red neon letters of a giant Coca-Cola sign silhouetted against the deepening blue of the sky; and then, below this 'false aurora borealis', a Muslim woman in full *chador* eating a hamburger in the window of a Q-Quick Restaurant. If this scene fires Rolin to keep exploring, it's not because it is picturesque or symbolic in a heavy-handed way, but because it gives some sort of access to the incongruities, discrepancies, contradictions and conflicts, that are part of the fabric of Paris and France in the very late twentieth century.

Rolin progressively comes to realize that the kind of reportage he practises in *Zones* depends entirely on the constraints — physical, mental, writerly — he places himself under. *Estranging* himself (however temporarily) is what enables him to see what he doesn't usually see. By making an incongruous 'journey' around the edges of his 'own' city he provisionally inhabits a zone that opens up other zones — the imbricated but often hermetically sealed worlds that politics, capital, and the society of the Spectacle (Rolin has learnt from Guy Debord and the Situationists) have created in Paris's old *quartiers populaires*, and in Nanterre, Bécon-les-Bruyères, Garge-lès-Goneses, Sarcelles, Ile Saint-Denis or Gennevilliers. Placing himself in a profoundly ironic situation, Rolin becomes a connoisseur of the ironies lurking in such quarters as the gaps between official discourse and urban realities (what is the point of anti-drug realities propaganda on a Flipper machine? Is the campaign against AIDS helped by ribbons on municipal trees?). He has a memorable encounter with Stéphane, one of several denizens of the strangely countrified area (rabbits, foxes) that is the building site for the future *Grand Stade*, where lucky (and wealthy) spectators of the Word Cup Final 1998 will no doubt be oblivious of the syringes and other detritus underneath (*déchets* is a key word in *Zones*).

If irony is a dominant mode in *Zones*, self-irony gives the work much of its strength and appeal. In its lucid self-consciousness, its emphasis on setting up a quasi-experimental situation, and sticking (mostly) to the rules, in its awareness of the difficulties of attending to a complex reality, Zones has affinities with such works as Francois Maspéro's *Les Passagers du Roissy-Express* or Annie Ernaux's *Journal du dehors*, as well as a poet like Jacques Réda. But Rolin has his own voice, and this excellent book has its own place in the new literature of Paris.

# 40

# Bataille, Sartre, Valéry, Breton

*Review of Suzanne Guerlac,* Literary Polemics: Bataille, Sartre, Valéry, Breton
*(Stanford, CA: Stanford University Press, 1997)*

*Enfin!* At last, a profoundly serious analysis that rocks the Good Ship Theory not by conservative retrenchment but by making real waves which expose the uncharted reefs, depths and shallows below the calm surface of received ideas. At last, a book which radically questions the routine elevation of Bataille at the expense of Breton; which rescues Valéry from the stereotype of outmoded neoclassicism and the fetishizing of artistic form; which recognizes the nonreferential, anti-realist slant of Sartre's 'myth of prose' in *Qu'est-ce que la Littérature?*. Working backwards from *Tel Quel's* appropriation of the notion of transgression, Suzanne Guerlac shows how literary polemics foster myths of incompatibility (Bataille/Breton, engagement/ pure art) which obscure hidden proximities. There was nothing new about *Tel Quel's* erasure of earlier twentieth-century movements: Sartre and Bataille had already found it expedient to bury Surrealism, just as Breton had sought to inter the author of *La Jeune Parque*. But if Bretonian automatism can be seen to have more in common with Valéry's account of the workings of poetic creation than first appears, so Sartrean engagement can be seen to rest on a not un-Valéryan cult of literature (as Sartre acknowledged in *Les Mots*); while Bataille's defence of Baudelaire (and poetry) against Sartre in the 1940s reveals affinities with Breton. Guerlac's book is remarkable for the way close textual reading reveals the dynamic play of poetry vs. action, form vs. content, pure art vs. engagement, at work in conceptual worlds generally held to be mutually exclusive. Avoiding the adoption of a new orthodoxy (but insisting on the need to quash the embargo on Breton and Surrealism) Guerlac seeks to unblock channels between bodies of ideas that evolved in dynamic interaction with each other, and whose real differences need re-mapping. A key operator in this project is the disinterring of Bergsonian subtexts. Bergson is a quintessential victim of erasure, his extraordinary renown succeeded by total obliteration (a fate from which Deleuze has latterly sought to rescue him). But Guerlac shows, convincingly on the whole, that the Bergsonian intertext in the work of her four main protagonists can serve to reveal their lost, if relative, commonality. Tracing the vitalist current in Valéry's poetics reveals its accentuation of the dynamics of interiority to be in harmony with key aspects of Surrealist automatism. In turn, automatism can be illuminated when the Surrealist 'resolution' of antinomies is read not in terms of Hegel's dialectic but of Bergsonian *reconnaissance*, rooted in the dynamic interaction of perception and memory. Sartre's Bergsonism can be located in his theory of reading, and in his view of action which is vitalist in its stress on process and the *vécu*. In Bataille's case, vitalist thinking is channelled through ethnography, and informs the 'sacred sociology' that makes an absolute of inner experience. Often adventurous and provocative, Guerlac's readings are admirably detailed and nuanced. *Literary Polemics* brilliantly exemplifies the new kinds of literary history the twenty-first century needs.

# 41

# The Material and the Real

*Review of Susan Harrow,* The Material, the Real and the Fractured Self:
Subjectivity and Representation from Rimbaud to Réda
*(Toronto: University of Toronto Press, 2004)*

In this admirable study, Susan Harrow revitalizes the study of modern French
poetry — scandalously under-researched despite the treasures displayed here
on every vivid page — by using ideas from cultural theory, autobiography
theory and art history. The prime focus is on the interaction between embodied
subjectivity and the materiality of the real, with language's own material riches as
indispensable go-between. Throughout, Harrow shows how poetry works to resist
the homogenizing pressures of modern capitalist society. Three of the four poets
examined are canonical, but in each case the critic shows them in a new light.
Stressing the 'hyperactive outwardness' of his project, Harrow sees Rimbaud as
a poet of mess and debris as well as sensation and colour, whose texts, crammed
with discordant and fragmentary discourses, embrace the body's dissident priorities.
In Apollinaire, the tensions between materiality and subjectivity are probed in a
brilliant new account of the war poems in *Calligrammes*. Far from representing
indifference to the horrors of war, Apollinaire's poetic performances — read as
autobiographical fantasy — embody poetry's resistance to ready-made responses,
enacting the anxiety and irresolution fostered by participation in historical
calamity. 'Combining the roles of participant, ethnographer, and memorialist of
war', Apollinaire creates verbal and visual artefacts that render the soldier-self's
negotiations with the real. Drawing on ethnographies of the everyday, Harrow
develops a superb reading where 'the obsessive naming of parts' and 'pleasurable
immersion in small things' offset the terrible generalities of war, providing small
havens of agency. Renderings of colloquial speech likewise indicate how lexical
inventiveness and homosocial bonding serve to shore up collective self-identity, as
do pervasive references to the feminine and the erotic, which Harrow treats with
considerable insight. In Ponge's writing, Harrow, with considerable originality,
considers the configuration of the cultural, the material and the subjective,
drawing on recent theoretical reorientations that have (partially) reinstated the
human subject. Analysing the alienated subjectivity behind the mordant social
critique of the early *Douze petits écrits*, Harrow goes on to explore the attention to
bodily (often oral, erotic) experience in Ponge's famous celebrations of mundane
things. Thereafter, through close readings, she shows that Ponge's attention to the

overlooked is restorative with regard to the self as well as the world. This lays ideal foundations for a fourth poet, Jacques Réda, given his first extensive treatment in English. In Réda, as in Ponge, we encounter a subject in process, constantly made and unmade in negotiations with the outside world. In Réda's case, this pliancy (a key notion developed by Harrow) is exercised amidst the sights and sounds of city or suburb, traversed endlessly on foot or Solex. Harrow views Réda as an 'artisan of the everyday', making parallels with Michel de Certeau, notably with regard to walking in the city and to the quotidian as a zone of resistance (an excellent comparison is also made with Agnès Varda's film, *Les Glaneurs et la glaneuse*). Exploring the embodied, kinetic character of Réda's 'excursive desire', Harrow investigates his treatment of ordinary 'micro-practices' identified in the apparently nondescript. A final section, linking back to Rimbaud and Ponge, shows how in Réda attempts to articulate nuances of colour betoken the movements of desiring subjectivity. Beautifully written, engaged without being rhapsodic, always to the point, Susan Harrow's fine book will be a major reference-point for many years to come.

# 42

# Survival and Resurgence of the Avant-Garde, or the Influence of Pierre Alferi on André Breton

In 1977 the poet Jacques Roubaud, one of the editors of the review *Change*, the great (or, let us not exaggerate, small) rival of the *Tel Quel* group, which was at this point in its Maoist phase, brought out *Autobiographie chapitre dix* [Autobiography Chapter Ten]. The back cover reads as follows:

> Il m'est arrivé en 1918 *la première aventure céleste de monsieur Antipyrine*, en 1919 *la deuxième*; en 1918 encore *la lucarne ovale* de Pierre Reverdy, en 1923 *Rrose Sélavy* de Marcel Duchamp et Robert Desnos...
>
> De tous ces poèmes, composés dans les dix-huit années (1914–1932) qui précédèrent ma naissance, j'ai fait ce livre, chapitre dixième d'une autobiographie: *la vie est unique*, mais les paroles d'avant la mémoire font ce qu'on en dit.[1]

> [*The First Adventure of Monsieur Antipyrine* happened to me in 1918, *The Second...* in 1919; also in 1918, *The Oval Skylight* by Pierre Reverdy, then *Rrose Sélavy* by Marcel Duchamp and Robert Desnos in 1923...
>
> From all of these poems, composed in the eighteen years (1914–1932) before my birth, I have made this book, the tenth chapter of my autobiography: *Life is unique*, but what we say about it is made up of words that precede memory.]

By appropriating these works by Tristan Tzara, Pierre Reverdy, Marcel Duchamp and Robert Desnos, Roubaud affirmed the legacy of 'words that precede memory' within the weave of his own poetic utterance. The tests in question clearly belong to the avant-garde. *La première aventure céleste de monsieur Antipyrine*, a pure product of Zurich Dada, was Tzara's first book. *La Lucarne ovale*, whose first edition actually appeared in 1916, is the first major collection of a poet linked to several branches of the avant-garde, particularly Cubism and Surrealism, and whose *Nord-Sud* (1917–18) is the very epitome of an avant-garde review. 'Rrose Sélavy' was, as we know, originally the alter ego of Marcel Duchamp photographed in drag by Man Ray in 1921. However, in 1922, during the famous 'époque des sommeils' [the period of sleeps], when he showed his astonishing aptitude for 'speaking fluent surrealist', spontaneously forging poetic spoonerisms, Robert Desnos took on the character of 'Rrose' — who subsequently became the incarnation of this form of poetic creation — and publicized his complicity with Duchamp, who was in New York at the time, with one of these poetic aphorisms: 'Rrose Sélavy connaît bien le marchand du sel' [Rrose Sélavy knows the salt seller (a spoonerism of Marcel Duchamp) well]. Most of Roubaud's 317 texts combine quotations from one or several poets (Breton, Aragon, Eluard, Peret, Soupault, Cendrars, Picabia, Huidobro...), often 'trafiquées' [tampered with]: (Breton's *Mont de piété* becomes 'Pont de mi-été' [Midsummer Bridge] and *Le Revolver à cheveux blancs* becomes 'Le Browning aux tresses noires' [The black-haired Browning], with elements concocted by Roubaud, sometimes purportedly lifted from previous works (for example the diary of his walk along the Mississippi).

What is the meaning of Roubaud's gesture? Insofar as the avant-garde texts he manipulated harked back to a prehistory, must we conclude that here the avant-garde is mummified, filed away, even dismissed? Does the clear presence of irony, and the fact that the poems appropriated by Roubaud, dating from 1918 to 1932, are a part of his past and warrant their place in his autobiography, mean that this practice simply references, for the record as it were, the *history* of the avant-garde? Or would it not be just as plausible to see here the reappropriation of discursive traits harking back to a French 'modernism', to be aligned with works by Ezra Pound, T. S. Eliot, or James Joyce that are also often seen in different ways — as works of the avant-garde, as the pillars of 'High Modernism', yet at the same time, in recent readings, as works that are already — always-already — postmodern?[2] Should we apply the label 'postmodern' to Roubaud's 'citational' gesture? Or is it rather the reverse: in allowing himself to mix these lifted quotations with the ingredients of his life, is Roubaud, the admirer of Aby Warburg,[3] not in fact celebrating the 'survival', the enduring efficacy, the longevity, of the avant-garde?

★   ★   ★   ★   ★

Perhaps it all boils down to the interaction of three terms — *avant-garde(s)*; *modernism(s)*; *post-modernism(s)* — all three in the singular and in the plural. And perhaps we are concerned essentially with the space between two pitfalls. Firstly, that of historicism, which believes in befores and afters. On a historicist view, the avant-gardes become the 'historic avant-gardes', to be docketed and archived; modernism is seen to centre on the 'High Noon' of 'High Modernism' (Eliot, Proust, Pound, Woolf...); and the postmodern is reduced to the supposed end of 'grands récits' and the coming of an era in which we are still caught up. Secondly, the pitfall of nominalism, which consists in the belief that there is an essence, even a quintessence, of each of our categories. From this perspective, the avant-garde involves a pure gesture of destruction or derision; modernism fosters the 'religion of art'; postmodernism, with the supposed death of those 'grands récits' (no doubt 'much exaggerated', like the false rumour of Mark Twain's demise), parades an intrinsic lack of essence.

Confronted with the first pitfall, I am tempted to replace Fredric Jameson's famous apothegm, 'Always historicize'[4] with an adage of my own invention: 'Never historicize', which does not come down to recognizing a supra-historical existence in the phenomenon in question, but simply to noting the indigence of historicist approaches which are all more or less deterministic. Confronted with the second pitfall, the nominalist or essentialist error, I shall brandish the recollection of a 'spoof' by Tom Wolfe in which, at a conference on the modern art market, the 'new journalist' parodied a common type of statement in bottom-of-the-range art criticism, phrases such as: 'sur ces entrefaites, les Fauves firent leur entrée fracassante sur la scène parisienne' [meanwhile, the Fauves make their thunderous entrance onto the Parisian stage], or 'le constructivisme mena tambour battant' [constructivism took the lead, all guns blazing]. Wolfe nailed these excessive personifications which with the slogan 'the trend that walks like a man'...

'Avant-garde', 'modern', 'post-modern': how can we triangulate these notions without reducing them to straw men, abstractions, caricatures? How can we avoid being grave-diggers of the avant-gardes, curators (or taxidermists) of modernism, pedants always ready to raise an eyebrow at improper uses of the term 'postmodern'? Firstly, one should no doubt be wary of straight lines: in 'avant-garde speak', all in watchwords, our slogans should be: multiply the links, complicate chronologies, look for side-alleys, perfect the arabesque, revere curves, vary the geometry. In short, when it comes to the avant-gardes, suppress the desire to 'reset the pendulum', and instead follow the advice of W. H. Auden in a poem made notorious by its reincarnation in a popular film, *Four Weddings and a Funeral*: 'Stop all the clocks'! And, confronted with nominalism, do the same: de-compartmentalize, cultivate variety, cherish nuances and family resemblances, throw out Occam's razor and revel in nuances and differences, recognize only what's singular, tell yourself that any space can turn out to be a Borgesian 'Garden of Forking Paths'...

Discourses on the death, or end of the avant-gardes, as on the end of history, clash with a more salubrious trend that consists in pointing out what Karl Popper called 'the poverty of historicism'. How often, in respect of artistic styles and currents, must we resist the lure of the single track? After all, so many voices tempt us to resist the siren call of historical orderliness: Warburgian 'survivals', Benjamin's 'dialectical images', Bergsonism renewed by Deleuze, the 'paradigm shifts' and 'epistemes' of Kuhn and Foucault, Kosseleck's 'presents past', Hartog's 'regimes of historicicity'.

★   ★   ★   ★   ★

I would therefore like to propose, on the basis of a case that seems exemplary, that of Pierre Alferi, born in 1963, a series of untimely considerations on the difficulty of satisfactorily triangulating the three spheres: of the avant-garde, modernism, and postmodernism. Faced with Pierre Alferi's work which comprises, or rather combines, poetry, manifestos and theoretical reflections, films and film criticism, drawings, performances, it is difficult to pick out the elements that come from avant-gardist traditions (sweeping declarations, a fondness for the 'gestural'), from modernism (the constant comparisons with cinema, considered as a sort of childhood of art, as Godard put it), and the postmodern (strong presence of the topos of the virtual, as in Deleuze). In other words, Alferi's work — though it seems to me that we could say the same of many other artists, for instance Georges Perec — simultaneously sets the three machines of the avant-garde, the modern and the post-modern into motion, with their congenital and inextricable elements. And, through this, the reader-spectator is required to be capable of appreciating the mixture of elements and vectors emanating from these three living sources, whose longevity and fertility rely on their manifold ways of interconnecting. One could of course retort that an avant-garde that consorts with other trends is merely a second-hand avant-garde, fed on by the organisms that have incorporated it. To which one could reply that this process is the very matter of art, of aesthetic work in its temporal dimension. What do we find in reading Rimbaud, Marinetti, Apollinaire, Breton, or Bataille, if not the creators of discourses which quote and 'process' the past? Are we not aware that the pre-Romantic poet, Edward Young, author of *Night-Thoughts*, was revived thanks to the *Manifeste du surréalisme* in which it is written that 'Les *Nuits* d'Young sont surréalistes d'un bout à l'autre' [Young's *Night-Thoughts* are surrealist through and through]?[5] It is true that Young studied at All Souls College, Oxford, the college of departed souls, as the great modernist poet W. B. Yeats, in his spiritualist poem 'All Souls Night' — and the postmodern novelist Javier Marías in his novel, *All Souls* — both acknowledged.

★   ★   ★   ★   ★

Pierre Alferi's first book, a study of the English philosopher and theologian William of Ockham,[6] based on a philosophy thesis, was followed by a sort of poetic treatise-manifesto: *Chercher une phrase*,[7] and by a collection of poems whose title, *Les Allures naturelles*[8] [natural gaits] referred back to the images of the late nineteenth-century photographer, Jules Marey, which captured bodies in motion and placed emphasis on question of posture, place, and tactic in poetic enunciation. In 1995 and 1996 he published two large collective volumes with Olivier Cadiot which have many characteristics of avant-garde productions (mixing manifestos, formal texts, quotations from favoured predecessors — Gertrude Stein, Jacques Roubaud et al...).[9]

Alferi's second book of poetry, *Le chemin familier du poisson combatif*[10] [The familiar path of the fighting fish] flaunts its avant-garde credentials right down to its title and its various paratexts. The back cover introduces the notion of experimentation. The book records an 'aventure' [adventure], a series of experiments or experiences, quite banal or everyday in nature since they concern themselves with very simple acts, to which the narrator would subject himself:

> Le narrateur se soumet à quatre épreuves. La première est de sortir. La deuxième, de passer le temps. La troisième, de rentrer chez soi. La quatrième, de regarder.
> Récit d'une aventure.

> [The narrator subjects himself to four ordeals. The first is to go out. The second, to pass the time. The third, to go back home. The fourth, to watch. The story of an adventure.]

To fit with the idea of the 'épreuve' [ordeal], the text takes the form of an elaborated structure, and a ritual or set of protocols, meaning that after the writer, it is the reader who becomes the guinea pig: the reader too is asked to give him- or herself over to an experiment, a programme, an inquiry. Each of the four parts, after its title (that of the first part is eponymous, the others, along the same lines, are: 'Le mouvement de l'escargot' [The snail's movement], 'Demeure et territoire de l'épinoche' [The home and territory of the stickleback], and 'La même rue pour un œil de mouche' [The same road from a fly's perspective], is preceded by a bizarre diagram, and a description of a strange experiment involving an animal — fish, snail, stickleback, fly. A 'Note' at the end of the book recalls the work of ethologist Jacob von Uexküll, father of biosemiotics, whose experiments, aiming to demonstrate that each species has its own world, its *Umwelt*, aroused lively interest from the 1920s in a number of writers and philosophers, including Rilke and Heidegger, and later Merleau-Ponty, Deleuze and Guattari.[11] If we take the trouble to consult the book of von Uexküll's to which Alferi is referring, we notice that the texts where he describes the four experiments 'détournent' [subvert] passages from the ethologist's text, and are in fact almost collages. Yet, when we approach Alferi's texts, we notice that the experimental subject in them is a human being, rather than an animal. The subject of these four 'séquences' [sequences] in free verse, each of around a dozen pages, reports 'en direct' [live], by means of monologue, on rather everyday experiences, in each of which we can recognize one of the great themes of modernism — a walk around Paris (the city, urban experiences, with its chance collisions); the course of a single day (as in Joyce's *Ulysses*, Woolf's *Mrs Dalloway*, Apollinaire's 'Zone'); domestic space (as in Georges Perec, we find descriptions of bedrooms); the phenomenological experience of sight — the flow of perception. Among other elements of the structure and procedure, we find the insistent presence of elements of parascientific discourse — indicating that the subject of this 'promenade méthodique' [methodological stroll][12] tries to load his perceptions with often ill-digested scientific knowledge. The first text comprises asides such as: 'lu sans comprendre grand-chose | un article de mathématiques sur les chaos déterministes, | l'expression m'a frappé' [read without understanding much | an article on the mathematics of deterministic chaos, | the expression appealed to me],[13] 'lu un rapport sur les abeilles et les automates acentrés' [read a report on bees and acentric automata].[14] Likewise, we find the following instructions in an untitled preliminary note, referring to certain passages in each of the four texts: 'ces "reprises" sont faites pour être lues deux fois. Leur premier vers est en capitales; dans la dernière séquence, leur fin est signalée par un tiret' [these 'reruns' are made to be read twice. Their first lines are in capitals; in the final sequence, the end is signposted with a hyphen]. Here is an extract from the first sequence, in which the capitals indicate that it is one of the 'reprises' [reruns] that should be read twice:

> AUX LIGNES DROITES ET AUX BOUCLES (AUX AVENUES ET AUX PLACES)
> on préfère un réseau et au boulevard périphérique (au polygone)
> les rues et leur fuite en avant (un arbre ou ce qui paraît tel
> parce qu'en repartant de plus haut à chaque impasse
> (selon le progrès de la sève dans les nervures d'une feuille)
> il croît sans arrière-pensée par la pointe des branches)
> du moins si l'on bat son quartier (une battue s'achève

lorsqu'on a parcouru tous les segments de rue
(dans les deux sens) pour se prouver en suivant une règle
à chaque fourche (ne jamais emprunter le même dans le même)
et une stratégie à courte vue (celle d'Ariane Folle
entraîne sans cesse dans de nouveaux détours (ouvrir et dérouler)
ou bien (clore et rembobiner) celle d'Ariane Sage
pousse à revenir au plus vite sur ses pas)
qu'il est possible d'explorer (d'épuiser les possibles)
sans supposer de centre[15]

[TO STRAIGHT LINES AND LOOPS (TO AVENUES AND PLACES)
we prefer a network and to the peripheral boulevards (to the polygon)
the streets and their forward rush (a tree or what looks like one
because in setting off higher at every dead end
(according to the spreading of sap through the veins of a leaf)
It grows by the tips of the branches without ulterior motives)
at least if you go on a hunt in your neighbourhood (a hunt concludes
when each segment of street has been embraced
(in both directions) to prove to yourself by following a rule
at each fork (never take the same within the same)
and a short-sighted strategy (that of Mad Ariadne
continuously leads to new detours (open and unwind)
or else (close and rewind) that of Wise Ariadne
incites you to retrace your steps as quickly as possible)
that it is possible to explore (exhausting all possibilities)
without assuming there's a centre]

At the heart of this piece is a motif dear to Apollinaire, the surrealists and their descendants: 'les rues et leur fuite en avant' [the streets and their forward rush], meaning a practice of walking that favours chance and unexpected encounters, with a predilection for crossed paths rather than straight lines or predictable loops. If we decipher this labyrinthine text, firstly eliminating the many parentheses and sub-parentheses, as well as the forks and shortcuts (a modernist treatment of punctuation), we find an underlying sentence, which we could be tempted to call the main proposition, were it not for the fact that it does not pre-exist its interruptions; one must 'chercher' [seek out] this sentence (*Chercher une phrase*), to see where it goes. Here it is:

AUX LIGNES DROITES ET AUX BOUCLES (...) on préfère un réseau et au boulevard périphérique (...) les rues et leur fuite en avant (... (...) ...) du moins si l'on bat son quartier (...) pour se prouver en suivant une règle | à chaque fourche (...) et une stratégie à courte vue (... (...) ... (...) ...) qu'il est possible d'explorer (...) | sans supposer de centre.

(TO STRAIGHT LINES AND LOOPS (...) we prefer a network and to the peripheral boulevards (...) the streets and their forwards rush (... (...) ...) at least if you go on a hunt in your neighbourhood (...) to prove to yourself by following a rule | at each fork (...) and a short-sighted strategy (... (...) ... (...) ...) that it is possible to explore (...) | without assuming there's a centre.)

The parentheses are either single, double (parentheses within parentheses), or triple (parentheses within parentheses within parentheses — later on in the text it will go up to eight or nine — as in ee cummings, Gertrude Stein, John Ashbery or Jacques Roubaud). We can also note the metaphor of the sap and veins of a leaf, and that of a hunt ('battue', which recurs throughout the four sequences, also means beating the bushes to force out the game, recalling the place of hunting in Carlo Ginzburg's 'evidential paradigm', where Sherlock Holmes and Sigmund Freud stand alongside Morelli as exemplary and intrepid hunters of meaning.[16] Let us also note the motif of the thread and the labyrinth, with its two Ariadnes — Mad and Wise: classical references laced with folklore. A constantly resourceful and open-ended process of hybridization and mixing and matching governs a textual process that takes every opportunity to feed off the multiple meanings of words and phrases. The joint motifs of spatial wandering and the production of meaning also combine in the idea that exploration comes down to 'épuiser des possibles' [exhausting possibilities], in the manner of Perec in his 'Tentatives d'épuisement' [Attempts at Exhausting] various types of urban space.[17] We may also note the definition, or rather the recipe, of a 'battue' (hunt): 'parcour[ir] tous les segments de rue | (dans les deux sens)' [embrace every segment of street | (in both directions)].

How, in a text of this genre (but of what genre, exactly?), can we sort out what comes from the avant-garde, from modernism, or from postmodernism? An obvious temptation is to opt for the label 'postmodern' on the pretext that all the parameters of this poetic structure, the 'effects' it deploys, even when we can attach them to moments from the past, must be attributed to postmodernism since it is not only about citation (a modernist trait as much as a postmodern one), but recycling. But why settle for this solution? Is this not to fall into the most obvious nominalist trap, or, worse, simply to allow oneself to be guided by simple chronology, forgetting that temporal linearity — according to which what comes after is necessarily different from, and either better or worse than, what came before — is not always appropriate? Prioritizing the postmodern option amounts to making a choice among the range of possibilities that abound in this text, and claiming the existence of watertight categories, denying the longevity of the relationships between, firstly, the so-called historical avant-gardes, secondly, modernism — whose living force and influence should be recognized, rather than its 'legacy' — as if it remained inert[18] — and, thirdly, a postmodern vision that is wholly capable of affirming its autonomy, but which, in the case of an Alferi, refuses this option so as, rather, to revitalize itself, by retaining links with the currents of the past — including the radical force of the avant-garde gesture, and the rigorous demands of the great modernists? According to what criteria do we allow ourselves to deny this text its participation in, and its innovation through, something that partake of the avant-garde, if not the assumption that the avant-gardes are to be tidied away into a trinket shop, on the grounds that they are nothing but memorial places, historical monuments? Why follow in the footsteps of Peter Bürger, according to whom, since the alleged end of the avant-gardes, all art that calls itself avant-garde is in fact merely 'neo-avant-garde', condemned to repeat 'historical' gestures in the void, and doomed to fail?[19] Let us lean more towards Hal Foster, who sees in the artistic practices of the 1960s, apparently belonging to a 'neo-avant-garde', the true and therefore first iteration of the transformative force harboured by these avant-garde aesthetics.[20]

★　★　★　★　★

Let us conduct an experiment.

Here are extracts from a poem by Alferi, taken from the collection *Sentimentale journée*, dating from 1997.

ALLEGRIA
*Quel est cet élan*
*C'est un mouvement de mort*
*Mais c'est aussi*
*Une jouissance pure de contenu.*

Quel est cet élan que tu prends dévalant,
L'escalier, marches enjambées du souffle habituel
Quand tu aspires 'hi' expires 'han' jusqu'au tremplin
De la rue? —
[...]
— À l'instant où tu rebondis
Sur le trottoir après la dernière marche
Tu n'es qu'un photogramme et le paysage avec toi
Gelé par la touche 'pause' du magnétoscope
Mais qui ne veut pas s'arrêter, tremble comme une feuille
Ou un rongeur piégé qui gigote pour rejoindre
Ses semblables. L'image aussi veut rentrer dans la danse
Des images/seconde. Quel est cet élan qui
Frappe de vanités tous les dépôts, voitures garées
Immeubles rescapés du bombardement de la nuit
Et résolutions du réveil? A tout point de vue,
[...]
C'est un mouvement de mort, escalade et dégringolade
Une soif inextinguible, un appel répété
Au sacrifice (et j'en rajoute exprès), une surenchère
Dans la dévastation. — Mais c'est aussi
Tout le contraire cet aller simple
Que rien ne justifie. Pas un plaisir
Car ça ne donne rien et chaque instant te dépossède
Du spectacle emballé par le rétroviseur
En rivant ton regard au tronçon de route qui fonce
Vers toi. Une jouissance pure de contenu:
L'idée visible de la danse dans le miroir
Qui a mangé le mur derrière la rampe et vide
La piste de ses cavaliers apprentis trop inquiets
De leur pied droit sur place (temps faibles) et du gauche
En arrière de côté (temps forts) pour s'admirer
Évoluant. Disparus corps et biens comme toi
Les Parisiens d'une photo longtemps posée d'Atget
Par excès de vitesse ont-ils au moins connu l'orgasme
Dans un éternuement? — Le stroboscope les ressuscite

En danseurs, en fugitifs, en fantômes pris sur le fait
Le temps de reconnaître en eux tes frères d'armes
Puis il faudra glaner d'autres images combustibles
Brûler les meubles jusqu'à retrouver le dosage
Explosif de l'absence, de la joie et du mouvement[21]

[ALLEGRIA
*What is this impulse*
*It's an annihilating movement*
*But it's also*
*Joy stripped of content.*

What is this impulse that sends you hurtling down
The stairs, missing out the steps of regular breath
When breathing in 'hee', breathing out 'haw' until you reach the
springboard
Street? —
[...]
— At the moment you rebound
From the pavement following the last step
You're no more than a photogram and the landscape with you
Frozen by the pause button on the videotape player
But one that doesn't want to stop, trembles like a leaf
Or a trapped rodent struggling to rejoin
Its fellows. The image too wants to enter into the dance
Of images | second. What is this impulse that
Outmodes all deposits, parked cars
Buildings unharmed by the night's bombardments
And waking resolutions? From any point of view,
[...]
It's an annihilating movement, climb and abject fall
An inextinguishable thirst, a repeated call
For sacrifice (and I add this on purpose), it accelerates
Devastation. — But it's also
Just the opposite this one-way trip
That nothing can justify. Not a pleasure
For it gets you nothing and each moment deprives you
Of the spectacle wrapped into the rear-view mirror
Gaze fixed on the stub of road lunging
At you. Joy stripped of content:
The visible idea of dance in the mirror
That has consumed the wall behind the projectors emptying
The floor of its dancers in training too concerned
About where their right foot is (upbeat) and their left
At the back and to the side (downbeat) to admire their own
Twirls. Gone for good like you
Parisians of a long-exposed photo by Atget
Speeding did they at least experience orgasm
In a sneeze? — The stroboscope resuscitates them
As dancers, fugitives, ghosts caught on the run
Time enough to recognize them as brothers in arms

> Then we'll have to pick up other combustible images
> Burn the furniture until we find the explosive
> Dose of absence, joy and movement][22]

And here is a poem by André Breton, taken from *Le Revolver à cheveux blancs* dating from 1932. A gap of sixty-five years, or around two generations, separates the Breton poem form Alferi's.

> NŒUD DES MIROIRS
> Les belles fenêtres ouvertes et fermées
> Suspendues aux lèvres du jour
> Les belles fenêtres en chemise
> Les belles fenêtres aux cheveux de feu dans la nuit noire
> Les belles fenêtres de cris d'alarmes et de baisers
> Au-dessus de moi au-dessous de moi derrière moi il y en a
> moins qu'en moi
> Où elles ne font qu'un seul cristal bleu comme les blés
> Un diamant divisible en autant de diamants qu'il en faudrait
> pour se baigner à tous les bengalis
> Et les saisons qui ne sont pas quatre mais quinze ou seize
> En moi parmi lesquelles celle où le métal fleurit
> Celle dont le sourire est moins qu'une dentelle
> Celle où la rosée du soir unit les femmes et les pierres
> Les saisons lumineuses comme l'intérieur d'une pomme dont
> on a détaché un quartier
> Ou encore comme un quartier excentrique habité par des
> êtres qui sont de mèche avec le vent
> Ou encore comme le vent de l'esprit qui la nuit ferre d'oiseaux
> sans bornes les chevaux à naseaux d'algèbre
> Ou encore comme la formule
>
> Teinture de passiflore    {
> Teinture d'aubépine    {    aa 50 cent. cubes
>
> Teinture de gui 5 cent. cubes
> Teinture de scille 3 cent. cubes
>
> qui combat le bruit de galop
> Les saisons remontent maille par maille leur filet brillant de l'eau vive
> de mes yeux
> Et dans ce filet il y a ce que j'ai vu c'est la spire d'un fabuleux coquillage
> Qui me rappelle l'exécution en vase clos de l'empereur Maximilien
> Il y a ce que je connais bien que je connais si peu que prête-moi
> tes serres vieux délire
> Pour m'élever avec mon cœur le long de la cataracte
> Les aéronautes parlent de l'efflorescence de l'air en hiver[23]
>
> [KNOT OF MIRRORS
> The beautiful windows open and closed
> Suspended from the lips of the day
> The beautiful windows in shirtsleeves
> The beautiful windows with fiery hair in the black night
> The beautiful windows of cries of alarm and of kisses

Above me beneath me behind me they are
fewer than those within me
Where they make just one crystal as blue as the wheat fields
A diamond divisible into as many diamonds you would need
to swim amid the flares of strawberry finches
And the seasons of which there are not four but fifteen or sixteen
In me among which the one where metal flowers
The one whose smile is less than lace
The one where the evening dew unites women and rocks
Seasons bright as the inside of an apple from which
one has cut off a quarter
Or else like an eccentric quarter inhabited by
beings who are in league with the wind
Or else like the wind of the mind which at night gives the horses with
algebraic nostrils hooves made up of endless birds
Or else like the formula
Tincture of Passionflower    {
Tincture of Hawthorne    {    aa 50 cubic cents

Tincture of Mistletoe 5 cubic cents
Tincture of Spring squill 3 cubic cents

That slows your galloping heart
The seasons pull up link by link their net sparkling with the bright water
of my eyes
And in this net there is what I have seen it is the whorl of a fabulous shell
Which reminds me of the execution in camera of Emperor Maximilian
There is what I know well what I know so little that lend me
your talons old delirium
To hoist me with my heart along the length of the waterfall
Balloonists speak of the efflorescence of the air in winter)

Revealing many similarities, these two poetic works possess above all a 'family resemblance': blank verse, with a capital letter on the left; a lack of stanza breaks or other comparable formal traits; lengths considerably exceeding the shorter formats such as the sonnet often favoured since the Symbolists, but not looking to expand excessively; dimensions that favour lyrical-narrative development — a lyrical-autobiographical first person that addresses a 'tu' [you] in Alferi's case — as in Apollinaire's 'Zone': a modernist trait — while in Breton the 'je' [I] describes itself, throughout the poem, as at once a space, 'nœud' [knot], a locus or receptacle, and site of a perpetual work where sensation is the source of knowledge (ce que j'ai vu [...] ce que je connais' [what I have seen [...] what I know]; rapid discourse, spurred on less by an ordinary narrative logic than by an energy fuelled by work at a lexical level, making it difficult, and no doubt useless, in the two cases, to try to situate the 'action' in any part of the world as we know it; a title which, after reading, turns out to be rhematic — that is to say not, or not only, pertaining to the theme of the poem, but to its discursive or performative nature.[24]

In Alferi, the title 'Allegria' relates as much to the container as the content, to the poem itself as an exhilarating celebration. Similarly, Breton's 'Nœud des miroirs' is both the 'I' of which Breton's poem extols the capacities (an 'I' that relates to all the windows it opens onto, the outsides that it allows itself to be modelled by); and the poem, to the extent that the 'I' is more a subject formed via a relationship with language and with the process of signification. It is the poem itself which is a 'Nœud des miroirs' [Knot of mirrors]: thanks to its generativity — demonstrated by the word 'quartier' which, like other words in the poem, generates a referential context that is then swiftly replaced by another, generated by another sense of the word that then takes over — the language 'prête [son] délire' [lends [its] delirium], in other words its freedom, to the subject which, as a result, turns out to be capable of sharing this emancipation, to access this essential plasticity, to sense its multiple dimensions. Thus, as in the case of Alferi's 'Allegria', the title of Breton's poem refers to the experiment, the adventure, the shock that the poem, in its generativity, brings about in the domain of subjectivity. 'Nœud des miroirs' conjures up a subjectivity that experiences its euphoric multiplicity; that conceives itself as a series of reflective surfaces, relating to the world in a multiplicity of ways — truly a 'nœud des miroirs'!

Furthermore, one only has to glance at the table of contents of each collection to realize that in Breton as in Alferi most of the titles have a rhematic side to them. Thus, in Breton, the poem and the subject (or the adventures of the subject) have as their setting an 'Hôtel d'étincelles' [Hotel of sparks], take on '[D]es attitudes spéctrales' [Spectral attitudes], wait for a 'Dernière levée' [Final post]; while in Alferi the titles often refer back to the poem as a space for communication or comparison: 'Vous êtes invités' [You are invited], 'Ne coupez pas' [Don't hang up], 'Suite à notre conversation' [Following our conversation]. One could argue that in Breton's case this is a modernist, a post-Mallarméan, trait, involving the self-reflexive dimension of the poetic text. What if we find the 'same' trait, the same acquired characteristic, in Alferi? Does it necessarily change its status, reversing its vector to become — in the poem now deemed 'postmodern' — citational, ironic, sarcastic? Or is it not, rather, that in its flamboyant avant-gardeness Breton's poem, modernist as it may be in many ways, finds its surrealist *force de frappe* reinforced, not weakened, by the effects of its proximity to Alferi, that enable us to read it afresh (this might be Hal Foster's argument)?

As for 'Allegria', must we necessarily read this text from a postmodern perspective, taking our cues, for example, from the disposition towards citation that is present from the start in the highlighted lines cited as epigraph? But, rather than referring back to a previous text, the words of this epigraph are taken from the poem that we are about to read, for which it creates a sort of trailer, delivering the salient points in advance. The snippets that form it are found scattered within the poem: we will discover them while reading the text. And, as a result, the reader will hear or see echoes of what has already been heard or seen. Then, if we reread the text we will have the pleasure of identifying these fragments, even of anticipating them, spotting them out of the corner of our eye as they are about come up. We may end up highlighting them in colour, and then — why not? —comparing the various uses of this method in the collection (each poem in *Sentimentale journée* has its own abridged version, its 'trailer', with the level of distribution and dissemination of the poem's elements subject to variation). Certainly, citation and fragmentation are modernist traits (we may think of Eliot, Pound, Apollinaire), but recycling these same elements in a 'homeostatic' system such as this can make us opt for the postmodern. But it is here that we once again note that the categories of the avant-garde, the modern and the postmodern (or of the neo-avant-garde) apply less to traits that we can identify in texts than to procedures we can apply while reading them, and thus to choices we can make when attributing meaning to them.

'Allegria' ponders the nature of an 'élan' [momentum] at once that of the subject that propels itself outside, 'dévalant | L'escalier' [hurtling down | The stairs] to land in the street, and that of the enunciation carrying the poem (the 'élan' [momentum] of the poetic discourse at the heart of *Chercher une phrase*).[25] Placed as epigraph, the abridged version of the poem gets straight to the point. 'Cet élan' [This impulse] could equally be 'un mouvement de mort' [an annihilating movement], meaning the elimination of full and sovereign subjectivity — more 'rien' [nothing] than something — and, at the same time, 'une jouissance pure de contenu' [Joy stripped of content]. More discreetly, the full poem takes on the appearance of a conversation (many of the poems in the collection comprise elements of the 'poem-conversation' as practised by Apollinaire), filled with interruptions, digressions, breaks in the flow, where all kinds of methods of communication or modern technologies portray a subject stamped with the virtual (which 'n'es[t] qu'un photogramme ... | Gelé par la touche 'pause' du magnétoscope' [no more than a photogram | Frozen by the pause button on the videotape player]; or like 'Les Parisiens d'une photo longtemps posée d'Atget [que] | Le stroboscope [...] ressuscite | En danseurs, en fugitifs, en fantômes pris sur le fait' [Parisians of a long-exposed photo by Atget | [which] the stroboscope resuscitates | As dancers, fugitives, ghosts caught on the run].) But if this momentum seems lethal, an 'escalade et dégringolade [...] appel répété au sacrifice' [climb and abject fall [...] a repeated call | For sacrifice],

> c'est aussi
> Tout le contraire cet aller simple
> Que rien ne justifie. Pas un plaisir
> Car ça ne donne rien et chaque instant te dépossède
> [...] Une jouissance pure de contenu

> [But it's also
> Just the opposite this one-way trip
> That nothing can justify. Not a pleasure
> For it gets you nothing and each moment deprives you
> [...] Joy stripped of content]

The momentum that the poem seeks to pinpoint is connected to an experience firmly anchored in the body, an 'athlétisme affectif' [emotional athleticism], as Artaud would say, linked to the descent of a flight of stairs, to a pace, a cadence which implies an eclipse of self — 'Une jouissance pure de contenu' [joy stripped of content], and at the same time the quest for the 'dosage | explosif de l'absence, de la joie et du mouvement' [explosive | dose of absence, joy and movement]. In this we can certainly hear — or project — the sound of a Deleuzian bell, a po-mo note, but why not at the same time hear the bugle of the avant-gardes, in their wish to eliminate the boundary between art and life, to transform human existence? And moreover, is this Deleuzian ring not, in a rather neat way, also wholly present, or virtual, in Breton's poem?

★   ★   ★   ★   ★

It would not be difficult to propose an avant-gardist or modernist reading of 'Nœud des Miroirs', depending on which traits one chose to highlight. But in the twenty-first century, a postmodern reading would be just as valid, and was perhaps already, twenty or thirty years ago. It will all depend on our interpretation of Breton's poetic mindset, and the spirit in which the reader decides which traits to deem pertinent; it is we who decide on the mixture of various elements in the text, through reading and re-reading. Or rather coming down to choice, all may depend on our varying iterations of the poem, the shape our reading gives it, on this day, at this hour. If there is enough in 'Nœud des Miroirs' to satisfy a reader who is keen on avant-gardism, or well-versed in modernist finesse, there is as much, if not more, for a passionate reader of Deleuze or Nancy, an enthusiast for Deguy rather than Bonnefoy, for Catherine Malabou rather than Jean-Pierre Richard. Yes, this celebration of internal 'saisons', 'quinze ou seize en moi' [fifteen or sixteen in me], can be understood in terms of a widening of the sphere of Romantic subjectivity, and of a passion for perceptual experience that has displaced other methods of contemplating the human person, perhaps especially those linked to individual psychology. But read alongside 'Allegria', and after Lacan among others, we can be more sensitive, in 'Nœud des Miroirs' as with every poem in *Revolver à cheveux blancs*, to the way the poem demonstrates this apprehension of the multiplicity and the plasticity of the subject, which of course permeates all Breton's poetry and thought. Are there not states in Breton that are just as *extimate* as they are intimate, which testify to a 'mouvement de mort' [annihilating movement] and a 'jouissance pure de contenu' [joy stripped of content] as much as Alferi's poem? In '[s']élev[ant] avec [s]on cœur le long de la cataracte' [ris[ing] with [his] heart along the length of the waterfall] Breton remains in the Romantic sublime; however, the reference to this 'efflorescence de l'air' [efflorescence of the air], which balloonists have reported, seems postmodern, 'Alferian' even — in its brevity and its enthusiasm for modern methods of transport or communication — and projects the experience of the subject into another domain. And we may recall that the advertising announcement for *Ralentir Travaux* written jointly by Breton, Éluard and Char in 1930, displayed this phrase — rhematic to a degree — 'le sujet de ce livre est un être mobile' [the subject of this book is a mobile being].[26]

★   ★   ★   ★   ★

One might retort that this supposedly postmodern reading of a surrealist (modernist) poem merely reveals the lack of reliable criteria for demarcating the modern and the postmodern, at least when we are grappling with a verbal or pictorial work. Quite so. But that is where the banner of the good-old — and eternal? — avant-garde seems always to be at the ready. Because 'Nœud des Miroirs' has been, still is, and always will be, it seems to me, a poem of the avant-garde. Look at the beautiful collage it displays at its centre, a found object, a *readymade* consisting in a recipe for a homeopathic remedy made from dyes from different plants with pretty names — passionflower, hawthorn, mistletoe, spring squill — to combat the 'bruit de galop' [galloping heart], in other words cardiac arrhythmia.[27]

But let us not insist too much on this point, since it is more interesting to come back to the family resemblance between Breton's poem and Alferi's, written sixty years later, and to ask ourselves whether, alongside its modernist and postmodernist traits, Alferi's poem could not also be seen in some way as a poem of the avant-garde? Since it seems to me that if the avant-gardes of course have a history (just like every phenomenon), we must not see this historic being of the avant-gardes (the life and death of groups and sub-groups, shocking manifestos and, above all, highly performative works, whose sphere of action or application goes far beyond the usual parameters of literature or the art market) as a millstone that would prevent the actions and gestures of the avant-garde from being endlessly susceptible of reanimation and re-enactment. This is not because I want to distil a spirit of pure avant-gardism transcending all particular manifestations, but rather because the essential historicity of the avant-gardes is rooted in the perennial character of certain recurrent traits. And, if there is a common history, which would tie both Alferi and Breton's poems to an art of the avant-garde, it lies in the wider context of contemporary aesthetics where direct and indirect links with the great period of the avant-gardes are legion. If this period belongs to the past, it is a past that is not yet over, a history whose story continues, a past that survives via all sorts of channels, ties, underground (or aerial) trails, all sorts of linkages whose flexibility should be tested, trails that should be retraced (taking, for example, the city, the everyday, or the archive as investigatory grounds).

Avant-gardes are often held to comprise the following traits: a desire to eliminate the boundary between art and life; a programmatic bent (but also a desire to 'deprogramme', to invent new and unheard of pathways); a desire to shake up the spectator/reader; the artist's solidarity with collective enterprises, whether or not they have political ambitions, and whether or not this aligns the artist with established groups; the ambition to get out of the ivory tower; a desire to escape the past as a dead weight, often by diverting past energies and turning them towards the future; an experimental attitude: art as a project, an experiment; a conceptual dimension: the defetishization of the work, which is conceived as activity or process rather than product; to recognize a pragmatic, performative character in the artistic gesture, in the artist's stance. But is this list of criteria not just as applicable, step by step, to the landscape of contemporary creation in its multifarious manifestations, where, to confine ourselves to the 'literary', there emerges a Pierre Alferi, an Olivier Cadiot or a Valère Novarina? And, a fortiori, in the 'visual' arts, dominated by performance, the 'site-specific', installations, the experiential, the material, the immaterial, 'self-technologies', archives? Must we really deny all these people the status of avant-garde artist and condemn them to the nothingness of the neo?

Some of course say: that's all nostalgia, imitation, pastiche, retro. This line was taken in a double article in *Le Monde du Samedi*, entitled 'Rétro, c'est trop. Quand la création carbure au passé' [Retro: it's too much. When creation runs on the past].[28] On the basis of an English book, *Retromania* by Simon Reynolds, dedicated to the retro trend in music — a preference for vinyl, the 'vintage explosion' — the authors of this article, Nathalie Herzberg and Aureliano Tonet, initially look for examples of their own — the covering by French artist Red of an entire album by Leonard Cohen; the roaring success of *Mad Men* or *The Artist*. Their aim? To pin down the so-called 'epidemic' or 'contagious disease' constituted by an all-pervasive *passéisme* [past-ism]. Then, in order to magnify and stretch the frame of their argument they cite works or interviews with, randomly, the author of an essay on hits, the 'film-palimpsest', *Holy Motors*, by Leos Carax, which covers the entire history of cinema and recycles a song by Gérard Manset called 'Revivre'; a recent book, also named *Revivre*, by the Bergsonist, Frédéric Worms. Remarks by the literary critic Dominique Viart on the return to the real and the debt to the past (and the library) that has characterized French literature since 1980, blend with those of the editors of *Schnock*, a 'quarterly review' for old gentlemen of all ages (!), and those of the 'anarcho-dandy' authors of the *Manifeste Chap* who encourage 'la révolution non pas par le tweet mais par le tweed' [revolution not by tweet but by tweed]...

If not everything in it is false, this article in *Le Monde* betrays a profound misunderstanding of the relationship with the past in contemporary creativity. In this domain, the parallels and convergences between the fields of the visual and the written are of themselves signs of the strength of the traits which have characterized avant-gardes from their beginning. The way in which the poems of Jacques Roubaud or Pierre Alferi cite, recycle, replay and update moments from the avant-gardist past has nothing to do with a predilection for old LPs, nostalgia for Zippo lighters, or the desire to quit actuality by finding a haven in the past. Collecting and archiving, *détournement* and parody, performance and event, the multi-tracking of utterance and the shaking up of linguistic proprieties, the scrambling of registers and temporalities: these are just some of the driving forces in contemporary art. Just as they were driving forces in the avant-gardes, both those now labelled 'historical' and those which, until further notice, we may call current.

## Notes

1. *Autobiographie, chapitre dix: poèmes avec des moments de repos en prose* (Paris: Gallimard, 1977).
2. See as a symptomatic example, Kevin J. H. Dettmar, *The Illicit Joyce of Postmodernism: Reading against the Grain* (Madison: Wisconsin University Press, 1996).
3. See Jacques Roubaud, *La Bibliothèque de Warburg* (Paris: Seuil, 2002).
4. *The Political Unconscious: Narrative as a Socially Symbolic Act* (London: Methuen, 1981).
5. Breton, *Œuvres complètes*, ed. by Marguerite Bonnet, 4 vols (Paris: Gallimard, 1988–2008), I, 329.
6. *Guillaume d'Ockham le singulier* (Paris: Minuit, 1989).
7. *Chercher une phrase* (Paris: Christian Bourgois, 1991).
8. Paris: P.O.L., 1991.
9. *Revue de la littérature générale*, I: *La Mécanique lyrique* (Paris: P.O.L., 1995), and *Revue de la littérature générale*, II: *Digest* (Paris: P.O.L., 1996).

10. Paris: P.O.L., 1992.

11. See my 'Pierre Alferi and Jakob von Uexküll: Experience and Experiment in *Le Chemin familier du poisson combatif*', in the present volume.

12. *Le Chemin familier*, p. 21.

13. Ibid, p. 17.

14. Ibid, p. 21.

15. Ibid, p. 22.

16. Carlo Ginzburg, 'Traces: racines d'un paradigme indiciaire', in *Mythes, emblèmes, traces: morphologue et histoire* (Paris: Flammarion, 1989), pp. 139–80.

17. See Michael Sheringham, *Everyday Life: Theories and Practices from Surrealism to the Present* (Oxford: Oxford University Press, 2006), pp. 221–78.

18. See my 'Omvormingen van het Modernisme: De stad, het alledaagse, het archief' [Transmutations of Modernism: The City, the Everyday, and the Archive], in *De Erfenis van het Modernisme*, ed. by Jan Baetens, Sjef Houppermans, Arthur Langeveld and Peter Liebregts (Amsterdam: Rozenberg, 2010), pp. 15–33.

19. Peter Bürger, *Theorie der Avantgarde* (Frankfurt: Suhrkamp, 1974).

20. Hal Foster, 'What's Neo about the Neo-Avant-Garde?', *October*, 70 (1994), 5–32.

21. *Sentimentale journée* (Paris: P.O.L., 1997), 97–99.

22. Pierre Alferi, 'Allegria', trans. by Kate Lermitte Campbell, in *Substance*, 123 (2010), 24–25.

23. André Breton, *Œuvres complètes*, II, 87–88.

24. See Gérard Genette, *Seuils* (Paris: Seuil, 1987).

25. *Chercher une phrase* (Paris: Christian Bourgois, 2007), p. 30.

26. André Breton, *Œuvres complètes*, II, 1312.

27. It is amusing to find the opinion of a pharmacist on the internet: see Thierry Lefevre, 'Surréalisme et pharmacie', *Revue d'histoire de la pharmacie*, 337 (2003), 180–83.

28. 16 June 2012.

# 43

# Pierre Alferi, 'Une défense de la poésie'

UNE DÉFENSE DE LA POÉSIE

*Cela se passe*
*Ici*
*Entre la sensation aiguë et le sentiment latent*
*Entrant tu*
*As troublé le vieux jeu de l'âme*
*Et du paysage*
*Alors j'ai bien besoin de toi pour avancer.*

Quel bonheur te voir surmarcher
Mon territoire, échanger quelques mots
Insignifiants de passe avec les nains
Du jardin. Les figures humaines s'étaient tues
Dans la partie construite du domaine
À la frontière à peine un vieillard retenait-

Il l'attention en tranchant la queue d'une banane
Affublée d'un code-barre avec un couteau suisse.
Oui, dès la première sensation
La face visible annonce la couleur
Le code du jour: la nature
De son lien avec la cachée. Cela se passe
Ici, non pas dans le 'non-dit'

Mais entre les vues du moment
Du quartier tout à fait fidèles
Et ce qu'elles couvrent qu'il faut dire.
Un vérin hydraulique soutient la galerie
Je m'y appuie, j'éprouve sa résistance
À chaque ligne. Chaque ligne mesure
La distance entre le décor
Constat que l'on dresse et son ombre
Inventaire que l'on couche par écrit —
Entre la sensation aiguë et le sentiment latent, entre
Entre. Or cette proportion capricieuse qui règle
Mon débit maladif, le rythme, le débite
Avait gelé dans les lieux familiers. Tout un pan
Gagné par le désert et ses nuits froides
Et son vent-fou-que-nul-n'écoute-impunément.

Le même manège: regards d'habitués qui s'évitent
Préfèrent se rendre la monnaie des paroles de profil

Murs et chaussée lustrés par la rêverie
Pour la rêverie, sketches mille fois répétés
Devant une assemblée de chaises. Entrant tu
As troublé le vieux jeu de l'âme
Et du paysage. L'air que tu déplaces en marchant
A regonflé les figures de cartes d'ici.
    — Cela nous fait un peu beaucoup d'images
Non? De quoi parlait le téléfilm hier soir?
Même pas compris si c'était un docudrama
Ou quoi. — Oui, tout se mêle ce matin
Plutôt se juxtapose, une vue clap une autre
Dosages inégaux de soleil, passants, voitures, ciment
Que rien ne lie sinon l'analogie dont la raison
Fuit dans la vue suivante. — Au moins j'espère
Qu'en les cousant tu cernes un peu mieux
Ce qu'elles couvrent dans ta pauvre petite tête.
    — En deux mots j'appelle ça le sentimental
Alors j'ai bien besoin de toi pour avancer
D'une comparaison à l'autre ironiquement
Naïvement dans cette lumière indirecte
Cette 'réalité' qui se cite elle-même
Et se distance. Car derrière elle, loin derrière
Le réalisme et l'imagination piétinent
Dans un mortel docudrama. — C'est tout?
    — C'est tout, j'ai trop parlé, c'est de ta faute.
Maintenant changeons de terrasse
Cherchons du silence mais dehors.

[*It's happening*
*Here*
*Between the acute sensation and the latent feeling*
*Coming in*
*You disturbed the old game of the soul*
*And the landscape*
*So I really need you so I can make headway*

What fun seeing you cruising over
My territory, swapping a few innocuous
Pass words with the garden
Gnomes. The human figures had quietened down
In the built-up bit of the domain
At the border an old guy scarcely
Attracted attention as he hacked into a banana
Sporting a barcode with a Swiss Army knife.
Yes, no sooner the first sensation
The visible side of things shows its colours
Today's code: the nature
Of its link with the hidden. It's happening
Here, not in the 'un-said'

But between the views at this moment
Of the neighbourhood quite faithful

And what they hide that must be said.
A hydraulic jack props up the gallery
I lean against it, feeling its resistance
At every line. Each line measures
The distance between the décor
An agreed statement and its shadow
Inventory laid out in writing
Between the acute sensation and the latent feeling, between
Between. In fact this capricious proportion that regulates
My sickly delivery, that provides its rhythm, trots it out
Had frozen up in the usual places. A whole swathe
Taken over by the desert and its cold nights
And its mad-wind-that-no-one listens to unscathed.
The same merry-go-round: the glances of the regulars avoiding
one another
Preferring to give talk's loose change in profile
Walls and roadway smoothed by reverie
And for reverie, sketches repeated a thousand times
Before an audience of chairs. Coming in
You disturbed the old game of the soul
And the landscape. The air you displace as you walk
Has pumped up again the cardboard figures hereabouts.
    — That's a few too many images
Isn't it? What was last night's telefilm about?
Didn't grasp if it was a drama-documentary
Or what. — Yes, it's all getting mixed up this morning
Or rather getting juxtaposed, one view, action, another view
Uneven doses of sun, passers-by, cars, cement
That nothing links except analogy whose rationale
Disperses in the next take. — I hope at least
That in sewing them together you fathom a bit better
What they cover up in your poor little head.
In two words I call this the sentimental
So I really need you so I can make headway
From one comparison to another ironically
Naively in this indirect light
This 'reality' that keeps quoting itself
And takes its distance. Because behind it, way behind
Realism and imagination are treading water
In a deadly docudrama. — Is that all?
    — That's all, I've said too much, it's your fault.
Now let's change location
Let's look for silence but outside]

From *Sentimentale journée*

The title of Alferi's poem, from his 1997 collection *Sentimentale journée*,[1] links it with innumerable poems about poetry, such as Verlaine's 'Art poétique', but alludes most directly to Shelley's 1821 treatise, *A Defence of Poetry*, which claimed that poetry 'purges from our inward sight the film of familiarity which obscures from us the wonder of our being'.[2] In fact, most poems in *Sentimentale journée* can be said to be 'about' poetry since, as in 'Une défense de la poésie', Alferi repeatedly confronts the reader with hyperactive linguistic performances that include, among many other things, commentary on their own status and progress. With everything moving so fast it is often hard to see what is going on: items stand out momentarily before being swept away in a helter-skelter of words and images. As Alferi has observed, the 'flux' of poetic language necessarily engenders a certain 'flou'. His back-cover text for *Sentimentale journée* invokes the improvisatory arts of conversation and soccer: in these poems 'on voit en gros de quoi ils parlent... mais pas très bien ce qu'ils veulent dire' [one can see broadly what they're talking about... but not very clearly what they mean]; meaning is kicked around like a football: 'ils repoussent le sens d'une image à l'autre, qu'ils défont, d'une phrase à l'autre, qu'ils coupent, un peu comme on frappe dans un ballon' [they put off meaning from one image to the other, they undo, from one sentence to another, they cut, a little like one kicks a ball].[3] The word 'image' here also points to cinema, an art form constantly invoked by Alferi. Like talk, football, and film, poetry is a 'chemin de la | Coupe':[4] cutting in, cutting across, and cutting up find their equivalents in the segmentation of utterance and vision accomplished by poetic lineation, especially when heightened by the frequent enjambment that is central to Alferi's poetics.

Each poem in *Sentimentale journée* has an epigraph made up of fragments of the text to follow. These 'edited highlights' constitute a sort of 'trailer'-poem, a speeded-up version that singles out certain topics whilst allowing the same words to function differently. Here, we zoom in to the enjambment of ll. 12–13, pared down to a stark assertion of 'hereness': 'Cela se passe | Ici', and we then jump to a truncated version of l. 23, which locates 'Ici' as an intermediate realm ('Entre...'). We then speed along to the double enjambment of ll. 33–35 which refer to the upsetting of a traditional balance between inner and outer worlds, and finally land at l. 48 which points to the role of interlocution and exchange. Filtering out most of its details and loops, the 'trailer' highlights the main poem's ongoing concern with its own mechanisms, with whatever 'se passe | Ici'. Yet this concern with poetry itself is far from exclusive. On the contrary, Alferi's poetic practice, like that of others of his generation (Anne Portugal, Olivier Cadiot, Nathalie Quintane) associates poetic language directly with the processes of everyday existence. In many respects, including a passion for cinema and multimedia inventiveness, Alferi harks back to the avant-garde movements of earlier twentieth-century Modernism where linguistic and visual experimentation sought to be directly experiential and to break down the barriers between expression and reality, thus capturing the processes of perception. To be sure, the Modernist belief in art's capacity to transform life would be alien to Alferi's sceptical postmodern temper. But by contrast with the emphasis on a heroic struggle between language and being, or the disjunction between word and world, which has often marked modern poetry from Char and Ponge to Bonnefoy and Dupin, Alferi's work — taking cues in this regard from Deguy and Roubaud — questions demarcations between self and language, and between language and world. In so doing, it promotes the capacity for poetic, or more broadly literary, language to sponsor perceptual processes that are generally discouraged by routine and convention.

From start to finish, 'Une défense de la poésie' puts language on display. If we encounter a motley array of familiar things, including garden gnomes, bananas, Swiss Army knives, hydraulic jacks, and TV movies; and familiar types of utterance, including first-person narration, *style indirect libre*, dialogue, and rumination, the poem has a pervasive air of suspended reality. Alferi's aesthetic, as articulated in his treatise, *Chercher une phrase*, affirms a belief in the creative and heuristic power of defamiliarization. This does not operate through unusual combinations of words, or clusters of images, but through sentences. For Alferi, literariness occurs at the level of the sentence because sentences demarcate syntactic structures, while syntax establishes rhythm, the balances, ratios and vectors that produce meaning: 'le sens d'une phrase est l'effet global de son rythme' [the meaning of a sentence is the global effect of its rhythm].[5] Literature, and poetry in particular, where the sentence is characteristically a group of lines making up a sequence, offers the possibility of new sentences. If anything is primal for Alferi it is 'l'élan de la profération' [the momentum of proclamation] (*CP* 27),[6] a propensity for utterance that does not channel desire or crave meaning but articulates life itself as an embodied process. In each of us this 'élan' can remain on fixed pathways, giving us the same old types of experience. Poetry, however, can reroute it, offering us, temporarily at least, through the dual process of writing and reading, new encounters with reality. One way it can do this is by fostering a verbal flow where rhythm is not the regular return of the same but a constant, open-ended mixing and matching, operating at every level of signification, where familiar things are made both recognizable and strange: 'la phrase met en rythme les choses. Elle est une expérience' [the sentence puts things in rhythm. It is an experience] (*CP* 35). This kind of 'mise en rythme', favouring the dislocating agency of enjambment, can produce a convergence of the referential and the hallucinatory (Alferi's terms are 'référence' and 'apparition'). Through the curving paths of syntax, 'la phrase fait scintiller la référence: elle crée ainsi un flottement dans les choses' [the sentence makes reference sparkle: it thus creates a wavering in things] (*CP* 38); but this disorientation is followed by recognition: 'la phrase s'achève en les [les choses] laissant se poser de nouveau, s'offrir comme pour la première fois' [the sentence comes to an end by letting things come up again, and offer themselves as for the first time] (*CP* 40). The poem constantly gives the illusion that it is describing a pre-existing state of affairs, whilst in reality 'la phrase invente une expérience', constructing in its wake an 'antérieur absolu' (*CP* 14). Everything in the poem — including its way of making our ordinary world visible to us in new ways — is the outcome of this sentence-making activity, of its 'élan': nothing was there, but retrospectively a world is created.

Conversational in tone, and making frequent reference to the language and technology of filmmaking, most of the poems in *Sentimentale journée* feature quick-changing scenarios where a protagonist, who often adopts a succession of (dis)guises, undergoes a series of strange experiences that can often seem to mirror the poetic activity that generates them. 'Une défense de la poésie' is one of the poems that makes this most explicit. From the start, the speaker comments approvingly on a force, addressed as 'tu', that affects what the world looks like, and in the course of the poem he (like Alferi, the protagonist is male) will seek to pin down the modus operandi of this 'tu', locating it outside or between various types of representation — 'entre' is a key word throughout. Put very crudely, this identifies the 'tu' as poetry itself; and in the course of the poem it becomes evident that the speaker's disquisition concerns his own activity, which makes him the poet, or rather a subject in the throes of what poetry does. In the last segment (from l. 37), another voice enters the poem (heralded by the dash indicating speech), and challenges the primary speaker to express himself more clearly. The ensuing cut-and-thrust dialogue resembles a comedy sketch in which a creative artist is pestered by a sceptical down-to-earth friend.

The poem is in *vers libres*, with a capital letter at the head of each line, and a norm of eight to eleven syllables. Lineation frequently replaces punctuation, favouring parataxis and appositional constructions with few commas. This highlights the frequent enjambment (ll. 1, 2, 3, 6, 11, 12, 14, etc.), which in turn draws attention to the segmentation whereby sentences generally end in mid-line, creating a mixture of staccato jerkiness and fluidity. The poem falls naturally into three sequences (ll. 1–16, 17–36 and 37–57), marked at ll. 16 and 36 by two of the infrequent end-stopped lines. Other end-stopped lines (at ll. 8 and 28) provide a caesura in mid-sequence, without interrupting the rhetorical shape.

In the first sequence the speaker ascribes the euphoric experience of a change in his perception to a sort of 'trans-coding' that happens to his 'territoire' when it is 'surmarch[é]'. This neologism, with its comic echo of 'supermarché' (which surfaces later in the 'code-barre'), suggests walking in the air, floating just above the surface, and feeds into the various bits of scenario that follow, where artifice and a blurring of familiar categories predominate, and where everything seems to hover between reality and unreality. The matter-of-fact tone is belied by the constant incongruities, befitting the way these are generated by the discourse. The syntax parallels '*surmarcher* | Mon territoire' and '*échanger* quelques mots', while the enjambment at ll. 2/3 separates the components of the phrase 'mots de passe' so that 'Insignifiants' becomes ambiguous. Making us strongly aware of the language, this 'stuttering' effect, where a word is followed by two predicates, or is repeated with a different sense, will recur repeatedly in the poem, often in connection with enjambment (e.g. ll. 10–11, 11–12, 14–15, 19, 23–24, 31–32). Familiar binaries (nature/culture, animate/inanimate, human/inhuman, reality/artifice) are toyed with by the syntax. For example, the *rejet* 'Du jardin' (varied in 'du domaine' (l. 5)) is juxtaposed with the periphrastic 'partie construite', which, if it connotes civilization, sounds more like a stage or film set, just as the 'figures humaines' seem more like 'figurants' than ordinary mortals. In this conjuncture (implicitly that of 'poetry') what grabs attention is situated 'À la frontière' (l. 6): *between* realms. The 'vieillard' (l. 6) would be unexceptional were it not for the way poetic language zooms in on the tiny barcode on his banana ('affublée', suggesting a theatrical prop, underlines the artifice), and for his rather theatrical way of slicing the fruit with his penknife.

Beginning with a discursive and approbatory 'Oui', the second half (ll. 9–16) of the first sequence has a similar structure (two sentences, winding syntax), and reflects meditatively on the 'experience' recounted in the first, picking up the question of attention and the visible, and the idea of codes. Through brilliantly performative language, ll. 9–12 ruminate on the connections between the seen and the unseen, while ll. 12–16, focusing on representation and the links between the said and the unsaid, affirm that '[ce] qu'il faut dire' is to be found between them rather than in either of the two. Line 9 links the unsettling of customary appearances with the field of sensory experience: 'la première sensation' and 'jour' suggest morning awakening and the beginning of the day's stream of perceptions (the 'journée' is a common motif in Alferi's writing). The idiomatic phrase 'annonce la couleur', meaning to lay one's cards on the table (card games recur further on), fits the day's new colours but cleverly suggests the plain 'literality' of 'la face visible'. Syntactical ambiguity first allows 'annonce la couleur' to stand alone, and then, via the kind of 'stuttering' I referred to, allows for an enjambment where 'Le code du jour' is a second object of 'annonce', reinforcing the neutral quality of the 'face visible' by construing 'la couleur' as a 'code'. This is further reinforced, but then questioned, via repetition of the same device: l. 11 initially stands alone, reaffirming 'codedness' by associating the visible with the natural, but enjambment then makes a bridge, opening up a 'lien' between the 'face visible' and — the word is cunningly made invisible — '[la face] cachée' (l. 12).

In ll. 12–16 the opposition between the merely visible and the possibly invisible is replayed in terms of banal 'vues' that are firstly momentary glimpses, 'vues du moment', but then, via more 'stuttering' at ll. 14–15, more like picture postcards: ('[vues] Du quartier tout à fait fidèles'). But a bid is made to locate the real 'action' — 'Cela se passe' — neither in the codedly visible, nor in some symbolic 'non-dit' that would lie beneath the cover of visibility, but rather 'entre'. This is '[ce] qu'il faut dire'.

The middle segment of the poem (ll. 17–36) maintains the mix of linguistic play, fabulation and rumination that is characteristic of Alferi's poetry. Here, as elsewhere, it is as if the poetic voice were constantly trying to account for the strange contraption it constructs as it proceeds. The 'élan de la profération' manifests itself in linguistic performances, and syntax weaves together different discursive modes: meta-poetry and poetry are wired into the same circuitry. Lines 17–19 seem initially to re-specify the physical location as some sort of mine or cave where tunnelling ('galerie') is jacked up hydraulically. Hitherto only implicit, the pronoun 'Je' (l. 18) now briefly places the speaker in the diegesis: as wielder of the jack he feels the force needed to create the space in which he finds himself (the comma in l. 18 emphasizes 'j'éprouve' by lengthening the vowel sound). But the repetition of 'ligne' in l. 19 dissolves the diegetic space and lays bare the metaphorical play where 'ligne', linked to 'mesure', can allude to the verbal structure of the poem. The connection with engineering is consistent with Alferi's view of poetry as a 'mécanique lyrique'.[7] Here, the poem engineers equivalence between its structure of lines and a hollowed-out, subterranean or adjacent space. This culminates in the enjambment and repetitive stuttering of ll. 23–24, where the first 'entre' is a preposition designating interstitial spaces between the manifest and the latent, and the second 'entre' is an imperative inviting us to enter this space (a homophone, 'antre', is flickeringly perceptible here). Lines 20–24, where the word 'entre' occurs four times, echo the specifications regarding 'Ici' and '[ce] qu'il faut dire' in ll. 12–16. The 'space' of poetry is connected with a resistance to and a distance from other constructions of experienced reality. It lies between the purely objective, dispassionate 'constat' of observation (l. 21), and any fastidious verbal 'Inventaire' (l. 22) that could register this (the paralleling of the verbs 'dresser' and 'coucher' is apt). But as l. 23 asserts, poetic space is not to be confused with extreme sensations or buried (unconscious) feeling. As l. 23 insists once again, with its 'entre' at either end, and a further 'Entre' as its *rejet*, the space of the poetic is between.

Alferi's poetry is insistently present-tense, as it manifests its own becoming, but it often generates flashbacks that help to situate the 'action', creating different time zones within a single poem. Here, ll. 24–33, starting with 'Or', constitute an analeptic excursus that conjures up a sterile universe of noncommunication connected with a time when the speaker's mode of utterance, his 'débit maladif', had lost its capacity to find the right 'proportion capricieuse' between the various factors (objectivity, emotion, etc.) that seek to regulate or monopolize it. In the first scenario, 'Les lieux familiers' (l. 26) become a kind of arctic wasteland (the portmanteau word in l. 28 suggests the artifice of a theatrical or cinematic wind-machine, whose job is to add portentous symbolism). In the second (ll. 29–33) we have people habitually ('le même manège') avoiding verbal exchange (l. 29), a transaction given negative connotations via the expression 'se rendre la monnaie' (to reciprocate) which, in another instance of 'stuttering', linking it to both 'des paroles' and 'de profil', seems more of a snub than a greeting. Equally, the 'stuttering' in ll. 31–32 associates reverie with an activity that is anaesthetizing rather than enlivening, like addressing an audience of empty chairs (l. 33). In ll. 33–36 the scenario of a sterile, dysfunctional, bogusly stricken world, is curtailed by the advent of 'tu' — of poetry or something like it — which effects a reanimation or re-enchantment by disrupting the 'old game' where 'l'âme' found its image in the 'paysage' — the pathetic fallacy, inherited from Romanticism. The poetry defended in Alferi's poem subverts a traditional symbolic order — one where self and world mirror each other in a specular relationship without any real outside ('dehors' will be the poem's last word). Line 35 links the animating force of poetry with walking (a recurrent motif in Alferi), a bodily activity that effects constant displacement. And the slipstream this creates is credited metaphorically with the capacity literally to inject breath ('regonfler') into figures as lifeless as playing cards, and to return us 'ici' (l. 36), to the here and now.

Amusingly, the chaotic piling-up of metaphors does not go unremarked. In the last sequence (ll. 37–57), a dialogue strikes up between the main speaker and a heckling friend who insists on clarification, colloquially bemoaning the poem's plethora of images, and then asking whether last night's made-for-TV film was a 'docudrama' (ll. 37–40). As the speaker strives to clarify what he has been saying,

Alferi's poem closes its defence of poetry with a consideration of genre. In his opening rejoinder (ll. 40–44), he affirms that, 'ce matin' (as in the famous opening sequence of Apollinaire's 1913 poem, 'Zone', the new day stands for the present, the 'now' of perceptual experience), reality consists of a juxtaposition of items in 'uneven doses' — sunlight, passers-by, cars, cement. This 'material' could be edited together in such a way as to deliver an underlying 'non-dit', an unstated, allegorical meaning — 'ce qu'elles [the 'vues'] couvrent dans ta pauvre petite tête' (l. 46), as the friend puts it, revealing his appetite for conventional verisimilitude. But being run through the mill of generic conventions would destroy the content of experience, turning what was live perception into the inert elements of a 'mortel docudrama', dominated by the coded verisimilitude of conventional realism or a conventional 'imaginary' (l. 53). (The colloquial 'mortel' in l. 54, meaning 'dead boring', cleverly enfolds the deathlier meaning.) By contrast, this stream of perceptions can be left in its raw unedited state, as 'rushes', (the 'clap' of a clapper board in l. 41 invokes the discontinuity of film shooting). If so, the link between one percept and another will be analogical rather than symbolic: 'Dosages... Que rien ne lie sinon l'analogie', notes l. 43, with a nice internal rhyme. Provisional and momentary, such linkages dissolve, as one 'vue' succeeds another. Pressed by his interlocutor, the speaker offers a definition of this analogical successiveness (his way of 'sewing' (l. 45) the images together). 'En deux mots', he avers sententiously, it is 'le sentimental'. The joke here is that any idea of conventional sentiment or sentimentality seems wide of the mark in this context. But the word 'sentimental' could be stretched to make 'deux mots', and 'le senti-mental' would suggest the intermingling of feeling and intellection, the physical and the mental, that characterizes the kind of poetry this poem wants to defend. We are referred implicitly here to the title of the volume, *Sentimentale journée*, and to the end of another poem that clarifies the bilingual pun *journée/journey*, and the allusion to Laurence Sterne's eighteenth-century travel narrative, *A Sentimental Journey*.[8] The span of a *journée* can be seen as an unbroken journey of perception. But this is where poetry comes in, for it takes a particular form of utterance, always involving an addressee ('j'ai besoin de toi', l. 48), to invoke a mode in which 'reality' is not turned into something other than itself but apprehended or appropriated in its unfolding. It takes the ironies and naïveties of poetic analogy-making (l. 49), its 'lumière indirecte' (l. 50), to enact 'Cette "réalité" qui se cite elle-même' (l. 51). In the poetry defended, or celebrated, here the entities we encounter are not representations of reality but, momentarily at least, before language's headlong progress drags our attention forwards — so that what was 'there' a micro-second ago recedes into distance — citations or samples of the real. In Alferi's hands the dual *journée/journey* is uniquely exhilarating, but the need to move on is pressing: 'Maintenant changeons de terrasse' (l. 56).

## Notes

1. Pierre Alferi, *Sentimentale journée* (Paris: P.D.L., 1997), pp. 53–55.
2. P. B. Shelley, *Selected Poetry, Prose and Letters* (London: Nonesuch Press, 1951), p. 1052.
3. Alferi, *Sentimentale journée*, back cover.

4. Ibid., p. 21.

5. Pierre Alferi, *Chercher une phrase* (Paris: Christian Bourgois, [1991]; rev. edn 2007), p. 30. Hereafter, page references will be given in the text, following the abbreviation *CP*.

6. See the poem 'Allegria', in Alferi, *Sentimentale journée*, pp. 97–99.

7. See the issue of *Revue de littérature générale*, co-edited by Pierre Alferi and Olivier Cadiot (Paris: P.O.L., 1995).

8. Alferi, *Sentimentale journée*, p. 20.

# 44

# Pierre Alferi and Jakob von Uexküll: Experience and Experiment in *Le Chemin familier du poisson combatif*

This article focuses on Alferi's second book of poetry, *Le Chemin familier du poisson combatif* [*The Fighting Fish's Familiar Path*], published in 1992. It is a companion piece to my article, 'Pierre Alferi and the Poetics of the Dissolve', examining his 1997 collection, *Sentimentale journée*, which appears in this volume. The notion of the dissolve links two things that are crucial in Alferi: first, the way sense keeps forming and dispersing in his poems through a variety of means mirrored by frequent references to cinema and other technological media: as in cinema, rupture and continuity are both essential to the process. Second, the way his poetic language, working through processes of disruption or interruption, and favouring a thematics of cognitive experiment and bewilderment in everyday contexts, offers an image of subjective experience or identity that stresses the pleasures and pains of self-dissolution. What I call a 'poetics of the dissolve' is bound up with the consistently experimental — or *faux*-experimental — bias of Alferi's work, its play with procedures and modes of conjecture associated with different kinds of scientific inquiry. Devising or simulating an experimental situation can be seen as recapping — with a few twists of irony — aspects of the avant-garde tradition, including the project of questioning not only the division between various art forms in favour of a more generalized set of practices, but also the border between art and life, art practice and the everyday. Alferi works in ways that fit with the recent prevalence of an 'art of the project', where the artwork is the residue of an experiment, a setting up of certain conditions, a report.[1]

The back cover text of *Le Chemin familier du poisson combatif* reads as follows:

> Le narrateur se soumet à quatre expériences. La première est de sortir. La deuxième, de passer le temps. La troisième, de rentrer chez soi. La quatrième, de regarder.
> Récit d'une aventure.

> [The narrator submits himself to four experiments. The first is going out. The second, passing time. The third, coming home. The fourth, watching. || An adventure story.]

At the end of the book a note informs us that it draws on information from *The*

*Oxford Companion to Animal Behaviour*, that it cites a definition from a book on wild mammals, and a sentence from Henry James, and that it borrows four diagrams and their captions from a book called *Mondes animaux et monde humain, suivi de Théorie de la signification* [*Animal Worlds and the Human World, followed by A Theory of Signification*], by Jakob von Uexküll, published in 1965.[2] This helps explain why the four parts of *Le Chemin familier* have titles relating to animals. In each case the title is followed by a strange diagram, evidently borrowed from Uexküll, followed, in the first three parts, by an italicized preamble set out as a poem, beginning with the words — '*pour faire cette expérience*' [*to carry out this experiment*], and outlining a bizarre set of practical instructions. In the first part instructions relate to the arrangement of a fish-tank and the likely responses of a Siamese fighting fish when confronted with a barrier constructed in a certain way. In part four this preamble is omitted, but the text begins with the words 'Pour faire cette expérience il n'est besoin d'aucun procès | technique [...]' [Carrying out this experiment requires no technical trial] (*Chemin*, p. 79). Following the preamble, each of the book's parts consists in some twenty pages of text divided into unnumbered and untitled sections, where every other section begins with a first line in capital letters that serves as a sort of title and, along with other features, notably a switch from the first-person *je* to the anonymous *on*, marks these as more autonomous poems.[3] A note at the beginning identifies these segments as 'Reprises' — reruns, revivals, or repeats. It reads as follows:

> Les 'reprises' sont faites pour être lues deux fois de suite. Leur premier vers est en capitales; dans la dernière séquence, leur fin est signalée par un tiret. (ibid., p. 7)

> [The 'reprises' are made to be read twice in a row. Their first line is capitalized; in the final sequence, their end is signalled by a dash.]

At the end of the book we find an index of all the 'reprise' texts or poems, in alphabetical order, which accentuates their different status. As we read the four parts of the poem, we may or may not follow the instruction to read these portions twice, but we notice that in many cases they do 'reprise', restate, or otherwise echo the more loosely structured and discursive first-person text that immediately precedes them. Following the end of each of the first three parts of the book a sentence — in italics like the instructions at the outset — 'sums up' each experiment, and serves as a kind of 'envoi'. The first reads rather gnomically:

> *On peut donc dire que le chemin familier se présente comme un filet fluide à l'intérieur d'une masse visqueuse* (p. 29)

> [*We can therefore say that the familiar path shows up as a thin fluid current within a viscous mass.*]

If we do some homework we discover that this is more or less a direct quotation from the book by Uexküll cited by Alferi in his 'Note' at the end; and that the four parts of the text are also derived from Uexküll's work on animal worlds. First we have the eponymous 'Le Chemin familier du poisson combatif', then 'Le Moment de l'Escargot' [The Snail's Moment], followed by 'Habitat et Territoire de l'épinoche' [Habitat and Territory of the Stickleback], and finally, 'La même rue, pour un œil une mouche' [The same street, for a fly's eye]. The *envois* of the second and third texts are:

> *Il nous est permis de conclure que le temps perceptif d'un escargot s'écoule à la cadence de trois à quatre moments par seconde. (Chemin, p. 51)*
>
> [*We may conclude that the perceptive time of a snail passes at the rate of three to four moments per second.*]
>
> *Hors de son territoire l'épinoche n'est jamais victorieuse.* (ibid., p. 73)
>
> [*The stickleback is never victorious outside of its territory.*]

Despite this predominance of references to animal life in the poem's multiple paratexts (titles, liminary instructions, envois), when we read the main body of the four parts or sequences (each comprising seven segments followed by its 'reprise', giving a text of 56 segments), we are firmly in the *human* world, in fact in the first-person world of an individual experimenting in the field of his own experiences.

If we knew nothing about studies of animal behaviour (but everyone knows a little), and in particular nothing about Uexküll, Alferi has provided enough pointers for us to read his work in the light of an experimental framework where the initial focus is on animal behaviour. The moment we find out more about Uexküll — effectively carrying out part of the text's programme — we discover many ways of enhancing and enriching our reading. Let us initially examine the first, eponymous, section of the poem, concerned with the activity of 'going out' and which, as we shall see, draws on Uexküll's notion of an animal's habitual pathway or 'chemin familier'. Each of the text's seven leading segments (echoed by the seven 'reprises') begins with a past participle, and these form a sequence:

> 'Sorti' (15); 'Rentré' (17); 'Tourné' (19); 'Perdu' (20); 'Descendu' (22); 'Remonté' (24); 'Parti' (26).
>
> ['Gone out'; 'Returned'; 'Turned'; 'Lost'; 'Gone down'; 'Come back up'; 'Departed'.]

In the first segment, the word 'Sorti' is followed by 37 lines of free verse that report on the speaker's decision to look at his daily itinerary as if it were a sort of experiment (he calls himself a 'cobaye autonome' [an autonomous guinea pig] (p. 16), and later in the poem he refers to a 'promenade méthodique' (p. 21)). His initial comments refer to phases of his walk that seem qualitatively different in terms of the processes of consciousness — pauses, or blanks, sudden 'coups de rame' [oarstrokes] (p. 15), sequences where it is as if one had one's eyes closed: 'Et même dans les tournants prévus, | toute une géométrie, une négociation inconscientes' [And even in the foreseen turnings, | a whole unconscious geometry and negotiation] (ibid.). At one point the speaker compares the walk with his memories of it later in the day, noting that 'le fonds de l'art de la mémoire' [the art of memory's permanent collection] — the pegs onto which perceptual experiences are hung — is based on spaces, visual clues and impressions (such as that of the interminable wall of a particular building, the Institut des Jeunes Sourds). Walking, making one's way, is seen to be as tactile as it is visual: 'ici le modèle est le tact, non la vue' [the model here is touch, not sight] (ibid.).

In the last quarter of this first segment, we find a feature that will recur quite often: after references to specialized forms of knowledge (topology and zoology) the past participle 'Lu' [Read] introduces citations of back-up reading on the experimenter's part — in this case articles in scientific journals on the human sense of direction. One article referred to an 'algorithme local', another spoke of a kind of 'flair de tout le corps, notamment musculaire' [sense of smell belonging to the whole body, and particularly to the muscles] (ibid., p. 16). But, as in later instances of such citations, these scientific contributions are viewed ironically: remote from concrete reality, they do not capture the subject's actual perceptual experience.

Let us now consider the man who seems to have inspired Alferi's way of exploring everyday patterns of behaviour and experience — Jakob von Uexküll, referred to in the last part of Alferi's book as 'le patron de ce livre' (ibid., p. 84). Von Uexküll was born in Estonia in 1864, studied at the University of Tartu, and worked initially on muscular physiology. He developed a strong opposition to the mechanistic and teleological approaches to animal behaviour of his contemporaries and started trying to understand how each individual species related to its own environment. On the strength of his development of the key concept of *Umwelt*, designating the 'subjective spatial-temporal world' of each animal, and of his view of nature as a kind of musical composition based on the combination and counterpoint of different motifs, Uexküll is often seen as a founder of modern ecology. Shunned by the scientific establishment, he worked independently until financial ruin in World War I forced him to find a rather lowly position at the University of Hamburg. He later returned to the family villa in Capri where he died in 1944.

Uexküll's work was admired by many contemporary writers and thinkers, including Cassirer, Scheler and Ortega y Gasset. The semiotician Thomas Sebeok hailed him as the inventor of biosemiotics and drew significantly on his writings (much of Uexküll's work is concerned with signs). Heidegger engages with Uexküll in *Being and Time* in 1925, and at length in his 1929–30 lectures on *The Foundations of Metaphysics*. In his 2002 book *The Open: Man and Animal*,[4] Giorgio Agamben explores Heidegger's deployment and critique of Uexküll, as well as connections with Rilke's eighth *Duino Elegy*, where animals are seen as apprehending a wider sphere of being that the poet calls 'the open'. Agamben shows how Heidegger chose to read Uexküll and Rilke in a way that in fact clearly demarcated man and animal, seeing the latter as *weltlos* — 'poor in world'. This study fits in with Agamben's own project of exploring what is at stake in our preoccupation with the interface between humanity and animality, which is also the perspective of Derrida's late work on the animal.[5] In France, Uexküll was rediscovered through the translation of two key texts, dating from 1930 and 1934 respectively: *Mondes animaux et monde humain* and *Théorie de la signification*. Published together in a widely available paperback series in 1965 and often reprinted (it is the text referenced by Alferi), this volume is referred to and cited in the work that has done most to make Uexküll's name present in contemporary culture (and which is without doubt the origin of Alferi's own interest in Uexküll) — Deleuze and Guattari's *Mille Plateaux*.[6] Here, and in other writings (for example their late text *Qu'est-ce que la philosophie?*

[*What is Philosophy?*]) Deleuze and Guattari express huge admiration for Uexküll, and the ethologist's ideas underpin some of the key motifs and terms in their writing, notably, habitat and territory, lines of flight, and the *ritournelle* or refrain. For example, Chapter 3 of *Mille Plateaux* (subtitled 'Pour qui elle se prend, la terre?' [Who does the earth think she is?]), develops the idea of the associated or annexed *milieu* — a micro-environment constituted by a particular set of connections between heterogeneous items. In the preface to *Mondes animaux* Uexküll insisted that animals are not objects but subjects, and that they construct worlds though their actions and perceptions. Each animal's particular array of organs determines its sphere or capacity for action and perception, and hence its *Umwelt*, which is distinct from the wider, objective reality within which it operates (the *Umgebung*). Within that wider world, common to all, including human beings, each species, according to its constitution, carves out a *milieu*, or 'lived world', and it is these worlds — those of the tick, the fly, the spider, and many other creatures — that Uexküll seeks to describe and celebrate, inviting us to find ways of making an incursion into their micro-universes, however hard they may be to perceive. Each of these worlds is a totality — Uexküll often uses the metaphor of the 'bubble' — but this does not mean they are totally separate from one another. The world-bubble each animal constructs and inhabits is made up of elements (albeit in different combinations) that are shared with other animals. Inviting us to take a walk through a meadow on a sunny day, Uexküll devoted a famous passage (*U* 89) to the stalk of a flower, which is one thing for a young girl who picks it for her corsage, another thing for an ant who uses it as a handy route towards its food (the petals); something else again for the cicada who pumps the stem for a liquid out of which to make its home; or for the cow who takes a whole bunch into its muffle and chomps on it. For Uexküll, a wide array of entities and qualities in the wider world — objects, shapes, colours, textures, materials, vectors — act as carriers of meaning, and thus as semiotic building blocks for different animals in the construction of their separate but overlapping worlds. If each animal's milieu is a unity,

> chaque partie est déterminée par la signification qu'elle reçoit pour le sujet de ce milieu. Tout objet qui entre dans l'orbite d'un milieu est modulé et transformé jusqu'à ce qu'il devienne un porteur de signification utilisable ou bien reste totalement négligé. (*U* 90)

> [each part is determined by the meaning that it receives for the subject of this milieu. Every object which comes into the orbit of a milieu is adjusted and transformed so that it becomes a useable bearer of meaning, or else remains entirely neglected.]

In a set of illustrated plates, Uexküll, by using shading and colour, gives us different views of the same street scene, as seen by a human, a fly, and a mollusc. The last part of Alferi's poem, 'La même rue, pour un œil de mouche', refers to this sequence of illustrations and its captions.

Deleuze and Guattari refer to Uexküll's 'unforgettable' account of the milieu of the tick which climbs into a tree after mating and waits for an opportunity to drop onto a passing animal so as to feed on its blood:

Ce brigand de grand chemin, aveugle et sourd, perçoit l'approche de ses proies par son odorat. L'odeur de l'acide butyrique, que dégagent les follicules sébacés de tous les mammifères, agit sur lui comme un signal qui le fait quitter son poste de garde et se lâcher en direction de sa proie. S'il tombe sur quelque chose de chaud (ce que décèle pour lui un sens affiné de la température), il a atteint sa proie, animal à sang chaud, et n'a plus besoin que de son sens tactile pour trouver une place aussi dépourvue de poils que possible, et s'enfoncer jusqu'à la tête dans le tissus cutané de celle-ci. Il aspire alors lentement à lui un flot de sang chaud. (*U* 17)

[This highwayman, blind and deaf, perceives its prey approaching by its sense of smell. The smell of butyric acid, which is given off by the sebaceous follicles of all mammals, acts as a signal which makes it leave its guard-post and set off in the direction of its prey. If it comes across something hot (revealed to it by a highly refined sense of temperature), it has reached its prey, a warm-blooded animal, and now needs only its tactile sense to find a spot with as few hairs as possible, and to bury itself up to the head in the cutaneous tissues. It then slowly draws towards itself a flow of warm blood.]

A useful characteristic of ticks, given the rather aleatory nature of this feeding process, is that they have been known to go for as long as eighteen years without a meal!

Drawing on Uexküll, Deleuze and Guattari focus on the process whereby milieux are woven out of heterogeneous ingredients, so that even if they are different and in a sense autonomous, they are interrelated and composed of combinations of the same elements. Combining this with concepts relating to genetic coding, Deleuze and Guattari develop the idea of a process of constant territorialization, through which milieux are constructed; and deterritorialization, whereby the same item is resignified and conscripted to serve in a different role in a different milieu. Looking at this in an evolutionary perspective, but also, like Uexküll, in a perspective that sees animals as subjects and thus as having to contend with local circumstances that may not fit with their predispositions, thus forcing them to adapt, they develop the notion of the 'line of flight' that allows the animal to retreat to its territory if conditions are unpropitious, or to deal with disasters, for example the destruction of its habitat. Crucially, Deleuze and Guattari see 'lignes de fuite' as instances of creativity, and view territorialities as being inseparable from the lines of flight that traverse them (*Mille Plateaux*, p. 72).

In a later chapter (Ch. 11) of *Mille Plateaux*, on the *ritournelle* or refrain, Deleuze and Guattari further insist on the movement of flight as central to the process though which territories are formed. Territories are now seen as distinct from milieux: a territory is constituted by the process that allows milieux to be constructed — a sort of bricolage of signifying elements — but it is an act or process rather than a stable entity. Milieux themselves are 'mobile' and provisional because the same elements are always playing different parts, being coded in different ways. Drawing on Uexküll, Deleuze and Guattari identify a process of 'transcodage' (ibid., p. 396) that works rhythmically and keeps milieux, so to speak, 'vibrating'. Deleuze and Guattari (and later, Alferi) allude to Uexküll's famous account of how the spider's web is shaped in a way that is 'fly-shaped' in the sense that it bears the imprint or code of the fly that is its prey. And they also borrow from Uexküll the analogy with music, particularly the idea of the musical score ('il y a donc une partition originelle pour la mouche, comme il en existe une pour l'araignée' [there is thus an original score for the fly, as there is one too for the spider] (*U* 106)), along with the idea of counterpoint or complementarity, and of nature as a kind of symphony made up of the different scores of each animal. They observe that 'J. von Uexküll a fait une admirable théorie de ces transcodages, en découvrant dans les composantes autant de mélodies qui se feraient contrepoint, l'une servant de motif à l'autre et réciproquement: la Nature comme Musique' [J. von Uexküll developed a fine theory of these transcodings, discovering in the component parts so many melodies counterpointing each other, one acting as the motif for the other and *vice versa*: Nature as Music] (*Mille Plateaux*, p. 386). This image of musical harmony was one of the aspects of Uexküll's work that Merleau-Ponty had commended in his lecture courses on Nature, given in 1956–60, but published only in 1995 (after *Mille Plateaux* and Alferi's *Le Chemin familier*). For Merleau-Ponty, Uexküll's vision of animal worlds as a series of singular fields, co-ordinated through a grammar of differential qualities, has parallels with the way languages can generate a multiplicity of sentences (a perspective that fits with Alferi's fascination with syntax and sentences).[7]

A key term for Deleuze and Guattari is rhythm, not in the sense of cadence or repetition but as an open-ended process of combination based on constant counterpoint and switching of codes.[8] They write that:

> Le territoire est en fait un acte, qui affecte les milieux et les rythmes, qui les 'territorialise'. [...] un territoire emprunte à tous les milieux, il mord sur eux, il les prend à bras le corps [...] Il est construit avec des aspects ou des portions de milieux. Il comporte en lui-même un milieu extérieur, un milieu intérieur, un intermédiaire, un annexé. (ibid., p. 386)

> [Territory is in fact an act, one which affects milieux and rhythms, one which 'territorializes' them. [...] a territory takes from all milieux, sinks its teeth into them, takes hold of them bodily [...] It is made up from aspects or portions of milieux. It contains in itself an exterior milieu, an interior milieu, an intermediary one, an annexed one.]

Like Uexküll, Deleuze and Guattari have much to say about the components out of which milieux are made — many aspects of the environment, and many qualities, including colours, shapes, and vectors, all of which take on the character of 'signatures' — not of individual identities but of domains and habitats (Deleuze and Guattari refer, like Uexküll and Alferi, to the zig-zagging movements of the stickleback) (ibid., p. 390). 'Le territoire', they write,

> c'est d'abord la distance critique entre deux êtres de même espèce: marquer ses distances. Ce qui est mien, c'est d'abord ma distance, je ne possède que des distances. (ibid, p. 393)

> [Territory is first of all the critical distance between two beings of the same species — marking one's distances. What is mine is first of all my distance; I possess only distances.]

What is essential is the gap between the code and the territory. The territory is formed at the level of a certain decoding (or scrambling) of codes. What Deleuze and Guattari call the *ritournelle*, a little snatch of song, or a little bit of code, is defined as:

> Tout ensemble de matières d'expression qui trace un territoire, et qui se développe en motifs territoriaux, en paysages territoriaux (il y a des ritournelles motrices, gestuelles, optiques, etc.). (ibid., p. 397)

> [Every collection of expressive material which describes a territory, and which grows in territorial motifs, in territorial landscapes (there are motivating *ritournelles*, gestural ones, optical ones, etc.]

★    ★    ★    ★    ★

In turning back to Alferi's poem, let us take stock. It is clear that the use Alferi makes of Uexküll in *Le Chemin familier* is partly mediated through Deleuze and Guattari. For example, the way the first eponymous sequence in Alferi treats Uexküll's theme of the 'familiar path', by focusing on the act of going out — from one's habitat into one's territory — could serve as illustration of a passage near the beginning of the chapter on the *ritournelle* where Deleuze and Guattari, having linked the *ritournelle* first to a protective inward turn (the child humming a tune to ward of darkness or chaos, creating the familiar within the unfamiliar), and second, to the way a habitat or lived environment holds off chaos by constituting a circle, a round of harmonious ingredients made of different qualities, invoke a third context, crucial to their concept of the refrain and the territory: the way it includes what is outside its circle:

> III. Maintenant enfin, on entrouvre le cercle, on l'ouvre, on laisse entrer quelqu'un, on appelle quelqu'un, ou bien on va soi-même au-dehors, on s'élance. On n'ouvre pas le cercle du côté où presse les anciennes forces du chaos, mais dans une région, créée par le cercle lui-même. Comme si le cercle tendait lui-même à s'ouvrir sur un futur, en fonction des forces en œuvre qu'il abrite. Et cette fois c'est pour rejoindre des forces de l'avenir, des forces cosmiques. On s'élance, on risque une improvisation. Mais improviser, c'est rejoindre le Monde, ou se confondre avec lui. On sort de chez soi au fil d'une chansonnette. Sur les lignes motrices, gestuelles, sonores qui marquent le parcours coutumier d'un enfant, se greffent ou se mettent à bourgeonner des 'lignes d'erre', avec des boucles, des nœuds, des vitesses, de mouvements, des gestes et des sonorités différents. (ibid., pp. 382–83)

> [III. Now, finally, the circle is partially opened, one opens it, one lets someone enter, one calls to someone, or else one goes outside oneself, one sets forth. One does not open the circle at the point where the ancient forces of chaos exert pressure, but in a region created by the circle itself. It is as if the circle tended to open itself onto a future, as a function of the active forces which it shelters. And in doing so this time it meets the forces of the future, cosmic forces. One sets forth, taking a chance on an improvisation. But to improvise is to meet the World, or to confuse oneself with it. One leaves one's home following the thread of a little song. Along the motivating, gestural, and aural lines which mark out the child's typical trajectory, 'lines of wandering' are grafted on or begin to bud, with loops, knots, speeds, different gestures and sonorities.]

Yet even if his starting point and some of his inspiration are Deleuzean, Alferi in fact has his own take on Uexküll, borrowing and playing with elements derived from his reading of *Mondes animaux* particularly, and then combining them with other materials. Thus, in the first text, Alferi makes a number of direct references to Uexküll's discussion of 'Chemins familiers', but mixes this with references to, among other things, Surrealist and Situationist accounts of wandering in the city, a combination that 'estranges' both sources and produces a weird and compelling effect. Chapter nine of Uexküll's *Mondes animaux* consists of a four-page discussion of the 'chemin familier'. Nothing, claims Uexküll, better illustrates the multiplicity of milieux than the way in which an individual animal constructs and negotiates its regular itineraries by dint of a semiotic process, where the animal's steps are orientated by perceptual clues or signs it has internalized, and which it thus follows apparently blindly or automatically. Alferi imports concepts and terminology poached from Uexküll into his own account of wandering around the fifth and sixth *arrondissements* of Paris — for example the discussion of different kinds of sign, the term 'pas d'orientation' (*Chemin*, p. 17), and the preoccupation with paces, steps, legwork, and the tendency to repeat the same behavioural patterns. Significant aspects of Alferi's poem, a monologue in which a human animal tries to register its own behaviour, can be seen as illustrating a passage such as this in Uexküll:

> Quand nous parcourons plusieurs fois une certaine distance nous gardons en mémoire comme signe de direction l'élan impulsé dans la marche, si bien que nous nous arrêtons involontairement au même endroit, même si nous n'avons pas prêté attention aux caractères perceptifs optiques. Ce sont donc les signaux de direction qui jouent un rôle prépondérant dans le chemin familier. (*U* 58)

> [When we cross a certain distance several times we retain in our memory as a signpost the momentum which impelled us in walking, so much that we stop involuntarily at the same place we did before, even if we have paid no attention to its perceptive optical characteristics. Direction markers, then, have a determining role to play in the familiar path.]

In the eponymous first section of *Le Chemin familier du poisson combatif*, Alferi's liminal text in italics is preceded by a version of Uexküll's diagram (*Chemin*, p. 11):

Alferi begins by adapting Uexküll's brief account of research with Siamese fighting fish (*U* 60), omitting the first part of the experiment (which simply showed the fishes' disquiet when presented with a change in their environment), and focusing on the more elaborate experiment, illustrated by the diagram, which demonstrates that a fish will stick to its known, familiar, itinerary even when it is unnecessary for it to do so to get at its food. Alferi's highly elliptical version uses the word 'proie' for 'nourriture' and introduces the notions of a 'ronde' and a 'détour', where Uexküll just refers to the fish going the familiar long way round. Uexküll writes:

> Si l'on montre la nourriture du côté de la séparation, le poisson parcourt simplement le chemin familier, même si la cloison est disposée de telle façon que le poisson eût pu atteindre la nourriture sans tenir compte de cet écran. (*U* 61)

[If one shows the food on the walled-off side, the fish simply takes the familiar path, even if the wall is positioned so that the fish could reach the food without taking this screen into account.]

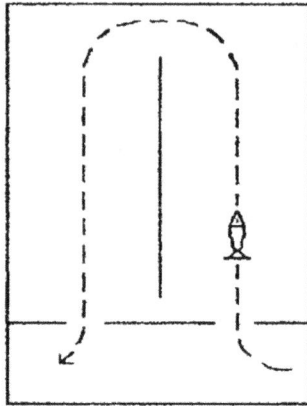

Which in Alferi becomes:

> [...] *Alors*
> *En lui montrant une proie*
> *On entraîne un poisson combatif*
> *Par le premier passage*
> *le long de la seconde cloison*
> *par le second passage*
> *dans une ronde. Ensuite*
> *voyant des proies à sa portée*
> *il refera tout le détour* [...] (*Chemin*, p. 13)

> [...] *Then | By showing him a target | One leads a fighting fish | Through the first passage | along the second wall | through the second passage | full circle. Then | seeing its targets within its reach | it makes the whole detour once more* [...]

Uexküll's text goes on to indicate what the experiment proves, in terms that will be closely echoed in the body of Alferi's poem: 'Le chemin familier est déterminé dans ce cas par des caractères perceptifs, optiques, directionnels, et peut-être aussi par des pas d'orientation' [The familiar path is in these cases determined by perceptive, optical, and directional characteristics, and perhaps also by orienting steps] (*U* 61). But Alferi's liminal text works very differently, and in mid-line, or rather, through an enjambment (his favourite device, central to his poetics of the sentence), he abruptly 'pastes in' a reference to Uexküll's earlier example of a 'chemin familier' also accompanied by an illustration (not reproduced by Alferi): the way young jackdaws ('choucas'), instead of flying in a full circle around a house, turn around and retrace their path — now familiar — but fail to recognize their starting point when seeing it from the opposite direction. Uexküll writes:

> Comme on le voit, le choucas vole autour de la maison, mais ensuite il fait demi-tour pour emprunter le chemin inverse, qu'il connaît pour l'avoir déjà parcouru à l'aller. Ainsi il retourne à son point de départ, qu'il n'a pas reconnu en arrivant par l'autre côté (*U* 59–60).

[As we can see, the jackdaw flies around the house, but then turns around in order to take the opposite path, which he knows, having already travelled it on the way out. It thus returns to its starting point, which it did not recognize when it arrived from the other side.]

In Alferi this becomes:

> [...] *il refera tout le détour. Ainsi*
> *le jeune choucas retourne*
> *à son point de départ*
> *qu'il n'avait pas reconnu*
> *en venant par l'autre côté* (*Chemin*, p. 13)

> [...] *it will take the whole detour once more. Thus | the young jackdaw returns | to its starting point | which it did not recognize | coming from the other side*

Alferi's cutting-and-pasting, his collage-like treatment of Uexküll's text (matched in the other liminal texts, which feature similar abrupt fusions or confusions), points to the dual way he treats the material he derives from Uexküll — both as a serious source of inspiration, and as no more than found material, ready-made stuff out of which to compose his poem, as a bird constructs its nest. This duality or ambivalence is an essential feature of Alferi's poem.

Uexküll's chapter on the 'chemin familier' ends with a sentence following immediately after the passage quoted above, which reads: 'Dans l'ensemble, on peut dire que le chemin familier se présente comme un filet fluide à l'intérieur d'une masse visqueuse' [In general, we can say that the familiar path shows up as a thin fluid current within a viscous mass] (*U* 61). Alferi saves this for the end, adopting it, with a slight variation as his *envoi*, 'On peut donc dire que le chemin familier se présente comme un filet fluide à l'intérieur d'une masse visqueuse' (*Chemin*, p. 29). However, by this point the reader is no longer at the threshold of a text, but at the end of thirteen pages devoted not to the behaviour of an exotic fish in a tank but to capturing the experiences of a human being in the streets of Paris (*Chemin*, pp. 15–28). In fact, variations on this sentence, which articulates Uexküll's fundamental idea that each singular, individual member of an animal species creates its own 'bubble', figure at the end of both the first segment of Alferi's poem and of the 'reprise' that follows it. After the reference to the scientific articles on the sense of direction we read:

> Je monologue en route sur le ton contraint de la science
> amusante, un cobaye autonome. La rue des Feuillantines,
> la rue Saint-Jacques jusqu'à l'église Saint-Jacques-du-Haut-Pas,
> la rue de l'Abbé-de-L'Epée jusqu'au jardin du Luxembourg
> forment une gaine visuelle étanche qui m'imprime
> le mouvement qui lui manque (*Chemin*, p. 16)

> [I soliloquize along the way in the constrained tone of fun science, | an autonomous guinea pig. The rue des Feuillantines, | the rue Saint-Jacques up to the church of Saint-Jacques-du-Haut-Pas, | the rue de l'Abbé-de-L'Épée up to the Luxembourg Gardens/ form an impermeable visual sheath which impresses on me | the movement it lacks]

In the context of this walk, a very precise Parisian topography is recast as an experimental space where an itinerary, because it is familiar or habitual, is seen as a mobile array of tacit perceptual stimuli. Uexküll's final sentence is further recast at the end of the 'reprise' where the metaphor of the 'gaine étanche' is replaced by that of a capillary tube:

> LE REGARD TATE LES PAROIS
> la ville n'a pas de plan, on ne voit pas le plan
> les signes de piste sont précis et discrets
> on retient des images actives et leur ordre
> tout peut s'apprendre ainsi par cœur
> on avance mais on se demande, à certains moments, si vraiment
> on avance mais on se demande, à certains moments, si vraiment
> une enjambée vaut une phrase
> le trajet n'a pas de dessin, on ne voit pas le dessin
> les pas d'orientation sont des calculs myopes
> on avance dans un tube capillaire onduleux
> tout est compact opaque autour (*Chemin*, pp. 16–17)

[THE REGARD FEELS THE WALLS | the city has no plan, one cannot see the plan | the spoor is precise and discreet | one retains the active images and their order | everything can thus be learned by heart | one moves forward but asks oneself, from time to time, if truly | one moves forward but asks oneself, from time to time, if truly | a stride is worth a sentence | the journey has no outline, one cannot see the outline | the orienting steps are short-sighted calculations | one moves forward in a sinuous capillary tube | everything around is compact opaque]

Here, as in all the 'reprises', first-person monologue is replaced by anonymizing third-person grammatical constructions that generalize and objectify the same experiential material initially presented as an autobiographical narrative. Rather than a monologue, the poem — designed to be read twice — gives a meditative cast to topics from Uexküll: signals, learning by heart, references to steps, including the phrase 'pas d'orientation'. The stuttering, repeated line ('on avance mais...') seems to have to do with the experimenter's difficulty in trying to capture and record actions that are supposed to be more or less unconscious. The final image, of the 'capillary tube', echoes the many ways of visualizing the subject's itinerary that arise in the course of the poem. Another example would be the way in the second segment the poem begins by envisaging a visual transcription of the day's toing and froing, but then worries about how to represent the hesitation, the constant 'tremblement léger' [slight trembling] (*Chemin*, p. 17) induced first by the fact that the outing has been assigned no more than the vague, paradoxical goal of meeting someone one doesn't know, and second, by the numerous bifurcations whose cause, if any, remains obscure. After a reference to reading a mathematical article on chaos theory, and a few others 'sans comprendre grand-chose' [without understanding much] (ibid.), the poet recalls being struck by an illustration that suggested that if you plotted all the movements of an individual ('les déplacements d'un quidam') over a period of about a month you would get a kind of cat's cradle with two or three nodal points, some big gaps, and a few one-off lines (ibid.). This can only be a reference to a famous diagram executed in 1952 by the urban sociologist Paul-Henri Chombart de Lauwe, which illustrated in similar fashion the movements of a Parisian student.[9] The diagram was subsequently used to illustrate the theory and practice of *dérive* — the situationists' revamp of surrealist *errance* — in Guy Debord's hugely influential text 'Théorie de la dérive' and was reproduced in the second issue of the Situationist journal *L'Internationale Situationniste* in 1958.

The 'reprise poem' then plays with the motif of ravelling and unravelling, of parallel and divergent lines induced by minute variations (half-recognizing a face, being diverted by a shop window, forgetting one's keys). It ends with a reference to '...le même coin | prenant, vu au travers d'un peu de temps, la profondeur | louche d'un film en 3D' [...the same corner | taking on, when seen across a little time, the seedy depth | of a 3D film] (*Chemin*, p. 19), an instance of Alferi's habitual references to film and other audiovisual technologies that can be linked to Uexküll's frequent allusions to the way photography — and especially cinema — have helped bring a new visibility to many aspects of the natural world, for example by the use of long exposures and slow or fast motion.[10]

In the third segment (*Chemin*, pp. 19–20), Alferi alludes to how a glimpse of someone we know can suddenly superimpose another timescale onto an itinerary, folding and thickening it, and how our regular haunts — like a café where the poet is known by his first name — produce 'identical sensations' (p. 19). The fourth segment (pp. 20–22) covers the experience of losing one's bearings, of feeling lost for a moment, and introduces the image of the labyrinth, associated here with the grid of the city's A–Z plan (square Q-17 of the *Indispensable* guide is referred to) and, in connection with moments of recognition — 'so that's where it was' — or of misremembering the exact position of things. Here we find what is almost certainly a passing reference to the passage in *Nadja* where André Breton reported on how, in the same neighbourhood, he and Philippe Soupault, one Sunday afternoon, found that they were able to predict the position, in a given street, of the wood and coal merchant, before turning the corner, even when they were unsure of their precise location.[11] '...Ainsi le marchand de bois & charbon, | rue du Puits-de-l'Ermite, et donc la rue elle-même | m'ont toujours paru soit trop hauts, soit trop bas' [...Thus the wood & coal merchant, | on the rue de Puits-de-l'Ermite, and so the street itself | have always seemed to me too far up or too far down] (*Chemin*, p. 21). The fifth segment (pp. 22–24), featuring a ride on the metro, further develops the labyrinth motif, and the sixth (pp. 24–26), where the poet Visits the zoo in the Jardin des Plantes, allows for explicit allusions to animals (plentiful throughout the poem) and parallels with animal behaviour. The seventh and last segment (pp. 26–28) picks up earlier allusions to hunting and tracking animals, to depositing traces and scents, and these are then extended in the dense and dynamic 'reprise' poem that brings this first part of the book to its conclusion:

> TRAIT HATIF SINUEUX
> nécessaire
> cheminant c'est-à-dire inventant son chemin comme suivi
> ou le suivant comme inventé
> alternative que disent le 'son'
> la courte rémanence

Celle d'une courbe décrite en l'air par le bout brûlant d'un bâton
Le 'trac' de tout à trac c'est-à-dire la poursuite
du poursuivi, du poursuivant
deux en un fil tendu, tout en muscles
Un corps et sa coulée c'est-à-dire son passage dans l'herbe
à travers une haie, ses foulées imprimées
Dans les feuilles mortes, imprévisible
à peine visible malgré qu'il y laissât des plumes
Des poils, des excréments
bave nacrée, épreintes et fientes, laissées, fumées
et des empreintes
marches, traces, pieds
le pas réglé sur le rythme précaire de teintes
d'odeurs subliminales
de minuscules changements internes
dans la peur, l'improvisation (*Chemin*, pp. 27–28)

[QUICK SINUOUS STROKE | necessary | making its way that is inventing its
way as though followed | or following it as though invented | an alternative
said by 'sound' | the brief afterglow | That of a curve described in the air by
the burning end of a stick | The 'trac' of *tout à trac* that is the pursuit | of the
pursued, of the pursuer | two in one thread pulled tight, muscled all over |
A body and its path that is its passage through the grass | across a hedge, its
strides impressed | In dead leaves, unforeseeable | hardly visible despite having
left feathers there | Hairs, excrement | pearly drool, droppings and scat, left,
smoked | and imprints | steps, traces, feet | pace regulated by the precarious
rhythm of tints | of subliminal odours | of miniscule internal changes | in
fear, improvisation]

The walker's itinerary is compared to a graphic line (reminiscent of Paul Klee's
remark about 'taking a line for a walk') that is sinuous and rapid, but also possesses
its own logic and necessity. Prompting the question of agency, this raises a crucial
aspect of the 'chemin familier'. If the path has become completely habitual, so that
one could follow it blindfolded, whose path is it? Is it the walker's? Or does the
path itself determine the walker's steps? This alternative is played out, in the poem
just cited, first through two pairs of words: 'inventant/inventé ', 'suivi/suivant';
then through a visual image: the evanescent line traced in the night air by a fire
brand that is retained briefly on the retina; and then by two linguistic cruxes: the
ambiguity of the possessive adjective 'son' (which can refer to the walker or to
the *chemin*); and the word *trac*, which derives from a word for trace or track, and
means fear, especially stage fright, but which, in the expression 'tout à trac' means
to blurt out, to speak without preparation, to extemporize, to improvise. The
idiom of tracking leads into another pair: 'poursuivi/poursuivant', and then ushers
in a brilliant development relating to hunting, where the notion of the animal is
vividly present in an account of the walker and his path. The pivotal line, 'deux
en un fil tendu, tout en muscles' goes from the idea of doubleness to that of a
body and its traces, 'un corps et sa coulée'. The switch to a rural environment as a
metaphor for the city (in the tradition of Eugène Sue's *Les Mohicans de Paris*) imports
a whole range of terms from hunting, very much in the spirit of Carlo Ginzburg's

famous essay on clues, where the comparable methods of Morelli, Freud and
Sherlock Holmes were seen to share a common origin in the 'conjectural model'
of hunting.[12] Alferi's poem gives us a long chain of words related to the depositing
of traces by an animal, through the secretion of smells and fluids, though the
marking of natural phenomena, through excretion, and so forth. And he brilliantly
maintains a triple context: animal movement in the country; human movement in
the city; leaving and interpreting traces as involving language ('foulées imprimées'
cleverly turns on two meanings of the verb *imprimer*: to print as in newsprint, and
to leave an impression). In the last four lines we find ourselves very close indeed to
Uexküll: all the terms in the lines 'le pas reglé sur le rythme précaire de teintes |
d'odeurs sublimales' allude to aspects of Uexküll's thought and case studies relating
to the ways the different semiotic universes of various animals are configured. And
in the last two lines, alluding to the rhythm of minuscule changes, the poem clearly
articulates the Deleuzean angle on Uexküll, right down to the key word, with
which the poem ends: 'improvisation'. For Deleuze, as we saw, the *ritournelle* is an
improvisation ventured in the kinds of foray that create a territory — an affective
construct rooted in fear or apprehensiveness, but also a creative act: 'on s'élance, on
tente une improvisation' [one sets forth, one tries an improvisation] (*Mille Plateaux*,
p. 383).

★　★　★　★　★

Let us now see how the other three parts of *Le Chemin familier du poisson combatif*
use Uexküll's ideas: Part II, 'Le Moment de l'escargot', reflects Uexküll's discussion
of 'Le temps perceptif' where he argues that time, rather than being uniform
and objective, 'est un produit du sujet' (*U* 37). Uexküll argues that experimental
evidence shows that in a given stretch of time, species experience, or live through,
different numbers of moments, with a moment being the smallest 'receptacle' of
time. Cinema, Uexküll claimed, has shown that in human beings, the rhythm of
visual perception is in units of an eighteenth of a second: anything happening in
less than this interval is imperceptible to us. But other animals experience moments
that are longer or shorter than ours. One example developed by Uexküll, with the
aid of a diagram (reproduced by Alferi, *Chemin*, p. 33), is the snail:

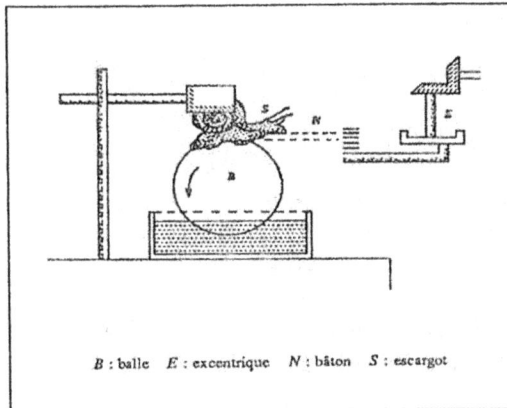

B : balle　E : excentrique　N : bâton　S : escargot

This bizarre experiment — where a snail is placed on top of a rubber ball floating in a tank of water, but held by a clamp so that it can practise its habitual mode of locomotion yet in fact stay put — is designed to demonstrate the fact that in the snail's milieu movements occur much more quickly than in that of humans. The experiment involves waving a stick under the snail and it demonstrates that if you wave the stick up to three times a second the snail won't notice it, but if you wave it at a rate of four times a second it will start to climb along the stick. As Alferi puts it in his liminal account of the experiment: '*Au rythme | de trois vibrations par seconde | l'escargot reste sur la balle. Au rythme | de quatre par seconde | il se lance car le bâton | pour lui est immobile*' [*At a rate | of three vibrations per second | the snail stays on the ball. At the rate | of four per second | it sets out because the rod | is in its eyes immobile*] (p. 35). But at this point Alferi, as in the liminal text to the eponymous first part, suddenly switches to a different example, that of the 'poisson combatif'. Uexküll argues that if you show a fighting fish its own image eighteen times in a second it will not recognize it. It only recognizes its image if you show it at least thirty times a second. Here, in Uexkull's text, the translator adds the following footnote: 'la *betta splendens* [Latin name for this species of fish] se prépare à la lutte [hence its nickname] dès qu'il perçoit l'image d'un de ses congénères' [the *betta splendens* prepares for battle from the moment that it perceives the image of one of its fellows] (U 39). Alferi cites this, in slightly modified form, at the end of his liminal text, apparently randomly tacking this reference to fish behaviour on to the end of the experiment, which of course involves a snail, not a fish, as reflected in Alferi's title for this section of the poem: 'Le Moment de l'escargot'. In the envoi Alferi quotes more or less verbatim this sentence from Uexküll: '*Il nous est permis de conclure que le temps perceptif d'un escargot s'écoule à la cadence de trois a quatre moments par seconde*' (*Chemin*, p. 51). Accordingly, 'Le Moment de l'escargot', part II of Alferi's poem, switches from the spatial concerns of part I ('Le Chemin familier') to a concern with time. Here the seven segments relate to different moments in the unfolding of a day, from waking at 9 a.m., to trying to get to sleep at midnight. Alferi devises a whole host of ways of illustrating and amplifying Uexküll's point about the subjective experience of time, stressing primarily the many different rates at which humans experience various kinds of intervals, depending on mood, circumstances, and bodily conditions such as tiredness, etc. In passing Alferi alludes to theories about circadian and other bodily rhythms, using the technical term *Zeitgeber* (*Chemin*, p. 40), and so on.

★    ★    ★    ★    ★

Part III, 'Demeure et territoire de l'épinoche', derives from the tenth chapter of Uexküll's *Mondes animaux*, entitled 'Demeure et territoire' (Dwelling and territory) (U 61–66), which argues that many animals have a territory that stretches well beyond the confines of their dwelling. His first example is the male stickleback, which builds a nest whose entrance is often marked by a coloured thread, possibly as an aid to its young.

This diagram, reproduced by Alferi (p. 55), shows an aquarium in which two sticklebacks have made nests in opposite corners, and the experiment shows that

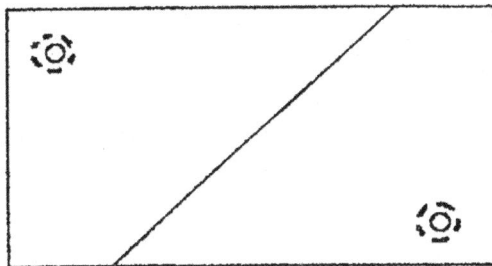

each stickleback will vigorously and successfully defend the territory on its side of an invisible line dividing it from that of its neighbour. Uexküll's point is that a territory is 'une création purement subjective' (U 61) that could not be detected by simply looking at the surroundings. Alferi's liminary text dramatizes Uexküll's account, embroidering a little:

> si l'une s'aventure au-delà
> d'une oblique fantomatique
> l'autre la repousse aussitôt
> avec énergie et succès
> quelle qu'en soit la taille (p. 57)

[*if one strays beyond | an oblique, spectral line | the other repels it right away | energetically and successfully | however big it is*]

But, as in the two previous instances, Alferi switches abruptly to another of Uexküll's examples, illustrating a slightly different point — the way some birds of prey leave a 'neutral zone' between home and hunting ground — a trait some ornithologists explain by the fact that this obviates the danger of the bird attacking its own offspring in the areas round the nest. Alferi's more sardonic version ends:

> [...] *Ainsi*
> L'on suppose qu'elle évite
> De se dévorer elle-même (*Chemin*, p. 57)

[*Thus | We suppose that it avoids | Devouring itself*]

And his envoi at the end involves a somewhat redundant logical extrapolation:

> Hors de son territoire l'épinoche
> N'est jamais victorieuse (73)

[*Outside its territory the stickleback | Is never victorious*]

In connection with the question of territory, Alferi's poem, again in seven segments with seven 'reprises', focuses this time on a series of rooms (inspired perhaps by Georges Perec's project, outlined in *Espèces d'espaces* [*Species of spaces*],[13] of compiling an inventory of all the rooms he had slept in). Beginning with that of the infant, and continuing chronologically through other phases, these rooms are seen as separate 'bulles' (Alferi uses Uexküll's word, 'bubbles'), each a world of its own. In this part of the poem, the segments begin with the words 'Première chambre', 'Deuxième chambre', and so on, and in the last few lines of each there is a reference to 'le premier acte', 'le deuxième acte', etc. In the case of the second room, corresponding to the phase of being a student, the corresponding 'acte' seems to have to do with negotiating the borderline between solitude and community. In the case of the third room, the issue seems to be that of constructing one's own living space for the first time. In the fourth and fifth rooms, the context is living abroad provisionally and being able to generate new ghostly identities. Some lines are italicized, including the following:

> *Habiter ou hanter, host ou ghost peut se dire*
> *De toi comme du rectangle clair sur le mur jaune* (Chemin, p. 67)

> [*To inhabit or to haunt, one can say host or ghost* | *Of you as of the bright rectangle on the yellow wall*]

The seventh and last room is our current habitat, which encompasses all the rooms one has been in before (still present in one's bodily memory) and is therefore a constantly changing space. And in this segment Alferi plays with Uexküll and Deleuze's distinction between habitat and surrounding territory, as well as citing the idea of an intermediate 'zone franche' [free zone].

★   ★   ★   ★   ★

The fourth and last part of the text, 'La même rue, pour un œil de mouche', starts with the photograph treated by Uexküll to show how a fly's vision compares with that of a human being and a mollusc (Chemin, p. 77).

Uexküll used photographic technology to demonstrate the rudimentary 'visual space' or milieu of the fly and to make the point that within it the threads of a spider's web are invisible. More generally, Uexküll explains the disparity between visual space and tactile (or haptic) space, and makes parallels with the human sphere. In a passage explicitly alluded to in Alferi's poem, Uexküll writes:

> De même que la main dans son exploration tactile, l'œil dans son exploration visuelle étend sur tous les objets du milieu une fine mosaïque de lieux dont la finesse dépend du nombre des éléments optiques qui saisissent la même portion de l'entourage. (U 33)

[Like the hand's tactile exploration, the eye's visual exploration spreads over all the objects in the milieu a precise mosaic of items, the precision of which depends on the number of optical elements which grasp the same portion of the surrounding area.]

In Alferi's poem we read:

> Le champ épouse une mosaïque de lieux plus ou moins fine
> Tachiste pour le mollusque impressionniste pour la mouche (pp. 80–81)

[The field weds a mosaic of items, more or less subtle | Tachist for the mollusc impressionist for the fly]

In this fourth and last part of Alferi's poem (about a quarter longer than each of the other three) there is no liminal text, and no corresponding *envoi*. Rather than clear divisions into seven segments and seven 'reprises', Alferi uses various means to create a sense of a fluid continuum. He dispenses with punctuation and uses spacing to create different effects — for example, by starting lines close to the right margin or by inserting space within the line. The 'reprises' are maintained but they are now integrated into the overall flow of the poem: signalled by a brief phrase, or a single word in capitals: LE MONDE (p. 80), L'IMAGE (p. 82), ANAGLYPHE (p. 89). More like a title than a first line, the 'reprise' sequences end with an em dash, followed by the resumption of the ongoing discursivity of the main poetic meditation.

Although it maintains some elements of first-person narrativity, 'La même rue, pour un œil de mouche' is more meditative and philosophical than the preceding three parts of the poem. The beginning indicates that the investigation of sight or vision does not require elaborate experimental conditions: a few days of holiday will do; and so we find ourselves in what seems to be a sunny Mediterranean landscape (cypress trees, etc.), which the narrator comically affects to dislike:

> combien je hais les paysages combien
> les descriptions m'ennuient surtout si l'auteur y a mis
> de la ferveur par sympathie pour les choses du monde
> visible                    où était la rue [...] (*Chemin*, p. 79)

[how I hate landscapes how | descriptions bore me above all if the author has put | enthusiasm into it out of a liking for the things of the visible world where was the street [...]]

On his return to Paris at the end he claims to experience 'une paix déflagrante' in the Luxembourg Gardens (p. 95).

Without the clear segmentation of the preceding sections (the seven facets of taking a walk, the seven moments of a day, the seven rooms), we are presented with ruminations on the paradoxes of vision, which embrace theories of mind and of colour, wave-theory, semiotics, parallax, comparisons with the other senses, three-dimensionality, distant and close-up Vision, doubles, the physiology of the eye, photography and cinema, and so on. The narrator observes that 'la nature physique et morale de la vue m'intriguait' [the physical and moral nature of sight intrigued me] (p. 81). The first occurrence of a running phrase — 'la vue est un piège' [sight is a trap] — introduces a sequence reviewing the ideas of Galen, Spinoza, Democritus, and the Jesuit Christoph Scheiner, who experimented on the severed eye of a cow and saw for the first time the inverted image of the world that appears on the retina. This leads into the first of two passages where Jakob von Uexküll is explicitly mentioned for the first time in the poem. Uexküll is referred to as 'le patron de ce livre' (p. 84), but is chided for having had a condescending view of the sight of familiar animals, although the poet enthusiastically commends the passage (*U* 56) where Uexküll used colour coding on the diagram of a room to show how it would be perceived by a dog as opposed to a human 'mais sa chambre du chien où tous les meubles verdissent | quoiqu'elle ait de schématique et de fabuleux persuade [...]' (*Chemin*, p. 84). Recurring references to flies work to hold the last section of *Le Chemin familier* together, reminding us of its Uexküllian framework and title. But here the flies are not just illustrations, but real elements of a Mediterranean summer: in a sequence concerned with seeing things in the distance, a fly buzzes around the writer's manuscript ('la mouche qui se pose | sans arrêt sur cette page' [the fly which lands | ceaselessly on this page] (*Chemin*, p. 90). And this leads into another mention of the book's patron. Distant space is amorphous,

> comme la bulle transparente dont Jakob von Uexküll
> dit qu'elle entoure dans un pré chaque vache ou bien comme
> la liste sidérale des émotions et des pensées
> dont chacun entend parler qu'il se sait incapable
> de sentir (*Chemin*, p. 91)

[like the transparent bubble which Jakob von Uexküll | says surrounds in a field each cow or else like | the sidereal list of emotions and thoughts | which each hears spoken of which he knows he is incapable | of feeling]

All through Alferi's disquisition on sight we feel his fascination with the nature of vision, and particularly with the numerous aspects of seeing, made manifest through comparisons with animals. Alferi's fascination is both shared with and distinct from Uexküll, since Alferi is more philosophical and poetic. In a fine passage, he watches the colours change as the sun goes down:

> la journée finissait déjà
> et sans ciller je regardais le soleil bas outrer
> des teintes absurdement qui passeraient comme les autres
> au bleu et puis du bleu au noir et je raisonnais contre
> tout ce que je voyais non pour gagner par le détour
> d'un savoir de seconde main et pauvre un au-delà
> plus vrai du paysage mais me rêver à la place
> d'un autre animal spectateur car pour aimer la vue
> faire profession de voir en oubliant l'heure et le lieu
> encore faut-il et d'autant plus qu'elle est plus intérieure
> aimer son propre point de vue ne pas y soupçonner
> un piège et je voulais tenter de contourner le mien
> sinon de le défaire en me prêtant d'autres regards
> me fussent-ils aussi contraires que le jour à la nuit
> et que les sons émis par son ennemi au papillon
> qui les capte fort bien alors que d'autre part le monde

se tait pour lui ou mieux encore en me représentant
celui de l'araignée vu depuis celui de la mouche
qui n'ont aucune intersection l'araignée voyant flou
au-delà de sa toile qui demeure elle absolument
invisible à sa proie (*Chemin*, pp. 85–86)

[the day was already ending | and without blinking I watched the low sun
absurdly exaggerate | shades which would change like the others | to blue
and then from blue to black and I reasoned against | all I saw not in order to
win by the detour | of a poor second-hand knowledge a truer beyond | to the
landscape but to dream of myself in the place | of another animal spectator
for to love sight | to profess that one sees forgetting the hour and the place |
requires moreover and so much more the more interior it is | that one love
one's own point of view not suspect | a trap in it and I wanted to try to bypass
my own | if not to undo it by giving myself other gazes | even if they are as
opposed to me as day to night | and that the sounds emitted to the butterfly
by its enemy | which receives them loud and clear while on the other hand the
world | is silent for it or better yet by picturing to myself | that of the spider
seen from that of the fly | which in no way intersect the spider's vision blurring
| beyond its web which itself remains absolutely | invisible to its prey]

The beauty of the imperceptibly changing shades, as night slowly falls, inspires a
desire to 'see differently': not in order to see through or beyond the landscape, but
so as to separate seeing from ratiocination, and to forget the contingencies of place
and time. The project (inspired by Uexküll and using some of his examples) of
'borrowing' the point of view of a spectating animal ('me [prêter] d'autres regards')
is in fact to overcome the 'piège' of scepticism, and to gain access to one's own
inner 'point de vue'. The spirit here, as in *Le Chemin familier* as a whole, is that
of the counterfactual thought experiment. The perceptual fields of the butterfly
that hears only the sounds emitted by its enemy, or those of the spider and the fly,
which are totally divergent (the spider cannot see anything clearly beyond its web,
while for the fly the spider's web, in which it always risks being caught, is invisible)
may be wholly contrary to our own, but to witness nightfall in Tuscany is to
undergo a complex and contradictory sequence of visual experiences. For example,
as the continuation of the passage indicates, with contrasting reference to the
monochrome and infra-red sight of creatures like bats and owls, human sight finds
darkness threatening, when the sky, lit by stars, suddenly becomes more familiar
than the earth which seethes with apparently formless motion. By playing off the
kinds of ecstatic and epiphanic experiences of vision that we may all experience in
certain favoured circumstances, moments and locales (for example in the Tuscan
countryside; Alferi refers to Tuscan painters, and the Italian landscape seems very
present here) with thought experiments that we can conduct by comparing our
sight to that of other creatures, as well as by blinking, closing our eyes, or going out
in the dark, Alferi draws on Uexküll to explore the ontology of vision.

★    ★    ★    ★    ★

As the concluding section of *Le Chemin familier* makes clear, Alferi's overall
project is to further modern poetry's long-standing engagement with the relation

between mind and world by devising hugely inventive new avenues of enquiry. While questions of language are not absent, it is noticeable that in *Le Chemin familier* the framework of para-scientific and site-specific experimentation tends to keep linguistic experimentation in the background. In Alferi's subsequent work, *Sentimentale journée* for example, the animal worlds of Uexküll will be replaced — as a presiding framework or sounding board — by the world of twentieth-century audiovisual technologies, from silent cinema onwards, and various devices will serve to sound out the relations between poetic language and the Visual languages of our era, a project furthered in Alferi's own experimentation with what he calls 'ciné-poèmes'. I hope, however, to have shown that Alferi's use of Uexküll is not simply adventitious. It fits into a tradition of 'onto-ethology',[14] where Uexküll is an inspiration to such figures as Heidegger, Merleau-Ponty and Deleuze. If modern poetry is concerned with our relation to the world, Alferi, like Rilke, Lawrence or Hughes, is a poet for whom the animal world is an important source of inspiration. Secondly, Alferi's way of continuing to work with some of the parameters of the twentieth-century avant-garde tradition, not least in maintaining the idiom of existential experiment on the borderline between art and life, which marked Dada, Surrealism and many other subsequent movements and moments, imbues *Le Chemin familier du poisson combatif* with a playfulness, but also a vitality and variety, that are immensely stimulating. Lastly, through its battery of idioms and devices (including diagrams, quotations, instructions, reprises, indexes and notes), and its formal variety (particularly the alternation between discursive first-person *vers libre* and rhythmically tighter, dense and powerful 'reprises', often brilliant poems in their own right), Alferi's second book of poetry is as formally pleasing and innovative as it is conceptually and intellectually challenging.

## Notes

1. On this see *The Art of the Project*, ed. by Johnnie Gratton and Michael Sheringham (Oxford: Berghahn, 2005).
2. All page references for quotations from Alferi and Uexküll will be given in the text. '*Chemin*' will refer to *Le Chemin familier du poisson combatif* (Paris: P.O.L., 1992). The abbreviation *U* will refer to Jakob von Uexküll, *Mondes animaux et monde humain* (Paris: Gonthier, 1965).
3. For a brief account of *Le Chemin familier* see Eric Pesty, 'Pierre Alferi: "Pas un geste inutile | pas un qui ne soit libre"', *Critique*, 735–36 (Aug.–Sept. 2008), 612–24.
4. *The Open: Man and Animal*, trans. by Kevin Attell (Stanford, CA: Stanford University Press, 2004).
5. See Jacques Derrida, *L'Animal que donc je suis* (Paris: Galilée, 2006).
6. Paris: Minuit, 1980.
7. On this see Brett Buchanan, *Onto-Ethologies: The Animal Environments of Uexküll, Heidegger, Merleau-Ponty and Deleuze* (Albany: SUNY, 2008). Buchanan points out that Uexküll already featured in one of Merleau-Ponty's earliest works, *La Structure du comportement* (1943). See also Jean-Christophe Bailly, *Le Versant animal* (Paris: Bayard, 2007), especially pp. 95–104. On Deleuze and Uexküll see Elizabeth Grosz, *Chaos, Territory, Art: Deleuze and the Framing of the Earth* (New York: Columbia University Press, 2008), pp. 40–45.
8. See Michael Sheringham, 'Everyday Rhythms, Everyday Writings: Réda with Deleuze and Guattari' in the present volume.
9. See Simon Sadler, *The Situationist City* (Boston: MIT Press, 1988), p. 94.

10. For example, in several places Uexküll mentions a film by Arndt that showed the growth of a type of mushroom in slow motion (*U* 95, 98, 117, 139).

11. André Breton, *Nadja* (1928; Paris: Gallimard, 1972), p. 29.

12. Carlo Ginzburg, 'Morelli, Freud, and Sherlock Holmes: Clues and Scientific Method', *History Workshop Journal*, 9 (1980), 5–36.

13. Georges Perec, *Espèces d'espaces* (Paris: Galilée, 1974).

14. See Buchanan, *Onto-Ethologies*.

# 45

# Pierre Alferi and the Poetics of the Dissolve: Film and Visual Media in *Sentimentale Journée*

The vocabulary and technology of film, from silent cinema, through genre films, to special effects and video, figure prominently in the poetry of Pierre Alferi, notably in such collections as *Sentimentale Journée* [A Day's Journey] (1997) and *La Voie des airs* [Airway] (2004). In the last ten years Alferi has written extensively on film. *Des enfants et des monstres* [Children and Monsters] (2004) collects pieces on horror movies he wrote for *Cahiers du cinéma*; whilst *Le Cinéma des familles* [Family Cinemas] (1999) is a novel or *auto-fiction* where a childhood is viewed through the prisms of a number of films including Charles Laughton's *Night of the Hunter* (1955) and Robert Flaherty and Zoltan Korda's *Elephant Boy* (1937).[1] Alferi started doing public readings from *Le Cinéma des familles* while extracts from the films were projected behind him with soundtrack material remixed by the musician Rodolphe Burger. Then, in 2002, he produced a DVD called *Cinépoèmes et films parlants* [Cinepoems and Talking Films] comprising short film works he had made himself since 2000.[2] The four *films parlants* consist of sequences from existing films, including *Night of the Hunter* and *Elephant Boy*, which Alferi re-edits, reordering, slowing down, and repeating bits of the original. He then adds a text he has written himself which is supplied either through subtitles or voice-over. In the six *Cinépoèmes* he combines words and images more directly, using animation and other devices to make words appear and disappear before our eyes, creating rhythms of reading that illuminate the operations of poetic language.

The focus here will be on *Sentimentale Journée*, and my aim is to suggest how the endless coagulation and dissolution of meaning in Alferi's poems, with their concomitant exploration of what we could call 'dissolved subjectivity', can be related to cinema, the filmic apparatus, film spectatorship and, more broadly, audiovisual technologies. *Sentimentale Journée* offers constant evidence of a predilection for modes of language that bring about, on the one hand, a 'mise à plat et à distance' [flattening and distancing] (*SJ* 69) of the real, often associated with the dislocating, derealizing effects of twentieth-century media and technologies; and on the other hand, a liberation from the shackles of fixed identity, thematized by free-wheeling and frequently comic scenarios, often derived from cinema, where narratives untrammelled by *vraisemblance* evince the transgressive, euphoric, boundary-crossing potential of what Michel de Certeau calls 'delinquent' narratives.[3]

Articulated at the outset of his career in a remarkable treatise, *Chercher une phrase* [Looking for Sentences] (1991), Alferi's poetics confer agency on the workings of the sentence, on the performative power of literary utterances: 'les phrases, en disant quelque chose, font quelque chose' [in saying something, sentences do something].[4] Rather than simulating or representing reality, literarity asserts its independence from customary codifications of the real by becoming the vehicle of a fundamentally indeterminate, indescribable energy: 'l'élan de la profération' [the *élan* of utterance] (p. 27). Literature does not describe this *élan* but can seek to enshrine it: 'rythmant l'élan, la phrase le met en scène. Mais elle ne le représente pas' [turning the *élan* into rhythm, the sentence makes it performative but does not represent it] (p. 28). 'La phrase invente une expérience' [the sentence invents an experience] (p. 41). Once articulated, an utterance seems to refer to a pre-existent state of affairs, but that state of affairs did not exist, was only virtual, until it was uttered. And certain forms of language retain this virtuality. Both metaphorically and materially, film can abet poetry in a jubilant process of liberation where identities and meanings dissolve.

One of the things that links poetry and film for Alferi is his vision of poetry as a form of experimental practice, bearing on immediate experience, on what it is like to be out in the everyday world.[5] He sees his filmmaking as an extension of his poetic activity:

> J'écris pour [...] mettre en mouvement les choses alentour, corps et mots, que les mots vidés redeviennent moteurs. Il s'agit de se déplacer en regardant, de respirer, de ressentir et d'adopter la juste pulsation. [...] La pulsation la plus intime, dans le langage, est celle du sens, partout tremblé, mouvant. À partir d'elle, la poésie, le récit — toute fiction écrite — produit des rythmes de vie, des flux et des caillots de sensation.
> On y façonne le temps à toutes les échelles.[6]

> [I write to get the things around me, bodies and words, moving, so that empty words are reactivated. The idea is to keep shifting the angle of vision, to breathe, to feel and adopt the right wavelength. The most intimate pulsation in language is that of meaning, which is always trembling, in motion. From this, poetry, narrative — any written fiction — produces living rhythms, flows and clots of sensation.
> Time is shaped there at every level.]

By shaping time, poetry and film open up the experience of temporality itself, fired by 'cette ancienne illusion de pouvoir agir sur le temps — le ralentir, l'accélérer, le morceler ou le suspendre, s'installer dans un instant' [that old illusion of being able to fashion time — slow it down, speed it up, fragment or suspend it, inhabit the moment] (p. 11). Allusions to 'l'éclat du présent pur' [the glare of the pure present] (*SJ*, p. 66), or to the 'violence' (p. 59) of the present, occur frequently in the poems of *Sentimentale Journée*, where we are confronted with

> une existence entière
> Dans ce laps de présent extrême (pp. 43–44)

> [a whole existence In the extreme present of this moment]

homing in on 'Le laps de temps le plus dense, le plus gribouillé' [the densest, the most scribbled passage of time] (p. 78), where 'l'événement [est] consommé sur place' [the event is consumed on the spot] and we may benefit from 'l'élasticité modeste mais réelle de l'instant' [the modest but real elasticity of the moment] (p. 84).

The following text appears on the back cover of *Sentimentale Journée*:

> Ce sont des poèmes improvisés comme une conversation. Un exergue extrait un sujet. Donc on voit en gros de quoi ils parlent (d'amour, du jour et de la nuit, de temps, de cinéma, de mouvement), et précisément ce qu'ils disent, mais pas très bien ce qu'ils veulent dire. Ils prennent à revers la 'communication': ils repoussent le sens d'une image à l'autre, qu'ils défont, d'une phrase à l'autre, qu'ils coupent, un peu comme on frappe un ballon. Peut-être qu'ils riment à rien. Peut-être qu'ils sont fidèles à un 'sentiment monstre', à une expérience du présent où 'aucun flou n'est évitable'.

> [These are poems that are improvised like a conversation. An epigraph highlights a topic. So one can see more or less what they are about (love, day and night, time, cinema, movement), and precisely what they say, but not very clearly what they mean. They approach 'communication' from the other end: they bounce meaning from one image to the next, which they undo, from one sentence to the next, which they cut, like when you kick a ball around. Perhaps they don't connect with anything. Perhaps they are faithful to 'monstrous feelings', an experience of the present where 'no blurring is avoidable'.]

This is a good description of what it is like to read these poems: we are confronted with a mass of details and referents, and a powerful sense of momentum, but it is hard to figure out what's going on, what it is all about. Constellations of meaning recur — love, day and night, film — and 'experiencing the present' — but the sense of 'flou' [blurring] is pervasive. The analogies with improvisation, conversation and football conjure up the way these poems, rather than communicating a message, keep on spinning a thread that just about survives endless deferrals and metamorphoses.

A reference in one of the poems indicates that the title of the collection involves a bilingual pun on Laurence Sterne's eighteenth-century travel narrative, *A Sentimental Journey*. But it also references the famous Doris Day song from the 1940s Big Band era, 'Sentimental Journey'. The motif of the *journée* — a day as a span of time — crops up frequently.[7] If a *journée* can be thought of as a journey, it is not because it is *sentimentale* in the psychological sense, but rather because it is a sequence of sentiments and sensations; the 'matter' of the day is displaced from what pertains to an individual psychological agent, to what pertains to a sentient being: a *journée* and a journey are necessarily some-body's — in other words experienced, 'vécu' [lived] — but the somebody in question is also every-body, no one in particular.

References to film thematize the modes of embodied mental activity and experience in time that these poems seek to enact. Like most of the thirty pieces, the opening poem, 'Vous êtes invités' [We invite you] (*SJ*, pp. 7–10), features a voice that spins meditative riffs, often dialoguing with an alter ego, as it appears to reflect on experience; but the content of that experience is generally made up of second-hand elements, often borrowed from popular culture and media, including cinema.

It is as if giving any substance to the elusive flow of the present involved traducing it, converting it into something borrowed and artificial. The whole apparatus of film figures this artifice. All through the poem there is an opposition between the immediacy of the present, its pristine quality, and the second-handness of experience the moment it has ceased to be present. Everything that is *then* — even *just then* — as opposed to now is to some degree fake, 'truqué' [artificial]. The virtual possibilities harboured by every moment — while it is still present — are annulled as soon as they solidify into an event we take cognisance of, necessarily in retrospect. Alferi's art consists in trying to delay the betrayal of the virtual by the actual.

> Et la journée s'avance masquée
> Sur des rails trop étroits. Décidément
> Elle ne fait pas son âge (p. 7)

> [And the day wears its mask
> As it advances on rails that are too narrow. It really
> Doesn't show its age]

From its beginning, at daybreak, the day advances both on the narrow rails of the moment-by-moment, and also in masked form (there is a play here on Descartes's motto *Larvatus prodeo* [I come forward, masked].[8] The day's first avatar is as a person who does not show his or her age, or get older, even if the shopping seems to get heavier. Popular culture, and by implication cinema, enter the poem via the image of a big band that incarnates the soundtrack of the day,

> La rumeur
> De la ville tend la perche de minute en minute
> À la journée dans son chorus qui paraît frêle
> Par des riffs de cuivres huilés. L'arrangement
> Sent la sueur et le big band en smokings pathétiques
> Imite un orchestre classique (p. 7)

> [Minute by minute
> The city's buzz with its brassy riffs
> Hooks up with the day's chorus that seems so fragile
> The arrangement
> Is a bit stale and the big band in worn tuxedos
> Imitates a classical orchestra]

We are put in mind of big band scenes in movies, as the poem conjures up a customer and his neighbour at an adjacent table who are both concerned with capturing the present. The neighbour says that what he enjoys is

> La sensation, la plus forte et la plus subtile,
> Comme un parfum traverse la salle sur des talons
> Aiguilles, de l'aujourd'hui. Plus tard
> Quand je ferai sauter le bouchon je sais
> (Et ce savoir ajoute une tuile à mon plaisir
> Un peu vert pour l'instant) qu'elle sera là
> Millésimée (p. 8)

> [The feeling — as strong and subtle as can be

> Like a perfume that crosses the room on high
> Heels — of today. Later
> When I pop the cork I know
> (And this knowledge adds a little extra to my pleasure
> Which is a bit green at first) that it will be there
> Stamped with its date]

For this speaker, experience is like a heavy scent, something to be savoured after the event, stored up for later like a good vintage. For his interlocutor on the other hand, the 'sensation [...] de l'aujourd'hui' is not linked to memory but to the immediacy of minute sensations like the sudden hissing of the coffee as it starts to percolate; or the sun moving across a carpet; or the way the cat goes crazy when it hears the ring of the fork against the tin of cat-food. For him 'me sentir' [to experience myself] or

> sentir
> Tout court (p. 8)
>
> [Just
> Experience]

is not to be aligned with the cultivation of the self through culture. He does not keep his Polaroids in the freezer: unlike some people he has no desire to 'retarder l'éffacement' [delay erasure]. For him, stuff that happens is mobile and mutable: it does not need cooking, it never comes raw in the first place:

> Le temps ne coule incolore qu'à température
> Ambiante. (p. 8)
>
> [Time only flows colourlessly
> At ambient temperatures.]

— a wonderfully gnomic piece of poetic sententiousness. But, like everything ambient, the ambient temperature is ever-changing. As the lights go down in the bar we shift to a different setting or scenario that will predominate in the second half of the poem. The 'changement de tarif' [change of tariff] marks the switch from the diurnal to the nocturnal and the oneiric, beautifully articulated here as it often is in Alferi:

> Bonne nuit, dors bien mon amour. — Si c'est un ordre
> Sache que je vais me mutiner. Le capitaine est à fond de cale.
> Dans cette mélasse une chatte ne retrouverait pas ses petits
> Et le port de départ ni celui vers quoi nous voguons
> N'est en vue. Hier m'a posé un lapin. Demain
> Demain (*Autant en emporte le vent*)
> Est un autre jour. La nuit, quelle violence
> Inouïe, tu ne trouves pas? (p. 9)
>
> [Good night, sleep tight baby. — If that's an order
> You'd better know I'll mutiny. The captain is down in the hold
> In this murk a cat wouldn't find its kittens
> And neither the port we left nor the one we're headed for
> Are in sight. Yesterday didn't show up. Tomorrow
> Tomorrow (*Gone with the Wind*)

Is another day. Nightfall, so amazingly
Violent, don't you think?]

Night and sleep are seen to bring a hiatus that dissolves continuity, uncoupling yesterday from tomorrow and disjoining disparate planes of experience. The motif of cinema is present initially via references to specific films and then via a switch into scenarios derived from cinematic materials. First, 'Bonne nuit, dors bien mon amour' is a phrase from a song, 'The Lullaby of Broadway', that features in a Busby Berkeley film, *Gold Diggers of 1935*, where, over shots of party girls getting home in the morning, we hear:

Good night, baby,
Good night, milkman's on his way.
Sleep tight, baby,
Sleep tight, let's call it a day!

(One of Alferi's *films parlants* — *La Berceuse de Broadway* — on the *Cinépoèmes* DVD re-edits this sequence.) Second, 'Tomorrow is another day' — Scarlett O'Hara's closing line from the film, *Gone with the Wind* — is reinterpreted as a comment on the 'violent' disruption wrought by night, making yesterday unrecoverable, and tomorrow a fresh start. The motif of the maritime journey, with its references to the captain down in the hold, and later a ship's bridge, a night watch, an engine room, and a cabin-boy, works to convey an image of night as a perilous passage where 'les rouages de la la veille' [the mechanism of yesterday] is exposed to 'la discontinuité amorphe des heures' [the amorphous discontinuity of hours], inducing an unease that is said to be less akin to Heideggerean anguish than to nauseous heterogeneity:

un bazar, un medley sadique
Des plus mauvaises chansons sur Radio Nostalgie (p. 9)

[a bazaar, a sadistic medley
Of the worst songs on Radio Nostalgia]

The genre of the disaster movie is then referenced, as the ship scenario, picking up an earlier reference to an iceberg, brings on the *Titanic*, via a conspiracy theory — another genre — according to which the real *Titanic* did not sink but was replaced *in extremis* by another ship, so that the 'real' *Titanic* is still tucked away in a safe haven. As it meditates on time, the virtual, experience, parallel worlds, and as it manifests language's capacity to grasp and enact the multiple paradoxes at play here, the poem throws up provisional frameworks that draw massively on a repertoire of representations where cinema is especially prominent, along with other related mèdia, including photography. The poem ends with a reference to a postcard — bearing an invitation to the opening of a new restaurant — with the image of a half-sunk ship (the *Cabiria* — shades of Fellini — or the *Caribbean* — pirate films again) and bearing the legend 'Vous êtes invités'. In the poem's last lines the speaker identifies with this 'bateau débaptisé privé de son big band' [ship deprived of its name and its big band] that is eternally sinking and not sinking, and the last line — 'Tu l'as gagné à la sueur de ton sommeil' [You earned it with the sweat of your sleep] links the postcard image to the in-between state of dreams, but also implicitly to poetic language and its analogue, film.

We have yet to consider a key feature of all the poems in *Sentimentale Journée* that can be related to cinema: the italicized epigraph, referred to in Alferi's blurb as the 'exergue [qui] dégage un sujet' [an epigraph [that] highlights a topic].

> *La journée s'avance masquée*
> *La sensation, la plus forte et la plus subtile*
> *De l'aujourd'hui*
> *La nuit*
> *On y voit nus les rouages*
> *L'encombrement du temps*
> *On fait eau, on va droit*
> *Sur l'iceberg.* (p. 7)

> [*The day wears its mask as it advances*
> *The sensation, as strong and subtle as can be*
> *Of Today*
> *Night*
> *When you can see the workings exposed*
> *The piling up of time*
> *There's a leak, you're heading straight*
> *For the iceberg.*]

This is a speeded-up version of the poem itself, a set of edited highlights that constitute a kind of trailer. At the same time it is a poem in its own right, a remix that produces different meanings. Each of the thirty poems features — and plays brilliant variations on — this brilliant, essentially cinematographic device. In one case the lines picked out are consecutive in the original poem, but in all other cases the trailer-poem tends, as in this instance, to zoom us from some point in the first half of the poem, not necessarily the beginning, to some later point (not unusually the end). In 'Vous êtes invités', the trailer-poem zooms us from the *journée* in the first line, via the 'sensation [...] De l'aujourd'hui' to 'la nuit' and its 'rouages' (which in the main poem are in fact the 'rouages de la veille') — the phrase has been cropped and re-edited, before picking up l'encombrement du temps' and finally the iceberg scenario.

In many of the poems in *Sentimentale Journée*, film is one of a range of communications media invoked in connection with apprehending the real. 'Mettez une voix sur sa prose' [Put a voice to her prose] (*SJ*, pp. 11–13) starts off from the idea of putting a name to a voice, developing, as usual in Alferi, a number of overlapping contexts, including how to pin down what is going on in a narrative. A sequence towards the end features a dancer or actress who might have known that 'dans un film de ce genre' [in this type of film] (p. 13) her role was likely to be short-lived, and to consist mostly of the sound of footsteps (no doubt courtesy of the Foley artists who do sound effects), and an off-screen murder in the style, it is suggested, of Val Lewton, head of the RKO Horror unit and producer of such films as *Cat People* (1942). The next poem, 'Ne coupez pas' [Don't hang up] (*SJ*, pp. 14–17), explores the idea of being *in medias res*, and always having the feeling that one somehow missed the beginning of whatever seems to be going on. But in one sequence the speaker wonders why, on a particular morning, the usual haphazard events in the café and market seem to display 'la cohésion d'un film' [the cohesiveness of a film] (p. 15), deciding that it is not something tacked on like heavy-handed film music, but more the rhythm of events themselves:

> Une prosodie plutôt
> Improvisée qui fait aussi retour
> Sur soi nonchalamment (p. 15)

> [A sort of
> Improvised prosody that nonchalantly recurs]

Film then comes in again to illustrate moments of experience that seem to have no before or after. The poem offers us bits of scenario from a gangster film and an adventure film involving explorers, and then comments:

> De telles choses arrivent dans la vie: à mi-course
> Dans la zone indécise où pour quelques instants encore
> Tout peut tout pénétrer (p. 16)

> [Such things happen in life mid-way
> In the uncertain zone where for a few moments longer
> Everything could merge with everything else]

This feeling of potential is linked with the way in cinema 'd'anonymes bienfaiteurs assurent la soudure' [anonymous benefactors manage the transitions] (p. 16): by dressing the sets differently, or through editing, technicians produce different versions of reality. Alferi's poems are full of moments of virtuality, expectancy, anticipation, when things can go in any direction: film and the art of filmmaking provide analogues for this, or in some cases counter-examples, as in 'Suite à notre conversation' [Following our conversation] (SJ, pp. 29–37) where a telephonic exchange prompts the observation:

> ce ne sera pas
> Comme les mauvais films où l'on voit au débit
> De l'acteur récitant les points de suspension du script
> Qu'il parle dans le vide. (p. 32)

> [it won't be
> like in bad films where the actor's
> way of reciting the ellipses in the script
> reveals that he's speaking into the void]

Beginning with the great line 'L'amour est un effet spécial' [Love is a special effect], 'Les fiancés' [Engaged couple] (SJ, pp. 50–52) draws on the famous film *The Thief of Bagdad* to deconstruct the phases of a relationship, linking them to a variety of special effects —

> ficelles
> Crochets et diversions: des mensonges bénins (p. 50)

> [bits of know-how
> hooks and diversions: benign lies]

that keep love on track.⁹ As the trailer-poem puts it, fusing two disparate moments in the poem:

> Le truc c'est qu'il n'y ait pas de sortilège
> Le charme
> Est mécanique (p. 50)

> [*The trick is that there is no magic spell*
> *the charm*
> *is mechanical*]

The artifices of fantasy cinema become metaphors for the special moments that fuel a love affair, helping it to keep up its momentum. The main thing is that the lovers should follow instructions:

> Ne posez pas trop la question, plus vous réclamez plus
> Vous réduisez vos chances. Il vous suffira de savoir
> Que cela roule sur un artifice assez simple.
> Décidez une fois du placement de la caméra
> Et ne lâchez plus l'œilleton, laissez travailler le petit
> Prodige des effets spéciaux (*SJ*, p. 52)

> [Don't ask questions, the more you ask for
> The slimmer your chances. All you need to know
> Is that it all works by simple artifice.
> Decide once and for all where to place the camera
> And don't drop the viewfinder, let that little
> Wizard from special effects do his job]

or the desired result — marriage — to be achieved, a supporting cast of well-wishers and assistants, including a guardian angel, is seen to be desirable. And the poem ends, charmingly, with a child as the fruit of this union.

'Fay Wray rencontre Buster Brown' [Fay Wray meets Buster Brown] (*SJ*, pp. 68–71) links the iconic heroine of the silent film *King Kong* with the young hero of a hugely successful American strip cartoon. The poem explores the idea that reality consists in a repertoire of stock situations, roles, expressions and emotions:

> Le stock d'incarnations
> Déborde. Les reflets ruissellent (p. 68)

> [The stock of incarnations
> Spills over. The reflections stream]

There are references to the 'album' of a matrimonial agency and to a casting dictionary where you can pick the facial expressions you like — Fay Wray's face is said to be no more than

> un nom pour 'effrayée'
> Le contrechamp d'un monstre. (p. 69)

> [a word for 'scared'
> reaction shot to a monster]

The poem presents discrete 'morceau[x] de signification' [bits of meaning] (p. 68), and the sequence concerning Buster Brown describes one of the comic strips where the last frame gives the lie to the previous images where naughty Buster, a rebellious child accompanied by a little dog, had feigned repentance. Alferi revels in the 'cadrages nickel' [ace framings] (p. 69) of both film and cartoons, allying them with his poetics, where enjambment allows each line to constitute a discrete flash of meaning instantly modified by its qualification in the following line, just as the next image in a film, or the next box in a strip cartoon, impacts on the preceding one without destroying its momentary uniqueness. Another poem, 'Aventures sous les tropiques' [Tropical adventures] (*SJ*, pp. 76–78), concerned with the discrepancy between time as a flow and time as series of instants, and between images and narrativity, references Winsor McCay (p. 78), another pioneering cartoonist and inventor of the Little Nemo character, and especially *Nemo in Slumberland*, where the character always wakes up in the last frame of the strip, revealing the story to have been a dream. McCay went on to make animated films that were to be a major influence on Walt Disney.

Two poems towards the end of *Sentimentale Journée* explicitly use references to visual media, including cinema, to explore the connections between poetry and the dissolution or multiplication of the self that are central to Alferi. 'Vies parallèles' [Parallel lives] (*SJ*, pp. 100–05) is concerned with the ramifications — 'l'arbre exponentiel' [exponential branching] (p. 101) — of 'Des tranches de vie translucides' [translucent slices of life], and the trailer-version urges us not to choose between the virtual lives, the forking paths that each instant offers us: '*Toute action enclenche une vie parallèle*' [*every act sets off a parallel life*] (p. 100). There are references to all the B movies an actor has played in, to the different rig-outs an actor might wear — diving suit, evening dress, uniforms — and the 'identités d'emprunt' [borrowed identities] (p. 103) they offer. An aspect of filmmaking is then used to explore further the notion of multiple parallel lives: film is

> un déroulement
> Commandé par le mot action (p. 103)
>
> [a sequence
> determined by the word action]

but there are moments in films when we get a sense of all the other films that could have been made, if the actors had not heeded the word 'Cut' and had continued to act, with the same sets, the same voices, but in a 'different' movie.

The poem titled 'Allegria' (*SJ*, pp. 97–99), joyousness, festivity, *joie de vivre*, muses on the status of an *élan* that, right from the start — as someone runs down stairs and then bounds along, by virtue of the 'tremplin | De la rue' [springboard of the street] (p. 97) — mixes bodily rhythm and poetic rhythm. 'Quel est cet élan' [what is this *élan*?], the poem asks?

> C'est un mouvement de mort
> Mais c'est aussi
> Une jouissance pure de contenu
>
> [It's a movement towards death
> But it's also
> A pure rapture without content]

The *élan* is deathly because it plays with fire, involves an endless sacrifice of self. But it is also

> Tout le contraire cet aller simple
> Que rien ne justifie (p. 98)

> [The opposite: a one-way ticket
> That nothing justifies].

It is not *plaisir* [pleasure], but *jouissance* [rapture], and it is content-free and simple. Visual media are invoked to convey firstly the sense of virtuality: in the instant when the protagonist emerges into the street, he is like an image momentarily arrested by the pause button of a VCR, which is frozen, but also flickers or trembles like a leaf or a trapped animal, anxious to

> [...] rentrer dans la danse
> Des images seconde (p. 98)

> [re-enter the dance
> of images and seconds].

Secondly, the last sequence of the poem uses the motifs of a dance lesson, where the dancers are supposed to view themselves in the parallel universe of a mirror that seems to swallow them up, and of a stroboscope where the moving images appear as a succession of freeze frames, as if, we are told, the Parisians in an Atget photograph had been resuscitated, 'En danseurs, en fugitifs, en fantômes pris sur le fait' [as dancers, as fugitives, as ghosts caught in the act] — epithets that make them the poet's brothers-in-arms as he seeks to work out

> le dosage
> Explosif de l'absence, de la joie et du mouvement (p. 99)

> [the explosive dose
> of absence, joy and movement]

For Alferi, cinema is a dream machine in which a highly material and often cumbersome technology produces fantasies and illusions. The constant switching between the artificial and the real, and the combination of different codes and technologies (notably sound and image), and the way these work with time to produce sequences of experience that are both real and virtual, make cinema poetry's significant other. Many aspects of film production are cited in the poems, including movie acting where you have to shoot scenes without having read the whole script; body doubles; sounds that need to be simulated, eradicated or laboriously captured; artificial sets and film lots; editing, with its ellipses, flashbacks and rhythms that process and package experience in different ways; montage, which works, as poetry so often does, by selection, combination and juxtaposition. Exploring the endless plasticity of experience, which can be processed and replayed in innumerable ways, Alferi manages to work in such aspects of cinema as material left on the cutting-room floor — which could be surreptitiously edited into an alternative version — and the idea of not having the final cut, which means that actions could turn out to have very different resolutions from those anticipated. Often, the deployment of the cinematic in the poems alludes to established connections between film and psychoanalysis, or film and the nature of memory, or film and narrativity. Alferi often brings in film as one of the frameworks that are operative within a poem, but combines it with other frameworks such as travel or ethnographic exploration (which fits well with the idiom of experimentation in the field of present experience). But the sequences built around travel or anthropological enquiries often involve scenarios that are cinematic, or handled in terms of film idioms and clichés. And of course the switching of locales and of story strands, plot and sub-plot, story and back-story, is one of the features of the novel that classic cinema amplified and codified.

Alferi's poems hook up cinema with many other modes of language, communication, recording and information systems including telephones and the internet, as well as *verlan* [reverse slang]: in one poem, 'À donf dans la drepou' (*SJ*, pp. 33–36), which is *verlan* for 'À fond dans la poudre' [Flat out in the powder], the powder is both snow and a psychotropic drug. These media are then constantly put into contact with poetic language, and with the activity of converting experience into words, or of using language as an antenna to foment or guide experience. Above all, perhaps, cinema mediates between two interconnected realms — words and events — whose essential quality is to be pure movement or momentum. In Alferi, film in all its ramifications colours and gives body to the contours of language and experience.

## Notes

1. Pierre Alferi, *Sentimentale Journée* (Paris: POL, 1997), hereafter abbreviated in the text as *SJ*; *La Voie des airs* (Paris: POL, 2004); *Des enfants et des monstres* (Paris: POL, 2004); *Le Cinéma des familles* (Paris: POL, 1999).
2. Pierre Alferi, *Cinépoèmes et films parlants* (Les Laboratoires d'Aubervilliers, 2003) [on DVD].
3. Michel de Certeau, *L'Invention du quotidien*, 2 vols (Paris: Folio, 1990), I, 190. See Michael Sheringham, 'Trajets quotidiens et récits délinquants', *Temps zéro: Revue d'étude des écritures contemporaines*, 1 (2007) <http://tempszero.contemporain.info/document79>.
4. Pierre Alferi, *Chercher une phrase*, 2nd edn (Paris: Christian Bourgois, 2007), p. 13.
5. See my articles 'Pierre Alferi and Jakob von Uexkiill: Experience and Experiment in *Le Chemin familier du poisson combatif*' and 'Pierre Alferi: "Une défense de la poésie"', both in this volume.
6. Pierre Alferi, *Intime: les carnets de l'espace* (Belfort: Espace multimedia Gartner/Conseil général Territoire de Belfort, 2002), pp. 9–10.
7. On the motif of the day in modern writing see Michael Sheringham, 'Une journée à soi', *Conférence*, 25 (Autumn 2007).
8. René Descartes, 'Cogitationes privatae (janvier 1619)', in *Œuvres de Descartes*, ed. by Charles Adam and Paul Tannery, 11 vols (Paris: Librairie philosophique Vrin, 1983), X, 213.
9. *The Thief of Bagdad*: 1924 version with Douglas Fairbanks, directed by Raoul Walsh; 1940 version with Conrad Veidt, directed by Michael Powell.

# INDEX

❖

www.ingramcontent.com/pod-product-compliance
Lightning Source LLC
Chambersburg PA
CBHW080540090426
42734CB00016B/3158